Fundamental FINANCIAL ACCOUNTING Concepts

First Canadian Edition

Fundamental FINANCIAL ACCOUNTING Concepts

First Canadian Edition

Thomas P. Edmonds
University of Alabama – Birmingham

Frances M. McNair
Mississippi State University

Edward E. Milam
Mississippi State University

Philip R. Olds
Virginia Commonwealth University

Carole Bowman
Sheridan College

Donna P. Grace
Sheridan College

Toronto Montréal Boston Burr Ridge, IL Dubuque, IA Madison, WI New York San Francisco St. Louis Bangkok Bogotá Caracas Kuala Lumpur Lisbon London Madrid Mexico City Milan New Delhi Santiago Seoul Singapore Sydney Taipei

McGraw-Hill
Ryerson Limited

*A Subsidiary of The **McGraw-Hill** Companies*

Fundamental Financial Accounting Concepts
First Canadian Edition

ISBN: 0-07-090522-3

1 2 3 4 5 6 7 8 9 10 TCP 0 9 8 7 6 5 4 3

Printed and bound in Canada.

Vice President, Editorial and Media Technology: Pat Ferrier
Executive Editor: Nicole Lukach
Sponsoring Editor: Lenore Gray Spence
Developmental Editor: Katherine Goodes
Director of Marketing: Jeff MacLean
Senior Supervising Editor: Margaret Henderson
Copy Editors: Valerie Adams; Matthew Kudelka
Production Coordinator: Madeleine Harrington
Composition: VISU*TronX* Services
Cover Design: Greg Devitt
Cover Image: Chris McElcheran/Masterfile
Printer: Transcontinental Printing Group

National Library of Canada Cataloguing in Publication Data

Edmonds, Thomas P.
Fundamental financial accounting concepts / Thomas P. Edmonds, Carole Bowman, Donna P. Grace. -- 1st Canadian ed.

Includes index.
ISBN 0-07-090522-3

1. Accounting. I. Grace, Donna P. II. Bowman, Carole III. Title.

HF5635.E35 2002 657 C2002-901854-4

Thomas P. Edmonds

Thomas P. Edmonds, Ph.D. holds the Friends and Alumni Professorship in the Department of Accounting at the University of Alabama at Birmingham (UAB). He has been actively involved in teaching accounting principles throughout his academic career. Dr. Edmonds has coordinated the accounting principles courses at the University of Houston and UAB. He currently teaches introductory accounting in mass sections that frequently contain more than 180 students. Dr. Edmonds has received five prestigious teaching awards including the UAB President's Excellence in Teaching Award and the distinguished Ellen Gregg Ingalls Award for excellence in classroom teaching. He has written numerous articles that have appeared in many publications including *Issues in Accounting*, the *Journal of Accounting Education*, *Advances in Accounting Education*, *Accounting Education: A Journal of Theory, Practice and Research*, the *Accounting Review*, *Advances in Accounting*, the *Journal of Accountancy*, *Management Accounting*, the *Journal of Commercial Bank Lending*, the *Banker's Magazine*, and the *Journal of Accounting, Auditing, and Finance*. He has published four textbooks, five practice problems (including two computerized problems), and a variety of supplemental materials including study guides, work papers, and solutions manuals. Dr. Edmonds' work experience and academic training has enabled him to bring a unique user perspective to this textbook.

Frances M. McNair

Frances M. McNair, Ph.D., CPA holds the KPMG Peat Marwick Professorship in Accounting at Mississippi State University (MSU). Dr. McNair has been involved in teaching principles of accounting for the past twelve years and currently serves as the coordinator for the principles of accounting courses at MSU. She has authored various articles that have appeared in the *Journal of Accountancy*, *Management Accounting*, *Business and Professional Ethics Journal*, *The Practical Accountant*, *Taxes*, and is currently serving on committees of the American Taxation Association, The American Accounting Association, and the Institute of Management Accountants as well as numerous School of Accountancy and University committees.

Edward E. Milam

Edward E. Milam, Ph.D., CPA is a Professor of Accounting at Mississippi State University (MSU). He has served as President of the Federation of Schools of Accountancy, on the Standards Committee of AACSB (Business and Accounting Accrediting Association), as Treasurer/Secretary of the American Taxation Association, on the Board of Directors of the Mississippi Tax Institute, and on various committees of the ATA, FSA, AICPA, American Accounting Association, and the Mississippi Society of Certified Public Accountants. He has authored numerous articles that appeared in publications including *Journal of Accountancy*, *Taxes*, *Management Accounting*, *Financial Executive*, *Estate Planning*, *Trusts and Estates*, the *CPA Journal*, and others. He has also co-authored seven books.

Philip R. Olds

Philip R. Olds, Ph.D., CPA is an Associate Professor of Accounting at Virginia Commonwealth University (VCU) where he has taught since 1981. He serves as the coordinator of the introduction to accounting courses at VCU and is a CPA in the State of Virginia. In 1989 he was recognized with an Outstanding Faculty Vice-President Award by the national Beta Alpha Psi organization. Professor Olds has published articles in various professional journals and presented papers at national and regional conferences.

Carole Bowman

Carole Bowman, B.B.A., is foundation year coordinator at Sheridan College (Brampton campus), responsible for the first-year business students and the curriculum development for their foundation year. She received her B.B.A. from Wilfrid Laurier University with a major in accounting and a minor in economics. She is an alumnus of Arthur Andersen and Co., where she gained extensive knowledge in accounting and taxation of small businesses. Her designation as a certified management accountant helped her build a successful accounting and tax practice. Since 1989, Carole has taught many accounting courses at Sheridan including introductory accounting, intermediate accounting, advanced accounting and cost accounting. Other courses include income tax and computer software systems. Realizing the need for a different approach in accounting to improve student success for both accounting and non-accounting majors, she readily accepted the opportunity to co-author this exciting, new accounting textbook with its unique approach to learning accounting.

Donna Pothier Grace

Donna P. Grace, M.B.A., has a background in finance and accounting that began in American financial institutions. Her B.B.A. degree is with a concentration in accounting and she earned her M.B.A., majoring in finance, from Eastern Illinois University. Donna is a professor of Accounting and Finance at Sheridan, School of Business, Brampton, Ontario. In addition to twenty years as a lecturer, Donna has served as Chairperson in the School of Business and is Coordinator of the Accounting program. She has worked as a consultant to external agencies, including Canada Customs and Revenue Agency. Donna has been published as a supplements contributor and secondary author of several accounting texts. She is quite enthusiastic about the innovative approach this text follows with the use of the "financial statements model" as a method of teaching introductory accounting.

Brief Contents

Contents

Chapter 5 Accounting for Merchandising Businesses 188

Chapter 6 Internal Control and Accounting for Cash 234

Chapter 7 Accounting for Accruals—Advanced Topics: Receivables and Payables 276

Chapter 8 Asset Valuation: Accounting for Inventories 328

Chapter 9 Long-Term Operational Assets 364

Chapter 10 Accounting for Long-Term Debt 410

Chapter 11 Accounting for Equity Transactions 458

Chapter 12 Cash Flow Statement 488

Welcome to the first Canadian edition of *Fundamental Financial Accounting Concepts*. This is a conceptually based, user-oriented book that stresses meaningful learning over rote memorization. More specifically, the text focuses on the relationships between business events and financial statements. **The primary objective is for students to develop and explain how a particular business event can affect the income statement, balance sheet, and cash flow statement.** Did the event cause assets to increase, decrease, or stay the same? Similarly, what was its effect on liabilities, equity, revenue, expense, gains, losses, net income, and dividends? Furthermore, how did the event affect cash flow? These are the *big picture* relationships that both accounting majors and general business students need to understand to function effectively in the business world. The text contains numerous innovative features that are designed to facilitate the students' comprehension of the *events affecting financial statements*.

Innovative Features

A Horizontal Financial Statements Model Is the Primary Teaching Platform

A horizontal financial statements model replaces the accounting equation as the predominant teaching platform. The model enables students to visualize the simultaneous effects of a single business event on the income statement, balance sheet, and cash flow statement by arranging the statements horizontally across a single line of text in the following manner:

Event No.	Balance Sheet							Income Statement					Cash Flow Statement	
	Cash	+	Acc. Rec.	=	Com. Sh.	+	Ret. Earn.	Rev.	−	Exp.	=	Net Inc.		
1	NA	+	600	=	NA	+	600	600	−	NA	=	600	NA	
2	400	+	NA	=	NA	+	400	400	−	NA	=	400	400	OA
3	(350)	+	NA	=	NA	+	(350)	NA	−	NA	=	NA	(350)	FA
4	NA	+	NA	=	225	+	(225)	NA	−	NA	=	NA	NA	
Totals	50	+	600	=	224	+	425	1,000	−	NA	=	1,000	50	NC

One of the more powerful explanatory features of the horizontal statements model is derived from the specific events that are recorded directly in the financial statements. Traditionally, a series of events is recorded in accounts, and additional information is presented in the financial statements. Therefore, students do not observe the **effects of individual events on the financial statements**. The horizontal statements model teaches students to record statement effects transaction by transaction. For example, Event No. 1 in Exhibit 1 (see above) demonstrates that the recognition of revenue on account affects the balance sheet and income statement but not the cash flow statement. These effects are visibly isolated from the effects of other events. The horizontal statements model also provides an effective means for comparing the effects of one transaction with another. By comparing Event No. 1 with Event No. 2, students can see how the recognition of cash revenue differs from the recognition of revenue on account. Similarly, a comparison of Event No. 3 and No. 4 highlights differences between the effects of cash dividends versus stock dividends. Note that students are also required to identify cash flows as being financing activities (FA), investing activities (IA), or operating activities (OA) by placing the appropriate letters in the Cash Flow Statement column.

A Separate Section of Innovative End-of-Chapter Materials Encourages Students to Analyze, Think, Communicate

An innovative section entitled Analyze, Think, Communicate (ATC) has been added to the end-of-chapter materials. This section is composed of business applications cases, writing assignments, group exercises, Excel spreadsheet applications, ethics cases, and Internet assignments. Corresponding icons have been included in the text as shown below. These activities permit the user to emphasize either a user- or a preparer-oriented approach to accounting education. Furthermore, the material in this section enables you to stress computer applications to the extent you deem appropriate. Although the text is not designed to teach spreadsheet technicalities, Excel problems and exercises do include instructional tips that facilitate the students' ability to use spreadsheets.

By focusing on the materials in the ATC section, you can place heavy emphasis on a user orientation or on computer technology. Indeed, you can even teach the course without debits and credits if you are inclined to do so. However, the text includes a healthy supply of problems that require the use of debits and credits, journal entries, T-accounts, and other technical recording procedures. Therefore, you can emphasize the preparer approach by selectively choosing the end-of-chapter materials that contain the traditional requirements. The ATC section of the end-of-chapter materials permits you to emphasize those areas you consider to be most important for your particular academic environment. An example of an ATC case from Chapter 2 follows, and an example of an ATC Excel assignment from Chapter 5 is also shown.

REAL-WORLD CASE *Examining Annual Reports* **ATC 2–3**

Using the most current annual reports from these Web sites, answer the questions listed below.

www.royalbank.ca
www.magnaint.com
www.esso.ca

Required

a. In the asset section of its balance sheet, the Royal Bank reported "Securities." What did these securities consist of?
b. In the asset section of its balance sheet, Magna International, reported "Inventories." What were the items that were included in inventories?
c. In the asset section of its balance sheet, Imperial Oil Company reported "Goodwill" and "Other Intangible Assets." What was reported as an example of these assets?

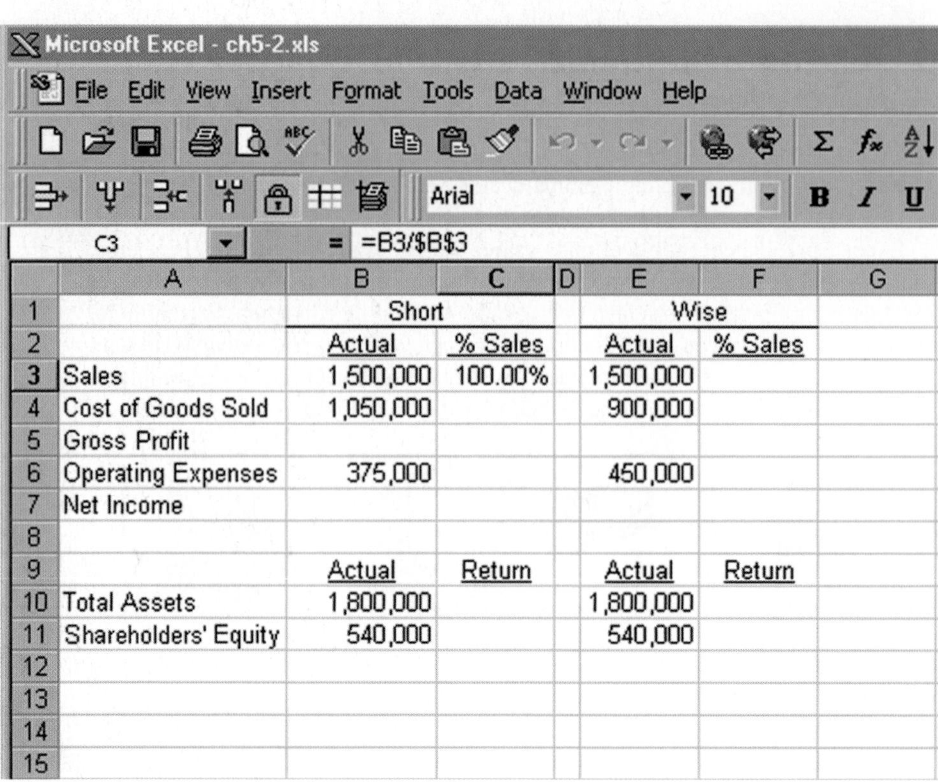

	A	B	C	D	E	F	G
1		Short			Wise		
2		Actual	% Sales		Actual	% Sales	
3	Sales	1,500,000	100.00%		1,500,000		
4	Cost of Goods Sold	1,050,000			900,000		
5	Gross Profit						
6	Operating Expenses	375,000			450,000		
7	Net Income						
8							
9		Actual	Return		Actual	Return	
10	Total Assets	1,800,000			1,800,000		
11	Shareholders' Equity	540,000			540,000		
12							
13							
14							
15							

Financial Statement Effects Are Demonstrated over Multiple Accounting Cycles

The text also uses a **vertical statements model**, which presents the statements in an upright pattern from the top to the bottom of the page. The income statement is presented first, the balance sheet directly after the income statement, and the cash flow statement directly after the balance sheet. Financial data for a sequence of accounting cycles are displayed in adjacent columns. An example of a vertical statements model from Chapter 9 follows.

Exhibit 9–2 *Financial Statements under Straight-Line Amortization*

DRYDEN ENTERPRISES
Financial Statements

	2004	2005	2006	2007	2008
Income Statements					
Rent Revenue	$ 8,000	$ 8,000	$ 8,000	$ 8,000	$ 0
Amortization Expense	(5,000)	(5,000)	(5,000)	(5,000)	0
Operating Income	3,000	3,000	3,000	3,000	0
Gain	0	0	0	0	500
Net Income	$ 3,000	$ 3,000	$ 3,000	$ 3,000	$ 500
Balance Sheets					
Assets					
Cash	$ 9,000	$17,000	$25,000	$33,000	$37,500
Van	24,000	24,000	24,000	24,000	0
Accumulated Amortization	(5,000)	(10,000)	(15,000)	(20,000)	0
Total Assets	$28,000	$31,000	$34,000	$37,000	$37,500
Shareholders' Equity					
Common Shares	$25,000	$25,000	$25,000	$25,000	$25,000
Retained Earnings	3,000	6,000	9,000	12,000	12,500
Total Shareholders' Equity	$28,000	$31,000	$34,000	$37,000	$37,500
Cash Flow Statements					
Operational Activities					
Inflow from Customers	$ 8,000	$ 8,000	$ 8,000	$ 8,000	$ 0
Investing Activities					
Outflow to Purchase Van	(24,000)	0	0	0	0
Inflow from Sale of Van	0	0	0	0	4,500
Financing Activities					
Inflow from Share Issue	25,000	0	0	0	0
Net Change in Cash	9,000	8,000	8,000	8,000	4,500
Beginning Cash Balance	0	9,000	17,000	25,000	33,000
Ending Cash Balance	$ 9,000	$17,000	$25,000	$33,000	$37,500

The vertical statements model enables the instructor to link related events over **multiple accounting cycles**. A student can see how expense recognition is spread over an asset's useful life. Furthermore, since a full set of statements is presented on a single page, the student can visually contrast expense recognition with cash flow. Similarly, the vertical statements model enables a student to observe the multi-cycle effects of transactions. An important difference between a vertical statements model and the traditional comparative financial statements is that the vertical statements model is presented in a simplified form on a single page of paper. Students cannot understand the link between the financial statements as easily when the statements and/or accounting periods are shown on separate pages.

The statement models are presented for instructional purposes. They are very helpful in understanding how accounting events affect financial statements. Therefore, statement models are used extensively in this text. Notice, however, that the models are not intended to represent the formal presentation formats that appear in annual reports. For example, although a full set of four financial statements is normally presented in published financial statements, the horizontal model shows only a particular set of statements. Similarly, the vertical instructional model may vary in form and content, depending on the learning task. Since the statements are presented in aggregate, the description of dates ("as of" versus "for the period ended") cannot be used to distinguish periodic from cumulative data. When using this text, keep in mind that statement models are intended to facilitate learning tasks. They do not conform to the detailed requirements of formal reporting practices.

Effects of Cash Flows Are Shown throughout the Entire Text

Coverage of the cash flow statement begins in the first chapter and continues throughout the text. Students can be taught to prepare a cash flow statement in the first chapter of an introductory accounting text by having them analyze the Cash account. When the Cash account is used as the data source, preparing a cash flow statement is simply a matter of learning how to classify events as operating, investing, or financing activities. This approach provides a logical learning environment that facilitates an understanding of the essential differences between cash flow and accrual-based income. More complicated topics such as the indirect method and a T-account approach for the conversion of accruals to cash are covered in a separate chapter at the end of the text.

Accounting Concepts Are Introduced in a Logical Stepwise Fashion

Students can get confused when too many new concepts are introduced simultaneously. Most books overwhelm students by introducing cash, accrual, and deferral events in the first chapter. This text introduces these components in a logical stepwise manner. Cash transactions are discussed in Chapter 1, accruals are introduced in Chapter 2, and deferrals are covered in Chapter 3. Nontechnical terminology (increase/decrease) is used to discuss the effects of events on the elements of financial statements in the first three chapters of the text. Recording procedures including debits and credits are demonstrated in Chapter 4. Accordingly, technical details are delayed until students have grasped the *big picture* relationships associated with financial statements.

An Appropriate Balance between Theory and Practice Is Maintained

A conceptual foundation enables students to think instead of memorize. Students who understand concepts are better able to communicate ideas and are more effective at solving unstructured problems. Therefore, **this text addresses the issues raised by the accounting education change movement**. It is important to note, however, that the call for change in accounting education is not a call for the abandonment of technical competence. Instead, the enhancement of communication and thinking skills must accompany technical proficiency. Practising accountants continue to book transactions, and real-world communication requires non-accountants to possess an adequate technical vocabulary. Although the coverage of recording procedures has been significantly reduced, it has not been eliminated. We cover the basic components of double-entry bookkeeping, including debits and credits, journal entries, T-accounts, and trial balances. Therefore, **it is not necessary to change your intermediate accounting course if you adopt this book**. Indeed, students may be better prepared for intermediate accounting than they were under the traditional approach.

Business Transactions Are Classified into Four Logical Categories

Instead of attempting to memorize transactions, students learn to identify events as belonging to one of four conceptual categories. More specifically, students learn to classify transactions as being (1) asset sources, (2) asset uses, (3) asset exchanges, or (4) claims exchanges.

A Consistent Point of Reference Is Provided

Do you ever wonder why good students sometimes have so much trouble grasping the simplest concepts? For example, why do so many students have difficulty distinguishing the effects of an owner investment from those of a business investment? A participant in a recent introductory accounting workshop provided the answer that enabled us to avoid a common pitfall that needlessly confuses so many students. Normally, accounting events are described from the perspective of the business entity. For example, we say that the business borrowed money, purchased assets, earned revenue, or incurred expenses. However, for equity transactions, we say that the owners contributed capital, provided cash, or invested assets in the business. From the perspective of the business, these are capital acquisitions, not owner investments. To understand how this *reference shift* affects the entry-level accounting student, try it on a different type of transaction. Suppose that we say, "A customer purchased services from a business." What kind of transaction is this? It is a revenue transaction, of course. How about "a supplier provides services to the business"? This is just a more confusing way of saying the business incurred an expense. Likewise, an owner investment is just a more confusing way of saying the business acquired assets from the owner. Your students will certainly appreciate the fact that this text uses the business entity as a consistent point of reference in the description of all accounting events. We steadfastly use the terminology "the business acquired cash from the issue of shares" rather than saying "the owner invested in the business" when describing equity events.

Content That Is Manageable and Relevant

Accounting is a dynamic discipline. It changes to reflect new and emerging business practices. As academics, we are certainly obligated to keep current and to introduce our students to the latest developments. As teachers, however, we must also recognize the limited ability of our students to meaningfully process an ever-increasing supply of information. **Remember that information overload equals memorization.** This first Canadian edition eliminates alternative recording procedures, meaningless details, and subject matter that is too advanced for introductory accounting students. As a result, it contains only 12 chapters.

Stimulating Student Interest

A good textbook must be more than pedagogically sound. It must be designed in a manner that motivates student interest. Toward this end, we have included several features that highlight real-world applications. Each chapter of the text opens with a scenario entitled **The Curious Accountant**. Each scenario poses a question regarding a real-world accounting issue. The question is answered in a separate box a few pages after the question. Pictures that stimulate interest are included. An example of The Curious Accountant feature follows. The text contains other real-world features such as actual financial statements, footnote quotations, and management analyses drawn from the **annual reports of well-known Canadian and North American companies**. As well, the end-of-chapter material includes real-world cases requiring the use of the **World Wide Web**.

the *curious* accountant

In January 2001, Air Canada and Canadian Airlines were amalgamated to form one company, known as Air Canada. The financing of this merger plus existing debt (totalling $11 billion) requires the company to pay almost $1 million in interest per day. The terrorist attacks of September 11, 2001, have placed further stresses on the company's financial position. Before September 2001, the airline had expected to achieve its financial targets. In late September 2001, the company issued a news release stating that it would need to substantially reduce its earnings projections for the next quarter. The price of the stock declined from $20 per share in mid-2000 to under $3 per share by October 2001. To help it through this difficult time, the company has hired a financial advisor (BMO Nesbitt Burns) to identify alternatives. If you were the advisor, what kind of advice would you give?

The successful operation of a business enterprise requires control. How can upper management of a major retailer such as Wal-Mart know that all its stores will open at a certain time? How can the presi-

answer to the *curious* accountant

Air Canada is struggling under its current debt load. The company needs to obtain additional cash flows to remain financially viable. Cash can be generated through increased revenues. However, since September 11, 2001, revenues have drastically fallen off. The projected revenue picture is for a marked decline in air travel, and this is not expected to change in the near future. Therefore, revenue generation probably won't be an answer to Air Canada's cash flow problems. Cost control is the next consideration. The events have already forced layoffs of personnel from all areas of the company, a reduction in the number of flights (which saves costs but also decreases revenues), and the sale of airplanes. This will allow for a reduction of operating costs and will reduce cash outlays, thus providing more cash. However, it won't provide enough to meet the company's cash needs. A further option may be to replace some of the debt with equity financing. This would reduce the interest charges for the company and allow the generation of more positive cash flow. Finally, the government may decide to provide cash on a temporary basis, but discussions to date indicate that Air Canada will have to restructure the company first and show the government that this downturn is only temporary in nature. Air Canada has received financial support from the government in prior years, and the government cannot afford to keep providing additional cash resources if the company does not show that its financial position will be turned around.

Finally, financial ratios introduced throughout the book are logically related to the chapter material. For example, accounts receivable turnover is introduced in the chapter that covers bad debts, and the times-interest-earned ratio is discussed in the bonds chapter. Industry data are shown to provide students with a basis for establishing a sense of normalcy regarding business practice. The 2001 annual report for Bombardier Inc. is included in Appendix B, and the "Analyze, Think, Communicate" section that relates directly to the annual report is in the end-of-chapter material.

Supplemental Material

The text is supported by a complete package of supplements. The author team has been involved with the development of many of these materials. Accordingly, you can rest assured that the supplements match the text. The package includes the following items:

For Instructors

Solutions Manual (ISBN 0-07-090517-7)

Prepared by Carole Bowman and Donna P. Grace, Sheridan College. The Solutions Manual has been prepared by the authors and contains the complete answers to all questions, exercises, problems, and cases. It has been tested using a variety of quality-control procedures to ensure accuracy. It was proofed and checked for accuracy.

Test Bank (ISBN 0-07-090516-9)

Prepared by Michael Lee, Humber College. The Test Bank includes an expansive array of true/false, multiple-choice, short discussion questions, and open-ended problems. The material is coded by learning objective and level of difficulty.

Instructor's CD-ROM (ISBN 0-07-090518-5)

This integrated CD allows instructors to customize their own classroom presentations. It contains key supplements such as:

- **Instructor's Manual**. **Prepared by Doug Ringrose, Grant MacEwen Community College.** The text is suitable to teaching approaches such as group dynamics and active pedagogy. The Instructor's Manual provides step-by-step, explicit instructions as to how the text can be used to implement these alternative teaching methodologies. Guidance is also provided for those instructors who choose to use the traditional lecture method. The Instructor's Manual includes lesson plans and demonstration problems with student work papers, as well as solutions for them.
- **Computerized Test Bank**. **Prepared by Michael Lee, Humber College.** A computerized version of the Test Bank, this supplement is a valuable resource for instructors who prepare their own quizzes and examinations.
- **Solutions Manual**. Prepared in Microsoft Word, these files are downloadable.
- **PowerPoint® Slides**. **Prepared by Michael Hockenstein, Vanier College.** These slides may be used in class as presentation material and to review chapter concepts.
- **SPATS**. **Prepared by Elizabeth Zaleschuk, Douglas College.** Available in Instructor version and Student version, Spreadsheet Application Templates make it easier for students to solve problems using Excel®.

Combining these resources, this Instructor's CD makes it easy for instructors to create multimedia presentations.

Online Learning Centre (www.mcgrawhill.ca/college/edmonds)

The textbook's Online Learning Centre includes valuable instructor resources, including the following:

- A "B" set of exercises mirroring the "A" set in the textbook, to be used as additional reinforcement for student learning.
- Supplemental topics covering the *CICA Handbook* and payroll.
- Downloadable supplements including the Instructor's Manual, Solutions Manual, PowerPoint® slides, and SPATS.

Grade Summit

Prepared by Michael Hockenstein, Vanier College. This new feature gives your students an edge! Grade Summit is not a student study guide. It is an Internet-based assessment service that:

- provides a variety of ways for students to analyze what they know and don't know.
- gives students the ability to evaluate how effectively they are absorbing the key concepts.
- contains hundreds of unique questions written by professors and peer-reviewed for accuracy and quality.
- provides an excellent tool for students, allowing them spend their limited time more efficiently and effectively.

See your McGraw-Hill Ryerson representative for more details.

Primis Online

McGraw-Hill's Primis Online, the world's largest and best resource, is available at your fingertips, literally! Select from our online database of over 350,000 pages of content, including the first edition of Edmonds, *Fundamental Financial Accounting Concepts*. With a few mouse clicks, create customized learning tools simply and affordably. When you adopt a Primis Online text, you decide the best medium for your students: printed textbooks or electronic e-books.

WebCT/Blackboard

For faculty requiring online content, *Fundamental Financial Accounting Concepts* is available in two of the most popular delivery platforms: WebCT and Blackboard. These platforms are designed for instructors who want complete control over course content and how it is presented to students. They provide instructors with more user-friendly and highly flexible teaching tools that enhance interaction between students and faculty.

PageOut

PageOut is a McGraw-Hill online tool that enables instructors to create and post class-specific Web pages simply and easily. No knowledge of HTML is required.

For Students

Student Study Guide (ISBN 0-07-090519-3)

Prepared by Michael Hockenstein, Vanier College. An essential study aid for students, each chapter of the Study Guide includes a review and an explanation of the chapter's learning objectives, as well as multiple-choice problems and short exercises. Also included is a series of articulation problems that require students to indicate how accounting events affect (i.e., increase, decrease, no effect) the elements of financial statements. They not only reinforce the student's understanding of how events affect statements but also help them to understand how the income statement, balance sheet, and cash flow statement interrelate.

Working Papers (ISBN 0-07-090527-4)

Prepared by Carole Bowman and Donna P. Grace. These Working Papers provide forms that are useful in the completion of both exercises and problems. Working Papers for exercises provide headings and prerecorded example transactions that enable students to get started quickly and to work in an efficient manner. The forms provided for the problems can be used with either series A or B problems.

Grade Summit

Grade Summit is not a student study guide. Prepared by Michael Hockenstein, Vanier College, it is an Internet-based assessment service that:

- provides a variety of ways for students to analyze what they know and don't know.
- gives students the ability to evaluate how effectively they are absorbing the key concepts.
- contains hundreds of unique questions written by professors and peer reviewed for accuracy and quality.
- provides an excellent tool for students, allowing them to spend their limited time more efficiently and effectively.

See your instructor for more information on Grade Summit.

Student Solutions Manual (ISBN 0-07-090521-5)

Extracted from the Instructor's Solutions Manual prepared by Carole Bowman and Donna P. Grace, the Student Solutions Manual contains solutions to odd-numbered exercises and problems in the text. The large text makes solutions easily readable.

Online Learning Centre (www.mcgrawhill.ca/college/edmonds).

The Student Online Learning Centre follows the text chapter-by-chapter. Students will find:

- **SPATS**. Prepared by Elizabeth Zaleschuk, Douglas College. Identified by the following logo, these Spreadsheet Application Templates make it easier for students to solve problems using Excel®.

- **PowerPoint® Slides**. Prepared by Michael Hockenstein, Vanier College. These slides may be used to review each chapter's concepts.
- A "B" set of exercises mirroring the "A" set in the textbook, to be used as additional reinforcement for student learning.
- Numerous other self-assessment quizzes.
- Learning objectives and their explanations.
- Key terms.
- Check figures.
- Internet exercises.

Acknowledgments

We are indebted to many individuals who have contributed to the development of the textbook. The text underwent an extensive review process that included a diverse group of instructors across the country. The comments and suggestions of the reviewers have significantly influenced the adaptation and Canadianization of this text. Our efforts to establish a meaningful but manageable level of content was greatly influenced not only by their suggestions regarding what to include but also by their opinions regarding what to leave out. Our sincere appreciation is extended to:

Brian Winter, *Southern Alberta Institute of Technology*

Jim Chambers, *St. Clair College*

Michael Lee, *Humber College*

Christopher Burnley, *Malaspina College*

Cecile Ashman, *Algonquin College*

Dennis Wilson, *Centennial College*

Gary Earle, *Loyalist College*

Cathie Hurlie, *University of New Brunswick*

Karen Cramm, *Keyano College*

Marie Madill-Payne, *George Brown College*

Albert Ganesh, *Seneca College*

Joe Pidutti, *Durham College*

Peter Richter, *John Abbott College*

Dennis Ralph, *Georgian College*

Elizabeth Zaleschuk, *Douglas College*

McGraw-Hill Ryerson

Online Learning Centre

McGraw-Hill Ryerson offers you an online resource that combines the best content with the flexibility and power of the Internet. Organized by chapter, the EDMONDS Online Learning Centre (OLC) offers the following features to enhance your learning and understanding of Accounting:

- Self-Assessment Quizzes
- Microsoft® Excel® Templates
- SPATS and Microsoft® PowerPoint® Presentations
- Internet Application Questions

By connecting to the "real world" through the OLC, you will enjoy a dynamic and rich source of current information that will help you get more from your course and improve your chances for success, both in the course and in the future.

For the Instructor

Downloadable Supplements

All key supplements are available, password-protected for instant access!

PageOut

Create your own course Web page for free, quickly and easily. Your professionally designed Web site links directly to OLC material, allows you to post a class syllabus, offers an online gradebook, and much more! Visit www.pageout.net

Primis Online

Primis Online gives you access to our resources in the best medium for your students: printed textbooks or electronic ebooks. There are over 350,000 pages of content available from which you can create customized learning tools from our online database at www.mhhe.com/primis

WebCT/Blackboard

If you require online content, **Fundamental Financial Accounting Concepts** is available in two of the most popular delivery platforms: WebCT and Blackboard. These platforms are designed to give you complete control over course content and how you present it to your students. These user-friendly and highly flexible teaching tools enhance interaction between you and your students.

Higher Learning. Forward Thinking.™

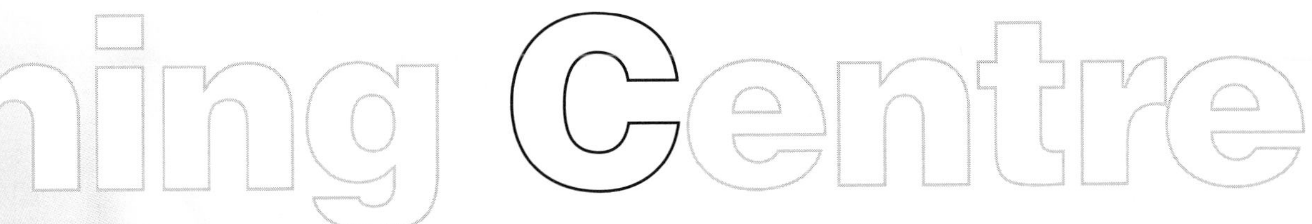

For the Student

Online Quizzes

Do you know the material? You can consult the Key terms for each chapter as well as having handy access to the Learning Objectives. Need some practice? Work through the eLearning Sessions contained in every chapter. If that isn't enough for you, test your knowledge with the Multiple Choice quizzes to maximize the effect of the time spent reviewing text concepts.

SPATS and Microsoft® PowerPoint® Presentations

View and download presentations created for each chapter, then work through selected Technology problems from the text with the Spreadsheet Application Template Software (SPATS).A great way to improve your skills while preparing for class or for post-class review.

Internet Application Questions

Go online to learn how companies use the Internet in their day-to-day activities. Answer questions based on current organization Web sites and strategies.

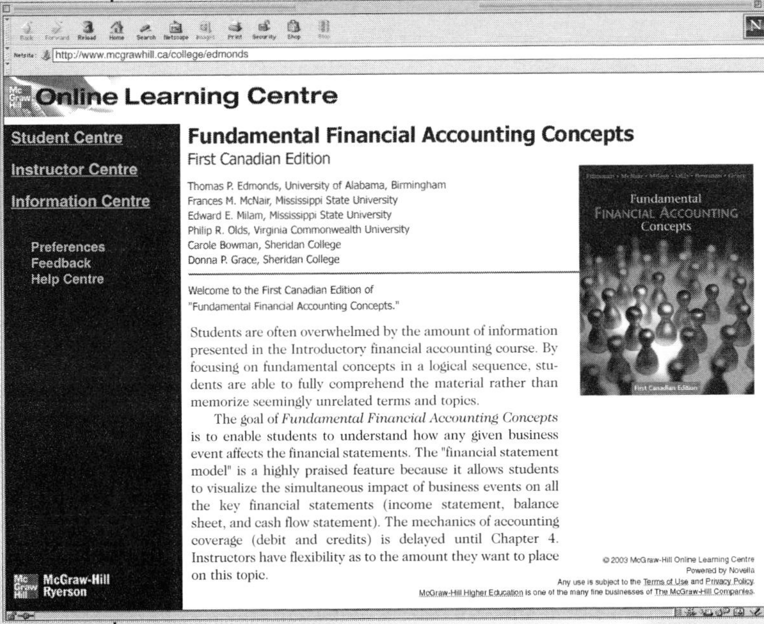

Your Internet companion to the most exciting educational tools on the Web!

The Online Learning Centre can be found at:
www.mcgrawhill.ca/college/edmonds

Chapter 1

Elements of Financial Statements

Learning Objectives

After completing this chapter, you should be able to:

1. Describe the main characteristics of a sole proprietorship, partnership, and corporation.
2. Distinguish between financial and managerial accounting.
3. Explain the need for measurement rules (generally accepted accounting principles [GAAP]).
4. Identify, describe, and prepare the four basic financial statements.
5. Identify the major elements of financial statements.
6. Describe the relationships expressed in the accounting equation.
7. Record business events in a financial statements model.
8. Classify business events as asset source, use, or exchange transactions.
9. Record business events in general ledger accounts.
10. Identify the steps in the accounting cycle, including the closing process.
11. Calculate, and explain the meaning of, the price-earnings ratio.
12. Identify the major components of real-world annual reports and some of the technical terms used in them.

the *curious* accountant

Who owns Shoppers Drug Mart? Who owns the Canadian Cancer Society (CCS)? Besides the owners, many other people and organizations have an interest in the operations of Shoppers Drug Mart and the CCS. Parties with an interest in the operations of an organization are called *stakeholders*. They include lenders, employees, suppliers, customers, benefactors, research institutions, hospitals, doctors, patients, lawyers, bankers, financial analysts, and government agencies such as the Canadian Customs and Revenue Agency (CCRA) and the Ontario Securities Commission. Organizations communicate information to stakeholders through documents called *financial reports*. How will the financial reports of Shoppers Drug Mart differ from those of the CCS? For an answer, see page 21.

Why should you study accounting? Because it can help you succeed in business. In fact, your chances of success are pretty dismal if you are ignorant about accounting. Imagine trying to play a game such as football or monopoly when you do not know how to keep score. Accounting is how you keep score in business. Make no mistake: business is highly competitive, and if you do not know the rules of the game, you will be at a severe disadvantage.

***Accounting** is information. Accountants do not make or sell goods; rather they provide information services to their clients. More specifically, they provide information that helps their clients make better decisions. Do not underestimate the importance of reliable information. Think of the money you could make if you had reliable information regarding the winner of next year's Grey Cup. Likewise, reliable information about a company's earnings potential could make you a wealthy Bay Street investor.*

The parties that use accounting information are frequently called ***stakeholders****. Stakeholders (****users****) can have a direct or an indirect interest in the organizations that issue accounting reports. Stakeholders that have a direct interest include owners, managers, creditors, suppliers, and employees. These individuals are directly affected by what happens to the business. For example, owners and employees of a business prosper when the business makes money. Likewise, they suffer when the business incurs losses. Stakeholders with an indirect interest in the reporting company include financial analysts, brokers, lawyers, government regulators, and news reporters. These individuals use information in financial reports to advise and influence their clients. For example, financial analysts often advise clients to buy or sell shares of companies they do not personally own.*

Clearly, accounting is a dynamic discipline. It affects a wide range of individuals and organizations. Accounting is so important that it has been called the language of business. *Indeed, accounting affects not only individual businesses but also society as a whole.*

Formation of Business Organizations

The three major forms of business organization are the *sole proprietorship*, the *partnership*, and the *corporation*. These business structures were developed to meet the specific needs of society at different times. The most basic form is the **sole proprietorship**. Sole proprietorships are owned by one person and are usually fairly small.

The proprietorship was the main form of business for many years. Gradually, businesspeople realized the benefits of joining together as partners to share their talents, their capital, and the risks of business. The **partnership** form is many thousands of years old. However, the real development of partnerships began around the thirteenth century.

The roots of the **corporation** lie in the exploration of the New World. The need for large amounts of capital led to the sale of shares in trading companies such as the Dutch East India Company. Later, the Industrial Revolution of the nineteenth century spurred the growth of the corporate form of business. Vast sums of capital were needed to keep pace with increasing technology and mass production.

Ownership Agreements

LO1 Describe the main characteristics of a sole proprietorship, partnership, and corporation.

Proprietorships are owned by a single individual, so there are no disputes about who is ultimately responsible for deciding how profits will be distributed. Therefore, a sole proprietorship can usually be established simply by obtaining a business licence from the local government. In contrast, partnerships require that it be made clear how authority, risks, and profitability will be shared among the partners. To minimize misunderstandings and conflict, most partnerships are based on a **partnership agreement**. This is a legal document that defines the responsibilities of each partner and describes the division of income and losses. The formation and operation of a partnership may require the services of accounting professionals as well as lawyers. The distribution of profits is certainly affected by how these profits are measured. Therefore, partnerships may require the services of independent public accountants who ensure that records are kept in accordance with GAAP.

Establishing a corporation usually requires the help of legal and accounting professionals. Although individuals can file the documents necessary to start a corporation, the process involves completing a fairly complex set of forms containing technical terms. So for routine filings, legal and accounting services are usually well worth the cost.

A corporation is considered a legal entity separate and distinct from its owners. It may be incorporated federally, under the Canada Business Corporation Act, or provincially, under a province's business corporation act. Corporations created under federal laws can carry on business in every province or territory. A provincially incorporated company must obtain a licence to operate in other provinces or territories.

The first step toward incorporation is the filing of an application. This document is called the **articles of incorporation**, and contains all the information required by law. The most common information items required are (1) the name of the corporation and proposed date of incorporation; (2) the purpose of the corporation; (3) the location of the business and its expected life (which can be perpetuity, meaning "endless"); (4) provisions for share capital (the certificates that evidence an ownership interest in the corporation); and (5) the names and addresses of the members of the first board of directors (the designated group of individuals with the ultimate authority for operating the business).

Regulation

Very few laws apply specifically to proprietorships and partnerships. Corporations are a different story. The regulations applied to corporations depend on the size of the company's ownership interest. The ownership interest in a corporation is normally reflected in **share certificates**. When owners contribute assets to a corporation, they receive share certificates that describe the rights and privileges accompanying the ownership interest. Since shares are proof of ownership, owners are often called **shareholders**.

Ownership can be transferred from one individual to another by the exchange of share certificates. As long as exchanges (the buying and selling of shares) are limited to transactions between individuals, the company is defined as a **privately held corporation**. However, once a corporation reaches a certain size, it may list its shares on a stock exchange such as the Toronto Stock Exchange or the Vancouver Stock Exchange. Privately held corporations are fairly free from regulation; companies whose shares are traded on the exchanges face extensive rules and regulations.

Advantages and Disadvantages of Different Forms of Business Organization

LO1 Describe the primary characteristics of a sole proprietorship, partnership, and corporation.

The owners of proprietorships and partnerships are held *personally accountable* for the actions they take in the name of their businesses. A partner is responsible not only for his or her own actions but also for the actions that any other partner takes on behalf of the partnership. Corporations are legal entities separate from their owners. Therefore, corporations bear the responsibility for actions taken in the name of the company. These different levels of responsibility provide a unique set of advantages and disadvantages for each type of business structure as discussed below.

Double Taxation

Because the corporation is an entity in itself, its profits are taxed by provincial and federal governments. This often gives rise to *double taxation*. **Double taxation** refers to the fact that any corporate profits distributed to owners are taxed twice—first when the income appears on the corporation's income tax return, and again when the dividends appear on the individual's return. For example, assume that a corporation in a 30 percent tax bracket earns pretax income of $100,000. The corporation is required to pay income tax of $30,000 ($100,000 × 0.30). If the corporation distributes the after-tax income of $70,000 ($100,000 − $30,000) to an individual who is also taxed at a 30 percent rate, that individual has to report the dividends on her or his income tax return and has to pay $21,000 ($70,000 × 0.30) of income taxes. Thus, a total of $51,000 of tax has to be paid on $100,000 of earned income. This equates to an effective tax rate of 51 percent ($51,000 ÷ $100,000).

Partnerships and proprietorships are not separate legal entities, so they do not earn income in the names of their companies. Instead, the income generated by these businesses is considered to be earned by the owners and therefore is taxed only at the individual owner's tax rate. This is true whether the income is retained in the business or is distributed to the owners.

Regulation

Corporations are "artificial" in the sense that they are created by government authorities. These authorities may restrict corporations from engaging in certain activities. Also, authorities often require corporations to make public disclosures that are not required of proprietorships or partnerships. For example, the Ontario Securities Commission requires large publicly traded corporations to make a full set of audited financial statements available for public review. Following the rules that apply to corporations can be complicated and expensive. Clearly, government regulation is a disadvantage of the corporate form of business organization.

Limited Liability

Given the consequences of double taxation and increased regulation, you may wonder why anyone would choose the corporate form of business structure over a partnership or proprietorship. One major reason is that the corporate form limits an investor's liability when he or she obtains an ownership interest in a business venture. Because a corporation is responsible for its own actions, creditors cannot lay claim to the owners' personal assets as payment for the company's debts. Any lawsuits are filed against the corporation, not against its owners. Thus, the most that any owner of a corporation can lose is the amount that she or he has invested in the company. In contrast, the owners of proprietorships and partnerships are *personally liable* for actions taken in the names of their companies. **Limited liability** is one of the main benefits of the corporate form of business organization.

Continuity

Partnerships and proprietorships end when an owner leaves; in contrast, a corporation's life may extend well beyond the time at which any particular shareholder retires or sells his or her shares. This **continuity** allows corporations formed in the 1800s to continue to thrive in today's economy.

Transferability

Since the ownership of a corporation is divided into small units called shares, **transferability** of ownership is easily accomplished. Millions of shares representing ownership in corporations are bought and sold on the major stock exchanges daily. The firm's operations are usually unaffected by the transfers. The owners of corporations do not have to find willing buyers for their business, as do the owners of proprietorships and partnerships. For example, compare selling $1 million of Petro-Canada shares versus selling a privately owned gas station. The shares could be sold on the Toronto Stock Exchange to a variety of investors within minutes. In contrast, it could take years to find an individual who is financially capable of and interested in owning a gas station.

Management Structure

Partnerships and proprietorships are usually managed by their owners. In contrast, there are three levels of management authority in a corporation. The *owners* (shareholders) are at the highest level. These shareholders *elect* a **board of directors** to oversee the operations of the corporation. The directors then *hire* executives who manage the company. Since large corporations are able to offer high salaries and challenging career opportunities, these companies can often attract highly capable managers.

Ability to Raise Capital

Because corporations can be owned by millions of individuals, they have more opportunities to raise capital. Few individuals have the financial ability to establish a telecommunications network such as

Bell Canada or a marketing distribution system such as Wal-Mart. However, by pooling the resources of many individuals through public stock and bond offerings, corporations can generate billions of dollars. In contrast, the capital capacity of proprietorships and partnerships is bound by the financial condition of a handful of private owners. Although these types of businesses can increase their resource base by borrowing, the amount that creditors are willing to lend them is usually limited by the size of the owners' net worth. Corporations can raise large amounts of capital; this is a big reason why they can develop and market expensive new technologies more effectively than individuals operating other forms of business.

Types of Accounting Information

LO2 Distinguish between financial and managerial accounting.

Accounting information that is designed to satisfy the needs of external resource providers is called **financial accounting**. Since resource providers are viewed as entities that are separate from the business, they are often called *external users* of accounting information. Another branch of accounting, known as **managerial accounting**, provides information that is useful in operating a business. Since managers and employees are responsible for operating the business, they are commonly called *internal users* of accounting information. The information needs of these two user groups often overlap. For example, both external and internal users are interested in how much income a business earns. However, managerial accounting information is usually more detailed than financial information. An investor wants to know whether Wendy's or Burger King produces more income relative to risk; in contrast, a regional manager of Wendy's wants to know which of the restaurants under her control produces the highest amount of earnings. Also, a manager is interested in many nonfinancial measures, such as the number of employees needed to operate a restaurant, the number of parking spaces needed, and the times at which customer demand is highest, as well as the measures of cleanliness and customer satisfaction.

Measurement Rules

LO3 Comprehend the need for measurement rules (GAAP).

Accountants have established rules that businesspeople can apply to ensure that they are talking about the same thing. Suppose a store sells a CD player in December to a customer who agrees to pay for it in January. Should the storeowner recognize the sale in December or in January? Recognition when the sale occurred in December is an *accrual accounting* rule. A *cash accounting* rule requires recognition when cash is collected in January. Whether the storeowner uses the accrual or the cash rule is not important as long as a third rule is established that requires the owner to disclose which method he uses. Even when different reporting rules are used, clear communication can be established through full and fair disclosure.

Communication would be easier if only one measurement method were used to report each type of business activity. However, world economies have not yet evolved to allow this.

A well-educated businessperson must be able to understand and interpret accounting information that has been prepared using a variety of measurement rules. The rules of measurement for accounting used in Canada are called **generally accepted accounting principles (GAAP)**. This textbook introduces you to these principles so that you will be able to understand business activity as it is presented in accounting reports.

Reporting Entities

We begin our study of accounting by discussing the reports that accountants prepare to summarize business activities. First, you must understand that accounting reports summarize the activities of particular organizations or individuals, known as **reporting entities**. Each entity is treated as a separate reporting unit. For example, a business is a reporting entity that is separate from its owners and creditors. Furthermore, a business, the person who owns the business, and a bank that loans money to the business are three separate reporting entities. In this case, accountants prepare a separate set of reports to describe the economic activities of each of the three entities. Thus, the first step in understanding accounting reports is to identify the reporting entity.

Our study is directed from the perspective of a business entity. This point of view likely requires you to make a mental adjustment in your view of the world. You are accustomed to thinking from a customer perspective. For example, as a customer you think that a sales discount is a great thing. The view is different for the business granting the discount. A sales discount means that the item did not sell at the expected price. To move the item, the business has had to settle for less money than it expected to make. Therefore, the sales discount is not a good thing. To understand accounting, it will be helpful for you to retrain yourself to consider the business rather than the consumer.

Check Yourself 1.1

In a recent business transaction, land was exchanged for cash. Did the amount of cash increase or decrease?

Answer The answer depends on the reporting entity to which the question pertains. One entity sold land. The other entity bought land. For the entity that sold land, cash increased. For the entity that bought land, cash decreased.

Financial Statements[1]

LO4 Identify, describe, and prepare the four basic financial statements.

Business entities communicate information to the public through a process known as *financial reporting*. The central feature of external financial reporting is a set of **financial statements**. Therefore, financial statements are the principal means for communicating economic information to individuals and institutions outside the reporting enterprise. The four general-purpose financial statements are the (1) income statement, (2) statement of equity, (3) balance sheet, and (4) cash flow statement.

The statements can have other names. For example, the income statement can be called a *statement of operations* or an *earnings statement*. Similarly, alternative names exist for the other statements. The balance sheet is also known as a *statement of financial position*. The statement of equity can also be called a *capital statement* or *statement of shareholders' equity*.[2]

[1] This text book will focus on the corporate form of business. Proprietorships and partnerships will be covered in more detail in Chapter 11.

[2] Many companies in Canada use the *statement of retained earnings* and disclose changes in ownership through the notes to the financial statements. We have chosen to combine these items in one statement referred to as the *statement of shareholders' equity*. This should help you follow the changes that affect the shareholders' equity section of the balance sheet. Note that Bombardier, Inc., included in Appendix B, uses the *statement of shareholders' equity*, not the *statement of retained earnings*.

Elements of Financial Statements

LO5 Identify the major elements of financial statements.

The items reported in financial statements are organized into classes or categories known as **elements**. The following elements are discussed in this chapter: assets, liabilities, equity, revenues, and expenses. Gains and losses will be discussed in a later chapter. In practice, many different titles are used to identify the elements of financial statements. For example, *net income*, *net earnings*, and *net profit* are used interchangeably to describe the same element. Similarly, *contributed capital* can be called *common shares*, *owner's capital*, or *partners' equity*. Furthermore, *dividends*, *withdrawals*, and *distributions* all describe the transfer of assets from a business to its owners. Think of accounting as a language. Be prepared for the fact that different terms can be used to describe the same business event.

The elements represent broad classifications as opposed to specific items. In other words, cash, equipment, buildings, and land are particular economic resources. They should not be identified as elements; rather, they represent specific items or subclassifications of the element known as *assets*. The subclassifications of the elements are often called **accounts**. The accounts appear in the financial statements under the broader classifications that have been identified as elements. For example, the balance sheet contains the element assets, which includes accounts that describe specific items such as cash, inventory, equipment, and land.

How many accounts does a business use? The number depends on the company's information-gathering objectives. Companies create and use the number of accounts that they require to store the information they need in order to make decisions. Some managers want very detailed information; others want highly summarized data. Thus, the number of accounts used in an accounting system varies from company to company.

Elements of the Accounting Equation

LO6 Describe the relationships expressed in the accounting equation.

The resources that a business uses to produce earnings are called **assets**. Assets include land, buildings, equipment, materials, and supplies. Generally accepted accounting principles require assets to be recognized in financial statements only when they result from historical events. For example, if a business owns a truck that was purchased in a past transaction, the truck is an asset of the business. However, a truck that a business *plans* to purchase in the future is not considered an asset of that business, no matter how certain the future purchase might be.

The assets of a business belong to the resource providers, who are said to have **claims** on the assets. The relationship between the assets and the claims on those assets is known as the **accounting equation**:

$$\text{Assets} = \text{Claims}$$

The creditors have first claim on the assets; the *owners* are said to have a **residual interest**. This means that in the case of a business liquidation, the owners receive the assets that are left after the debts to creditors have been paid. The equation shows the relationship among the assets, creditors' claims (called **liabilities**), and owners' claims (called **equity**).

$$\text{Assets} = \frac{\text{Claims}}{\text{Liabilities} + \text{Equity}}$$

Liabilities can also be viewed as *obligations of the enterprise*. When the obligations are settled in the future, the business probably will have to use some of its assets (pay off its debts with cash), provide services to its creditors (work off its debts), or accept other obligations (trade short-term debt for long-term debt).

Algebraically, total assets minus total liabilities equals the *equity*. Since equity equals the net difference between the assets and the liabilities, it is also called **net assets**. Therefore, *equity*, *net assets*, and *residual interest* are synonyms for the ownership interest in the business. To illustrate, assume that Hagan Company has assets of $500, liabilities of $200, and equity of $300. These amounts appear in the accounting equation as follows:

$$\text{Assets} = \frac{\text{Claims}}{\text{Liabilities} + \text{Equity}}$$

$$\$500 = \$200 + \$300$$

Given the equality expressed in the accounting equation, the equity (net assets or residual interest) can be computed as follows:

$$\text{Assets} - \text{Liabilities} = \text{Equity}$$
$$\$500 - \$200 = \$300$$

Asset Sources

The claims side of the accounting equation (liabilities plus equity) can be viewed as a list of the sources of assets. For example, when a bank loans assets (cash) to a business, it establishes a claim for the return of those assets at some future date. In other words, the bank has a claim on the assets because it provided them to the business. As a result, liabilities can sometimes be viewed as sources of assets.

Equity can also be viewed as a source of assets. In fact, equity is composed of two distinct sources of assets. First, a business might acquire assets from its owners. To acknowledge the receipt of assets from owners, businesses often issue certificates known as **common shares**. Expanding this terminology, the owners of the business are often called *shareholders*, and the ownership interest in the business is called **shareholders' equity**. Second, a business might obtain assets through its earnings activities (the business acquires assets by working for them). Assets that have been earned by the business can be either distributed to the owners or kept in the business. The portion of assets that have been provided by earnings activities is called **retained earnings**. An accounting equation that depicts the three sources of assets (liabilities, common shares, and retained earnings) follows:

$$\text{Assets} = \text{Sources or Claims}$$
$$\text{Assets} = \text{Liabilities} + \text{Common Shares} + \text{Retained Earnings}$$

The combination of common shares and retained earnings is called shareholders' equity. Therefore, the accounting equation also can be written as follows:

$$\text{Assets} = \text{Liabilities} + \text{Shareholders' Equity}$$
$$\text{Assets} = \text{Liabilities} + \text{Common Shares} + \text{Retained Earnings}$$

Introduction to Financial Statements

LO4 Identify, describe, and prepare the four basic financial statements.

Recall that accountants communicate information through four financial statements: a balance sheet, an income statement, a cash flow statement, and a statement of shareholders' equity. In the following section we briefly explain the balance sheet, income statement, and cash flow statement. Later in this chapter we discuss the statement of equity.

Balance Sheet

The *balance sheet* draws its name from the *accounting equation*; it lists the assets of a business and the corresponding claims on those assets. The assets must balance with (be equal to) the sources of those assets. Balance sheets are normally divided into two sections. The first section lists the company's assets, and the second shows the sources of those assets (liabilities and shareholders' equity).

Try to create a balance sheet that describes your personal financial condition. List your assets first and then your liabilities. Determine the amount of your equity by subtracting your liabilities from your assets.

Answer Answers for this exercise will vary depending on each student's particular assets and liabilities. Some common types of personal assets include automobiles, computers, stereos, TVs, phones, CD players, and clothes. Common types of liabilities include car loans, mortgages, and credit card debt. The difference between the assets and the liabilities is the equity.

Income Statement

Businesses use assets to generate increased quantities of other assets. The **income statement** measures the difference between the asset increases and the asset decreases associated with operating a business.[3] Asset increases resulting from operating activities are called **revenues**. Asset decreases incurred to generate revenues are called **expenses**. If revenues are greater than expenses, the difference between these two elements is called **net income** (or *profit* or *earnings*). If expenses exceed the revenues, the difference is referred to as a **net loss**. Net income indicates that a company has succeeded in earning more assets than it used. A net loss shows that a business used more assets than it earned. Note that assets transferred from a business to its owners are called **dividends**. Cash dividends paid to shareholders are not expenses because the asset decrease (cash) was not incurred to generate revenue. Therefore, dividends are not shown on the income statement.

Mahoney, Inc., was started when it issued common shares to its owners for $300,000. In its first year of operation, Mahoney received $523,000 in cash for providing services to customers. Mahoney paid $233,000 cash to employees and cash advertising costs of $102,000. Other cash operating expenses amounted to $124,000. Finally, Mahoney paid a $25,000 cash dividend to its shareholders. What amount of net income would Mahoney report on its earnings statement for the year?

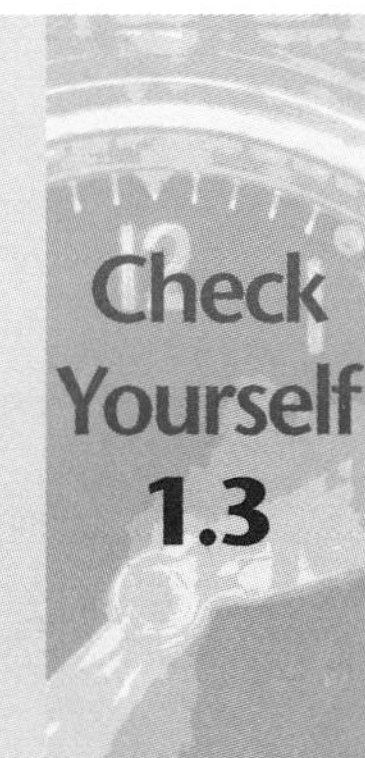

Answer Mahoney would report net income of $64,000 ($523,000 revenue − $233,000 salary expense − $102,000 advertising expense − $124,000 other operating expenses). The cash received from issuing shares is not revenue because it did not result from earnings activities. In other words, the business did not work (perform services) for this money. Likewise, the cash dividends are not expenses because they were not paid for the purpose of generating revenue. Instead, cash dividends (which decrease cash) represent a transfer of wealth to the owners.

Cash Flow Statement

The **cash flow statement** explains how a company obtained and used *cash* during the accounting period (usually one year). The sources of cash are called *cash inflows*, and the uses are known as *cash outflows*. The statement classifies cash receipts (inflows) and payments (outflows) into three categories: financing activities, investing activities, and operating activities.

Businesses normally start with an idea. For example, suppose that you notice a shortage of apartment rental space and decide to build an apartment complex. Implementing the idea usually requires cash. In this case, you would need cash to build the apartments. The efforts to acquire cash to start a business are called **financing activities**. Specifically, financing activities include obtaining cash from (cash inflows) or paying cash to (cash outflows) owners, including dividends. Also, borrowing cash from (cash inflows) or repaying principal to (cash outflows) creditors is shown in the financing activities section. Note, however, that interest paid to creditors is treated as an expense and so is included in the operating activities section of the cash flow statement.

Once you have obtained cash from financing activities, you invest it in the productive assets that will be used to operate the business. The cash paid for (cash outflows) productive assets and the cash received from (cash inflows) the sale of productive assets are shown in the **investing activities** section of the cash flow statement. **Productive assets** are sometimes called *long-term assets* because they are normally used for more than one accounting period. For example, cash outflows to purchase land and cash inflows from selling a building are reported in the investing activities section of the cash flow statement. In contrast, cash spent to purchase supplies goes in the operating activities section because the supplies represent short-term assets that are generally used within a single accounting period.

[3] This description of the income statement is expanded in subsequent chapters as additional relationships among the elements of the financial statement are introduced.

Exhibit 1–1 *Cash Flow Statement Classification Scheme*

Cash Flows from Operating Activities
Cash receipts (inflows) from revenue (including interest)
Cash payments (outflows) for expenses (including interest)

Cash Flows from Investing Activities
Cash receipts (inflows) from the sale of long-term assets
Cash payments (outflows) for the purchase of long-term assets

Cash Flows from Financing Activities
Cash receipts (inflows) from borrowed funds
Cash receipts (inflows) from the issue of common shares
Cash payments (outflows) to repay borrowed funds
Cash payments (outflows) for dividends

Once the productive assets have been acquired and put into place, you begin to operate the business. The cash received from revenue (cash inflows) and the cash paid for expenses (cash outflows) are reported in the **operating activities** section of the cash flow statement.

The main cash inflows and outflows associated with each type of business activity are shown in Exhibit 1–1. The exhibit and the preceding discussion are limited to the business events discussed in this chapter. As later chapters introduce new events, their effects on the cash flow statement will be added to the exhibit.

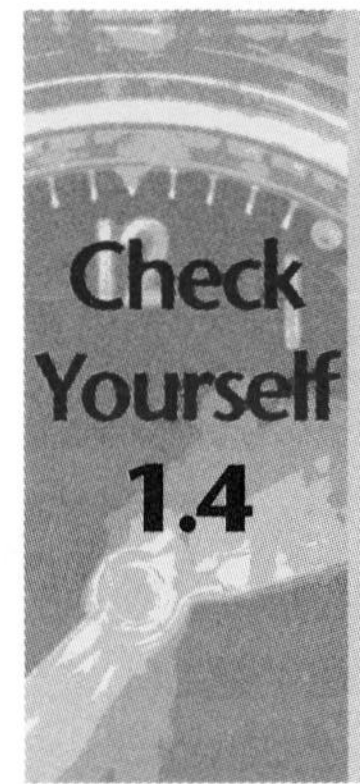

Classify each of the following cash flows as an operating, investing, or financing activity.

1. Cash acquired from owners.
2. Cash borrowed from creditors.
3. Cash paid to purchase land.
4. Cash earned as revenue.
5. Cash paid for salary expenses.
6. Cash paid for dividends.
7. Cash paid for interest.

Answer (1) financing activity; (2) financing activity; (3) investing activity; (4) operating activity; (5) operating activity; (6) financing activity; (7) operating activity.

Accounting Equation Summary

The accounting equation is the basis of accounting. It is used to create the financial statements for an entity as follows:

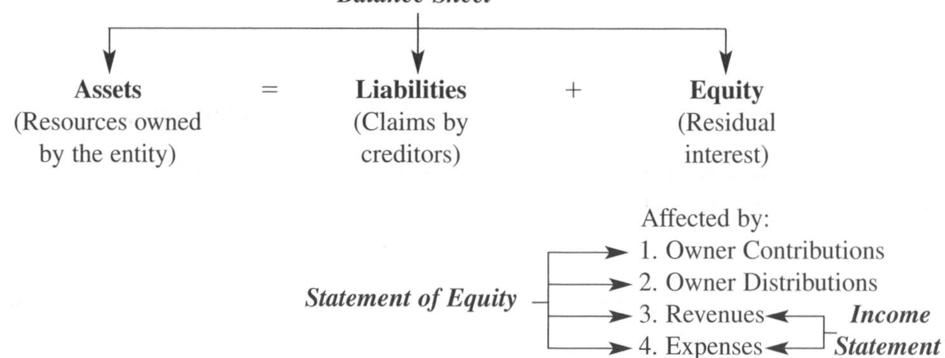

As you can see, the *income statement* and the *statement of equity* are simply substatements of the *balance sheet*. They provide specific details relating to the events that affected the equity section of the balance sheet.

Horizontal Statements Model

LO7 Record business events in a financial statements model.

The **horizontal statements model** is so named because it arranges financial statement information horizontally across a single page of paper. It presents the balance sheet first, followed by the income statement, and then the cash flow statement. An example of a financial statements model follows. Note that the elements have been divided into subclassifications known as *accounts*. For example, the element *assets* has been divided into two *accounts* (Cash and Land). Recall that the number of accounts a company uses depends on the nature of its business and the level of detail that management needs to operate the business. For example, Sears Canada would have a Cost of Goods Sold account, but SunLife Insurance would not. This is so because Sears sells goods (merchandise), but SunLife does not.

Balance Sheet					Income Statement	Cash Flow Statement
Assets	=	Liab.	+	Shareholders' Equity		
Cash + Land	=	N. Pay	+	C. Sh. + Ret. Ear.	Rev. − Exp. = Net Inc.	

Rustic Camp Sites Inc. Illustration: Events for 2004

An **accounting event** is an economic occurrence that causes changes in an enterprise's assets, liabilities, and/or equity. Events can be internal, such as using raw materials or equipment to produce goods or services. Events can also be external, such as an exchange of goods or services with another company. A **transaction** is a particular type of event that involves the transfer of something of value between two entities. Transactions include acquiring assets from owners, borrowing funds from creditors, and purchasing or selling goods and services. In the next section we explain how several different types of accounting events affect a company's financial statements.

Asset Source Transactions

Businesses obtain assets in three main ways: they acquire assets from owners, they borrow them from creditors, and they earn them through their operations. Asset source transactions increase total assets and total claims.

Event 1

Rustic Camp Sites Inc. (RCS) is formed on January 1, 2004, when it acquires $120,000 cash from the issue of common shares.

When RCS issued shares, it received cash and gave the investors share certificates as receipts. Since this transaction provided $120,000 of assets (Cash) to the enterprise, it is an **asset source transaction**. It increases the business's assets (Cash account) and its shareholders' equity (Common Shares account). Notice that the business did not work (perform earnings activities) for this money, but acquired the money by issuing shares. Since the business did not work for the money, this transaction does not affect the income statement. The cash inflow resulted from a financing activity (acquisition from owners). In the Cash Flow Statement column, activity classifications are identified with a simple two-letter designation: cash flow from operating activities with OA; investing activities with IA; and financing activities with FA. The designation "NA" indicates that an account is not affected by an event. These effects are shown in the following financial statements model:

Balance Sheet									Income Statement					Cash Flow Statement
Assets			=	Liab.	+	Shareholders' Equity								
Cash	+	Land	=	N. Pay	+	C. Sh.	+	Ret. Ear.	Rev.	−	Exp.	=	Net Inc.	
120,000	+	NA	=	NA	+	120,000	+	NA	NA	−	NA	=	NA	120,000 FA

Notice that this single transaction is recorded in the balance sheet twice, once as an asset (Cash) and a second time as the source of that asset (Common Shares). All later transactions will be recorded at least twice in the balance sheet accounts. The **double-entry bookkeeping** system derives its name from this practice.

Event 2 RCS acquires an additional $400,000 of assets by borrowing cash from creditors.

This transaction would also be classified as an asset source transaction. It acts to increase assets (Cash) and liability claims (Notes Payable). The account title Notes Payable derives its name from the fact that the borrower is normally required to issue a promissory note to the creditors (a bank). A promissory note, among other things, describes the amount of interest that will be charged and the length of time for which the money will be borrowed. The event did not result from operating the business (performing work), so the income statement is not affected. The event provided a cash inflow from financing activities. These effects on the financial statements follow:

Balance Sheet									Income Statement					Cash Flow Statement
Assets			=	Liab.	+	Shareholders' Equity								
Cash	+	Land	=	N. Pay	+	C. Sh.	+	Ret. Ear.	Rev.	−	Exp.	=	Net Inc.	
400,000	+	NA	=	400,000	+	NA	+	NA	NA	−	NA	=	NA	400,000 FA

Asset Exchange Transactions

Businesses often trade one asset for another. In this case, the amount of one asset decreases and the amount of another asset increases. Total assets are not affected by asset exchange transactions. The following event introduces asset exchange transactions.

Event 3 RCS pays $500,000 cash to purchase land.

This asset exchange transaction reduces the asset account Cash and increases the asset account Land. The amount of total assets is not affected. An asset exchange transaction simply notes the change in the makeup of assets. In this case, the company traded cash for land. Therefore, the amount of cash decreased by $500,000, and the amount of land increased by the same amount. The income statement is not affected because the business did not engage in earnings activities. However, the cash flow statement shows a $500,000 cash outflow from investing activities. Note that we have followed the standard of using parentheses to show decreases in account balances and cash outflows.

Balance Sheet									Income Statement					Cash Flow Statement
Assets			=	Liab.	+	Shareholders' Equity								
Cash	+	Land	=	N. Pay	+	C. Sh.	+	Ret. Ear.	Rev.	−	Exp.	=	Net Inc.	
(500,000)	+	500,000	=	NA	+	NA	1	NA	NA	−	NA	=	NA	(500,000) IA

Another Asset Source Transaction

Event 4 RCS obtains $85,000 cash by leasing campsites to customers.

An *increase in assets* obtained from earnings activities (providing customers with goods and services) is called *revenue*. Revenue transactions are also viewed as *asset source transactions*. In this case, the asset account, Cash, increases. This increase is balanced by an increase in the retained earnings section of shareholders' equity (revenue increases the amount of earnings that can be retained in the business). The income statement is affected because the increase in assets resulted from earnings activities. The cash flow statement shows an $85,000 inflow from operating activities. The effects of this transaction on the financial statements follow:

Balance Sheet									Income Statement					Cash Flow Statement
Assets			=	Liab.	+	Shareholders' Equity								
Cash	+	Land	=	N. Pay	+	C. Sh.	+	Ret. Ear.	Rev.	−	Exp.	=	Net Inc.	
85,000	+	NA	=	NA	+	NA	+	85,000	85,000	−	NA	=	85,000	85,000 OA

Asset Use Transactions

Businesses use assets for many purposes. For example, they can use assets to pay off liabilities. Similarly, businesses can transfer assets to the owners. Businesses also can use assets to generate earnings. All asset use transactions result in decreases in the total amount of assets and the total amount of claims on assets (liabilities or shareholders' equity).

RCS paid $50,000 cash for operating expenses such as salaries, rent, and interest. (Separate accounts could be established for each type of expense. However, RCS's management team does not desire to have this level of detail. Remember, the number of accounts that a business uses depends on the level of information that is needed to make decisions.) **Event 5**

Normally, a business consumes some of its assets in the process of trying to obtain other assets. The assets acquired by operating activities are called *revenues*; the assets used in generating the revenues are called *expenses*. Since the owners bear the ultimate risk and reap the rewards of operating the business, revenues increase shareholders' equity (Retained Earnings), and expenses decrease retained earnings. In this case, the asset account, Cash, decreases. This decrease is balanced by a decrease in the retained earnings section of shareholders' equity (expenses decrease the amount of earnings that can be retained in the business). Since the assets were used to generate earnings, the income statement reflects an increase in expenses and a decrease in net income. The cash flow statement shows a cash outflow from operating activities. The effect of this asset use transaction on the financial statements is as follows:

Balance Sheet									Income Statement					Cash Flow Statement
Assets			=	Liab.	+	Shareholders' Equity								
Cash	+	Land	=	N. Pay	+	C. Sh.	+	Ret. Ear.	Rev.	−	Exp.	=	Net Inc.	
(50,000)	+	NA	=	NA	+	NA	+	(50,000)	NA	−	50,000	=	(50,000)	(50,000) OA

The minus sign in front of the Expenses column does not mean that expenses decreased. Indeed, in this case, expenses increased by $50,000. Instead, the minus sign points out that expenses are subtracted from revenues to find out the amount of net income.

RCS pays a $4,000 cash dividend to its owners. **Event 6**

The enterprise's *net assets* have increased by $35,000 ($85,000 revenue – $50,000 expense) as a result of its earnings activities. Since the risks and rewards of operating a business rest with its owners, the owners are entitled to the assets that are created through earnings activities. The enterprise can keep the additional assets in the business, or it can transfer them to the owners. If the business chooses to transfer some or all of the earned assets to the owners, the transfer is called a *dividend*. Since assets given to owners are not used for creating revenue, the income statement is not affected. In other words, *dividends are wealth transfers, not expenses*. The cash outflow appears in the financing activities section of the cash flow statement. The effect on the financial statements is as follows:

Balance Sheet									Income Statement					Cash Flow Statement
Assets			=	Liab.	+	Shareholders' Equity								
Cash	+	Land	=	N. Pay	+	C. Sh.	+	Ret. Ear.	Rev.	−	Exp.	=	Net Inc.	
(4,000)	+	NA	=	NA	+	NA	+	(4,000)	NA	−	NA	=	NA	(4,000) FA

A dividend and an expense have the same effect on the accounting equation. Both cause a decrease in assets and a matching decrease in shareholders' equity (Retained Earnings). The difference between expenses and dividends arises from the reason for the decline in assets. An *expense* is recognized when assets decline because of a firm's efforts to earn revenue. A *dividend* occurs when assets decline because of transfers of wealth from the business to its owners. In summary, expenses are incurred to produce revenue, and dividends are wealth transfers made to satisfy the owners.

Types of Transactions

LO8 Classify business events as asset source, use, or exchange transactions.

The transactions just described have been classified into one of three categories: (1) asset source transactions, (2) asset exchange transactions, and (3) asset use transactions. A fourth category, claims exchange transactions, will be introduced in a later chapter. As noted earlier, *asset source transactions result in an increase in the total amount of assets and an increase in the total amount of claims*. In its first year of operation, RCS received assets from three sources. First, it acquired assets from owners (Event 1). Next, RCS borrowed assets (Event 2). Finally, it obtained assets through earnings activities (Event 4). *Asset exchange transactions result in a decrease in one asset account and an increase in another asset account. The total amount of assets is not affected by asset exchange transactions.* RCS experienced one asset exchange transaction when it used cash to purchase land (Event 3). *Asset use transactions cause the amount of total assets and total claims to decrease.* RCS used assets to pay expenses (Event 5) and to pay dividends (Event 6). We encourage you to practise classifying transactions into one of the four categories. Businesses engage in thousands of transactions every day. It is far better to learn how to classify the transactions into meaningful categories than it is to attempt to memorize the effects of thousands of transactions.

Summary of Transactions

LO9 Recording events in ledger accounts.

We are using the horizontal statements model for instructional purposes. It is very useful for showing how accounting events affect financial statements. However, this model does *not* reflect the presentation formats found in accounting practice. For example, although a full set of four financial statements is normally presented in published financial statements, the horizontal model shows only a partial set of statements.

For your review of the RCS illustration, the six business events the company experienced in 2004 are summarized here:

1. RCS acquired $120,000 cash from the owners.
2. RCS borrowed $400,000 cash.
3. RCS paid cash to purchase $500,000 worth of land.
4. RCS earned $85,000 of cash revenue.
5. RCS paid $50,000 for cash expenses.
6. RCS paid a $4,000 cash dividend to the owners.

In practice, accountants record transactions in accounts. The full collection of accounts is called the **general ledger**. The information in the ledger accounts is used to prepare the financial statements. The general ledger accounts that contain the transaction data for RCS's 2004 accounting period are shown in Exhibit 1–2. The accounts have been organized under the accounting equation. To promote communication, we follow this practice throughout the text. Because of space limitations the revenue, expense, and dividend accounts are shown in the Retained Earnings column. The titles of these accounts are shown immediately to the right of the monetary amounts that appear in the Retained Earnings column.

Exhibit 1–2 *General Ledger Accounts Organized under the Accounting Equation*

	Assets		=	Liabilities	+	Shareholders' Equity		
Event No.	**Cash**	**+ Land**	**=**	**Notes Payable**	**+**	**Common Shares**	**+ Retained Earnings**	**Other Account Titles**
Bal.	$ 0	$ 0		$ 0		$ 0	$ 0	
1	120,000					120,000		
2	400,000			400,000				
3	(500,000)	500,000						
4	85,000						85,000	Revenue
5	(50,000)						(50,000)	Expense
6	(4,000)						(4,000)	Dividend
	$51,000	$500,000		$400,000		$120,000	$31,000	

LO4 Identify, describe, and prepare the four basic financial statements.

Elements Presented in Financial Statements

The *income statement*, *statement of shareholders' equity* (or *statement of retained earnings*), and *cash flow statement* provide unique perspectives on the performance of the enterprise *during some span of time*, which is called the *accounting period*. The *balance sheet* provides information about the financial condition of the enterprise *at a particular point in time*.

Exhibit 1–3

RUSTIC CAMP SITES INC.
Income Statement
For the Year Ended December 31, 2004

Revenue *(asset increases)*	$85,000
Operating Expenses *(asset decreases)*	(50,000)
Net Income *(change in net assets)*	$35,000

Income Statement

The income statement for RCS is shown in Exhibit 1–3. Observe the phrase *For the Year Ended December 31, 2004*, in the heading of the income statement. Income is measured over a span of time called the **accounting period**. The length of the accounting period is usually one year, but is not always required. Indeed, income can be measured weekly, monthly, quarterly, semiannually, or over any other time period that the users deem appropriate in relation to their needs for information.

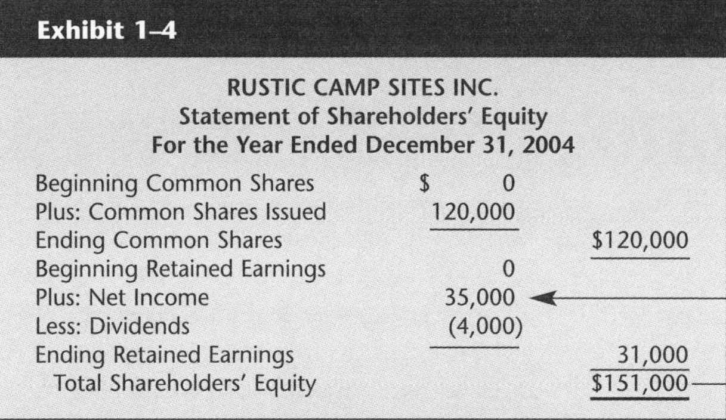

Exhibit 1–4

RUSTIC CAMP SITES INC.
Statement of Shareholders' Equity
For the Year Ended December 31, 2004

Beginning Common Shares	$ 0	
Plus: Common Shares Issued	120,000	
Ending Common Shares		$120,000
Beginning Retained Earnings	0	
Plus: Net Income	35,000	
Less: Dividends	(4,000)	
Ending Retained Earnings		31,000
Total Shareholders' Equity		$151,000

Statement of Shareholders' Equity

The **statement of shareholders' equity** is used to explain the effects of transactions on shareholders' equity during the accounting period. It includes the beginning and ending balances for the amount of common shares and reflects any new shares issued during the accounting period. It also shows the portion of the net earnings retained in the business. Exhibit 1–4 shows the statement of shareholders' equity for RCS. This statement is also dated with the phrase *For the Year Ended December 31, 2004*, because it describes what happened to shareholders' equity over that span of time.

Exhibit 1–5

RUSTIC CAMP SITES INC.
Balance Sheet
December 31, 2004

Assets		
Cash	$ 51,000	
Land	500,000	
Total Assets		$551,000
Liabilities		
Notes Payable		$400,000
Shareholders' Equity		
Common Shares	120,000	
Retained Earnings	31,000	
Total Shareholders' Equity		151,000
Total Liabilities and Shareholders' Equity		$551,000

Balance Sheet

The statement that lists the assets and the corresponding claims on those assets is called the **balance sheet**. Exhibit 1–5 shows the balance sheet for RCS. The total claims (liabilities plus shareholders' equity) equal the total assets. Note also the order of the assets in the balance sheet. Cash appears first, followed by the Land account. Assets are displayed in the balance sheet according to their level of **liquidity**; that is, assets are listed in order of how rapidly they can be converted to cash. Finally, note that the balance sheet is dated *December 31, 2004*. This indicates that it describes the company's financial condition at that particular point in time.

Exhibit 1–6

RUSTIC CAMP SITES INC. Cash Flow Statement For the Year Ended December 31, 2004		
Cash Flows from Operating Activities		
Cash Receipts from Revenue	$ 85,000	
Cash Payments for Expenses	(50,000)	
Net Cash Flow from Operating Activities		$ 35,000
Cash Flows from Investing Activities		
Cash Payments to Purchase Land		(500,000)
Cash Flows from Financing Activities		
Cash Receipts from Borrowed Funds	400,000	
Cash Receipts from Issue of Common Shares	120,000	
Cash Payments for Dividends	(4,000)	
Net Cash Flow from Financing Activities		516,000
Net Increase in Cash		51,000
Plus: Beginning Cash Balance		0
Ending Cash Balance		$ 51,000

Cash Flow Statement

Exhibit 1–6 shows the cash flow statement for RCS. The cash flow statement explains the change between the beginning and ending cash balances during the accounting period. In this case, the amount of cash increased by $51,000. The beginning balance in the Cash account was zero; adding the $51,000 increase results in a $51,000 ending balance. The $51,000 ending balance equals the amount of cash shown on the December 31 year-end balance sheet. The statement of cash flows is dated with the phrase *For the Year Ended December 31, 2004*, because it describes what happened to cash over that span of time.

Closing Process

LO10 Identify the steps in the accounting cycle, including the closing process.

Accounting is a cyclical activity. This means that the recognition of business activities is divided into time periods called *cycles,* which follow one after the other. The process continues for as long as the accounting entity exists. The information for balance sheet items (assets, liabilities, common shares, and retained earnings) is cumulative. Thus, last period's ending balances become next period's beginning balances. Since RCS had $551,000 of assets at the end of 2004, it begins the 2005 cycle with $551,000 of assets. Because of their continuing nature, balance sheet accounts are sometimes called **permanent accounts**.

In contrast, revenue, expense, and dividend accounts are **temporary accounts** that are used to collect information about a single cycle (one accounting period only). Because they are temporary, they are referred to as **nominal accounts**. After the amounts in the nominal accounts (revenues, expenses, and dividends) are used to prepare the financial statements, the account balances are then transferred to the retained earnings account. The process of removing the balances from the revenue, expense, and dividend accounts is called **closing the accounts**, or **closing**. Since the balances in the nominal accounts are removed at the end of each accounting period, these accounts always have a zero balance at the beginning of each accounting period. In contrast, the Retained Earnings account is a summary account that contains cumulative data regarding revenues, expenses, and dividends that have existed from the company's inception. Accordingly, the 2004 ending balance in the Retained Earnings account becomes the 2005 beginning balance for that account.

Rustic Camp Sites Inc.: Events for Second Cycle

Next we demonstrate the cyclical nature of the accounting process. Assume that RCS experienced the following events during its second accounting period. Then, the second cycle is the 2005 calendar year. Assume that all transactions involve the payment or receipt of cash.

1. RCS acquired $20,000 cash by issuing common shares.
2. RCS provided services to customers and received $96,000.
3. RCS paid $12,000 for salaries expenses.
4. RCS paid a $5,000 cash dividend to the owners.
5. RCS paid the bank $70,000 to reduce its note payable liability.
6. RCS paid $40,000 for other operating expenses.

The effects of these events are shown in the general ledger accounts in Exhibit 1–7. The names of the nominal accounts are shown to the right of the monetary amounts that appear in the Retained Earnings column.

Exhibit 1–7 *General Ledger Accounts for RCS*

	Assets			=	Liabilities	+	Shareholders' Equity			
Event No.	Cash	+	Land	=	Notes Payable	+	Common Shares	+	Retained Earnings	Other Account Titles
	$51,000		$500,000		$400,000		$120,000		$31,000	
1	20,000						20,000			
2	96,000								96,000	Revenue
3	(12,000)								(12,000)	Salary Exp.
4	(5,000)								(5,000)	Dividend
5	(70,000)				(70,000)					
6	(40,000)								(40,000)	Other Operating Exp.
	$40,000	+	$500,000	=	$330,000	+	$140,000	+	$70,000	

Financial Statements for 2005

The 2005 income statement for RCS is shown in Exhibit 1–8. Notice that the amounts of revenue and expense shown on the income statement apply only to 2005. Remember that revenue and expense items relating to 2004 have been transferred to the Retained Earnings account through the closing process. Accordingly, the beginning balances in these accounts were zero. In contrast, the amounts in the balance sheet accounts contain cumulative information. For example, the ending Cash balance ($40,000) was determined by adding the current period changes (2005 data) to the beginning Cash balance.

Exhibit 1–8

RUSTIC CAMP SITES INC. Income Statement For the Year Ended December 31, 2005	
Revenue *(asset increase)*	$96,000
Salary Expense *(asset decrease)*	(12,000)
Other Operating Expenses *(asset decrease)*	(40,000)
Net Income *(change in net assets)*	$44,000

The 2005 statement of shareholders' equity is shown in Exhibit 1–9. This period's net income of $44,000 and the $5,000 dividend were combined with the $31,000 beginning Retained Earnings account balance, resulting in an ending Retained Earnings balance of $70,000. Total shareholders' equity at the end of the period amounted to $210,000 ($140,000 in common shares + $70,000 retained earnings).

Exhibit 1–9

RUSTIC CAMP SITES INC.
Statement of Shareholders' Equity
For the Year Ended December 31, 2005

Beginning Common Shares	$120,000	
Plus: Common Shares Issued	20,000	
Ending Common Shares		$140,000
Beginning Retained Earnings	31,000	
Plus: Net Income	44,000	
Less: Dividends	(5,000)	
Ending Retained Earnings		70,000
Total Shareholders' Equity		$210,000

Exhibit 1–10

RUSTIC CAMP SITES INC.
Balance Sheet
December 31, 2005

Assets		
Cash	$ 40,000	
Land	500,000	
Total Assets		$540,000
Liabilities		
Notes Payable		$330,000
Shareholders' Equity		
Common Shares	$140,000	
Retained Earnings	70,000	
Total Shareholders' Equity		210,000
Total Liabilities and Shareholders' Equity		$540,000

Exhibit 1–11

RUSTIC CAMP SITES INC.
Cash Flow Statement
For the Year Ended December 31, 2005

Cash Flows from Operating Activities		
Cash Receipts from Revenue	$ 96,000	
Cash Payments for Expenses	(52,000)	
Net Cash Flow from Operating Activities		$ 44,000
Cash Flows from Investing Activities		0
Cash Flows from Financing Activities		
Cash Paid to Reduce Debt	(70,000)	
Cash Receipts from Share Issue	20,000	
Cash Payments for Dividends	(5,000)	
Net Cash Flow from Financing Activities		(55,000)
Net Decrease in Cash		(11,000)
Plus: Beginning Cash Balance		51,000
Ending Cash Balance		$ 40,000

The 2005 balance sheet is shown in Exhibit 1–10. This balance sheet shows that the company has $540,000 of assets, of which $330,000 was borrowed from creditors, $140,000 was acquired from owners, and $70,000 was earned and retained in the business.

The 2005 cash flow statement is shown in Exhibit 1–11. The operating activities section shows that $96,000 cash was received from revenue and $52,000 was paid for expenses. The net result was a $44,000 ($96,000 − $52,000) net cash inflow from operating activities. There were no investing activities. The financing activities section describes a $70,000 cash outflow to reduce debt, a $20,000 inflow from the issue of shares, and a $5,000 cash outflow for dividends paid to the owners. Accordingly, the net cash outflow for financing activities amounted to a $55,000 decrease [($70,000) + $20,000 + ($5,000)]. As a result, the net change in cash during 2005 was a decrease of $11,000 [$44,000 + ($55,000)]. The beginning cash balance of $51,000 minus the 2005 net decrease of $11,000 explains the ending cash balance of $40,000.

Stages of an Accounting Cycle

The complete accounting cycle has several stages. So far we have identified three distinct stages. Specifically, accounting data are recorded in accounts, the data are then used to make financial statements, and finally the nominal accounts are closed. After these three stages have been completed, a new cycle begins. We will introduce other stages later in the text. The three stages of the accounting cycle discussed to this point are depicted in the following illustration.

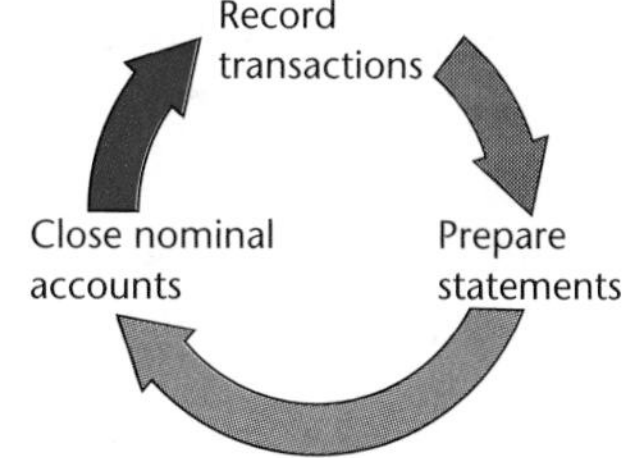

Vertical Statements Model

As its name implies, the **vertical statements model** arranges a full set of financial statement information on a single page, with account titles arranged vertically from the top to the bottom of

answers to the *curious* accountant

Anyone who owns "shares" in Shoppers Drug Mart owns a part of the company. Shoppers has many owners. In contrast, nobody actually owns the Canadian Cancer Society (CCS). The CCS has a board of directors that is responsible for overseeing its operations, but the board is not the owner.

Ultimately, the purpose of a business entity is to increase the wealth of its owners. To this end, it "spends money to make money." The expense that Shoppers incurs for drugs is a cost incurred in the hope that it will generate revenues when the drugs are sold. The financial statements of a business show, among other things, if and how the company made a profit during the current year.

The CCS is a "not-for-profit" entity. It operates to provide services to society at large, not to make a profit. It cannot increase the wealth of its owners because it has no owners. When the CCS spends money on research to find the cause of cancer, it does not spend this money in the expectation that it will generate "revenues." The revenues of the CCS come from contributors who wish to support efforts related to reducing cancer. Because the CCS does not spend money to make money, there is no reason for it to prepare an *income statement* like that of Shoppers Drug Mart.

Not-for-profit entities prepare financial statements that are similar in appearance to those of commercial enterprises. The financial statements of not-for-profit entities are called the *statement of resources*, the *statement of financial activities*, and a *cash flow statement*.

the page. The income statement is presented first, and the statement of shareholders' equity follows it. The balance sheet is presented directly below the statement of shareholders' equity. Finally, the cash flow statement is shown directly below the balance sheet. The 2004 and 2005 financial statements for RCS are illustrated in the vertical statements model in Exhibit 1–12.

The vertical statements model allows you to visualize several important interrelationships among the financial statements over the two accounting cycles. Notice that the amount of net income is transferred to the statement of shareholders' equity, where it becomes part of the computation of the amount of ending retained earnings. The ending retained earnings is then shown on the balance sheet. By tracing these relationships, you can see how net income increases retained earnings. Also observe that last year's ending balances become this year's beginning balances. For example, the 2004 ending balance in the Retained Earnings account ($31,000) becomes the beginning balance for 2005. Finally, notice that the ending cash balance on the balance sheet is validated by the computations shown in the cash flow statement. Specifically, the net change in cash is added to the beginning cash balance to produce the ending cash balance.

Assessment of the Price of a Share

LO11 Calculate, and explain the meaning of, the price-earnings ratio.

When you buy a share of a company, what do you really get? The share certificate you receive is evidence of your right to share in the earnings of the company. The more the company earns, the more your wealth increases. This fact is evidenced by the willingness of investors to pay higher prices for companies with higher earnings potential. Indeed, the **price-earnings ratio**, often called the *P/E ratio*, is the most commonly reported measure of a company's value.

Exhibit 1–12 *Vertical Statements Model*

RUSTIC CAMP SITES INC.
Financial Statements

For the Years	2004	2005
Income Statements		
Revenue	$ 85,000	$ 96,000
Expense	(50,000)	(52,000)
Net Income	$ 35,000	$ 44,000
Statements of Shareholders' Equity		
Beginning Common Shares	$ 0	$120,000
Plus: Contributions	120,000	20,000
Ending Common Shares	120,000	140,000
Beginning Retained Earnings	0	31,000
Plus: Net Income	35,000	44,000
Less: Dividends	(4,000)	(5,000)
Ending Retained Earnings	31,000	70,000
Total Shareholders' Equity	$151,000	$210,000
Balance Sheets		
Assets		
Cash	$ 51,000	$ 40,000
Land	500,000	500,000
Total Assets	$551,000	$540,000
Liabilities		
Notes Payable	$400,000	$330,000
Shareholders' Equity		
Common Shares	120,000	140,000
Retained Earnings	31,000	70,000
Total Shareholders' Equity	151,000	210,000
Total Liabilities and Shareholders' Equity	$551,000	$540,000
Cash Flow Statements		
Cash Flows from Operating Activities		
Cash Receipts from Revenue	$ 85,000	$ 96,000
Cash Payments for Expenses	(50,000)	(52,000)
Net Cash Flows from Operating Activities	35,000	44,000
Cash Flows from Investing Activities		
Cash Payments to Purchase Land	(500,000)	0
Cash Flows from Financing Activities		
Cash Receipts (Payments) for Borrowed Funds	400,000	(70,000)
Cash Receipts from Issue of Common Shares	120,000	20,000
Cash Payments for Dividends	(4,000)	(5,000)
Net Cash Flows from Financing Activities	516,000	(55,000)
Net Change in Cash	51,000	(11,000)
Plus: Beginning Cash Balance	0	51,000
Ending Cash Balance	$ 51,000	$ 40,000

Price-Earnings Ratio

The P/E ratio is computed by dividing the market price per share by the earnings per share (EPS).[4] To illustrate, assume that Western Company's shares are selling at $54 per share and that it produces earnings of $3 per share. In this case, Western's shares are selling at a P/E ratio of 18 ($54 investment ÷ $3 EPS). What does a P/E ratio of 18 mean? If Western continues to earn $3 per share and pays all earnings out in the form of cash dividends, it will take an investor 18 years to recover the price paid to obtain the shares. For comparison, assume that the Eastern Company's shares sell for $48 per share while its earnings per share are $4. This yields a P/E ratio of 12 ($48 investment ÷ $4 EPS). In these circumstances, investors buying Eastern Company shares will get their money back 6 years more quickly (18 − 12) than investors who bought Western Company shares.

Why would investors buy a share with a P/E ratio of 18 (Western Company) when they could buy one with a P/E ratio of 12 (Eastern Company)? If Western Company's earnings grow faster than Eastern's earnings, the higher P/E ratio could be justified. For example, suppose that Western Company's earnings double to $6 per share while Eastern's hold at $4 per share. Now the P/E ratio of Western drops to 9 ($54 investment ÷ $6 per share) while Eastern's P/E ratio holds at 12 ($48 investment ÷ $4 earnings per share). This explains why high-growth companies sell for higher P/E multiples than do low-growth companies.

Measurement of Growth through Percentage Analysis

An analysis of the 2002 and 2003 income statements of Cammeron, Inc., shows that earnings increased by $4.2 million. Comparable data for Diller Enterprises indicate earnings growth of $2.9 million. Does this mean that Cammeron is a better-managed company than Diller? Not necessarily. It could mean that Cammeron is simply a larger company than Diller. Investors often use percentage analysis to compare companies of differing sizes on a level playing field. To illustrate, consider the following actual earnings data for the two companies:

	2002*	2003*	Growth†
Cammeron	$42.4	$46.6	$4.2
Diller	9.9	12.8	2.9

*Earnings data shown in millions.
†Growth calculated by subtracting 2002 earnings from 2003 earnings.

The growth in earnings between 2002 and 2003 for the two companies can be measured in terms of a percentage by the following formula:

$$\frac{\text{Alternative year earnings} - \text{Base year earnings}}{\text{Base year earnings}} = \text{Percentage growth rate}$$

Cammeron, Inc.:

$$\frac{\$46.6 - \$42.4}{\$42.4} = 9.9\%$$

Diller Enterprises:

$$\frac{\$12.8 - \$9.9}{\$9.9} = 29.3\%$$

[4] The amount of earnings per share is provided in the company's annual report. In its simplest form, it is computed by dividing the company's net income (net earnings) by the number of outstanding common shares.

reality bytes

What is GAAP?

This chapter introduces the fact that financial reporting is a measurement and communication discipline based on a set of rules referred to as *generally accepted accounting principles (GAAP)*. Business students must be aware that the accounting rules that are the primary focus of this course are based on Canadian GAAP. Not all economies throughout the world use the same accounting rules. Although there are many similarities among the GAAP used in different countries, there are also major differences. There have been attempts to create international accounting standards and even North American standards, but individual countries have retained the authority to establish their own GAAP; there is no single "global GAAP." Throughout this book, we present examples of how financial reporting in other countries differs from Canadian reporting.

Accounting rules differ among countries due to a variety of factors, including the economic and legal environments that exist in each country and how the GAAP in that country are established. In Canada, GAAP is established mainly by the **Canadian Institute of Chartered Accountants (CICA).** The CICA is a nongovernmental rule-making body that was established by the accounting profession.

The process of creating new generally accepted accounting principles involves the views of the CICA, the comments and suggestions of the corporations affected, opinions of Canada's professional accountants, and our tax authority, the Canada Customs and Revenue Agency (CCRA).

Canada and the United States have strong economic and geographic ties. So we are greatly influenced by what happens south of the border. The U.S. GAAP also influences what happens in Canadian GAAP. The Financial Accounting Standards Board (FASB) and the U.S. tax authority, the Internal Revenue Service (IRS), determine GAAP in the United States.

This analysis shows that although Cammeron is a larger company, Diller is growing much more quickly. If this trend continues, Diller will eventually become a larger company with higher earnings than Cammeron. For this reason, investors value fast-growing companies. Indeed, the P/E ratios of real-world companies are highly correlated with their growth rates.

Real-World Financial Reports

LO12 Identify the major components of real-world annual reports and some of the technical terms used in them.

Organizations exist in many different forms. As noted earlier, two major classifications are *business* and *not-for-profit* entities. Business entities can be further subdivided into three categories: service, merchandising, and manufacturing. As the name implies, **service organizations** provide services to consumers. Service providers include doctors, lawyers, accountants, dry cleaners, and maids. **Merchandising businesses** are sometimes called *retail* or *wholesale companies*; they sell goods that other entities make. **Manufacturing companies** make goods and often sell them to customers. Some businesses include combinations of these three categories. For example, an automotive repair shop might change oil (service function), sell parts such as oil filters (retail function), and rebuild engines or other parts (manufacturing function).

The nature of the reporting **entity** affects the form and content of the information contained in its financial statements. Therefore, you should expect some degree of diversity when viewing real-world financial statements.

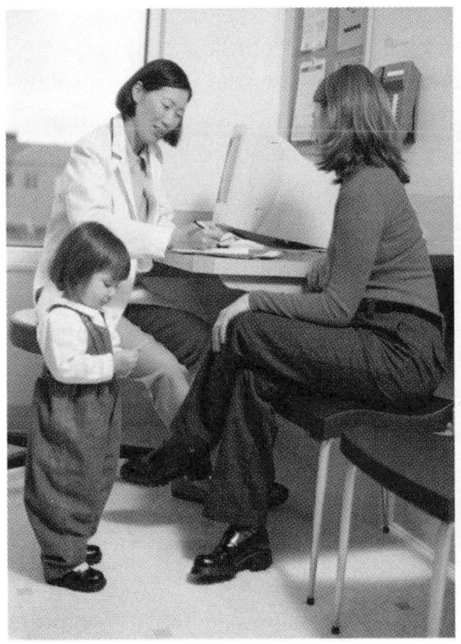

Annual Report for Bombardier, Inc.

Organizations normally provide information, including financial statements, to *stakeholders* yearly in a document known as an **annual report**. Appendix B provides the annual report for Bombardier, Inc. This report contains the company's financial statements (see pages 69–72 of the report). Immediately following the statements are footnotes that provide more detailed information about the items described in the statements (see pages 79–105 of the report). Besides financial statements, the annual report contains the *auditor's report*, discussed in Chapter 2. Annual reports also include written commentary that describes management's assessment of significant events that affected the company during the reporting period. This section of an annual report, called *management's discussion and analysis* (MD&A), is discussed in Chapter 4.

Special Terms in Real-World Reports

The financial statements of real-world companies contain many items relating to advanced topics that are not covered in introductory accounting textbooks. Do not let this discourage you from browsing through real-world annual reports. Indeed, your learning will significantly improve if you look at many annual reports and attempt to identify all the items your current knowledge permits. As your academic knowledge grows, most likely you will experience a corresponding increase in interest in real-world financial reports and the business practices they describe. We encourage you to look up annual reports in your local library or ask your employer for a copy of your company's report. The Internet is another excellent source of annual reports. Most companies provide links on their home pages that lead to their annual reports. Look for links that are titled "about the company" or "investor relations" or something similar. The best way to learn accounting is to become involved. Look at accounting information, and ask questions about things you do not understand. Accounting is the language of business. Learning the language will serve you well in almost any area of business you pursue.

a look back

In this chapter we discussed the role of accounting in society and business. Accounting's role is to provide information that enables an organization to evaluate its performance. Accounting is a measurement discipline. To facilitate communication, it is necessary to attain agreement on the rules of measurement. *Generally accepted accounting principles (GAAP)* are the rules used by the accounting profession in Canada to promote consistency in financial reporting. GAAP are always evolving.

The chapter has described and discussed eight elements of financial statements: *assets, liabilities, equity, common shares (contributed capital), revenue, expenses, dividends,* and *net income*. The elements represent broad classifications of information that appear on financial statements. Four basic financial statements appear in public reports: the *balance sheet*, the *income statement*, the *statement of shareholders' equity*, and the *cash flow statement*. The chapter discussed the form and content of each statement as well as the interrelationships among the statements.

This chapter introduced a *horizontal financial statements model* as a tool to facilitate your understanding of how business events affect a set of financial statements. This model will be used throughout the text. Accordingly, you should carefully study this model before proceeding to Chapter 2.

a look forward

To keep matters simple and to focus attention on the interrelationships among financial statements, this chapter considered only cash events. Obviously, many real-world events do not involve an immediate cash exchange. An example of a noncash event is a customer's use of telephone service throughout the month without paying for it until the end of the month. As mentioned briefly in this chapter, events such as this are called *accruals*. The effects that accrual events have on the financial statements are the subject of Chapter 2.

SELF-STUDY REVIEW PROBLEM

During 2006, Rustic Camp Sites experienced the following transactions.

1. RCS acquired $32,000 cash by issuing common shares.
2. RCS received $116,000 cash for providing services to customers.
3. RCS paid $13,000 cash for salaries expenses.
4. RCS paid a $9,000 cash dividend to the owners.
5. RCS sold land that had cost $100,000 for $100,000 cash.
6. RCS paid $47,000 cash for other operating expenses.

Required

a. Record the transaction data in a horizontal financial statements model like the following one. In the Cash Flow Statement column, classify the cash flows as operating activities (OA), investing activities (IA), or financing activities (FA). The beginning balances have been recorded as an example. They are the ending balances shown on RCS's December 31, 2005, financial statements illustrated in the chapter.

	Balance Sheet									Income Statement					Cash Flow Statement
	Assets			=	Liab.	+	Shareholders' Equity								
Event No.	Cash	+	Land	=	N. Pay	+	C. Sh.	+	Ret. Ear.	Rev.	−	Exp.	=	Net Inc.	
Bal.	40,000	+	500,000	=	330,000	+	140,000	+	70,000	NA	−	NA	=	NA	NA

b. Explain why there are no beginning balances in the Income Statement columns.
c. What amount of net income will RCS report on the 2006 income statement?
d. What amount of total assets will RCS report on the December 31, 2006, balance sheet?
e. What amount of retained earnings will RCS report on the December 31, 2006, balance sheet?

f. What amount of net cash flow from operating activities will RCS report on the 2006 cash flow statement?
g. Assume that RCS has 20,000 common shares outstanding, which are selling at a market price of $33.60 per share. Determine the company's P/E ratio.

Answer

a.

	Balance Sheet					Income Statement			Cash Flow Statement	
	Assets		= Liab.	+ Shareholders' Equity						
Event No.	Cash +	Land =	N. Pay +	C. Sh. +	Ret. Ear.	Rev. −	Exp. =	Net Inc.		
Bal.	40,000 +	500,000 =	330,000 +	140,000 +	70,000	NA −	NA =	NA	NA	
1	32,000 +	NA =	NA +	32,000 +	NA	NA −	NA =	NA	32,000	FA
2	116,000 +	NA =	NA +	NA +	116,000	116,000 −	NA =	116,000	116,000	OA
3	(13,000) +	NA =	NA +	NA +	(13,000)	NA −	13,000 =	(13,000)	(13,000)	OA
4	(9,000) +	NA =	NA +	NA +	(9,000)	NA −	NA =	NA	(9,000)	FA
5	100,000 +	(100,000) =	NA +	NA +	NA	NA −	NA =	NA	100,000	IA
6	(47,000) +	NA =	NA +	NA +	(47,000)	NA −	47,000 =	(47,000)	(47,000)	OA
Totals	219,000 +	400,000 =	330,000 +	172,000 +	117,000	116,000 −	60,000 =	56,000	179,000	NC*

* The letters NC on the last line of the column designate the net change in cash flow.

b. The revenue and expense accounts are temporary accounts used to capture data for a single accounting period. They are closed (amounts removed from the accounts) at the end of the accounting period and therefore always have zero balances at the beginning of the accounting cycle.
c. RCS will report net income of $56,000 on the 2006 income statement. Compute this amount by subtracting the expenses from the revenue ($116,000 Revenue − $13,000 Salaries expenses − $47,000 Other operating expense).
d. RCS will report total assets of $619,000 on the December 31, 2006, balance sheet. Compute total assets by adding the cash amount to the land amount ($219,000 Cash + $400,000 Land).
e. RCS will report retained earnings of $117,000 on the December 31, 2006, balance sheet. Compute this amount using the following formula: Beginning retained earnings + Net income − Dividends = Ending retained earnings. In this case, $70,000 + $56,000 − $9,000 = $117,000.
f. Net cash flow from operating activities is the difference between the amount of cash collected from revenue and the amount of cash spent for expenses. In this case, $116,000 cash inflow from revenue − $13,000 cash outflow for salaries expenses − $47,000 cash outflow for other operating expenses = $56,000 net cash inflow from operating activities.
g. Earnings per share = Net earnings ÷ Number of shares outstanding = $56,000 ÷ 20,000 shares = $2.80 per share. Price/Earning ratio = Market price per share ÷ Earnings per share = $33.60 ÷ $2.80 = 12 times.

KEY TERMS

account *9*
accounting *3*
accounting equation *9*
accounting event *13*
accounting period *17*
annual report *25*
articles of incorporation *5*
asset *9*
asset source transaction *13*
balance sheet *18*
board of directors *6*
Canadian Institute of Chartered Accountants (CICA) *24*
cash flow statement *11*
claims *9*
closing the accounts *18*
common shares *10*
continuity *6*
corporation *4*
dividend *11*
double-entry bookkeeping *14*
double taxation *5*
elements *9*
entity *24*
equity *9*
expenses *11*
financial accounting *7*
financial statements *8*
financing activities *11*

general ledger *16*
generally accepted accounting principles (GAAP) *8*
horizontal statements model *13*
income statement *11*
investing activities *11*
liabilities *9*
limited liability *6*
liquidity *18*
managerial accounting *7*
manufacturing companies *24*
merchandising businesses *24*
net assets *9*
net income *11*
net loss *11*
nominal accounts *18*
operating activities *12*
partnership *4*
partnership agreement *4*
permanent accounts *18*
price-earnings ratio *21*
privately held corporation *5*
productive assets *11*
reporting entities *8*
residual interest *9*
retained earnings *10*
revenue *11*
service organizations *24*
share certificate *5*
shareholders *5*
shareholders' equity *10*
sole proprietorship *4*
stakeholders *4*
statement of shareholders' equity *17*
temporary accounts *18*
transaction *13*
transferability *6*
users *4*
vertical statements model *20*

QUESTIONS

1. Explain the term *stakeholder*. Distinguish between stakeholders with a direct versus an indirect interest in the companies that issue accounting reports.
2. Why is accounting called the *language of business*?
3. What are the three major forms of business organizations? Describe each.
4. How are sole proprietorships formed?
5. Discuss the purpose of a partnership agreement. Is such an agreement necessary for partnership formation?
6. What is meant by the phrase *separate legal entity*? To which type of business organization does it apply?
7. What is the purpose of the articles of incorporation? What information do they provide?
8. What is the function of the share certificate?
9. What are the advantages and disadvantages of the corporate form of business organization?
10. How does the term *double taxation* apply to corporations? Give an example of double taxation.
11. What is the difference between contributed capital and retained earnings for a corporation?
12. Why is it easier for a corporation to raise large amounts of capital than it is for a partnership?
13. How do financial and managerial accounting differ?
14. What are the Canadian rules of accounting information measurement called?
15. What body has the main responsibility for establishing GAAP in Canada?
16. Distinguish between elements of financial statements and accounts.
17. What is the most basic form of the accounting equation?
18. What role do assets play in business profitability?
19. To whom do the assets of a business belong?
20. What is the nature of creditors' claims on assets?
21. What does *residual interest* mean? Identify two other terms that describe the residual interest.
22. What term describes creditors' claims on the assets of a business?
23. What is the accounting equation? Describe each of its three components.
24. Who ultimately bears the risk and collects the rewards associated with operating a business?
25. What does a *double-entry bookkeeping system* mean?
26. Identify the four types of accounting transactions. Provide an example of each type of transaction, and explain how it affects the accounting equation.
27. How does acquiring capital from owners affect the accounting equation?
28. What is the difference between assets that are acquired by issuing common shares and those that are acquired using retained earnings?
29. How does earning revenue affect the accounting equation?
30. Which accounts are closed at the end of an accounting period?
31. What are the three primary sources of assets?
32. What is the source of retained earnings?
33. How does distributing assets (paying dividends) to owners affect the accounting equation?
34. What are the similarities and differences between dividends and expenses?
35. What four general-purpose financial statements do business enterprises use?
36. Which of the general-purpose financial statements provides information about the enterprise at a specific designated date?

37. Explain why revenue, expense, and dividend accounts have zero balances at the beginning of each accounting period.
38. What causes a net loss?
39. What three categories of cash receipts and cash payments do businesses report on the cash flow statement? Explain the types of cash flows reported in each category.
40. How are asset accounts usually arranged in the balance sheet?
41. What is the difference between a permanent account and a nominal account?
42. What type of information does a business typically include in its annual report?
43 Identify and discuss the three stages of an accounting cycle that this chapter introduced.

EXERCISES

EXERCISE 1–1 *Identifying Financial Statements* L.O. 2, 4

Accounting reports prepared for public use normally include four financial statements.

Required
Provide the names of the four financial statements and alternative names for any statements that have them.

EXERCISE 1–2 *Forms of Organization* L.O. 1

Required
Compare and contrast the three forms of organization structures.

EXERCISE 1–3 *Components of the Accounting Equation* L.O. 6

Required
The following three requirements are independent of each other.

a. Wilson Auto Parts has assets of $6,200 and net assets of $1,200. What is the amount of liabilities? What is the amount of claims?
b. Clarke Juices, Inc., has liabilities of $1,200 and equity of $4,400. What is the amount of assets? What is the amount of net assets?
c. Ted's Tennis Shop has assets of $56,700 and liabilities of $32,300. What is the amount of its equity? What is the amount of its net assets?

EXERCISE 1–4 *Distributions in a Business Liquidation* L.O. 3

Assume that McNeal Company acquires $400 cash from creditors and $600 cash from investors (shareholders). The company then has an operating loss of $500 cash and goes out of business.

Required

a. Define the term *business liquidation*.
b. What amount of cash will McNeal's creditors receive?
c. What amount of cash will McNeal's investors (shareholders) receive?

EXERCISE 1–5 *Effect of Events on the Accounting Equation* L.O. 6

Solar Enterprises experienced the following events during 2006.

1. Acquired cash from the issue of common shares.
2. Provided services to clients for cash.
3. Paid operating expenses with cash.
4. Borrowed cash.
5. Purchased land with cash.
6. Paid a cash dividend to the shareholders.

Required

Explain how each of these events affects the accounting equation by writing the letter I for increase, the letter D for decrease, and NA for no effect under each of the components of the accounting equation. The first event is shown as an example.

Event Number	Assets	=	Liabilities	Equity: Common Shares	Equity: Retained Earnings
1	I		NA	I	NA

L.O. 9 EXERCISE 1–6 *Effect of Events on a Horizontal Financial Statements Model*

Greer Consulting Services experienced the following events during 2006.

1. Acquired cash by issuing common shares.
2. Collected cash for providing tutoring services to clients.
3. Paid cash for operating expenses.
4. Borrowed cash from a local government small business foundation.
5. Purchased land for cash.
6. Paid a cash dividend to the shareholders.

Required

Use a horizontal statements model to show how each event affects the balance sheet, income statement, and cash flow statement. Indicate whether the event increases (I), decreases (D), or does not affect (NA) each element of the financial statements. Also, in the Cash Flow Statement column, classify the cash flows as operating activities (OA), investing activities (IA), or financing activities (FA). The first transaction is shown as an example.

Event No.	Balance Sheet									Income Statement					Cash Flow Statement	
	Cash	+	Land	=	N. Pay	+	C. Shares	+	Ret. Ear.	Rev.	−	Exp.	=	Net Inc.		
1.	I	+	NA	=	NA	+	I	+	NA	NA	−	NA	=	NA	I	NA

L.O. 6, 7 EXERCISE 1–7 *Effects of Issuing Shares*

Chia Company was started in 2009 when it acquired $12,000 cash by issuing common shares. The cash acquisition was the only event that affected the business in 2009.

Required

Write an accounting equation, and record the effects of the share issue under the appropriate general ledger account headings.

L.O. 4, 5, 7 EXERCISE 1–8 *Effects of Borrowing*

Northern Rockies Company was started in 2007 when it issued a note to borrow $7,200 cash.

Required

Write an accounting equation, and record the effects of the borrowing transaction under the appropriate general ledger account headings.

L.O. 5, 7 EXERCISE 1–9 *Effects of Revenue, Expense, and Dividend Events*

Kwon Company was started on January 1, 2005. During 2005, the company experienced the following three accounting events: (1) earned cash revenues of $9,500, (2) paid cash expenses of $5,800, and (3) paid a $700 cash dividend to its shareholders. These were the only events that affected the company during 2005.

Required

a. Write an accounting equation, and record the effects of each accounting event under the appropriate general ledger account headings.
b. Prepare an income statement for the 2005 accounting period and a balance sheet at the end of 2005 for Kwon Company.
c. What is the name of the practice of transferring the balances from the revenue, expense, and dividend accounts to the Retained Earnings account at the end of an accounting period?

EXERCISE 1–10 *Record Events in the Horizontal Statements Model* L.O. 3, 9

Maulder Mechanics was started in 2007. During 2007, the company (1) acquired $7,000 cash from the issue of common shares, (2) earned cash revenue of $14,000, (3) paid cash expenses of $6,800, and (4) paid a $1,000 cash dividend to the shareholders.

Required

a. Record these four events in a horizontal statements model. Also, in the Cash Flow Statement column, classify the cash flows as operating activities (OA), investing activities (IA), or financing activities (FA). The first event is shown as an example.

Event No.	Balance Sheet								Income Statement					Cash Flow Statement	
	Cash	=	N. Pay	+	C. Shares	+	Ret. Ear.		Rev.	−	Exp.	=	Net Inc.		
1.	7,000	=	NA	+	7,000	+	NA		NA	−	NA	=	NA	7,000	NA

b. What does the income statement tell you about the assets of this business?

EXERCISE 1–11 *Classifying Items for the Cash Flow Statement* L.O. 5

Required

Indicate how each of the following would be classified on the cash flow statement as operating activities (OA), investing activities (IA), financing activities (FA), or not applicable (NA).

a. Paid $2,000 cash for salary expense.
b. Borrowed $5,000 cash from Scotiabank.
c. Received $25,000 cash from the issue of common shares.
d. Purchased land for $6,000 cash.
e. Performed services for $12,000 cash.
f. Paid $2,400 cash for utilities expense.
g. Sold land for $4,000 cash.
h. Paid a cash dividend of $1,000 to the shareholders.
i. Hired an accountant to keep the books.
j. Paid $2,000 cash on the loan from Scotiabank.

EXERCISE 1–12 *Effect of Transactions on General Ledger Accounts* L.O. 4, 7

At the beginning of 2005, Sani Service Company's accounting records had the following general ledger accounts and balances.

Sani Service Company
Accounting Equation

Event	Assets		=	Liabilities	+	Equity		Acct. Titles for RE
	Cash	Land		Notes Payable		Common Shares	Retained Earnings	
Balance 1/1/2005	25,000	50,000		35,000		30,000	10,000	

Sani completed the following transactions during 2005:

1. Purchased land for $10,000 cash.
2. Acquired $15,000 cash from the issue of common shares.
3. Received $55,000 cash for providing services to customers.
4. Paid cash operating expenses of $38,000.
5. Paid $20,000 cash to creditors.
6. Paid a $3,000 cash dividend to the shareholders.

Required

a. Record the transactions in the appropriate general ledger accounts. Record the amounts of revenue, expense, and dividends in the Retained Earnings column. Provide the appropriate titles for these accounts in the last column of the table.
b. Determine the amount of net income for the 2005 period.
c. What is the amount of total assets at the end of 2005? What is the amount of net assets at the end of 2005?

L.O. 4, 6, 9 EXERCISE 1–13 *Preparing Financial Statements*

Kerry Company experienced the following events during 2006:

1. Acquired $25,000 cash from the issue of common shares.
2. Paid $9,000 cash to purchase land.
3. Borrowed $5,000 cash.
4. Provided services for $12,000 cash.
5. Paid $500 cash for rent expense.
6. Paid $7,000 cash for other operating expenses.
7. Paid a $2,000 cash dividend to the shareholders.

Required

a. The January 1, 2006, general ledger account balances are shown in the following accounting equation. Record the seven events in the appropriate general ledger accounts. Record the amounts of revenue, expense, and dividends in the Retained Earnings column. Provide the appropriate titles for these accounts in the last column of the table. The first event is shown as an example.

Kerry Company Accounting Equation									
Event	Assets			=	Liabilities	+	Equity			Acct. Titles for RE
	Cash	+	Land	=	Notes Payable	+	Common Shares	+	Retained Earnings	
Balance 1/1/2006	2,000		16,000		0		10,000		8,000	
1.	25,000						25,000			

b. Prepare an income statement, statement of shareholders' equity, year-end balance sheet, and cash flow statement for the 2006 accounting period.
c. What are the balances in the revenue, expense, and dividend accounts on January 1, 2007?

L.O. 3, 9 EXERCISE 1–14 *Effect of Events on a Horizontal Statements Model*

Tax Time, Inc., was started on January 1, 2004. The company experienced the following events during its first year of operation:

1. Acquired $30,000 cash from the issue of common shares.
2. Paid $9,000 cash to purchase land.
3. Received $28,000 cash for providing tax services to customers.
4. Paid $9,500 cash for salary expenses.

5. Acquired $5,000 cash from the issue of additional common shares.
6. Borrowed $10,000 cash from the bank.
7. Purchased additional land for $5,000 cash.
8. Paid $6,000 cash for other operating expenses.
9. Paid a $2,800 cash dividend to the shareholders.

Required

a. Record these events in a horizontal statements model. Also, in the Cash Flow Statement column, classify the cash flows as operating activities (OA), investing activities (IA), or financing activities (FA). The first event is shown as an example.

Event No.	Balance Sheet									Income Statement					Cash Flow Statement	
	Cash	+	Land	=	N. Pay	+	C. Shares	+	Ret. Ear.	Rev.	−	Exp.	=	Net Inc.		
1.	30,000	+	NA	=	NA	+	30,000	+	NA	NA	−	NA	=	NA	30,000	FA

b. What is the net income earned in 2004?
c. What is the amount of total assets at the end of 2004?
d. What is the net cash flow from operating activities for 2004?
e. What is the net cash flow from investing activities for 2004?
f. What is the net cash flow from financing activities for 2004?
g. What is the cash balance at the end of 2004?

EXERCISE 1–15 *Titles and Accounts Appearing on Financial Statements*

L.O. 4, 5

Annual reports normally include an income statement, a statement of shareholders' equity, a balance sheet, and a cash flow statement.

Required

Identify the financial statements on which each of the following titles or accounts would appear. If a title or an account appears on more than one statement, list all statements that would include it.

a. Common Shares
b. Land
c. Ending Cash Balance
d. Beginning Cash Balance
e. Notes Payable
f. Retained Earnings
g. Revenue
h. Dividends
i. Financing Activities
j. Salary Expense

EXERCISE 1–16 *Closing the Accounts*

L.O. 3, 4

The following information was drawn from the accounting records of Pearson Company as of December 31, 2007, before the nominal accounts had been closed. The Cash balance was $3,000, and Notes Payable amounted to $2,500. The company had revenues of $4,000 and expenses of $2,500. The company's Land account had a $5,000 balance. Dividends amounted to $500. There was $1,000 of common shares outstanding.

Required

a. Identify which accounts would be classified as permanent and which accounts would be classified as nominal (temporary).
b. Assuming that Pearson's beginning balance (as of January 1, 2007) in the Retained Earnings account was $3,500, determine its balance after the nominal accounts were closed at the end of 2007.
c. What amount of net income would Pearson Company report on its 2007 income statement?

d. Explain why the amount of net income differs from the amount of the ending Retained Earnings balance.
e. What are the balances in the revenue, expense, and dividend accounts on January 1, 2008?

L.O. 10 EXERCISE 1–17 *Closing Accounts and the Accounting Cycle*

Required

a. Identify which of the following accounts are temporary (will be closed to Retained Earnings at the end of the year) and which are permanent.
   (1) Cash
   (2) Salaries Expense
   (3) Notes Payable
   (4) Utilities Expense
   (5) Service Revenue
   (6) Dividends
   (7) Common Shares
   (8) Land
   (9) Interest Revenue
   (10) Retained Earnings
b. List and explain the three stages of the accounting cycle. Which stage must be first? Which stage is last?

L.O. 8 EXERCISE 1–18 *Classifying Events as Asset Source, Use, or Exchange*

Jacobs Company experienced the following events during its first year of operations:

1. Acquired $6,000 cash from the issue of common shares.
2. Borrowed $8,000 cash from the Royal Bank.
3. Paid $3,000 cash to purchase land.
4. Received $4,500 cash for providing services.
5. Acquired an additional $2,000 cash from the issue of common shares.
6. Purchased additional land for $3,500 cash.
7. Paid $2,200 cash for salary expenses.
8. Signed a contract to provide additional services in the future.
9. Paid $1,000 cash for rent expense.
10. Paid a $1,000 cash dividend to the shareholders.

Required

Classify each event as an asset source, use, or exchange transaction or as not applicable (NA).

L.O. 8, 9 EXERCISE 1–19 *Types of Transactions and the Horizontal Statements Model*

Better Sports experienced the following events during its first year of operations, 2008:

1. Acquired cash by issuing common shares.
2. Provided services and collected cash.
3. Borrowed cash from a bank.
4. Paid cash for operating expenses.
5. Purchased land with cash.
6. Paid a cash dividend to the shareholders.

Required

a. Indicate whether each event is an asset source, use, or exchange transaction.
b. Use a horizontal statements model to show how each event affects the balance sheet, income statement, and cash flow statement. Indicate whether the event increases (I), decreases (D), or does not affect (NA) each element of the financial statements. Also, in the Cash Flow Statement column, classify the cash flows as operating activities (OA), investing activities (IA), or financing activities (FA). The first transaction is shown as an example.

	Balance Sheet									Income Statement					Cash Flow Statement	
Event No.	Cash	+	Land	=	N. Pay	+	C. Shares	+	Ret. Ear.	Rev.	−	Exp.	=	Net Inc.		
1.	I	+	NA	=	NA	+	I	+	NA	NA	−	NA	=	NA	I	FA

EXERCISE 1–20 *Relating Accounting Events to Entities* L.O. 5, 8

Dundee Company was started in 2004 when it acquired $80,000 cash by issuing common shares to Don Sinclair.

Required

a. Was this event an asset source, use, or exchange transaction for Dundee Company?
b. Was this event an asset source, use, or exchange transaction for Don Sinclair?
c. Was the cash flow an operating, investing, or financing activity on Dundee Company's 2004 cash flow statement?
d. Was the cash flow an operating, investing, or financing activity on Don Sinclair's 2004 cash flow statement?

EXERCISE 1–21 *Missing Information in the Accounting Equation* L.O. 6

Required

Calculate the missing amounts in the following table:

					Equity		
Company	**Assets**	=	**Liabilities**	+	**Common Shares**	+	**Retained Earnings**
A	$?		$48,000		$52,000		$36,000
B	90,000		?		25,000		40,000
C	87,000		15,000		?		37,000
D	102,000		29,000		42,000		?

EXERCISE 1–22 *Missing Information in the Accounting Equation* L.O. 6

As of December 31, 2005, Betts Company had total assets of $156,000, total liabilities of $85,600, and common shares of $48,400. During 2006 Betts earned $22,000 of cash revenue, paid $12,500 for cash expenses, and paid a $500 cash dividend to the shareholders.

Required

a. Determine the amount of retained earnings as of December 31, 2005.
b. Determine the amount of net income earned in 2006.
c. Determine the amount of retained earnings as of December 31, 2006.

EXERCISE 1–23 *Missing Information for Determining Net Income* L.O. 5, 6

The December 31, 2006, balance sheet for Trebing Company showed total shareholders' equity of $62,500. Total shareholders' equity increased by $53,400 between December 31, 2006, and December 31, 2007. During 2007 Trebing Company acquired $11,000 cash from the issue of common shares. Trebing Company paid an $8,000 cash dividend to the shareholders during 2007.

Required

Determine the amount of net income or loss Trebing reported on its 2007 income statement. (*Hint:* Remember that share issues, net income, and dividends all change total shareholders' equity.)

EXERCISE 1–24 *Price-Earnings Ratio* L.O. 11

The following information is available for two companies.

	Henry Company	**Pager Company**
Earnings per share	$ 1.05	$ 4.50
Market price per share	38.50	108.00

Required

a. Compute the price-earnings ratio for each company.
b. Explain why one company would have a higher price-earnings ratio than the other.

PROBLEMS—SERIES A

L.O. 1 PROBLEM 1–1A *Different Forms of Business Organization*

Shawn Bates was working to establish a business enterprise with four of his wealthy friends. Each of the five individuals would receive a 20 percent ownership interest in the company. A primary goal of establishing the enterprise was to minimize the amount of income taxes paid. Assume that the five investors are in a 36 percent personal tax bracket and that the corporate tax rate is 25 percent. Also assume that the new company is expected to earn $200,000 of cash income before taxes during its first year of operation. All earnings are expected to be immediately distributed to the owners as salary.

Required

Calculate the amount of after-tax cash flow available to each investor if the business is established as a partnership versus a corporation. Write a memo explaining the advantages and disadvantages of these two forms of business organization.

L.O. 9 PROBLEM 1–2A *Recording the Effect of Events in a Horizontal Statements Model*

Lighthouse Services experienced the following transactions during 2006:

1. Acquired cash by issuing common shares.
2. Borrowed cash from the local bank.
3. Received cash for performing services.
4. Paid cash expenses.
5. Purchased land for cash.
6. Paid cash to reduce the principal balance of the bank loan.
7. Paid a cash dividend to the shareholders.

Required

Use a horizontal statements model to show how each event affects the balance sheet, income statement, and cash flow statement. Indicate whether the event increases (I), decreases (D), or does not affect (NA) each element of the financial statements. Also, in the Cash Flow Statement column, classify the cash flows as operating activities (OA), investing activities (IA), or financing activities (FA). The first transaction is shown as an example.

	Balance Sheet									Income Statement					Cash Flow Statement	
Event No.	Cash	+	Land	=	N. Pay	+	C. Shares	+	Ret. Ear.	Rev.	−	Exp.	=	Net Inc.		
1.	I	+	NA	=	NA	+	I	+	NA	NA	−	NA	=	NA	I	FA

L.O. 5, 9 PROBLEM 1–3A *Recording Events in a Horizontal Statements Model*

Marx Company was started on January 1, 2007, and experienced the following events during its first year of operation:

1. Acquired $24,000 cash from the issue of common shares.
2. Borrowed $16,000 cash from a local bank.
3. Earned cash revenues of $36,000 for performing services.
4. Paid cash expenses of $25,000.
5. Paid a $4,000 cash dividend to the shareholders.
6. Acquired an additional $20,000 cash from the issue of common shares.
7. Paid $5,000 cash to reduce the principal balance of the bank note.
8. Paid $53,000 cash to purchase land.

Required

a. Record the preceding transactions in the horizontal statements model. Also, in the Cash Flow Statement column, classify the cash flows as operating activities (OA), investing activities (IA), or financing activities (FA). The first event is shown as an example.

	Balance Sheet									Income Statement					Cash Flow Statement	
Event No.	Cash	+	Land	=	N. Pay	+	C. Shares	+	Ret. Ear.	Rev.	−	Exp.	=	Net Inc.		
1.	24,000	+	NA	=	NA	+	24,000	+	NA	NA	−	NA	=	NA	24,000	FA

b. Determine the amount of total assets that Marx would report on the December 31, 2007, balance sheet.
c. Identify the sources of the assets that Marx would report on the December 31, 2007, balance sheet. Determine the amount of each of these sources.
d. Determine the net income that Marx would report on the 2007 income statement. Explain why dividends do not appear on the income statement.
e. Determine the net cash flows from operating activities, investing activities, and financing activities that Marx would report on the 2007 cash flow statement.

PROBLEM 1–4A *Preparing Financial Statements for Two Complete Accounting Cycles* **L.O. 4, 5, 6, 7**

Reynolds Consulting experienced the following transactions for 2006, its first year of operations, and 2007. *Assume that all transactions involve the receipt or payment of cash.*

Ex

Transactions for 2006

1. Acquired $25,000 by issuing common shares.
2. Received $72,000 for providing services to customers.
3. Borrowed $16,000 from creditors.
4. Paid expenses amounting to $50,000.
5. Purchased land for $44,000.

Transactions for 2007

1. Acquired an additional $24,000 from the issue of common shares.
2. Received $94,000 for providing services.
3. Paid $10,000 to creditors to reduce debt principal.
4. Paid expenses amounting to $71,500.
5. Paid a $6,000 dividend to the shareholders.

Required

a. Write an accounting equation, and record the effects of each accounting event under the appropriate headings for each year. Record the amounts of revenue, expense, and dividends in the Retained Earnings column. Provide appropriate titles for these accounts in the last column of the table.
b. Prepare an income statement, statement of shareholders' equity, year-end balance sheet, and cash flow statement for each year. Use the vertical format when you prepare the financial statements.
c. Examine the balance sheets for the two years. How did assets change from 2006 to 2007?
d. Determine the percentage growth in net earnings from 2006 to 2007.

PROBLEM 1–5A *Interrelationships among Financial Statements* **L.O. 4, 5**

Chase Enterprises started the 2006 accounting period with $30,000 of assets (all cash), $18,000 of liabilities, and $4,000 of common shares. During the year, Chase earned cash revenues of $36,000, paid cash expenses of $23,000, and paid a cash dividend to shareholders of $2,000. Chase also acquired $10,000 of additional cash from the sale of common shares and paid $6,000 cash to reduce the liability owed to a bank.

Required

Prepare an income statement, statement of shareholders' equity, period-end balance sheet, and cash flow statement for the 2006 accounting period. (*Hint*: Determine the amount of beginning retained earnings before considering the effects of the current period events. It also might help to record all events under an accounting equation before preparing the statements.)

PROBLEM 1–6A *Relating Titles and Accounts to Financial Statements* **L.O. 5**

Required

Identify the financial statements on which each of the following items (titles, date descriptions, and accounts) appears by placing a check mark in the appropriate column. If an item appears on more than one statement, place a check mark in every applicable column.

Item	Income Statement	Statement of Shareholders' Equity	Balance Sheet	Cash Flow Statement
Ending cash balance				
Salary expense				
Consulting revenue				
Dividends				
Financing activities				
Ending common shares				
Interest expense				
As of (date)				
Land				
Beginning cash balance				
Notes payable				
Beginning common shares				
Service revenue				
Utility expense				
Cash acquired from share issue				
Operating activities				
For the period ended (date)				
Net income				
Investing activities				
Net loss				

L.O. 3, 4, 5, 6 **PROBLEM 1–7A** *Closing the Accounts*

The following accounts and account balances were taken from the records of Green View Company. Except as otherwise indicated, all balances are as of December 31, 2004, before the closing entries had been recorded.

Cash Received from Common Shares Issued during 2004	$ 3,500
Cash	7,800
Revenue	7,400
Salary Expense	2,900
Cash Flow from Operating Activities	2,500
Notes Payable	2,000
Utility Expense	600
Dividends	1,200
Cash Flow from Financing Activities	2,300
Rent Expense	1,400
Land	20,200
Retained Earnings, January 1, 2004	14,700
Common Shares, December 31, 2004	10,000

Required

a. Prepare the income statement Green View would include in its 2004 annual report.
b. Identify the accounts that should be closed to the Retained Earnings account.

c. Determine the Retained Earnings account balance at December 31, 2004. Identify the reasons for the difference between net income and the ending balance in Retained Earnings.
d. What are the balances in the revenue, expense, and dividend accounts on January 1, 2005? Explain.

PROBLEM 1–8A *Missing Information in Financial Statements*

L.O. 4, 5

Required
Fill in the blanks (indicated by the letters in parentheses) in the following financial statements. Assume the company started operations on January 1, 2005.

	For the Years		
	2005	**2006**	**2007**
Income Statements			
Revenue (assume cash)	$ 700	$ 1,300	$ 2,000
Expense (assume cash)	(a)	(700)	(1,300)
Net Income (Loss)	$ 200	$ (m)	$ 700
Statements of Shareholders' Equity			
Beginning Common Shares	$ 0	$ (n)	$ 6,000
Plus: Common Shares Issued	5,000	1,000	2,000
Ending Common Shares	5,000	6,000	(t)
Beginning Retained Earnings	0	100	200
Plus: Net Income (loss)	(b)	(o)	700
Less: Dividends	(c)	(500)	(300)
Ending Retained Earnings	100	(p)	600
Total Shareholders' Equity	$ (d)	$ 6,200	$ 8,600
Balance Sheets			
Assets			
Cash	$ (e)	$ (q)	$ (u)
Land	0	(r)	8,000
Total Assets	$ (f)	$11,200	$10,600
Liabilities	$ (g)	$ 5,000	$ 2,000
Equity			
Common Shares	(h)	(s)	8,000
Retained Earnings	(i)	200	600
Total Shareholders' Equity	(j)	6,200	8,600
Total Liabilities and Shareholders' Equity	$8,100	$11,200	$ 10,600
Cash Flow Statements			
Cash Flows from Operating Activities			
Cash Receipts from Revenue	$ (k)	$ 1,300	$ (v)
Cash Payments for Expenses	(l)	(700)	(w)
Net Cash Flows from Operating Activities	200	600	700
Cash Flows from Investing Activities			
Cash Payments for Land	0	(8,000)	0
Cash Flows from Financing Activities			
Cash Receipts from Loan	3,000	3,000	0
Cash Payments to Reduce Debt	0	(1,000)	(x)
Cash Receipts from Share Issue	5,000	1,000	(y)
Cash Payments for Dividends	(100)	(500)	(z)
Net Cash Flows from Financing Activities	7,900	2,500	(1,300)
Net Change in Cash	8,100	(4,900)	(600)
Plus: Beginning Cash Balance	0	8,100	3,200
Ending Cash Balance	$8,100	$ 3,200	$ 2,600

L.O. 8 PROBLEM 1–9A *Classifying Events as Asset Source, Use, or Exchange*

The following unrelated events are typical of those experienced by business entities.

1. Acquire cash by issuing common shares.
2. Pay monthly rent on an office building.
3. Purchase land with cash.
4. Borrow cash from a bank.
5. Purchase equipment with cash.
6. Hire a new office manager.
7. Provide services for cash.
8. Acquire land by accepting a liability (financing the purchase).
9. Pay a cash dividend to shareholders.
10. Pay cash for operating expenses.
11. Pay an office manager's salary with cash.
12. Receive cash for services that have been performed.
13. Discuss plans for a new office building with an architect.
14. Repay part of a bank loan.
15. Pay cash to purchase a new office building.

Required

Identify each of the events as an asset source, use, or exchange transaction. If an event would not be recorded under generally accepted accounting principles, identify it as *not applicable* (NA). Also indicate for each event whether total assets would increase, decrease, or remain unchanged. Organize your answer according to the following table. The first event is shown in the table as an example.

Event No.	Type of Event	Effect on Total Assets
1	Asset source	Increase

L.O. 11 PROBLEM 1–10A *Price-Earnings Relationships*

Earnings per share and market price per share data for Advantage, Inc., and Hi-Lite, Inc., follow:

Advantage, Inc.	2005	2006	2007
Earnings per share	$ 4.22	$ 4.13	$ 4.18
Market price per share	50.64	45.43	45.98
Hi-Lite, Inc.	**2005**	**2006**	**2007**
Earnings per share	$ 3.27	$ 4.19	$ 5.81
Market price per share	98.10	129.89	220.78

Required

a. Calculate the annual growth rate in the earnings per share of each company from 2006 to 2007.
b. Calculate the price-earnings ratio for each company for all three years.
c. Explain what the price-earnings ratio means.
d. Why would the price-earnings ratios of the two companies be different?

PROBLEMS—SERIES B

PROBLEM 1–1B *Different Forms of Business Organization* L.O. 1

Paul Salvy established a partnership with Lisa Witlow. The new company, S&W Fuels, purchased coal directly from mining companies and contracted to ship the coal via waterways to a seaport, where it was delivered to ships that were owned and operated by international utilities companies. Salvy was primarily responsible for running the day-to-day operations of the business. Witlow negotiated the buy-and-sell agreements. She recently signed a deal to purchase and deliver $2,000,000 of coal to Solar Utilities. S&W Fuels purchased the coal on account from Miller Mining Company. After accepting title to the coal, S&W Fuels agreed to deliver the coal under terms FOB destination, Port of Halifax. Unfortunately, Witlow failed to inform Salvy of the deal in time for Salvy to insure the shipment. While in transit, the vessel carrying the coal suffered storm damage that rendered the coal virtually worthless by the time it reached its destination. S&W Fuels immediately declared bankruptcy. The company not only was responsible for the $2,000,000 due to Miller Mining Company but also was sued by Solar for breach of contract. Witlow had a personal net worth of virtually zero, but Salvy was a wealthy individual with a net worth approaching $2,500,000. Accordingly, Miller Mining and Solar filed suit against Salvy's personal assets. Salvy claimed that he was not responsible for the problem because Witlow had failed to inform him of the contracts in time to obtain insurance coverage. Witlow admitted that she was personally responsible for the disaster.

Required
Write a memo describing Salvy's risk associated with his participation in the partnership. Comment on how other forms of ownership would have affected his level of risk.

PROBLEM 1–2B *Recording the Effect of Events in a Horizontal Statements Model* L.O. 9

Belzio Company was started in 2001. It had existing balances in various permanent accounts at the start of 2006. The company experienced the following transactions during 2006.

1. Paid a cash dividend to the shareholders.
2. Acquired cash by issuing additional common shares.
3. Signed a contract to perform services in the future.
4. Performed services for cash.
5. Paid cash expenses.
6. Sold land for cash at an amount equal to its cost.
7. Borrowed cash from a bank.

Required
Use a horizontal statements model to show how each event affects the balance sheet, income statement, and cash flow statement. Indicate whether the event increases (I), decreases (D), or does not affect (NA) each element of the financial statements. Also, in the Cash Flow Statement column, classify the cash flows as operating activities (OA), investing activities (IA), or financing activities (FA). The first transaction is shown as an example.

	Balance Sheet									Income Statement					Cash Flow Statement	
Event No.	Cash	+	Land	=	N. Pay	+	C. Shares	+	Ret. Ear.	Rev.	−	Exp.	=	Net Inc.		
1.	D	+	NA	=	NA	+	NA	+	D	NA	−	NA	=	NA	D	FA

PROBLEM 1–3B *Recording Events in a Horizontal Statements Model* L.O. 5, 9

Foreman Company was started January 1, 2008, and experienced the following events during its first year of operation:

1. Acquired $32,000 cash from the issue of common shares.
2. Borrowed $20,000 cash from a local bank.
3. Earned cash revenues of $42,000 for performing services.
4. Paid cash expenses of $28,000.
5. Paid a $6,000 cash dividend to the shareholders.
6. Acquired an additional $10,000 cash from the issue of common shares.
7. Paid $15,000 cash to reduce the principal balance of the bank note.
8. Paid $45,000 cash to purchase land.

Required

a. Record the preceding transactions in the horizontal statements model. Also, in the Cash Flow Statement column, classify the cash flows as operating activities (OA), investing activities (IA), or financing activities (FA). The first event is shown as an example.

	Balance Sheet									Income Statement					Cash Flow Statement	
Event No.	Cash	+	Land	=	N. Pay	+	C. Shares	+	Ret. Ear.	Rev.	−	Exp.	=	Net Inc.		
1.	32,000	+	NA	=	NA	+	32,000	+	NA	NA	−	NA	=	NA	32,000	FA

b. Determine the amount of total assets that Foreman would report on the December 31, 2008, balance sheet.

c. Identify the sources of the assets that Foreman would report on the December 31, 2008, balance sheet. Determine the amount of each of these sources.

d. Determine the net income that Foreman would report on the 2008 income statement. Explain why dividends do not appear on the income statement.

e. Determine the net cash flows from operating activities, investing activities, and financing activities that Foreman would report on the 2008 cash flow statement.

L.O. 4, 5, 6, 7 PROBLEM 1–4B *Preparing Financial Statements for Two Complete Accounting Cycles*

Jim's Janitorial Services experienced the following transactions for 2006, the first year of operations, and 2007. *Assume that all transactions involve the receipt or payment of cash.*

Transactions for 2006

1. Acquired $60,000 by issuing common shares.
2. Received $100,000 for providing services to customers.
3. Borrowed $25,000 cash from creditors.
4. Paid expenses amounting to $70,000.
5. Purchased land for $40,000 cash.

Transactions for 2007

1. Acquired an additional $20,000 from the issue of common shares.
2. Received $120,000 for providing services in 2007.
3. Paid $10,000 to creditors.
4. Paid expenses amounting to $80,000.
5. Paid a $15,000 dividend to the shareholders.

Required

a. Write an accounting equation, and record the effects of each accounting event under the appropriate headings for each year. Record the amounts of revenue, expense, and dividends in the Retained Earnings column. Provide appropriate titles for these accounts in the last column of the table.

b. Prepare an income statement, statement of shareholders' equity, year-end balance sheet, and cash flow statement for each year. Use the vertical format when you prepare the financial statements.

c. Compare the information provided by the income statement with the information provided by the cash flow statement. Point out similarities and differences.

d. Determine the percentage growth in earnings from 2006 to 2007.

L.O. 4, 5 PROBLEM 1–5B *Interrelationships among Financial Statements*

Best Electronics started the accounting period with $10,000 of assets, $2,200 of liabilities, and $4,550 of retained earnings. During the period, the Retained Earnings account increased by $3,565. The bookkeeper reported that Best paid cash expenses of $5,010 and paid a $625 cash dividend to shareholders, but she could not find a record of the amount of cash that Best received for performing services. Best also paid $1,000 cash to reduce the liability owed to a bank, and the business acquired $2,000 of additional cash from the issue of common shares.

Required

Prepare an income statement, statement of shareholders' equity, year-end balance sheet, and cash flow statement for the accounting period. (*Hint*: Determine the beginning balance in the common share account before considering the effects of the current period events. It also might help to record all events under an accounting equation before preparing the statements.)

PROBLEM 1–6B *Relating Titles and Accounts to Financial Statements*

L.O. 5

A random list of various financial statement components follows: (1) Retained Earnings account ending balance, (2) Revenues, (3) Common Shares account beginning balance, (4) Common Shares account ending balance, (5) Assets, (6) Expenses, (7) Operating Activities, (8) Dividends, (9) Retained Earnings beginning balance, (10) Investing Activities, (11) Common Shares issued during the period, (12) Liabilities, and (13) Financing Activities.

Required

Set up a table with the following headings. Identify the financial statements on which each of the preceding components appears by placing the reference number for the component in the appropriate column. If an item appears on more than one statement, place the reference number in every applicable column. The first component is shown as an example.

Income Statement	Statement of Shareholders' Equity	Balance Sheet	Cash Flow Statement
	1	1	

PROBLEM 1–7B *Closing the Accounts*

L.O. 3, 4, 5, 6

The following accounts and account balances were taken from the records of Peaks View Company. Except as otherwise indicated, all balances are as of December 31, 2005, before the closing entries had been recorded.

Consulting Revenue	$14,500
Cash	28,500
Cash Received from Common Shares Issued during 2005	4,500
Travel Expense	1,100
Dividends	3,000
Cash Flow from Investing Activities	3,400
Rent Expense	1,800
Payment to Reduce Debt Principal	8,000
Retained Earnings, January 1, 2005	19,000
Salary Expense	6,900
Cash Flow from Operating Activities	1,500
Common Shares, December 31, 2005	10,000
Other Operating Expenses	2,200

Required

a. Identify the accounts that should be closed to the Retained Earnings account.
b. Prepare the income statement that Peaks View would include in its 2005 annual report.
c. Determine the Retained Earnings account balance at December 31, 2005. Explain how the company could pay cash dividends in excess of the amount of net income earned in 2005.
d. Name the stages of the accounting cycle in the order in which they normally occur.

PROBLEM 1–8B *Missing Information in Financial Statements*

L.O. 4, 5

Required

Fill in the blanks (indicated by the letters in parentheses) in the following financial statements. Assume the company started operations January 1, 2007.

	For the Years		
	2007	2008	2009
Income Statements			
Revenue (cash)	$ 400	$ 500	$ 800
Expense (cash)	(250)	(l)	(425)
Net Income (loss)	$ (a)	$ 100	$ 375
Statements of Shareholders' Equity			
Beginning Common Shares	$ 0	$ (m)	$ 9,100
Plus: Common Shares Issued	(b)	1,100	310
Ending Common Shares	8,000	9,100	(s)
Beginning Retained Earnings	0	25	75
Plus: Net Income (loss)	(c)	100	375
Less: Dividends	(d)	(50)	(150)
Ending Retained Earnings	25	(n)	300
Total Shareholders' Equity	$ (e)	$ 9,175	$ (t)
Balance Sheets			
Assets			
Cash	$ (f)	$ (o)	$ (u)
Land	0	(p)	2,500
Total Assets	$11,000	$11,650	$10,550
Liabilities	$ (g)	$ (q)	$ 840
Equity			
Common Shares	(h)	(r)	9,410
Retained Earnings	(i)	75	300
Total Shareholders' Equity	8,025	9,175	9,710
Total Liabilities and Shareholders' Equity	$11,000	$11,650	$10,550
Cash Flow Statements			
Cash Flows from Operating Activities			
Cash Receipts from Revenue	$ (j)	$ 500	$ (v)
Cash Payments for Expenses	(k)	(400)	(w)
Net Cash Flows from Operating Activities	150	100	375
Cash Flows from Investing Activities			
Cash Payments for Land	0	(5,000)	0
Cash Receipt from Sale of Land	0	0	2,500
Net Cash Flows from Investing Activities	0	(5,000)	2,500
Cash Flows from Financing Activities			
Cash Receipts from Borrowed Funds	2,975	0	0
Cash Payments to Reduce Debt	0	(500)	(x)
Cash Receipts from Share Issue	8,000	1,100	(y)
Cash Payments for Dividends	(125)	(50)	(z)
Net Cash Flows from Financing Activities	10,850	550	(1,475)
Net Change in Cash	11,000	(4,350)	1,400
Plus: Beginning Cash Balance	0	11,000	6,650
Ending Cash Balance	$11,000	$ 6,650	$ 8,050

L.O. 8 PROBLEM 1–9B *Classifying Events as Asset Source, Use, or Exchange*

The following unrelated events are typical of those experienced by business entities:

1. Acquire cash by issuing common shares.
2. Borrow cash from the local bank.
3. Paid office supplies expense.
4. Make plans to purchase office equipment.

5. Trade a used car for a computer with the same value.
6. Paid other operating supplies expense.
7. Agree to represent a client in a tax audit and to receive payment when the audit is complete.
8. Receive cash from customers for services rendered.
9. Pay employee salaries with cash.
10. Pay back a bank loan with cash.
11. Pay interest to a bank with cash.
12. Transfer cash from a chequing account to a money market account.
13. Sell land for cash at its original cost.
14. Pay a cash dividend to shareholders.
15. Learn that a financial analyst determined the company's price-earnings ratio to be 26.

Required

Identify each of the events as an asset source, asset use, or asset exchange transaction. If an event would not be recorded under generally accepted accounting principles, identify it as *not applicable* (NA). Also indicate for each event whether total assets would increase, decrease, or remain unchanged. Organize your answer according to the following table. The first event is shown in the table as an example.

Event No.	Type of Event	Effect on Total Assets
1	Asset source	Increase

PROBLEM 1–10B *Price-Earnings Relationships* **L.O. 11**

Beta One, Inc., is a pharmaceutical company heavily involved in research leading to the development of genealogy-based medicines. While the company has several promising research studies in progress, it has brought only two viable products to market during the last decade. Earnings per share and market price per share data for the latest three years of operation follow.

Beta One, Inc.	2003	2004	2005
Earnings per share	$ 1.22	$ 1.19	$ 1.20
Market price per share	85.40	84.49	87.60

Required

a. Calculate the company's annual growth rate in earnings per share for 2004 and 2005.
b. Calculate the company's price-earnings ratio for all three years.
c. Explain the size of the price-earnings ratio.

ANALYZE, THINK, COMMUNICATE

BUSINESS APPLICATIONS CASE *Bombardier's Annual Report* **ATC 1–1**

Required

Use the Bombardier financial statements in Appendix B to answer the following questions.

a. What was Bombardier's net income for 2002?
b. How does net income for 2002 compare to net income for 2001?
c. What was Bombardier's accounting equation for 2002?

GROUP ASSIGNMENT *Missing Information* **ATC 1–2**

The following selected financial information is available for H&R Block. Amounts are in millions of dollars.

Income Statements	1998	1997	1996	1995
Revenue	$1,307	$ (a)	$ 894	1,239
Cost and Expenses	(a)	(1,859)	(769)	(a)
Income from Continuing Operations	174	71	(a)	(b)
Unusual Items	218	(b)	(b)	0
Net Income	$ (b)	$ 47	$ 177	$ 107
Balance Sheets				
Assets				
Cash and Marketable Securities	$1,247	$ (c)	$ 419	$ 353
Other Assets	(c)	1,226	(c)	725
Total Assets	$2,904	$ (d)	$1,418	$1,078
Liabilities	$ (d)	$ 907	$ (d)	$ (c)
Equity				
Common Shares	356	(e)	313	(d)
Retained Earnings	(e)	684	(e)	(14)
Total Equity	1,342	(f)	1,040	686
Total Liabilities and Equity	$ (f)	$1,906	$1,418	$1,078

Required

a. Divide the class into groups of four or five students each. Organize the groups into four sections. Assign Task 1 to the first section of groups, Task 2 to the second section, Task 3 to the third section, and Task 4 to the fourth section.

Group Tasks

(1) Fill in the missing information for 1995.
(2) Fill in the missing information for 1996.
(3) Fill in the missing information for 1997.
(4) Fill in the missing information for 1998.

b. Each section should select two representatives. One representative is to put the financial statements assigned to that section on the board, underlining the missing amounts. The second representative is to explain to the class how the missing amounts were determined.

c. Each section should list events that could have caused the unusual item category on the income statement.

ATC 1–3 REAL-WORLD CASE

Required

Go to www.royalbank.ca. Using the most recent annual report of the Royal Bank, answer the following questions:

a. What is the year-end date for the Royal Bank?
b. What are the major asset categories on the Royal Bank's balance sheet?
c. Compute the percentage growth in the Royal Bank's *net income before income taxes* for the current year and the prior year.

ATC 1–4 BUSINESS APPLICATIONS CASE *Use of Real-World Numbers*

The following information was drawn from the annual report of Dofasco:

	For the Years (in thousands) 1999	2000
Income Statements		
Revenue	$3,142.3	$3,201.1
Operating Expenses	2,735.3	2,894.7
Income from Operations	407.0	306.4
Non-operating Expenses	146.2	117.7
Net Income	260.8	188.7
Balance Sheets		
Assets	$3,482.8	$3,523.6
Liabilities	$1,670.3	$1,671.1
Contributed Capital	843.8	804.8
Retained Earnings	968.7	1,047.7
Total Liabilities and Equity	$3,482.8	$3,523.6

Required

a. Compute the percentage change in net income from 1999 to 2000.
b. How would you explain the difference in retained earnings between 1999 and 2000?
c. What do you think contributed to Dofasco's decrease in net income between 1999 and 2000? (*Hint:* Think in terms of the elements that affect the income statement.)

WRITING ASSIGNMENT *Elements of Financial Statements Defined* ATC 1–5

Bob and his sister Marsha both attend university. As a reward for their successful completion of the past year (Bob had a 3.2 GPA in business, and Marsha had a 3.7 GPA in art), their father gave each of them 100 shares of the Walt Disney Company. They have just received their first annual report. Marsha does not understand what the information means and has asked Bob to explain it to her. Bob is currently taking an accounting course, and she knows he will understand the financial statements.

Required

Assume that you are Bob. Write Marsha a memo explaining the following financial statement items to her. In your explanation, describe each of the financial statements and explain the financial information each contains. Also define each of the elements listed for each financial statement and explain what it means.

Balance Sheet
Assets
Liabilities
Equity
Income Statement
Revenue
Expense
Net Income

ETHICAL DILEMMA *Loyalty versus the Bottom Line* ATC 1–6

Assume that Jones has been working for you for five years. He has had an excellent work history and has received generous pay raises in response. The raises have been so generous that Jones is quite overpaid for the job he is required to perform. Unfortunately, he is not qualified to take on other, more responsible jobs available within the company. A recent job applicant is willing to accept a salary $5,000 per year less than the amount currently being paid to Jones. The applicant is well qualified to take over Jones's duties and has a very positive attitude. The following financial statements were reported by your company at the close of its most recent accounting period.

Financial Statements		
Income Statement		
Revenue		$57,000
Expense		(45,000)
Net Income		$12,000
Statement of Shareholders' Equity		
Beginning Common Shares	$20,000	
Plus: Additional Shares Issued	5,000	
Ending Common Shares		$25,000
Beginning Retained Earnings	50,000	
Net Income	12,000	
Dividends	(2,000)	
Ending Retained Earnings		60,000
Total Equity		$85,000
Balance Sheet		
Assets		
Cash		$85,000
Shareholders' Equity		
Common Shares		$25,000
Retained Earnings		60,000
Total Shareholders' Equity		$85,000
Cash Flow Statement		
Operating Activities		
Inflow from Customers	$57,000	
Outflow for Expenses	(45,000)	
Net Inflow from Operations		$12,000
Investing Activities		0
Financing Activities		
Inflow from Common Shares Issued	5,000	
Outflow for Dividends	(2,000)	
Net Inflow from Financing Activities		3,000
Net Change in Cash		15,000
Plus: Beginning Cash Balance		70,000
Ending Cash Balance		$85,000

Required

a. Reconstruct the financial statements, assuming that Jones was replaced at the beginning of the most recent accounting period. Both Jones and his replacement are paid in cash. No other changes are to be considered.

b. Discuss the short- and long-term ramifications of replacing Jones. There are no right answers. However, assume that you are required to make a decision. Use your judgment and common sense to support your choice.

ATC 1–7 SPREADSHEET ASSIGNMENT *Using Excel*

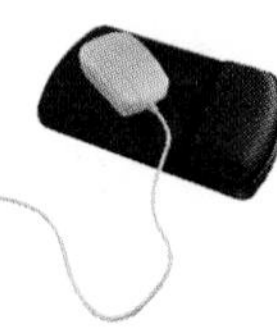

The financial statements for Simple Company are reported here using an Excel spreadsheet.

Required

Re-create the financial statements using your own Excel spreadsheet.

a. For each number with an arrow by it, enter a formula in that particular cell address to solve for the number shown. (Do not enter the arrow.)

b. When complete, print the spreadsheet with formulas rather than absolute numbers.

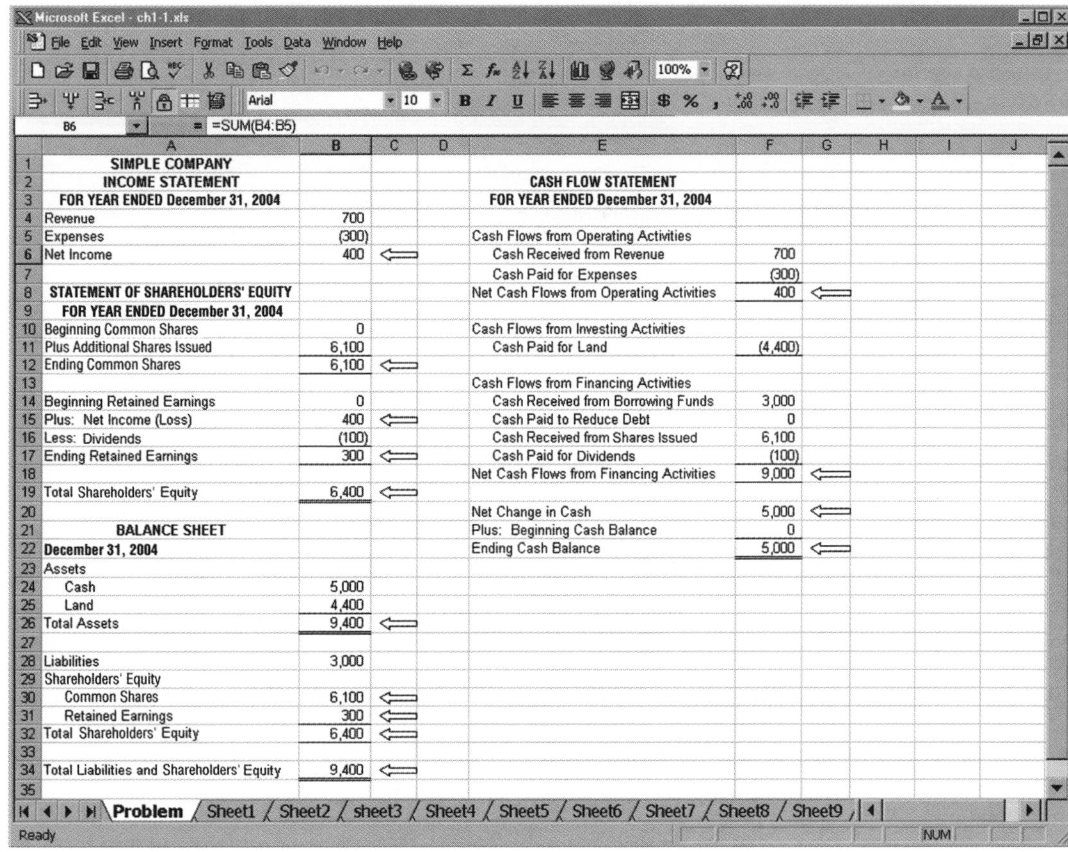
Microsoft Excel - ch1-1.xls

B6 = =SUM(B4:B5)

	A	B	C	D	E	F	G
1	SIMPLE COMPANY						
2	INCOME STATEMENT				CASH FLOW STATEMENT		
3	FOR YEAR ENDED December 31, 2004				FOR YEAR ENDED December 31, 2004		
4	Revenue	700					
5	Expenses	(300)			Cash Flows from Operating Activities		
6	Net Income	400	⇐		Cash Received from Revenue	700	
7					Cash Paid for Expenses	(300)	
8	STATEMENT OF SHAREHOLDERS' EQUITY				Net Cash Flows from Operating Activities	400	⇐
9	FOR YEAR ENDED December 31, 2004						
10	Beginning Common Shares	0			Cash Flows from Investing Activities		
11	Plus Additional Shares Issued	6,100			Cash Paid for Land	(4,400)	
12	Ending Common Shares	6,100	⇐				
13					Cash Flows from Financing Activities		
14	Beginning Retained Earnings	0			Cash Received from Borrowing Funds	3,000	
15	Plus: Net Income (Loss)	400	⇐		Cash Paid to Reduce Debt	0	
16	Less: Dividends	(100)			Cash Received from Shares Issued	6,100	
17	Ending Retained Earnings	300	⇐		Cash Paid for Dividends	(100)	
18					Net Cash Flows from Financing Activities	9,000	⇐
19	Total Shareholders' Equity	6,400	⇐				
20					Net Change in Cash	5,000	⇐
21	BALANCE SHEET				Plus: Beginning Cash Balance	0	
22	December 31, 2004				Ending Cash Balance	5,000	⇐
23	Assets						
24	Cash	5,000					
25	Land	4,400					
26	Total Assets	9,400	⇐				
27							
28	Liabilities	3,000					
29	Shareholders' Equity						
30	Common Shares	6,100	⇐				
31	Retained Earnings	300	⇐				
32	Total Shareholders' Equity	6,400	⇐				
33							
34	Total Liabilities and Shareholders' Equity	9,400	⇐				
35							

Problem / Sheet1 / Sheet2 / sheet3 / Sheet4 / Sheet5 / Sheet6 / Sheet7 / Sheet8 / Sheet9

Spreadsheet Tips

(1) Widen a column by positioning the cursor on the vertical line between two column headings until a crosshair appears. Either double click to automatically widen or click and drag the crosshair to the desired width.

(2) Negative numbers can be parenthesized by choosing Format and then Cells. Under Category, choose Custom, and under Type, choose the first option containing parentheses.

(3) The SUM function is one way to add a series of numbers. For example, the formula for net income in cell B6 is SUM(B4:B5).

(4) Single and double lines can be drawn using the Borders icon.

(5) Print a spreadsheet on one page by choosing File, Page Setup, and Fit to 1.

(6) Print without gridlines by choosing File, Page Setup, and Sheet and uncheck Gridlines. Another option is to choose Tools and Options and uncheck Gridlines.

(7) Print formulas by choosing Tools, Options, and Formulas.

SPREADSHEET ASSIGNMENT *Mastering Excel* ATC 1–8

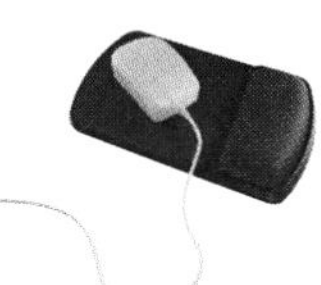

Required

a. Enter the following headings for the horizontal statements model onto a blank spreadsheet.

Microsoft Excel - ch1-2.xls

File Edit View Insert Format Tools Data Window Help

O6 = =B6

	A	B	C	D	E	F	G	H	I	J	K	L	M	N	O	P
1					Balance Sheet						Income Statement				Cash Flow	
2		Assets			Liabilities	Shareholders' Equity									Statement	
3	Event				Loan	Common	Retained						Net			
4	Number	Cash	Land	=	Payable	Shares	Earnings		Revenue	-	Expense	=	Income		Amount	Activity
5																
6	1	$6,100				$6,100									$6,100	Financing
7	2															
8	3															
9	4															
10	5															
11	6															
12																
13	Totals	$6,100	$0		$0	$6,100	$0		$0		$0		$0		$6,100	
14																
15			$6,100		$6,100											
16			Total		Total											
17			Assets		Claims											
18																
19																
20																

b. Under the appropriate headings, record the effects of each of the following accounting events for the first month of operations. The first event has been recorded as an example.
   (1) Acquired $6,100 from the issue of common shares.
   (2) Paid $4,400 to purchase land.
   (3) Borrowed $3,000 cash.
   (4) Provided services to customers and received $700 in cash.
   (5) Paid $300 for expenses.
   (6) Paid a $100 dividend to the shareholders.
   (*Note:* The amounts on the cash flow statement can be referenced to the Cash account on the balance sheet. In other words, recording the cash amounts twice is not necessary. Instead enter formulas in the Cash Flow Statement column equating those cell addresses to the respective cell in the Cash column. Notice that the formula in cell O6 (cash flow statement) is set equal to cell B6 (cash on the balance sheet). Once the formula is completed for cell O6, it can be easily copied to cells O7 through O11.)

c. Using formulas, sum each of the quantitative columns to arrive at the end-of-month amounts reported on the financial statements.

Spreadsheet Tips

(1) Centre the heading Balance Sheet across columns by entering the entire heading in cell B1. Position the cursor on B1 until a fat cross appears. Click and drag the cursor across B1 through G1. Click on the Merge and Centre icon (it is highlighted in the screen in the computer display).

(2) Enter arithmetic signs as headings by placing an apostrophe in front of the sign. For example, to enter the equals sign in cell D4, enter '=.

(3) Copy cells by positioning the cursor in the bottom right corner of the cell to copy from (such as cell O6) until a thin cross appears. Click and drag the cursor down through the desired locations to copy to (through cell O11).

(4) To enter the dollar sign, choose Format, Cells, and Currency.

Chapter 2

Accounting for Accruals

Learning Objectives

After completing this chapter, you should be able to:

1. Explain the concept of accrual versus cash accounting.

2. Explain how accrual transactions (as well as cash transactions introduced in Chapter 1) affect the financial statements of a business.

3. Demonstrate how events are recorded under an accounting equation.

4. Prepare simple financial statements for a business that uses cash and accrual transactions.

5. Define *revenue* and *expense* as they relate to assets and liabilities.

6. Explain the effects of end-of-period adjustments related to accruals.

7. Explain the auditor's role in financial reporting.

8. Understand the importance of a code of ethics.

9. Classify accounting events into one of four categories, including
   a. asset source transactions.
   b. asset use transactions.
   c. asset exchange transactions.
   d. claims exchange transactions.

the *curious* accountant

Suppose a company located in Calgary, Alberta, needs to ship goods to a customer located 3,000 km away in Montreal, Quebec. The company agrees to pay the CN Corporation $1,500 to deliver the goods by rail. When should CN report that it has earned revenue? More specifically, should the revenue be recognized before, during, or after the delivery of the goods? For the answer, turn to page 59.

All of the transactions shown in Chapter 1 had direct cash consequences. For example, revenue was recorded at the time cash was collected, and expenses were recorded at the time cash was paid. Such exact coincidence seldom occurs in business practice. Indeed, a "buy-now, pay-later" philosophy is common in all major industrialized economies. Customers often purchase services in one accounting period and pay for them in a different period. ***Accrual accounting*** *recognizes the effects of revenue and expense events in the period in which they occur, regardless of when cash is exchanged. The generally accepted accounting principles that apply to accrual accounting specifically are (1) the revenue recognition principle and (2) the matching principle. Suppose a business provides services in 2005 but collects cash for those services in 2006. Under accrual accounting, the business recognizes the revenue in 2005 (revenue recognition principle). Similarly, if a business consumes resources in 2005 that are paid for in 2006, an expense is recognized in 2005 even though the cash payment is made in 2006 (matching principle).*

Accrual accounting distinguishes between the recognition of accounting events and the realization of cash receipts or payments. ***Recognition*** *means recording an event in the financial records.* ***Realization*** *usually refers to the collection or payment of cash. Revenues or expenses can be recognized (recorded) before or after cash is realized (collected or paid).*

Accrual accounting uses both accruals and deferrals. The term ***accrual*** *applies to earnings events that are recognized before cash is exchanged. For example, revenue may be recognized in 2005 although the associated cash is collected in 2006. The term deferral applies to earnings events that are recognized after cash has been exchanged. To illustrate, assume that supplies are purchased with cash in 2005 but are used in 2006. The supplies expense would be recognized in 2006 even though cash was paid in 2005. This chapter introduces the most common types of accruals. Deferrals will be explained in Chapter 3.*

Accrual Accounting Illustrated

LO1 Explain the concept of accrual versus cost accounting.

Beth Conner started a consulting practice called Conner Consultants that specializes in developing and delivering quality training programs. The business began operations on January 1, 2005. Since the training programs take place on the client's premises, Conner's clients provide office space and secretarial support. As a result, she is able to avoid many operating expenses. However, Conner does incur salary expenses for one instructor who is a part-time employee. During 2005, Conner experienced the following business events.

Effect of Events on Financial Statements

This section of the text describes seven events that Conner Consultants experienced in its first year of operation (2005). The effects of each event will be shown in a horizontal statements model.

Event 1 The business was started when it acquired $5,000 cash by issuing common shares.

LO2 Explain how accrual transactions (as well as cash transactions introduced in Chapter 1) affect the financial statements of a business.

The $5,000 share issue is an **asset source transaction**. It increases the business's assets (Cash) and its equity (Common Shares). Because the event did not result from business operations, the transaction did not affect the income statement. The cash inflow is classified as a financing activity (acquisition from owners). These effects are shown in the following financial statements model:

Assets	=	Liab.	+	C. Sh.	+	Ret. Ear.	Rev.	−	Exp.	=	Net Inc.	Cash Flow Statement
5,000	=	NA	+	5,000	+	NA	NA	−	NA	=	NA	5,000 FA

Event 2 During 2005 Conner Consultants provided $84,000 of consulting services to its clients. The work has been performed and bills have been sent to the clients, but Conner has not yet collected any cash. This type of transaction is often referred to as *providing services on account.*

Accrual accounting requires recognizing $84,000 of assets and the corresponding revenue in the 2005 accounting period (the period in which the work was done). The fact that cash has not been *collected* does not affect the amount of assets and revenue to be *recognized.* The specific asset that increases is called **Accounts Receivable**. As its name suggests, the receivables account represents amounts of future cash receipts that are due from customers (amounts that are expected to be collected in the future). The revenue recognition transaction is an *asset source transaction*. Its effect on the financial statements follows:

Assets			=	Liab.	+	Equity								Cash Flow Statement
Cash	+	Acc. Rec.	=	Liab.	+	C. Sh.	+	Ret. Ear.	Rev.	−	Exp.	=	Net Inc.	
NA	+	84,000	=	NA	+	NA	+	84,000	84,000	−	NA	=	84,000	NA

The event affects the income statement but not the cash flow statement. Accrual accounting recognizes revenue in the period it is earned (when the work is done), regardless of when cash is collected.

Conner collected $60,000 cash from customers in partial settlement of its accounts receivable. **Event 3**

The conversion of $60,000 of accounts receivable to cash is an **asset exchange transaction**. The amount in the Cash account increases, and the amount in the Accounts Receivable account decreases. The amount of total assets is unchanged. The effect of the $60,000 collection of receivables on the financial statements is as follows:

Assets			=	Liab.	+	Equity								Cash Flow Statement
Cash	+	Acc. Rec.	=	Liab.	+	C. Sh.	+	Ret. Ear.	Rev.	−	Exp.	=	Net Inc.	
60,000	+	(60,000)	=	NA	+	NA	+	NA	NA	−	NA	=	NA	60,000 OA

Note that collecting the cash did not affect the income statement. The full $84,000 of revenue was recognized at the time the work was done. Revenue would be double counted if it were recognized again when the cash is collected. The cash flow statement reflects a cash inflow from operating activities.

The instructor earned a salary of $16,000. No cash has yet been paid to the employee. **Event 4**

This event illustrates the common circumstance of recognizing expenses before paying cash. In this case, the $16,000 of salary expenses is offset by an increase in a liability account called *Salaries Payable*. As its name suggests, the **Salaries Payable** account represents amounts of future cash payments owed to the employee. The effect of the expense recognition on the financial statements follows:

Assets			=	Liab.	+	Equity								Cash Flow Statement
Cash	+	Acc. Rec.	=	Sal. Pay.	+	C. Sh.	+	Ret. Ear.	Rev.	−	Exp.	=	Net Inc.	
NA	+	NA	=	16,000	+	NA	+	(16,000)	NA	−	16,000	=	(16,000)	NA

This event is a **claims exchange transaction**. The claims of creditors (liabilities) increase, and the claims of owners (retained earnings) decrease by $16,000. Total claims stay the same. The expense is recognized on the income statement although cash has not been paid.

Do not confuse liabilities with expenses. True, liabilities are sometimes affected when expenses are recognized, but they are not the same thing as expenses. Expenses are economic sacrifices incurred in an effort to produce revenue. More specifically, expenses are decreases in assets or increases in liabilities that result from earnings activities. Expenses always reduce equity. In contrast, liabilities are obligations (amounts owed to another party). They can arise from acquiring assets or from recognizing expenses. For example, if a business borrows money from a bank, it recognizes a liability (an obligation to repay the bank). Here, assets and liabilities both increase. Expenses are not affected. In summary, expenses are economic sacrifices that reduce equity; liabilities are obligations. Expenses are reported on the income statement; liabilities are reported on the balance sheet.

Conner paid $10,000 to the instructor in partial settlement of salaries payable. **Event 5**

Cash payments to creditors are **asset use transactions**. When Conner pays the instructor, the asset account Cash and the liability account Salaries Payable both decrease by $10,000. The effect of this transaction on the financial statements follows:

Assets			=	Liab.	+	Equity								Cash Flow Statement
Cash	+	Acc. Rec.	=	Sal. Pay.	+	C. Sh.	+	Ret. Ear.	Rev.	−	Exp.	=	Net Inc.	
(10,000)	+	NA	=	(10,000)	+	NA	+	NA	NA	−	NA	=	NA	(10,000) OA

The actual cash payment did not involve recognizing an expense. The expense was recognized in full at the time the employee did the work. Double counting would occur if it were recognized again when the cash payment is made. The cash flow statement would reflect a cash outflow from operating activities.

Event 6 Conner paid $2,000 cash for advertising costs.

Cash payments for expenses are asset use transactions. Both the asset account Cash and the equity account Retained Earnings decrease by $2,000. Recognizing the expense decreases net income on the income statement. Since the expense was paid with cash, the cash flow statement would reflect a cash outflow from operating activities. These effects on the financial statements follow:

Assets			=	Liab.	+	Equity								Cash Flow Statement
Cash	+	Acc. Rec.	=	Sal. Pay.	+	C. Sh.	+	Ret. Ear.	Rev.	−	Exp.	=	Net Inc.	
(2,000)	+	NA	=	NA	+	NA	+	(2,000)	NA	−	2,000	=	(2,000)	(2,000) OA

Event 7 Conner signed contracts for $42,000 of consulting services to be performed in 2006.

The contracts for $42,000 of consulting services to be performed in 2006 are not recognized in the 2005 financial statements. Assets increase as the result of work that has actually been performed, not work that is expected to be performed. Since no work has been done on these contracts, assets have not increased and revenue has not been earned. Revenue is not recognized before the work is performed no matter how likely its future performance may be. As indicated, this event does not affect any of the financial statements.

Assets			=	Liab.	+	Equity								Cash Flow Statement
Cash	+	Acc. Rec.	=	Sal. Pay.	+	C. Sh.	+	Ret. Ear.	Rev.	−	Exp.	=	Net Inc.	
NA	+	NA	=	NA	+	NA	+	NA	NA	−	NA	=	NA	NA

During 2004, Anwar Company earned $345,000 of revenue on account and collected $320,000 cash from accounts receivable. Expenses amounted to $300,000 and were paid with cash. Anwar paid a $12,000 cash dividend. Determine the amount of net income Anwar should report on the 2004 income statement and the amount of cash flow from operating activities Anwar should report on the 2004 cash flow statement.

Answer Net income equals revenue minus expenses ($345,000 − $300,000 = $45,000). The cash flow from operating activities equals the amount of revenue collected in cash (collection of accounts receivable) minus the cash paid for expenses ($320,000 − $300,000 = $20,000). Dividend payments are classified as financing activities and do not affect either the determination of net income or cash flow from operating activities.

Summary of Transactions

LO3 Demonstrate how events are recorded under an accounting equation.

Event 1 The business acquired $5,000 cash by issuing common shares.
Event 2 Conner provided $84,000 of consulting services on account.
Event 3 Conner collected $60,000 cash from customers in partial settlement of its accounts receivable.
Event 4 Conner recognized $16,000 of salary expense on account.
Event 5 Conner paid $10,000 to the part-time employee in partial settlement of the salary payable.
Event 6 Conner paid $2,000 cash for advertising costs.
Event 7 Conner signed contracts for $42,000 of consulting services to be performed in 2006.

56.76

The general ledger accounts used to record the transaction data for Conner Consultants' 2005 accounting period are shown in Exhibit 2–1. Event 7 is not shown in the illustration because it does not affect the balances in any of the ledger accounts. The data in the accounts are used to prepare the financial statements. Because of space limitations, the revenue and expense accounts are shown in the Retained Earnings column. The titles of these accounts are shown just to the right of the monetary amounts.

Exhibit 2–1 *Transaction Data Recorded in Accounts*

	Assest			=	Liabilities	+	Shareholders' Equity			
Event No.	Cash	+	Accounts Receivable	=	Salaries Payable	+	Common Shares	+	Retained Earnings	Account Titles
Beg. Bal.	$ 0		$ 0		$ 0		$ 0		$ 0	
1	5,000						5,000			
2			84,000						84,000	Consulting Revenue
3	60,000		(60,000)							
4					16,000				(16,000)	Salary Expense
5	(10,000)				(10,000)					
6	(2,000)								(2,000)	Advertising Expense
End Bal.	$ 53,000	+	$ 24,000	=	$6,000	+	$ 5,000	+	$ 66,000	

2005 Financial Statements

Conner Consultants' financial statements for 2005 are shown in a vertical statements model in Exhibit 2–2.

LO2 Explain how accrual transactions (as well as cash transactions introduced in Chapter 1) affect the financial statements of a business.

Income Statement

The income statement explains the changes in shareholders' equity from all sources other than transactions with the owners of an enterprise. As such, it represents the change in net assets resulting from operating the business. In the case of Conner Consultants, the net income ($66,000) represents the net economic benefit of owning the business. In other words, the wealth of the business increased as a result of performing consulting activities. Net income increases owner claims on business assets and enhances the wealth of the owners.

LO4 Prepare simple financial statements for a business that uses cash and accrual transactions.

Recognizing salaries expense in the Conner illustration expands the definition of expenses used in Chapter 1. In that chapter, expenses were defined as economic sacrifices resulting in asset decreases. In the Conner illustration, the recognition of salaries expense coincided with an increase in liabilities (Salaries Payable). So expenses actually can be defined as decreases in assets *or* increases in liabilities resulting from operating activities undertaken to generate revenue. Similarly, revenue recognition can coincide with decreases in liabilities. For example, a person could work off a debt rather than pay cash to the creditor; this would decrease the liability and increase revenue. As a result, the definition of revenue can be expanded as follows: an increase in assets or a decrease in liabilities resulting from the operating activities of a business enterprise.

LO5 Define *revenue* and *expense* as they relate to assets and liabilities.

Statement of Shareholders' Equity

The statement of shareholders' equity reports the effects on equity of issuing common shares, earning net income, and paying dividends to shareholders. It identifies how an entity's equity increased and decreased as a result of transactions with owners and operating the business. In the Conner case, the statement shows that equity increased when the business acquired $5,000 cash by issuing common shares. The same statement indicates that equity increased by $66,000 as a result of earning income and that none of the $66,000 of net earnings was distributed to owners (no dividends were paid), so the amount of ending equity is $71,000 ($5,000 + $66,000).

Exhibit 2–2 *Vertical Statements Model*

CONNER CONSULTANTS
Financial Statements
For the 2005 Accounting Period*

Income Statement		
Consulting Revenue		$ 84,000
Salary Expense		(16,000)
Advertising Expense		(2,000)
Net Income		$ 66,000
Statement of Shareholders' Equity		
Beginning Common Shares	$ 0	
Plus: Common Shares Issued	5,000	
Ending Common Shares		$ 5,000
Beginning Retained Earnings	0	
Plus: Net Income	66,000	
Less: Dividends	0	
Ending Retained Earnings		66,000
Total Shareholders' Equity		$ 71,000
Balance Sheet		
Assets		
Cash	$ 53,000	
Accounts Receivable	24,000	
Total Assets		$ 77,000
Liabilities		
Salaries Payable		$ 6,000
Shareholders' Equity		
Common Shares	5,000	
Retained Earnings	66,000	
Total Shareholders' Equity		71,000
Total Liabilities and Shareholders' Equity		$ 77,000
Cash Flow Statement		
Cash Flows from Operating Activities		
Cash Receipts from Customers	$ 60,000	
Cash Payments for Salary Expense	(10,000)	
Cash Payments for Advertising Expenses	(2,000)	
Net Cash Flow from Operating Activities		$ 48,000
Net Cash Flow from Investing Activities		0
Net Cash Flow from Financing Activities		
Cash Receipt from Issuing Common Shares		5,000
Net Change in Cash		53,000
Plus: Beginning Cash Balance		0
Ending Cash Balance		$ 53,000

* As previously indicated, the vertical model format does not distinguish individual statement date characteristics ("as of" versus "for the year ended"). This practice is used through the text whenever the four financial statements are presented simultaneously. In real-world annual reports, financial statements are normally presented separately with appropriate descriptions of the date to indicate whether the statement applies to the entire accounting period or a specific point in time.

answers to the *curious* accountant

The accrual concept requires a company to recognize revenue when it is "earned" rather than when it collects cash. In some business operations, it is not always easy to know precisely when the revenue is earned. CN Corporation, a very large transportation company, recognizes revenue "proportionately as shipments move from origin to destination."

This means that if CN agrees to ship goods 3,000 km for $1,500, it recognizes approximately $0.50 of revenue for every kilometre the goods are moved. If you are thinking that this must require a very sophisticated computer system, you are correct!

Notice that the "recognize-as-you-go" practice does not violate the rule that revenue cannot be recognized before it is earned. CN cannot recognize the entire $1,500 until the point of destination has been reached. However, the company can recognize the revenue in proportion to the amount of the trip that is completed. If one-half of the trip is completed, one-half of the revenue can be recognized.

Balance Sheet

The balance sheet provides information about an entity's assets, liabilities, and shareholders' equity at a particular time. It reports the economic resources (assets) that the enterprise can use for its operating activities. It also reports the claims on those resources. Conner Consultants had two assets at the end of the 2005 accounting period: Cash of $53,000 and Accounts Receivable of $24,000. These assets are listed on the balance sheet according to their respective levels of liquidity. Of the total $77,000 of assets, creditors have a $6,000 claim; the remaining $71,000 represents owner interests.

Cash Flow Statement

The cash flow statement explains the change in cash from one accounting period to the next. It can be prepared by analyzing the Cash account. Since Conner Consultants was established in the 2005 accounting period, its beginning cash balance was zero. By the end of the period, the balance had increased to $53,000. The cash flow statement explains this increase. Specifically, the Cash account balance increased by $60,000 from consulting activities (operating the business). Furthermore, $12,000 was paid for expenses. As a result, Conner experienced a net cash inflow from operating activities of $48,000. Also, the business acquired $5,000 cash by issuing common shares. This combination of activities explains the $53,000 (or $48,000 + $5,000) increase in cash during the 2005 accounting period.

Closing the Accounts

Recall from Chapter 1 that the balances in the nominal accounts (revenues, expenses, and dividends) are transferred out of those accounts at the end of each accounting period through a process known as *closing the accounts*. Exhibit 2–3 shows the general ledger accounts for Conner Consultants after the revenue and expense accounts have been closed to Retained Earnings. In this case, there were three **closing entries**, which transferred the balances of the nominal accounts to the Retained Earnings account at the end of the accounting period. These entries are labelled Cl.1, Cl.2, and Cl.3. The first closing entry (Cl.1) transferred the balance in the Consulting Revenue account to the Retained Earnings account. The second (Cl.2) and third (Cl.3) transferred the balances in the expense accounts to the Retained Earnings account. As a result of the closing entries, the balances for these revenue and expense accounts will be zero at the beginning of the 2006 accounting period. The balances from these accounts are now summarized in Retained Earnings. The Retained Earnings account reflects the cumulative effect of revenues, expenses, and dividends since the company was founded.

Exhibit 2–3 *General Ledger Accounts for Conner Consultants*

Assets = Liabilities + Equity

Assets

Cash	
[1]	5,000
[3]	60,000
[5]	(10,000)
[6]	(2,000)
Bal.	53,000

Accounts Receivable	
[2]	84,000
[3]	(60,000)
Bal.	24,000

Liabilities

Salaries Payable	
[4]	16,000
[5]	(10,000)
Bal.	6,000

Equity

Common Shares	
[1]	5,000

Retained Earnings	
Cl.1	84,000
Cl.2	(16,000)
Cl.3	(2,000)
Bal.	66,000

Consulting Revenue	
[2]	84,000
Cl.1	(84,000)
Bal.	0

Salary Expense	
[4]	(16,000)
Cl.2	16,000
Bal.	0

Advertising Expense	
[6]	(2,000)
Cl.3	2,000
Bal.	0

Matching Principle

Businesses must make economic sacrifices (incur expenses) to produce economic benefits (earn revenues). A business succeeds when the benefits exceed the sacrifices. Accrual accounting measures the success (profitability) of a business by matching expenses (sacrifices) with the revenues (benefits) they produce. The income statement reports the result of the matching process.

In the case of Conner Consultants, the instructor's salary expense can be matched easily with the revenue the teaching activity generated. Advertising expense presents a more challenging matching issue. The advertising cost can generate revenue in future accounting periods as well as the present period. For example, a prospective customer could save an advertising brochure for several years. At some future date when he needs training services, he might retrieve the brochure and call Conner to perform those services. In such cases, where the relationship between the expense and the corresponding revenue is vague, common practice is to match the expense with the period in which it is incurred. With respect to Conner's advertising cost, the entire $2,000 is matched with (recognized in) the 2005 accounting period even though some of that cost might generate revenue in future accounting periods. Expenses that are matched with the period in which they were incurred are often called **period costs**.

Second Accounting Cycle

Assume that the following accounting events apply to the operations of Conner Consultants during 2006:

Event 1 Conner Consultants acquired $25,000 cash by issuing common shares.

Event 2 During the period, $96,000 of revenue was recognized on account.

Event 3 Conner collected $102,000 of cash from accounts receivable.

reality bytes

Under the accrual system, accountants recognize revenue after the work has been done but before the cash is collected. Investors are more aggressive than accountants with respect to income recognition. They recognize income even before the work is done. This explains why shares (ownership) of some companies sell for more than shares of other companies. Investors buy shares because they want to participate in the profit (net income) that the company earns. Therefore, investors are willing to pay more for a company whose future earnings potential is significantly greater than average. For example, since Microsoft operates in an industry with significant growth potential, its shares may sell for 40 times earnings while Petro-Canada's are selling for only 10 times earnings. This means if Microsoft and Petro-Canada were earning $1 per share, Microsoft's shares would be selling for $40 while Petro-Canada's shares would be selling for $10. In other words, investors are basing their purchases on the companies' potential to earn future profits rather than their past earnings history as depicted in the companies' financial statements. Does this mean that financial statements are not useful in making investment decisions? The answer is no. Past earnings provide insight into the future. In other words, a company that has a history of earnings that grow at a rate of 30 percent per year is more likely to continue to experience rapid growth than a company with a 10 percent historical growth rate. Therefore, financial statements that are based on accrual accounting can provide insight into the future even though they are historically based.

Conner accrued $22,000 of salary expense. **Event 4**

Cash paid toward the settlement of salaries payable was $20,000. **Event 5**

Conner paid a $10,000 cash dividend to shareholders. **Event 6**

These events are conceptually identical to transactions that were discussed earlier. The effects of these events on the general ledger accounts are shown in Exhibit 2–5 on page 63. If you have difficulty understanding these effects, review the previous material.

On March 1, 2006, Conner invested $60,000 in a term deposit (TD). **Event 7**

LO2 Explain how accrual transactions (as well as cash transactions introduced in Chapter 1) affect the financial statements of a business.

The purchase of the term deposit is an asset exchange transaction. It represents an **investment** made by Conner. The event decreases the asset account Cash and increases the asset account Term Deposit. Total assets stay the same. The income statement is not affected. The cash flow statement shows an outflow from investing activities. The effects of this transaction on the financial statements are shown here:

Assets			=	Liab.	+	Equity								Cash Flow Statement
Cash	+	TD	=	Liab.	+	C. Sh.	+	Ret. Ear.	Rev.	−	Exp.	=	Net Inc.	
(60,000)	+	60,000	=	NA	+	NA	+	NA	NA	−	NA	=	NA	(60,000) IA

Adjusting the Accounts

On December 31, 2006, Conner adjusted the books to recognize interest revenue earned on the term deposit. The term deposit had a 6 percent annual rate of interest and a one-year term to maturity. Interest is due in cash on the maturity date (February 28, 2007). **Event 8**

When Conner invested in (purchased) the term deposit, the company, in effect, loaned the bank money. In exchange for the privilege of using Conner's money, the bank agreed to return the money (principal) and an additional 6 percent of the principal amount (interest) to Conner one year from the date it borrowed the funds. In other words, in exchange for receiving $60,000 on March 1, 2006, the bank agreed to pay Conner $63,600 (or $60,000 + [0.06 × $60,000]) on February 28, 2007. Conner will receive $3,600 (0.06 × $60,000) per year as compensation for letting the bank use its cash.

Note that interest is earned continually even though the full amount of cash is not collected until the maturity date. In other words, the amount of interest due increases proportionally as time passes. Without sophisticated computer equipment, recording (recognizing) interest continually is impossible.

As a practical matter, many businesses let interest accrue without recognition until it is time to prepare financial statements. The accounts are then *adjusted* to reflect the amount of interest due as of the date of the financial statements. For example, when Conner purchased the term deposit on March 1, 2006, it recorded the asset exchange immediately (see Event 7). However, it would not recognize the interest earned on the term deposit until the date of the financial statements, December 31, 2006. At that time, Conner would make an entry to recognize all of the interest it had earned during the previous 10 months (March 1 through December 31). This entry is called an **adjusting entry** because it updates (adjusts) the account balances before financial statements are prepared.

The amount of interest is computed by multiplying the face value (purchase price) of the TD by the annual interest rate and by the length of time for which the term deposit has been outstanding.

Principal	×	Annual interest rate	×	Time outstanding	=	Interest revenue
$60,000	×	0.06	×	(10/12)	=	$3,000

The effects of the adjusting entry on the financial statements follow:

Assets						=	Liab.	+	Equity								Cash Flow Statement
Cash	+	TD	+	Int. Rec.		=	Liab.	+	C. Sh.	+	Ret. Ear.	Rev.	−	Exp.	=	Net Inc.	
NA	+	NA	+	3,000		=	NA	+	NA	+	3,000	3,000	−	NA	=	3,000	NA

The interest is treated as revenue in 2006 although the cash will not be collected until 2007. This practice is consistent with the **matching principle**. Interest revenue is recognized in (matched with) the period in which it is earned, regardless of when the associated cash is collected. The adjusting entry is an asset source transaction. The asset account Interest Receivable increases, and the shareholders' equity account Retained Earnings increases. The income statement shows an increase in revenue and net income. The cash flow statement is not affected because cash will not be collected until the maturity date (February 28, 2007).

Summary of Account Names

You must identify the appropriate element (asset, liability, or equity) affected by a business event; even more importantly, you need to determine the specific account name. To build your vocabulary of generally accepted account names, see Exhibit 2–4.

Exhibit 2–4 *Summary of Account Names*

Assets	=	Liabilities	+	Equity	
Cash		Accounts Payable		1) Owner's Contributions	**Common Shares**
Accounts Receivable		Notes Payable		2) Dividends	**Retained Earnings**
Interest Receivable		Salary Payable		3) Revenues	
Term Deposits		Interest Payable		4) Expenses	

Mei Company purchased a $36,000 term deposit (TD) from a local bank on October 1, 2004. The TD had a 5 percent annual interest rate and a two-year term to maturity. The interest is to be collected in cash on the maturity date. Determine the amount of interest revenue Mei would report on the 2004 income statement and the amount of cash flow from operating activities Mei would report on the 2004 cash flow statement.

Answer Mei would report interest revenue of $450 on the 2004 income statement (see the following calculation). There would be no cash flow from operating activities to report on the 2004 cash flow statement because Mei will not collect any cash for the interest until the TD matures on September 30, 2006. (Mei *would* report a $36,000 cash outflow in 2004 for the TD purchase as an investing activity, not an operating activity.)

Principal	×	Annual interest rate	×	Time outstanding	=	Interest revenue
$36,000	×	0.05	×	(3/12)	=	$450

Because the interest rate is 5 percent *per year*, the denominator for the *time outstanding* is 12 months although the note has a 24-month term. Mei will earn 5 percent interest each year, a total of 10 percent for the full 24-month term.

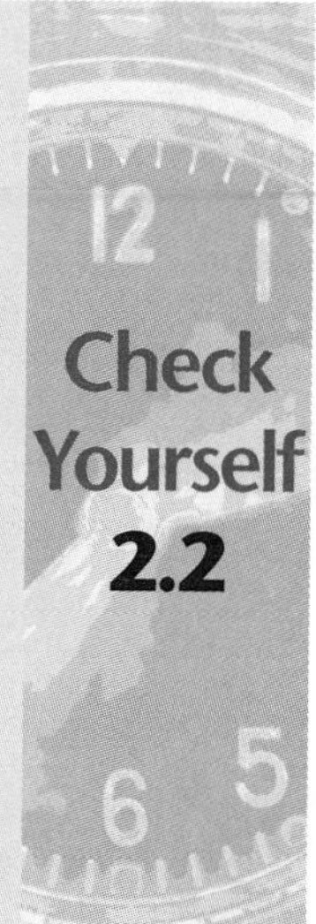

Summary of Transactions

LO3 Demostrate how events are recorded under an accounting equation.

Event 1 Conner Consultants acquired $25,000 cash by issuing common shares.
Event 2 During the period, Conner recognized $96,000 of revenue on account.
Event 3 Conner collected $102,000 of cash from accounts receivable.
Event 4 Accrued salary expenses amounted to $22,000.
Event 5 Cash paid toward the settlement of salaries payable was $20,000.
Event 6 Conner paid a $10,000 cash dividend to shareholders.
Event 7 On March 1, 2006, Conner invested $60,000 in a term deposit (TD).
Event 8 On December 31, 2006, Conner adjusted the books to recognize interest revenue earned on the term deposit. The term deposit had a 6 percent annual rate of interest and a one-year term to maturity. Interest is due in cash on the maturity date (February 28, 2007).

The general ledger accounts used to record the transaction data for Conner Consultants' 2006 accounting period are shown in Exhibit 2–5. The data in the accounts are used to prepare the financial statements. Because of space limitations, the revenue and expense accounts are shown in the Retained Earnings column. The titles of these accounts are shown immediately to the right of the monetary amounts.

Exhibit 2–5 ***Transaction Data Recorded in Accounts***

	Assets								=	Liabilities	+	Shareholders' Equity			
Event No.	Cash	+	Accounts Receivable	+	Interest Receivable	+	Term Deposit		=	Salaries Payable	+	Common Shares	+	Retained Earnings	Account Titles
Beg. Bal.	$ 53,000		$ 24,000		$ 0		$ 0			$ 6,000		$ 5,000		$ 66,000	
1	25,000											25,000			
2			96,000											96,000	Consulting Revenue
3	102,000		(102,000)												
4										22,000				(22,000)	Salary Expense
5	(20,000)									(20,000)					
6	(10,000)													(10,000)	Dividends
7	(60,000)						60,000								
8					3,000									3,000	Interest Revenue
End Bal.	$ 90,000	+	$ 18,000	+	$ 3,000	+	$ 60,000		=	$ 8,000	+	$ 30,000	+	$ 133,000	

2006 Financial Statements

LO4 Prepare simple financial statements for a business that uses cash and accrual transactions.

The ledger account balances shown in Exhibit 2–5 are used to prepare the financial statements shown in Exhibit 2–6. The relationships among the statements are discussed in the following section of the chapter.

Exhibit 2–6 *Vertical Statements Model*

CONNER CONSULTANTS
Financial Statements
For the 2006 Accounting Period

Income Statement		
Consulting Revenue	$ 96,000	
Interest Revenue	3,000	
Total Revenue		$ 99,000
Salary Expense		(22,000)
Net Income		$ 77,000
Statement of Shareholders' Equity		
Beginning Common Shares	$ 5,000	
Plus: Common Shares Issued	25,000	
Ending Common Shares		$ 30,000
Beginning Retained Earnings	66,000	
Plus: Net Income	77,000	
Less: Dividends	(10,000)	
Ending Retained Earnings		133,000
Total Shareholders' Equity		$163,000
Balance Sheet		
Assets		
Cash	$ 90,000	
Accounts Receivable	18,000	
Interest Receivable	3,000	
Term Deposit	60,000	
Total Assets		$171,000
Liabilities		$ 8,000
Shareholders' Equity		
Common Shares	30,000	
Retained Earnings	133,000	
Total Shareholders' Equity		163,000
Total Liabilities and Shareholders' Equity		$171,000
Cash Flow Statement		
Cash Flows from Operating Activities		
Cash Receipts from Revenue	$102,000	
Cash Payments for Salaries Expense	(20,000)	
Net Cash Flow from Operating Activities		$ 82,000
Cash Flows from Investing Activities		
Cash Payment to Purchase TD		(60,000)
Cash Flows from Financing Activities		
Cash Receipt from Common Shares Issued	25,000	
Cash Payment for Dividends	(10,000)	
Net Cash Flow from Financing Activities		15,000
Net Change in Cash		37,000
Plus: Beginning Cash Balance		53,000
Ending Cash Balance		$ 90,000

Income Statement

Note that the amount of net income ($77,000) is not a cash-equivalent figure. The cash flow from operating activities is $82,000, as shown in the cash flow statement. Although $96,000 of consulting revenue was recognized, $102,000 of cash was collected from customers because some of the revenue recognized in 2005 was actually collected in 2006. Also, the income statement reports recognition of $3,000 of interest revenue. None of this revenue was collected during 2006. Accordingly, the total amount of cash collected from revenue transactions was $102,000. Finally, although the amount of salary expense recognized was $22,000, the amount paid was only $20,000. Accordingly, the net cash inflow from operating activities was $82,000 ($102,000 − $20,000). In contrast, the income statement displays the amount of net income recognized ($96,000 + $3,000 − $22,000 = $77,000).

Statement of Shareholders' Equity

The beginning balances for the Common Shares and Retained Earnings accounts equal last year's ending balances. The $25,000 share issue is added to the $5,000 beginning Common Shares balance to arrive at the $30,000 ending balance. Of the $77,000 of net income, $10,000 was distributed to the shareholders. Accordingly, Retained Earnings increases by $67,000 ($77,000 net income − $10,000 dividend) from a beginning balance of $66,000 to an ending balance of $133,000. The ending balance in total shareholders' equity amounts to $163,000 ($30,000 common shares + $133,000 retained earnings).

Balance Sheet

Two additional asset accounts appear on the 2006 balance sheet; however, all assets are still listed according to their respective levels of liquidity. Total assets amount to $171,000, which equals the claims of $171,000. The claims are divided into the claim associated with creditors (salaries payable) of $8,000 and the shareholders' claim of $163,000.

Cash Flow Statement

The $82,000 net cash inflow from operating activities is discussed in the section about the income statement. Besides this amount, an analysis of the Cash account discloses a $60,000 cash outflow from purchasing the term deposit. Also, a further $25,000 cash inflow resulted from issuing common shares. Finally, a $10,000 cash outflow occurred in the form of a dividend paid to the shareholders. Accordingly, the net change in cash was a $37,000 increase ($82,000 − $60,000 + $15,000). This increase can be verified by comparing the Cash balance at the beginning of the period ($53,000) with the Cash balance at the end of the period ($90,000). The difference is a $37,000 increase.

LO6
Explain the effects of end-of-period adjustments related to accruals.

Accounting Cycle

The adjusting process described earlier applies to many types of accounting events. Many of these events will be discussed in later chapters. Adjusting the accounts is an integral part of the **accounting cycle**. So far, we have discussed four stages of the accounting cycle: (1) recording transactions, (2) adjusting the accounts, (3) preparing financial statements, and (4) closing the accounts. Stage 1 occurs throughout the accounting period. Stages 2, 3, and 4 normally occur at the end of the accounting period. Other stages will be added in the following chapters.

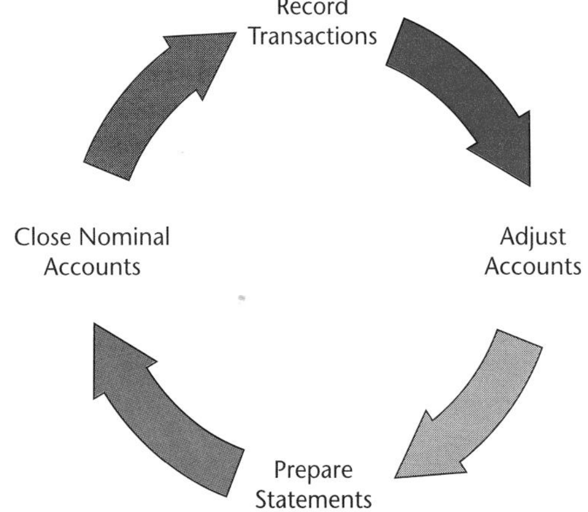

Accounting for Notes Payable

This section describes how borrowing funds from a bank affects a company's financial statements. Conner most likely engaged in many transactions during its 2007 and 2008 accounting periods, but we limit our discussion to the transactions associated with borrowing. The specific transactions discussed are shown in the following statements model.

Assets		=	Liab.			+	Equity									
Date	Cash	=	Note Pay.	+	Int. Pay.	+	C. Sh.	+	Ret. Ear.	Rev.	−	Exp.	=	Net Inc.	Cash Flow Statement	
09/01/07	90,000	=	90,000	+	NA	+	NA	+	NA	NA	−	NA	=	NA	90,000	FA
12/31/07	NA	=	NA	+	2,700	+	NA	+	(2,700)	NA	−	2,700	=	(2,700)	NA	
08/31/08	NA	=	NA	+	5,400	+	NA	+	(5,400)	NA	−	5,400	=	(5, 400)	NA	
08/31/08	(8,100)	=	NA	+	(8,100)	+	NA	+	NA	NA	−	NA	=	NA	(8,100)	OA
08/31/08	(90,000)	=	(90,000)	+	NA	+	NA	+	NA	NA	−	NA	=	NA	(90,000)	FA

LO2

Explain how accrual transactions (as well as cash transactions introduced in Chapter 1) affect the financial statements in a business.

On September 1, 2007, Conner borrowed money by issuing a $90,000 note to a local bank. This is an asset source transaction. The asset account Cash increases by $90,000, and the liability account **Note Payable** increases by the same amount. The account title Note Payable is used because the bank normally requires the borrower to sign a note that describes the loan terms. Typical items included in the note are the rate of interest, the term to maturity, and any collateral pledged to secure the loan. The borrower issues (gives) the note to the bank and receives money from the bank. The borrower is the **issuer of a note**, and the bank is the *creditor* or *lender*. Borrowing funds is a financing activity that is reported on the cash flow statement. The income statement is not affected by the borrowing activity.

The note had a 9 percent annual rate of interest and a one-year term. An *adjusting entry* is necessary to recognize the interest that accrued from September 1 through December 31. In this case four months of interest accrued by the closing date, December 31, 2007. The accrued interest is $2,700 ($90,000 × 0.09 × [4/12]). The entry to record the accrued interest reflects a claims exchange. The liability account Interest Payable increases, and the equity account Retained Earnings decreases. The income statement reflects interest expense although no cash was paid in 2007.

Three events recorded in the statements model are dated August 31, 2008 (the maturity date). The first entry records the $5,400 of interest that accrued in 2008 between January 1 and August 31 ($90,000 × 0.09 × [8/12]). This entry parallels the adjusting entry made on December 31, 2007. It is used to reflect the balance of the accrued interest on the note.

The second entry on August 31, 2008, reflects the cash paid for interest. This is an asset use transaction that reduces the Cash and Retained Earnings accounts by $8,100 ($90,000 × 0.09 × [12/12]). In other words, the entire amount of interest (four months accrued in 2007 and eight months accrued in 2008) is paid on August 31, 2008. There is no effect on the income statement because the interest expense was recognized earlier. The cash flow statement shows the cash outflow resulting from operating activities.

The final entry dated August 31, 2008, reflects the repayment of principal. This is an asset use transaction. The Cash account and the Notes Payable account decrease by $90,000. The income statement is not affected because repaying a loan is not an earnings activity. The cash flow statement shows a $90,000 cash outflow from financing activities. Note that the interest payment is classified as an operating activity while the principal repayment is treated as a financing activity.

Because this section discussed only a limited selection of transactions that occurred in 2007 and 2008, a full set of financial statements is not presented for these accounting periods.

Trent, Incorporated, borrowed $120,000 by issuing a note to a local bank on November 1, 2004. The note had a 12 percent annual interest rate and a one-year term to maturity. Determine the amount of interest expense and the cash flow from operating activities Trent would report on the 2004 and 2005 financial statements.

Answer The amount of interest expense Trent would recognize each year is computed as follows:

	Principal	×	Annual interest rate	×	Time outstanding	×	Interest expense
2004	$120,000	×	0.12	×	(2/12)	=	$ 2,400
2005	$120,000	×	0.12	×	(10/12)	=	$12,000

Because Trent will pay the total amount of interest ($120,000 × 0.12 × 12/12 = $14,400) on the maturity date (October 31, 2005), there is no cash flow from operating activities to report in 2004 and a $14,400 cash outflow from operating activities in 2005.

---

a look back

Chapters 1 and 2 have introduced four types of transactions. It is helpful to identify transactions by type. Although businesses engage in an infinite variety of transactions, all transactions can be classified into one of four types. By learning to identify transactions by type, you can learn how to incorporate unfamiliar events within the bounds of a conceptual framework. The four types of transactions follow:

LO9 Classify accounting events into one of four categories.

1. *Asset source transactions:* An asset account increases, and a corresponding claims account increases.
2. *Asset use transactions:* An asset account decreases, and a corresponding claims account decreases.
3. *Asset exchange transactions:* One asset account increases, and another asset account decreases.
4. *Claims exchange transactions:* One claims account increases, and another claims account decreases.

Also, the definitions of revenue and expense have been expanded. The complete definitions of these two elements are as follows:

1. **Revenue:** Revenue is the *economic benefit* associated with operating the business. Its recognition is triggered by an increase in assets or a decrease in liabilities that results from the normal operating activities of the business.
2. **Expense:** An expense is an *economic sacrifice* incurred in the process of generating revenue. Its recognition is triggered by a decrease in assets or an increase in liabilities that results from an effort to produce revenue.

This chapter has also introduced the *accrual accounting* concept. When this concept is applied, significant differences arise in the amount of revenues and expenses reported on the income statement and in the amount of cash flow from operating activities on the cash flow statement. Review the following transactions and the corresponding statements model. To improve your understanding, set up a statements model on a piece of paper and try to record the effects of each event before you look at the explanation provided.

List of Events

1. Provided $600 of services on account.
2. Collected $400 cash from accounts receivable.
3. Accrued $350 of salary expense.
4. Paid $225 cash in partial settlement of salaries payable.

Event No.	Balance Sheet							Income Statement					Cash Flow Statement	
	Cash	+	Acc. Rec.	=	S. Pay.	+	Ret. Earn.	Rev.	−	Exp.	=	Net Inc.		
1	NA	+	600	=	NA	+	600	600	−	NA	=	600	NA	
2	400	+	(400)	=	NA	+	NA	NA	−	NA	=	NA	400	OA
3	NA	+	NA	=	350	+	(350)	NA	−	350	=	(350)	NA	
4	(225)	+	0	=	(225)	+	NA	NA	−	NA	=	NA	(255)	OA
Totals	175	+	200	=	125	+	250	600	−	350	=	250	175	NC

Notice that the amount of net income ($250) is different from the amount of cash flow from operating activities ($175). A review of the entries in the statements model should make the reasons clear. Although $600 of revenue is recognized, only $400 of cash was collected. The remaining $200 is expected to be collected later and is currently shown on the balance sheet as Accounts Receivable. Also, although $350 of salary expense is recognized, only $225 was paid in cash. The remaining $125 is expected to be paid later. This obligation is shown as Salaries Payable on the balance sheet. Study these relationships carefully to develop a clear sense of how accrual accounting affects financial reporting.

a look forward

Chapter 3 continues the examination of accrual accounting. Besides accruals, the accrual system involves deferrals. *Deferrals* result when a company receives or pays cash before it recognizes the related revenue or expense. A magazine subscription is an example of a deferral event because magazine companies receive the cash before they provide magazines to their customers. The cash is collected in advance, but the revenue is not recognized until the magazines are delivered. Chapter 3 also reinforces what you have learned about asset source, use, and exchange transactions and claims exchange transactions. Also, you will broaden your understanding of how business events affect financial statements.

APPENDIX

LO7 Explain the auditor's role in financial reporting.

Role of the Independent Auditor

The four basic financial statements presented in annual reports are the income statement, statement of shareholders' equity, balance sheet, and cash flow statement. As noted earlier, these statements are prepared in accordance with certain rules, called *generally accepted accounting principles*, or *GAAP*. Thus, when Bombardier, Inc., publishes its financial statements, it is saying not only "here are our financial statements," but more specifically, "here are our financial statements prepared according to GAAP." As discussed throughout this course, the application of GAAP requires considerable judgment and calls for some interpretation, estimation, and assumption making. How can users of financial statements be sure that a company really did follow GAAP and exercised reasonable judgment and good faith in applying GAAP to its financial reporting practices? Users rely on **audits** conducted by professional accountants.

The following sections discuss in detail the roles and responsibilities of an independent auditor. Briefly, the independent auditor performs several functions:

1. Conducts a financial audit, which is a detailed examination of a company's financial statements and documents.
2. Assumes both legal and professional responsibilities to the public, not to the company paying the auditor.
3. Guarantees that financial statements are materially correct rather than absolutely correct.
4. Presents conclusions in an audit report, which includes an opinion resulting from the audit. When necessary, the auditor issues a disclaimer.
5. Maintains professional confidentiality with clients. However, this does not exempt the auditor from legal obligations such as testifying in court.

The Financial Audit

What is an audit? First, you must realize that there are several different types of audits. The type most relevant to this course is called a **financial audit**, which is a detailed examination of a company's financial statements and the documents that support the information presented in those statements. The audit includes a verification process that tests the reliability of the underlying accounting system used to produce the financial reports. A financial audit is conducted by an accountant who is known as the **independent auditor**.

Understanding the role of an independent auditor is almost as important as understanding what a financial audit is. Normally, the term *independent auditor* designates a firm of professional accountants. These may be chartered accountants (CAs), certified general accountants (CGAs), or certified management accountants (CMAs) depending on provincial requirements. The accountants who perform financial audits are paid by the companies they audit. However, they are not employees of those companies. In fact, neither the accountant nor their immediate family members may own shares or have any other type of investment in the companies they audit. Also, payments to the accountant are not based on the outcome of the audit. The accountants are to be as independent of the companies they audit as is reasonably possible.

Independent auditors are chosen by, paid by, and can be fired by the company they are auditing; however, the auditors are responsible mainly to *the public*. In fact, auditors have a legal responsibility to those members of the public who have a financial interest in the company being audited. If investors in a company lose money, they sometimes sue the independent auditors in an attempt to recover their losses. This is more likely to occur if the loss was due to something dramatic, such as the company's filing for bankruptcy. The lawsuit will succeed only if it can be shown that the auditors failed in their professional responsibilities when conducting the audit. The fact that a company declares bankruptcy does not imply that the auditors can be sued successfully. In the real world, auditors are not sued very often, given the number of audits they perform.

Auditors' professional responsibility is to ensure that the company properly reports its financial situation, whether good or bad. Auditors get into trouble when a company has a problem that is not properly reported and the auditors do not detect the improper reporting practice. For example, a company might overstate its net income. If the auditors allow the incorrect amount to be reported and the size of the error is material, the auditors create a problem for which they may suffer legal consequences.

Materiality and Financial Audits

Now things get a bit fuzzy. What is a **material error**? An error, or other reporting problem, is considered *material* if knowing about the problem would affect the decisions of an *average prudent investor*. Thus, the concept of materiality is very subjective. All of this means that the auditors are not guaranteeing that the financial statements are absolutely correct—only that they are *materially* correct. If General Motors inadvertently overstated its sales by $1 million, would this be material? In 2000, GM had approximately US$185 billion of sales! A $1 million error in computing sales at GM is like a $1 error in computing the pay of a person who makes $185,000 per year—not material at all!

A financial audit is not concerned with absolute precision, and it is not looking mainly for fraud on the part of the company's employees. Even so, auditors must provide *reasonable assurance* that their audits will detect material misstatements (fraud). Also, auditors are responsible for ensuring that internal control procedures (explained in Chapter 6) are in place to help prevent fraud. If fraud is widespread in a company, normal audit procedures should detect it.

Accounting majors take at least one and often two or more courses in auditing to understand how to conduct an audit to detect material accounting problems. Obviously, there is not enough time in this course to explain auditing techniques, but at least be aware that auditors do not review how the company accounted for every transaction. Along with other methods, auditors use statistical sampling to review company records.

Types of Audit Opinions

Once an audit is complete, the auditors present their conclusions in an audit report, which includes an *audit opinion*. There are three basic types of audit opinions, with variations.

An **unqualified opinion**, despite its negative-sounding name, is the best that auditors can give. It means that the auditor believes the financial statements are in compliance with GAAP without qualification, reservation, or exception.

The most negative report that an auditor can issue is an **adverse opinion**. This means that something in the financial statements is not in compliance with GAAP and the auditors think it would be material to the average prudent investor. The auditor's report explains the unacceptable accounting practice(s) that resulted in the adverse opinions. Adverse opinions are very rare. To avoid receiving an adverse opinion, a company usually corrects the accounting issue that concerns the auditors.

A **qualified opinion** falls between an unqualified and an adverse opinion. A qualified opinion means that for the most part, the company's financial statements are in compliance with GAAP, but the auditors are concerned about something in the statements or have some other reason not to give a fully unqualified opinion. At least an entire chapter could be written about reasons to issue qualified opinions, but typically they result from the auditors' need to bring special attention to some accounting attribute in the financial statements. A qualified opinion usually does not imply a serious accounting problem, but users should read the auditors' report and draw their own conclusions about the relevance of the issues involved. The auditors' report explains why a qualified opinion is being issued.

If an auditor cannot perform the audit procedures necessary to determine whether the statements are prepared in accordance with GAAP, the auditor cannot issue an opinion on the financial statements. Instead, the auditor issues a **disclaimer of audit opinion**. A disclaimer is neither negative nor positive; it simply means that the auditor cannot obtain enough information to confirm compliance or noncompliance with GAAP.

It is vital to understand that the ultimate responsibility for the financial statements rests with the executives of the reporting company. Just like auditors, managers can be sued by investors who believe that they lost money due to improper financial reporting. This is one reason why nonaccounting businesspeople should understand accounting fundamentals.

Confidentiality

The code of ethics for professional accountants forbids auditors from **voluntarily disclosing** information they have acquired as a result of their accountant–client relationships. However, accountants may be required to testify in a court of law. In general, federal law does not recognize an accountant–client privilege as it does with lawyers and clergy. Even so, federal courts have taken exception to this position, especially as it applies to tax cases. The law varies with respect to its treatment of accountant–client privilege. Furthermore, auditors who terminate a client relationship because of ethical or legal disagreements and who are later contacted by a successor accountant may be required to inform the successor of the reasons for the termination. Also, the circumstances surrounding the case must be considered when assessing the appropriateness of making such a disclosure. Given the legal diversity with respect to the issue of accountant–client confidentiality, it is wise to seek legal counsel before making any disclosures of information obtained in an accountant–client relationship.

To illustrate, assume that Joe Smith, CA, discovers that his client Jane Doe is making misrepresentations in her financial statements. Smith tries to convince Doe to change her practices, but she refuses to cease and desist. Smith is required by the code of ethics to end his relationship with Doe. However, Smith is not permitted to disclose Doe's dishonest reporting practices unless he is called on to provide testimony in a legal hearing or is responding to an inquiry by Doe's successor accountant.

With respect to the discovery of significant fraud, the auditor is required to inform management at one level above the position of the employee who is engaged in the fraud and to notify the board of directors of the company. Suppose that Joe Smith, CA, discovers that Jane Doe, employee of Western Company, is embezzling money from Western. Smith is required to inform Doe's supervisor and to notify Western's board of directors. However, Smith cannot speak publicly about the fraud.

Importance of Ethics

LO8 Understand the importance of a code of ethics.

Accountants cannot perform their role in society unless they establish trust and credibility. For example, tax and consulting advice is useless if it emanates from a source that lacks credible competence. Because of the high ethical standards required by the profession, the accountant assumes an obligation of self-discipline above and beyond requirements of laws and regulations. The importance of ethical conduct is universally recognized across a broad spectrum of accounting organizations. In Canada, these include the Canadian Institute of Chartered Accountants, the Society of Management Accountants, and the Certified General Accountants Association. Each accounting organization has a **code of professional conduct**. The codes stipulate and bind accountants to the highest level of care, duty, and responsibility to their clients, the public, and their fellow professionals.

People who become involved in unethical or criminal behaviour usually do so unwittingly. They start with small indiscretions that evolve into more serious violations of trust. Therefore, awareness is a key to avoiding unethical or illegal conduct. Professional accountants are expected to be able to (1) identify ethical issues, (2) analyze both the positive and negative sides of options available to resolve the issue, and (3) choose the best solution after weighing all the options.

Accountants establish policies and procedures for reducing the opportunities for fraud. These policies and procedures are commonly called **internal controls**. Specific internal control procedures are tailored to meet the individual needs of particular businesses. For example, a bank may use vaults, but a university has little use for this type of equipment. Chapter 6 discusses internal control procedures in more detail. At this point, simply recognize that accountants are aware of the need to reduce the opportunity for unethical and criminal activities.

Ethical misconduct is a serious offence in the accounting profession. Accountants must realize that in this arena, their careers are vulnerable to a single mistake. If you are caught in white-collar crime, you normally lose the opportunity to hold a white-collar job. Second chances are rarely granted; it is extremely important that you learn how to recognize and avoid ethical misconduct. To help you prepare for the real-world situations you are likely to encounter, we include an ethical dilemma in the end-of-chapter materials.

SELF-STUDY REVIEW PROBLEMS

Walberg Company experienced the following accounting events during 2008.

1. Started operations in January 2008 when it acquired $22,000 cash by issuing common shares.
2. During the 2008 period, recognized $246,000 of revenue on account.
3. Collected $222,000 cash from accounts receivable.
4. Paid operating expenses of $205,000 in cash.
5. Paid a $14,000 cash dividend to shareholders.
6. On April 1, 2008, borrowed $18,000 by issuing a note to a local bank.
7. On December 31, 2008, adjusted the accounting records to recognize interest expense incurred on the note it had issued to the bank. The note had a 10 percent annual interest rate and a one-year term to maturity. Interest is due in cash on the maturity date (March 31, 2009).

Walberg Company experienced the following accounting events during 2009.

1. Accrued the remaining interest expense on the note payable through March 31, 2009.
2. Paid cash for the amount of interest payable as of March 31, 2009.
3. Paid cash to repay the principal due on the note payable as of March 31, 2009.
4. Recognized $259,000 of revenue on account.
5. Collected $262,000 cash from accounts receivable.
6. Paid operating expenses of $211,000 in cash.
7. Paid a $24,000 cash dividend to shareholders.

Required

a. Record the events in a financial statements model like the following one. The first event is recorded as an example.

Event No.	Assets		=	Liab.	+	Equity						
	Cash	+ Acc. Rec.	=	Note Pay.	+	Int. Pay.	+ C. Sh.	+ Ret. Earn.	Rev.	− Exp.	= Net Inc.	Cash Flow Statement
1	22,000 +	NA	=	NA	+	NA	+ 22,000 +	NA	NA	− NA	= NA	22,000 FA

b. What amount of interest expense would Walberg report on the 2008 and 2009 income statements?
c. What amount of cash outflow for interest would Walberg report in the operating activities sections of the 2008 and 2009 cash flow statements?
d. What are the 2009 opening balances for the revenue and expense accounts?
e. What amount of total assets would Walberg report on the 2008 balance sheet?
f. What claims on assets would Walberg report on the 2008 balance sheet?
g. Explain what caused the cash balance to change between December 31, 2008, and December 31, 2009.

Solution to Requirement a

The financial statements model follows:

Event No.	Assets		= Liabilities		+ Equity					Cash Flow Statement
	Cash	+ Acc. Rec.	= Note Pay.	+ Int. Pay	+ C. Sh.	+ Ret. Earn.	Rev.	− Exp.	= Net Inc.	
1	22,000	NA	NA	NA	22,000	NA	NA	NA	NA	22,000 FA
2	NA	246,000	NA	NA	NA	246,000	246,000	NA	246,000	NA
3	222,000	(222,000)	NA	NA	NA	NA	NA	NA	NA	222,000 OA
4	(205,000)	NA	NA	NA	NA	(205,000)	NA	205,000	(205,000)	(205,000) OA
5	(14,000)	NA	NA	NA	NA	(14,000)	NA	NA	NA	(14,000) FA
6	18,000	NA	18,000	NA	NA	NA	NA	NA	NA	18,000 FA
7*	NA	NA	NA	1,350	NA	(1,350)	NA	1,350	(1,350)	NA
Totals	43,000	24,000	18,000	1,350	22,000	25,650	246,000	206,350	39,650	43,000 NC
	Asset, Liability, and Equity Account Balances Carry Forward						Rev. & Exp. Accts. Are Closed			
Bal.	43,000	24,000	18,000	1,350	22,000	25,650	NA	NA	NA	NA
1†	NA	NA	NA	450	NA	(450)	NA	450	(450)	NA
2	(1,800)	NA	NA	(1,800)	NA	NA	NA	NA	NA	(1,800) OA
3	(18,000)	NA	(18,000)	NA	NA	NA	NA	NA	NA	(18,000) FA
4	NA	259,000	NA	NA	NA	259,000	259,000	NA	259,000	NA
5	262,000	(262,000)	NA	NA	NA	NA	NA	NA	NA	262,000 OA
6	(211,000)	NA	NA	NA	NA	(211,000)	NA	211,000	(211,000)	(211,000) OA
7	(24,000)	NA	NA	NA	NA	(24,000)	NA	NA	NA	(24,000) FA
Totals	50,200	21,000	0	0	22,000	49,200	259,000	211,450	47,550	7,200 NC

*Accrued interest expense for 2008 = $\$18,000 \times 0.10 \times 9/12 = \$1,350$.
†Accrued interest expense for 2009 = $\$18,000 \times 0.10 \times 3/12 = \$450$.

Solution to Requirements b–g

b. Walberg would report interest expense on the 2008 and 2009 income statements of $1,350 and $450, respectively.

c. Walberg made no cash interest payments in 2008. All cash for interest was paid in 2009. Walberg would report zero cash outflow for interest on the 2008 cash flow statement and $1,800 cash outflow for interest on the 2009 statement.

d. Because all revenue and expense accounts are closed at the end of each accounting period, the beginning balances for revenue and expense accounts are always zero.

e. The total asset balance on the 2008 balance sheet would be $67,000 (Cash $43,000 + Accounts Receivable $24,000).

f. Creditors have a $19,350 (Note Payable $18,000 + Interest Payable $1,350) claim. Owners (investors) have a $47,650 (Common Shares $22,000 + Retained Earnings $25,650) claim on the assets. Total claims of $67,000 ($19,350 + $47,650) are equal to total assets.

g. The net cash inflow from operating activities was $49,200 ($262,000 revenue − $1,800 interest expense − $211,000 operating expense). There were no investing activities. The net cash outflow from financing activities was $42,000 ($18,000 debt payment + $24,000 dividends). The net change in cash was a $7,200 cash inflow ($49,200 from operating activities − $42,000 used by financing activities).

KEY TERMS

QUESTIONS

1. What does accrual accounting try to accomplish?
2. Define *recognition*. How is it independent of collecting or paying cash?
3. What does *asset source transaction* mean?
4. What effect does issuing common shares have on the accounting equation?
5. How does recognizing revenue on account (accounts receivable) affect the income statement compared to its effect on the cash flow statement?
6. Give an example of an asset source transaction. What is the effect of this transaction on the accounting equation?
7. When is revenue recognized under accrual accounting?
8. Give an example of an asset exchange transaction. What is the effect of this transaction on the accounting equation?
9. What effect does expense recognition have on the accounting equation?
10. What does *claims exchange transaction* mean?
11. What type of transaction is a cash payment to creditors? How does this type of transaction affect the accounting equation?
12. When are expenses recognized under accrual accounting?
13. Why may net cash flow from operating activities on the cash flow statement be different from the amount of net income reported on the income statement?
14. What is the relationship between the income statement and changes in assets and liabilities?
15. What does *net assets* mean?
16. How does net income affect the shareholders' claims on the business's assets?
17. What does *expense* mean?
18. What does *revenue* mean?
19. What is the purpose of the statement of shareholders' equity?
20. What is the main purpose of the balance sheet?
21. Why is the balance sheet dated *as of* a specific date when the income statement, statement of shareholders' equity, and cash flow statement are dated with the phrase *for the period ended*?
22. In what order are assets listed on the balance sheet?
23. What does the cash flow statement explain?
24. When is interest earned on an investment recognized?
25. What does *adjusting entry* mean? Give an example.
26. What type of entry is the entry to record accrued interest revenue? How does it affect the accounting equation?
27. What type of entry is the entry to record accrued interest expense? How does it affect the accounting equation?
28. Is land purchased in 1920 reported on a current balance sheet at its current value? If not, at what value is it shown?
29. What is the historical cost concept of accounting measurement?
30. Do all countries use historical cost for accounting measurement? Why or why not?
31. What types of accounts are closed at the end of the accounting period? Why must accounts be closed?
32. Give several examples of period costs.
33. Give an example of a cost that can be matched directly with the revenue produced by an accounting firm from preparing a tax return.
34. List and describe the four stages of the accounting cycle discussed in Chapter 2.
35. What is a financial audit? Who is qualified to perform it?
36. What is an independent auditor? Why must auditors be independent?
37. What makes an error in the financial statements material?
38. What three basic types of auditors' opinions can be issued on audited financial statements? Describe each.
39. What are the implications of an unqualified audit opinion?
40. When might an auditor issue a disclaimer on financial statements?
41. In what circumstances can an auditor disclose confidential information about a client without the client's permission?

EXERCISES

Where applicable in all exercises, round computations to the nearest dollar.

L.O. 1, 2, 3 EXERCISE 2–1 *Effect of Earning Revenue on Account on the Financial Statements*

W. Harder started a computer training centre in 2004. The only accounting event in 2004 was the recognition of $7,500 of service revenue earned on account.

Required

Use the following horizontal statements model to show how this event affects the balance sheet, income statement, and cash flow statement. Indicate whether the event increases (I), decreases (D), or does not affect (NA) each element of the financial statements. Also, in the Cash Flow Statement column, designate the cash flows using the letters OA for operating activities, IA for investing activities, and FA for financing activities.

Balance Sheet							Income Statement					Cash Flow Statement
Cash	+	Acc. Rec.	=	Com. Sh.	+	Ret. Earn.	Rev.	−	Exp.	=	Net Inc.	

L.O. 1, 2, 3 EXERCISE 2–2 *Effect of Collecting Accounts Receivable on the Accounting Equation and Financial Statements*

Gayoso Company earned $4,500 of service revenue on account during 2008. The company collected $3,000 cash from accounts receivable during 2008.

Required

Based on this information alone, determine the following. (*Hint:* Record the events in general ledger accounts under an accounting equation before satisfying the requirements.)

a. The balance of the accounts receivable that Gayoso would report on the December 31, 2008, balance sheet.
b. The amount of net income that Gayoso would report on the 2008 income statement.
c. The amount of net cash flow from operating activities that Gayoso would report on the 2008 cash flow statement.
d. The amount of retained earnings that Gayoso would report on the 2008 balance sheet.
e. Why are the answers to Requirements *b* and *c* different?

L.O. 1, 2, 6 EXERCISE 2–3 *Effects of Recognizing Accrued Interest on Financial Statements*

Gail Rogers started Rogers Company on January 1, 2005. The company experienced the following events during its first year of operation:

1. Earned $400 of cash revenue for performing services.
2. Borrowed $1,500 cash from the bank.
3. Adjusted the accounting records to recognize accrued interest expense on the bank note. The note, issued on September 1, 2005, had a one-year term and an 8 percent annual interest rate.

Required

a. What is the amount of interest expense in 2005?
b. What amount of cash was paid for interest in 2005?
c. Use a horizontal statements model to show how each event affects the balance sheet, income statement, and cash flow statement. Indicate whether the event increases (I), decreases (D), or does not affect (NA) each element of the financial statements. Also, in the Cash Flow Statement column, designate the cash flow as operating activities (OA), investing activities (IA), or financing activities (FA). The first transaction has been recorded as an example.

Event No.	Balance Sheet									Income Statement					Cash Flow Statement
	Cash	=	Note Pay.	+	Int. Pay.	+	Com. Sh.	+	Ret. Earn.	Rev.	−	Exp.	=	Net Inc.	
1	I	=	NA	+	NA	+	NA	+	I	I	−	NA	=	I	I OA

EXERCISE 2–4 *Net Income versus Changes in Cash* L.O. 2, 3

In the period 2004, Abbot Inc. billed its customers $75,000 for services performed. The company later collected $68,000 of the amount billed. Abbot incurred $59,000 in other operating expenses but paid cash for only $50,000 of that amount. Abbot acquired $20,000 cash from the issue of common shares. The company invested $15,000 cash in the purchase of land.

Required

Use the preceding information to answer the following questions. (*Hint:* Identify the six events described in the paragraph and record them in general ledger accounts under an accounting equation before attempting to answer the questions.)

a. What amount of revenue will Abbot report on the 2004 income statement?
b. What amount of cash flow from revenue will Abbot report on the cash flow statement?
c. What is the net income for the period?
d. What is the net cash flow from operating activities for the period?
e. Why is the amount of net income different from the net cash flow from operating activities for the period?
f. What is the amount of net cash flow from investing activities?
g. What is the amount of net cash flow from financing activities?
h. What amounts of total assets, liabilities, and equity will Abbot report on the year-end balance sheet?

EXERCISE 2–5 *Effect of Accounts Receivable and Accounts Payable Transactions on Financial Statements* L.O. 1, 2, 6

The following events apply to Jones and Reed, a public accounting firm, for the 2004 accounting period:

1. Performed $85,000 of services for clients on account.
2. Performed $25,000 of services for cash.
3. Incurred $32,000 of other operating expenses on account.
4. Paid $15,000 cash to an employee for salary.
5. Collected $73,000 cash from accounts receivable.
6. Paid $28,000 cash on accounts payable.
7. Paid a $5,000 cash dividend to the shareholders.
8. Accrued salaries of $1,250 at the end of 2004.

Required

a. Show the effects of the events on the financial statements using a horizontal statements model like the following one. In the Cash Flow Statement column, use OA to designate operating activity, IA for investment activity, FA for financing activity, and NC for net change in cash. Use NA to indicate that the element is not affected by the event. The first event is recorded as an example.

Event No.	Assets			=	Liabilities			+	Equity						Cash Flow Statement
	Cash	+	Acc. Rec.	=	Acc. Pay.	+	Sal. Pay	+	Ret. Earn.	Rev.	−	Exp.	=	Net Inc.	
1	NA	+	85,000	=	NA	+	NA	+	85,000	85,000	−	NA	=	85,000	NA

b. What is the amount of total assets at the end of 2004?
c. What is the balance of accounts receivable at the end of 2004?
d. What is the balance of accounts payable at the end of 2004?
e. What is the difference between accounts receivable and accounts payable?
f. What is net income for 2004?
g. What is the amount of net cash flow from operating activities for 2004?

EXERCISE 2–6 *Effect of Accruals on the Financial Statements* L.O. 2, 3, 4

John Carroll, Inc., experienced the following events in 2003, the first year of operation:

1. Received $10,000 cash from the issue of common shares.
2. Performed services on account for $35,000.

3. Paid the utility expense of $700.
4. Collected $26,000 of the accounts receivable.
5. Recorded $12,000 of accrued salaries at the end of the year.
6. Paid a $2,000 cash dividend to the shareholders.

Required

a. Record the events in general ledger accounts under an accounting equation. In the last column of the table, provide appropriate account titles for the Retained Earnings amounts. The first transaction has been recorded as an example.

JOHN CARROLL, INC. General Ledger Accounts								
Event	Assets		=	Liabilities	+	Equity		Acct. Titles for RE
	Cash	Accounts Receivable		Salaries Payable		Common Shares	Retained Earnings	
1.	10,000					10,000		

b. Prepare the income statement, statement of shareholders' equity, balance sheet, and cash flow statement for the 2003 accounting period.
c. Why is the amount of net income different from the amount of net cash flow from operating activities?

L.O. 1, 2, 6 EXERCISE 2–7 *Recognizing Accrued Interest Revenue*

N&J Company invested $80,000 in a term deposit (TD) on May 1, 2006. The term deposit had a 6 percent annual rate of interest and a one-year term to maturity.

Required

a. What amount of interest revenue will N&J recognize for the year ending December 31, 2006?
b. Show how the December 31, 2006, adjusting entry to recognize the accrued interest revenue affects the accounting equation.
c. What amount of cash will N&J collect for interest revenue in 2006?
d. What is the amount of interest receivable as of December 31, 2006?
e. What amount of cash will N&J collect for interest revenue in 2007, assuming it does not renew the TD?
f. What amount of interest revenue will N&J recognize in 2007, assuming it does not renew the TD?
g. What is the amount of interest receivable as of December 31, 2007, assuming it does not renew the TD?

L.O. 1, 2, 6 EXERCISE 2–8 *Recognizing Accrued Interest Expense*

Carroll Corporation borrowed $80,000 from the bank on November 1, 2003. The note had a 7.5 percent annual rate of interest and matured on April 30, 2004. Interest and principal were paid in cash on the maturity date.

Required

a. What amount of interest expense was paid in cash in 2003?
b. What amount of interest expense was reported on the 2003 income statement?
c. What amount of total liabilities was reported on the December 31, 2003, balance sheet?
d. What total amount of cash was paid to the bank on April 30, 2004, for principal and interest?
e. What amount of interest expense was reported on the 2004 income statement?

L.O. 9 EXERCISE 2–9 *Identifying Source, Use, and Exchange Transactions*

Indicate whether each of the following transactions is an asset source (AS), asset use (AU), asset exchange (AE), or claims exchange (CE) transaction.

Required

a. Collected cash from accounts receivable.
b. Invested cash in a term deposit.
c. Purchased land with cash.
d. Acquired cash from the issue of shares.

e. Paid a cash dividend to the shareholders.
f. Paid cash on accounts payable.
g. Incurred other operating expenses on account.
h. Paid cash for rent expense.
i. Performed services for cash.
j. Performed services for clients on account.

EXERCISE 2–10 *Identifying Asset Source, Use, and Exchange Transactions* L.O. 9

Required

a. Name an asset source transaction that will *not* affect the cash flow statement.
b. Name an asset source transaction that will affect the income statement.
c. Name an asset use transaction that will *not* affect the income statement.
d. Name an asset exchange transaction that will affect the cash flow statement.
e. Name an asset exchange transaction that will *not* affect the cash flow statement.
f. Name an asset source transaction that will *not* affect the income statement.

EXERCISE 2–11 *Effect of Transactions on the Balance Sheet* L.O. 2, 3, 6

Sun Corp. was formed on January 1, 2007. The business acquired $85,000 cash from the issue of common shares. The business performed $250,000 of services on account and collected $200,000 of the amount due. Other operating expenses incurred on account amounted to $215,000. By the end of 2007, $190,000 of that amount had been paid with cash. The business paid $30,000 cash to purchase land. Sun borrowed $25,000 cash from the bank. On December 31, 2007, there was $1,250 of accrued interest expense.

Required

Using the preceding information, answer the following questions. (*Hint:* Identify the eight events described in the preceding paragraph and record them in general ledger accounts under an accounting equation before answering the questions.)

a. What is the cash balance at the end of 2007?
b. What is the balance of accounts receivable at the end of 2007?
c. What is the amount of total assets at the end of 2007?
d. What is the amount of total liabilities at the end of 2007?
e. What is the amount of common shares at the end of 2007?
f. What is the amount of retained earnings at the end of 2007?

EXERCISE 2–12 *Effects of Revenue and Expense Recognition on the Income Statement and Cash Flow Statement* L.O. 1, 2

The following transactions pertain to the operations of Clark & Co.

1. Acquired $100,000 cash from the issue of common shares.
2. Performed accounting services and billed clients $80,000.
3. Paid a $10,000 cash dividend to the shareholders.
4. Collected $75,000 cash from accounts receivable.
5. Paid $55,000 cash for other operating expenses.
6. Performed accounting services for $6,000 cash.

Required

a. Identify which of these transactions result in revenue and expense recognition for Clark & Co.
b. Based on your response to Requirement *a*, determine the amount of net income Clark will report on its income statement.
c. Identify which of the preceding transactions affect(s) cash flow from operating activities.
d. Based on your response to Requirement *c*, determine the amount of net cash flow from operating activities Clark will report on the cash flow statement.

EXERCISE 2–13 *Complete Accounting Cycle* L.O. 2, 3, 6

The following information is available for Zig Co. for the year 2006:

1. Acquired $65,000 cash from the issue of common shares.
2. Performed $175,000 of services on account.

3. Incurred other operating expenses on account in the amount of $105,000.
4. Purchased land for $25,000 cash.
5. Collected $95,000 cash from accounts receivable.
6. Paid $50,000 cash on accounts payable.
7. Performed services for $15,000 cash.
8. Paid $5,000 cash for salaries expense.
9. Paid a $10,000 cash dividend to the shareholders.
10. Borrowed $20,000 cash from a local bank.

Information for Adjusting Entry

11. Accrued interest expense at the end of the accounting period was $900.

Required

a. Explain how each of the transactions affects the elements of the accounting equation by placing a + for *increase*, − for *decrease*, and NA for *not affected* under each of the elements. Also record the dollar amount of the effect of each event on the accounting equation. In the last column of the table, provide appropriate account titles for Retained Earnings accounts. The first event is recorded as an example.

					Equity				
Event No	Assets	=	Liabilities	+	Common Shares	+	Retained Earnings	+	Acct. Title for RE
1	+65,000	=	NA		+65,000	+	NA		

b. What is the amount of net income for 2006?
c. What is the amount of total assets at the end of 2006?
d. What is the amount of total liabilities at the end of 2006?

L.O. 2, 4 EXERCISE 2–14 *Classifying Events on the Cash Flow Statement*

The following transactions pertain to the operations of Smoltz Company for 2005:

1. Acquired $18,000 cash from the issue of common shares.
2. Provided $25,000 of services on account.
3. Incurred $15,000 of other operating expenses on account.
4. Collected $20,000 cash from accounts receivable.
5. Paid a $2,000 cash dividend to the shareholders.
6. Paid $10,000 cash on accounts payable.
7. Performed services for $4,000 cash.
8. Paid $600 cash for rent expense.

Required

a. Classify the cash flows from these transactions as operating activities (OA), investing activities (IA), or financing activities (FA). Use NA for transactions that do not affect the cash flow statement.
b. Prepare a cash flow statement. (There is no beginning cash balance.)

L.O. 2, 4, 5 EXERCISE 2–15 *Evaluating Cash Management*

The data in the following table apply to DeChow, Incorporated.

	2003	2004
Accounts receivable	$ 24,600,000	$ 27,060,000
Sales	332,700,000	382,606,000
Accounts payable	15,800,000	18,644,000
Operating expenses	257,300,000	285,603,000

Required

a. What is the percentage growth in the Accounts Receivable, Sales, Accounts Payable, and Operating Expenses accounts from 2003 to 2004?
b. Companies must incur interest expense to obtain cash. To minimize interest expense, companies attempt to collect cash from receivables as quickly as possible and to delay the payment of cash to settle payables as long as possible. Based on your answers to Requirement *a*, comment on DeChow's cash management.

EXERCISE 2–16 *Relation of Elements to Financial Statements* L.O. 4

Required

Identify whether each of the following items would appear on the income statement (IS), statement of shareholders' equity (SE), balance sheet (BS), or cash flow statement (CF). Some items may appear on more than one statement; if so, identify all applicable statements. If an item would not appear on any financial statement, label it NA.

a. Note Payable
b. Notes Receivable
c. Accounts Receivable
d. Retained Earnings
e. Interest Receivable
f. Utilities Payable
g. Auditor's Opinion
h. Land
i. Interest Revenue
j. Dividends
k. Salaries Expense
l. Net Income
m. Interest Payable
n. Ending Cash Balance
o. Cash Flow from Investing Activities

EXERCISE 2–17 *Matching Concept* L.O. 6

Companies make sacrifices known as *expenses* to obtain benefits called *revenues*. The accurate measurement of net income requires that expenses be matched with revenues. In some circumstances matching a particular expense directly with revenue is difficult or impossible. In these circumstances, the expense is matched with the period in which it is incurred.

Required

a. Identify an expense that could be matched directly with revenue.
b. Identify a period expense that would be difficult to match with revenue. Explain why.

EXERCISE 2–18 *Closing Entries* L.O. 2, 6

Required

Which of the following accounts are closed at the end of the accounting period?

a. Cash
b. Accounts Receivable
c. Service Revenue
d. Advertising Expense
e. Accounts Payable
f. Term Deposit
g. Notes Payable
h. Interest Expense
i. Interest Payable
j. Dividends
k. Retained Earnings
l. Utilities Expense

PROBLEMS—SERIES A

L.O. 2, 3, 4 PROBLEM 2–1A *Effect of Events on the Financial Statements*

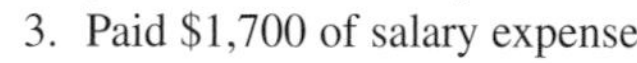

A-1 Auto experienced the following transactions during 2004:

1. Provided services to customers and billed them $8,600.
2. Borrowed $8,000 from the bank on September 1, 2004. The note had a 9 percent annual interest rate and a one-year term to maturity.
3. Paid $1,700 of salary expense.
4. Provided services to customers and collected $3,200 cash.
5. Incurred $3,900 of other operating expenses on account.
6. Collected $7,500 of the accounts receivable.
7. Paid $3,400 of the accounts payable.
8. Recognized the accrued interest on the note payable at December 31, 2004.

Required

a. Show the effects of the transactions on the financial statements using a horizontal statements model like the following one. In the Cash Flow Statement column, use the letters OA for operating activity, IA for investing activity, FA for financing activity, and NC for net change in cash. Use NA to indicate accounts not affected by the transaction. The first one is recorded as an example.

Event No.	Balance Sheet											Income Statement					Cash Flow Statement
	Assets			=	Liabilities					+	Equity						
	Cash	+	Acc. Rec.	=	Accts. Pay.	+	Note Pay	+	Int. Pay	+	Ret. Earn.	Rev.	−	Exp.	=	Net Inc.	
1	NA	+	8,600	=	NA	+	NA	+	NA	+	8,600	8,600	−	NA	=	8,600	NA

b. What is the ending balance of Retained Earnings? What is the amount of net income? Why are these amounts the same in this problem? Is the balance in Retained Earnings likely to be the same as the amount of net income at the end of 2005? Explain your answer.

L.O. 3 PROBLEM 2–2A *Effect of Events on the Accounting Equation*

Required

Explain how each of the following independent accounting events would affect the accounting equation by writing the letter I for increase, the letter D for decrease, and NA for no effect under the appropriate columns. The effects of the first event are shown for you.

Letter of Event	Assets	=	Liabilities	+	Common Shares	+	Retained Earnings
a	I		NA		I		NA

a. Acquired cash from the issue of common shares.
b. Paid cash for salary expense.
c. Performed services for clients on account.
d. Incurred operating expenses on account.
e. Collected cash from accounts receivable.
f. Paid a cash dividend to the shareholders.
g. Performed services for cash.
h. Paid cash to creditors on account.
i. Bought equipment by issuing a note payable.
j. Paid monthly rent expense.
k. Accrued interest expense on a note payable.
l. Repaid note payable and interest with cash.

PROBLEM 2–3A *Effect of Accrued Interest on Financial Statements*

L.O. 2, 3

Marshall Co. borrowed $12,000 from the local bank on May 1, 2008, when the company was started. The note had a 10 percent annual interest rate and a one-year term to maturity. Marshall Co. recognized $28,000 of revenue on account in 2008 and $34,000 of revenue on account in 2009. Cash collections from accounts receivable were $22,000 in 2008 and $32,000 in 2009. Marshall Co. paid $15,000 of salaries expense in 2008 and $18,000 of salaries expense in 2009. (*Hint:* Record the events in general ledger accounts under an accounting equation before answering the questions.)

Required

Based on the preceding information, answer the following questions.

a. What amount of net cash flow from operating activities would Marshall report on the 2008 cash flow statement?
b. What amount of interest expense would Marshall report on the 2008 income statement?
c. What amount of total liabilities would Marshall report on the December 31, 2008, balance sheet?
d. What amount of retained earnings would Marshall report on the December 31, 2008, balance sheet?
e. What amount of cash flow from financing activities would Marshall report on the 2008 cash flow statement?
f. What amount of interest expense would Marshall report on the 2009 income statement?
g. What amount of cash flows from operating activities would Marshall report on the 2009 cash flow statement?
h. What amount of total assets would Marshall report on the December 31, 2009, balance sheet?
i. What amount of cash flow from investing activities would Marshall report on the 2009 cash flow statement?
j. If Marshall Co. paid a $700 dividend during 2009, what retained earnings balance would it report on the December 31, 2009, balance sheet?

PROBLEM 2–4A *Two Complete Accounting Cycles*

L.O. 3, 4

Ex

The following accounting events apply to Tri-City Company.

Accounting Events for 2003

1. The company started when it acquired $40,000 cash from the issue of common shares.
2. Recognized $97,000 of revenue on account during the period for services performed.
3. Collected $75,000 cash from accounts receivable.
4. Paid an $8,000 cash dividend.
5. Paid $32,000 cash for salaries expense.
6. Paid $21,000 cash for other operating expenses.
7. Invested $24,000 in a term deposit with an 18-month term.

Information for Adjusting Entries (Books are closed on December 31)

8. Accrued salaries expense of $3,000.
9. Recorded accrued interest on the term deposit. The term deposit was purchased on June 30, 2003, and had a 5 percent annual rate of interest.

Accounting Events for 2004

1. Made cash payment of $3,000 for salaries payable.
2. Borrowed $40,000 from a local bank.
3. Received an additional $6,000 cash from the issue of common shares.
4. Recognized $120,000 of revenue on account during 2004 for services performed.
5. Collected $112,000 of cash on accounts receivable during the period.
6. Purchased land for the company that cost $50,000 cash. A few months later, the land was appraised at $60,000.
7. Paid a $12,000 cash dividend to the shareholders of the company.
8. Received the principal amount plus the interest earned on the term deposit. (See Event No. 7 in year 2003 for details regarding the original investment.)
9. Paid cash of $40,000 for salaries expense.
10. Paid $33,000 cash for other operating expenses.

Information for Adjusting Entries

11. Accrued salaries expense of $7,000.
12. Recorded accrued interest expense on the bank note (see Event No. 2 in 2004). The note was issued to the bank on June 1, 2004. It had a 12 percent annual rate of interest and a two-year term to maturity.

Required

a. Record the effect of each of the events in general ledger accounts under an accounting equation for the 2003 and 2004 fiscal years. In the last column of the table, provide appropriate account titles for Retained Earning accounts.
b. Prepare an income statement, statement of shareholders' equity, balance sheet, and cash flow statement for the 2003 and 2004 calendar years.

L.O. 4 PROBLEM 2–5A *Identifying and Arranging Elements on Financial Statements*

The following information was drawn from the records of Simmons & Associates at December 31, 2008:

Consulting Revenue	$60,000	Notes Payable	$24,000
Land	52,000	Salaries Payable	6,500
Dividends	8,000	Salary Expense	36,000
Cash Flow from Fin. Activities	33,000	Common Shares Issued	17,000
Interest Revenue	3,000	Beginning Common Shares	19,000
Ending Retained Earnings	56,500	Accounts Receivable	31,000
Cash	42,000	Cash Flow from Inv. Activities	(50,000)
Interest Payable	2,000	Cash Flow from Oper. Activities	40,000
Interest Expense	6,000		

Required

Use the preceding information to construct an income statement, statement of shareholders' equity, balance sheet, and cash flow statement.

L.O. 2, 4 PROBLEM 2–6A *Classifying Events as Source, Use, or Exchange and Effect of Events on Financial Statements—Horizontal Statements Model*

The following transactions pertain to L&N Advisory Services for 2006:

1. Business started when it acquired $50,000 cash from the issue of common shares.
2. Paid $25,000 cash to purchase land.
3. Paid $3,600 cash for rent expense.
4. Performed services for clients and billed them $15,200. Expected to collect cash at a later date (the revenue was earned on account).
5. Incurred $9,600 of other operating expenses on account (expected to make cash payment at a later date).
6. Received an $800 bill for utilities. The amount due was payable within 30 days.
7. Paid $4,400 cash on the account payable created in Event No. 5.
8. Acquired an additional $7,000 cash from the issue of common shares.
9. Paid $5,200 cash on the balance of the account payable created in Event No. 5.
10. Performed additional services for $4,500 cash.
11. Paid a $1,800 cash dividend to the shareholders.
12. Collected $8,600 cash from accounts receivable.

Required

a. Classify each of L&N's transactions as asset source (AS), asset use (AU), asset exchange (AE), or claims exchange (CE).
b. Show the effects of the events on the financial statements using a horizontal statements model like the following one. In the Cash Flow Statement column, use the initials OA for operating activity, IA for investing activity, FA for financing activity, and NC for net change in cash. Use NA to indicate accounts not affected by the transaction. The first one is recorded as an example.

Event No.	Assets			=	Liab.	+	Equity						Cash Flow Statement
	Cash	+ Acc. Rec.	+ Land	=	Acct. Pay.	+	Com. Sh.	+ Ret. Earn.	Rev.	− Exp.	=	Net Inc.	
1	50,000	+ NA	+ NA	=	NA	+	50,000	+ NA	NA	− NA	=	NA	50,000 FA

c. What is the amount of net income for 2006?
d. What is the amount of net cash flow from operating activities for 2006?

PROBLEM 2–7A *Missing Information in Financial Statements*

L.O. 2, 3, 4

Lake Properties had the following assets at the beginning of the accounting period (January 1, 2006): Cash—$21,000, Accounts Receivable—$33,000, Term Deposit—$16,000, and Land—$62,000. The beginning balances in the liability accounts were Accounts Payable—$27,000 and Notes Payable—$20,000. A $51,000 balance was in Common Shares at the beginning of the accounting period. During the accounting period, service revenue earned on account was $44,000. The ending balance in the Accounts Receivable account was $31,000. Operating expenses incurred on account amounted to $29,000. There was $33,000 paid on accounts payable. In addition, there was $1,200 of accrued interest revenue and $1,700 of accrued interest expense as of the end of the accounting period (December 31, 2006). Finally, a $2,500 cash dividend was paid to the shareholders. (*Hint:* Record the events in general ledger accounts under an accounting equation before satisfying the requirements.)

Required

a. Determine the amount of cash collected from accounts receivable.
b. Prepare a balance sheet as of January 1, 2006.
c. Prepare an income statement, statement of shareholders' equity, balance sheet, and cash flow statement for 2006.
d. Determine the interest rate earned on the term deposit.
e. Determine the interest rate paid on the note payable.

PROBLEMS—SERIES B

Where applicable in all problems, round computations to the nearest dollar.

PROBLEM 2–1B *Effect of Events on the Financial Statements*

L.O. 2, 3, 4

Expert Services experienced the following transactions during 2003.

1. Provided services to customers and received $5,000 cash.
2. Paid $1,000 cash for other operating expenses.
3. Borrowed $15,000 from the bank on March 1, 2003. The note had an 8 percent annual interest rate and a one-year term to maturity.
4. Provided services to customers and billed them $20,000.
5. Incurred $6,000 of other operating expenses on account.
6. Collected $12,000 of accounts receivable.
7. Paid $3,100 of the amount due on accounts payable.
8. Recognized the accrued interest on the note payable at December 31, 2003.

Required

a. Show the effects of the transactions on the financial statements using a horizontal statements model like the following one. In the Cash Flow Statement column, use the letters OA for operating activity, IA for investing activity, FA for financing activity, and NC for net change in cash. Use NA to indicate accounts not affected by the transaction. The first one is recorded as an example.

Event No.	Balance Sheet										Income Statement					Cash Flow Statement
	Assets			=	Liabilities					+ Equity						
	Cash	+	Acc. Rec.	=	Accts. Pay.	+	Note Pay.	+	Int. Pay.	+ Ret. Earn.	Rev.	−	Exp.	=	Net Inc.	
1	5,000	+	NA	=	NA	+	NA	+	NA	+ 5,000	5,000	−	NA	=	5,000	5,000 OA

b. What is the ending balance of retained earnings? What is the amount of net income? Why are these amounts the same in this problem? Give an example of a transaction that would cause these amounts to be different.

L.O. 3 PROBLEM 2–2B *Effect of Events on the Accounting Equation*

Required

Explain how each of the following independent accounting events would affect the accounting equation by writing the letter I for increase, the letter D for decrease, and NA for no effect under the appropriate columns. The effects of the first event are shown for you.

Letter of Event	Assets	=	Liabilities	+	Common Shares	+	Retained Earnings
a	I		NA		I		NA

a. Received cash from the issue of common shares.
b. Paid cash for interest expense accrued in a previous period.
c. Purchased land with cash.
d. Repaid borrowed funds with cash.
e. Collected cash from accounts receivable.
f. Paid cash for salaries.
g. Recognized service revenue on account.
h. Received utility bill; cash payment will be made in the future.
i. Borrowed cash from creditors.
j. Paid a cash dividend to the shareholders.
k. Accrued interest expense on note payable at the end of the accounting period.

L.O. 2, 3 PROBLEM 2–3B *Effect of Accrued Interest on Financial Statements*

Diamond Enterprises borrowed $18,000 from a local bank on July 1, 2006, when the company was started. The note had a 10 percent annual interest rate and a one-year term to maturity. Diamond Enterprises recognized $42,500 of revenue on account in 2006 and $45,000 of revenue on account in 2007. Cash collections of accounts receivable were $36,000 in 2006 and $35,000 in 2007. Diamond paid $24,000 of other operating expenses in 2006 and $28,000 of other operating expenses in 2007.

Required

Based on this information, answer the following questions. (*Hint:* Record the events in the general ledger accounts under an accounting equation before answering the questions.)

a. What amount of interest expense would Diamond report on the 2006 income statement?
b. What amount of net cash flow from operating activities would Diamond report on the 2006 cash flow statement?
c. What amount of total liabilities would Diamond report on the December 31, 2006, balance sheet?
d. What amount of retained earnings would Diamond report on the December 31, 2006, balance sheet?
e. What amount of net cash flow from financing activities would Diamond report on the 2006 cash flow statement?
f. What amount of interest expense would Diamond report on the 2007 income statement?
g. What amount of net cash flow from operating activities would Diamond report on the 2007 cash flow statement?
h. What amount of total assets would Diamond report on the December 31, 2007, balance sheet?
i. What amount of net cash flow from investing activities would Diamond report on the 2007 cash flow statement?
j. If Diamond Enterprises paid a $1,500 dividend during 2007, what retained earnings balance would it report on the December 31, 2007, balance sheet?

L.O. 3, 4 PROBLEM 2–4B *Two Complete Accounting Cycles*

The following accounting events apply to Maples Machine Co.

Accounting Events for 2007

1. Business started when it acquired $80,000 cash from the issue of common shares.
2. Recognized $190,000 of service revenue on account.
3. Collected $166,000 cash from accounts receivable.
4. Paid the shareholders a $10,000 cash dividend.
5. Paid $92,000 cash for salaries expense.
6. Invested $48,000 cash in a 12-month term deposit.

Information for December 31, 2007, End-of-Year Adjusting Entries

7. Accrued salary expense of $6,000.
8. Recorded accrued interest on the term deposit. The TD was purchased on July 1, 2007, and had a 10 percent annual rate of interest.

Accounting Events for 2008

1. Paid cash for salaries payable of $6,000.
2. Received an additional $60,000 cash from the issue of common shares.
3. Earned service revenue on account of $210,000 for the year.
4. Collected $224,000 cash from accounts receivable.
5. Paid a $30,000 cash dividend.
6. Paid $70,000 cash for salaries expense.
7. Purchased for $280,000 cash a plot of land on May 31, 2008. The value of the land rose to $300,000 by December 31.
8. Borrowed on June 1, 2008, $84,000 cash on a two-year, 8 percent note issued to a local bank.
9. Received cash for the principal and interest due on the term deposit of $52,800 when it matured on June 30, 2008.

Information for Adjusting Entries

10. Accrued salary expenses of $10,000.
11. Recorded accrued interest expense on the bank note (see Event No. 8 in 2008).

Required

a. Record the effect of each of the events in general ledger accounts under an accounting equation for the 2007 and 2008 fiscal years. In the last column of the table, provide appropriate account titles for Retained Earnings accounts.

b. Prepare an income statement, statement of shareholders' equity, balance sheet, and cash flow statement for the 2007 and 2008 fiscal years.

PROBLEM 2–5B *Identifying and Arranging Elements on Financial Statements* L.O. 4

The following information was drawn from the records of Vickers & Associates at December 31, 2004:

Land	$97,500	Common Shares Issued	$10,000
Salaries Payable	17,000	Salary Expense	22,500
Interest Expense	1,375	Beginning Common Shares	12,000
Accounts Receivable	20,600	Ending Retained Earnings	60,500
Notes Payable	35,000	Cash Flow from Inv. Activities	(7,700)
Cash Flow from Oper. Activities	30,800	Interest Payable	300
Cash	16,700	Interest Revenue	375
Service Revenue	51,000	Dividends	2,000
Cash Flow from Fin. Activities	(8,400)		

Required

Use the preceding information to construct an income statement, statement of shareholders' equity, balance sheet, and cash flow statement.

PROBLEM 2–6B *Classifying Events as Source, Use, or Exchange and Effect of Events on Financial Statements—Horizontal Statements Model* L.O. 2, 4

The following transactions pertain to Bunyard Financial Services for 2004:

1. Business started when it acquired $10,000 cash from the issue of common shares.
2. Paid $1,200 cash for rent expense.
3. Performed services for clients and billed them $8,000. Expected to collect cash at a later date (the revenue was earned on account).
4. Incurred $1,750 of other operating expenses on account (expected to make cash payment at a later date).

5. Paid $1,400 cash on the account payable created in Event No. 4.
6. Acquired $1,500 cash from the issue of additional common shares.
7. Paid $350 cash on the balance of the account payable created in Event No. 4.
8. Performed additional services for $3,500 cash.
9. Paid a $500 cash dividend to the shareholders.
10. Collected $7,250 cash from accounts receivable.

Required

a. Classify each of Bunyard's transactions as asset source (AS), asset use (AU), asset exchange (AE), or claims exchange (CE).
b. Show the effects of the events on the financial statements using a horizontal statements model like the following one. In the Cash Flow Statement column, use the initials OA for operating activity, IA for investing activity, FA for financing activity, and NC for net change in cash flow. Use NA to indicate accounts not affected by the transaction. The first one has been recorded as an example.

Event No.	Assets			=	Liab.	+	Equity								Cash Flow Statement
	Cash	+	Acc. Rec.	=	Acc. Pay.	+	Common Shares	+	Ret. Earn.	Rev.	−	Exp.	=	Net Inc.	
1	10,000	+	NA	=	NA	+	10,000	+	NA	NA	−	NA	=	NA	10,000 FA

c. What is the amount of net income for 2004?
d. What is the amount of net cash flow from operating activities for 2004?

L.O. 2, 3, 4 PROBLEM 2–7B *Missing Information in Financial Statements*

Dudley Properties had the following assets at the beginning of the accounting period (January 1, 2007): Cash—$1,600, Accounts Receivable—$2,400, Term Deposit—$5,000, and Land—$20,000. The beginning balances in the liability accounts were Accounts Payable—$1,000, and Notes Payable—$8,000. A $5,400 balance was in the Common Shares account at the beginning of the accounting period. During the accounting period, $3,600 of service revenue was earned on account. The ending balance in the Accounts Receivable account was $3,800. Operating expenses incurred on account amounted to $2,100. There was $2,600 paid on accounts payable. In addition, there was $400 of accrued interest revenue and $700 of accrued interest expense as of the end of the accounting period (December 31, 2007). Finally, an $800 cash dividend was paid to the shareholders. (*Hint:* Record the events in general ledger accounts under an accounting equation before satisfying the requirements.)

Required

a. Determine the amount of cash collected from accounts receivable.
b. Prepare a balance sheet as of January 1, 2007.
c. Prepare an income statement, statement of shareholders' equity, balance sheet, and cash flow statement for December 31, 2007.
d. Determine the interest rate earned on the term deposit.
e. Determine the interest rate charged on the note payable.

ANALYZE, THINK, COMMUNICATE

ATC 2–1 BUSINESS APPLICATIONS CASE *Bombardier's Annual Report*

Required

Using the Bombardier financial statements in Appendix B, answer the following questions:

a. Who are the independent auditors for Bombardier?
b. On what date does it appear the independent auditors completed the audit work related to Bombardier's 2002 financial statements?
c. Does the auditors' report give any information about how the audit was conducted? If so, what does it suggest was done?
d. Who is responsible for the financial information provided in the annual report?
e. What is the auditor responsible for?

GROUP ASSIGNMENT *Missing Information* ATC 2–2

Tricon, Inc., is a company composed of KFC, Pizza Hut, and Taco Bell. The following information, taken from the annual report, is available for the years 2000, 1999, and 1998.

	2000	1999	1998
Revenue	$ 7,093,000	$ 7,822,000	$ 8,479,000
Operating Expenses	6,233,000	6,582,000	7,451,000
Interest Expense	176,000	202,000	272,000

Required

a. Divide the class into groups of four or five students. Organize the groups into three sections. Assign each section of groups the financial data for one of the preceding accounting periods.

Group Tasks

(1) Determine the amount of net income for the year assigned.
(2) How does the result in Requirement *a*(1) affect the retained earnings of the company?
(3) If the average interest rate is 7 percent, what is the average amount of debt for the year?
(4) Have representatives from each section put the income statement for their respective year on the board.

Class Discussion

b. Have the class discuss the trend in revenue and net income. The company has new leadership teams and new management processes that will make Tricon a company "that stands for growth." If this is true, what actual results would you expect to see from the company in 2001?

REAL-WORLD CASE *Examining Annual Reports* ATC 2–3

Using the most current annual reports from these Web sites, answer the questions listed below.

www.royalbank.ca
www.magnaint.com
www.esso.ca

Required

a. In the asset section of its balance sheet, the Royal Bank reported "Securities." What did these securities consist of?
b. In the asset section of its balance sheet, Magna International, reported "Inventories." What were the items that were included in inventories?
c. In the asset section of its balance sheet, Imperial Oil Company reported "Goodwill" and "Other Intangible Assets." What was reported as an example of these assets?

BUSINESS APPLICATIONS CASE *Effects of Errors* ATC 2–4

The accounting firm of Espey & Davis, CAs, has recently completed the audits of three separate companies. During these audits, the following events were discovered, and Espey & Davis is trying to determine the effect, if any, each event has on the numbers provided.

1. In 2003, Foxx Company reported service revenues of $1,000,000 and net earnings of $80,000. Because of an accounting error, the company recorded $6,000 as revenue in 2003 for services that will not be performed until early 2004.
2. Guzza Company plans to report a cash balance of $70,000. This balance includes the president's bonus that was incorrectly recorded as $82,000. The bonus cheque received and cashed by the president was for $87,000. Guzza also plans to report total assets of $4,000,000 and net earnings of $415,000.
3. Jeter Company's 2003 balance sheet shows a cash balance of $200,000 and total assets of $9,000,000. For 2003, the company had a net income of $750,000. These balances include $5,000 for business travel expenses that were claimed by the president of the company. In fact, the president had charged the cost of personal vacations for himself and his family on the company's credit card.

Required

Write a memorandum to the partners of Espey & Davis, explaining how each of these events, if properly recorded, would affect the numbers provided.

ATC 2–5 BUSINESS APPLICATIONS CASE *Limitations of Audit Opinion (Appendix)*

The statement of financial position (balance sheet) of Trident Company reports assets of $4,500,000. Jan Lewis advises you that a major accounting firm has audited the statements and attested that they were prepared in accordance with generally accepted accounting principles. She tells you she can buy the total owner's interest in the business for only $2,750,000 and is seriously considering the opportunity. She says the auditor's unqualified opinion validates the $4,500,000 value of the assets. Lewis believes she would be foolish to pass up the opportunity to purchase the assets for only $2,750,000.

Required

a. What part of the accounting equation is Lewis failing to consider?
b. Comment on Lewis's misconceptions regarding the auditor's role in providing information that is useful in making investment decisions.

ATC 2–6 WRITING ASSIGNMENT *Definition of Elements of Financial Statements*

Putting "yum" on people's faces around the world is the mission of Tricon, Inc., a new company that resulted from a spin-off from PepsiCo. The company is composed of KFC, Pizza Hut, and Taco Bell. A spin-off occurs when a company separates its operations into two or more distinct companies. In this case, the Tricon restaurants were operated as part of PepsiCo prior to the spin-off, which was financed by having Tricon borrow $4.55 billion. These funds were used to pay PepsiCo for the value of the fast-food restaurants. Tricon's net income for 2000 was $413 million after taxes, and the long-term debt was down to $2.397 billion.

Required

a. If Tricon's debt remains constant at $2.397 billion for 2001, how much interest will Tricon incur in 2001, assuming that the average interest rate is 7 percent?
b. Does this amount of debt seem excessive compared with the amount of net income? Explain.

ATC 2–7 ETHICAL DILEMMA *Now It Is Your Turn to Cover for Me (Appendix)*

Johnny Travera and Tim Sanders were unusual friends. Travera came from a background of poverty while Sanders had an extremely affluent family. Indeed, the two would have never known each other except for an unusual set of events. Sanders's parents bought him a new car for his 16th birthday. Not being used to the new vehicle, Sanders misjudged a curve and wrecked the car. Travera happened to see the accident and helped Sanders get out of the vehicle. Sanders was unhurt but extremely distraught. He told Travera that his parents would never trust him again. When the police arrived, Travera told them he had seen a child run in front of Sanders's car and that Sanders had swerved off the road to save the child's life. Upon hearing the story, Sanders's parents considered him a hero. The insurance company bought a new car, and Sanders made a friend for life.

Sanders went to college and became a CGA in his father's accounting firm. Travera worked for several restaurants and finally managed to start one of his own. The restaurant succeeded, and Travera turned the accounting work over to Sanders. Having no formal education, Travera had little knowledge of technical business practices.

At the beginning of 2006, Travera's balance sheet included cash of $10,000, other assets amounting to $380,000, liabilities of $80,000, and common shares of $25,000. Sanders provided Travera with accounting services for several years and was reasonably certain as to the accuracy of these figures. Since Sanders always advised Travera on financial matters, Sanders was aware that during 2006 Travera had paid cash to purchase $50,000 of restaurant equipment. Also, Travera had been able to repay $15,000 cash on a note payable that evidenced the restaurant's liability to a bank. Finally, Travera had received a $20,000 cash dividend from the restaurant. Travera made no contributions to the business during 2006. Even so, the records that Travera provided Sanders for 2006 indicated that the restaurant earned $200,000 in cash revenues and incurred $175,000 in cash expenses. The ending balance in the Cash account was $12,000.

After analyzing the data, Sanders became convinced that Travera was not reporting accurate information to him for the determination of net income. He confronted Travera with the issue, and Travera admitted that he was not reporting all sales information. He said he did not report some of the cash sales because he did not feel the income tax system was fair and he did not want to pay any more taxes than he had to pay. He defended himself by saying, "I'm only doing what everybody else does. Your dad's biggest client, Billy Abbott, has been skimming a million a year off his chain of restaurants. He's been doing it for the last five years. I know; I used to work for him. Even so, you and your dad give him an unqualified audit opinion every year. So why won't you do the same thing for me?

I'm supposed to be your friend, and you keep telling me you think this Abbott guy is a real jerk." Indeed, Travera became so indignant that he told Sanders, "Either you sign my tax return, or I find a new accountant and a new friend to boot. I've always stood up for you, and this is the thanks I get."

Required

a. Based on the information provided in the case, determine the amount of Travera's unreported income. (*Hint:* The beginning balances were correct, but the entries for the current year transactions were recorded incorrectly. It may help to use an accounting equation with the beginning balances provided in the case, and record the current period's transactions under the equation. Assume that the ending cash balance is an accurate measure of cash on hand at the end of the accounting period. The amount of unrecorded cash equals the amount of unrecorded income.)

b. Explain how Travera's failure to report cash revenue will affect the elements of financial statements by indicating whether each element will be overstated, understated, or not affected by the reporting omission. The elements to consider are assets, liabilities, common shares, retained earnings, revenue, expenses, net income, and dividends.

c. If you were Sanders, would you sign Travera's tax return as Travera presented it to you?

d. Assume that you are Sanders, that you refuse to sign Travera's tax return, and that some other CGA without knowledge of Travera's deceitful reporting practice signs his tax return. Would you report Travera to the Canadian Customs and Revenue Agency (CCRA)?

e. Suppose that you are Sanders and that you investigate Travera's charges regarding Abbott. You find that Abbott is in fact underreporting income to the extent that Travera accused him of so doing. Would you report Abbott to the CCRA?

SPREADSHEET ASSIGNMENT *Using Excel*

ATC 2–8

Required

a. Refer to Problem 2–5A. Use an Excel spreadsheet to construct the required financial statements. To complete Requirement *b*, use formulas where normal arithmetic calculations are made within the financial statements (in particular the statement of shareholders' equity).

b. It is interesting to speculate about what would happen if certain operating results change for better or worse. After completing Requirement *a*, change certain account balances for each of the following independent operating adjustments. After each adjustment, notice how the financial statements would differ if the change in operations were to occur. After noting the effect of each adjustment, return the data to the original amounts in Problem 2–5A and then go to the next operating adjustment.

In the following table, note the new amounts on the financial statements for the various operating changes listed.

Original	1	2	3	4	5
Net Income					
Total Assets					
Total Liabilities					
Total Shareholders' Equity					
Total Liabilities & Shareholders' Equity					

Independent Operating Adjustments

1. Revenue and the related Accounts Receivable increased $10,000.
2. Revenue and the related Accounts Receivable decreased $10,000.
3. Salary Expense and the related Salaries Payable decreased $4,000.
4. Salary Expense and the related Salaries Payable increased $4,000.
5. Dividends paid decreased $500 and cash changed accordingly.

SPREADSHEET ASSIGNMENT *Mastering Excel*

ATC 2–9

Refer to Problem 2–6A. Complete Requirements *b*, *c*, and *d* using an Excel spreadsheet. Refer to Chapter 1 problem ATC 1–8 for ideas on how to structure the spreadsheet.

Chapter 3

Accounting for Deferrals

Learning Objectives

After completing this chapter, you should be able to:

1. Provide a more complete explanation of the accrual accounting system.
2. Identify business events that involve deferrals.
3. Demonstrate how events are recorded under an accounting equation.
4. Prepare financial statements that include cash, accrual, and deferral events.
5. Explain how deferral events affect the financial statements.
6. Explain the effects of end-of-period adjustments related to deferrals.
7. Distinguish between a cost that is an asset and a cost that is an expense.
8. Distinguish gains and losses from revenues and expenses.
9. Analyze financial statements and make meaningful comparisons between companies using ratios.
10. Record deferral events in a financial statements model.

the *curious* accountant

If a person wishes to subscribe to *Reader's Digest* for one year (12 issues), the subscriber must pay for the magazines before they are actually published. Suppose Paige Long sends $12 to the Reader's Digest Association in September 2003 for a one-year subscription; she will receive her first issue in October. How should Reader's Digest account for the receipt of this cash? How would this event be reported on Reader's Digest's December 31, 2003, financial statements?

In Chapter 2, we defined accruals *as the recognition of revenue and expense* before *the receipt or payment of cash. In this chapter, you will learn that accrual accounting is a much broader concept that includes not only accruals but also deferrals and allocations. A* ***deferral*** *involves the recognition of revenue or expense at some time* after *cash has been collected or paid. For example, a business may collect cash in 2003 for services performed in 2004. In this case, revenue is recognized in 2004 even though the cash was collected in 2003. In summary, when recognition comes before cash flow, it is called an* accrual. *When recognition comes after cash flow, it is called a* deferral.

When deferred amounts are spread over several accounting periods, the process of assigning a portion of the total amount to each accounting period is called an ***allocation****. To illustrate, assume that a lawyer received a retainer fee of $30,000 from a client at the beginning of 2003. In exchange for the cash receipt, the lawyer agreed to act as a trustee for the client's children for the years 2003, 2004, and 2005. From the perspective of accrual accounting, the cash receipt obligates the lawyer to work for the three-year period. Because of this future obligation, a liability is established in 2003 when the cash is collected. The recognition of revenue is deferred until the lawyer's obligation*

LO1 Provide a more complete explanation of the accrual accounting system.

(liability) to work is satisfied. If the work were spread evenly over the three-year period, it would be reasonable to allocate *the $30,000 evenly so that $10,000 of revenue was recognized during each of the three accounting periods.*

Accounting for Deferrals Illustrated

LO2 Identify business events that involve deferrals.

Stephen Peck is a brilliant young advertising executive employed by Westberry Corporation. Peck's ad campaigns were credited with virtually doubling Westberry's sales over a three-year period. Peck always wanted to start his own advertising agency so he could be the boss. He believed that his recent success with Westberry gave him enough credibility to attract a respectable client base. He informed his employer of his plans and tendered his resignation. Westberry was stunned. The company's executives urged Peck to reconsider and offered a generous raise. Peck was grateful but refused the offer. In desperation, Westberry negotiated the following deal. Peck was free to start his own company. Indeed, Westberry agreed to become Peck's first client, paying him $72,000 in advance to develop ad campaigns for the company. Peck's company, Marketing Magic, Inc. (MMI), began operations on January 1, 2004. The company experienced the following accounting events during its first year of operation.

Event 1 MMI acquired $1,000 cash from the issue of common shares. The share issue is an *asset source* transaction. Its impact on the financial statements was discussed in previous chapters. If you have difficulty understanding the effects of this event, see Chapters 1 and 2.

The impact of the share issue on the financial statements follows:

Assets						=	Liab.	+	Equity								Cash Flow Statement
Cash	+	Off. Equip.	−	Acc. Amort.		=	Unear. Rev.	+	C. Sh.	+	Ret. Ear.	Rev.	−	Exp.	=	Net Inc.	
1,000	+	NA	−	NA		=	NA	+	1,000	+	NA	NA	−	NA	=	NA	1,000 FA

The statements model contains several accounts that have not been discussed previously. We will present a full description of these accounts as additional accounting events are introduced.

Event 2 MMI obtained a $72,000 cash receipt as an advance from Westberry for services to be performed between March 1, 2004, and February 28, 2005.

On January 1, 2004, Marketing Magic received $72,000 cash. In exchange, Marketing Magic agreed to provide advertising development services for the one-year period between March 1, 2004, and February 28, 2005. Revenue could not be recognized on January 1, 2004, because services had not been performed (no work had been done). Even though the cash had been received, the revenue recognition had to be *deferred* until after the services had been performed. The amount of the deferred revenue represents a liability to Marketing Magic because the company is *obligated* to perform services in the future. The term **unearned revenue** is used for the liability reported in Marketing Magic's accounting records. The cash receipt is an *asset source* transaction. The asset, Cash, increases, and the liability account, Unearned Revenue, increases by the same amount, $72,000. The income statement is not affected when the cash is collected because no work has been performed. The revenue will be shown on the income statement after the service has been rendered. The cash flow statement shows a $72,000 cash inflow from operating activities. The effects of this transaction on the financial statements are shown here:

Assets			=	Liab.	+	Equity			Rev. − Exp. = Net Inc.			Cash Flow Statement
Cash	+ Off. Equip.	− Acc. Amort.	=	Unear. Rev.	+	C. Sh.	+	Ret. Ear.	Rev.	− Exp.	= Net Inc.	
72,000	+ NA	− NA	=	72,000	+	NA	+	NA	NA	− NA	= NA	72,000 OA

Event 3

MMI obtained contracts to provide $58,000 of marketing services in 2005.

Notice that even though $58,000 of contracts were signed for services to be performed in 2005, no cash was exchanged. There is no historical activity to record in the financial statements. The contracts will be reported later, when cash is received or when service is performed. Since no service has been performed and no cash has been exchanged, there is no realization or recognition to report in the financial statements.

Assets			=	Liab.	+	Equity			Rev. − Exp. = Net Inc.			Cash Flow Statement
Cash	+ Off. Equip.	− Acc. Amort.	=	Unear. Rev.	+	C. Sh.	+	Ret. Ear.	Rev.	− Exp.	= Net Inc.	
NA	+ NA	− NA	=	NA	+	NA	+	NA	NA	− NA	= NA	NA

Event 4

MMI paid $12,000 cash to purchase office equipment.

The purchase of the equipment is an *asset exchange* transaction. The asset Cash decreases; and the asset Office Equipment increases. Total assets are unchanged. The income statement is not affected. An expense will be recognized later, after the equipment has been used. The cash flow statement shows a $12,000 outflow for investing activities. The effects of this transaction on the financial statements are shown here:

Assets			=	Liab.	+	Equity			Rev. − Exp. = Net Inc.			Cash Flow Statement
Cash	+ Off. Equip.	− Acc. Amort.	=	Unear. Rev.	+	C. Sh.	+	Ret. Ear.	Rev.	− Exp.	= Net Inc.	
(12,000)	+ 12,000	− NA	=	NA	+	NA	+	NA	NA	− NA	= NA	(12,000) IA

Event 5

MMI adjusted its accounts to recognize the revenue earned in 2004.

LO6 Explain the effects of end-of-period adjustments related to deferrals.

Marketing Magic must recognize the amount of revenue earned on the Westberry contract during the 2004 accounting period. Marketing Magic began earning revenue on the Westberry contract on March 1, 2004. Assuming that the work is distributed evenly throughout the contract period, the earnings process is continuous. Recording revenue as it is earned (continuously) is impractical, if not impossible. A more reasonable approach is to adjust the accounting records at the end of the accounting period by the amount of revenue earned for the entire accounting period. For example, the $72,000 of unearned revenue can be divided by 12 to determine the amount of revenue to recognize on a monthly basis ($72,000 ÷ 12 = $6,000). Since 10 months of service were performed in 2004, $60,000 (10 × $6,000) of revenue could be recognized in a single year-end adjustment. This adjustment is made by removing $60,000 from the Unearned Revenue account and placing it in the Revenue account. This entry represents a *claims exchange*, with the liability account, Unearned Revenue, decreasing and the equity increasing (recognizing the revenue will cause net income to increase and ultimately a corresponding increase in Retained Earnings). Total claims remain unchanged. The decrease in the liability account triggers the recognition of the revenue. As the company satisfies its obligation to perform services, the creditor's claim on the firm's assets decreases and the owner's claim increases. Recall that *revenue* is defined as an increase in assets or a *decrease* in liabilities. The effect of the revenue recognition on the financial statements follows:

Assets																				
		Assets			=	Liab.	+		Equity								Cash Flow Statement
Cash	+	Off. Equip.	−	Acc. Amort.	=	Unear. Rev.	+	C. Sh.	+	Ret. Ear.	Rev.	−	Exp.	=	Net Inc.	
NA	+	NA	−	NA	=	(60,000)	+	NA	+	60,000	60,000	−	NA	=	60,000	NA

Event 6 MMI adjusted its accounts to recognize an expense to reflect the portion of the computer equipment that was used during the 2004 accounting period. The equipment was purchased on January 1, 2004. It has an expected useful life of four years and a $2,000 residual value.

LO6 Explain the effects of end-of-period adjustments related to deferrals.

To assess the net economic benefit associated with running the business, we must determine how much of the computer equipment was used in the process of earning the revenue. Assuming that the equipment is used evenly over its four-year life, it is logical to allocate an equal amount as expense for each year that the equipment is operated. Recall that the equipment cost $12,000 and has an estimated **residual (salvage) value** of $2,000. Since the $2,000 residual value represents the portion of the cost that will likely be recovered at the end of its useful life, only $10,000 worth of the equipment is ultimately expected to be used. The amount of expense to be recognized in the 2004 accounting period is $2,500 ([$12,000 − $2,000] ÷ 4). This allocation plan is commonly referred to as the **straight-line method**. As this discussion implies, the formula for determining a straight-line allocation is *cost minus residual value, divided by the number of years of useful life*:

$$\text{Straight-line amortization} = \frac{\text{Cost} - \text{Residual value}}{\text{Useful life in years}}$$

The recognition of the use of a long-term, tangible asset is commonly called **amortization expense**. *Long term* is usually defined as a period longer than the typical accounting cycle (longer than one year). The recognition of amortization expense constitutes an *asset use* transaction. The use of the asset (decrease) triggers the expense recognition. Recall that an *expense* is defined as a *decrease* in assets or an increase in liabilities. The effects of the expense recognition on the financial statements are as follows:

		Assets			=	Liab.	+		Equity							Cash Flow Statement
Cash	+	Off. Equip.	−	Acc. Amort.	=	Unear. Rev.	+	C. Sh.	+	Ret. Ear.	Rev.	−	Exp.	=	Net Inc.	
NA	+	NA	−	2,500	=	NA	+	NA	+	(2,500)	NA	−	2,500	=	(2,500)	NA

Note that the asset account, Office Equipment, was not directly decreased. Rather, a **contra asset account** called **Accumulated Amortization** was used to show the reduction. This is the generally accepted approach for reporting the effects of amortization:

$$\text{Net book value} = \text{Cost} - \text{Accumlated Amortization}$$

The Accumulated Amortization account is subtracted from the original cost of the asset to determine the **net book value** (carrying value) of the asset. Both the **historical cost** (GAAP principle) of the asset and the Accumulated Amortization account are shown in the financial statements. This treatment is shown in the financial statements in Exhibit 3–1 on page 96.

Event 7 MMI paid a $50,000 cash dividend to the shareholders.

As discussed in Chapters 1 and 2, the dividend represents an *asset use* transaction. Its effect on the financial statements is shown here:

		Assets			=	Liab.	+		Equity							Cash Flow Statement
Cash	+	Off. Equip.	−	Acc. Amort.	=	Unear. Rev.	+	C. Sh.	+	Ret. Ear.	Rev.	−	Exp.	=	Net Inc.	
(50,000)	+	NA	−	NA	=	NA	+	NA	+	(50,000)	NA	−	NA	=	NA	(50,000) FA

Summary of Events and Ledger Accounts

Marketing Magic Inc. experienced seven business events in its 2004 accounting period. These events are summarized here:

1. Acquired $1,000 cash from the issue of common shares.
2. Obtained a $72,000 cash receipt as an advance from Westberry for services to be performed between March 1, 2004, and February 28, 2005.
3. Obtained contracts to provide $58,000 of marketing services in 2005.
4. Paid $12,000 cash to purchase office equipment.
5. Adjusted its accounts to recognize the revenue earned in 2004.
6. Adjusted its accounts to recognize an expense to reflect the portion of the computer equipment purchased on January 1, 2004, and used during the 2004 accounting period. It has an expected useful life of four years and a $2,000 residual value.
7. Paid a $50,000 cash dividend to the shareholders.

The accounting events have been recorded in the following ledger accounts. We have used the information in these accounts to prepare the financial statements shown in Exhibit 3–1.

Assets		= Liabilities	+ Equity	
Cash	**Office Equipment**	**Unearned Revenue**	**Common Shares**	**Retained Earnings**
(1) 1,000	(4) 12,000	(2) 72,000	(1) 1,000	0
(2) 72,000	**Accumulated Amortization**	(5) (60,000)		**Revenue**
(4) (12,000)	(6) (2,500)	Bal 12,000		(5) 60,000
(7) (50,000)				**Amortization Expense**
Bal 11,000				(6) (2,500)
				Dividend
				(7) (50,000)

The 2004 Financial Statements

LO4 Prepare financial statements that include cash, accrual, and deferral events.

Exhibit 3–1 contains the financial statements for Marketing Magic for the 2004 accounting period. By now you should be familiar with most of the components of the financial statements. However, it is important to trace the effects of all transactions to the financial statements. Pay special attention to the fact that deferrals as well as accruals cause differences between the amount of reported net income and the amount of cash flow from operations.

The income statement displays the allocations for revenue recognition ($60,000) and amortization expense ($2,500); it thus reported net income of $57,500. In contrast, the operating activities section of the cash flow statement shows the $72,000 of cash received from the Westberry contract. Note that the $12,000 cash paid for office equipment is shown in the investing activities section rather than the operating activities section. This treatment applies to the purchase or sale of any long-term asset.

Another item that should be reviewed is the treatment of the Accumulated Amortization account. Note that the full amount of the original cost is shown in the Office Equipment account. The amount of the accumulated amortization is subtracted from this amount to arrive at the carrying value (net book value) of the asset ($12,000 − $2,500 = $9,500). Net book value ($9,500) is then added to the other assets to arrive at the amount of total assets appearing on the balance sheet.

Exhibit 3–1 *Vertical Statements Model*

MARKETING MAGIC, INC.
Financial Statements
For the 2004 Accounting Period

Income Statement		
Service Revenue		$ 60,000
Amortization Expense		(2,500)
Net Income		$ 57,500
Statement of Shareholders' Equity		
Beginning Common Shares	$ 0	
Plus: Common Shares Issued	1,000	
Ending Common Shares		$ 1,000
Beginning Retained Earnings	0	
Plus: Net Income	57,500	
Less: Dividends	(50,000)	
Ending Retained Earnings		7,500
Total Shareholders' Equity		$ 8,500
Balance Sheet		
Assets		
Cash		$ 11,000
Office Equipment	$ 12,000	
Less: Accumulated Amortization	(2,500)	9,500
Total Assets		$ 20,500
Liabilities		
Unearned Revenue		$ 12,000
Shareholders' Equity		
Common Shares	$ 1,000	
Retained Earnings	7,500	
Total Shareholders' Equity		8,500
Total Liabilities and Shareholders' Equity		$ 20,500
Cash Flow Statement		
Cash Flows from Operating Activities		
Cash Receipt from Receivables		$ 72,000
Cash Flows from Investing Activities		
Cash Payment for Computer Equipment		(12,000)
Cash Flows from Financing Activities		
Cash Receipt from Issuing Common Shares	$ 1,000	
Cash Payment for Dividends	(50,000)	
Net Cash Outflow from Financing Activities		(49,000)
Net Increase in Cash		11,000
Plus: Beginning Cash Balance		0
Ending Cash Balance		$ 11,000

Sanderson & Associates received a $24,000 cash advance as a retainer to provide legal services to a client. The contract called for Sanderson to render services during a one-year period beginning October 1, 2006. Based on this information alone, determine the cash flow from operating activities Sanderson would report on the 2006 and 2007 cash flow statements. Also determine the amount of revenue Sanderson would report on the 2006 and 2007 income statements.

Answer Since Sanderson collected all of the cash in 2006, the 2006 cash flow statement would report a $24,000 cash inflow from operating activities. The 2007 cash flow statement would report zero cash flow from operating activities. Revenue is recognized in the period in which it is earned. Here revenue is earned at the rate of $2,000 per month ($24,000 ÷ 12 months = $2,000 per month). Sanderson rendered services for three months in 2006 and nine months in 2007. Sanderson would report $6,000 (3 months × $2,000) of revenue on the 2006 income statement and $18,000 (9 months × $2,000) of revenue on the 2007 income statement.

Key Accounting Concepts

You may have noticed that the amortization expense represented the part of the asset that was used during the period from January 1 to December 31, 2004. However, the revenue was recognized from a starting point on March 1, 2004. Therefore, it could be argued that the computer was used for purposes other than generating the revenue related to the Westberry contract. Sometimes, revenues and expenses do not perfectly match. As discussed in Chapter 2, many expenses are not directly related to particular revenues and are therefore matched with the period in which they are incurred. However, it does not make sense to recognize all of the cost of the equipment in the period in which it was purchased. Since the equipment will be used to produce revenue over a four-year period, it is logical to spread its cost over the four-year useful life. The process of spreading the cost over several accounting periods is often called a **systematic allocation**.

As the preceding discussion suggests, the **matching principle** (GAAP principle) is accomplished on three levels. First, possible costs are matched directly with the revenues they generate (expenses are recognized in the same period as the related revenue). Common examples include cost of land that has been sold and sales commissions. Second, the cost of items with short or undeterminable useful lives is matched with the period in which they are incurred (expenses are recognized in the period in which they are incurred). Examples of period expenses include advertising, rent, and utilities. Finally, the costs of long-term assets with definable useful lives are systematically allocated over the assets' useful lives (expenses are spread over the periods the assets are used). Amortization is an example of an expense that is recognized through the systematic allocation of cost.

The treatment of amortization highlights the fact that financial reports contain information from approximate, rather than exact, measures. Notice that the amounts of both the asset's residual value and its expected useful life are estimates. Thus, the amounts of amortization expense, net income, and retained earnings constitute estimated, rather than exact, amounts. Estimates and other slight imperfections are to be expected. Indeed, the **concept of materiality** (GAAP principle) recognizes the practical limitations in financial reporting. Proper treatment is required for material items only. An omission or misstatement of accounting information is considered material if the decision of a reasonable person would have been influenced by the omission or misstatement. Generally accepted accounting principles do not apply to items that would not affect the decisions of a reasonable person (immaterial items).

answers to the *curious* accountant

Because the Reader's Digest Association receives cash from customers before actually providing any magazines to them, the company has not earned any revenue when it receives the cash. Thus, Reader's Digest has a liability, which is called *unearned revenue*. If Reader's Digest closed its books on December 31, then $3 of Paige Long's subscription would be recognized as revenue in 2003. The remaining $9 would appear on Reader's Digest's balance sheet as a liability.

Reader's Digest actually ends its accounting year on June 30, each year. Exhibit 3–2 is a copy of the June 30, 2000, balance sheet for Reader's Digest. Notice the unearned revenue liability amounting to $289.4 million—this liability represented about 23 percent of Reader's Digest's total liabilities!

Will Reader's Digest need cash to pay off these subscription liabilities? Not exactly. The liabilities will not be paid off with cash. Instead, they will be satisfied by providing magazines to the subscribers. However, Reader's Digest will need cash to pay for the production and distribution of the magazines supplied to the customers. Even so, the amount of cash required to provide magazines will probably differ significantly from the amount of unearned revenues. In most cases, subscription fees do not cover the cost of producing and distributing magazines. Publishers collect significant advertising revenues that enable them to provide magazines to customers at prices well below the cost of publication. Accordingly, the amount of unearned revenue is not likely to represent the amount of cash needed to cover the cost of satisfying the company's obligation to produce and distribute magazines. Although the association between unearned revenues and the cost of providing magazines to customers is not direct, a knowledgeable financial analyst can use the information to make estimates regarding future cash flows and revenue recognition.

Exhibit 3–2 *Excerpt from the Reader's Digest 2000 Annual Report*

The Reader's Digest Association, Inc., and Subsidaries
Consolidated Balance Sheets (in millions $US)

	June 30, 2000	June 30, 1999
Assets		
Current Assets		
Cash and Cash Equivalents	$ 49.7	$ 413.4
Receivables, Net	285.3	319.9
Inventories, Net	120.3	94.9
Prepaid and Deferred Promotion Costs	115.5	109.0
Prepaid Expenses and Other Current Assets	201.7	193.5
Total Current Assets	772.5	1,130.7
Marketable Securities	173.5	20.9
Property, Plant and Equipment, Net	152.4	148.4
Intangible Assets, Net	438.8	68.5
Other Noncurrent Assets	221.6	248.0
Total Assets	$1,758.8	$1,616.5
Liabilities and Shareholders' Equity		
Current Liabilities		
Loans and Notes Payable	$ 89.4	$ 0.4
Accounts Payable	146.4	130.7
Accrued Expenses	309.6	352.2
Income Taxes Payable	38.7	56.0
Unearned Revenue	289.4	336.5
Other Current Liabilities	30.9	16.5
Total Current Liabilities	904.4	892.3
Postretirement and Postemployment Benefits Other than Pensions	142.3	146.9
Other Noncurrent Liabilities	207.8	195.8
Total Liabilities	1,254.5	1,235.0

Exhibit is continued on the following page.

Shareholders' Equity		
Capital Shares	28.9	24.8
Paid-In Capital	223.1	146.2
Retained Earnings	1,106.6	955.4
Accumulated Other Comprehensive Income (Loss)	31.0	(56.6)
Treasury Shares, at Cost	(885.3)	(688.3)
Total Shareholders' Equity	504.3	381.5
Total Liabilities and Shareholders' Equity	$1,758.8	$1,616.5

Second Accounting Cycle

Stephen Peck moved the offices of Marketing Magic Inc. to a new location on January 1, 2005. Westberry continued to be a client but decided to pay for services as rendered rather than in advance. Marketing Magic consummated the following transactions during the 2005 accounting period.

LO2 Identify business events that involve deferrals.

1. Acquired an additional $5,000 cash from the issue of more common shares.
2. Paid $400 cash for supplies.
3. Paid $1,200 cash for an insurance policy that covered the company for one year, beginning February 1, 2005.
4. Recognized revenue for services provided on account in the amount of $108,000.
5. Collected $89,000 of the receivables due from customers.
6. Recognized accrued operating expenses, other than supplies and insurance, charged on account in the amount of $32,000.
7. Paid suppliers $28,000 of the amount due on the accounts payable.
8. Paid a $70,000 cash dividend to shareholders.
9. Purchased land that cost $3,000 cash.

Adjusting Entries

10. Recognized the remainder of the unearned revenue. All services had been provided by February 28, 2005, as per the original contract.
11. Recognized amortization expense.
12. Recognized supplies expense; $150 of supplies was on hand at the close of business on December 31, 2005.
13. Recognized 11 months of insurance expense.

Exhibit 3–3 is a summary of the transactions on the accounting equation. The effects are referenced by the transaction number in parentheses to the left of the transaction amount. The beginning balances were carried forward from the last period's ending balances. Many of the transactions were introduced previously. New transactions are discussed in the following section.

LO3 Demonstrate how events are recorded under an accounting equation.

Effect of 2005 Transactions on the Accounting Equation and the Financial Statements

LO7 Distinguish between a cost that is an asset and a cost that is an expense.

Transaction 2 is a deferral. The cost of the supplies is first placed in an asset account (*asset exchange* transaction). The conversion of the asset to an expense is deferred until the supplies are used in the process of earning revenue. It is helpful at this point to distinguish clearly between *cost* and *expense*. A *cost* can be either an asset or an expense. If the item acquired has been used for earning revenue, its cost represents an *expense*. If the item will be used in the future to generate revenue, its cost represents an *asset*. The cost is held in the asset account (the expense recognition is deferred) until the item is used to

Exhibit 3–3 *Effect of 2005 Transactions on the Accounting Equation**

Assets = Liabilities + Equity

Assets

Cash	
Bal.	$ 11,000
(1)	5,000
(2)	(400)
(3)	(1,200)
(5)	89,000
(7)	(28,000)
(8)	(70,000)
(9)	(3,000)
Bal.	$ 2,400

Accounts Receivable	
Bal.	$ 0
(4)	108,000
(5)	(89,000)
Bal.	$ 19,000

Supplies	
Bal.	$ 0
(2)	400
(12)	(250)
Bal.	$ 150

Land	
Bal.	$ 0
(9)	3,000
Bal.	$ 3,000

Prepaid Insurance	
Bal.	$ 0
(3)	1,200
(13)	(1,100)
Bal.	$ 100

Office Equipment	
Bal.	$ 12,000

Accumulated Amortization	
Bal.	$ (2,500)
(11)	(2,500)
Bal.	$ (5,000)

Liabilities

Unearned Revenue	
Bal.	$ 12,000
(10)	(12,000)
Bal.	$ 0

Accounts Payable	
Bal.	$ 0
(6)	32,000
(7)	(28,000)
Bal.	$ 4,000

Equity

Common Shares	
Bal.	$ 1,000
(1)	5,000
Bal.	$ 6,000

Retained Earnings	
Bal.	$ 7,500

Service Revenue	
(4)	$ 108,000
(10)	12,000
Bal.	$ 120,000

Operating Expenses	
(6)	$ (32,000)

Amortization Expense	
(11)	$ (2,500)

Supplies Expense	
(12)	$ (250)

Insurance Expense	
(13)	$ (1,100)

Dividend	
(8)	$ (70,000)

* To conserve space, we have used columnar representations in this exhibit. These are not T-accounts.

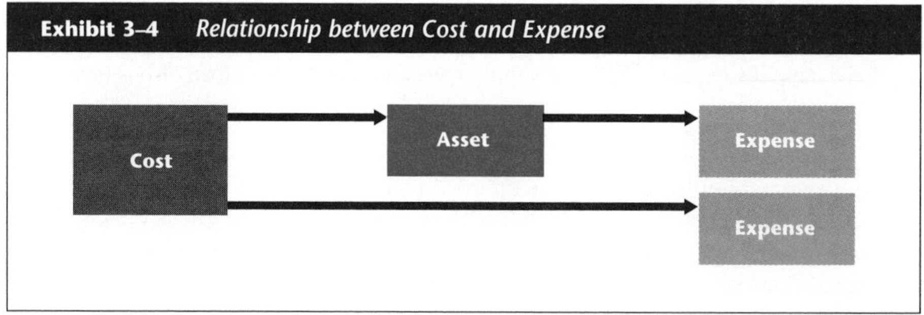

LO5 Explain how deferral events affect financial statements.

LO6 Explain the effects of end-of-period adjustments related to deferrals.

produce revenue. When the revenue is generated, the asset is converted to an expense to match revenues with their related expenses. Exhibit 3–4 demonstrates the relationship between a cost and an expense.

It is impractical to recognize supplies expense as the supplies are being used. For example, it is too tedious to record an expense every time a pencil, a piece of paper, or an envelope is used. Instead, normal practice is to recognize the total amount of supplies used during the entire accounting period in a single adjusting entry at the end of the accounting period. The amount of supplies used is determined by subtracting the amount of supplies on hand at the end of the period from the amount of supplies that were available for use. Since Marketing Magic had no supplies at the beginning of the period, the only supplies available for use were the $400 of supplies purchased during 2005. Transaction 12 states that

$150 of supplies was on hand at the end of the accounting period. In practice, this amount is determined by counting the supplies on hand at the end of the period. Based on the information provided in the case, $250 of supplies must have been used during the period ($400 − $150). This explains the year-end adjusting entry (Transaction 12) that removes the amount of the used supplies from the asset account and transfers it into the Supplies Expense account. Recall that an *expense* is defined as a decrease in assets or an increase in liabilities. In this case, the decrease in the asset, Supplies, triggers the expense recognition. The $150 of supplies on hand at the end of the accounting period is shown as an asset on the balance sheet. The parentheses surrounding the amounts in the expense and dividend accounts indicate that the business events acted to decrease the Retained Earnings equity account. Although events 6, 8, 11, 12, and 13 increase the amount of an expense or dividend account, they acted to decrease equity.

Note that the deferral causes a difference between the amount of expense recognized and the amount of cash flow. Although $400 of cash is paid for supplies, only $250 of this is recognized as an expense. The remaining $150 is deferred as an asset. The $400 appears as an outflow under the operating activities section of the cash flow statement, the $250 is reported as supplies expense on the income statement, and the $150 is displayed as an asset (supplies) on the balance sheet. Verify these effects by reviewing the financial statements shown in Exhibit 3–5.

Transaction 3 is also a deferral. The $1,200 cost of the insurance must be allocated between an asset account and an expense account. Since the insurance policy provided coverage for one year, the cost of coverage per month is $100 ($1,200 ÷ 12). By the end of the accounting period, 11 months of the coverage have been used and one month of coverage is available for use in 2006. Therefore, $1,100 ($100 × 11) should be charged to expense, and the remaining $100 represents an asset. Since the insurance is paid for in advance of its use, the title *Prepaid Insurance* is an appropriate name for the asset account.

As a practical matter, the full cost of the insurance is placed in the Prepaid Insurance account at the time of the purchase (see Transaction 3 in Exhibit 3–3). An adjusting entry is made at the end of the accounting period to recognize the amount of the insurance that has been used. The adjustment (Transaction 13) moves the amount of used insurance from the asset account to the expense account.

The deferral for the insurance cost causes a difference between the amount of insurance expense and the cash flow. The $1,200 cash cost is shown in the cash flow from operating activities section of the cash flow statement. The used portion of the cost is shown as an $1,100 expense on the income statement, and the remaining $100 is deferred as an asset, Prepaid Insurance, on the balance sheet. Verify this allocation and the effects of the remaining transactions by reviewing the financial statements in Exhibit 3–5.

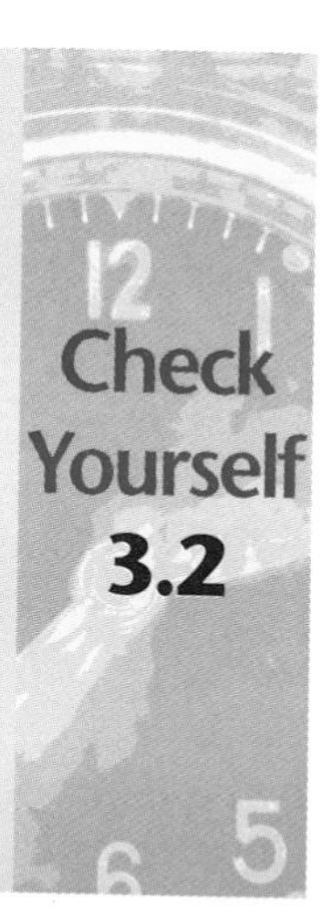

Rujoub, Inc., paid $18,000 cash for one year of insurance coverage that began on November 1, 2005. Based on this information alone, determine the cash flow from operating activities that Rujoub would report on the 2005 and 2006 cash flow statements. Also determine the amount of insurance expense Rujoub would report on the 2005 income statement and the amount of prepaid insurance (an asset) that Rujoub would report on the December 31, 2005, balance sheet.

Answer Since Rujoub paid all of the cash in 2005, the 2005 cash flow statement would report an $18,000 cash outflow from operating activities. The 2006 cash flow statement would report zero cash flow from operating activities. The expense would be recognized in the periods in which the insurance is used. In this case, insurance expense is recognized at the rate of $1,500 per month ($18,000 ÷ 12 months = $1,500). Rujoub used two months of insurance coverage in 2005 and so would report $3,000 (2 months × $1,500) of insurance expense on the 2005 income statement. Rujoub would report a $15,000 (10 months × $1,500) asset, prepaid insurance, on the December 31, 2005, balance sheet. The $15,000 of prepaid insurance would be recognized as insurance expense in 2006 when the insurance coverage is used.

Exhibit 3–5 *Vertical Statements Model*

MARKETING MAGIC, INC.
Financial Statements
For the 2005 Accounting Period

Income Statement

Service Revenue		$120,000
Operating Expenses	$ 32,000	
Amortization Expense	2,500	
Supplies Expense	250	
Insurance Expense	1,100	
Total Expenses		(35,850)
Net Income		$ 84,150

Statement of Shareholders' Equity

Beginning Common Shares	$ 1,000	
Plus: Common Shares Issued	5,000	
Ending Common Shares		$ 6,000
Beginning Retained Earnings	7,500	
Plus: Net Income	84,150	
Less: Dividends	(70,000)	
Ending Retained Earnings		21,650
Total Shareholders' Equity		$ 27,650

Balance Sheet

Assets		
Cash		$ 2,400
Accounts Receivable		19,000
Supplies		150
Prepaid Insurance		100
Office Equipment	$ 12,000	
Less: Accumulated Amortization	(5,000)	7,000
Land		3,000
Total Assets		$ 31,650
Liabilities		
Accounts Payable		$ 4,000
Shareholders' Equity		
Common Shares	$ 6,000	
Retained Earnings	21,650	
Total Shareholders' Equity		27,650
Total Liabilities and Shareholders' Equity		$ 31,650

Cash Flow Statement

Cash Flows from Operating Activities		
Cash Receipt from Receivables		$ 89,000
Cash Payment for Supplies	$ (400)	
Cash Payment for Insurance	(1,200)	
Cash Payment for Operating Expenses	(28,000)	
Total Cash Outflows from Operations		(29,600)
Net Cash Flow from Operating Activities		59,400
Cash Flows from Investing Activities		
Cash Outflow to Purchase Land		(3,000)
Cash Flows from Financing Activities		
Cash Receipt from Issuing Common Shares	5,000	
Cash Payment for Dividends	(70,000)	
Net Cash Outflow from Financing Activities		(65,000)
Net Decrease in Cash		(8,600)
Plus: Beginning Cash Balance		11,000
Ending Cash Balance		$ 2,400

Third Accounting Cycle

The following transactions occurred during the 2006 accounting period:

LO2 Identify business events that involve deferrals.

1. Acquired an additional $1,000 cash from the issue of common shares.
2. Sold the land that it owned for $2,500 cash.
3. Purchased $400 of supplies with cash.
4. Borrowed $20,000 from a local bank on February 1, 2006. The bank note carried a 9 percent annual rate of interest and a one-year term.
5. Paid $1,200 cash to renew the insurance policy for a one-year term beginning February 1, 2006.
6. Recognized revenue for services provided on account in the amount of $167,000.
7. Collected $129,000 of the receivables due from customers.
8. Recognized accrued operating expenses, other than supplies and insurance. These operating expenses were charged on account in the amount of $62,000.
9. Paid suppliers $65,000 of the amount due on the accounts payable.
10. Received advance payment of $18,000 cash from a customer. Marketing Magic agreed to provide marketing services to the customer for a one-year period beginning December 1, 2006.
11. An $80,000 cash dividend was paid to the shareholders.

Adjusting Entries

12. Recognized one month of the unearned revenue.
13. Recognized amortization expense.
14. Recognized supplies expense; $200 of supplies was on hand at the close of business on December 31, 2006.
15. Recognized 12 months of insurance expense.
16. Recognized the accrued interest on the bank note.

The effects of the 2006 accounting events are shown in Exhibit 3–6.

Effect of 2006 Transactions on the Accounting Equation and the Financial Statements

LO3 Demonstrate how events are recorded under an accounting equation.

LO8 Distinguish gains and losses from revenues and expenses.

The sale of the land resulted in the recognition of a $500 loss. Since the asset was carried on the books at $3,000 and was sold for $2,500, total assets decreased by $500. This decrease in assets is called a loss. **Losses** are similar to expenses in that they are defined as decreases in assets or increases in liabilities. Losses differ from expenses in that losses result from **peripheral (incidental) transactions**, rather than ordinary operating activities. In this case, Marketing Magic is not in the business of selling land. The sale is incidental to its normal operating activities. Therefore, the decrease in assets is labelled a *loss* rather than an *expense*. **Gains** are similar to revenues in that they are defined as increases in assets or decreases in liabilities. However, gains differ from revenues in that gains result from peripheral rather than ordinary operating activities.

The sale of the land results in an increase in the Cash account. Also, we must remove the amount in the Land account from the records and recognize the loss as a reduction in shareholders' equity. Recording the effects requires a $2,500 increase to the Cash account, a $3,000 decrease to the Land account, and a $500 reduction in Retained Earnings. These effects are shown in Exhibit 3–6, labelled as Transaction 2. The $500 loss is shown on the income statement as a separate line item after **income from operations**, which is determined by subtracting expenses from revenues. However, the loss does not measure the cash flow consequences of the sale. Recall that the land was sold for $2,500 cash. This amount is shown as a source (cash inflow) of funds under the investing activities section of the cash flow

Exhibit 3–6 *Effect of 2006 Transactions on the Accounting Equation**

Assets = Liabilities + Equity

Assets

Cash	
Bal.	$ 2,400
(1)	1,000
(2)	2,500
(3)	(400)
(4)	20,000
(5)	(1,200)
(7)	129,000
(9)	(65,000)
(10)	18,000
(11)	(80,000)
Bal.	$ 26,300

Accounts Receivable	
Bal.	$ 19,000
(6)	167,000
(7)	(129,000)
Bal.	$ 57,000

Supplies	
Bal.	$ 150
(3)	400
(14)	(350)
Bal.	$ 200

Land	
Bal.	$ 3,000
(2)	(3,000)
Bal.	$ 0

Prepaid Insurance	
Bal.	$ 100
(5)	1,200
(15)	(1,200)
Bal.	$ 100

Office Equipment	
Bal.	$ 12,000

Accumulated Amortization	
Bal.	$ (5,000)
(13)	(2,500)
Bal.	$ (7,500)

Liabilities

Accounts Payable	
Bal.	$ 4,000
(8)	62,000
(9)	(65,000)
Bal.	$ 1,000

Unearned Revenue	
Bal.	$ 0
(10)	18,000
(12)	(1,500)
Bal.	$ 16,500

Interest Payable	
(16)	$ 1,650

Notes Payable	
(4)	$ 20,000

Equity

Common Shares	
Bal.	$ 6,000
(1)	1,000
Bal.	$ 7,000

Retained Earnings	
Bal.	$ 21,650

Service Revenue	
(6)	$ 167,000
(12)	1,500
Bal.	$ 168,500

Operating Expense	
(8)	$ (62,000)

Amortization Expense	
(13)	$ (2,500)

Supplies Expense	
(14)	$ (350)

Insurance Expense	
(15)	$ (1,200)

Interest Expense	
(16)	$ (1,650)

Loss on Sale of Land	
(2)	$ (500)

Dividend	
(11)	$ (80,000)

* To conserve space, we have used column representations in this exhibit. These are not T-accounts.

statement. Cash flow from operations is not affected by the sale. Remember, the loss was associated with a *peripheral activity* rather than an ordinary operating activity. Verify these effects by reviewing the financial statements in Exhibit 3–7.

LO6 Explain the effects of end-of-period adjustments related to deferrals.

The amount of supplies expense is determined by the same approach as was used in 2005, except that in this case there is a beginning balance in the Supplies account. Since the Supplies account has a beginning balance of $150 and $400 of supplies is purchased during the period, $550 of supplies is available to be used. Given that $200 of supplies was on hand at December 31, 2006, then $350 of supplies must have been used during the accounting period. Accordingly, the year-end adjusting entry (Transaction 14) removes $350 from the asset account, Supplies, and places it in the Supplies Expense account. Note that the amount of supplies expense does not correspond to the amount of cash spent. The operating activities section of the cash flow statement displays the $400 cash outflow made to purchase supplies. Note that the beginning balances in the expense and dividend accounts are assumed to be zero because the prior year balances were closed (transferred) to the Retained Earnings account.

The Prepaid Insurance account increased as a result of $1,200 of insurance purchased on February 1, 2006 (Transaction 5). Given the $100 beginning balance in the Prepaid Insurance account, $1,300 of insurance is available to use over a 13-month period. Since 12 months of insurance were used in 2006, the year-end adjusting entry removes $1,200 from the Prepaid Insurance account and places it in the Insurance Expense account (Transaction 15).

Exhibit 3–7 *Vertical Statements Model*

MARKETING MAGIC, INC.
Financial Statements
For the 2006 Accounting Period

Income Statement		
Service Revenue		$168,500
Operating Expense	$ 62,000	
Amortization Expense	2,500	
Supplies Expense	350	
Insurance Expense	1,200	
Interest Expense	1,650	
Total Expenses		(67,700)
Net Operating Income		100,800
Less: Loss on Sale of Land		(500)
Net Income		$100,300
Statement of Shareholders' Equity		
Beginning Common Shares	$ 6,000	
Plus: Common Shares Issued	1,000	
Ending Common Shares		$ 7,000
Beginning Retained Earnings	21,650	
Plus: Net Income	100,300	
Less: Dividends	(80,000)	
Ending Retained Earnings		41,950
Total Equity		$ 48,950
Balance Sheet		
Assets		
Cash		$ 26,300
Accounts Receivable		57,000
Supplies		200
Prepaid Insurance		100
Office Equipment	$ 12,000	
Less: Accumulated Amortization	(7,500)	4,500
Total Assets		$ 88,100
Liabilities		
Accounts Payable	$ 1,000	
Unearned Revenue	16,500	
Interest Payable	1,650	
Notes Payable	20,000	
Total Liabilities		$ 39,150
Shareholders' Equity		
Common Shares	7,000	
Retained Earnings	41,950	
Total Shareholders' Equity		48,950
Total Liabilities and Shareholders' Equity		$ 88,100
Cash Flow Statement		
Cash Flows from Operating Activities		
Cash Receipt from Receivables	$129,000	
Cash Receipt from Advance Collections	18,000	
Cash Payment for Supplies	(400)	
Cash Payment for Insurance	(1,200)	
Cash Payment for Operating Expenses	(65,000)	
Net Cash Flow from Operating Activities		$ 80,400
Cash Flows from Investing Activities		
Cash Receipt from Sale of Land		2,500
Cash Flows from Financing Activities		
Cash Receipt from Bank Loan	20,000	
Cash Receipt from Issuing Common Shares	1,000	
Cash Payment for Dividends	(80,000)	
Net Cash Outflow from Financing Activities		(59,000)
Net Increase in Cash		23,900
Plus: Beginning Cash Balance		2,400
Ending Cash Balance		$ 26,300

The borrowed funds from the bank loan (Transaction 4) require the accrual of interest expense. The amount of interest is determined by multiplying the principal by the rate by the time ($20,000 × 0.09 × [11 ÷ 12] = $1,650). The accrued interest represents a liability to Marketing Magic as of December 31, 2006. The increase in liabilities requires that interest expense be recognized as shown in Transaction 16 in Exhibit 3–6.

The advance payment described in Transaction 10 is a deferral. The cash receipt is first recorded as a liability (*Unearned Revenue*). Assuming that the work associated with the contract is spread evenly over the one-year period, the monthly allocation for revenue recognition is $1,500 ($18,000 ÷ 12). Since one month of service has been provided by the close of business on December 31, 2006, the year-end adjusting entry (Transaction 12) removes $1,500 from the liability account and places it in the revenue account. This treatment is consistent with the definition of revenue as being a decrease in liabilities. The deferral causes a difference between the amount of revenue recognized on the income statement ($1,500 is included in the $168,500 of revenue reported on the income statement) and the amount of cash receipt shown in the operating activities section of the cash flow statement ($18,000). Trace the effect of these transactions to the financial statements.

The other transactions for 2006 should be familiar to you. However, it is worth tracing the results of each transaction to the related financial statements. We now encourage you to review in full all the effects of the transactions in Exhibit 3–6 and the financial statements in Exhibit 3–7.

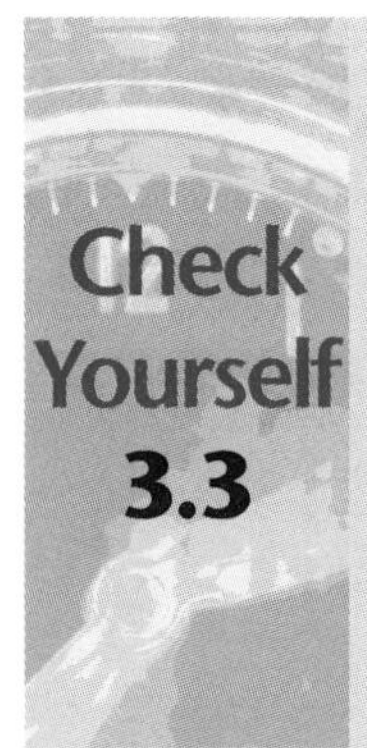

On January 1, 2006, Lambert Company paid $28,000 cash to purchase office furniture. The furniture has a $3,000 residual value and a five-year useful life. Explain how Lambert would report this asset purchase on the 2006 cash flow statement. Also, determine the amount of amortization expense and accumulated amortization Lambert would report in the 2008 financial statements.

Answer Lambert would report a $28,000 cash outflow in the investing activities section of the 2006 cash flow statement. During 2008 and every other year of the asset's useful life, Lambert would report $5,000 ([$28,000 − $3,000] ÷ 5 = $5,000) of amortization expense on the income statement. The accumulated amortization would increase by $5,000 each year of the asset's useful life. As of December 31, 2008, Lambert would report accumulated amortization on the balance sheet of $15,000 (3 years × $5,000 per year = $15,000).

Analysis of Financial Statements to Assess Managerial Performance

Assessment of the Effective Use of Assets

LO9 Analyze financial statements and make meaningful comparisons using ratios.

Suppose you are told that a company earned net income of $1,000,000. Has the company's performance has been good or bad? If the company is General Motors, the answer is probably "bad." If it is Al Bundy's shoe store, $1,000,000 indicates outstanding performance. Clearly, to evaluate performance we must consider the size of the investment required to produce the income. The relationship between the level of income and the size of the investment can be expressed in a single figure known as the **return on assets ratio**, which is defined as follows:

$$\text{Return on Assets} = \frac{\text{Net income}^{1}}{\text{Total assets}}$$

This ratio enables us to compare different-sized companies. To understand the importance of comparing ratios rather than absolute dollar values, consider the following comparison between Ford Motor

[1] The use of net income in this ratio does not consider the effects of debt financing and income taxation.

Company and Chrysler Corporation. Both Ford and Chrysler had positive net incomes in 1997. Ford's earnings for that year were US$6.9 billion, and Chrysler's were US$2.8 billion; thus Ford's earnings were more than double those of Chrysler. However, the return on asset ratios for the two companies reveal that Chrysler produced higher earnings relative to the amount of assets invested. Ford's ratio was 2.5 percent while Chrysler's was 4.6 percent. This suggests that even though Chrysler generated less income in total dollars, the company did a better job of managing its assets. Clearly, different companies cannot be compared fairly on the basis of absolute dollar values.

Other ratios besides this one can be computed to help us analyze financial statements. Two of these are discussed below.

Assessment of the Risk of Debt

Borrowing money can be risky. Assume that two companies have the following financial structures:

	Assets	=	Liabilities	+	Shareholders' Equity
Eastern Company	100	=	20	+	80
Western Company	100	=	80	+	20

Which company faces the greater financial risk? To answer, look at the financial structures that will exist if each company incurs a $30 loss.

	Assets	=	Liabilities	+	Shareholders' Equity
Eastern Company	70	=	20	+	50
Western Company	70	=	80	+	(10)

Clearly, Western Company is at greater risk. Notice that Eastern Company would survive a $30 loss that reduced assets and shareholders' equity. After such a loss, Eastern Company would still have a $50 balance in shareholders' equity and would still have more than enough assets ($70) to cover the creditor's $20 claim. In contrast, a $30 loss would throw Western Company into bankruptcy. The company would have a $10 deficit (negative) balance in shareholders' equity. Also, the remaining balance in assets ($70) would be insufficient to cover the creditor's $80 claim on assets.

The level of risk can be measured in part by computing a **debt to assets ratio**:

$$\frac{\text{Total debt}}{\text{Total assets}}$$

Eastern Company has a 20 percent debt to assets ratio ($20 ÷ $100) while Western Company has an 80 percent debt to assets ratio ($80 ÷ $100). Why would the owners of Western Company be willing to accept greater risk? To answer this question, assume that both companies produce $12 of revenue and must pay 10 percent interest on the money they have borrowed. Income statements for the two companies appear as follows:

	Eastern Company	Western Company
Revenue	$12	$12
Interest Expense	2	8
Net Income	$10	$ 4

At first glance, it seems that the owners of Eastern Company are still better off because that company produced higher net income. However, a closer look discloses that, in fact, the owners of Western Company are better off. Remember that the owners of Eastern Company had to put $80 of their own money into the business in order to get the $10 of income. Thus, the return on their invested funds is 12.5 percent ($10 ÷ $80). In contrast, the owners of Western Company needed to invest only $20 to obtain $4 of net income. Their return on invested funds amounts to 20 percent ($4 ÷ $20). In different terms, an $80 investment would buy four companies like Western Company or one like Eastern Company. Four companies like Western Company would produce $16 of net income ($4 income per company × 4 companies). This compares favourably to $10 of net income produced by Eastern Company. Clearly, Western Company is the more profitable investment. The relationship between the amount of net income and the shareholders' equity is called the **return on equity ratio**. As suggested, the return on equity ratio is:

$$\frac{\text{Net income}}{\text{Shareholders' equity}}$$

In business, the practice of using borrowed money to increase the return on shareholders' investment is called **financial leverage**. Financial leverage explains why companies are willing to accept the risk of debt. Companies borrow money to make money. If a company can borrow money at 10 percent and invest it at 12 percent, the owners will be better off by 2 percent of the amount borrowed. A business that does not use borrowed funds may be missing an opportunity to increase its return on equity.

Scope of Coverage

Throughout this text, in each chapter we introduce new ratios directly related to the topics being covered. Even so, we are introducing only a few of the many ratios available to users of financial statements. A more extensive examination of ratios and other topics related to financial statement analysis is part of most introductory finance courses. Many business programs include a course that focuses solely on financial statement analysis. These courses develop the students' capacity to make judgments regarding the ratio results that signal "good" or "bad" performance. However, the development of such judgment requires an understanding of how accounting policies and procedures can affect financial ratios. The ratios introduced in this text are designed to enhance your understanding of accounting and thereby give you the foundation that you will need to further your comprehension of business practice as you are introduced to more advanced topics in later courses.

---

a look back

LO10 Record deferral events in a financial statements model.

In this chapter we introduced the practice of deferring revenue and expense recognition. *Deferrals* involve recognizing revenue or expense at some time *after* cash has been collected or paid. Deferrals cause significant differences in the amount of revenue and expenses reported on the income statement and the amount of cash flow from operating activities. These differences become obvious when relevant events are recorded in a horizontal financial statements model. To illustrate, review the following transactions and the corresponding statements model that follows them. To understand better, draw a statements model on a piece of paper and try to record the effects of each event before you look at the explanation provided.

List of Events

1. Received an advanced payment of $1,200 cash for services to be performed in the future.
2. Provided $800 of the services agreed on in Event 1.
3. Paid $900 in advance for a one-year contract to rent office space.
4. Used eight months ($600) of the office space leased in Event 3.

Event No.	Balance Sheet									Income Statement	Cash Flow Statement
	Assets			=	Liab.	+	Equity			Rev. − Exp. = Net Inc.	
	Cash	+	P. Rent	=	U. Rev.	+	Ret. Earn.				
1	1,200	+	NA	=	1,200	+	NA			NA − NA = NA	1,200 OA
2	NA	+	NA	=	(800)	+	800			800 − NA = 800	NA
3	(900)	+	900	=	NA	+	NA			NA − NA = NA	(900) OA
4	NA	+	(600)	=	NA	+	(600)			NA − 600 = (600)	NA
Totals	300	+	300	=	400	+	200			800 − 600 = 200	300 NC

Note that the amount of net income ($200) is different from the amount of cash flow from operating activities ($300). A review of the entries in the statements model should make the reasons for this difference clear. Although $1,200 of cash was collected, only $800 of revenue was recognized. The remaining $400 will be recognized later when the work is done. The $400 obligation to perform the work in the future is currently shown on the balance sheet as unearned revenue. Also, although $900 cash was paid for rent, only $600 of rent expense was recognized. The remaining $300 is shown on the balance sheet as an asset called *prepaid rent*. In general, costs are **capitalized** (recorded) in asset accounts when cash is paid. Expense recognition is deferred until the time the assets (capitalized costs) are used to produce revenue. This practice is applied to many costs, including those incurred for supplies, insurance, equipment, and buildings. Study these relationships carefully to develop a clear understanding of how deferrals affect financial reporting.

To this point, we have used plus and minus signs to record the effects of business events on financial statements. In the real world, so many transactions occur that recording them with simple mathematical notations is impractical. In practice, accountants often maintain records under a system of rules known as *double-entry bookkeeping*. Chapter 4 introduces you to the basic components of this bookkeeping system. You will learn how to record business events using a debit/credit format. You will be introduced to ledgers, journals, and trial balances. When you finish Chapter 4, you will understand how accountants maintain records of business activity.

SELF-STUDY REVIEW PROBLEM

Gifford Company experienced the following accounting events during 2005:

1. Started operations on January 1 when it acquired $20,000 cash by issuing common shares.
2. On January 1 paid $15,000 cash to purchase computer equipment.
3. On March 1 collected $36,000 cash as an advance for services to be performed in the future.
4. Paid cash operating expenses of $17,000.
5. Paid a $2,700 cash dividend to the shareholders.
6. On December 31, 2005, adjusted the books to recognize the revenue earned by providing services related to the advance described in Event 3. The contract required Gifford to provide services for a one-year period starting March 1.
7. On December 31, 2005, Gifford adjusted the books to recognize amortization expense on the computer equipment. The equipment has a three-year useful life and a $3,000 residual value.

Gifford Company experienced the following accounting events during 2006:

1. Recognized $38,000 of cash revenue.
2. Paid cash operating expenses of $21,000.
3. Paid a $5,000 cash dividend to the shareholders.

4. On December 31, 2005, adjusted the books to recognize the remaining revenue earned by providing services related to the advance described in Event 3 of 2005.
5. On December 31, 2005, Gifford adjusted the books to recognize amortization expense on the computer equipment purchased in Event 2 of 2005. The equipment has a three-year useful life and a $3,000 residual value.

Required

a. Record the events in a financial statements model like the following one. The first event is recorded as an example.

Event No.	Assets: Cash	+ Comp. Equip.	− Acc. Amort.	= Liab.: Unear. Rev.	+ Equity: C. Sh.	+ Ret. Earn.	Rev.	− Exp.	= Net Inc.	Cash Flow Statement
1	20,000	NA	NA	NA	20,000	NA	NA	NA	NA	22,000 FA

b. What amount of amortization expense would Gifford report on the 2005 and 2006 income statements?
c. What amount of cash flow for amortization would Gifford report on the 2006 cash flow statement?
d. What amount of unearned revenue would Gifford report on the 2005 and 2006 year-end balance sheets?
e. What are the 2006 opening balances for the revenue and expense accounts?
f. What amount of total assets would Gifford report on the December 31, 2005, balance sheet?
g. What claims on the assets would Gifford report on the December 31, 2006, balance sheet?

Solution to Requirement a

The financial statements model follows:

Event No.	Assets: Cash	+ Comp. Equip.	− Acc. Amort.	= Liab.: Unear. Rev.	+ Equity: C. Sh.	+ Ret. Earn.	Rev.	− Exp.	= Net Inc.	Cash Flow Statement
1	20,000	NA	NA	NA	20,000	NA	NA	NA	NA	20,000 FA
2	(15,000)	15,000	NA	NA	NA	NA	NA	NA	NA	(15,000) IA
3	36,000	NA	NA	36,000	NA	NA	NA	NA	NA	36,000 OA
4	(17,000)	NA	NA	NA	NA	(17,000)	NA	17,000	(17,000)	(17,000) OA
5	(2,700)	NA	NA	NA	NA	(2,700)	NA	NA	NA	(2,700) FA
6*	NA	NA	NA	(30,000)	NA	30,000	30,000	NA	30,000	NA
7†	NA	NA	4,000	NA	NA	(4,000)	NA	4,000	(4,000)	NA
Bal.	21,300	15,000	4,000	6,000	20,000	6,300	30,000	21,000	9,000	21,300 NC
	Asset, Liability, and Equity Account Balances Carry Forward						Rev. & Exp. Accts. Are Closed			
Bal.	21,300	15,000	4,000	6,000	20,000	6,300	NA	NA	NA	NA
1	38,000	NA	NA	NA	NA	38,000	38,000	NA	38,000	38,000 OA
2	(21,000)	NA	NA	NA	NA	(21,000)	NA	21,000	(21,000)	(21,000) OA
3	(5,000)	NA	NA	NA	NA	(5,000)	NA	NA	NA	(5,000) FA
4*	NA	NA	NA	(6,000)	NA	6,000	6,000	NA	6,000	NA
5†	NA	NA	4,000	NA	NA	(4,000)	NA	4,000	(4,000)	NA
Bal.	33,300	15,000	8,000	0	20,000	20,300	44,000	25,000	19,000	12,000 NC

*Revenue is earned at the rate of $3,000 ($36,000 ÷ 12 months) per month. Revenue recognized in 2005 is $30,000 ($3,000 × 10 months). Revenue recognized in 2006 is $6,000 ($3,000 × 2 months).

† Amortizaion expense is $4,000 ([$15,000 − $3,000] ÷ 3 years) per year.

Solutions to Requirements b–g

b. Gifford would report amortization expense in 2005 of $4,000 ([$15,000 − $3,000] ÷ 3 years). This same amount would be recognized in 2005, 2006, and 2007.

c. There is no cash flow for amortization in 2006 or any other year. The total cash outflow from purchasing the computer equipment ($15,000) would be reported as a cash outflow from investing activities in the year in which the equipment was purchased.

d. The December 31, 2005, balance sheet will report $6,000 of unearned revenue, which is the amount of the cash advance less the amount of revenue recognized in 2005 ($36,000 − $30,000).

e. Since revenue and expense accounts are closed at the end of each accounting period, the beginning balances in these accounts are always zero.

f. Assets on the December 31, 2005, balance sheet consist of Gifford's cash at year end and the net book value (cost − accumulated amortization) of the computer equipment. Specifically, the amount of total assets is $32,300 ($21,300 + [$15,000 − $4,000]).

g. Since all unearned revenue would be recognized before the financial statements were prepared at the end of 2006, there would be no liabilities on the 2006 balance sheet. Common Shares and Retained Earnings would be the only claims as of December 31, 2006, for a claims total of $40,300 ($20,000 + $20,300).

KEY TERMS

accumulated amortization *94*
allocation *91*
amortization expense *94*
capitalized *109*
concept of materiality *97*
contra asset account *94*
debt to assets ratio *107*
deferral *91*
financial leverage *108*
gains *103*
historical cost *94*
income from operations *103*
losses *103*
matching principle *97*
net book value *94*
peripheral (incidental) transactions *103*
residual (salvage) value *94*
return on assets ratio *106*
return on equity ratio *108*
straight-line method *94*
systematic allocation *97*
unearned revenue *92*

QUESTIONS

1. What role do assets play in business profitability?
2. What does *deferral* mean?
3. If cash is collected in advance of performing services, when is the associated revenue recognized?
4. What does *residual value* mean?
5. What is the effect on the claims side of the accounting equation when cash is collected in advance of performing services?
6. What does *unearned revenue* mean?
7. How is straight-line amortization computed?
8. Define *amortization expense*. On what type of asset is amortization recognized?
9. Define *contra asset account*. What is an example?
10. How is the net book value of an asset determined?
11. If a piece of equipment originally cost $12,000, has an estimated residual value of $1,000, and has accumulated amortization of $10,000, what is the net book value of the equipment?
12. What does *financial leverage* mean?
13. In which section of the cash flow statement is cash paid for office equipment reported?
14. What is the difference between a cost and an expense?
15. When does a cost become an expense? Do all costs become expenses?
16. How and when is the cost of the *supplies used* recognized in an accounting period?
17. Give an example of an asset whose cost is systematically allocated over several accounting periods.
18. List the three ways in which expenses are matched with the revenues they produce.
19. Define *losses*. How do losses differ from expenses?
20. Define *gains*. How do gains differ from revenues?
21. How is income from operations computed?
22. What does *peripheral activity* mean?
23. Assume that Company A has revenues of $45,000, operating expenses of $36,000, and a gain from the sale of land of $12,500. What is the amount of income from operations? What is the amount of net income?
24. Explain the *concept of materiality*.
25. How is the return on assets ratio computed? How is this measure useful in comparing two companies?
26. How is the debt to assets ratio computed? What does this ratio measure?
27. How can financial leverage increase the return on equity ratio?

EXERCISES

L.O. 1 EXERCISE 3–1 *Transactions That Affect the Elements of Financial Statements*

Required

Give an example of a transaction that will do the following:

a. Increase an asset and increase equity (asset source event).
b. Increase a liability and decrease equity (claims exchange event).
c. Decrease an asset and decrease equity (asset use event).
d. Decrease an asset and decrease a liability (asset use event).
e. Decrease a liability and increase equity (claims exchange event).
f. Increase an asset and decrease another asset (asset exchange event).
g. Increase an asset and increase a liability (asset source event).

L.O. 2 EXERCISE 3–2 *Identifying Deferral and Accrual Events*

Required

Identify each of the following events as accruals, deferrals, or neither.

a. Provided services on account.
b. Recognized interest on a note payable before cash is paid.
c. Paid one year's rent in advance.
d. Purchased a computer with a three-year life.
e. Incurred other operating expenses on account.
f. Paid cash for utilities expense.
g. Collected $1,200 in advance for services to be performed over the next six months.
h. Paid cash to purchase supplies to be used over the next several months.
i. Recorded expense for salaries owed to employees at the end of the accounting period.
j. Issued common shares for cash.

L.O. 6 EXERCISE 3–3 *Effect of Deferrals on the Accounting Equation*

Required

For each of the following independent cases, show the effect on the accounting equation of both the deferral and the related December 31, 2007, adjustment.

a. Global Shipping paid $24,000 for a 12-month lease on warehouse space on August 1, 2007.
b. Unistar Services purchased a new computer system for $22,000 on January 1, 2007. The computer system has an estimated useful life of three years and a $1,000 residual value.
c. Tommy Holliman, CGA, accepted a $30,000 advance from his client on October 1, 2007, for services to be performed over the next six months.

EXERCISE 3–4 *Identifying Transaction Type and Effect on the Financial Statements*

Required

Identify whether each of the following transactions is an asset source (AS), asset use (AU), asset exchange (AE), or claims exchange (CE). Also show the effects of the events on the financial statements using the horizontal statements model. Indicate whether the event increases (I), decreases (D), or does not affect (NA) each element of the financial statements. In the Cash Flow Statement column, designate the cash flows as operating activities (OA), investing activities (IA), or financing activities (FA). The first two transactions have been recorded as examples.

						Equity									
Event No.	Type of Event	Assets	=	Liabilities	+	Common Shares	+	Retained Earnings	Rev.	−	Exp.	=	Net Inc.	Cash Flow Statement	
a	AS	I		I		NA		NA	NA	−	NA	=	NA	I	OA
b	AU	D		D		NA		NA	NA	−	NA	=	NA	D	OA

a. Received cash advance for services to be provided in the future.
b. Paid cash on accounts payable.
c. Acquired cash from the issue of common shares.
d. Purchased office equipment for cash.
e. Incurred other operating expenses on account.
f. Paid cash to purchase office supplies to be used in the future.
g. Performed services on account.
h. Paid cash advance for rent on office space.
i. Adjusted books to reflect the amount of prepaid rent expired during the period.
j. Paid cash for operating expenses.
k. Performed services for cash.
l. Paid a cash dividend to the shareholders.
m. Recorded accrued salaries.
n. Purchased a building with cash *and* issued a note payable.
o. Collected cash from accounts receivable.
p. Recorded amortization expense on office equipment.
q. Paid cash for salaries accrued at the end of a prior period.

EXERCISE 3–5 *Effect of Prepaid Rent on the Accounting Equation and Financial Statements* **L.O. 3, 4, 7**

The following events apply to 2007, the first year of operations of Management Consulting Services:
1. Acquired $12,000 cash from the issue of common shares.
2. Paid $9,000 cash in advance for one-year rental contract for office space.
3. Provided services for $18,000 cash.
4. Adjusted the records to recognize the use of the office space. The one-year contract started on February 1, 2007. The adjustment was made as of December 31, 2007.

Required
a. Write an accounting equation and record the effects of each accounting event under the appropriate general ledger account headings.
b. Prepare an income statement and cash flow statement for the 2007 accounting period.
c. Explain the difference between the amount of net income and amount of net cash flow from operating activities.

EXERCISE 3–6 *Effect of Supplies on the Financial Statements* **L.O. 3, 4, 7**

Quick Printing, Inc., started the 2005 accounting period with $5,000 cash, $2,000 of common shares, and $3,000 of retained earnings. Quick Printing was affected by the following accounting events during 2005:
1. Purchased $7,200 of paper and other supplies on account.
2. Earned and collected $15,000 of cash revenue.
3. Paid $5,000 cash on accounts payable.
4. Adjusted the records to reflect the use of supplies. A physical count indicated that $1,400 of supplies was still on hand on December 31, 2005.

Required
a. Show the effects of the events on the financial statements using a horizontal statements model like the following one. In the Cash Flow Statement column, use OA to designate operating activity, IA for investing activity, FA for financing activity, and NC for net change in cash. Use NA to indicate accounts not affected by the event. The beginning balances are entered in the following example.

Event No.	Assets		=	Liab.	+	Equity								Cash Flow Statement
	Cash	Supplies	=	Acct. Pay.	+	Com. Sh.	+	Ret. Earn.	Rev.	−	Exp.	=	Net Inc.	
Beg. Bal.	5,000	0	=	0	+	2,000	+	3,000	0	−	0	=	0	0

b. Explain the difference between the amount of net income and amount of net cash flow from operating activities.

L.O. 3, 4, 7 **EXERCISE 3–7** *Effect of Amortization on the Accounting Equation and Financial Statements*

The following events apply to Tasty Pizza for the 2008 fiscal year:

1. Started the company when it acquired $12,000 cash from the issue of common shares.
2. Purchased a new pizza oven that cost $11,000 cash.
3. Earned $8,000 in cash revenue.
4. Paid $2,000 for cash operating expenses.
5. Adjusted the records to reflect the use of the pizza oven. The oven, purchased on January 1, 2008, has an expected useful life of five years and an estimated residual value of $1,000. Use straight-line amortization. The adjusting entry was made as of December 31, 2008.

Required

a. Write an accounting equation and record the effects of each accounting event under the appropriate general ledger account headings.
b. What amount of amortization expense would Tasty Pizza report on the 2009 income statement?
c. What amount of accumulated amortization would Tasty Pizza report on the December 31, 2009, balance sheet?
d. Would the cash flow from operating activities be affected by amortization in 2009?

L.O. 3, 4 **EXERCISE 3–8** *Effect of Unearned Revenue on Financial Statements*

Kim Vanderbilt started a personal financial planning business when she accepted $72,000 cash as advance payment for managing the financial assets of a large estate. Vanderbilt agreed to manage the estate for a one-year period, beginning March 1, 2003. The company's year-end is December 31.

Required

a. Show the effects of the advance payment and revenue recognition on the 2003 financial statements using a horizontal statements model like the following one. In the Cash Flow Statement column, use OA to designate operating activity, IA for investing activity, FA for financing activity, and NC for net change in cash. Use NA if the account is not affected.

	Assets	=	Liab.	+	Equity	Rev. − Exp. = Net Inc.	Cash Flow Statement
Event No.	Cash		Unearn. Rev.		Ret. Earn.		

b. How much revenue would Kim recognize on the 2004 income statement?
c. What is the amount of cash flow from operating activities in 2004?

L.O. 8 **EXERCISE 3–9** *Effect of Gains and Losses on the Accounting Equation and Financial Statements*

On January 1, 2002, IBC purchased a parcel of land for $6,000 cash. At the time of purchase, the company planned to use the land for future expansion. In 2004, IBC Enterprises changed its plans and sold the land.

Required

a. Assume that the land was sold for $5,500 in 2004.
   (1) Show the effect of the sale on the accounting equation.
   (2) What amount would IBC report on the income statement related to the sale of the land?
   (3) What amount would IBC report on the cash flow statement related to the sale of the land?
b. Assume that the land was sold for $7,000 in 2004.
   (1) Show the effect of the sale on the accounting equation.
   (2) What amount would IBC report on the income statement related to the sale of the land?
   (3) What amount would IBC report on the cash flow statement related to the sale of the land?

EXERCISE 3–10 *Effect of Accounting Events on the Income Statement and Cash Flow Statement* L.O. 5, 6

Required

Explain how each of the following events and the related adjusting entry will affect the amount of *net income* and the amount of *cash flow from operating activities* reported on the year-end financial statements. Identify the direction of change (increase, decrease, or no effect) and the amount of the change. Organize your answers according to the following table. The first event is recorded as an example. If an event does not have a related adjusting entry, record only the effects of the event.

	Net Income		Cash Flows from Operating Activities	
Event No.	Direction of Change	Amount of Change	Direction of Change	Amount of Change
a	Increase	$12,000	Increase	$10,000

a. Earned $12,000 of revenue on account. Collected $10,000 cash from accounts receivable.
b. Paid $3,600 cash on November 1 to purchase a one-year insurance policy.
c. Accrued salaries amounting to $6,000.
d. Paid $20,000 cash to purchase equipment. The equipment, purchased on January 1, had an estimated residual value of $4,000 and an expected useful life of four years.
e. Purchased $1,600 of supplies on account. Paid $1,200 cash on accounts payable. The ending balance in the Supplies account, after adjustment, was $200.
f. Provided services for $5,400 cash.
g. Paid cash for other operating expenses of $2,000.
h. Collected $2,400 in advance for services to be performed in the future. The contract called for services to start on April 1 and to continue for one year.
i. Acquired $24,000 cash from the issue of common shares.
j. Sold land that cost $7,000 for $9,000 cash.

EXERCISE 3–11 *Effect of Accruals and Deferrals on Financial Statements: the Horizontal Statements Model* L.O. 10

R. Ross, Lawyer, experienced the following transactions in 2009, the first year of operations:

1. Accepted $15,000 on April 1, 2009, as a retainer for services to be performed evenly over the next 12 months.
2. Purchased $900 of office supplies on account.
3. Performed legal services for cash of $35,300.
4. Paid cash for salaries expenses of $21,400.
5. Paid a cash dividend to the shareholders of $4,000.
6. Paid $700 of the amount due on accounts payable.
7. Determined that at the end of the accounting period, $75 of office supplies remained on hand.
8. On December 31, 2009, recognized the revenue that had been earned for services performed in accordance with Transaction 1.

Required

Show the effects of the events on the financial statements using a horizontal statements model like the following one. In the Cash Flow Statement column, use the initials OA to designate operating activity, IA for investing activity, FA for financing activity, and NC for net change in cash. Use NA to indicate accounts not affected by the event. The first event has been recorded as an example.

Event No.	Assets			=	Liabilites			+	Equity	Rev.	−	Exp.	=	Net Inc.	Cash Flow Statement
	Cash	+	Supp.	=	Acct. Pay.	+	Unearn. Rev.	+	Ret. Earn.						
1	15,000	+	NA	=	NA	+	15,000	+	NA	NA	−	NA	=	NA	15,000 OA

L.O. 7 EXERCISE 3–12 *Distinguishing between an Expense and a Cost*

Mike Kosko tells you that the accountants where he works are real hair splitters. For example, they make a big issue over the difference between a cost and an expense. He says the two terms mean the same thing to him.

Required

a. Explain to Mike the difference between a cost and an expense from an accountant's perspective.
b. Explain whether each of the following events produces an asset or an expense.
   (1) Purchased equipment for cash.
   (2) Purchased supplies on account.
   (3) Used supplies to produce revenue.
   (4) Purchased equipment on account.
   (5) Recognized accrued interest.

L.O. 6 EXERCISE 3–13 *Matching Principle*

Required

Place a check mark in the appropriate cell of the following table to indicate whether each of the following costs would be expensed through (1) direct matching, (2) period matching, or (3) systematic allocation.

Cost	Matched Directly with Revenue	Matched with the Period Incurred	Systematically Allocated
Rent			
Office equipment			
Land that has been sold			
Utilities			
Sales commissions			
Furniture			
Advertising			

L.O. 5, 6 EXERCISE 3–14 *Effect of an Error on Financial Statements*

On March 1, 2007, Stotzy Corporation paid $7,200 to purchase a 24-month insurance policy. Assume that Stotzy records the purchase as an asset and that the books are closed on December 31.

Required

a. Provide the adjusting entry to record the 2007 insurance expense.
b. Assume that Stotzy Corporation failed to record the adjusting entry to reflect the expiration of insurance. How would the error affect the company's 2007 income statement and balance sheet?

L.O. 1 EXERCISE 3–15 *Revenue and Expense Recognition*

Required

a. Describe a revenue recognition event that results in a decrease in liabilities.
b. Describe a revenue recognition event that results in an increase in assets.
c. Describe an expense recognition event that results in an increase in liabilities.
d. Describe an expense recognition event that results in a decrease in assets.

L.O. 1, 5 EXERCISE 3–16 *Unearned Revenue Defined as a Liability*

Jacob Huron received $600 in advance for tutoring fees when he agreed to help Kev Saia with his introductory accounting course. Upon receiving the cash, Jacob mentioned that he would have to record the transaction as a liability on his books. Saia asked, "Why a liability? You don't owe me any money, do you?"

Required

Respond to Saia's question regarding Huron's liability.

PROBLEMS—SERIES A

PROBLEM 3–1A *Recording Events in a Horizontal Statements Model* L.O. 10

The following events pertain to Oshawa Company:

1. Acquired $8,000 cash from the issue of common shares.
2. Provided services for $2,000 cash.
3. Provided $10,000 of services on account.
4. Collected $7,500 cash from the account receivable created in Event 3.
5. Paid $800 cash to purchase supplies.
6. Had $150 of supplies on hand at the end of the accounting period.
7. Received $3,000 cash in advance for services to be performed in the future.
8. Performed $500 of the services agreed to in Event 7.
9. Paid $3,200 for salaries expense.
10. Incurred $1,200 of other operating expenses on account.
11. Paid $1,000 cash on the account payable created in Event 10.
12. Paid an $800 cash dividend to the shareholders.

Required

Show the effects of the events on the financial statements using a horizontal statements model like the following one. In the Cash Flow Statement column, use the letters OA to designate operating activity, IA for investing activity, FA for financing activity, and NC for net change in cash. Use NA to indicate accounts not affected by the event. The first event is recorded as an example.

Event No.	Assets						=	Liabilites			+	Equity				Rev.	−	Exp.	=	Net Inc.	Cash Flow Statement
	Cash	+	Acc. Rec.	+	Supp.		=	Acc. Pay.	+	Unearn. Rev.	+	Com. Sh.	+	Ret. Earn.							
1	8,000	+	NA	+	NA		=	NA	+	NA	+	8,000	+	NA		NA	−	NA	=	NA	8,000 FA

PROBLEM 3–2A *Effect of Deferrals on Financial Statements: Three Separate Single-Cycle Examples* L.O. 4, 5, 6

Required

a. On March 1, 2005, Wax Made was formed when it received $50,000 cash from the issue of common shares. On May 1, 2005, the company paid $48,000 cash in advance to rent office space for the coming year. The office space was used as a place to consult with clients. The consulting activity generated $65,000 of cash revenue during 2005. Based on this information alone, record the events in the general ledger accounts under the accounting equation. Determine the amount of net income and cash flows from operating activities for 2005.

b. On January 1, 2007, the accounting firm of Copeland & Associates Inc. was formed. On April 1, 2007, the company received a retainer fee (was paid in advance) of $21,000 for services to be performed monthly during the coming year. Assuming that this was the only transaction completed in 2007, prepare an income statement, statement of shareholders' equity, balance sheet, and cash flow statement for 2007.

c. Fashion Cents was started when it received $35,000 cash from the issue of common shares on January 1, 2008. The cash received by the company was immediately used to purchase a $35,000 asset that had a $5,000 residual value and an expected useful life of five years. The company earned $10,000 of cash revenue during 2008. Show the effects of these transactions on the financial statements using the horizontal statements model.

PROBLEM 3–3A *Effect of Adjusting Entries on the Accounting Equation* L.O. 3, 6

Required

Each of the following independent events requires a year-end adjusting entry. Show how each event and its related adjusting entry affects the accounting equation. Assume a December 31 closing date. The first event is recorded as an example.

Event/ Adjustment	Total Assets: Asset 1	+	Asset 2	=	Liabilities	+	Equity: Common Shares	+	Retained Earnings
a	(18,000)		18,000		NA		NA		NA
Adj.	NA		450		NA		NA		450

a. Invested $18,000 cash in a term deposit that paid 5 percent annual interest. The term deposit was acquired on July 1 and had a one-year term to maturity.
b. Paid $4,200 cash in advance on September 30 for a one-year insurance policy.
c. Purchased $2,000 of supplies on account. At year's end, $200 of supplies remained on hand.
d. Paid $9,000 cash in advance on March 1 for a one-year lease on office space.
e. Borrowed $10,000 by issuing a one-year note with 12 percent annual interest to a local bank on April 1.
f. Paid $19,000 cash to purchase a delivery van on January 1. The van was expected to have a three-year life and a $4,000 residual value. Amortization is computed on a straight-line basis.
g. Received a $6,000 cash advance for a contract to provide services in the future. The contract required a one-year commitment starting August 1.

L.O. 1, 3, 4 PROBLEM 3–4A *Events for Two Complete Accounting Cycles*

Nevada Drilling Company was formed on January 1, 2006.

Events Affecting the 2006 Accounting Period

1. Acquired cash of $40,000 from the issue of common shares.
2. Purchased office equipment that cost $17,000 cash.
3. Purchased land that cost $8,000 cash.
4. Paid $600 cash for supplies.
5. Recognized revenue on account of $16,000.
6. Paid $7,200 cash for other operating expenses.
7. Collected $10,000 cash from accounts receivable.

Information for Adjusting Entries

8. Incurred accrued salaries of $4,100 on December 31, 2006.
9. Had $100 of supplies on hand at the end of the accounting period.
10. Used the straight-line method to amortize the equipment acquired in Event 2. Purchased on January 1, it had an expected useful life of five years and a $1,000 residual value.

Events Affecting the 2007 Accounting Period

1. Acquired an additional $6,000 cash from the issue of common shares.
2. Paid $4,100 cash to settle the salaries payable obligation.
3. Paid $2,100 cash in advance to rent office facilities.
4. Sold the land that cost $8,000 for $7,500 cash.
5. Received $4,800 cash in advance for services to be performed in the future.
6. Purchased $1,000 of supplies on account during the year.
7. Provided services on account of $12,000.
8. Collected $13,000 cash from accounts receivable.
9. Paid a cash dividend of $1,000 to the shareholders.

Information for Adjusting Entries

10. The advance payment for rental of the office facilities (see Event 3) was made on May 1 for a one-year lease term.
11. The cash advance for services to be provided in the future was collected on August 1 (see Event 5). The one-year contract started August 1.
12. Had $120 of supplies on hand at the end of the period.
13. Recorded amortization on the office equipment for 2007.
14. Incurred accrued salaries of $4,000 at the end of the accounting period.

Required

a. Identify each event affecting the 2006 and 2007 accounting periods as asset source (AS), asset use (AU), asset exchange (AE), or claims exchange (CE). Record the effects of each event under the appropriate general ledger account headings of the accounting equation.
b. Prepare an income statement, statement of shareholders' equity, balance sheet, and cash flow statement for 2006 and 2007.

PROBLEM 3–5A *Effect of Events on Financial Statements* **L.O. 3, 5**

Topez Company had the following balances in its accounting records as of December 31, 2007:

Assets		Claims	
Cash	$ 70,000	Accounts Payable	$ 44,000
Accounts Receivable	41,000	Common Shares	80,000
Land	40,000	Retained Earnings	27,000
Totals	$151,000		$151,000

The following accounting events apply to Topez's 2008 fiscal year:

Jan. 1 Acquired an additional $10,000 cash from the issue of common shares.
1 Purchased a delivery van that cost $18,000 and that had a $3,000 residual value and a three-year useful life.
Mar. 1 Borrowed $8,000 by issuing a note that had a 12 percent annual interest rate and a one-year term.
May 1 Paid $3,900 cash in advance for a one-year lease for office space.
June 1 Paid a $1,000 cash dividend to the shareholders.
July 1 Purchased land that cost $16,000 cash.
Aug. 1 Made a cash payment on accounts payable of $7,000.
Sept. 1 Received $5,600 cash in advance as a retainer for services to be performed monthly during the next eight months.
Sept. 30 Sold land for $17,000 cash that had originally cost $20,000.
Oct. 1 Purchased $1,500 of supplies on account.
Nov. 1 Purchased a one-year $10,000 term deposit that paid a 6 percent annual rate of interest.
Dec. 31 Earned $45,000 of service revenue on account during the year.
31 Received $47,000 cash collections from accounts receivable.
31 Incurred $6,000 other operating expenses on account during the year.
31 Incurred accrued salaries expense of $2,000.
31 Had $100 of supplies on hand at the end of the period.

Required

Based on the preceding information, answer the following questions. All questions pertain to the 2008 financial statements. (*Hint:* Record the events in general ledger accounts under an accounting equation before answering the questions.)

a. What additional five transactions during the year need adjusting entries at the end of the year?
b. What amount of interest expense would Topez report on the income statement?
c. What amount of net cash flow from operating activities would Topez report on the cash flow statement?
d. What amount of rent expense would Topez report in the income statement?
e. What amount of total liabilities would Topez report on the balance sheet?
f. What amount of supplies expense would Topez report on the income statement?
g. What amount of unearned revenue would Topez report on the balance sheet?
h. What amount of net cash flow from investing activities would Topez report on the cash flow statement?
i. What amount of interest payable would Topez report on the balance sheet?
j. What amount of total expenses would Topez report on the income statement?
k. What amount of retained earnings would Topez report on the balance sheet?
l. What total amount of all revenues would Topez report on the income statement?
m. What amount of cash flows from financing activities would Topez report on the cash flow statement?

n. What is the amount of the loss on sale of land Topez would report on the income statement?
o. What amount of net income would Topez report on the income statement?

L.O. 4 **PROBLEM 3–6A** *Identifying and Arranging Elements on Financial Statements*

The following accounts and balances were drawn from the records of Highpoint Company:

Cash	$30,000	Cash Flow from Operating Act.	$ 15,000
Land	12,000	Beginning Retained Earnings	12,000
Insurance Expense	1,500	Beginning Common Shares	6,500
Dividends	2,500	Service Revenue	50,000
Prepaid Insurance	6,000	Cash Flow from Financing Act.	5,500
Accounts Payable	3,000	Issue Common Shares	28,000
Supplies	150	Accumulated Amortization	11,500
Supplies Expense	850	Cash Flow from Investing Act.	(20,000)
Amortization Expense	2,000	Operating Expenses	10,000
Accounts Receivable	18,000	Office Equipment	28,000

Required
Use the accounts and balances from Highpoint Company to construct an income statement, statement of shareholders' equity, balance sheet, and cash flow statement.

L.O. 4 **PROBLEM 3–7A** *Relationship of Accounts to Financial Statements*

Required
Identify whether each of the following items would appear on the income statement (IS), statement of shareholders' equity (SE), balance sheet (BS), or cash flow statement (CF). Some items may appear on more than one statement; if so, identify all applicable statements. If an item would not appear on any financial statement, label it NA.

a. Total Assets
b. Consulting Revenue
c. Amortization Expense
d. Supplies Expense
e. Salaries Payable
f. Notes Payable
g. Ending Common Shares
h. Interest Payable
i. Office Equipment
j. Interest Revenue
k. Land
l. Operating Expenses
m. Total Liabilities
n. Debt to Equity Ratio
o. Salaries Expense
p. Net Income
q. Service Revenue
r. Cash Flow from Operating Activities
s. Return on Assets Ratio
t. Interest Receivable
u. Salary Expense
v. Notes Receivable
w. Unearned Revenue
x. Cash Flow from Investing Activities
y. Insurance Expense
z. Ending Retained Earnings
aa. Accumulated Amortization
bb. Supplies
cc. Beginning Retained Earnings
dd. Term Deposit
ee. Cash Flow from Financing Activities
ff. Accounts Receivable
gg. Prepaid Insurance
hh. Cash
ii. Interest Expense
jj. Accounts Payable
kk. Beginning Common Shares
ll. Dividends

L.O. 3, 4 **PROBLEM 3–8A** *Missing Information in Financial Statements*

The following data are relevant to the revenue and expense accounts of Cornell Corporation during 2004. The Accounts Receivable balance was $45,000 on January 1, 2004. Consulting services provided to customers on account during the year were $128,000. The receivables balance on December 31, 2004, amounted to $28,000. Cornell received $21,000 in advance payment for training services to be performed over a 24-month period beginning March 1, 2004. Furthermore, Cornell purchased a $30,000 term deposit on September 1, 2004. The term deposit paid 15 percent interest, which was payable in cash on August 31 of each year. During 2004, Cornell recorded amortization expense of $18,000. Salaries earned by employees during 2004 were $25,000. The Salaries Payable account increased by $3,500 during the year. Other operating expenses paid in cash during 2004 amounted to $70,000. No other revenue or expense transactions occurred during 2004.

Required

a. Prepare an income statement, assuming that Cornell uses the accrual basis of accounting.
b. Determine the net cash flows from operating activities for 2004.

PROBLEM 3–9A *Using Accounting Information*

L.O. 1, 9

Louise Mayes is trying to decide whether to start a small business or put her capital into a savings account. To help her make a decision, two of her friends shared their investing experiences with her. Donna Everhart had started a small business three years ago. As of the end of the most recent year of operations, Everhart's business had total assets of $185,000 and net income of $11,220. The second friend, Analisa Harrison, had deposited $20,000 in a bank savings account that paid $900 in interest during the last year.

Required

a. Assume you are an investment counsellor. Show Mayes how the return on assets ratio shows whether Everhart's or Harrison's investment is producing a higher return.
b. Using your personal judgment, identify any other factors that Mayes should consider before she decides whether to start her own business or deposit her money in a savings account. Recommend to Mayes which alternative you think she should accept.

PROBLEMS—SERIES B

PROBLEM 3–1B *Recording Events in a Horizontal Statements Model*

L.O. 10

The following events pertain to Ice Land Ltd.:

1. Acquired $8,000 cash from the issue of common shares.
2. Provided $9,000 of services on account.
3. Provided services for $3,000 cash.
4. Received $2,500 cash in advance for services to be performed in the future.
5. Collected $5,600 cash from the account receivable created in Event 2.
6. Paid $1,100 for cash expenses.
7. Performed $1,400 of the services agreed to in Event 4.
8. Incurred $2,800 of expenses on account.
9. Paid $2,400 cash in advance for one-year contract to rent office space.
10. Paid $2,200 cash on the account payable created in Event 8.
11. Paid a $1,500 cash dividend to the shareholders.
12. Recognized rent expense for nine months' use of office space acquired in Event 9.

Required

Show the effects of the events on the financial statements using a horizontal statements model like the following one. In the Cash Flow Statement column, use the letters OA to designate operating activity, IA for investing activity, FA for financing activity, and NC for net change in cash. Use NA to indicate accounts not affected by the event. The first event is recorded as an example.

	Assets						=	Liabilites			+	Equity									
Event No.	Cash	+	Acc. Rec.	+	Prep. Rent		=	Acc. Pay.	+	Unearn. Rev.	+	Com. Sh.	+	Ret. Earn.		Rev.	−	Exp.	=	Net Inc.	Cash Flow Statement
1	8,000	+	NA	+	NA		=	NA	+	NA	+	8,000	+	NA		NA	−	NA	=	NA	8,000 FA

L.O. 4, 5, 6 **PROBLEM 3–2B** *Effect of Deferrals on Financial Statements: Three Separate Single-Cycle Examples*

Required

a. On February 1, 2006, Oliver Company was formed when it acquired $10,000 cash from the issue of common shares. On June 1, 2006, the company paid $2,400 cash in advance to rent office space for the coming year. The office space was used as a place to consult with clients. The consulting activity generated $5,200 of cash revenue during 2006. Based on this information alone, record the events in general ledger accounts under the accounting equation. Determine the amount of net income and cash flows from operating activities for 2006.

b. On August 1, 2005, the consulting firm of Cooper & Associates was formed. On September 1, 2005, the company received a $12,000 retainer (was paid in advance) for monthly services to be performed over a one-year period. Assuming that this was the only transaction completed in 2005, prepare an income statement, statement of shareholders' equity, balance sheet, and cash flow statement for 2005.

c. Eagle Company was started when it acquired $10,000 cash from the issue of common shares on January 1, 2004. The company immediately used the cash received to purchase a $10,000 machine that had a $2,000 residual value and an expected useful life of four years. The machine was used to produce $5,200 of cash revenue during the accounting period. Show the effects of these transactions on the financial statements using the horizontal statements model.

L.O. 3, 6 **PROBLEM 3–3B** *Effect of Adjusting Entries on the Accounting Equation*

Required

Each of the following independent events requires a year-end adjusting entry. Show how each event and its related adjusting entry affects the accounting equation. Assume a December 31 closing date. The first event is recorded as an example.

	Total Assets						Equity		
Event/ Adjustment	Asset 1	+	Asset 2	=	Liabilities	+	Common Shares	+	Retained Earnings
a	(3,600)		3,600		NA		NA		NA
Adj.	NA		(900)		NA		NA		(900)

a. Paid $3,600 cash in advance on October 1 for a one-year insurance policy.
b. Borrowed $20,000 by issuing a one-year note with 9 percent annual interest to a local bank on April 1.
c. Paid $19,000 cash to purchase a delivery van on January 1. The van was expected to have a four-year life and a $4,000 residual value. Amortization is computed on a straight-line basis.
d. Received a $1,800 cash advance for a contract to provide services in the future. The contract required a one-year commitment, starting April 1.
e. Purchased $800 of supplies on account. At year's end, $140 of supplies remained on hand.
f. Invested $8,000 cash in a term deposit that paid 6 percent annual interest. The term deposit was acquired on May 1 and had a one-year term to maturity.
g. Paid $7,200 cash in advance on August 1 for a one-year lease on office space.

PROBLEM 3–4B *Events for Two Complete Accounting Cycles*

Great Plains Company was formed on January 1, 2005.

Events Affecting the 2005 Accounting Period

1. Acquired $25,000 cash from the issue of common shares.
2. Purchased communication equipment that cost $6,000 cash.
3. Purchased land that cost $12,000 cash.
4. Paid $500 cash for supplies.
5. Recognized revenue on account of $9,000.
6. Paid $2,400 cash for other operating expenses.
7. Collected $7,000 cash from accounts receivable.

Information for Adjusting Entries

8. Incurred accrued salaries of $3,200 on December 31, 2005.
9. Had $100 of supplies on hand at the end of the accounting period.

10. Used the straight-line method to amortize the equipment acquired in Event 2. Purchased on January 1, the equipment had an expected useful life of four years and a $2,000 residual value.

Events Affecting the 2006 Accounting Period

1. Acquired $12,000 cash from the issue of common shares.
2. Paid $3,200 cash to settle the salaries payable.
3. Paid $6,000 cash in advance to rent computer equipment.
4. Sold the land that cost $12,000 for $18,000 cash.
5. Received $8,400 cash in advance for services to be performed in the future.
6. Purchased $2,000 of supplies on account during the year.
7. Provided services on account of $11,000.
8. Collected $9,000 cash from accounts receivable.
9. Paid a cash dividend of $2,000 to the shareholders.

Information for Adjusting Entries

10. The advance payment for rental of the computer equipment (see Event 3) was made on February 1 for a one-year term.
11. The cash advance for services to be provided in the future was collected on October 1 (see Event 5). The one-year contract started on October 1.
12. Had $200 of supplies remaining on hand at the end of the period.
13. Recorded amortization on the computer equipment for 2006.
14. Incurred accrued salaries of $6,000 at the end of the accounting period.

Required

a. Identify each event affecting the 2005 and 2006 accounting periods as an asset source (AS), asset use (AU), asset exchange (AE), or claims exchange (CE). Record the effects of each event under the appropriate general ledger account headings of the accounting equation.
b. Prepare an income statement, statement of shareholders' equity, balance sheet, and cash flow statement for 2005 and 2006.

PROBLEM 3–5B *Effect of Events on Financial Statements* L.O. 3, 5

Juan Company had the following balances in its accounting records as of December 31, 2003:

Assets		Claims	
Cash	$23,000	Accounts Payable	$ 5,000
Accounts Receivable	7,000	Common Shares	24,000
Land	42,000	Retained Earnings	43,000
Totals	$72,000	Total	$72,000

The following accounting events apply to Juan Company's 2004 fiscal year:

Jan. 1 Acquired $12,000 cash from the issue of common shares.
1 Purchased a truck that cost $22,000 and had a $2,000 residual value and a four-year useful life.
Feb. 1 Borrowed $10,000 by issuing a note that had a 9 percent annual interest rate and a one-year term.
1 Paid $3,000 cash in advance for a one-year lease for office space.
Mar. 1 Paid a $1,000 cash dividend to the shareholders.
April 1 Purchased land that cost $28,000 cash.
May 1 Made a cash payment on accounts payable of $2,000.
July 1 Received $5,400 cash in advance as a retainer for services to be performed monthly over the coming year.
Sept. 1 Sold land for $60,000 cash that had originally cost $42,000.
Oct. 1 Purchased $3,000 of supplies on account.
Nov. 1 Purchased a one-year $50,000 term deposit that paid a 6 percent annual rate of interest.
Dec. 31 Earned $35,000 of service revenue on account during the year.
31 Received cash collections from accounts receivable amounting to $40,000.
31 Incurred other operating expenses on account during the year that amounted to $6,000.
31 Incurred accrued salaries expense of $4,800.
31 Had $50 of supplies on hand at the end of the period.

Required

Based on the preceding information, answer the following questions. All questions pertain to the 2004 financial statements. (*Hint:* Enter items in general ledger accounts under the accounting equation before answering the questions.)

a. Based on the preceding transactions, identify five additional adjustments and describe them.
b. What amount of interest expense would Juan report on the income statement?
c. What amount of net cash flow from operating activities would Juan report on the cash flow statement?
d. What amount of rent expense would Juan report in the income statement?
e. What amount of total liabilities would Juan report on the balance sheet?
f. What amount of supplies expense would Juan report on the income statement?
g. What amount of unearned revenue would Juan report on the balance sheet?
h. What amount of net cash flow from investing activities would Juan report on the cash flow statement?
i. What amount of interest payable would Juan report on the balance sheet?
j. What amount of total expenses would Juan report on the income statement?
k. What amount of retained earnings would Juan report on the balance sheet?
l. What total amount of all revenues would Juan report on the income statement?
m. What amount of cash flows from financing activities would Juan report on the cash flow statement?
n. What is the amount of the gain on sale of land Juan would report on the income statement?
o. What amount of net income would Juan report on the income statement?

L.O. 4 PROBLEM 3–6B *Preparing Financial Statements*

The following accounts and balances were drawn from the records of Johnson Company:

Supplies	$ 300	Beginning Retained Earnings	$14,500
Cash Flow from Investing Act.	(7,800)	Cash Flow from Financing Act.	0
Prepaid Insurance	600	Amortization Expense	1,500
Service Revenue	45,450	Dividends	6,000
Operating Expenses	35,000	Cash	9,000
Supplies Expense	750	Accounts Receivable	7,000
Insurance Expense	1,800	Office Equipment	16,000
Beginning Common Shares	24,000	Accumulated Amortization	8,000
Cash Flow from Operating Act.	10,450	Land	36,000
Common Shares Issued	6,000	Accounts Payable	16,000

Required

Use the accounts and balances from Johnson Company to construct an income statement, statement of shareholders' equity, balance sheet, and cash flow statement.

L.O. 4 PROBLEM 3–7B *Relationship of Accounts to Financial Statements*

Required

Identify whether each of the following items would appear on the income statement (IS), statement of shareholders' equity (SE), balance sheet (BS), or cash flow statement (CF). If some items appear on more than one statement, identify all applicable statements. If an item will not appear on any financial statement, label it NA.

a. Amortization Expense
b. Interest Receivable
c. Term Deposit
d. Unearned Revenue
e. Service Revenue
f. Cash Flow from Investing Activities
g. Consulting Revenue
h. Interest Expense
i. Ending Common Shares
j. Total Liabilities
k. Debt to Assets Ratio
l. Cash Flow from Operating Activities
m. Operating Expenses
n. Supplies Expense
o. Beginning Retained Earnings
p. Beginning Common Shares
q. Prepaid Insurance
r. Salary Expense

s. Accumulated Amortization
t. Cash
u. Supplies
v. Cash Flow from Financing Activities
w. Interest Revenue
x. Ending Retained Earnings
y. Net Income
z. Dividends
aa. Office Equipment
bb. Return on Equity Ratio
cc. Land
dd. Interest Payable
ee. Salaries Expense
ff. Notes Receivable
gg. Accounts Payable
hh. Total Assets
ii. Salaries Payable
jj. Insurance Expense
kk. Notes Payable
ll. Accounts Receivable

PROBLEM 3–8B *Missing Information in Financial Statements* L.O. 3, 4

Deluxe Technology Company started the 2005 accounting period with $6,500 cash, accounts receivable of $8,000, prepaid rent of $4,500, supplies of $150, computers that cost $35,000, accumulated amortization on computers of $7,000, accounts payable of $10,000, and common shares of $15,000. During 2005, Deluxe recognized $93,000 of revenue on account and collected $84,000 of cash from accounts receivable. It paid $5,000 cash for rent in advance and reported $6,000 of rent expense on the income statement. Deluxe paid $1,000 cash for supplies, and the income statement reported supplies expense of $1,100.

Amortization expense reported on the income statement amounted to $3,500. It incurred $38,600 of operating expenses on account and paid $34,000 cash toward the settlement of accounts payable. The company acquired capital of $10,000 cash from the issue of common shares. A $700 cash dividend was paid. (*Hint:* Record the events under the general ledger accounts of an accounting equation before satisfying the requirements.)

Required

a. Determine the balance in the Retained Earnings account at the beginning of the accounting period.
b. Prepare an income statement, statement of shareholders' equity, balance sheet, and cash flow statement as of the end of the accounting period.

PROBLEM 3–9B *Using Accounting Information* L.O. 1

Marty Fairchild told his friend that he was very angry with his father. He had asked his father for a sports car, and his father had replied that he did not have the cash. Fairchild said that he knew his father was not telling the truth because he had seen a copy of his father's business records, which included a balance sheet that showed a Retained Earnings account of $650,000. He said that anybody with $650,000 had enough cash to buy his son a car.

Required

Explain why Fairchild's assessment of his father's cash position may be invalid. What financial statements and which items on those statements would enable him to make a more accurate assessment of his father's cash position?

ANALYZE, THINK, COMMUNICATE

BUSINESS APPLICATIONS CASE *Bommardier's Annual Report* ATC 3–1

Required

Using Bombardier's financial statements in Appendix B, answer the following questions:

a. What was Bombardier's debt to assets ratio for 2002?
b. What was Bombardier's return on assets ratio for 2002?
c. What was Bombardier's return on equity ratio for 2002?
d. Why was Bombardier's 2002 return on equity ratio greater than its 2002 return on assets ratio?

ATC 3–2 GROUP ASSIGNMENT *Missing Information*

Little Theatre Group is a local performing arts group that sponsors various theatre productions. The company sells season tickets for the regular performances. It also sells tickets to individual performances called *door sales*. The season tickets are sold in June, July, and August for the season that runs from September through April of each year. The season tickets package contains tickets to eight performances, one per month. The first year of operations was 2003. All revenue not from season ticket sales is from door sales. The following selected information was taken from the financial records for December 31, 2003, 2004, and 2005, at the company's year end:

	2003	2004	2005
Revenue (per income statement)	$450,000	$575,000	$625,000
Unearned Revenue (per balance sheet)	127,000	249,000	275,000
Operating Expense	231,000	326,000	428,000

Required

a. Divide the class into groups consisting of four or five students. Organize the groups into three sections. Assign the groups in each section the financial data for one of the preceding accounting periods.

Group Tasks

(1) Determine the total amount of season ticket sales for the year assigned.
(2) Determine the total amount of season door sales for the year assigned.
(3) Compute the net income for the year assigned.
(4) Have a representative of each section put its income statement on the board.

Class Discussion

b. Compare the income statements for 2003, 2004, and 2005. Discuss the revenue trend; that is, are door sales increasing more than season ticket sales? What is the company's growth pattern?

ATC 3–3 REAL-WORLD CASE *Different Numbers for Different Industries*

The following are the debt to assets, return on assets, and return on equity ratios for four companies from two different industries. The range of interest rates each company was paying on its long-term debt is provided. Each of these public companies is a leader in its particular industry, and the data are for the fiscal years ending in 2001. *All numbers are percentages.*

	Debt to Assets	Return on Assets	Return on Equity	Interest Rates
Banking Industry				
Royal Bank	95	0.7	16.8	5.1–11.75
Scotiabank	95	0.8	14.8	5.4–11.4
Automotive Industry				
General Motors	89	1.5	18.6	5.6–7.0
DaimlerChrysler	79	4.0	18.9	5.7–6.6

Required

a. Based only on the debt to assets ratios, the banking companies appear to have the most financial risk. Generally, lower interest rates are usually charged for companies that have lower financial risk. Given this, write a brief explanation as to why the banking companies can borrow money at lower interest rates than the automotive companies.

b. Explain why the Royal Bank's return on equity ratio is more than 20 times higher than its return on assets ratio, while DaimlerChrysler's return on equity ratio is less than 5 times higher than its return on assets ratio.

BUSINESS APPLICATIONS CASE *Using Ratio Analysis to Assess Financial Risk* **ATC 3–4**

The following information was drawn from the balance sheets of two companies:

Company	Assets	=	Liabilities	+	Equity
Men's Clothier	215,000		58,000		157,000
Women's Fashions	675,000		256,500		418,500

Required

a. Compute the debt to assets ratio to measure the level of financial risk of both companies.
b. Compare the two ratios computed in part a to determine whether Men's Clothier or Women's Fashions has the higher level of financial risk.

BUSINESS APPLICATIONS CASE *Using Ratio Analysis to Make Comparisons between Companies* **ATC 3–5**

At the end of 2007, the following information is available for El Greco Pizza and Athenian Pizza.

Statement Data	El Greco Pizza	Athenian Pizza
Total Assets	$127,000	$753,000
Total Liabilities	93,000	452,000
Shareholders' Equity	34,000	301,000
Net Income	8,000	45,000

Required

a. For each company, compute the debt to assets ratio and the return on equity ratio.
b. Determine what percentage of each company's assets was financed by the owners.
c. Which company had a higher level of financial risk?
d. Based on profitability alone, which company performed better?
e. Do the preceding ratios support the concept of financial leverage? Explain.

WRITING ASSIGNMENT *Effect of Land Sale on Return on Assets* **ATC 3–6**

Toyo Company is holding land that cost $900,000 for future use. However, plans have changed and the company may not need the land in the foreseeable future. The president is concerned about the return on assets. Current net income is $425,000 and total assets are $3,500,000.

Required

a. Write a memo to the company president explaining the effect of disposing of the land, assuming that it has a current value of $1,500,000.
b. Write a memo to the company president explaining the effect of disposing of the land, assuming that it has a current value of $600,000.

ETHICAL DILEMMA *What Is a Little Deceit among Friends?* **ATC 3–7**

Glenn's Cleaning Services Company is experiencing cash flow problems and needs a loan. Glenn has a friend who is willing to lend him the money he needs provided she can be convinced that he will be able to repay the debt. Glenn has assured his friend that his business is viable, but his friend has asked to see the company's financial statements. Glenn's accountant produced the following financial statements:

Income Statement		Balance Sheet	
Service Revenue	$ 38,000	Assets	$ 85,000
Operating Expenses	(70,000)	Liabilities	$ 35,000
Net Loss	$ (32,000)	Common Shares	82,000
		Retained Earnings	(32,000)
		Total Liabilities and Shareholders' Equity	$ 85,000

Glenn made the following adjustments to these statements before showing them to his friend. He recorded $82,000 of revenue on account from Barrymore Manufacturing Company for a contract to clean its headquarters office building that was still being negotiated for the next month. Barrymore had scheduled a meeting to sign a contract the following week, so he was sure that he would get the job. Barrymore was a reputable company, and Glenn was confident that he could ultimately collect the $82,000. Also, he subtracted $30,000 of accrued salaries expense and the corresponding liability. He reasoned that since he had not paid the employees, he had not incurred any expense.

Required

a. Reconstruct the income statement and balance sheet as they would appear after Glenn's adjustments. Comment on the accuracy of the adjusted financial statements.

b. Comment on the ethical implications of Glenn's actions. Before you answer, consider the following scenario. Suppose you are Glenn and the $30,000 you owe your employees is due next week. If you are unable to pay them, they will quit and the business will go bankrupt. You are sure you will be able to repay your friend when your employees perform the $82,000 of services for Barrymore and you collect the cash. However, your friend is risk averse and is not likely to make the loan based on the financial statements your accountant prepared. Would you make the changes that Glenn made to get the loan and thereby save your company? Defend your position with a rational explanation.

ATC 3–8 SPREADSHEET ASSIGNMENT *Using Excel*

Set up the following spreadsheet for Hubbard Company to calculate financial ratios based on given financial information.

Microsoft Excel - ch3-1.xls

B5 = =B3+B4

	A	B	C	D	E	F	G	H	I
1		Total		Total		Shareholders'		Net	
2		Assets	=	Liabilities	+	Equity		Income	
3	Original Amounts	100,000		40,000		60,000		20,000	
4	Transaction	10,000		0		10,000		0	
5	Revised Amounts	110,000		40,000		70,000		20,000	
6									
7	**Ratios**	Original		Revised					
8	Debt to Assets	40.00%		36.36%					
9	Debt to Equity	66.67%		57.14%					
10	Return on Assets	20.00%		18.18%					
11	Return on Equity	33.33%		28.57%					
12									
13									
14									

Steps to Prepare Spreadsheet

1. Enter the information in Column A.
2. Enter the headings in rows 1 and 2.
3. In row 3, enter the numbers for the Original Amounts.
4. In Column B, beginning with row 8, formulate the ratios based on the Original Amounts. Format the ratios as percentages.

5. The following independent transactions apply to Hubbard Corporation.
   a. Acquired $10,000 cash from the issue of common shares.
   b. Borrowed $10,000 cash.
   c. Earned $5,000 revenue and received cash.
   d. Accrued $3,000 of expenses.
   e. Incurred and paid $3,000 of expenses.

Required

a. In row 4, enter the effect of Transaction *a* on both the accounting equation and net income.
b. Formulate the revised amounts in row 5 for each heading after considering the effect of Transaction *a* on the original amounts.
c. Design formulas for the ratios in Column D based on the Revised Amounts.
d. Enter the ratios for the Original and Revised Transaction *a* amounts in the following table.

		Ratios for Various Transactions				
Ratios	**Original**	*a*	*b*	*c*	*d*	*e*
Debt to Assets						
Equity to Assets						
Return on Assets						
Return on Equity						

e. Delete the effect of Transaction *a* in row 4. Enter the effect of Transaction *b* in row 4. Notice that Excel automatically recalculates the Revised Amounts and Ratios on your spreadsheet as the result of the changed data.
f. Continue to delete transactions in row 4 as completed and enter the effect of each subsequent transaction, *c* through *e*, one at a time. Enter the ratios for each independent transaction in the preceding table.

Spreadsheet Tip

Format percentages by choosing Format, Cells, and Percentage.

SPREADSHEET ASSIGNMENT *Mastering Excel* ATC 3–9

a. Refer to Problem 3–6A. Using an Excel spreadsheet, prepare the financial statements as indicated. Use formulas where normal arithmetic calculations are made in the financial statements.
b. It is interesting to speculate what would happen if certain operating results change for better or worse. After completing Requirement *a*, change certain account balances for each of the following independent operating adjustments. After each adjustment, note how the financial statements would differ if the change in operations were to occur. After the effect of each adjustment is noted, return the data to the original amounts in Problem 3–6A, and then go to the next operating adjustment.

   In the following table, record the new amounts on the financial statements for the various operating changes listed.

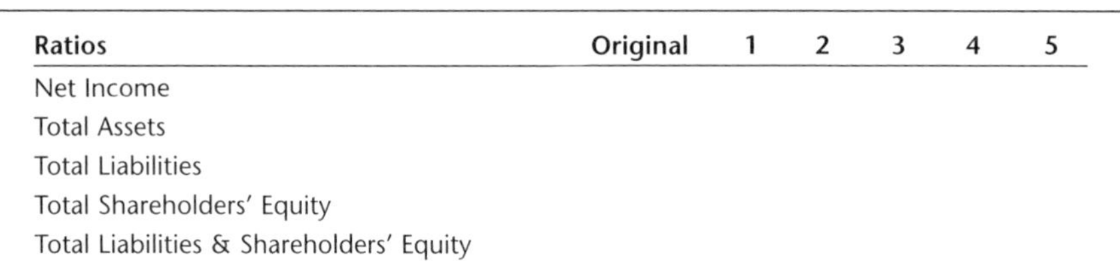

Ratios	**Original**	1	2	3	4	5
Net Income						
Total Assets						
Total Liabilities						
Total Shareholders' Equity						
Total Liabilities & Shareholders' Equity						

Independent Operating Adjustments

1. Service Revenue increased $7,500. Assume that all services are provided on account.
2. Insurance Expense decreased $500. The related Prepaid Insurance account changed accordingly.
3. Supplies Expense decreased $100. The related Supplies account changed accordingly.
4. Amortization Expense increased $300. The related Accumulated Amortization account changed accordingly.
5. Dividends paid decreased $1,000 and the Cash account changed accordingly.

Chapter 4

The Recording Process

Learning Objectives

After completing this chapter, you should be able to:

1 Explain the fundamental concepts associated with double-entry accounting systems.

2 Describe business events using debit/credit terminology.

3 Record transactions in T-accounts.

4 Identify the events that need adjusting entries and record them.

5 State the need for and record closing entries.

6 Prepare and interpret a trial balance.

7 Record transactions using the general journal format.

8 Describe the components of an annual report, including the management's discussion and analysis (MD&A) section and the notes to financial statements.

the *curious* accountant

As noted earlier, most companies prepare financial statements at least once a year. The year for which accounting records are maintained is called the company's **fiscal year**. This book usually assumes that the fiscal year is the same as a calendar year; that is, it ends on December 31. In practice, many companies have fiscal years that do not end on December 31. For example, Polo Ralph Lauren, a company that produces clothing, has a fiscal year that ends around March 31. The Limited, a company that also sells clothing, has a fiscal year that ends on January 31. Why do you think these companies choose these dates to end their fiscal years?

The task of accounting for business activity becomes more complex as the size of the business increases. Double-entry accounting systems provide the structure necessary to maintain the records for complex as well as simple business organizations. This chapter discusses the fundamentals of double-entry accounting systems.

*A simplified accounting form known as a **T-account** is a good starting point for learning the recording procedures used in double-entry accounting systems. The account title is placed above the horizontal bar of the T, and increases and decreases are placed on either side of the vertical bar. This account form omits the detailed information concerning a transaction and thus permits observers to focus on the accounting concepts. This is why the T-account form is often used in the classroom, in textbooks, and in business discussions. However, it does not appear in the formal records of a business. It should be viewed simply as a convenient format that enhances communication.*

Debit/Credit Terminology

LO1 Explain the fundamental concepts associated with double-entry accounting systems.

LO2 Describe business events using debit/credit terminology.

The left side of the T-account is called the **debit** side, and the right side is called the **credit** side. It is common practice to abbreviate the terms *debit* and *credit* with the initials Dr. and Cr., respectively. As well, it is said that an account has been *debited* when an amount is placed on the left side of the account and *credited* when an amount is entered on the right. For any given account, the difference between the debit and credit amounts is known as the **account balance**. An account can have either a debit or a credit balance.

The **double-entry accounting** system is designed so that total debits always equal total credits. This allows each transaction to be checked for accuracy by verifying that the debits and credits are equal. Also, the entire list of accounts can be checked by verifying that the total of all debit balances is equal to the total of all credit balances. However, this system cannot ensure complete accuracy. For example, although it may have been appropriate to make a debit entry, the accountant may select the wrong account when recording the debit. As a result, the debits and credits will be equal, but the records will be inaccurate. The system is not perfect, but it has proved very effective in eliminating or reducing incomplete entries, transposed or incorrect amounts, and inaccurate entries to accounts.

The double-entry accounting system has two basic equality requirements: (1) The equality of the basic accounting equation (assets = claims) must be maintained and (2) total debits must equal total credits. A recording method that maintains these two equalities is discussed now.

Suppose a company borrows $1,000 from a bank. In accordance with the first equality requirement, assets and liabilities increase; this maintains the equality of the accounting equation. If the increase in assets is recorded as a debit, the second equality rule (debits = credits) requires that the corresponding increase in liabilities be recorded as a credit. Thus, the financing activity is recorded as a debit to Cash and a credit to Notes Payable. Similarly, increases in all asset accounts are recorded as debits, and increases in liability and equity accounts are recorded as credits. Extending the logic requires that we record decreases in asset accounts as credits and decreases in liability and equity accounts as debits. The repayment of the $1,000 debt is recorded with a debit to Notes Payable and a credit to Cash.

It is useful to compare the requirements of the recording process with those of a simpler system, such as a traffic light. It makes no difference whether *red* is defined as *go* or *stop*; what is important is that the system's users agree on the definition. Similarly, the users of the double-entry accounting system must agree on the recording rules. In summary, these rules are as follows:

1. Debits increase assets and decrease liabilities and equity.
2. Credits increase liabilities and equity and decrease assets.

The rules for debits and credits are shown in T-account form here.

Assets		=	Claims				
			Liabilities		+	Equity	
Debit	Credit		Debit	Credit		Debit	Credit
+	−		−	+		−	+

Collins Consultants Inc. Case

LO3 Record transactions in T-accounts.

We will demonstrate the rules for debits and credits by recording the accounting events that affect a small business, Collins Consultants Inc. Assume that Raymond Collins started his consulting practice on January 1, 2005. The accounting equation reflects zero assets and zero claims at the beginning of the practice. The case utilizes the following format: Business events are introduced. Each event is described in debit/credit terminology and then demonstrated in T-account format. The effects of each event on the balance sheet, income statement, and cash flow statement are shown in a horizontal statements model. We number the events and then use the numbers as references. Recall that accounting events can be divided into four categories. The transactions used in the Collins Consultants case are organized according to the following categories:

1. Asset source transactions
2. Asset exchange transactions
3. Asset use transactions
4. Claims exchange transactions

Asset Source Transactions

A business obtains assets from three main sources: (1) acquired from the owners, (2) borrowed from creditors, or (3) produced through operating activities. The debit/credit recording method is identical for all three source transactions. They all result in an increase to an asset account (recorded with a debit entry) and a corresponding increase in a claims account (recorded with a credit entry).

Event 1 Owners Provide Assets

Collins Consultants Inc. (CCI) was established on January 1, 2005, when it acquired $15,000 cash from Collins in exchange for common shares.

This accounting event will increase assets and equity. The increase in assets (Cash) is recorded as a debit, and the increase in equity (Common Shares) as a credit. In T-account form, this transaction appears as follows:

Assets		=	Liabilities	+	Equity	
Cash					Common Shares	
Debit	Credit				Debit	Credit
+						+
(1) 15,000						15,000 **(1)**

The entry affects the elements of the financial statements as indicated:

Assets	=	Liab.	+	Equity	Rev.	−	Exp.	=	Net Inc.	Cash Flow Statement	
15,000	=	NA	+	15,000	NA	−	NA	=	NA	15,000	FA

Event 2 Creditor Provides Assets

On February 1, CCI borrowed $10,000 from a local bank.

CCI issued a note to the bank that obligated the company to pay 12 percent annual interest. The note carried a one-year term to maturity. Interest and principal were payable in cash at the maturity date. Since the party borrowing the money *issues* the note, that party is called the *issuer of a note*, as noted earlier. In this case, CCI is the issuer. From CCI's point of view, issuing the note in exchange for cash will increase assets and liabilities. The increase in assets (Cash) is recorded as a debit, and the increase in liabilities (Notes Payable) is recorded as a credit. After the transaction has been recorded, the T-accounts look like this:

Assets		=	Liabilities		+	Equity
Cash			Notes Payable			
Debit +	Credit		Debit	Credit +		
(2) 10,000				10,000 (2)		

Because space is limited, only the accounts affected by the event being analyzed are shown. Since Event 2 affects Cash and Notes Payable, these are the only two accounts shown. CCI's records still contain the Common Shares account created in Event 1, but that account is not shown here. Also, only the effects of the event being discussed are shown in the accounts. For example, even though the first transaction affected the Cash account, only the effects of the second transaction are shown in the T-account for Cash. The effects of each event are labelled with the event number shown in parentheses, in this case (2). We continue this practice throughout the chapter. Cumulative data for all accounts are shown later in this chapter.

The entry affects the elements of the financial statements as indicated:

Assets	=	Liab.	+	Equity	Rev.	−	Exp.	=	Net Inc.	Cash Flow Statement	
10,000	=	10,000	+	NA	NA	−	NA	=	NA	10,000	FA

Event 3 Creditor Provides Assets

On February 17, CCI purchased $850 of office supplies on account (agreed to pay for the supplies at a later date) from Morris Supply Company.

Purchasing the supplies on account will increase assets and liabilities. The increase in assets (Supplies) is recorded as a debit, and the increase in liabilities (Accounts Payable) is recorded as a credit. After the transaction is recorded, the T-accounts look like this:

Assets		=	Liabilities		+	Equity
Cash			Accounts Payable			
Debit +	Credit		Debit	Credit +		
(3) 850				850 (3)		

The entry affects the elements of the financial statements as indicated:

Assets	=	Liab.	+	Equity	Rev.	−	Exp.	=	Net Inc.	Cash Flow Statement
850	=	850	+	NA	NA	−	NA	=	NA	NA

Event 4 Creditor Provides Assets

On February 28, CCI agreed to review the internal control structure of Kendall Food Stores.

Kendall paid CCI $5,000 in advance for the services to be performed. CCI must provide services to the food store at some future date. Whenever a company receives cash in advance of providing a service, a liability is created. The liability is called *unearned revenue*. Recording the event increases assets and liabilities. The increase in assets (Cash) is recorded as a debit, and the increase in liabilities (Unearned Revenue) as a credit. After the transaction is recorded, the T-accounts look like this:

Assets	=	Liabilities	+	Equity
Cash		Unearned Revenue		
Debit + (4) 5,000 | Credit		Debit | Credit + 5,000 (4)		

The entry affects the elements of the financial statements as indicated:

Assets	=	Liab.	+	Equity	Rev.	−	Exp.	=	Net Inc.	Cash Flow Statement	
5,000	=	5,000	+	NA	NA	−	NA	=	NA	5,000	OA

Event 5
Creditor Provides Assets

On March 1, CCI received $18,000 as a result of signing a contract that required Collins to provide advice to Harwood Corporation over the coming year.

The event will increase assets and liabilities. The increase in assets (Cash) is recorded as a debit, and the increase in liabilities (Unearned Revenue) as a credit. After the transaction is recorded, the T-accounts look like this:

Assets	=	Liabilities	+	Equity
Cash		Unearned Revenue		
Debit + (5) 18,000 | Credit		Debit | Credit + 18,000 (5)		

The entry affects the elements of the financial statements as indicated:

Assets	=	Liab.	+	Equity	Rev.	−	Exp.	=	Net Inc.	Cash Flow Statement	
18,000	=	18,000	+	NA	NA	−	NA	=	NA	18,000	OA

Event 6
Operating Activity Provides Assets

On April 10, CCI provided services on account (agreed to receive payment at a future date) to Rex Company.

CCI sent Rex a bill for the amount of $2,000. Recognition of the revenue will increase assets and equity. The increase in assets (Accounts Receivable) is recorded as a debit, and the increase in equity (Consulting Revenue) as a credit. After the transaction is recorded, the T-accounts look like this:

Assets	=	Liabilities	+	Equity
Accounts Receivable				Consulting Revenue
Debit + (6) 2,000 | Credit				Debit | Credit + 2,000 (6)

The entry affects the elements of the financial statements as indicated:

Assets	=	Liab.	+	Equity	Rev.	−	Exp.	=	Net Inc.	Cash Flow Statement
2,000	=	NA	+	2,000	2,000	−	NA	=	2,000	NA

Event 7 Operating Activity Provides Assets

On April 29, Collins completed a two-week training seminar for which his company was paid $8,400 in cash.

Recognizing the revenue will increase assets and equity. The increase in assets (Cash) is recorded as a debit, and the increase in equity (Consulting Revenue) as a credit. After the transaction has been recorded, the T-accounts look like this:

Assets		=	Liabilities	+	Equity	
Cash					Consulting Revenue	
Debit +	Credit				Debit	Credit +
(7) 8,400						8,400 **(7)**

The entry affects the elements of the financial statements as indicated:

Assets	=	Liab.	+	Equity	Rev.	−	Exp.	=	Net Inc.	Cash Flow Statement	
8,400	=	NA	+	8,400	8,400	−	NA	=	8,400	8,400	OA

Summary of Asset Source Transactions

To help you understand how the rules of debits and credits are applied, we must remind you that each of the preceding transactions supplied assets to the business. In each case, an asset and a corresponding claims account increased. Since debits are used to increase assets and credits are used to increase equities, each transaction resulted in a debit to an asset account and an offsetting credit to a liability or equity account. Other transactions that provide assets to a business are recorded in much the same way.

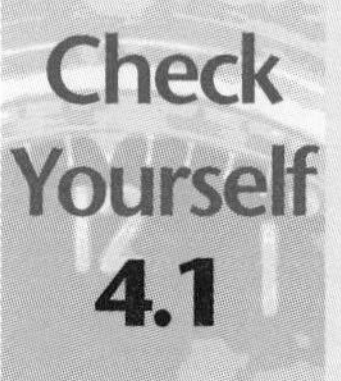

What are the three sources of assets? Which accounts are debited and credited when a business acquires an asset?

Answer The three sources of assets are creditors, investors, and earnings. When a company acquires an asset, the asset account is debited and the source account is credited. For example, if a company earns revenue on account, the receivables account is debited and the revenue account is credited.

Asset Exchange Transactions

Some transactions involve exchanging one asset for another. The decline in one asset account is offset by an increase in another asset account; this means the amount of total assets is unchanged by asset exchange transactions. Such transactions are recorded by crediting the account for the asset that decreased (the asset given) and debiting the account for the asset that increased (the asset obtained). In T-account form, the effects on the accounting equation look like this:

Assets				=	Claims
Asset 1		Asset 2			
Debit +	Credit	Debit	Credit −		

Event 8 Exchange Cash for Note Receivable

On May 1, CCI loaned Reston Company $6,000. Reston issued a one-year note to Collins and agreed to pay a 9 percent annual rate of interest.

From CCI's point of view, the loan represents an investment in Reston. Recognizing the loan (investment) will increase one asset account and decrease another. The increase in assets (Notes Receivable) is recorded as a debit, and the decrease in assets (Cash) is recorded as a credit. After the transaction is recorded, the T-accounts look like this:

Assets				=	Claims
Note Receivable		**Cash**			
Debit	Credit	Debit	Credit		
+			−		
(8) 6,000			6,000 **(8)**		

The entry would affect the elements of the financial statements as indicated:

Assets			=	Liab.	+	Equity	Rev.	−	Exp.	=	Net Inc.	Cash Flow Statement	
Cash	+	Note Rec.											
(6,000)	+	6,000	=	NA	+	NA	NA	−	NA	=	NA	(6,000)	IA

Event 9 Exchange Cash for Office Equipment

On June 30, CCI paid cash to purchase $42,000 of office equipment for the business.

The equipment was expected to have a five-year useful life and a $2,000 residual value. The purchase of equipment will increase one asset account and decrease another. The increase in assets (Office Equipment) is recorded as a debit, and the decrease in assets (Cash) as a credit. After the transaction is recorded, the T-accounts look like this:

Assets				=	Claims
Office Equipment		**Cash**			
Debit	Credit	Debit	Credit		
+			−		
(9) 42,000			42,000 **(9)**		

The entry affects the elements of the financial statements as indicated:

Assets			=	Liab.	+	Equity	Rev.	−	Exp.	=	Net Inc.	Cash Flow Statement	
Cash	+	Office Equip.											
(42,000)	+	42,000	=	NA	+	NA	NA	−	NA	=	NA	(42,000)	IA

Event 10 Exchange Cash for Prepaid Rent

On July 31, CCI entered into a contract with the owner of a building to rent office space.

CCI paid $3,600 cash in advance for rent for the coming year. The advance payment for rent will increase one asset account and decrease another. The increase in assets (Prepaid Rent) is recorded as a debit, and the decrease in assets (Cash) as a credit. After the transaction is recorded, the T-accounts look like this:

Assets				=	Claims
Prepaid Rent		**Cash**			
Debit	Credit	Debit	Credit		
+			−		
(10) 3,600			3,600 **(10)**		

The entry affects the elements of the financial statements as indicated:

Assets		=	Liab.	+	Equity	Rev.	−	Exp.	=	Net Inc.	Cash Flow Statement	
Cash	+ Pr Pd Rent											
(3,600)	+ 3,600	=	NA	+	NA	NA	−	NA	=	NA	(3,600)	OA

Event 11 Exchange Receivable for Cash

On August 8, CCI collected a $1,200 partial payment on the receivable from Rex Company (see Event 6).

The collection will increase one asset account and decrease another. The increase in assets (Cash) is recorded as a debit, and the decrease in assets (Accounts Receivable) as a credit. After the transaction is recorded, the T-accounts look like this:

Assets				=	Claims
Cash		Accounts Receivable			
Debit	Credit	Debit	Credit		
+			−		
(11) 1,200			1,200 (11)		

The entry affects the elements of the financial statements as indicated:

Assets		=	Liab.	+	Equity	Rev.	−	Exp.	=	Net Inc.	Cash Flow Statement	
Cash	+ Acct. Rec.											
1,200	+ (1,200)	=	NA	+	NA	NA	−	NA	=	NA	1,200	OA

Summary of Asset Exchange Transactions

Events 8–11 represent asset exchanges. In each case, one asset account is increased and another is decreased. The increase in the asset account is recorded with a debit entry, and the decrease in the other asset account with a credit entry. The amounts of total assets and total claims are unaffected by these transactions.

Asset Use Transactions

There are three main reasons to use assets. First, a company may use them to produce revenue. Recall that assets used to produce revenue are called *expenses*. Second, assets may be used to pay off liabilities. Third, a business may want to transfer to the owners some of the assets generated by its operating activities. Assets used for this purpose are called *dividends*. For all these asset use transactions, the debit/credit rules result in a credit to an asset account and a debit to a claims account. Both assets and claims decrease.

Event 12 Assets Used to Produce Revenue (Expenses)

On September 4, CCI paid $2,400 for salaries of employees who worked part-time for the company.

Recognizing the expense will decrease assets and equity. The decrease in assets (Cash) is recorded as a credit, and the decrease in equity (Salaries Expense) as a debit. After the transaction is recorded, the T-accounts look like this:

Assets		=	Liabilities	+	Equity	
Cash					Salaries Expense	
Debit	Credit − 2,400 **(12)**				Debit + Expense − Equity **(12)** 2,400	Credit

Note carefully that the debit entry has a dual effect on the equity elements. If Collins were to pay additional salaries, this amount would be added (debited) to the Salaries Expense account. Thus, debit entries will increase expense accounts. However, expenses will decrease equity. As a result, debits to expense accounts are considered additions to the ultimate reduction in equity. In summary, debits will increase expenses, and expenses will reduce equity.

The entry affects the elements of the financial statements as indicated:

Assets	=	Liab.	+	Equity	Rev.	−	Exp.	=	Net Inc.	Cash Flow Statement	
(2,400)	=	NA	+	(2,400)	NA	−	2,400	=	(2,400)	(2,400)	OA

Event 13
Assets Transferred to Owners (Dividends)

On September 20, CCI paid a $1,500 cash dividend to its shareholders.

Recognizing the dividend will decrease assets and equity. The decrease in assets (Cash) is recorded as a credit, and the decrease in equity (Dividend) as a debit. After the transaction is recorded, the T-accounts look like this:

Assets		=	Liabilities	+	Equity	
Cash					Dividend	
Debit	Credit − 1,500 **(13)**				Debit + Div'd. − Equity **(13)** 1,500	Credit

The debit entry can be viewed as an increase (+) in the dividends account or a decrease (−) in equity. Traditionally, the debit is viewed as an increase in the dividends account. Thus, it is said that debit entries increase the dividends account. The total balance in the dividends account then acts to reduce equity (Retained Earnings).

The entry affects the elements of the financial statements as indicated:

Assets	=	Liab.	+	Equity	Rev.	−	Exp.	=	Net Inc.	Cash Flow Statement	
(1,500)	=	NA	+	(1,500)	NA	−	NA	=	(NA)	(1,500)	FA

Event 14
Assets Used to Pay Liabilities

On October 10, CCI paid the $850 owed to Morris Supply Company (see Event 3).

Recognizing the cash payment will decrease assets and liabilities. The decrease in assets (Cash) is recorded as a credit, and the decrease in liabilities (Accounts Payable) as a debit. After the transaction is recorded, the T-accounts look like this:

Assets	=	Liabilities		+	Equity
Cash		Accounts Payable			
Debit	Credit	Debit	Credit		
	−	−			
	850 **(14)**	**(14)** 850			

The entry affects the elements of the financial statements as indicated:

Assets	=	Liab.	+	Equity	Rev.	−	Exp.	=	Net Inc.	Cash Flow Statement	
(850)	=	(850)	+	NA	NA	−	NA	=	NA	(850)	OA

Summary of Asset Use Transactions

Events 12–14 reduce assets and either liabilities or equity. Debit entries increased expense and dividends accounts. The total balances in these accounts then reduce equity. Each entry for asset use transactions required a debit to a liability or an equity account and a credit to an asset account.

Claims Exchange Transactions

Some transactions involve an exchange of one claims account for another claims account. The amount of total claims is not affected by these transactions because the decrease in one account is offset by an increase in another account. Such transactions are recorded by debiting one claims account and crediting the other.

Event 15 Recognition of Revenue (Unearned to Earned)

On November 15, Collins completed the work for the review of the internal control structure of Kendall Food Stores.

Kendall accepted Collins's report and expressed satisfaction with the services performed. The original contract price was $5,000. Recognition of the revenue decreases liabilities and increases equity. The decrease in liabilities (Unearned Revenue) is recorded as a debit, and the increase in equity (Consulting Revenue) as a credit. After the transaction is recorded, the T-accounts look like this:

Assets	=	Liabilities		+	Equity	
		Unearned Revenue			Consulting Revenue	
		Debit	Credit		Debit	Credit
		−				+
		(15) 5,000				5,000 **(15)**

The entry affects the elements of the financial statements as indicated:

Assets	=	Liab.	+	Equity	Rev.	−	Exp.	=	Net Inc.	Cash Flow Statement
NA	=	(5,000)	+	5,000	5,000	−	NA	=	5,000	NA

Event 16 Recognition of Expense

On December 18, CCI received a $900 bill from Creative Ads for advertisements placed in regional magazines. CCI plans to pay the bill later.

The event will increase liabilities and decrease equity. The increase in liabilities (Accounts Payable) is recorded as a credit, and the decrease in equity (Advertising Expense) as a debit. After the transaction is recorded, the T-accounts look like this:

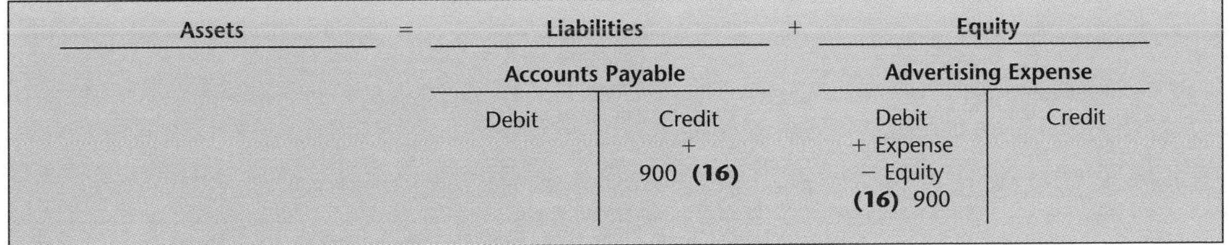

The entry affects the elements of the financial statements as indicated:

Assets	=	Liab.	+	Equity	Rev.	−	Exp.	=	Net Inc.	Cash Flow Statement
NA	=	900	+	(900)	NA	−	900	=	(900)	NA

Summary of Claims Exchange Transactions

The above two transactions reflect exchanges on the claims side of the accounting equation. In each case, one claims account was debited, and another claims account was credited. Total claims and total assets were not affected by the transactions.

Adjustments for Accruals

LO4 Understand the need for adjusting entries.

Assume that the above 16 events represent all the accounting events that affected CCI in 2005. As noted earlier, accrual accounting requires that revenues and expenses be recognized in the period in which they are earned or incurred, regardless of when cash changes hands. CCI's accounts were affected by three accruals during 2005. Since CCI has both notes receivable and notes payable that require accruals for interest, interest revenue and interest expense must be recognized in the adjusting process. Also, there is an unrecorded transaction for accrued salaries that is discussed in this section of the text.

Asset/Revenue Adjustments

When CCI loaned Reston Company $6,000, Reston agreed to pay CCI interest for the privilege of using the money. The interest is expressed as a percentage of the amount borrowed for a designated time. Thus, as time passes, the amount of interest due increases. The accrual increases assets and revenue on CCI's books. This is why the adjustment made to reflect the accrual of revenue is called an **asset/revenue adjustment**.

Adjustment 1 Accrual of Interest Revenue

CCI loaned Reston the $6,000 on May 1 at an annual interest rate of 9 percent.

Recall that the calculation for interest is the following:

$$i = Prt$$

where i = interest
P = principal
r = rate
t = time

As a result, CCI earned $360 ([$6,000 × 0.09] × [8/12]) in interest revenue in 2005. The required adjusting entry will increase assets and equity. The increase in assets (Interest Receivable) is recorded as a debit, and the increase in equity (Interest Revenue) as a credit. After the transaction has been recorded, the T-accounts would look like this:

Assets	=	Liabilities	+	Equity
Interest Receivable				**Interest Revenue**
Debit + / Credit				Debit / Credit +
(A1) 360				360 **(A1)**

Note that the transaction is labelled (A1). This notation is used to represent the first adjusting entry. The second adjusting entry is labelled (A2). Later entries follow this referencing method.

The adjustment affects the elements of the financial statements as indicated:

Assets	=	Liab.	+	Equity	Rev.	−	Exp.	=	Net Inc.	Cash Flow Statement
360	=	NA	+	360	360	−	NA	=	360	NA

Liability/Expense Adjustments

When CCI borrowed funds from a local bank, Collins agreed to pay the bank interest. As with interest revenue, interest expense increases with the length of time for which the money is borrowed. The increase in interest expense is offset by a corresponding increase in liabilities. This is why the adjustments made to reflect the accrual of expenses are called **liability/expense adjustments**.

Adjustment 2 Accrual of Interest Expense

On February 1, CCI borrowed $10,000 from a local bank at a 12 percent annual interest rate (see Event 2).

Interest expense on the note for the 2005 accounting period amounts to $1,100 ([$10,000 × 0.12] × [11/12]). The required adjusting entry will increase liabilities and decrease equity. The increase in liabilities (Interest Payable) is recorded as a credit, and the decrease in equity (Interest Expense) as a debit. After the transaction is recorded, the T-accounts look like this:

Assets	=	Liabilities	+	Equity
		Interest Payable		**Interest Expense**
		Debit / Credit +		Debit + Expense − Equity / Credit
		1,100 **(A2)**		**(A2)** 1,100

The adjustment affects the elements of the financial statements as indicated:

Assets	=	Liab.	+	Equity	Rev.	−	Exp.	=	Net Inc.	Cash Flow Statement
NA	=	1,100	+	(1,100)	NA	−	1,100	=	(1,100)	NA

Adjustment 3 Accrual of Salary Expense

Another common liability/expense adjustment involves accrued but unpaid salaries.

Note that the last time CCI paid salaries was on September 4 (see Event 12). Assume that CCI owes $800 to part-time employees for work they performed in 2005. CCI agreed to pay these salaries in 2006, when the projects on which the employees worked will be completed. The required adjusting entry increases liabilities and decreases equity. The increase in liabilities (Salaries Payable) is recorded as a credit, and the decrease in equity (Salaries Expense) as a debit. After the transaction is recorded, the T-accounts look like this:

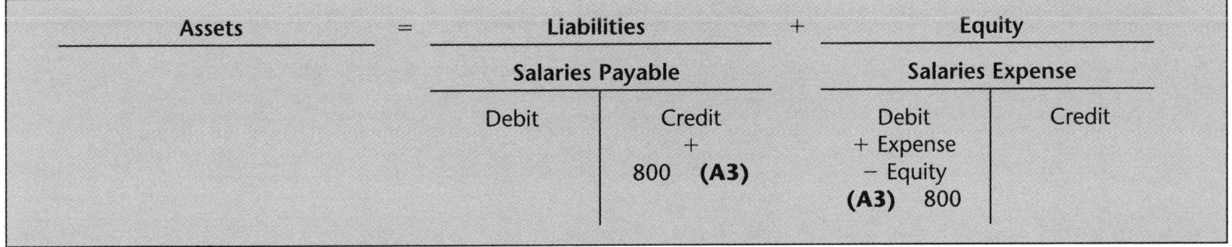

Assets	=	Liabilities		+	Equity	
		Salaries Payable			Salaries Expense	
		Debit	Credit + 800 **(A3)**		Debit + Expense − Equity **(A3)** 800	Credit

The adjustment affects the elements of the financial statements as indicated:

Assets	=	Liab.	+	Equity	Rev.	−	Exp.	=	Net Inc.	Cash Flow Statement
NA	=	800	+	(800)	NA	−	800	=	(800)	NA

Adjustments for Deferrals

As noted in Chapter 3, deferrals involve revenue and expense recognition that succeeds (comes after) the cash realizations. In 2005, CCI was affected by four deferrals. Cash was paid for office equipment, prepaid rent, and supplies, but no expenses were recognized to reflect the use of these resources during the accounting periods. Also, cash was collected for services provided, but revenue was not recognized. Each of these four deferrals requires adjustments on CCI's books to recognize revenue and expenses for the 2005 fiscal year.

Asset/Expense Adjustments

When CCI acquired the equipment, rent, and supplies, their costs were placed in asset accounts. At the end of the accounting period, the portion of the costs that represents used resources must be removed from the asset accounts and placed in expense accounts. Since each entry involves an asset account and an expense account, it is referred to as an **asset/expense adjustment**. Three asset/expense adjustments are shown next.

Adjustment 4 Equipment Used to Produce Revenue (Amortization Expense)

Since the office equipment was purchased on June 30, it was used for one-half of the year.

Accordingly, the amortization expense amounts to \$4,000 ([\$42,000 − \$2,000] ÷ 5 = \$8,000 ÷ 2 = \$4,000). The adjusting entry to record amortization will decrease assets and equity. The decrease in assets (Office Equipment) is recorded as a credit to the contra asset account Accumulated Amortization; and the decrease in equity (Amortization Expense) is recorded as a debit. After the transaction is recorded, the T-accounts look like this:

Assets		=	Liabilities	+	Equity	
Accumulated Amortization					Amortization Expense	
Debit	Credit + Acc. Amort. − Assets 4,000 **(A4)**				Debit + Expense − Equity **(A4)** 4,000	Credit

The plus sign in the Accumulated Amortization account indicates that the balance in this account increases when additional amounts of amortization are credited to the account. Therefore, credit entries will increase accumulated amortization. However, increases in the Accumulated Amortization account will reduce total assets. Since the Accumulated Amortization account has a balance that is opposite the normal asset balances, it is called a **contra account**.

The adjustment affects the elements of the financial statements as indicated:

Assets	=	Liab.	+	Equity	Rev.	−	Exp.	=	Net Inc.	Cash Flow Statement
(4,000)	=	NA	+	(4,000)	NA	−	4,000	=	(4,000)	NA

Adjustment 5 Office Space Used to Produce Revenue (Rent Expense)

On July 31, CCI paid $3,600 in advance for a one-year lease of office space.

The monthly rate of $300 ($3,600 ÷ 12 months) is multiplied by the five months for which the office was *used* in 2005 to determine the amount of rent expense ($300 × 5 = $1,500). Recognition of the rent expense decreases assets and equity. The decrease in assets (Prepaid Rent) is recorded as a credit, and the decrease in equity (Rent Expense) as a debit. After the transaction is recorded, the T-accounts look like this:

Assets		=	Liabilities	+	Equity	
Prepaid Rent					**Rent Expense**	
Debit	Credit − 1,500 **(A5)**				Debit + Expense − Equity **(A5)** 1,500	Credit

The adjustment affects the elements of the financial statements as indicated:

Assets	=	Liab.	+	Equity	Rev.	−	Exp.	=	Net Inc.	Cash Flow Statement
(1,500)	=	NA	+	(1,500)	NA	−	1,500	=	(1,500)	NA

Adjustment 6 Supplies Used to Produce Revenue (Supplies Expense)

Assume that a physical count indicates that $125 worth of supplies is on hand at the end of the accounting period.

Clearly, $725 ($850 − $125) of supplies must have been used in this period. Recognition of the supplies expense will decrease assets and equity. The decrease in assets (Supplies) is recorded as a credit and the decrease in equity (Supplies Expense) as a debit. After the transaction is recorded, the T-accounts look like this:

Assets		=	Liabilities	+	Equity	
Supplies					**Supplies Expense**	
Debit	Credit − 725 **(A6)**				Debit + Expense − Equity **(A6)** 725	Credit

The adjustment affects the elements of the financial statements as indicated:

Assets	=	Liab.	+	Equity	Rev.	−	Exp.	=	Net Inc.	Cash Flow Statement
(725)	=	NA	+	(725)	NA	−	725	=	(725)	NA

Liability/Revenue Adjustments

When the cash was received from Harwood Corporation in Event 5, Collins recorded the receipt as a liability to reflect the obligation to provide services over the one-year contract period. By the end of the accounting period, CCI would have provided some of the services that it was required to perform. Therefore, an amount of revenue representing the services provided must be recognized by transferring that amount from the liability to the revenue account. Since the entry involves a liability and a revenue account, it is called a **liability/revenue adjustment**.

Adjustment 7 Recognition of Revenue (Unearned to Earned)

On March 1, CCI received $18,000 as a result of signing a contract that required CCI to provide services to Harwood Corporation for a one-year period

By December 31, 2005, CCI would have provided Harwood services for 10 months. Therefore, $15,000 ($18,000 ÷ 12 = $1,500 × 10 = $15,000) of the obligation would have been satisfied in 2005. This amount must be removed from the Unearned Revenue account and placed in the Consulting Revenue account. The recognition of the revenue will decrease liabilities and increase equity. The decrease in liabilities (Unearned Revenue) is recorded as a debit, and the increase in equity (Consulting Revenue) as a credit. After the transaction is recorded, the T-accounts look like this:

Assets	=	Liabilities		+	Equity	
		Unearned Revenue			Consulting Revenue	
		Debit –	Credit		Debit	Credit +
		(A7) 15,000				15,000 (A7)

The adjustment affects the elements of the financial statements as indicated:

Assets	=	Liab.	+	Equity	Rev.	–	Exp.	=	Net Inc.	Cash Flow Statement
NA	=	(15,000)	+	15,000	15,000	–	NA	=	15,000	NA

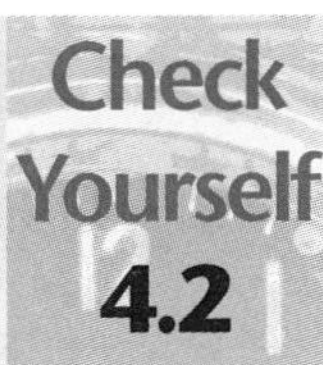

Can an asset exchange transaction be an adjusting entry?

Answer No. Adjusting entries always involve revenue or expense accounts. Since an asset exchange transaction involves only asset accounts, it cannot be an adjusting entry.

Debit/Credit Relationships

LO2 Describe business events using debit/credit terminology.

A review of the transactions presented in this chapter reveals the relationships shown in Panel A of Exhibit 4–1. These relationships are also depicted in T-account form in Panel B. Debit/credit terminology is essential to the communication of accounting information. Practise using the terminology until it becomes a natural part of your vocabulary. It is vital for you to establish a solid foundation early so you can easily add new concepts to your base of knowledge.

Summary of T-Accounts

LO3 Record transactions in T-accounts.

Exhibit 4–2 on page 147 is a summary of the accounts affected by the preceding transactions. It is important to verify that the recording method has satisfied the two equality requirements. In recording each transaction, debits were always equal to credits. Also, each transaction was recorded in accordance with the requirement that total assets equal total claims. As a result, the total of all asset balances amounted to $48,635, which is equal to the total amount of all balances in the liability and equity

Exhibit 4–1 *Debit/Credit Relationships*

Panel A

Account	Debits	Credits
Assets	Increase	Decrease
Contra Assets	Decrease	Increase
Liabilities	Decrease	Increase
Equity	Decrease	Increase
Common Shares	Decrease	Increase
Revenue	Decrease	Increase
Expenses	Increase	Decrease
Dividends	Increase	Decrease

Panel B

Assets		=	Liabilities		+	Equity	
Debit	Credit		Debit	Credit		Debit	Credit
+	−		−	+		−	+

Contra Assets	
Debit	Credit
+ Assets	− Assets
− Contra	+ Contra

Common Shares	
Debit	Credit
−	+

Revenue	
Debit	Credit
−	+

Expense	
Debit	Credit
− Equity	+ Equity
+ Exp.	− Exp.

Dividends	
Debit	Credit
− Equity	+ Equity
+ Div'd.	− Div'd.

accounts. Note that the balance of an account is located on the plus (increase) side of that account. As a result, asset, dividend, and expense accounts are said to carry *debit balances*; liability, equity, and revenue accounts are said to carry *credit balances*.

The Ledger

LO1 Explain the fundamental concepts associated with double-entry accounting systems.

A collection of accounts as in Exhibit 4–2 is referred to as a **ledger**. In manual systems, a ledger may be a book containing pages that represent accounts. Transaction information is recorded on the books by hand. In more sophisticated systems, a set of magnetic tapes may constitute the ledger. Input of transaction information to this type of ledger may be done through electronic keyboards or scanners. Ledger accounts are generally assigned a name and a number that describe certain classifications of data. The accounts are often listed in the ledger according to the sequence of their numbers. A list of the various accounts and their corresponding account numbers, which are contained in the ledger, is called a **chart of accounts**. Since it contains all accounts, the ledger is the main information source for the financial statements.

Exhibit 4–2 *Ledger Accounts*

Assets = Liabilities + Equity

Assets

Cash

	Debit	Credit	
(1)	15,000	6,000	(8)
(2)	10,000	42,000	(9)
(4)	5,000	3,600	(10)
(5)	18,000	2,400	(12)
(7)	8,400	1,500	(13)
(11)	1,200	850	(14)
Bal.	1,250		

Accounts Receivable

	Debit	Credit	
(6)	2,000	1,200	(11)
Bal.	800		

Supplies

	Debit	Credit	
(3)	850	725	(A6)
Bal.	125		

Prepaid Rent

	Debit	Credit	
(10)	3,600	1,500	(A5)
Bal.	2,100		

Notes Receivable

	Debit	Credit	
(8)	6,000		
Bal.	6,000		

Interest Receivable

	Debit	Credit	
(A1)	360		
Bal.	360		

Office Equipment

	Debit	Credit	
(9)	42,000		
Bal.	42,000		

Accumulated Amortization

	Debit	Credit	
		4,000	(A4)
		4,000	Bal.

Liabilities

Accounts Payable

	Debit	Credit	
(14)	850	850	(3)
		900	(16)
		900	Bal.

Unearned Revenue

	Debit	Credit	
(15)	5,000	5,000	(4)
(A7)	15,000	18,000	(5)
		3,000	Bal.

Notes Payable

	Debit	Credit	
		10,000	(2)
		10,000	Bal.

Interest Payable

	Debit	Credit	
		1,100	(A2)
		1,100	Bal.

Salaries Payable

	Debit	Credit	
		800	(A3)
		800	Bal.

Equity

Common Shares

	Debit	Credit	
		15,000	(1)
		15,000	Bal.

Consulting Revenue

	Debit	Credit	
		2,000	(6)
		8,400	(7)
		5,000	(15)
		15,000	(A7)
		30,400	Bal.

Interest Revenue

	Debit	Credit	
		360	(A1)
		360	Bal.

Salaries Expense

	Debit	Credit	
(12)	2,400		
(A3)	800		
Bal.	3,200		

Advertising Expense

	Debit	Credit	
(16)	900		
Bal.	900		

Interest Expense

	Debit	Credit	
(A2)	1,100		
Bal.	1,100		

Amortization Expense

	Debit	Credit	
(A4)	4,000		
Bal.	4,000		

Rent Expense

	Debit	Credit	
(A5)	1,500		
Bal.	1,500		

Supplies Expense

	Debit	Credit	
(A6)	725		
Bal.	725		

Dividends

	Debit	Credit	
(13)	1,500		
Bal.	1,500		

Total Assets	=	Total Liabilities	+	Total Equity
		15,800		32,835
48,635			Total Claims 48,635	

The General Journal

LO1 Explain the fundamental concepts associated with double-entry accounting systems.

As business activity expands, it becomes more and more difficult to enter transaction data directly into ledger accounts. For example, think about the number of entries that would be required to record a single day's cash transactions for a large grocery store. If customers were required to wait for the cashier to make a formal entry to ledger accounts for every food item sold, lines would become so long that shopping would be discouraged and the store would lose business. To simplify the record-keeping process, transaction data are usually recorded by nonaccounting personnel on general-purpose business documents before the data are transferred to the accounting department. For example, a salesclerk may record data about a sales transaction on a cash register tape. The tape then becomes a **source document**, which the accountant then uses to enter the transaction data into the accounting system. Other source documents are invoices, time cards, cheque stubs, and cash receipts.

Ledger accounts contain information about a particular part of a transaction. For example, a debit in the ledger account for Cash indicates that cash increased. However, it does not identify the cause of the increase, nor does it explain when the increase occurred relative to other transactions. To maintain a *complete chronological record* (a record arranged in order of time) of all business transactions, accountants first record the data from source documents in a **journal**. In other words, *information is recorded in journals before it is entered in the ledger accounts*. Thus, journals are often called **books of original entry**.

A company may use several different journals to maintain a chronological record of accounting events. Most transactions are recorded in a **general journal**. However, **special journals** could be used to record repetitive transactions that occur often. For example, a journal could be specially designed to record only transactions involving sales on account. A different journal could be used to record receipts of cash. Special journals are often named to be consistent with the types of transactions recorded in them. The journal used to record purchases on account may be called a *purchases journal*. Likewise, cash payments may be recorded in a *cash payments journal*. Exhibit 4–3 lists the commonly used special journals.

Exhibit 4–3 *Special Journals*

Sales Journal	Purchases Journal	Cash Receipts Journal	Cash Payments Journal	General Journal
Used to record all sales on account.	Used to record all purchases on account.	Used to record all cash received by the company.	Used to record all cash payments made by the company.	Used for any transactions that do not fit in the other four journals.

After complete transaction data have been recorded in a journal, portions of the data are summarized and transferred to the ledger accounts. For example, the total amount of many cash transactions that were recorded individually in a cash receipts journal may be posted as a single debit to the Cash account in the general ledger. The process of transferring information from journals to ledgers is called **posting**. After the information has been posted to the ledger accounts, the debit and credit balances of the accounts are determined and tested for equality. Finally, the ledger account balances are used to prepare financial statements. Thus, the recording process has five steps: (1) preparing and analyzing source documents, (2) journalizing the transaction data selected from the analysis of the source documents, (3) posting the transaction data from the journals to ledger accounts, (4) determining balances of the ledger accounts and testing the equality of debits and credits, and (5) using the ledger account balances to prepare financial statements.

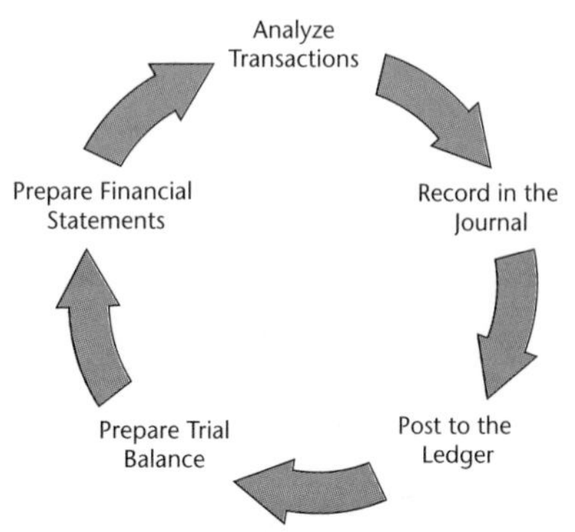

reality bytes

Do all accounting systems require the use of debits and credits? Definitely not. Many small businesses use a single-entry system. A chequebook constitutes a sufficient accounting system for many business owners. Deposits represent revenues, and payments constitute expenses. Many excellent automated accounting systems do not require data entry through a debit/credit recording method. Quick Books is a good example of this type of system. Data are entered into the Quick Books software program through a user-friendly computer interface that does not require knowledge of debit/credit terminology. Even so, the Quick Books program produces traditional financial reports such as an income statement, balance sheet, and cash flow statement. How is this possible? Before you become too ingrained in the debit/credit system, recall that throughout the first three chapters of this text, we maintained accounting records without using debits and credits. Financial reports can be produced in many ways without using a double-entry system. Having recognized this point, we also note that the vast majority of medium- to large-size companies use the double-entry system. Indeed, debit/credit terminology is a part of common culture. Most people have an understanding of what is happening when a business tells them that their account is being debited or credited. Therefore, it is important for you to embrace the double-entry system as well as other financial reporting systems.

More and more of companies are using computers to record transaction data and prepare financial statements. Although the computer can accomplish the required work at incredible speed and with unparalleled accuracy, it follows the same basic five-step sequence as a manual system. The analysis of a simple manual accounting system can provide significant insight into the more complex operations of computer-based systems. The following section demonstrates the recording procedures used in a simple manual accounting system.

LO7 Record transactions using the general journal format.

The illustration uses a general journal. While *special journals* can simplify the recording process, their use is not required. As in the case described later, all transactions can be recorded in the *general journal*. At a minimum, the general journal provides space for the date, account titles, and amount of each transaction. Exhibit 4–4 shows the typical format used in a general journal; it contains entries for all transactions discussed so far for CCI. The date of the transaction is recorded in the first column. The account to be debited is written first at the extreme left edge of the column provided for the account titles. The account to be credited is indented and placed on the line directly below the account to be debited. The money amount of the transaction is recorded in the Debit and Credit columns on the same lines with their respective account titles.

Financial Statements

The general ledger contains the information needed to prepare the financial statements for CCI. The income statement, statement of shareholders' equity, balance sheet, and cash flow statement are shown in Exhibits 4–5, 4–6, 4–7, and 4–8 on page 151.

Closing Entries

LO5 State the need for and record closing entries.

Exhibit 4–9 on page 152 shows the **closing entries** for CCI in general journal form. After the closing entries are posted to the ledger accounts, the revenue, expense, and dividends accounts have zero balances. The closing process clears the nominal accounts of all 2005 information and in this way readies them for use in the 2006 fiscal year.

Suppose that all companies close their books on December 31 of each year. In these circumstances, the demand for financial reporting services would cluster around one specific time period. Accountants, printers, lawyers, government agencies, and others who are involved in producing annual reports would be caught in a year-end bottleneck that would overburden their resources. Also, after the year-end rush

Exhibit 4-4 *General Journal*

Date		Account Titles	Debit	Credit
Jan.	1	Cash	15,000	
		Common Shares		15,000
Feb.	1	Cash	10,000	
		Notes Payable		10,000
	17	Office Supplies	850	
		Accounts Payable		850
	28	Cash	5,000	
		Unearned Revenue		5,000
Mar.	1	Cash	18,000	
		Unearned Revenue		18,000
April	10	Accounts Receivable	2,000	
		Consulting Revenue		2,000
	29	Cash	8,400	
		Consulting Revenue		8,400
May	1	Notes Receivable	6,000	
		Cash		6,000
June	30	Office Equipment	42,000	
		Cash		42,000
July	31	Prepaid Rent	3,600	
		Cash		3,600
Aug.	8	Cash	1,200	
		Accounts Receivable		1,200
Sept.	4	Salaries Expense	2,400	
		Cash		2,400
	20	Dividends	1,500	
		Cash		1,500
Oct.	10	Accounts Payable	850	
		Cash		850
Nov.	15	Unearned Revenue	5,000	
		Consulting Revenue		5,000
Dec.	18	Advertising Expense	900	
		Accounts Payable		900
		Adjusting Entries		
Dec.	31	Interest Receivable	360	
		Interest Revenue		360
	31	Interest Expense	1,100	
		Interest Payable		1,100
	31	Salaries Expense	800	
		Salaries Payable		800
	31	Amortization Expense	4,000	
		Accumulated Amortization		4,000
	31	Rent Expense	1,500	
		Prepaid Rent		1,500
	31	Supplies Expense	725	
		Supplies		725
	31	Unearned Revenue	15,000	
		Consulting Revenue		15,000

was over, there would be very little work to keep employees busy during the other parts of the year. In an effort to smooth the workload, companies have been encouraged to adopt a natural business year. A natural business year ends when the activities of an entity have reached the lowest point in an annual cycle. Often, the natural business year ends on December 31. However, as we indicated in the Curious Accountant, many companies have business cycles that end at times other than December 31.

Exhibit 4–5

COLLINS CONSULTANTS INC.
Income Statement
For the Year Ended December 31, 2005

Revenue		
Consulting Revenue	$30,400	
Interest Revenue	360	
Total Revenue		$30,760
Less Expenses		
Salaries Expense	3,200	
Advertising Expense	900	
Interest Expense	1,100	
Amortization Expense	4,000	
Rent Expense	1,500	
Supplies Expense	725	
Total Expenses		(11,425)
Net Income		$19,335

Exhibit 4–6

COLLINS CONSULTANTS INC.
Statement of Shareholders' Equity
For the Year Ended December 31, 2005

Beginning Common Shares	$ 0	
Plus: Common Shares Issued	15,000	
Ending Common Shares		$15,000
Beginning Retained Earnings	0	
Plus: Net Income	19,335	
Less: Dividends	(1,500)	
Ending Retained Earnings		17,835
Total Shareholders' Equity		$32,835

Exhibit 4–7

COLLINS CONSULTANTS INC.
Balance Sheet
December 31, 2005

Assets		
Cash	$ 1,250	
Accounts Receivable	800	
Supplies	125	
Prepaid Rent	2,100	
Notes Receivable	6,000	
Interest Receivable	360	
Office Equipment	42,000	
Less: Accumulated Amortization	(4,000)	
Total Assets		$48,635
Liabilities		
Accounts Payable	900	
Unearned Revenue	3,000	
Notes Payable	10,000	
Interest Payable	1,100	
Salaries Payable	800	
Total Liabilities		$15,800
Shareholders' Equity		
Common Shares	15,000	
Retained Earnings	17,835	
Total Shareholders Equity		32,835
Total Liabilities and Shareholders' Equity		$48,635

Exhibit 4–8

COLLINS CONSULTANTS INC.
Cash Flow Statement
For the Year Ended December 31, 2005

Cash Flow from Operating Activities		
Inflow from Customers*	$32,600	
Outflow for Rent	(3,600)	
Outflow for Salaries	(2,400)	
Outflow for Supplies	(850)	
Net Cash Inflow from Operations		$25,750
Cash Flow from Investing Activities		
Outflow for Loan	(6,000)	
Outflow to Purchase Equipment	(42,000)	
Net Cash Outflow from Investing		(48,000)
Cash Flow from Financing Activities		
Inflow from Issue of Common Shares	15,000	
Inflow from Borrowing	10,000	
Outflow for Dividends	(1,500)	
Net Cash Inflow from Financing		23,500
Net Change in Cash		1,250
Plus: Beginning Cash Balance		0
Ending Cash Balance		$ 1,250

* The sum of cash inflows from Events 4, 5, 7, and 11.

Trial Balance

LO6 Prepare and interpret a trial balance.

As noted earlier, the double-entry system checks on the accuracy of the recording and posting practices through a test of the equality of debits and credits. This test is commonly called a **trial balance**. A trial balance is a list of ledger account titles and their respective balances. The debit and credit balances are arranged in separate columns. Each column is totalled, and the two totals are compared to ensure equality. A failure to attain this equality signals an error in the recording process. Even if the debits balance with the credits, we must still be cautious regarding the level of assurance assigned to the "balance." For example, the trial balance does not reveal errors such as the failure to record an important transaction, misclassifications such as recording debits or credits to the wrong accounts, or counterbalancing errors such as overstating both debit and credit amounts of an entry. It follows that the attainment of equal debits and credits in the trial balance should be viewed as evidence, rather than proof, of accuracy in journalizing and posting transactions.

A trial balance should be prepared whenever the accountant feels it would be useful to test the equality of debits and credits. Some companies prepare a trial balance daily; others may prepare one monthly or quarterly. Exhibit 4–10 is a trial balance of the accounts of CCI after the closing entries have been posted to the ledger. This is often referred to as a **post-closing trial balance**.

Exhibit 4–9 *Closing Entries*

Date	Account Titles	Debit	Credit
	Closing Entries		
Dec. 31	Consulting Revenue	30,400	
	Interest Revenue	360	
	Retained Earnings		30,760
31	Retained Earnings	11,425	
	Salaries Expense		3,200
	Advertising Expense		900
	Interest Expense		1,100
	Amortization Expense		4,000
	Rent Expense		1,500
	Supplies Expense		725
31	Retained Earnings	1,500	
	Dividends		1,500

Exhibit 4–10 *Trial Balance*

Account Titles	Debit	Credit
Cash	$ 1,250	
Accounts Receivable	800	
Supplies	125	
Prepaid Rent	2,100	
Notes Receivable	6,000	
Interest Receivable	360	
Office Equipment	42,000	
Accumulated Amortization		$ 4,000
Accounts Payable		900
Unearned Revenue		3,000
Notes Payable		10,000
Interest Payable		1,100
Salaries Payable		800
Common Shares		15,000
Retained Earnings		17,835
Totals	$52,635	$52,635

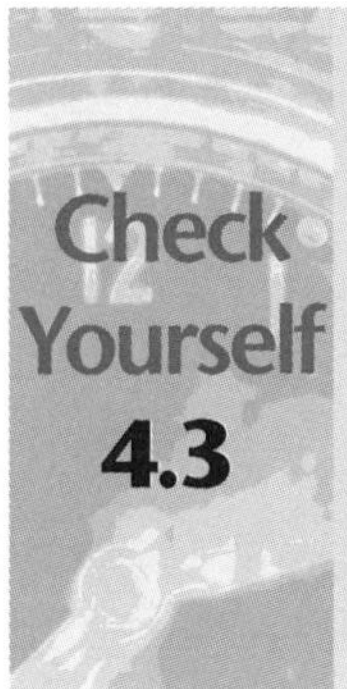

Describe an error that would not cause a trial balance to be out of balance.

Answer Many potential errors would not cause a trial balance to be out of balance, such as debiting or crediting the wrong account. For example, if revenue earned on account were recorded with a debit to Cash instead of Accounts Receivable, total assets would be correct and the totals in the trial balance would equal each other even though the balances in the Cash and Accounts Receivable accounts would be incorrect. Recording the same incorrect amount in both the debit and credit part of an entry also would not cause a trial balance to be out of balance. For example, if $20 of revenue earned on account were recorded as a $200 debit to Accounts Receivable and a $200 credit to Consulting Revenue, the totals in the trial balance would equal each other, but the Accounts Receivable and Consulting Revenue amounts would be incorrect.

answers to the *curious* accountant

Part 1

The process of closing the books and going through a year-end audit is time consuming for a business. Also, it is time spent that does not produce revenue. Thus, companies whose business is highly seasonal often choose "slow" periods to end their fiscal year. The Limited does heavy business during the Christmas season, so it might find December 31 an inconvenient time to close its books. Toward the end of January, business activity is slow, and inventory levels are at their low points. This is a good time to count the inventory and to assess the financial condition of the company. For these reasons, The Limited has chosen to close its books to end its fiscal year at the end of January.

Now that you know why a business like The Limited might choose to end its fiscal year at the end of January, can you think of a reason why Polo Ralph Lauren closes its books at the end of March?

Components of an Annual Report

LO8 Describe the components of an annual report.

Published annual reports, also called *financial reports*, usually are printed in colour on high-quality paper and contain lots of photographs. This is why accountants sometimes refer to them as the company's "glossies." Although this book focuses on financial statements, you should understand that accounting information involves much more than just the financial statements. Annual reports are often 40 or more pages long. The financial statements themselves require only four to six of these pages, so what are all those other pages for?

For the purposes of this course, the annual report of a large company can be divided into the following four major sections: (1) financial statements, (2) notes to the financial statements, (3) management's discussion and analysis, and (4) auditors' report. Earlier chapters introduced the financial statements and the auditors' report, but the bulk of the annual report actually consists of notes and management's discussion and analysis.

Notes to the Financial Statements

Notes to the financial statements help explain the information contained in the financial statements themselves. The need for this additional information will become clearer in future chapters, but for now, keep in mind that companies have to make estimates when performing accounting calculations. They also often have the option of accounting for a given transaction in different ways. Generally accepted accounting principles (GAAP) allow considerable flexibility. The notes explain some of the estimates that were made as well as which of the options available under GAAP were used. It would be foolish, and even dangerous, for a user to try to understand a company's financial statements without reading the notes. To emphasize this point, financial statements often place a statement at the bottom of the pages, such as "the accompanying notes are an integral part of these financial statements."

answers to the *curious* accountant

Part 2

Polo Ralph Lauren sells most of its clothes through retailers. Therefore, it must ship goods weeks before they will eventually be sold by stores such as The Limited. The end of March probably is a relatively slow time of year for Polo Ralph Lauren. The Christmas season has passed and most of the spring clothing probably has been shipped to retailers by the end of March, so this is a good time of year for clothing manufacturers to close their books. Tommy Hilfiger also closes its fiscal year at the end of March.

Management's Discussion and Analysis

Management's discussion and analysis (MD&A) is usually located at the beginning of the annual report. MD&A is the section of the annual report that management uses to explain many different aspects of the company's past performance and future plans. For example, MD&A typically discusses this year's sales compared to those of the past year and explains reasons for the changes. If the company is planning significant acquisitions of assets or other businesses, this information should be included in MD&A. Likewise, plans to dispose of part of the existing business should be discussed. Often, some events included in MD&A are also discussed in the notes.

Role of the Independent Auditor Revisited

The auditors' report was explained in Chapter 2. A well-educated businessperson should be aware that the auditor has a different role and responsibility for different parts of the annual report. Auditors have great responsibility for the financial statements and the notes to those statements. From an auditor's point of view, the notes are a part of the financial statements, which means that information in the notes is audited in the same manner as information in the balance sheet.

Auditors' responsibility for information in MD&A is less than that for the financial statements and notes; however, auditors do have some responsibility for this section of the annual report. Auditors *review* the MD&A section to be sure it does not contain comments that conflict with information in the financial statements. For example, if the current year's net income is down from last year's, management cannot say in MD&A that "earnings continue to grow."

However, MD&A often contains expressions of opinion not found in the financial statements or notes. If current earnings are down relative to last year's earnings, management could say, "We *believe* the decline to be temporary and expect substantial growth in the coming year." Management's opinion cannot be verified, or audited, in the same way as the balance in the Cash account can be.

---

a look back

This chapter introduced the *double-entry accounting system*, which has existed since at least the 1400s and is used by most companies that have formal bookkeeping systems. You should be familiar with the following components of the double-entry system.

1. Business events can be described using debit/credit terminology. *Debits* are used to record increases in asset accounts and decreases in liability and equity accounts. *Credits* are used to record decreases in asset accounts and increases in liability and equity accounts.
2. *T-accounts* are often used to communicate information. The account title is placed at the top of the horizontal bar of the T, and increases and decreases are placed on either side of the vertical bar. Debits are recorded on the left side and credits on the right side of a T-account.
3. To maintain a complete chronological record of all business events, accountants initially record data in journals. The *general journal* recording format is used not only for data entry but also to

communicate information. Each journal entry contains at least one debit and one credit. The entry is recorded in at least two lines with the debit recorded on the top line and the credit on the bottom line. The credit is indented to distinguish it from the debit. The general journal format is illustrated here:

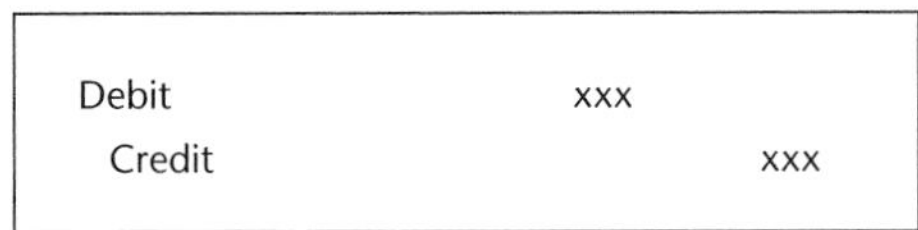

Debit	xxx	
Credit		xxx

4. Information is posted (transferred) from the journals to *ledger* accounts. The ledger accounts provide a means to summarize information for presentation in the financial statements.
5. *Trial balances* are used to check the accuracy of the recording process. Ledger accounts with their associated debit and credit balances are listed in the trial balance. The debit and credit amounts are totalled and compared. An equal amount of debits and credits provides evidence that transactions have been recorded correctly, although errors may still exist. A failure to attain a balance between debits and credits is proof that errors exist.

It is important to remember that the double-entry system is just another way to organize accounting data. No matter how we organize the data, the objective is to convert it into information that is useful for making decisions. Most decisions that are based on accounting data use information obtained from companies' financial statements. Therefore, whether data are organized using the horizontal model, a manual debit/credit system, or a computerized system, it is important that business managers understand how business events affect financial statements and the related ratios.

a look forward

If you think back on the types of businesses discussed in Chapters 1 through 4, you will realize that they are service enterprises. None of them sold a physical product. Obviously, in the real world, many businesses do sell products. The early chapters of this course used service businesses to keep matters relatively simple. Chapter 5 introduces some special accounting issues associated with companies that purchase and sell products. A word of caution is in order. If you do not understand Chapter 5, you cannot possibly understand Chapter 8, so give Chapter 5 careful attention.

SELF-STUDY REVIEW PROBLEM

The following events apply to the first year of operations for Mestro Financial Services Company:

1. Acquired $28,000 cash by issuing common shares on January 1, 2004.
2. Purchased $1,100 of supplies on account.
3. Paid $12,000 cash in advance for a one-year lease on office space.
4. Earned $23,000 of consulting revenue on account.
5. Incurred $16,000 of general operating expenses on account.
6. Collected $20,000 cash from receivables.
7. Paid $13,000 cash on accounts payable.
8. Paid a $1,000 cash dividend to the shareholders.

Information for Adjusting Entries

9. There was $200 of supplies on hand at the end of the accounting period.
10. The one-year lease on the office space was effective beginning on October 1, 2004.
11. There was $1,200 of accrued salaries at the end of 2004.

Required

a. Record the preceding events in ledger T-accounts.
b. Prepare an adjusted trial balance.
c. Prepare an income statement, statement of shareholders' equity, balance sheet, and cash flow statement.
d. Prepare the appropriate closing entries in general journal format.

Solution to Requirement a

MESTRO FINANCIAL SERVICES COMPANY
T-Accounts, 2003

Assets = Liabilities + Equity

Assets

Cash

	Debit		Credit
1.	28,000	3.	12,000
6.	20,000	7.	13,000
		8.	1,000
Bal.	22,000		

Supplies

	Debit		Credit
2.	1,100	9.	900
Bal.	200		

Prepaid Rent

	Debit		Credit
3.	12,000	10.	3,000
Bal.	9,000		

Accounts Receivable

	Debit		Credit
4.	23,000	6.	20,000
Bal.	3,000		

Liabilities

Accounts Payable

	Debit		Credit
7.	13,000	2.	1,100
		5.	16,000
		Bal.	4,100

Salaries Payable

	Debit		Credit
		11.	1,200
		Bal.	1,200

Equity

Common Shares

	Debit		Credit
		1.	28,000
		Bal.	28,000

Consulting Revenue

	Debit		Credit
		4.	23,000

General Operating Expenses

	Debit		Credit
5.	16,000		

Salaries Expense

	Debit		Credit
11.	1,200		

Supplies Expense

	Debit		Credit
9.	900		

Rent Expense

	Debit		Credit
10.	3,000		

Dividends

	Debit		Credit
8.	1,000		

Solution to Requirement b

MESTRO FINANCIAL SERVICES COMPANY
Adjusted Trial Balance
December 31, 2004

Account Titles	Debit	Credit
Cash	$22,000	
Accounts Receivable	3,000	
Supplies	200	
Prepaid Rent	9,000	
Accounts Payable		$ 4,100
Salaries Payable		1,200
Common Shares		28,000
Dividends	1,000	
Consulting Revenue		23,000
General Operating Expenses	16,000	
Salaries Expense	1,200	
Supplies Expense	900	
Rent Expense	3,000	
Totals	$56,300	$56,300

Solution to Requirement c

MESTRO FINANCIAL SERVICES COMPANY
Financial Statements
For 2004

Income Statement		
Consulting Revenue		$23,000
Expenses		
General Operating Expenses	$16,000	
Salaries Expense	1,200	
Supplies Expense	900	
Rent Expense	3,000	
Total Expenses		(21,100)
Net Income		$ 1,900

Statement of Shareholders' Equity		
Beginning Common Shares	$ 0	
Plus: Common Shares Issued	28,000	
Ending Common Shares		$28,000
Beginning Retained Earnings	0	
Plus: Net Income	1,900	
Less: Dividends	(1,000)	
Ending Retained Earnings		900
Total Shareholders' Equity		$28,900

Balance Sheet		
Assets		
Cash	$22,000	
Accounts Receivable	3,000	
Supplies	200	
Prepaid Rent	9,000	
Total Assets		$34,200
Liabilities		
Accounts Payable	$ 4,100	
Salaries Payable	1,200	
Total Liabilities		$ 5,300
Shareholders' Equity		
Common Shares	28,000	
Retained Earnings	900	
Total Shareholders' Equity		28,900
Total Liabilities and Shareholders' Equity		$34,200

Cash Flow Statement		
Cash Flows from Operating Activities		
Inflow from Customers	$20,000	
Outflow for Expenses	(25,000)	
Net Cash Flow from Operating Activities		$(5,000)
Cash Flows from Investing Activities		0
Cash Flows from Financing Activities		
Inflow from Issue of Common Shares	28,000	
Outflow for Dividends	(1,000)	
Net Cash Flow from Financing Activities		27,000
Net Change in Cash		22,000
Plus: Beginning Cash Balance		0
Ending Cash Balance		$22,000

Solution to Requirement d

Date		Account Titles	Debit	Credit
		Closing Entries		
Dec.	31	Consulting Revenue	23,000	
		Retained Earnings		23,000
Dec.	31	Retained Earnings	21,100	
		General Operating Expenses		16,000
		Salaries Expense		1,200
		Supplies Expense		900
		Rent Expense		3,000
Dec.	31	Retained Earnings	1,000	
		Dividends		1,000

KEY TERMS

account balance *132*
asset/expense adjustment *143*
asset/revenue adjustment *141*
books of original entry *148*
chart of accounts *146*
closing entries *149*
contra account *143*
credit *132*
debit *132*
double-entry accounting *132*
fiscal year *131*
general journal *148*
journal *148*
ledger *146*
liability/expense adjustment *142*
liability/revenue adjustment *145*
management's discussion and analysis (MD&A) *154*
notes to the financial statements *153*
post-closing trial balance *152*
posting *148*
source document *148*
special journals *148*
T-account *131*
trial balance *152*

QUESTIONS

1. What are the two basic equality requirements of the double-entry accounting system?
2. Define *debit* and *credit*. How are assets, liabilities, shareholders' equity, retained earnings, revenues, expenses, and dividends affected (increased or decreased) by debits and by credits?
3. How is the balance of an account determined?
4. What are the three primary sources of business assets?
5. What are the three primary ways a business may use assets?
6. Why is an adjusting entry necessary to record amortization expense? What accounts are affected? How are the account balances affected?
7. What is an asset/revenue adjustment? Give an example.
8. What is a liability/expense adjustment? Give an example.
9. Explain and give two examples of an asset/expense adjustment. What accounts are affected in your examples? Are the accounts debited or credited? Do the account balances increase or decrease?
10. Explain and give an example of a liability/revenue adjustment. What accounts are debited or credited in your example? Do the account balances increase or decrease?
11. How does a debit to an expense account ultimately affect retained earnings? Shareholders' equity?
12. What accounts normally have debit balances? What accounts normally have credit balances?
13. What is the primary source of information for preparing the financial statements?
14. What is the purpose of a journal?
15. What is the difference between the *general journal* and special journals?
16. What is a ledger? What is its function in the accounting system?
17. What are the five steps in the recording process?
18. What is the purpose of closing entries?
19. At a minimum, what information is recorded in the general journal?
20. What is the purpose of a trial balance?
21. When should a trial balance be prepared?
22. What does *posting* mean?
23. Where did *debit* and *credit* originate?
24. What type of information is found in the notes to the financial statements?
25. What type of information is found in the MD&A section of the annual report?

EXERCISES

EXERCISE 4–1 *Debit/Credit Rules* L.O. 1, 2

Debbie, Josh, and Deshonda, three accounting students, were discussing the rules of debits and credits. Debbie says that debits increase account balances and credits decrease account balances. Josh says that Debbie is wrong, that credits increase account balances and debits decrease account balances. Deshonda interrupts and declares that they are both correct.

Required
Explain what Deshonda meant and give examples of transactions where debits increase account balances, credits decrease account balances, credits increase account balances, and debits decrease account balances.

EXERCISE 4–2 *Matching Debit and Credit Terminology with Accounts* L.O. 2

Required
Complete the following table by indicating whether a debit or credit is used to increase or decrease the balance of the following accounts. The appropriate debit/credit terminology has been identified for the first account as an example.

Account Category	Used to Increase This Account	Used to Decrease This Account
Cash	Debit	Credit
Notes Payable		
Common Shares		
Equipment		
Other Operating Expense		
Accumulated Amortization		
Dividends		
Service Revenue		
Retained Earnings		
Rent Expense		

EXERCISE 4–3 *Matching Debit and Credit Terminology with Account Titles* L.O. 2

Required
Indicate whether each of the following accounts normally has a debit balance or a credit balance.

a. Cash
b. Common Shares
c. Amortization Expense
d. Accumulated Amortization
e. Notes Payable
f. Unearned Revenue
g. Service Revenue
h. Dividends
i. Land
j. Prepaid Rent

EXERCISE 4–4 *Identifying Increases and Decreases in T-Accounts* L.O. 2, 4

Required
For each of the following T-accounts, indicate the side of the account that should be used to record an increase or decrease in the accounting element.

Assets		=	Liabilities		+	Equity	
Debit	Credit		Debit	Credit		Debit	Credit

Contra Assets	
Debit	Credit

Revenue	
Debit	Credit

Expense	
Debit	Credit

L.O. 2 EXERCISE 4–5 *Applying Debit/Credit Terminology to Accounting Events*

Required

In parallel columns, list the accounts that would be debited and credited for each of the following unrelated transactions:

a. Acquired cash from the issue of common shares.
b. Provided services for cash.
c. Paid cash for salaries expense.
d. Borrowed cash from a local bank.
e. Incurred other operating expense on account.
f. Purchased land for cash.
g. Provided services on account.
h. Recorded accrued interest expense at the end of the accounting period.

L.O. 2, 3 EXERCISE 4–6 *T-Accounts and the Accounting Equation*

Required

Record each of the following Chandler Co. events in T-accounts and then explain how the event affects the accounting equation.

a. Received $10,000 cash by issuing common shares.
b. Purchased supplies for $500 on account.
c. Purchased land for $20,000, paying $5,000 cash and issuing a note payable for the balance.
d. Performed services on account for $4,000.

L.O. 3 EXERCISE 4–7 *Recording Transactions in T-Accounts*

The following events apply to Magnum Parcel Co. for 2006.

1. Received cash of $24,000 from the issue of common shares.
2. Purchased a delivery van for $15,000 cash. The delivery van has a residual value of $3,000 and a three-year useful life.
3. Performed $65,000 of services on account.
4. Paid $24,000 cash for salaries expense.
5. Incurred $5,000 of other operating expenses on account.
6. Collected $47,000 of accounts receivable.
7. Performed $6,200 of services for cash.
8. Paid $3,400 of the accounts payable.
9. Paid a $3,000 dividend to the shareholders.
10. Recorded amortization expense for the year on the delivery van.

Required

a. Record these events in the appropriate T-accounts and determine the ending balance in each account.
b. Determine the amount of total assets at the end of 2006.
c. Determine the amount of net income for 2006.

L.O. 2 EXERCISE 4–8 *Debit/Credit Terminology*

Required

For each of the following independent events, identify the account that would be debited and the account that would be credited. The accounts for the first event are identified as an example.

Event	Account Debited	Account Credited
a	Cash	Common Shares

a. Received cash by issuing common shares.
b. Provided services on account.
c. Paid cash for operating expenses.

d. Received cash for services to be performed in the future.
e. Recognized amortization expense.
f. Paid salaries payable.
g. Repaid principal balance on note payable.
h. Recognized revenue for services completed; collected the cash in Event d.
i. Paid accounts payable.
j. Received cash in payment of accounts receivable.
k. Purchased office equipment with cash.
l. Recognized accrued interest expense.
m. Recognized accrued interest revenue.
n. Paid cash dividends to the shareholders.
o. Purchased supplies on account.

EXERCISE 4–9 *Identifying Transaction Type, Its Effect on the Accounting Equation, and Whether the Effect Is Recorded with a Debit or Credit* L.O. 1, 2

Required

Identify whether each of the following transactions is an asset source (AS), asset use (AU), asset exchange (AE), or claims exchange (CE). Also explain how each event affects the accounting equation by placing a + for *increase*, − for *decrease*, and NA for *not affected* under each of the components of the accounting equation. Finally, indicate whether the effect requires a debit or credit entry. The first event is recorded as an example.

						Equity		
Event	Type of Event	Assets	=	Liabilities	+	Common Shares	+	Retained Earnings
a	AS	+ Debit		NA		NA		+ Credit

a. Provided services on account.
b. Purchased land by issuing a note.
c. Paid interest payable.
d. Borrowed cash by issuing a note.
e. Received cash in payment of accounts receivable.
f. Repaid principal balance on note payable.
g. Paid cash in advance for one-year's rent.
h. Received cash for services to be performed in the future.
i. Recognized accrued interest expense.
j. Incurred other operating expense on account.
k. Paid salaries payable.
l. Recognized revenue for services completed; cash collected previously.
m. Recognized accrued interest revenue.
n. Paid a cash dividend to the shareholders.
o. Recognized amortization expense on the equipment.

EXERCISE 4–10 *Recording Events in the General Journal* L.O. 7

Required

Record each of the following transactions in general journal form.

a. Received $5,000 cash for services to be performed at a later date.
b. Purchased supplies for $900 cash.
c. Performed $16,000 of services on account.
d. Purchased equipment that cost $36,000 by paying $8,000 cash and issuing a $28,000 note for the balance.
e. Charged $1,700 repairs made on equipment on account.
f. Sold land that cost $18,000 for $21,500.
g. Collected $12,200 cash on accounts receivable.

h. Paid $800 on accounts payable.
i. Paid $5,400 cash in advance for an insurance policy on the equipment.
j. Recorded accrued interest expense of $1,800.
k. Recorded $6,000 amortization expense on the equipment.
l. Recorded the adjusting entry to recognize $4,800 of insurance expense.

L.O. 6 EXERCISE 4–11 *Preparing a Trial Balance*

Required
On December 31, 2005, Huang Company had the following account balances in its general ledger. Use this information to prepare a trial balance.

Account	Balance
Cash	$30,000
Service Revenue	63,000
Dividends	5,000
Amortization Expense	4,500
Prepaid Insurance	5,400
Land	12,500
Rent Expense	18,000
Accounts Payable	4,000
Common Shares	15,000
Salaries Expense	11,000
Office Supplies	1,800
Advertising Expense	1,500
Retained Earnings, Jan. 1, 2005	11,200
Unearned Revenue	22,000
Office Equipment	25,000
Accounts Receivable	8,500
Accumulated Amortization	8,000

L.O. 5, 7 EXERCISE 4–12 *Preparing Closing Entries*

The following financial information was taken from the books of Refresh Day Spa.

Partial List of Account Balances as of December 31, 2008	
Accounts Receivable	$28,000
Accounts Payable	7,500
Advertising Expense	2,500
Accumulated Amortization	12,500
Cash	18,300
Term Deposit	22,000
Common Shares	20,000
Amortization Expense	4,800
Dividends	2,000
Equipment	30,000
Interest Receivable	400
Interest Revenue	1,800
Notes Payable	10,000
Prepaid Rent	3,200
Rent Expense	9,600
Retained Earnings	6,800
Salaries Expense	26,000
Salaries Payable	5,000
Service Revenue	85,500
Supplies	400
Supplies Expense	1,900

Required

a. Prepare the necessary closing entries at December 31, 2008, for Refresh Day Spa.
b. What is the balance in the Retained Earnings account after the closing entries are posted?

EXERCISE 4–13 *Recording Events in T-Accounts and Preparing an Adjusted Trial Balance* L.O. 3, 6

The following events apply to Custom Computer Services:

1. Received $20,000 cash from the issue of common shares.
2. Earned $20,000 of revenue on account.
3. Incurred $12,500 of operating expenses on account.
4. Borrowed $16,000 from a local bank.
5. Paid $4,000 cash to purchase office equipment.
6. Collected $18,000 of cash from accounts receivable.
7. Received an $8,200 cash advance for services to be provided in the future.
8. Purchased $800 of supplies on account.
9. Made an $8,000 payment on accounts payable.
10. Paid a $1,000 cash dividend to the shareholders.
11. Recognized $600 of supplies expense.
12. Recognized $4,000 of revenue for services provided to the customer in Event 7.
13. Recorded accrued interest expense of $1,500.
14. Recognized $1,200 of amortization expense.

Required

a. Record the events in T-accounts and determine the ending account balances.
b. Test the equality of the debit and credit balances of the T-accounts by preparing an adjusted trial balance.

EXERCISE 4–14 *Determining the Effect of Errors on the Trial Balance* L.O. 6

Required

Explain how each of the following posting errors affects a trial balance. State whether the trial balance will be out of balance because of the posting error, and indicate which side of the trial balance will have a higher amount after each independent entry is posted. If the posting error does not affect the equality of debits and credits shown in the trial balance, state that the error will not cause an inequality and explain why.

a. The collection of $800 of accounts receivable was posted to Accounts Receivable twice.
b. An $1,800 credit to Accounts Payable was posted as a credit to Cash.
c. A $900 credit to Notes Payable was not posted.
d. A $400 debit to Cash was posted as a $4,000 debit.
e. A $1,500 debit to Prepaid Rent was debited to Rent Expense.

EXERCISE 4–15 *Recording Events in the General Journal, Posting to T-Accounts, and Preparing Closing Entries* L.O. 3, 5, 7

At the beginning of 2005, Advanced Lawn Care had the following balances in its accounts:

Account	Balance
Cash	$15,000
Accounts Receivable	9,500
Accounts Payable	6,200
Common Shares	12,000
Retained Earnings	6,300

The following events apply to Advanced for 2005:

1. Provided $80,000 of services on account.
2. Incurred $5,600 of other operating expenses on account.
3. Collected $82,000 of accounts receivable.
4. Paid $42,000 cash for salaries expense.

5. Paid $6,500 cash as a partial payment on accounts payable.
6. Paid a $5,000 cash dividend to the shareholders.

Required

a. Record these events in a general journal.
b. Open T-accounts, and post the beginning balances and the preceding transactions to the appropriate accounts. Determine the balance of each account.
c. Record the beginning balances and the events in a horizontal statements model such as the following one:

Assets			=	Liab.	+	Equity			Rev. − Exp. = Net Inc.	Cash Flow Statement
Cash	+	Accts. Rec.	=	Accts. Pay.	+	Common Shares	+	Ret. Earn.		

d. Record the closing entries in the general journal and post them to the T-accounts. What is the amount of net income for the year?
e. What is the amount of *change* in retained earnings for the year? Is the change in retained earnings different from the amount of net income? If so, why?

L.O. 3, 5 EXERCISE 4–16 *Recording Receivables and Identifying Their Effect on Financial Statements*

Hubbard Company performed services on account for $45,000 in 2006, its first year of operations. Hubbard collected $32,000 cash from accounts receivable during 2006 and the remaining $13,000 in cash during 2007.

Required

a. Record the 2006 transactions in T-accounts.
b. Record the 2006 transactions in a horizontal statements model like the following one:

Assets			=	Liab.	+	Equity	Rev. − Exp. = Net Inc.	Cash Flow Statement
Cash	+	Accts. Rec.	=	NA	+	Ret. Earn.		

c. Determine the amount of revenue Hubbard would report on the 2006 income statement.
d. Determine the amount of cash flow from operating activities Hubbard would report for 2006.
e. Open a T-account for Retained Earnings, and close the 2006 Service Revenue account to the Retained Earnings account.
f. Record the 2007 cash collection in the appropriate T-accounts.
g. Record the 2007 transaction in a horizontal statements model like the one shown in Requirement *b*.
h. Assuming no other transactions occur in 2007, determine the amount of net income and the net cash flow from operating activities for 2007.

L.O. 3–6 EXERCISE 4–17 *Recording Supplies and Identifying Their Effect on Financial Statements*

Maria Cortez started and operated a small family consulting firm in 2005. The firm was affected by two events: (1) Cortez provided $12,000 of services on account, and (2) she purchased $2,000 of supplies on account. There were $400 of supplies on hand as of December 31, 2005.

Required

a. Open T-accounts and record the two transactions in the accounts.
b. Record the required year-end adjusting entry to reflect the use of supplies.
c. Record the above transactions in a horizontal statements model like the following one:

Assets			=	Liab.	+	Equity	Rev. − Exp. = Net Inc.	Cash Flow Statement
Accts. Rec.	+	Supp.	=	Accts. Pay.	+	Ret. Earn.		

d. Explain why the amount of net income and the net cash flow from operating activities differ.
e. Record and post the required closing entries, and prepare a post-closing trial balance.

EXERCISE 4–18 *Recording Prepaids and Identifying Their Effect on Financial Statements* L.O. 4, 7

Sudbury Mining began operations by issuing common shares for $70,000. The company paid $54,000 cash in advance for a one-year contract to lease machinery for the business. The lease agreement was signed on March 1, 2005, and was effective immediately. Sudbury Mining earned $75,000 of cash revenue in 2005.

Required

a. Record the March 1 cash payment in general journal format.
b. Record in general journal format the asset/expense adjustment required as of December 31, 2005.
c. Record all 2005 events in a horizontal statements model like the following one:

Assets			=	Liab.	+	Equity	Rev. − Exp. = Net Inc.	Cash Flow Statement
Cash	+	PrPd. Rent				Ret. Earn.		

d. What amount of net income would Sudbury Mining report on the 2005 income statement? What is the amount of net cash flow from operating activities for 2005?
e. Determine the amount of prepaid rent Sudbury Mining would report on the December 31, 2005, balance sheet.

EXERCISE 4–19 *Recording Accrued Salaries and Identifying Their Effect on Financial Statements* L.O. 4, 7

On December 31, 2008, Big Ben Company had accrued salaries of $6,500.

Required

a. Record in general journal format the expense/liability adjustment required as of December 31, 2008.
b. Determine the amount of net income Big Ben would report on the 2008 income statement, assuming that Big Ben earns $12,000 of cash revenue. What is the amount of net cash flow from operating activities for 2008?
c. What amount of Salaries Payable liability would Big Ben report on the December 31, 2008, balance sheet?

EXERCISE 4–20 *Recording Amortization and Identifying Its Effect on Financial Statements* L.O. 3, 4

On January 1, 2007, Swan bought a computer for $28,000 cash. The computer had a useful life of four years and a residual value of $4,000.

Required

a. Record in T-accounts Swan's purchase of the computer.
b. Record in T-accounts the asset/expense adjustment required on December 31, 2007.
c. Determine the net book value of the computer Swan would report on the December 31, 2007, balance sheet.
d. Determine the amount of net income Swan would report on the 2007 income statement, assuming that Swan earned $12,000 of cash revenue in 2007.
e. What is the amount of net cash flow from operating activities for 2007?
f. What amount of amortization expense would Swan report on the 2008 income statement?
g. Determine the net book value of the computer Swan would report on the December 31, 2008, balance sheet.

EXERCISE 4–21 *Recording a Note Payable and Identifying Its Effect on Financial Statements* L.O. 3, 4

On May 1, 2005, Brody Company borrowed $80,000 from a local bank. The note had a 9 percent annual interest rate and a one-year term to maturity.

Required

a. Identify the transaction type (asset source, use, or exchange or claims exchange), and record in T-accounts the entries for the financing event on May 1, 2005.
b. Identify the transaction type, and record in T-accounts the liability/expense adjustment as of December 31, 2005.
c. Determine the amount of net income on the 2005 income statement, assuming Brody Company earned $25,000 of cash revenue.

d. What is the amount of net cash flow from operating activities for 2005?
e. Determine the total liabilities on the December 31, 2005, balance sheet.
f. Record (1) the 2006 accrual of interest and (2) the cash payment of principal and interest on May 1, 2006.
g. Are the May 1, 2006, transactions asset source, asset use, asset exchange, or claims exchange transactions?

L.O. 3, 4 EXERCISE 4–22 *Recording Unearned Revenue and Identifying Its Effect on Financial Statements*

Shaw received a $72,000 cash advance payment on March 1, 2005, for legal services to be performed in the future. Services were to be provided for a one-year term beginning March 1, 2005.

Required

a. Record the March 1 cash receipt in T-accounts.
b. Record in T-accounts the liability/revenue adjustment required as of December 31, 2005.
c. Record the preceding transaction and related adjustment in a horizontal statements model like the following one:

Assets	=	Liab.	+	Equity	Rev.	−	Exp.	=	Net Inc.	Cash Flow Statement

d. Determine the amount of net income on the 2005 income statement. What is the amount of net cash flow from operating activities for 2005?
e. What amount of Unearned Revenue liability would Shaw report on the December 31, 2005, balance sheet?

L.O. 3 EXERCISE 4–23 *Using a T-Account to Determine Cash Flow from Operating Activities*

Baird, Inc., began the accounting period with a $57,000 debit balance in its Accounts Receivable account. During the accounting period, Baird earned revenue on account of $126,000. The ending accounts receivable balance was $49,000.

Required

Based on this information alone, determine the amount of cash inflow from operating activities during the accounting period. (*Hint*: Use a T-account for Accounts Receivable. Enter the debits and credits for the given events, and solve for the missing amount.)

L.O. 3 EXERCISE 4–24 *Using a T-Account to Determine Cash Flow from Operating Activities*

Bell Company began the accounting period with a $20,000 credit balance in its Accounts Payable account. During the accounting period, Bell incurred expenses on account of $75,000. The ending Accounts Payable balance was $22,000.

Required

Based on this information, determine the amount of cash outflow for expenses during the accounting period. (*Hint*: Use a T-account for Accounts Payable. Enter the debits and credits for the given events, and solve for the missing amount.)

PROBLEMS—SERIES A

L.O. 2 PROBLEM 4–1A *Identifying Debit and Credit Balances*

Required

Indicate whether each of the following accounts normally has a debit or credit balance.

a. Supplies Expense
b. Prepaid Rent
c. Accumulated Amortization
d. Equipment
e. Interest Payable
f. Service Revenue
g. Supplies
h. Accounts Payable
i. Amortization Expense
j. Unearned Revenue
k. Retained Earnings
l. Prepaid Insurance

m. Truck
n. Operating Expense
o. Dividends
p. Interest Receivable
q. Land
r. Notes Payable
s. Salaries Expense
t. Term Deposit
u. Interest Revenue
v. Rent Expense
w. Common Shares
x. Cash
y. Salaries Payable
z. Accounts Receivable
aa. Insurance Expense

PROBLEM 4–2A *Transaction Type and Debit/Credit Terminology* L.O. 2

The following events apply to Huff Enterprises.

1. Acquired $20,000 cash from the issue of common shares.
2. Paid salaries to employees, $3,000 cash.
3. Collected $18,400 cash for services to be performed in the future.
4. Paid cash for utilities, $600.
5. Recognized $18,000 of revenue on account.
6. Purchased equipment costing $100,000 by paying cash of $20,000 and borrowing the balance from a local bank by issuing a four-year note.
7. Paid a $3,000 cash dividend to the shareholders.
8. Purchased $1,500 of supplies on account.
9. Received $12,000 cash for services rendered.
10. Paid cash to rent office space for the next 12 months, $13,200.
11. Made a $10,000 principal payment on the bank note.
12. Paid cash of $10,000 for other operating expenses.
13. Paid creditor on account payable, $1,500.
14. Paid cash to purchase office furniture, $2,000.
15. Recognized $20,000 of amortization expense.
16. Recognized $8,800 of rent expense that had been paid in cash in a prior transaction (see Event 10).
17. Recognized $12,200 of revenue for services performed for which cash had been previously collected (see Event 3).
18. Recognized $4,000 of accrued interest expense.

Required

Identify each event as asset source (AS), asset use (AU), asset exchange (AE), or claims exchange (CE). Also identify the account to be debited and the account to be credited when the transaction is recorded. The first event is recorded as an example.

Event No.	Type of Event	Account Debited	Account Credited
1	AS	Cash	Common Shares

PROBLEM 4–3A *Recording Adjusting Entries in General Journal Format* L.O. 4, 7

Required

Each of the following independent events requires a year-end adjusting entry. Record each event and the related adjusting entry in general journal format. The first event is recorded as an example. Assume a December 31 closing date.

Date		Account Titles	Debit	Credit
Oct.	1	Prepaid Rent	3,500	
		Cash		3,500
Dec.	31	Rent Expense	875	
		Prepaid Rent		875

a. Paid $3,500 cash in advance on October 1 for a one-year lease on office space.
b. Borrowed $60,000 cash by issuing a note to a local bank on April 1. The note had a one-year term and a 7 percent annual rate of interest.

c. Paid $31,000 cash to purchase equipment on October 1. The equipment was expected to have a five-year useful life and a $5,000 residual value. Amortization is computed on a straight-line basis.
d. Invested $12,500 cash in a term deposit that paid 4 percent interest annually. The term deposit was acquired on April 1 and had a one-year term to maturity.
e. Purchased $2,400 of supplies on account on June 15. At year end, $250 of supplies remained on hand.
f. Received an $8,100 cash advance on July 1 for a contract to provide services for one year.
g. Paid $2,400 cash in advance on March 1 for a one-year insurance policy.

L.O. 1 PROBLEM 4–4A *One Complete Accounting Cycle*

The following events apply to Travel Company's first year of operations:

1. Acquired $12,500 cash from the issue of common shares on January 1, 2005.
2. Purchased $500 of supplies on account.
3. Paid $3,400 cash in advance for a one-year lease on office space.
4. Earned $16,000 of revenue on account.
5. Incurred $10,200 of other operating expenses on account.
6. Collected $14,500 cash from accounts receivable.
7. Paid $8,000 cash on accounts payable.
8. Paid a $1,200 cash dividend to the shareholders.

Information for Adjusting Entries

9. There was $110 of supplies on hand at the end of the accounting period.
10. The lease on the office space covered a one-year period beginning October 1.
11. There was $1,400 of accrued salaries at the end of the period.

Required

a. Record these transactions in general journal form.
b. Post the transaction data from the journal to ledger T-accounts.
c. Prepare an adjusted trial balance.
d. Prepare an income statement, statement of shareholders' equity, a balance sheet, and a cash flow statement.
e. Close the nominal accounts (Revenue, Expense, and Dividends) to Retained Earnings.
f. Post the closing entries to the T-accounts, and prepare a post-closing trial balance.

L.O. 3–7 PROBLEM 4–5A *Two Complete Accounting Cycles*

Northeast Welding experienced the following events during 2007:

1. Started operations by acquiring $20,000 of cash from the issue of common shares.
2. Paid $3,000 cash in advance for rent during the period from February 1, 2007, to February 1, 2008.
3. Received $2,400 cash in advance for services to be performed evenly over the period from September 1, 2007, to September 1, 2008.
4. Performed services for customers on account for $38,500.
5. Incurred operating expenses on account of $17,000.
6. Collected $32,500 cash from accounts receivable.
7. Paid $12,000 cash for salaries expense.
8. Paid $14,500 cash as a partial payment on accounts payable.

Adjusting Entries

9. Made the adjusting entry for the expired rent. (See Event 2.)
10. Recognized revenue for services performed in accordance with Event 3.
11. Recorded $1,600 of accrued salaries at the end of 2007.

Events for 2008

1. Paid $1,600 cash for the salaries accrued at the end of the previous year.
2. Performed services for cash, $20,100.
3. Borrowed $15,000 cash from the local bank by issuing a note.
4. Paid $12,500 cash to purchase land.
5. Paid $3,600 cash in advance for rent during the period from February 1, 2008, to February 1, 2009.

6. Performed services for customers on account for $64,000.
7. Incurred operating expenses on account of $35,200.
8. Collected $42,500 cash from accounts receivable.
9. Paid $32,000 cash as a partial payment on accounts payable.
10. Paid $28,000 cash for salaries expense.
11. Paid a $5,000 cash dividend to the shareholders.

Adjusting Entries

12. Recognized revenue for services performed in accordance with Event 3 in 2007.
13. Made the adjusting entry for the expired rent. (*Hint:* Part of the rent was paid in 2007.)
14. Recorded accrued interest. The note was issued on March 1, 2008, for a one-year term and had an interest rate of 9 percent (see Event 3).

Required

a. Record the events and adjusting entries for 2007 in general journal form.
b. Post the events to T-accounts.
c. Prepare an adjusted trial balance.
d. Prepare an income statement, statement of shareholders' equity, balance sheet, and cash flow statement for 2007.
e. Record the entries to close the nominal accounts to Retained Earnings in the general journal and post to the T-accounts.
f. Prepare a post-closing trial balance for December 31, 2007.
g. Repeat Requirements *a* through *f* for 2008.

PROBLEM 4–6A *Identifying Accounting Events from Journal Entries*

L.O. 7

Required

The following information is from the records of Bennett's Design Group. Write a brief description of the accounting event represented in each of the general journal entries.

Date		Account Titles	Debit	Credit
Jan.	1	Cash	12,500	
		Common Shares		12,500
Feb.	15	Cash	13,000	
		Unearned Revenue		13,000
Mar.	10	Supplies	1,550	
		Accounts Payable		1,550
Apr.	1	Office Equipment	17,000	
		Cash		4,000
		Note Payable		13,000
May	1	Prepaid Rent	10,200	
		Cash		10,200
	20	Accounts Receivable	18,400	
		Commission Revenue		18,400
June	15	Salaries Expense	6,100	
		Cash		6,100
Aug.	28	Cash	9,300	
		Commission Revenue		9,300
	30	Dividends	3,000	
		Cash		3,000
Sept.	19	Cash	16,000	
		Accounts Receivable		16,000
Oct.	31	Property Tax Expense	3,000	
		Cash		3,000
Dec.	31	Amortization Expense	2,700	
		Accumulated Amortization		2,700
	31	Supplies Expense	2,025	
		Supplies		2,025
	31	Rent Expense	6,400	
		Prepaid Rent		6,400
	31	Unearned Revenue	8,500	
		Commission Revenue		8,500

L.O. 3–6 PROBLEM 4–7A *Recording Events in Statements Model and T-Accounts and Preparing a Trial Balance*

The following accounting events apply to Chen Enterprises for the year 2006:

Asset Source Transactions

1. Began operations when the business acquired $10,000 cash from the issue of common shares.
2. Purchased $3,250 of equipment on account.
3. Performed services and collected cash of $600.
4. Collected $3,000 of cash in advance for services to be provided over the next 12 months.
5. Provided $6,500 of services on account.
6. Purchased supplies of $650 on account.

Asset Exchange Transactions

7. Purchased $5,000 of equipment for cash.
8. Collected $5,500 of cash from accounts receivable.
9. Loaned $500 to Ted Marples, who issued a 12-month, 9 percent note.
10. Purchased $400 of supplies with cash.
11. Purchased a $2,400 term deposit that had a six-month term and paid 5 percent annual interest.

Asset Use Transactions

12. Paid $2,500 cash for salaries of employees.
13. Paid a cash dividend of $1,500 to the shareholders.
14. Paid for the equipment that had been purchased on account (see Event 2).
15. Paid $650 for supplies that had been purchased on account.

Claims Exchange Transactions

16. Placed an advertisement in the local newspaper for $125 and agreed to pay for the ad later.
17. Incurred utilities expense of $100 on account.

Adjusting Entries

18. Recognized $2,100 of revenue for performing services. The collection of cash for these services occurred in a prior transaction. (See Event 4.)
19. Recorded $40 of interest revenue that had accrued on the note receivable from Marples (see Event 9).
20. Recorded $45 of interest revenue that had accrued on the term deposit (see Event 11).
21. Recorded $450 of accrued salary expense at the end of 2006.
22. Recognized $750 of amortization on the equipment (see Events 2 and 7).
23. Recorded supplies expense. Had $75 of supplies on hand at the end of the accounting period.

Required

a. Use a horizontal statements model to show how each event affects the balance sheet, income statement, and cash flow statement. Indicate whether the event increases (+), decreases (−), or does not affect (NA) each element of the financial statements. Also, in the Cash Flow Statement column, use the letters OA to designate operating activity, IA for investing activity, and FA for financing activity. The first event is recorded as an example.

Assets	=	Liab.	+	Equity	Rev.	−	Exp.	=	Net Inc.	Cash Flow Statement	
+		NA		+	NA		NA		NA	+	FA

b. Record each of the preceding transactions in T-accounts and determine the balance of each account.

c. Prepare an adjusted trial balance.

PROBLEM 4–8A *Effect of Journal Entries on Financial Statements* L.O. 7

Entry No.	Account Titles	Debit	Credit
1	Cash	XXX	
	Common Shares		XXX
2	Accounts Receivable	XXX	
	Commission Revenue		XXX
3	Salaries Expense	XXX	
	Cash		XXX
4	Cash	XXX	
	Commission Revenue		XXX
5	Dividends	XXX	
	Cash		XXX
6	Cash	XXX	
	Unearned Revenue		XXX
7	Supplies	XXX	
	Accounts Payable		XXX
8	Office Equipment	XXX	
	Cash		XXX
	Note Payable		XXX
9	Prepaid Rent	XXX	
	Cash		XXX
10	Cash	XXX	
	Accounts Receivable		XXX
11	Property Tax Expense	XXX	
	Cash		XXX
12	Amortization Expense	XXX	
	Accumulated Amortization		XXX
13	Supplies Expense	XXX	
	Supplies		XXX
14	Rent Expense	XXX	
	Prepaid Rent		XXX
15	Unearned Revenue	XXX	
	Commission Revenue		XXX

Required

The preceding 15 different accounting events are presented in general journal format. Use a horizontal statements model to show how each event affects the balance sheet, income statement, and cash flow statement. Indicate whether the event increases (+), decreases (−), or does not affect (NA) each element of the financial statements. Also, in the Cash Flow Statement column, use the letters OA to designate operating activity, IA for investing activity, and FA for financing activity. The first event is recorded as an example.

Assets	=	Liab.	+	Equity	Rev.	−	Exp.	=	Net Inc.	Cash Flow Statement	
+		NA		+	NA		NA		NA	+	FA

PROBLEM 4–9A *Effect of Errors on the Trial Balance* L.O. 6

Required

Consider each of the following errors independently (assume that each is the only error that has occurred). Complete the following table. The first error is recorded as an example.

Error	Is the Trial Balance Out of Balance?	By What Amount?	Which Is Larger, Total Debits or Credits?
a	yes	90	debit

a. A credit of $430 to Accounts Payable was recorded as $340.
b. A credit of $620 to Accounts Receivable was not recorded.

c. A debit of $700 to Rent Expense was recorded as a debit of $700 to Salaries Expense.
d. An entry requiring a debit of $325 to Cash and a credit of $325 to Accounts Receivable was not posted to the ledger accounts.
e. A credit of $2,000 to Prepaid Insurance was recorded as a debit of $2,000 to Prepaid Insurance.
f. A debit of $200 to Cash was recorded as a credit of $200 to Cash.

L.O. 6 PROBLEM 4–10A *Effect of Errors on the Trial Balance*

The following trial balance was prepared from the ledger accounts of Forbes, Inc.:

FORBES, INC.
Trial Balance
May 31, 2006

Account	Title Debit	Credit
Cash	$ 1,100	
Accounts Receivable	1,770	
Supplies	420	
Prepaid Insurance	2,400	
Office Equipment	10,000	
Accounts Payable		$ 1,500
Notes Payable		1,000
Common Shares		1,800
Retained Earnings		4,000
Service Revenue		19,600
Rent Expense	3,600	
Salaries Expense	9,000	
Operating Expense	2,500	
Dividends	400	
Totals	$31,190	$27,900

The accountant for Forbes, Inc., made the following errors during May 2006:

1. The cash purchase of a $2,110 typewriter was recorded as a $2,200 debit to Office Equipment and a $2,110 credit to Cash.
2. An $800 purchase of supplies on account was properly recorded as a debit to the Supplies account but was incorrectly recorded as a credit to the Cash account.
3. The company provided services valued at $7,500 to a customer. The accountant recorded the transaction in the proper accounts but in the incorrect amount of $17,500.
4. A $500 cash receipt for a payment on an account receivable was not recorded.
5. A $300 cash payment of an account payable was not recorded.
6. The May utility bill, which amounted to $600 on account, was not recorded.

Required

a. Identify the errors that would cause a difference in the total amounts of debits and credits that would appear in a trial balance. Indicate whether the Debit or Credit column would be larger as a result of the error.
b. Indicate whether each of the preceding errors would overstate, understate, or have no effect on the amount of total assets, liabilities, and equity. Your answer should take the following form:

Event No.	Assets	=	Liabilities	+	Equity
1	Overstate		No effect		No effect

c. Prepare a corrected trial balance.

PROBLEM 4–11A *Comprehensive Problem: Single Cycle*

L.O. 3–7

The following transactions pertain to Atwood Corporation for 2005:

Jan.	1	Began operations when the business acquired $60,000 cash from the issue of common shares.
Mar.	1	Paid rent for office space for two years, $19,200 cash.
Apr.	1	Borrowed $40,000 cash from a local bank. The note issued had a 10 percent annual rate of interest and matured in one year.
	14	Purchased $600 of supplies on account.
June	1	Paid $30,000 cash for a computer system. The computer system had a five-year useful life and no residual value.
	30	Received $36,000 cash in advance for services to be provided over the next year.
July	5	Paid $400 of the accounts payable from April 14.
Aug.	1	Billed a customer $6,600 for services provided during July.
	8	Completed a job and received $4,000 cash for services rendered.
Sept.	1	Paid employee salaries of $24,000 cash.
	9	Received $5,000 cash from accounts receivable.
Oct.	5	Billed customers $18,400 for services rendered on account.
Nov.	2	Paid an $800 cash dividend to the shareholders.
Dec.	31	Adjusted records to recognize the services provided on the contract of June 30.
	31	Recorded the accrued interest on the note to a local bank. (See April 1.)
	31	Recorded amortization on the computer system used in the business. (See June 1.)
	31	Recorded $1,800 of accrued salaries as of December 31.
	31	Recorded the rent expense for the year. (See March 1.)
	31	Physically counted supplies; $50 was on hand at the end of the period.

Required

a. Record the preceding transactions in the general journal.
b. Post the transactions to T-accounts and calculate the account balances.
c. Prepare an adjusted trial balance.
d. Prepare the income statement, statement of shareholders' equity, balance sheet, and cash flow statement.
e. Prepare the closing entries at December 31.
f. Prepare a trial balance after the closing entries are posted.

PROBLEM 4–12A *Comprehensive Problem: Two Cycles*

L.O. 3–7

This is a two-cycle problem. The second cycle is in Problem 4–12B. The first cycle *can* be completed without referring to the second cycle.

Sam and Barb organized a rental shop that began operations on April 1, 2007. Hawkins Rentals completed the following transactions during the first month of operation:

April	1	Acquired $40,000 to establish the company, $20,000 from the issue of common shares, and $20,000 from issuing a bank note. The note had a five-year term and a 9 percent annual interest rate. Interest was payable in cash on March 31 of each year.
	1	Paid $3,600 in advance rent for a one-year lease on office space.
	1	Paid $30,000 to purchase wedding décor. The décor was expected to have a useful life of five years and a residual value of $3,000.
	6	Purchased supplies for $220 cash.
	9	Received $500 cash as an advance payment from Donna Oreen to reserve wedding décor to be used in May.
	10	Recorded rentals to customers. Cash receipts were $850, and invoices for rentals on account were $1,200.
	15	Paid $960 cash for employee salaries.
	16	Collected $450 from accounts receivable.
	23	Received monthly utility bills amounting to $233. The bills will be paid during May.
	25	Paid advertising expense for advertisements run during April, $240.
	30	Recorded rentals to customers. Cash receipts were $1,150 and invoices for rentals on account were $1,600.
	30	Paid $960 cash for employee salaries.

Additional Data as of April 30

1. Counted the supplies inventory. Had $80 of supplies on hand.
2. Make adjustments for interest expense, rent expense, and amortization expense.

Required

a. Record the transactions for April in general journal format.
b. Open a general ledger, using T-accounts, and post the general journal entries to the ledger.
c. Prepare an unadjusted trial balance.
d. Record and post the appropriate adjusting entries.
e. Prepare an adjusted trial balance.
f. Prepare an income statement, statement of shareholders' equity, balance sheet, and cash flow statement.
g. Record and post the closing entries.
h. Prepare a post-closing trial balance.

PROBLEMS—SERIES B

L.O. 2 PROBLEM 4–1B *Identifying Debit and Credit Balances*

Required

Tell whether each of the following accounts normally has a debit or credit balance.

a. Common Shares
b. Retained Earnings
c. Term Deposit
d. Interest Expense
e. Accounts Receivable
f. Interest Revenue
g. Insurance Expense
h. Interest Payable
i. Cash
j. Dividends
k. Unearned Revenue
l. Operating Expense
m. Accumulated Amortization
n. Accounts Payable
o. Office Equipment
p. Amortization Expense
q. Service Revenue
r. Notes Payable
s. Notes Receivable
t. Supplies
u. Utilities Payable
v. Consulting Revenue
w. Interest Receivable
x. Supplies Expense
y. Salaries Expense
z. Equipment
aa. Salaries Payable
bb. Land
cc. Prepaid Insurance

PROBLEM 4–2B *Transaction Type and Debit/Credit Terminology*

The following events apply to Tank Enterprises:

1. Acquired $25,000 cash from the issue of common shares.
2. Paid salaries to employees, $1,750 cash.
3. Collected $8,100 cash for services to be performed in the future.
4. Paid cash for utilities, $402.
5. Recognized $22,500 of revenue on account.
6. Purchased equipment costing $15,000 by paying cash of $3,000 and borrowing the balance from a local bank by issuing a four-year note.
7. Paid a $1,250 cash dividend to the shareholders.
8. Purchased $1,600 of supplies on account.
9. Received $6,250 cash for services rendered.
10. Paid cash to rent office space for the next 12 months, $6,000.
11. Made a $3,750 principal payment on the bank note.
12. Paid cash of $8,750 for other operating expenses.
13. Paid creditor on account payable, $876.
14. Paid cash to purchase office furniture, $5,000.

15. Recognized $3,750 of amortization expense.
16. Recognized $1,500 of rent expense. Cash had been paid in a prior transaction (see Event 10).
17. Recognized $2,500 of revenue for services performed. Cash had been previously collected (see Event 3).
18. Recognized $376 of accrued interest expense.

Required

Identify each event as asset source (AS), asset use (AU), asset exchange (AE), or claims exchange (CE). Also identify the account that is to be debited and the account that is to be credited when the transaction is recorded. The first event is recorded as an example.

Event No.	Type of Event	Account Debited	Account Credited
1	AS	Cash	Common Shares

PROBLEM 4–3B *Recording Adjusting Entries in General Journal Format*

L.O. 4, 7

Required

Each of the following independent events requires a year-end adjusting entry. Record each event and the related adjusting entry in general journal format. The first event is recorded as an example. Assume a December 31 closing date.

Event No.	Date	Account Titles	Debit	Credit
a	Sept. 1	Prepaid Rent	15,000	
		Cash		15,000
a	Dec. 31	Rent Expense	5,000	
		Prepaid Rent		5,000

a. Paid $15,000 cash in advance on September 1 for a one-year lease on office space.
b. Borrowed $22,500 cash by issuing a note to a local bank on October 1. The note had a one-year term and an 8 percent annual rate of interest.
c. Paid $9,700 cash to purchase equipment on September 1. The equipment was expected to have a five-year useful life and a $2,500 residual value. Amortization is computed on a straight-line basis.
d. Invested $11,000 cash in a term deposit that paid 6 percent interest annually. The term deposit was acquired on June 1 and had a one-year term to maturity.
e. Purchased $2,000 of supplies on account on April 15. At year-end, $300 of supplies remained on hand.
f. Received a $3,600 cash advance on July 1 for a contract to provide services for one year.
g. Paid $5,100 cash in advance on February 1 for a one-year insurance policy.

PROBLEM 4–4B *One Complete Accounting Cycle*

L.O. 3–7

The following events apply to Copeland Company's first year of operations:

1. Acquired $20,000 cash from issuing common shares on January 1, 2006.
2. Purchased $600 of supplies on account.
3. Paid $12,000 cash in advance for a one-year lease on office space.
4. Earned $17,000 of revenue on account.
5. Incurred $8,970 of other operating expenses on account.
6. Collected $5,900 cash from accounts receivable.
7. Paid $6,500 cash on accounts payable.
8. Paid a $700 cash dividend to the shareholders.

Information for Adjusting Entries

9. There was $100 of supplies on hand at the end of the accounting period.
10. The lease on the office space covered a one-year period beginning September 1, 2006.
11. There was $2,200 of accrued salaries at the end of the period.

Required

a. Record these transactions in general journal form.
b. Post the transaction data from the journal to ledger T-accounts.

c. Prepare an adjusted trial balance.
d. Prepare an income statement, statement of shareholders' equity, a balance sheet, and a cash flow statement.
e. Close the nominal accounts (Revenue, Expense, and Dividends) to Retained Earnings.
f. Post the closing entries to the T-accounts, and prepare a post-closing trial balance.

L.O. 3–7 PROBLEM 4–5B *Two Complete Accounting Cycles*

Bricker Enterprises experienced the following events for 2006, the first year of operation:

1. Began operations by acquiring $13,000 cash from the issue of common shares.
2. Paid $4,000 cash in advance for rent. The payment was for the period April 1, 2006, to March 31, 2007.
3. Performed services for customers on account for $27,000.
4. Incurred operating expenses on account of $13,500.
5. Collected $25,150 cash from accounts receivable.
6. Paid $8,500 cash for salary expense.
7. Paid $11,500 cash as a partial payment on accounts payable.

Adjusting Entries

8. Made the adjusting entry for the expired rent. (See Event 2.)
9. Recorded $900 of accrued salaries at the end of 2006.

Events for 2007

1. Paid $900 cash for the salaries accrued at the end of the prior accounting period.
2. Performed services for cash of $8,500.
3. Borrowed $6,000 from the local bank by issuing a note.
4. Paid $4,500 cash in advance for rent. The payment was for one year beginning April 1, 2007.
5. Performed services for customers on account for $42,000.
6. Incurred operating expense on account of $19,250.
7. Collected $40,500 cash from accounts receivable.
8. Paid $20,000 cash as a partial payment on accounts payable.
9. Paid $14,000 cash for salary expense.
10. Paid a $6,000 cash dividend to the shareholders.

Adjusting Entries

11. Made the adjusting entry for the expired rent. (*Hint:* Part of the rent was paid in 2006.)
12. Recorded accrued interest. The note was issued on September 1, 2007, for a one-year term and had an interest rate of 9 percent. (See Event 3.)

Required

a. Record the events and adjusting entries for 2006 in general journal form.
b. Post the events to T-accounts.
c. Prepare an adjusted trial balance.
d. Prepare an income statement, statement of shareholders' equity, balance sheet, and cash flow statement for 2006.
e. Record the entries to close the nominal accounts to Retained Earnings in the general journal and post to the T-accounts.
f. Prepare a post-closing trial balance for December 31, 2006.
g. Repeat requirements *a* through *f* for 2007.

L.O. 7 PROBLEM 4–6B *Identifying Accounting Events from Journal Entries*

Required

The following information is from the records of lawyer Steve Ray. Write a brief description of the accounting event represented in each of the general journal entries.

Date		Account Titles	Debit	Credit
Jan.	1	Cash	20,000	
		Common Shares		20,000
Feb.	10	Cash	4,000	
		Unearned Revenue		4,000
Mar.	5	Supplies	2,000	
		Cash		2,000
Apr.	10	Office Equipment	12,000	
		Cash		2,000
		Note Payable		10,000
Apr.	30	Prepaid Rent	800	
		Cash		800
May	1	Accounts Receivable	24,000	
		Fees Revenue		24,000
June	1	Salaries Expense	2,000	
		Cash		2,000
Aug.	5	Accounts Receivable	12,000	
		Fees Revenue		12,000
	10	Dividends	1,000	
		Cash		1,000
Sept.	10	Cash	4,400	
		Accounts Receivable		4,400
Oct.	1	Property Tax Expense	3,000	
		Cash		3,000
Dec.	31	Amortization Expense	1,000	
		Accumulated Amortization		1,000
	31	Supplies Expense	800	
		Supplies		800
	31	Rent Expense	4,400	
		Prepaid Rent		4,400
	31	Unearned Revenue	6,240	
		Fees Revenue		6,240

PROBLEM 4–7B *Recording Events in Statements Model and T-Accounts and Preparing a Trial Balance* L.O. 3–6

The following accounting events apply to Mickey's Diner for the year 2007:

Asset Source Transactions

1. Began operations by acquiring $40,000 of cash from the issue of common shares.
2. Purchased $14,000 of equipment on account.
3. Performed services and collected cash of $2,000.
4. Collected $12,000 of cash in advance for services to be provided over the next 12 months.
5. Provided $24,000 of services on account.
6. Purchased supplies of $3,000 on account.

Asset Exchange Transactions

7. Purchased $8,000 of equipment for cash.
8. Collected $14,000 of cash from accounts receivable.
9. Loaned $4,800 to José, who gave Mickey's Diner a 12-month, 7 percent note in return.
10. Purchased $1,260 of supplies with cash.
11. Purchased a $9,600 term deposit. The TD had a six-month term and paid 4 percent annual interest.

Asset Use Transactions

12. Paid $8,000 cash for salaries of employees.
13. Paid a cash dividend of $4,000 to the shareholders.
14. Paid for the equipment that had been purchased on account (see Event 2).
15. Paid off $1,260 of the accounts payable with cash.

Claims Exchange Transactions

16. Placed an advertisement in the local newspaper for $1,600 to be billed.
17. Incurred utility expense of $1,200 on account.

Adjusting Entries

18. Recognized $8,800 of revenue for performing services. The collection of cash for these services occurred in a prior transaction. (See Event 4.)
19. Recorded $200 of interest revenue that had accrued on the note receivable from José. (See Event 9.)
20. Recorded $336 of interest revenue that had accrued on the term deposit. (See Event 11.)
21. Recorded $3,000 of accrued salary expense at the end of 2007.
22. Recognized $2,800 of amortization on the equipment. (See Events 2 and 7.)
23. Recorded supplies expense. Had $1,200 of supplies on hand at the end of the accounting period.

Required

a. Use a horizontal statements model to show how each event affects the balance sheet, income statement, and cash flow statement. Indicate whether the event increases (+), decreases (−), or does not affect (NA) each element of the financial statements. Also, in the Cash Flow Statement column, use the letters OA to designate operating activity, IA for investing activity, and FA for financing activity. The first event is recorded as an example.

Assets	=	Liab.	+	Equity	Rev.	−	Exp.	=	Net Inc.	Cash Flow Statement
+		NA		+	NA		NA		NA	+ FA

b. Record each of the preceding events in T-accounts.
c. Prepare an adjusted trial balance.

L.O. 7 PROBLEM 4–8B *Effect of Journal Entries on Financial Statements*

Entry No.	Account Titles	Debit	Credit
1	Cash	XXX	
	Common Shares		XXX
2	Office Equipment	XXX	
	Cash		XXX
	Note Payable		XXX
3	Prepaid Rent	XXX	
	Cash		XXX
4	Dividends	XXX	
	Cash		XXX
5	Utility Expense	XXX	
	Cash		XXX
6	Accounts Receivable	XXX	
	Service Revenue		XXX
7	Salaries Expense	XXX	
	Cash		XXX
8	Cash	XXX	
	Service Revenue		XXX
9	Cash	XXX	
	Unearned Revenue		XXX
10	Supplies	XXX	
	Accounts Payable		XXX
11	Amortization Expense	XXX	
	Accumulated Amortization		XXX
12	Cash	XXX	
	Accounts Receivable		XXX
13	Rent Expense	XXX	
	Prepaid Rent		XXX
14	Supplies Expense	XXX	
	Supplies		XXX
15	Unearned Revenue	XXX	
	Service Revenue		XXX

Required

The preceding 15 different accounting events are presented in general journal format. Use a horizontal statements model to show how each event affects the balance sheet, income statement, and cash flow statement. Indicate whether the event increases (+), decreases (−), or does not affect (NA) each element of the financial statements. Also, in the Cash Flow Statement column, use the letters OA to designate operating activity, IA for investing activity, and FA for financing activity. The first event is recorded as an example.

Assets	=	Liab.	+	Equity	Rev.	−	Exp.	=	Net Inc.	Cash Flow Statement
+		NA		+	NA		NA		NA	+ FA

PROBLEM 4–9B *Effect of Errors on the Trial Balance* L.O. 6

Required

Consider each of the following errors independently (assume that each is the only error that has occurred). Complete the following table. The first error is recorded as an example.

Error	Is the Trial Balance Out of Balance?	By What Amount?	Which Is Larger, Debits or Credits?
a	no	NA	NA

a. A debit of $800 to Supplies Expense was recorded as a debit of $800 to Rent Expense.
b. A credit of $500 to Consulting Revenue was not recorded.
c. A credit of $360 to Accounts Payable was recorded as $680.
d. A debit of $3,000 to Cash was recorded as a credit of $3,000 to Cash.
e. An entry requiring a debit to Cash of $850 and a credit to Accounts Receivable of $850 was not posted to the ledger accounts.
f. A debit of $4,200 to Prepaid Rent was recorded as a credit of $4,200 to Prepaid Rent.

PROBLEM 4–10B *Effect of Errors on the Trial Balance* L.O. 6

The following trial balance was prepared from the ledger accounts of Kona Company.

When the trial balance failed to balance, the accountant reviewed the records and discovered the following errors:

1. The company received $470 as payment for services rendered. The credit to Service Revenue was recorded correctly, but the debit to Cash was recorded as $740.
2. A $430 receipt of cash that was received as a payment on accounts receivable was not recorded.
3. A $450 purchase of supplies on account was properly recorded as a debit to the Supplies account. However, the credit to Accounts Payable was not recorded.

KONA COMPANY
Trial Balance
April 30, 2006

Account Title	Debit	Credit
Cash	$ 7,150	
Accounts Receivable	40,000	
Supplies	2,400	
Prepaid Insurance	3,200	
Equipment	56,800	
Accounts Payable		$ 8,950
Notes Payable		32,000
Common Shares		96,000
Retained Earnings		56,720
Service Revenue		40,000
Rent Expense	7,200	
Salaries Expense	26,400	
Operating Expense	65,240	
Dividends	6,000	
Totals	$214,390	$233,670

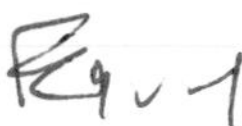

4. Equipment valued at $10,000 was contributed to the business in exchange for common shares. The entry to record the transaction was recorded as a $10,000 credit to both the Equipment account and the Common Shares account.
5. A $200 rent payment was properly recorded as a credit to Cash. However, the Salaries Expense account was incorrectly debited for $200.

Required

Based on this information, prepare a corrected trial balance for Kona Company.

L.O. 3–7 PROBLEM 4–11B *Comprehensive Problem: Single Cycle*

The following transactions pertain to Moon Walk Company for 2008:

Jan.	30	Established the business when it acquired $75,000 cash from the issue of common shares.
Feb.	1	Paid rent for office space for two years, $24,000 cash.
Mar.	1	Borrowed $20,000 cash from a local bank. The note issued had a 9 percent annual rate of interest and matured in one year.
Apr.	10	Purchased $5,300 of supplies on account.
June	1	Paid $27,000 cash for a computer system which had a three-year useful life and no residual value.
July	1	Received $50,000 cash in advance for services to be provided over the next year.
	20	Paid $1,800 of the accounts payable from April 10.
Aug.	15	Billed a customer $32,000 for services provided during July.
Sept.	15	Completed a job and received $19,000 cash for services rendered.
Oct.	1	Paid employee salaries of $20,000 cash.
	15	Received $25,000 cash from accounts receivable.
Nov.	16	Billed customers $37,000 for services rendered on account.
Dec.	1	Paid a dividend of $6,000 cash to the shareholders.
	31	Adjusted records to recognize the services provided on contract of July 1.
	31	Recorded the accrued interest on the note to a local bank. (See March 1.)
	31	Recorded amortization on the computer system used in the business. (See June 1.)
	31	Recorded $4,500 of accrued salaries as of December 31.
	31	Recorded the rent expense for the year. (See February 1.)
	31	Physically counted supplies; $480 was on hand at the end of the period.

Required

a. Record the preceding transactions in the general journal.
b. Post the transactions to T-accounts and calculate the account balances.
c. Prepare an adjusted trial balance.
d. Prepare the income statement, statement of shareholders' equity, balance sheet, and cash flow statement.
e. Prepare the closing entries at December 31.
f. Prepare a trial balance after the closing entries are posted.

L.O. 3–7 PROBLEM 4–12B *Comprehensive Problem: Two Cycles*

This problem extends Problem 4–12A involving Hawkins Rentals and *should not* be attempted until that problem has been completed. The transactions consummated by Hawkins Rentals during May 2007 (the company's second month of operation) consisted of the following:

May	1	Recorded rentals of wedding décor to customers. Cash receipts were $420, and invoices for rentals on account were $1,200.
	2	Purchased supplies on account that cost $300.
	7	Collected $2,500 cash from customer accounts receivable.
	8	Donna Oreen picked up the wedding décor that had been paid for in advance (see April 9 in Problem 4–12A).

May 10 Paid the utility company for the monthly utility bills that had been received in the previous month, $233.
15 Paid $2,100 cash for employee salaries.
15 Purchased a one-year insurance policy that cost $1,200.
16 Paid $300 on the account payable that was established when supplies were purchased on May 2.
27 Received monthly utility bills amounting to $310. The bills would be paid during the month of June.
31 Recorded rentals of wedding décor to customers. Cash receipts were $625, and invoices for rentals on account were $1,100.
31 Paid $2,100 cash for employee salaries.
31 Counted the supplies inventory. Had $40 of supplies on hand.

Required

a. Open a general ledger with T-accounts, using the ending account balances computed in Problem 4–12A.
b. Record the preceding transactions directly into the T-accounts.
c. Record the adjusting entries directly into the T-accounts. (Note: Refer to Problem 4–12A to obtain all the information needed to prepare the adjusting entries.)
d. Prepare an income statement, statement of shareholders' equity, balance sheet, and cash flow statement.
e. Record the closing entries directly into the T-accounts.
f. Answer the following questions.
   (1) Why is the amount in the May 31, 2007, Retained Earnings account not equal to the amount of net income or loss for the month of May?
   (2) Why is the amount of Accumulated Amortization on the May 31, 2007, balance sheet not equal to the amount of amortization expense for the month of May?

ANALYZE, THINK, COMMUNICATE

BUSINESS APPLICATIONS CASE *Bombardier's Annual Report* ATC 4–1

Required

Using the Bombardier financial statements in Appendix B, answer the following questions:

a. On January 31, 2002, Bombardier had a balance of $2,785.3 million in Retained Earnings. On January 31, 2001, the balance in Retained Earnings was $2,660.0 million. Explain the change in Retained Earnings during the year.
b. What is the nature of Bombardier's business; that is, what does it produce and sell?
c. Could Requirement *b* be answered by examining only Bombardier's income statement, balance sheet, and cash flow statement?

GROUP ASSIGNMENT *Financial Statement Analysis* ATC 4–2

The account balances for Collins Company were as follows:

	January 1		
	2006	2007	2008
Cash	$12,000	$ 5,800	$29,400
Accounts Receivable	6,000	10,000	6,000
Equipment	25,000	25,000	25,000
Accumulated Amortization	(12,000)	(13,200)	(14,400)
Prepaid Rent	0	1,000	1,400
Accounts Payable	4,000	3,000	7,000
Notes Payable	12,000*	0	0
Interest Payable	300	0	0
Salaries Payable	0	0	2,100
Common Shares	10,000	10,000	10,000
Retained Earnings	4,700	15,600	28,300

*Funds were originally borrowed on October 1, 2005, with an interst rate of 10%.

Collins Company experienced the following events for the accounting periods 2006, 2007, and 2008:

2006

1. Performed services for $36,000 on account.
2. Paid rent of $6,000 for the period March 1, 2006, to March 1, 2007.
3. Incurred operating expense of $18,000 on account.
4. Collected $32,000 of accounts receivable.
5. Paid $19,000 of accounts payable.
6. Paid note and interest due on October 1.
7. Recorded expired rent.
8. Recorded amortization expense of $1,200.

2007

1. Performed services on account of $48,000.
2. Paid rent of $8,400 for the period March 1, 2007, to March 1, 2008, and recorded the expired rent for the period January 1, 2007, to March 1, 2007.
3. Incurred operating expenses of $24,000 on account.
4. Collected $52,000 of accounts receivable.
5. Paid $20,000 of accounts payable.
6. Recorded expired rent.
7. Recorded accrued salaries of $2,100.
8. Recorded amortization expense of $1,200.

2008

1. Paid accrued salaries.
2. Performed services on account of $56,000.
3. Paid rent of $9,000 for the period March 1, 2008, to March 1, 2009, and recorded the expired rent for the period January 1, 2008, to March 1, 2008.
4. Incurred operating expenses of $32,000 on account.
5. Collected $55,000 of accounts receivable.
6. Paid $33,000 of accounts payable.
7. Sold equipment for $2,000; the equipment had a cost of $5,000 and accumulated amortization of $4,000.
8. Recorded expired rent.
9. Recorded amortization expense of $1,000.

Required

a. Divide the class into groups consisting of four or five students. Organize the groups into three sections. Assign each section of groups the financial data for one of the preceding accounting periods.

Group Task

(1) Prepare an income statement, balance sheet, and cash flow statement. It may be helpful to open T-accounts and post transactions to these accounts before attempting to prepare the statements.

Class Discussion

b. Review the cash flows associated with the collection of receivables and the payment of payables. Comment on the company's collection and payment strategy.
c. Explain why amortization decreased in 2008.
d. Did net income increase or decrease between 2006 and 2007? What were the primary causes?
e. Did net income increase or decrease between 2007 and 2008? What were the primary causes?

REAL-WORLD CASE *Fiscal Year-Ends* ATC 4–3

Consider the following brief descriptions of three companies, listed alphabetically, from different industries. Agricore, Ltd., one of Canada's leading grain companies, develops new varieties of seeds, such as corn, and sells them to farmers. IntraWest, Inc., operates several ski resorts in Canada, including Whistler/Blackcomb in BC and Mont Tremblant in Quebec. Toys "R" Us, Inc., is the well-known international retailer of toys.

This chapter explained that companies often choose to close their books when business usually is slow. Each of these companies ends its fiscal year on a different date. The closing dates, listed chronologically, are as follows:

January 31
June 30
July 31

Required

a. Try to determine which fiscal year end matches which company. Write a brief explanation to explain the reason for your decisions.
b. Because many companies choose to prepare their financial statements at a slow time of year, try to identify problems this may present for someone trying to analyze the balance sheet for Toys "R" Us. Write a brief explanation of the issues you identify.

BUSINESS APPLICATIONS CASE *Components of Financial Statements* ATC 4–4

A stockbroker handed Dr. Nguyen a set of financial statements for a company the broker described as a "sure bet" for a major increase in share price. The broker assured Nguyen that the company was a legitimate business. As proof, she stated that the company was listed with the Ontario Securities Commission (OSC) and on the Toronto Stock Exchange (TSE). After looking of over the financial statements, Nguyen wanted additional information. He has an Internet connection and can access the latest information for the company.

Required

Name the financial statements that Nguyen should review. In particular, what specific items within those financial statements would Nguyen want to analyze? What other nonfinancial information might he wish to obtain?

BUSINESS APPLICATIONS CASE *Components of Financial Statements* ATC 4–5

Beth Hughes just finished reading the annual report of Muncy Company. Hughes is enthusiastic about the possibility of investing in the company. In the management's discussion and analysis section of the report, Muncy's new president, Bill Karn, stated that he was committed to an annual growth rate of 25 percent over the next five years. Hughes tells you that the company's financial statements received an unqualified audit opinion from a respected firm of CAs. Based on the audit report, Hughes concluded that the auditors agree with Karn's forecast of a five-year, 25 percent growth rate. She tells you, "These accountants are usually very conservative. If they forecast 25 percent growth, actual growth is likely to be close to 35 percent. I'm not going to miss an opportunity like this. I am buying the shares."

Required

Comment on Hughes's understanding of the relationship between the auditors' report and management's discussion and analysis in a company's annual report.

WRITING ASSIGNMENT *Fiscal Closing Date* ATC 4–6

Assume you are the auditor for Metro Auto Sales. Metro currently has a December 31 year end as of which you perform the audit. You would like for Metro to change the year end to another time (almost any time except December 31).

Required

Write a memo to the owners of Metro Auto Sales and propose a new year end. In the memo explain why it would be reasonable or better to have a different year end and specify what the year end would be. Also, give reasons that the change would be beneficial from your perspective.

ATC 4–7 ETHICAL DILEMMA *Choice of Brothers: Ethics, Risk, and Accounting Numbers in a Medieval Setting*

In the late 1400s, a wealthy land owner named Caster was trying to decide which of his twin sons, Rogan or Argon, to designate as the first heir to the family fortune. He decided to set up each son with a small farm consisting of 300 sheep and 20 hectares of land. Each twin would be allowed to manage his property as he deemed appropriate. After a designated period, Caster would call his sons before him to account for their actions. The heir to the family fortune would be chosen on the basis of which son had produced a larger increase in wealth during the test period.

On the appointed day of reckoning, Argon boasted that he had 714 sheep under his control while Rogan had only 330. Furthermore, Argon stated that he had increased his land holdings to 27 hectares. The seven-hectare increase resulted from two transactions: first, on the day the contest started, Argon used 20 sheep to buy 10 additional hectares; and second, he sold three of these hectares for a total of 9 sheep on the day of reckoning. Also, Argon's flock had produced 75 newborn sheep during the period of accounting. He had been able to give his friends 50 sheep in return for the help that they had given him in building a fence, thereby increasing not only his own wealth but the wealth of his neighbours as well. Argon boasted that the fence was strong and would keep his herd safe from predatory creatures for five years (assume the fence had been used for one year during the contest period). Rogan countered that Argon was holding 400 sheep that belonged to another herder. Argon had borrowed these sheep on the day that the contest had started. Furthermore, Argon had agreed to return 424 sheep to the herder. The 24 additional sheep represented consideration for the use of the herder's flock. Argon had agreed to return the sheep immediately after the day of reckoning.

During the test period, Rogan's flock had produced 37 newborn sheep, but 2 sheep had gotten sick and died during the accounting period. Rogan had also lost 5 sheep to predatory creatures. He had no fence, and some of his sheep strayed from the herd, thereby exposing themselves to danger. Knowing that he was falling behind, Rogan had taken a wife in order to boost his productivity. His wife owned 170 sheep on the day they were married; her sheep had produced 16 newborn sheep since the date of her marriage to Rogan. Argon had not included the wife's sheep in his count of Rogan's herd. If his wife's sheep had been counted, Rogan's herd would contain 516 instead of the 330 sheep suggested by Argon's count.

Argon charged that seven of Rogan's sheep were sick with symptoms similar to those exhibited by the two sheep that were now dead. Rogan interjected that he should not be held accountable for acts of nature such as illness. Furthermore, he contended that by isolating the sick sheep from the remainder of the herd, he had demonstrated prudent management practices that supported his case to be designated first heir.

Required

a. Prepare an income statement, balance sheet, and sheep flow (cash flow) statement for each twin, using current accounting standards. Note that you have to decide whether to include the sheep owned by Rogan's wife when making his financial statements (what is the accounting entity?). (*Hint*: Use the number of sheep rather than the number of dollars as the common unit of measure.)

b. Refer to the statements you prepared in Requirement *a* to answer the following questions:
   (1) Which twin has more equity at the end of the accounting period?
   (2) Which twin produced the higher net income during the accounting period?
   (3) Which son should be designated heir based on conventional accounting and reporting standards?

c. What is the difference in the value of the land of the twins if the land is valued at market value (three sheep per hectare) rather than historical cost (two sheep per hectare)?

d. Did Argon's decision to borrow sheep increase his profitability? Support your answer with appropriate financial data.

e. Was Argon's decision to build a fence financially prudent? Support your answer with appropriate financial data.

f. Assuming that the loan resulted in a financial benefit to Argon, identify some reasons that the shepherd who owned the sheep may have been willing to loan them to Argon.

g. Which twin is likely to take risks to improve profitability? What would be the financial condition of each twin if one-half of the sheep in both flocks died as a result of illness? How should such risk factors be reported in financial statements?

h. Should Rogan's decision to "marry for sheep" be considered from an ethical perspective, or should the decision be made solely on the basis of the bottom-line net income figure?

i. Prepare a report that recommends which twin should be designated heir to the family business. Include a set of financial statements that supports your recommendation. Since this is a managerial report that will not be distributed to the public, you are not bound by generally accepted accounting principles.

SEDAR DATABASE *Investigating Bombardier's Annual Report*

ATC 4–8

Many companies must file financial reports with the Ontario Securities Commission (OSC). Many of these reports are available electronically through the SEDAR database. SEDAR is an acronym for System for Electronic Document Analysis and Retrieval, and it is accessible through the World Wide Web on the Internet. Instructions for using SEDAR are in Appendix A.

Using the most current annual report available on SEDAR, answer the following questions about Bombardier.

a. In what year did Bombardier begin operations?
b. What products does Bombardier sell?
c. How many employees does Bombardier have?
d. Describe, in dollar amounts, Bombardier's accounting equation at the end of the most recent year.
e. Has Bombardier's performance been improving or deteriorating over the past two years? Explain your answer.

SPREADSHEET ASSIGNMENT *Use of Excel*

ATC 4–9

Adams Company started operations on January 1, 2008. Six months later on June 30, 2008, the company decided to prepare financial statements. The company's accountant decided to problem solve for the adjusting journal entries and the final adjusted account balances by using an electronic spreadsheet. Once the spreadsheet is complete, she will record the adjusting entries in the general journal and post to the ledger. The accountant has started the following spreadsheet but wants you to finish it for her.

Required

a. On a blank spreadsheet, enter the following trial balance in Columns A through C. Also enter the headings for Columns E through I.

Microsoft Excel - ch4-1.xls

I10 = =C10-E10+G10

	A	B	C	D	E	F	G	H	I	J
1		Trial Balance			Adjusting Journal Entries			Adjusted Trial Balance		
2	Account Titles	Debit	Credit		Debit		Credit	Debit	Credit	
3	Cash	1,500								
4	Term Deposit	10,000								
5	Accounts Receivable	12,000								
6	Supplies	1,500								
7	Prepaid Rent	12,000								
8	Office Equipment	9,000								
9	Accounts Payable		2,500							
10	Unearned Revenue		5,000	(1)	3,000				2,000	
11	Common Shares		20,000							
12	Retained Earnings		0							
13	Service Revenue		35,000			(1)	3,000			
14	Salaries Expense	12,000								
15	Operating Expense	4,500								
16										
17	Totals	62,500	62,500		3,000		3,000	0	2,000	
18										
19										
20										

b. Each of the following events requires an adjusting journal entry. Instead of recording entries in general journal format, record the adjusting entries in the Debit and Credit columns under the heading Adjusting Journal Entries. Entry (1) has already been recorded as an example. Be sure to number your adjusting entries on the spreadsheet. It will be necessary to insert new accounts for the adjustments. Recall that the accounting period is for six months.
   (1) Received a $5,000 cash advance on April 1 for a contract to provide five months of service.
   (2) Had accrued salaries on June 30 amounting to $1,500.
   (3) On January 1 invested in a one-year, $10,000 term deposit that had a 5 percent interest rate.
   (4) On January 1 paid $12,000 in advance for a one-year lease on office space.
   (5) Received in the mail a utility bill dated June 30 for $150.
   (6) Purchased $1,500 of supplies on January 1. As of June 30, $700 of supplies remained on hand.
   (7) Paid $9,000 for office equipment on January 1. The equipment was expected to have a four-year useful life and a $1,000 residual value. Amortization is computed on a straight-line basis.

c. Develop formulas to sum both the Debit and Credit columns under the Adjusting Journal Entries heading.

d. Develop formulas to derive the adjusted balances for the adjusted trial balance. For example, the formula for the ending balance of Unearned Revenue is =C10-E10+G10. In other words, a credit balance minus debit entries plus credit entries equals the ending balance. Once an ending balance is formulated for one credit account, that formula can be copied to all other credit accounts; the same is true for debit accounts. Once an ending balance is formulated for a debit account, that formula can be copied to all other debit accounts.

e. Develop formulas to sum both the Debit and Credit columns under the Adjusted Trial Balance heading.

Spreadsheet Tips

1. Rows and columns can be inserted by positioning the mouse on the immediate row or column after the desired position. Click on the *right* mouse button. With the *left* mouse button, choose Insert and then either Entire Column or Entire Row. Use the same method to delete columns or rows.
2. Enter the sequential numbering of the adjusting entries as labels rather than values by positioning an apostrophe in front of each entry. The first adjusting entry should be labelled '(1).

SPREADSHEET ASSIGNMENT *Mastery of Excel*

ATC 4–10

At the end of the accounting period, Adams Company's general ledger contained the following adjusted balances.

Microsoft Excel - ch4-2.xls

File Edit View Insert Format Tools Data Window Help

B25 = =SUM(B3:B23)

	A	B	C	D	E	F	G	H	I	J
1		Adjusted Trial Balance			Closing Entries			Post-closing Trial Balance		
2	Account Titles	Debit	Credit		Debit		Credit	Debit	Credit	
3	Cash	1,500								
4	Term Deposit	10,000								
5	Interest Receivable	250								
6	Accounts Receivable	12,000								
7	Supplies	700								
8	Prepaid Rent	6,000								
9	Office Equipment	9,000								
10	Accumulated Amortization		1,000							
11	Accounts Payable		2,650							
12	Salaries Payable		1,500							
13	Unearned Revenue		2,000							
14	Common Shares		20,000							
15	Retained Earnings		0							
16	Service Revenue		38,000							
17	Interest Revenue		250							
18	Salaries Expense	13,500								
19	Rent Expense	6,000								
20	Utilities Expense	150								
21	Supplies Expense	800								
22	Amortization Expense	1,000								
23	Operating Expense	4,500								
24										
25	Totals	65,400	65,400							
26										

Required

a. Set up the preceding spreadsheet format. (The spreadsheet tips for ATC 4–9 also apply for this problem.)

b. Record the closing entries in the Closing Entries column of the spreadsheet.

c. Compute the Post-closing Trial Balance amounts.

Chapter 5

Accounting for Merchandising Businesses

Learning Objectives

After completing this chapter, you should be able to:

1 Distinguish between service and merchandising businesses.

2 Distinguish between product costs and selling and administrative costs.

3 Show how product costs affect financial statements.

4 Compare and contrast the perpetual and periodic inventory methods.

5 Understand the main features of the perpetual inventory method.

6 Explain the meaning of terms used to describe transportation costs, cash discounts, and returns or allowances.

7 Compare and contrast single- and multistep income statements.

8 Understand how lost, damaged, or stolen inventory affects financial statements.

9 Use common size financial statements to evaluate managerial performance.

10 Use ratio analysis to evaluate managerial performance.

11 Understand the cost of financing inventory.

12 Name the main features of the periodic inventory method.

the *curious* accountant

Suppose you go into a Sears department store to buy perfume as a gift for a friend. The fragrance, produced by Estee Lauder, costs $50. Using the income statements for Sears and Estee Lauder that are presented in Exhibit 5–1 on page 191, what did it cost Estee Lauder to make this product?

Previous illustrations and problems assumed that businesses generated revenue by providing services to their customers. Another large form of business activity generates revenue by selling goods to customers. Companies that sell goods normally accumulate a supply of those goods, which they use for delivery when sales are made. This supply is called ***inventory****.*

Inventory includes goods that are in the process of being made (unfinished goods) as well as goods that are finished and ready for sale. For example, unprocessed lumber, partially assembled tables, and finished goods stored in a warehouse would all be included in the inventory of a furniture manufacturer. The term inventory *also describes stockpiles of goods that are used indirectly in the process of selling merchandise or providing services, such as supplies, stamps, stationery, cleaning materials, and so on.*

At this point, it is helpful to note that many businesses concentrate on reselling finished goods. These businesses buy merchandise from a supplier and resell that merchandise to their customers. When the merchandise is resold, it is essentially in the same condition as it was when it was purchased from the supplier. Finished goods held for resale are commonly called ***merchandise inventory****. Companies that buy and sell merchandise inventory are called* ***merchandising businesses****. Merchandising businesses include* ***retail companies*** *(companies that sell goods to the final consumer) and* ***wholesale companies*** *(companies that sell to other businesses).*

A Service Business versus a Merchandising Business

LO1 Distinguish between service and merchandising businesses.

A service business sells services, whereas a merchandising business sells finished goods. Service businesses include the Royal Bank, Canada Post, WestJet Airlines, and accounting firms like PricewaterhouseCoopers and Ernst & Young. Merchandising businesses concentrate on the resale of goods. Some good examples are Wal-Mart, Canadian Tire, Costco, and Sears Canada.

Product Costs versus Selling and Administrative Costs

LO2 Distinguish between product costs and selling and administrative costs.

Inventory costs are capitalized in (accumulated in) the Merchandise Inventory account and shown as an asset on the balance sheet. Any cost incurred to acquire goods or to ready them for sale should be included in the Inventory account. Examples of inventory costs incurred by merchandising companies include the price of goods purchased, transportation or packaging costs associated with obtaining merchandise, storage costs, and transit insurance. Note that all of these costs are associated with products. As a result, inventory costs are often referred to as **product costs**. Costs that cannot be directly traced to products are usually classified as **selling and administrative costs**. Typical selling and administrative costs include advertising, administrative salaries, insurance, and interest. Since selling and administrative costs are usually recognized as expenses *in the period* in which they are incurred, they are sometimes called **period costs**. Product costs are expensed when the inventory is sold regardless of when it was purchased. In other words, product costs are matched directly with sales revenue, but selling and administrative costs are matched with the period in which they are incurred.

Allocation of Inventory Cost between Asset and Expense Accounts

LO3 Show how product costs affect financial statements.

The total inventory cost for any given accounting period is determined by adding the cost of inventory on hand at the beginning of the period to the cost of inventory purchased during the period. The total cost (beginning inventory plus purchases) is called the **cost of goods available for sale**. The cost of goods available for sale is allocated between an asset account called *Merchandise Inventory* and an expense account called *Cost of Goods Sold*. The cost of the items that have not been sold (Merchandise Inventory) is shown as an asset on the balance sheet, and the cost of the items sold (**Cost of Goods Sold**) is expensed on the income statement. The difference between the sales revenue and the cost of goods sold is called the **gross profit** or *gross margin*. The selling and administrative expenses (period costs) are subtracted from the gross profit to obtain the net income.

Exhibit 5–1 contains income statements drawn from the annual reports of Sears Canada and Estee Lauder, Inc. For each company, review the most current income statement and determine the amount of gross profit. The gross profit for Sears must be computed. Using data from the 2000 income statement, we determine gross profit to be $14,038 million ($40,937 million in sales − $26,899 million in cost of goods sold). No computation is necessary to determine the amount of the gross profit for Estee Lauder because its report includes the computation directly in its income statement. Estee Lauder's 2000 income statement shows a gross profit of $3,394.7 million.

Exhibit 5–1 *Consolidated Statements*

SEARS CANADA
Consolidated Statements of Earnings (partial)
Years Ended December 31
(dollars in thousands)

	2000	1999	1998
Net Sales	$40,937	$39,484	$39,953
Costs and Expenses			
Cost of Sales and Related Buying and Occupancy	26,899	25,627	25,794
Selling, General and Administrative	8,642	8,416	8,412
Interest, net	1,248	1,268	1,423
Service Charge Income and Other, net	251	41	352
Provision for Uncollectible Accounts	884	871	1,287
Depreciation and Amortization	826	848	830
Total Costs and Expenses	38,750	37,071	38,098
Earnings before Income Taxes	$ 2,187	$ 2,413	$ 1,855

THE ESTEE LAUDER COMPANIES INC.
Consolidated Statements of Earnings (partial)
Years Ended June 30
(dollars in millions)

	2000	1999	1998
Net Sales	$4,366.8	$3,961.5	$3,618.0
Cost of Sales	972.1	899.9	819.5
Gross Profit	3,394.7	3,061.6	2,798.5
Selling, General and Administrative Expenses			
Selling, General and Administrative	2,845.7	2,572.1	2,357.6
Related-Party Royalties	33.2	32.6	31.8
	2,878.9	2,604.7	2,389.4
Operating Income	515.8	456.9	409.1
Interest Income (Expense), net	(17.1)	(16.7)	(6.3)
Earnings before Income Taxes	$ 498.7	$ 440.2	$ 402.8

Inventory Cost Recorded

LO4 Compare and contrast the perpetual and periodic inventory methods.

Inventories are accounted for under either the perpetual or the periodic method. The **perpetual inventory method** derives its name from the fact that the balance in the Inventory account is adjusted perpetually (continually). Each time merchandise is purchased, the Inventory account is increased; each time it is sold, the Inventory account is decreased. In contrast, the **periodic inventory method** adjusts the Inventory balance only at the end of the accounting period. The Inventory account is unaffected by purchases or sales of inventory during the period. Note that the two methods represent alternative procedures for reporting the same information. The amount of cost of goods sold and ending inventory reported on the financial statements will be the same regardless of whether the perpetual or periodic procedures are applied.

The chief advantage of the periodic method is recording efficiency. Recording inventory transactions occasionally (periodically) requires less work than recording them on a continuous basis (perpetually). Think of the number of transactions that a typical grocery store would have to record every business day under a perpetual system. The recording advantage of the periodic system must be weighed against the control advantage inherent in the perpetual system. Since the perpetual system increases and decreases the Inventory account balance when purchases and sales are made, the book balance of inventory should agree with the amount of inventory on hand. Therefore, the amount of lost, damaged, destroyed, or stolen inventory can be determined by checking the book balance against a physical count of inventory. Also, reorder decisions and profitability assessments are made easier by the availability of immediate feedback.

Fortunately, the advent of computer technology has removed most of the practical constraints associated with recording inventory transactions on a continual basis. Electronic scanners can capture accounting information rapidly and efficiently. Computer programs that access the data captured by the scanners can update the accounting records instantaneously. As a result, the use of the perpetual inventory system has increased rapidly in recent years. Continued growth in the application of the perpetual method can be expected as technology advances. Therefore, this book concentrates on the perpetual inventory method.

Perpetual Inventory Method

LO5 Understand the main features of the perpetual inventory method.

Most modern companies maintain their inventory records under the *perpetual inventory method*. The following illustration demonstrates the basic features of the perpetual inventory method.

June Gardener was appropriately named. She loved plants, and they grew for her as they did for no one else. At the encouragement of her friends, Gardener decided to start a small retail plant store. She started June's Plant Shop Co. (JPS) on January 1, 2007. During the first year of operation, the company experienced the following business events.

1. Acquired $15,000 cash through the issue of common shares.
2. Made a $14,000 cash purchase of inventory.
3. Sold inventory that cost $8,000 for $12,000 cash.
4. Made a $1,000 cash payment for selling expenses.

Effect of Events on Financial Statements

The effect of each of these events on the financial statements is discussed here.

Event 1 JPS acquired $15,000 cash from the issue of common shares.

This event is an asset source transaction. The $15,000 acquisition of cash acts to increase assets (Cash) and equity (Common Shares). The income statement is not affected. The cash flow statement shows a $15,000 cash inflow from financing activities. These effects follow:

Cash	+	Merchandise Inventory	=	Common Shares	+	Ret. Ear.	Rev.	−	Exp.	=	Net Inc.	Cash Flow Statement
15,000	+	NA	=	15,000	+	NA	NA	−	NA	=	NA	15,000 FA

Event 2 JPS paid $14,000 cash to purchase inventory.

The Merchandise Inventory account is increased when goods are purchased. Since cash is used to purchase the goods, the purchase constitutes an asset exchange. The asset account Cash decreases, and the asset account Merchandise Inventory increases; the total amount of assets is unchanged. The income

an answer for the *curious* accountant

The income statement data suggest that the goods sold by Sears cost it about 66 percent of the store's selling price ($26,899 ÷ $40,937). This analysis suggests that the perfume you purchased for $50 cost Sears approximately $33 ($50 × 0.66). Similarly, Estee Lauder's income statement suggests that it cost Estee Lauder only 22 percent of its selling price to make the fragrance ($972.1 ÷ $4,366.8). Based on these numbers, we can determine that it cost Estee Lauder approximately $7.26 ($33 × 0.22) to make the perfume it sold to Sears. Thus, it appears that it cost approximately $7.26 to make the perfume you bought for $50. Keep in mind, however, the many other costs of operating a business in addition to the direct cost of making a product. For example, Estee Lauder spent $1,195.8 million (27 percent of sales) on advertising during the 2000 fiscal year.

statement is not affected by this event. Product costs are expensed when the goods are sold, not when they are purchased. However, the $10,000 cash outflow is shown in the operating activities section of the cash flow statement. These effects follow:

Cash	+	Merchandise Inventory	=	Common Shares	+	Ret. Ear.	Rev.	−	Exp.	=	Net Inc.	Cash Flow Statement
(14,000)	+	14,000	=	NA	+	NA	NA	−	NA	=	NA	(14,000) OA

JPS recognized $12,000 of cash revenue on the sale of inventory that cost $8,000. **Event 3a**

This event is composed of two transactions. The *first transaction* is an asset source transaction (cash is acquired by generating sales revenue). As with other revenue transactions, sales transactions increase assets (Cash) and equity (Retained Earnings). The sales revenue increases net income on the income statement. Also, the $12,000 cash inflow from the sale is shown in the operating activities section of the cash flow statement. These effects are shown here:

Cash	+	Merchandise Inventory	=	Common Shares	+	Ret. Ear.	Rev.	−	Exp.	=	Net Inc.	Cash Flow Statement
12,000	+	NA	=	NA	+	12,000	12,000	−	NA	=	12,000	12,000 OA

JPS recognized $8,000 of cost of goods sold. **Event 3b**

The second transaction associated with the sale of inventory is an asset use transaction. An expense (Cost of Goods Sold) is recognized because the asset, Inventory, was used to produce the sales revenue. Thus, $8,000 of cost must be transferred from the asset account, Merchandise Inventory, to the expense account, Cost of Goods Sold. The effect on the balance sheet is to reduce assets (Inventory) and equity (Retained Earnings). On the income statement, the expense, Cost of Goods Sold, will reduce net income. This event does not affect the cash flow statement. The cash outflow occurred when the goods were bought, not when they were sold. These effects follow:

Cash	+	Merchandise Inventory	=	Common Shares	+	Ret. Ear.	Rev.	−	Exp.	=	Net Inc.	Cash Flow Statement
NA	+	(8,000)	=	NA	+	(8,000)	NA	−	8,000	=	(8,000)	NA

Event 4 JPS paid $1,000 cash for selling expenses.

This event is an asset use transaction. The payment decreases assets (Cash) and equity (Retained Earnings). The increase in selling expenses decreases net income. The $1,000 cash outflow is shown in the operating activities section of the cash flow statement. These effects are shown here:

Cash	+	Merchandise Inventory	=	Common Shares	+	Ret. Ear.	Rev.	−	Exp.	=	Net Inc.	Cash Flow Statement
(1,000)	+	NA	=	NA	+	(1,000)	NA	−	1,000	=	(1,000)	(1,000) OA

Ledger T-Accounts

Exhibit 5–2 shows the ledger T-accounts containing the transaction data for the 2007 accounting period. Recall that the company experiences the following four accounting events:

1. Acquired $15,000 cash through the issue of common shares.
2. Made a $14,000 cash purchase of inventory.

3a. Recognized $12,000 cash revenue from sales.
3b. Recognized $8,000 of cost of goods sold.

4. Made a $1,000 cash payment for selling expenses.

For easy reference, the ledger accounts contain the event numbers shown in parentheses. The closing entry, which is designated by *cl*, is necessary to transfer the balances in the revenue and expense accounts to the Retained Earnings account. The closing entry is a claims exchange transaction, with some equity accounts decreasing while others increase. The amount of total equity is not affected by the closing entry.

The ledger account balances are used to prepare the financial statements shown in Exhibit 5–3. To confirm your understanding of the statement preparation, trace the ledger account balances to the financial statements.

Phambroom Company began 2006 with $35,600 in its Inventory account. During the year, it purchased inventory costing $356,800 and sold inventory that had cost $360,000 for $520,000. Based on this information alone, determine (1) the inventory balance as of December 31, 2006, and (2) the amount of gross profit Phambroom would report on its 2006 income statement.

Answer

1. Beginning inventory + Purchases = Goods available − Ending inventory = Cost of goods sold
   $35,600 + $356,800 = $392,400 − Ending inventory = $360,000
   Ending inventory = $32,400
2. Sales revenue − Cost of goods sold = Gross profit
   $520,000 − $360,000 = $160,000

Exhibit 5–2 *General Ledger*

Cash

	Debit	Credit	
(1)	15,000	14,000	(2)
(3a)	12,000	1,000	(4)
Bal.	12,000		

=

Liabilities

	Debit	Credit	
		0	Bal.

+

Common Shares

	Debit	Credit	
		15,000	(1)
		15,000	Bal.

Merchandise Inventory

	Debit	Credit	
(2)	14,000	8,000	(3b)
Bal.	6,000		

Retained Earnings

	Debit	Credit	
		3,000	(cl.)
		3,000	Bal.

Sales Revenue

	Debit	Credit	
(cl.)	12,000	12,000	(3a)
		0	Bal.

Cost of Goods Sold

	Debit	Credit	
(3b)	8,000	8,000	(cl.)
Bal.	0		

Selling Expenses

	Debit	Credit	
(4)	1,000	1,000	(cl.)
Bal.	0		

Exhibit 5–3 *Financial Statements*

Income Statement

Sales Revenue	$12,000
Cost of Goods Sold	(8,000)
Gross Profit	4,000
Less: Operating Exp.	
Selling and Admin. Exp.	(1,000)
Net Income	$ 3,000

Balance Sheet

Assets		
Cash	$12,000	
Merchandise Inventory	6,000	
Total Assets		$18,000
Liabilities		0
Shareholders' Equity		
Common Shares	$15,000	
Retained Earnings	3,000	
Total Shareholders' Equity		$18,000

Cash Flow Statement

Operating Activities		
Inflow from Customers	$ 12,000	
Outflow for Inventory	(14,000)	
Outflow for Selling & Admin.	(1,000)	
Net Cash Outflow from Operations		$ (3,000)
Investing Activities		0
Financing Activities		
Inflow from Share Issue		15,000
Net Change in Cash		12,000
Plus: Beginning Cash Balance		0
Ending Cash Balance		$12,000

Other Events Affecting Inventory Purchases

LO6 Explain the meaning of terms used to describe transportation costs, cash discounts, and returns or allowances.

Three other accounting events often affect inventory purchases: (1) incurring transportation costs, (2) returning inventory or accepting purchase allowances, and (3) receiving cash discounts. The effects of these events are demonstrated by analyzing JPS's operating activities during its second accounting cycle. The closing balances for the 2007 fiscal year became the opening balances for the 2008 calendar year. Accordingly, the beginning balances are: Cash, $12,000; Inventory, $6,000; Common Shares, $15,000; and Retained Earnings, $3,000.

Effect of Events on Financial Statements

JPS experienced the following events during its 2008 accounting period.

Event 1 JPS purchased $8,000 of merchandise inventory on account.

The effect of the purchase on the balance sheet is to increase assets (Inventory) and liabilities (Accounts Payable). The income statement is not affected by this event. Revenue and expense recognition occurs at the point of sale rather than at the time of purchase. Since the goods were purchased on account, cash flow was not affected. These effects on the financial statements are as follows:

Cash	+	Accts. Rec.	+	Merch. Inv.	=	Accts. Pay.	+	Note Pay.	+	Com. Sh.	+	Ret. Earn.	Rev.	−	Exp.	=	Net Inc.	Cash Flow Statement
NA	+	NA	+	8,000	=	8,000	+	NA	+	NA	+	NA	NA	−	NA	=	NA	NA

Event 2 JPS paid $300 cash for freight cost required to obtain goods purchased in Event 1.

The party responsible for transportation costs is designated by the terms **FOB shipping point** and **FOB destination point**. An easy way to interpret the terms is to note that the seller's responsibility ends at the point designated in the terms. If goods are shipped FOB shipping point, the seller's responsibility ends at the point of shipment and the buyer must pay the freight costs. On the other hand, if goods are shipped FOB destination, the seller retains ownership until the goods reach the destination point and is therefore responsible for the transportation costs. The following diagram summarizes the parties responsible for freight costs:

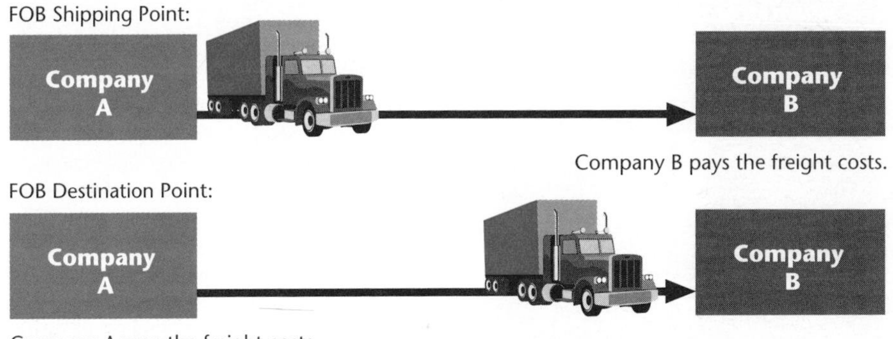

The cost of freight on goods purchased under terms FOB shipping point is called **transportation-in** or **freight-in**. Since transportation costs are a necessary part of obtaining inventory, they are added to the Inventory account. Assuming that the goods purchased in Event 1 were delivered under terms FOB shipping point, the buyer (JPS) is responsible for the freight. The freight costs will increase the balance in the Inventory account and decrease the balance of the Cash account. The income statement is not affected by this transaction. Since the freight costs are included in the Inventory account, they will be expensed as part of *costs of goods sold* when the inventory is sold to customers, not when it is delivered to JPS. However, the cash paid for freight at the time of delivery is shown as an outflow in the operating activities section of the cash flow statement. The effects of *transportation-in* costs on the financial statements follow:

Cash	+	Accts. Rec.	+	Merch. Inv.	=	Accts. Pay.	+	Note Pay.	+	Com. Sh.	+	Ret. Earn.	Rev.	−	Exp.	=	Net Inc.	Cash Flow Statement
(300)	+	NA	+	300	=	NA	+	NA	+	NA	+	NA	NA	−	NA	=	NA	(300) OA

JPS returned $1,000 of goods purchased in Event 1. **Event 3**

"Satisfaction or your money back" is a guarantee commonly offered in today's economy. Goods may be returned because the buyer becomes dissatisfied with a product's size, colour, design, and so on. Recall that the Inventory account is increased when goods are purchased. The reverse applies when goods are returned. In the case of JPS, the $1,000 purchase return acts to decrease assets (Inventory) and liabilities (Accounts Payable). The income statement and the cash flow statement are not affected. These effects on the financial statements follow:

Cash	+	Accts. Rec.	+	Merch. Inv.	=	Accts. Pay.	+	Note Pay.	+	Com. Sh.	+	Ret. Earn.	Rev.	−	Exp.	=	Net Inc.	Cash Flow Statement
NA	+	NA	+	(1,000)	=	(1,000)	+	NA	+	NA	+	NA	NA	−	NA	=	NA	NA

It is sometimes advantageous to appease the buyer by negotiating a reduction in the selling price of certain goods instead of accepting their return. Such reductions, called **allowances**, are often granted to buyers who receive defective goods or goods that are of a lower quality than the customer ordered. Purchase allowances affect the financial statements exactly the same as purchase returns do.

JPS received a cash discount on goods purchased in Event 1. **Event 4**

Assume that the goods described in Event 1 were purchased under terms 2/10, n/30. The terms **2/10, n/30** mean that the seller will give the purchaser a 2 percent discount on the account payable if the purchaser pays cash for the merchandise within 10 days from the date of purchase. The amount not paid within the first 10 days is due at the end of 30 days from the date of purchase. **Cash discounts** are extended to encourage prompt payment. Assuming that JPS pays for the goods within the discount period, the company will receive a $140 purchase discount (original cost of $8,000 − purchase return of $1,000 = $7,000 balance due × 0.02 discount = $140). The discount reduces the cost of the inventory and thereby lowers the amount due on the account payable. As a result, the **purchase discount** reduces the asset account, Inventory, and the liability account, Accounts Payable. Recall that product costs are expensed when inventory is sold. The income statement will be affected when goods are sold, not when the discount is acquired. Therefore, this transaction does not affect the income statement. The purchase discount will affect future cash flows, but it has no immediate impact. As a result, the discount event does not affect the cash flow statement. The effects of the purchase discount on the financial statements are shown here:

Cash	+	Accts. Rec.	+	Merch. Inv.	=	Accts. Pay.	+	Note Pay.	+	Com. Sh.	+	Ret. Earn.	Rev.	−	Exp.	=	Net Inc.	Cash Flow Statement
NA	+	NA	+	(140)	=	(140)	+	NA	+	NA	+	NA	NA	−	NA	=	NA	NA

JPS paid remaining balance of $6,860 due on account payable. **Event 5**

The effect of the payment on the balance sheet is to reduce assets (Cash) and liabilities (Accounts Payable), but the event does not affect the income statement. However, the $6,860 ($8,000 original cost − $1,000 purchase return − $140 cash discount) cash outflow is shown in the operating activities section of the cash flow statement. The effects on the financial statements follow:

Cash	+	Accts. Rec.	+	Merch. Inv.	=	Accts. Pay.	+	Note Pay.	+	Com. Sh.	+	Ret. Earn.	Rev.	−	Exp.	=	Net Inc.	Cash Flow Statement
(6,860)	+	NA	+	NA	=	(6,860)	+	NA	+	NA	+	NA	NA	−	NA	=	NA	(6,860) OA

Event 6 JPS borrowed $5,000 from a local bank.

JPS issued an interest-bearing note with a six-month term and a 10 percent annual interest rate. The borrowing event increased assets (Cash) and liabilities (Note Payable). The income statement is not affected. The $5,000 inflow is classified as a financing activity on the cash flow statement. These effects follow:

Cash	+	Accts. Rec.	+	Merch. Inv.	=	Accts. Pay.	+	Note Pay.	+	Com. Sh.	+	Ret. Earn.	Rev.	−	Exp.	=	Net Inc.	Cash Flow Statement
5,000	+	NA	+	NA	=	NA	+	5,000	+	NA	+	NA	NA	−	NA	=	NA	5,000 FA

Event 7a JPS recognized $24,750 of cash revenue on the sale of merchandise that cost $11,500.

The sale increases assets (Cash) and equity (Retained Earnings). The revenue recognition causes the net income to increase. Also, the $24,750 cash inflow from the sale is shown in the operating activities section of the cash flow statement. These effects follow:

Cash	+	Accts. Rec.	+	Merch. Inv.	=	Accts. Pay.	+	Note Pay.	+	Com. Sh.	+	Ret. Earn.	Rev.	−	Exp.	=	Net Inc.	Cash Flow Statement
24,750	+	NA	+	NA	=	NA	+	NA	+	NA	+	24,750	24,750	−	NA	=	24,750	27,450 OA

Event 7b JPS recognized $11,500 of cost of goods sold.

Recall that when goods are sold, the product cost—*including a proportionate share of transportation-in and adjustments for purchase returns and allowances*—is taken out of the Merchandise Inventory account and placed into the Cost of Goods Sold expense account. The recognition of the cost of goods sold decreases assets (Inventory) and equity (Retained Earnings). The expense recognition for cost of goods sold causes the net income to decrease. Cash flow is not affected. These effects are shown here:

Cash	+	Accts. Rec.	+	Merch. Inv.	=	Accts. Pay.	+	Note Pay.	+	Com. Sh.	+	Ret. Earn.	Rev.	−	Exp.	=	Net Inc.	Cash Flow Statement
NA	+	NA	+	(11,500)	=	NA	+	NA	+	NA	+	11,500	NA	−	11,500	=	(11,500)	NA

Event 8 Event 8 JPS incurred $450 of freight costs on goods delivered to customers.

Assume that the merchandise sold in Event 7 was delivered under terms FOB destination. The freight cost of $450 was paid in cash. Recall that FOB destination means the seller is responsible for the merchandise until it reaches its destination. JPS is responsible for the freight costs in this case. If the seller is responsible for the freight costs, the cost is considered to be an operating expense, which is shown on the income statement after the computation of gross profit. This treatment is logical because the cost of freight on goods delivered to customers is incurred *after* the goods are sold and, therefore, cannot be considered as part of the costs of obtaining goods or making them ready for sale. The freight cost for goods delivered to customers under terms of FOB destination is called **transportation-out**, **freight-out**, or **delivery expense**. When paid in cash, transportation-out is an expense that reduces assets (Cash) and equity (Retained Earnings). The event increases operating expenses and therefore reduces net income. The $450 cash outflow is shown in the operating activities section of the cash flow statement. These effects follow:

Cash	+	Accts. Rec.	+	Merch. Inv.	=	Accts. Pay.	+	Note Pay.	+	Com. Sh.	+	Ret. Earn.	Rev.	−	Exp.	=	Net Inc.	Cash Flow Statement
(450)	+	NA	+	NA	=	NA	+	NA	+	NA	+	(450)	NA	−	450	=	(450)	(450) OA

Event 9

JPS purchased $14,000 of merchandise inventory under credit terms 2/10, n/30.

The goods were shipped under freight terms FOB destination. The party responsible paid freight costs of $400 in cash. *Since the freight terms are FOB destination, the seller is responsible, and JPS's accounts are not affected.* Therefore, Merchandise Inventory and Accounts Payable will increase by $14,000. Net income and cash flow are not affected. These effects are shown here:

Cash	+	Accts. Rec.	+	Merch. Inv.	=	Accts. Pay.	+	Note Pay.	+	Com. Sh.	+	Ret. Earn.	Rev.	−	Exp.	=	Net Inc.	Cash Flow Statement
NA	+	NA	+	14,000	=	14,000	+	NA	+	NA	+	NA	NA	−	NA	=	NA	NA

Event 10

JPS paid interest on funds borrowed in Event 6.

Assume that the six-month term on the note issued in Event 6 has expired. JPS must determine the amount of interest expense and pay this amount to the bank. Recall that the face value was $5,000, the term six months, and the interest rate 10 percent per year. The amount of interest expense is $250 ($5,000 × 0.10 × 6/12). Since the term has expired, the interest is payable in cash. The payment reduces assets (Cash) and equity (Retained Earnings). The recognition of interest expense causes a corresponding decrease in net income. The cash outflow is shown in the operating activities section of the cash flow statement. These effects follow:

Cash	+	Accts. Rec.	+	Merch. Inv.	=	Accts. Pay.	+	Note Pay.	+	Com. Sh.	+	Ret. Earn.	Rev.	−	Exp.	=	Net Inc.	Cash Flow Statement
(250)	+	NA	+	NA	=	NA	+	NA	+	NA	+	(250)	NA	−	250	=	(250)	(250) OA

Event 11

JPS repaid the principal on funds borrowed in Event 6.

The repayment of the principal requires a $5,000 cash disbursement. This disbursement reduces assets (Cash) and liabilities (Note Payable). The repayment does not affect the income statement. The $5,000 cash outflow is shown in the financing activities section of the cash flow statement. These effects are shown here:

Cash	+	Accts. Rec.	+	Merch. Inv.	=	Accts. Pay.	+	Note Pay.	+	Com. Sh.	+	Ret. Earn.	Rev.	−	Exp.	=	Net Inc.	Cash Flow Statement
(5,000)	+	NA	+	NA	=	NA	+	(5,000)	+	NA	+	NA	NA	−	NA	=	NA	(5,000) FA

Event 12a

JPS recognized $16,800 of revenue on account on the sale of merchandise that cost $8,660.

Assume that the freight terms were FOB shipping point and that the party responsible paid freight costs of $275 in cash. The effect of the revenue recognition on the balance sheet is to increase assets (Accounts Receivable) and equity (Retained Earnings). The event increases revenue and net income. Since the sale was made on account, cash flow is not affected. These effects are as follows:

Cash	+	Accts. Rec.	+	Merch. Inv.	=	Accts. Pay.	+	Note Pay.	+	Com. Sh.	+	Ret. Earn.	Rev.	−	Exp.	=	Net Inc.	Cash Flow Statement
NA	+	16,800	+	NA	=	NA	+	NA	+	NA	+	16,800	16,800	−	NA	=	16,800	NA

Event 12b JPS recognized $8,660 of cost of goods sold.

To recognize the expense associated with the goods sold, $8,660 must be transferred from the Merchandise Inventory account to the Cost of Goods Sold account. The effect of the expense recognition on the balance sheet is to decrease assets (Inventory) and equity (Retained Earnings). The expense, Cost of Goods Sold, increases and net income decreases. Cash flow is not affected. *Since the goods were delivered FOB shipping point, the buyer is responsible for the freight costs and JPS's accounts are not affected.* These effects are shown here:

Cash	+	Accts. Rec.	+	Merch. Inv.	=	Accts. Pay.	+	Note Pay.	+	Com. Sh.	+	Ret. Earn.	Rev.	−	Exp.	=	Net Inc.	Cash Flow Statement
NA	+	NA	+	(8,660)	=	NA	+	NA	+	NA	+	(8,660)	NA	−	8,660	=	(8,660)	NA

Event 13 JPS made a $7,000 cash payment in partial settlement of the account payable generated in Event 9.

Assume that the payment was made after the discount period expired. JPS will not obtain a purchase discount from the supplier. The effect of the event on the balance sheet is to decrease assets (Cash) and liabilities (Accounts Payable). The income statement is not affected. The $7,000 cash outflow is included in the operating activities section of the cash flow statement. These effects follow:

Cash	+	Accts. Rec.	+	Merch. Inv.	=	Accts. Pay.	+	Note Pay.	+	Com. Sh.	+	Ret. Earn.	Rev.	−	Exp.	=	Net Inc.	Cash Flow Statement
(7,000)	+	NA	+	NA	=	(7,000)	+	NA	+	NA	+	NA	NA	−	NA	=	NA	(7,000) OA

Event 14 Event 14 JPS paid cash for selling and administrative expenses amounting to $8,000.

The effect of the event on the balance sheet is to decrease assets (Cash) and equity (Retained Earnings). The recognition of the selling and administrative expenses decreases net income. The $8,000 cash outflow is shown in the operating activities section of the cash flow statement. These effects are as follows:

Cash	+	Accts. Rec.	+	Merch. Inv.	=	Accts. Pay.	+	Note Pay.	+	Com. Sh.	+	Ret. Earn.	Rev.	−	Exp.	=	Net Inc.	Cash Flow Statement
(8,000)	+	NA	+	NA	=	NA	+	NA	+	NA	+	(8,000)	NA	−	8,000	=	(8,000)	(8,000) OA

General Ledger Accounts

Exhibit 5–4 shows the journal entries and Exhibit 5–5 (p. 202) shows the ledger T-accounts that reflect the accounting events just described. A summary of these events is provided here for your convenience. To confirm your understanding of the accounting process, trace the event data to the ledger account balances. The ledger account balances are used to prepare the 2008 financial statements, which are shown in Exhibit 5–6 (p. 203). It is useful to trace the ledger account balances to the financial statements.

Event 1 Purchased $8,000 of inventory on account.
Event 2 Paid $300 cash for transportation-in cost required to obtain goods purchased in Event 1.
Event 3 Returned $1,000 of goods purchased in Event 1.
Event 4 Received cash discount on goods purchased in Event 1.
Event 5 Paid remaining balance of $6,860 due on the account payable associated with Event 1.
Event 6 Borrowed $5,000 from a local bank.
Event 7a Recognized $24,750 of sales revenue.
Event 7b Recognized $11,500 of cost of goods sold.

Exhibit 5–4 *General Jounal Entries*

Event No.	Account Title	Debit	Credit
1	Inventory	8,000	
	Accounts Payable		8,000
2	Inventory	300	
	Accounts Payable		300
3	Accounts Payable	1,000	
	Inventory		1,000
4	Accounts Payable	140	
	Inventory		140
5	Accounts Payable	6,860	
	Cash		6,860
6	Cash	5,000	
	Note Payable		5,000
7(a)	Accounts Receivable	26,200	
	Sales Revenue		26,200
7(b)	Cost of Goods Sold	12,300	
	Inventory		12,300
8	Transportation-out	450	
	Cash		450
9	Inventory	14,000	
	Accounts Payable		14,000
10	Interest Expense	250	
	Cash		250
11	Note Payable	5,000	
	Cash		5,000
12(a)	Accounts Receivable	16,800	
	Sales Revenue		16,800
12(b)	Cost of Goods Sold	8,660	
	Inventory		8,660
13	Accounts Payable	7,000	
	Cash		7,000
14	Selling Expenses	8,000	
	Cash		8,000

Event 8 Incurred $450 of transportation-out cost on goods delivered to customers.
Event 9 Purchased $14,000 of inventory under credit terms 2/10, n/30.
Event 10 Paid interest on funds borrowed in Event 6.
Event 11 Repaid principal on funds borrowed in Event 6.
Event 12a Recognized $16,800 of sales revenue on account.
Event 12b Recognized $8,660 of cost of goods sold.
Event 13 Made a $7,000 cash payment in partial settlement of the account payable generated in Event 9.
Event 14 Paid cash for selling and administrative expenses amounting to $8,000.

Financial Statements

LO7 Compare and contrast single- and multistep income statements.

Carefully observe the format of the income statement shown in Exhibit 5–6. It provides more information than a simple comparison of revenues and expenses. It matches particular expenses with particular revenues. More specifically, the computation of gross profit provides information about the relationship between the cost of goods sold and the selling price. This information improves comparisons between companies or between stores within the same company. Such comparisons permit investors and managers to assess the competitiveness of pricing strategies, to evaluate the effectiveness of

Exhibit 5–5 *Ledger Accounts*

Assets = Liabilities + Equity

Assets

Cash

	Debit	Credit	
Bal.	12,000	300	(2)
(6)	5,000	6,860	(5)
(7a)	24,750	450	(8)
		250	(10)
		5,000	(11)
		7,000	(13)
		8,000	(14)
Bal.	13,890		

Accounts Receivable

	Debit	Credit	
(12a)	16,800		
Bal.	16,800		

Merchandise Inventory

	Debit	Credit	
Bal.	6,000	1,000	(3)
(1)	8,000	140	(4)
(2)	300	11,500	(7b)
(9)	14,000	8,660	(12b)
Bal.	7,000		

Liabilities

Accounts Payable

	Debit	Credit	
(3)	1,000	8,000	(1)
(4)	140	14,000	(9)
(5)	6,860		
(13)	7,000		
		7,000	Bal.

Note Payable

	Debit	Credit	
(11)	5,000	5,000	(6)
		0	Bal.

Equity

Common Shares

	Debit	Credit	
		15,000	Bal.

Retained Earnings

	Debit	Credit	
		3,000	Bal.
		12,690	(cl)
		15,690	Bal.

Sales Revenue

	Debit	Credit	
(cl)	41,550	24,750	(7a)
		16,800	(12a)
		0	Bal.

Cost of Goods Sold

	Debit	Credit	
(7b)	11,500	20,160	(cl)
(12b)	8,660		
Bal.	0		

Transportation-out

	Debit	Credit	
(8)	450	450	(cl)
Bal.	0		

Selling and Admin. Expenses

	Debit	Credit	
(14)	8,000	8,000	(cl)
Bal.	0		

Interest Expense

	Debit	Credit	
(10)	250	250	(cl)
Bal.	0		

Total Assets	=	Total Liabilities	+	Total Equity
$37,690		$7,000		$30,690

management, and to anticipate the likelihood of continued performance. The income statement in Exhibit 5–6 also distinguishes regular operating activities from peripheral, nonoperating activities. The separation of operating from nonoperating activities promotes financial statement analysis. Analysts are able to distinguish recurring operating activities from items such as gains and losses, discontinued operating activities, and extraordinary items that are not likely to be repeated. Income statements that show these additional relationships are called **multistep income statements**. This title distinguishes them from **single-step income statements**, which display a single comparison of total revenues and total expenses.

Note that interest is classified as a nonoperating item on a *multistep income statement*. This treatment is inconsistent with the way interest is reported on the cash flow statement. Recall that interest is reported as an operating activity on the *cash flow statement*.

Exhibit 5–6 *Financial Statements*

Income Statements	
Net Sales	$41,550
Cost of Goods Sold	(20,160)
Gross Margin	21,390
Less: Operating Exp.	
Sell. And Admin. Exp.	(8,000)
Transportation-out	(450)
Operating Income	12,940
Non-operating Items	
Interest Expense	(250)
Net Income	$12,690

Balance Sheet	
Assets	
Cash	$13,890
Accounts Rec.	16,800
Merchandise Inv.	7,000
Total Assets	$37,690
Liabilities	
Accounts Payable	$ 7,000
Shareholders' Equity	
Common Shares	15,000
Retained Earnings	15,690
Total Shareholders' Equity	30,690
Total Liab. and Shareholders' Equity	$37,690

Cash Flow Statement	
Operating Activities	
Inflow from Customers	$24,750
Outflow for Inventory	(14,160)
Outflow for Trans.-out	(450)
Outflow for S&A Exp.	(8,000)
Outflow for Interest	(250)
Net Cash Inflow from Oper.	1,890
Investing Activities	0
Financing Activities	
Inflow from Note Pay.	5,000
Outflow to Repay Debt	(5,000)
Net Cash Flow from Fin.	0
Net Change in Cash	1,890
Beginning Cash Bal.	12,000
Ending Cash Bal.	$13,890

Events Affecting Sales

Returns, allowances, and cash discounts also affect sales. To illustrate, assume JPS engages in the following events in January 2009.

1. Sells merchandise for $8,500 under terms 1/10, net/30.
2. Recognizes cost of goods sold amounting to $4,800.
3. Accepts $500 of returned merchandise.
4. The cost of the returned merchandise referenced in Event 3 amounted to $300.
5. Grants a sales discount on the remaining account receivable when it is collected within the 30-day discount period. The amount of the discount is $80 ([$8,500 − $500] × 0.01).
6. Recognizes the cash collection of the remaining receivables balance ($8,500 sale − $500 return − $80 discount = $7,920).

The effects of these transactions on the financial statements follow:

Event No.	Cash	+	Accts. Rec.	+	Merch. Inv.	=	Accts. Pay.	+	Note Pay.	+	Com. Sh.	+	Ret. Earn.	Rev.	−	Exp.	=	Net Inc.	Cash Flow Statement
Bal.	13,890	+	16,800	+	7,000	=	7,000	+	0	+	15,000	+	15,690	NA	−	NA	=	NA	NA
1		+	8,500	+		=		+		+		+	8,500	8,500	−		=	8,500	NA
2		+		+	(4,800)	=		+		+		+	(4,800)		−	4,800	=	(4,800)	NA
3		+	(500)	+		=		+		+		+	(500)	(500)	−		=	(500)	NA
4		+		+	300	=		+		+		+	300		−	(300)	=	300	NA
5		+	(80)	+		=		+		+		+	(80)	(80)	−		=	(80)	NA
6	7,920	+	(7,920)	+		=		+		+		+			−		=		7,920 OA
Bal.	21,810	+	16,800	+	2,500	=	7,000	+	0	+	15,000	+	19,110	7,920	−	4,500	=	3,420	7,920 NC

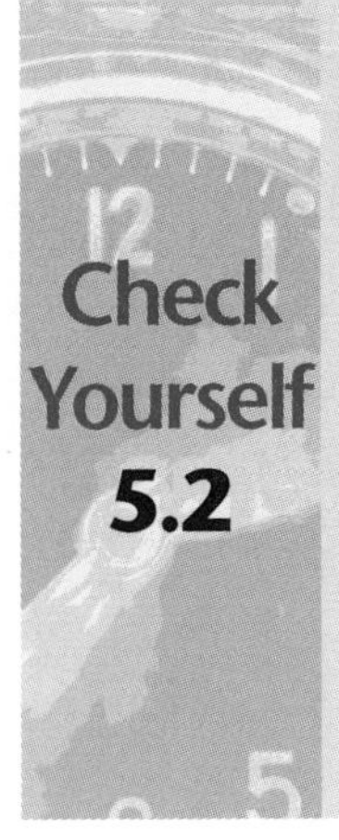

Choi Company purchased $24,000 of inventory on account with payment terms of 2/10, n/30 and freight terms FOB shipping point. Freight costs were $1,200. Choi paid $18,000 of the accounts payable within the 10-day discount period and the remaining $6,000 within 30 days. Choi sold all of the inventory for $32,000. Based on this information, determine the amount of gross profit Choi would report on the income statement.

Answer The cost of the inventory is determined as follows:

List price	$24,000
Less: Purchase discount ($18,000 × .02)	(360)
Plus Transportation-in	1,200
Total cost	$24,840

The gross profit is $7,160, the sales price less cost of goods sold ($32,000 − $24,840 = $7,160).

Lost, Damaged, or Stolen Merchandise

LO8 Understand how lost, damaged, or stolen inventory affects financial statements.

The *perpetual inventory method* is designed to capture information as it occurs. However, some events are not detectable at the time of occurrence. For example, when a shoplifter steals merchandise, the loss cannot be recorded until it is discovered, which is usually sometime after the theft occurred. Also, customers or employees may not report damage to merchandise when it happened. Finally, merchandise may be lost or misplaced. Again, the loss cannot be recorded until it is discovered. Lost, damaged, or stolen merchandise is usually discovered when a physical count of the merchandise on hand is taken at the end of the accounting period and those figures are compared with the book balance in the Inventory account.

When a discrepancy between the book balance and the physical count of inventory is discovered, an adjusting entry is needed to correct the book balance. If goods have been lost, damaged, or stolen, the book balance will be higher than the actual amount of inventory on hand. In this case, the adjusting entry acts to reduce assets and equity. More specifically, the Inventory account is reduced, and an expense for the amount of the lost, damaged, or stolen inventory is recognized.

Adjustment for Lost, Damaged, or Stolen Inventory

To illustrate, assume that Midwest Merchandising Company uses the perpetual inventory method. The end-of-period physical count reveals $23,500 of merchandise on hand while the Inventory account contains a $24,000 balance. The effect of the inventory write-down on the financial statements is shown here. The event decreases assets (Inventory) and equity (Retained Earnings). The write-down increases expenses and thereby decreases net income. Cash flow is not affected.

Assets	=	Liab.	+	Equity	Rev.	−	Exp.	=	Net Inc.	Cash Flow Statement
(500)	=	NA	+	(500)	NA	−	500	=	(500)	NA

The following entry is used to record the transaction in the general journal:

Account Title	Debit	Credit
Inventory Loss (Cost of Goods Sold)	500	
Inventory		500

reality bytes

"Closed for Inventory Count" is a sign you often see on retail stores sometime during the month of January. When companies use a perpetual inventory system, the amount of inventory on hand may be unknown because of lost, damaged, or stolen goods. The only way to determine the amount of inventory on hand is to count it. Why count it in January? Christmas shoppers and many after-Christmas sales shoppers are finished by mid-January, leaving the stores low on both merchandise and customers. Therefore, stores have less merchandise to count and "lost sales" are minimized during January. Companies that do not depend on seasonal sales (e.g., a plumbing supplies wholesale business) may choose to count inventory at some other time during the year. Indeed, counting inventory is not a revenue-generating activity. It is a necessary evil that should be conducted when it least disrupts operations.

Theoretically, the inventory loss is an operating expense. However, such losses are normally immaterial in amount and for internal reporting purposes are treated as additions to the amount of cost of goods sold.

Financial Analysis for Merchandising Companies

Merchandising companies face a highly competitive environment. A consulting enterprise may shelter itself from competition by hiring personnel whose expertise cannot be duplicated. A manufacturing company may hold a patent to a product that gives the company exclusive rights to produce it. In contrast, merchandising companies usually sell products that are available for sale by other companies. Merchandise sold at Wal-Mart usually is sold at Zellers as well, and many customers shop where the prices are lowest. Because of this competition, merchandising companies watch their *margins* very carefully. One such margin is the *gross profit*, introduced earlier in the chapter.

Common Size Financial Statements

LO9 Use common size financial statements to evaluate managerial performance.

Chapter 3 introduced ratios as a meaningful way to compare a large company's accounting information with that of a small company. It was shown that raw accounting numbers alone can be misleading. Suppose that Smith Company has a 10 percent return on assets while Jones Company returns only 8 percent. Also, assume that Smith Company has $1,000,000 of assets while Jones Company has $2,000,000. In these circumstances, Smith Company would report less income ($1,000,000 × 0.10 = $100,000) than Jones Company ($2,000,000 × 0.08 = $160,000) even though Smith Company was doing a better job of investing its assets. Similar problems can arise when a company tries to compare its financial statements from the current period with those of prior periods. How good is a $1,000,000 increase in net income? Certainly not as good if the company were Intel as it would be if the company were a small local computer store. To simplify comparisons between companies or between periods, we can use ratios to prepare financial statements on a percentage basis. Such statements are called **common size financial statements**. In this chapter we focus on *common size income statements*.

When a common size income statement is prepared, each account balance on the statement, or at least those of interest, is converted to a percentage of sales. Usually companies base common size income statements on net sales, which is sales minus sales returns and allowances and sales discounts. Thus, net sales become the base figure representing the 100 percent mark. Next, the cost of goods sold is divided by net sales to determine the cost of goods sold percentage, and so on down the income statement, with each item being converted to a percentage by dividing it by net sales. Exhibit 5–7 demonstrates a common size income statement using data from the 2008 income statement shown in Exhibit 5–6 for JPS.

Exhibit 5–7

JUNE'S PLANT SHOP
Common Size Income Statement
For the Year Ended 2008

Net Sales	$41,550	100%
Cost of Goods Sold	(20,160)	(49)
Gross Profit	21,390	51
Less: Operating Expenses		
Selling and Administrative Expenses	(8,000)	(19)
Transportation-out	(450)	(1)
Operating Income	12,940	31
Nonoperating Items		
Interest Expense	(250)	(1)
Net Income	$12,690	30%

Gross Profit Percentage

Perhaps the most important percentage on the common size income statement is the one for gross profit. Users of accounting information often compute this ratio even when common size statements are not prepared. It is often called the **gross profit percentage** and is defined as

$$\frac{\text{Gross profit}}{\text{Net sales}}$$

The gross profit percentage can indicate a lot about a retailer. For example, it provides some indication as to a company's pricing strategy. Companies with low margins have a small spread between their cost and their sales price. In other words, they price their merchandise low relative to its cost. For example, assume that two stores purchase the same type of inventory item for resale. Suppose that the item costs $100. Store A sells the item for $130 while Store B charges $140. The gross profit percentage for Store A is 23 percent ($30 ÷ $130) and for Store B it is 29 percent ($40 ÷ $140). Clearly, lower margins suggest lower sales prices.

Real-World Data

LO10 Use ratio analysis to evaluate managerial performance.

Exhibit 5–8 shows the 2000 gross profit percentages and return on sales ratios for six companies. Three companies sell a variety of consumer goods; the other three companies mine raw materials.

The upscale retailer Tommy Hilfiger has a much higher gross profit margin than the discount retailer Wal-Mart. Due to its size, Wal-Mart can usually obtain favourable pricing through quantity discounts (price reductions given when a customer buys large quantities of goods). Lower prices should translate into higher sales. Indeed, Wal-Mart has experienced phenomenal growth in sales recently. Note that all six companies have a wide range of gross profit percentages.

The following sales data are from the records of two retail sales companies. All amounts are in thousands.

	Company A	Company B
Sales	$21,234	$43,465
Cost of goods sold	14,864	34,772
Gross profit	$ 6,370	$ 8,693

One company is an upscale department store, and the other is a discount sales store. Which company is the upscale department store?

Answer The gross profit percentage for Company A is approximately 30 percent ($6,370 ÷ $21,234). The gross profit percentage for Company B is approximately 20 percent ($8,693 ÷ $43,465). These percentages suggest that Company A is selling goods with a higher markup than Company B, which implies that Company A is the upscale department store.

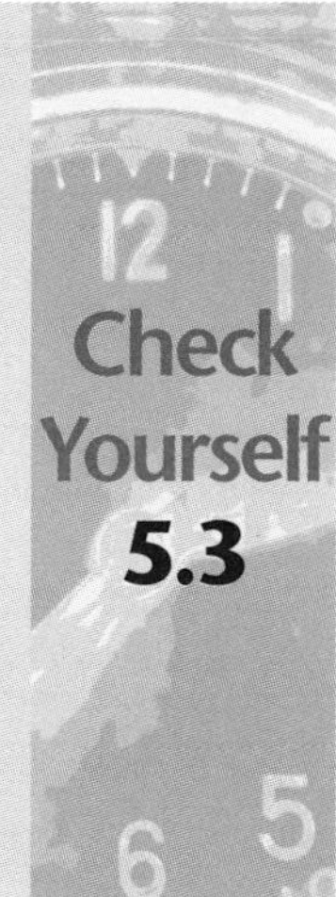

Return on Sales

Exhibit 5–8

Industry/Company	Gross Profit %	Return on Sales
Retail		
Wal-Mart	21%	3%
The Gap	37%	11%
Tommy Hilfiger	41%	7%
Mining		
INCO (Nickel)	20%	4%
De Beers (Diamonds)	40%	14%
Barrick Gold Mines	36%	23%

Low prices motivate high sales, but there is a limit as to how low a company can go. The gross profit percentage must be high enough to cover the cost of other expenses that are necessary to operate the stores. Employees must be paid. A retailer must also pay for utilities, rent, office equipment, furnishings, taxes, and a variety of other operating activities that consume resources. If Wal-Mart sells its goods at lower prices, it will have less money to pay for other expenses. Does this mean Wal-Mart will also have relatively lower profits? Another ratio from the common size income statement that can help answer this question is the **net income percentage**. The net income percentage (sometimes called **return on sales**) is determined as follows:

$$\frac{\text{Net income}}{\text{Net sales}}$$

Even though Tommy Hilfiger had a slightly higher gross profit percentage than The Gap (41 percent versus 37 percent) in 2000, The Gap had a higher return on sales (11 percent versus 7 percent). Regarding the three mining companies, the return on sales ratios for De Beers and Barrick Gold are higher than that for INCO. Gold and diamonds have a much higher selling price than nickel! Also, the data suggest that Wal-Mart can sell its products for lower prices, and can do so by exercising strong control over its operating expenses.

Use of Common Size Financial Statements

LO11 Understand the cost of financing inventory.

The above discussion focused on the use of common size income data to make comparisons among companies. Investors, creditors, and managers also find it useful to compare a particular company's performance over different periods. To illustrate, assume that June's Plant Shop decides to relocate to an upscale shopping mall with a wealthier customer base. June realizes she will have to pay more for rent but believes she will be able to cover the higher cost by selling her merchandise at higher prices. June changes location on January 1, 2009. Exhibit 5–9 shows common size income statements for 2008 and 2009. Comparisons between these two income statements can provide insight as to whether June's strategy was successful.

Exhibit 5–9

JUNE'S PLANT SHOP
Common Size Income Statement*

	2008		2009	
Net Sales	$ 41,550	100%	$ 49,860	100%
Cost of Goods Sold	(20,160)	(49)	(19,944)	(40)
Gross Profit	21,390	51	29,916	60
Less: Operating Expenses				
Selling and Administrative Expenses	(8,000)	(19)	(12,465)	(25)
Transportation-out	(450)	(1)	(500)	(1)
Operating Income	12,940	31	16,951	34
Nonoperating Items				
Interest Expense	(250)	(1)	(400)	(1)
Net Income	$ 12,690	30%	$ 16,551	33%

* All percentages have been rounded to the nearest whole percentage point.

An analysis of the common size statements suggests that June's strategy did indeed increase the profitability of her business. By increasing prices, June increased the absolute dollar value of sales by $8,310 ($49,860 − $41,550). Notice that operating expenses increased as expected. They now constitute 25 percent of sales instead of 19 percent. This 6 percent increase in operating expenses is more than offset by the increase in the gross profit rate. Gross profit percentage in 2009 was 9 percent higher than in 2008 (60 percent − 51 percent), which verifies that June was able to raise her prices. Transportation cost remained relatively stable. Interest costs were higher, implying June had to borrow more funds to support the higher operating expenses. However, neither transportation nor interest costs changed drastically enough to affect the measurement in percentage terms. The new strategy's overall impact is apparent in the net income percentage, which increased from 30 to 33 percent. Therefore, profitability increased as expected.

Financing of Merchandise Inventory

Suppose a store purchases inventory in October to sell during the Christmas season. Assume sales are made on account so that cash from the sale is collected in January or February of the next year. Since the cash from the sale is collected three or four months after the goods were purchased, how will the company get the money to pay for the inventory? One answer is to borrow the money. The company could pay for the merchandise in October with money borrowed from a bank. The bank could be repaid when the cash collections from sales come in during January and February.

The obvious drawback to obtaining a loan to pay for inventory is that it incurs interest expense on the borrowed funds. However, other alternative sources of financing inventory would also be expensive. If the owner uses his or her own money, then these funds cannot be invested elsewhere. For example, the owner's money could be deposited in an interest-earning savings account. The loss of interest earned is called an **opportunity cost**; it is effectively a financing cost that is just as real as the interest expense. Net income falls regardless of whether a business incurs expenses or loses revenue.

A third alternative is to purchase the inventory on account. However, when purchases are made on account, the seller usually charges the buyer an interest fee. This charge may be "hidden" in the form of higher prices. So while interest costs are lower, the cost of goods sold is higher. As pointed out earlier in this chapter, many companies recognize financing costs by offering buyers the opportunity to receive cash discounts by paying for purchases within a short time immediately following the sale. In summary, any way you look at it, merchandisers incur significant inventory-financing costs.

There is no way to eliminate the cost of financing inventory, but accounting information can help companies minimize this cost. As much as possible, businesses should reduce the time for which goods stay in inventory before being sold. Ratios that help manage inventory turnover are explained in Chapter 8. Companies should also try to shorten the time it takes to get customers to pay for the goods they purchase. This relates to managing accounts receivable turnover, which is explained in Chapter 7. In later chapters we discuss efforts to control inventory costs; this chapter provided a clear explanation of the need for such control.

---

a look back

This chapter introduced accounting for *merchandising companies*, which earn a profit by selling inventory at a price higher than the cost of goods. Merchandising companies include *retail companies* (which sell goods to the final consumer) and *wholesale companies* (which sell to other merchandising companies). The term for the products sold by merchandising companies is *inventory*. The costs to purchase the inventory, to receive it, and to make inventory ready for sale are known as *product costs*. These are first accumulated in an inventory account (balance sheet asset account) and then recognized as cost of goods sold (income statement expense account) in the period goods are sold. The purchase and sale of inventory can be recognized when goods are bought and sold (perpetual method) or at the end of the accounting period (periodic method).

Accounting for inventory includes the treatment of cash discounts, transportation costs, and returns and allowances. The cost of inventory is the list price less any *cash discount* offered by the seller. The cost of freight paid to acquire inventory (*transportation-in*) is considered a product cost. The cost of freight paid to deliver inventory to customers (*transportation-out*) is a selling expense. *Sales returns and allowances* and *sales discounts* are subtracted from sales revenue to determine the amount of *net sales* shown on the income statement. Purchase returns and allowances reduce product cost. Theoretically, the cost of lost, damaged, or stolen inventory is an operating expense. However, these costs are usually immaterial in amount and are often reported as part of cost of goods sold on the income statement.

Some companies show product costs separately from general, selling, and administrative costs on the income statement. Cost of goods sold is subtracted from sales revenue to determine the *gross profit*. General, selling, and administrative expenses are subtracted from gross profit to determine the amount of income from operations. This format is called a *multistep income statement*. Other companies report income under a *single-step format*. In this case, the cost of goods sold is listed along with general, selling, and administrative items in a single expense category that is subtracted in total from revenue to determine income from operations.

Merchandising businesses face a highly competitive environment. They must manage their operations closely to remain profitable. Managers of merchandising businesses often use *common size financial statements* (statements presented on a percentage basis) and ratio analysis to monitor their operations. Percentages (common size financial statements) permit comparisons among companies of different size. Although a $1 million increase in sales may be good for a small company and bad for a large company, a 10 percent increase represents an increment that is common to any size company. The two most common ratios used by merchandising companies are the *gross profit percentage* (gross profit ÷ net sales) and the *net income percentage* (net income ÷ net sales). Interpreting these ratios requires an understanding of industry practice. For example, a discount store such as Wal-Mart would be expected to have a much lower gross profit percentage than an upscale store such as Tommy Hilfiger.

Managers should be aware of the financing cost associated with carrying inventory. When it invests funds in inventory, a firm loses the opportunity to invest them in interest-bearing assets. This is why the financing cost of inventory is often called an *opportunity cost*. To minimize financing costs, a company should minimize the amount of inventory it carries, the length of time it holds the inventory, and the time it requires to collect accounts receivable.

a look forward

To this point, we have covered the basic accounting cycle for service and merchandising businesses. The rest of the book takes a closer look at specific accounting issues. For example, Chapter 6 examines internal control and accounting for cash. In Chapter 6 you will learn the accounting practices and procedures that companies use to protect their cash and other assets. You will learn to account for petty cash (small disbursements of cash) and to prepare a bank reconciliation. You will also learn to classify assets as short or long term. Finally, you will learn to use a ratio to assess the liquidity (the ability to meet short-term obligations) of a business.

APPENDIX

Periodic Inventory Method

LO12 Name the main features of the periodic inventory method.

Under certain conditions, it is impractical to record inventory transactions as they occur. For example, consider the operations of a fast-food restaurant. If records were maintained perpetually, it would be necessary to transfer costs from the Inventory account to the Cost of Goods Sold account each time a hamburger, order of fries, soft drink, or any other food item was sold. Obviously, recording each item at the point of sale would be impractical without the availability of sophisticated computer equipment. The *periodic inventory method* offers a practical approach to recording inventory transactions in a low-technology, high-turnover environment.

Under the periodic method, the cost of goods sold is determined at the end of the period rather than at the point of sale. Indeed, the Inventory account is *not* affected by purchases or sales of inventory. When goods are purchased, the cost is recorded in a Purchases account, and no entry is made to reduce inventory when goods are sold. Purchase returns and allowances, purchase discounts, and transportation-in are recorded in separate accounts. The amount of cost of goods sold is determined by subtracting the amount of ending inventory from the total cost of goods available for sale. The amount of ending inventory is determined by making a year-end physical count. Goods that are not in stock at the end of the period are assumed to have been sold. This is the same logic used in earlier chapters to determine the amount of supplies used during an accounting period.

It is important to note that the perpetual and periodic inventory systems represent alternative procedures for recording the same information. The amounts of cost of goods sold and ending inventory reported in the financial statements will be the same regardless of which method is applied. For comparative purposes, Exhibit 5–10 shows the general journal entries used under the periodic inventory method to record the accounting events for JPS for the 2008 accounting period. Observe carefully that the amount of cost of goods sold is recorded in an adjusting entry. This entry transfers the various product costs to the Cost of Goods Sold account and adjusts the Inventory account to reflect the amount of inventory on hand at the end of the accounting period. As its name implies, accountants using the *periodic inventory method* record changes in the balance of the Inventory and Cost of Goods Sold accounts at the end of the accounting period.

Schedule of Cost of Goods Sold

Since under the periodic method the cost of goods sold is not determined at the point of sale, it must be computed at the end of the period. The following logic is used to make the computation. First, calculate the cost of goods available for sale. This computation includes the amount of beginning inventory, plus the cost of all purchases, less any purchase returns and allowances, less purchase discounts, plus the cost of transportation-in. The result represents the total cost of all merchandise inventory that *could* have been sold to customers (the *cost of goods available for sale*). The next step is to subtract the amount of inventory that is on hand at the end of the accounting period from the cost of goods available for sale. The result is the amount of *cost of goods sold.*

Exhibit 5–11 is the computation of cost of goods sold for JPS's 2008 accounting period. The **schedule of cost of goods sold** is used for internal reporting purposes and is not shown in the formal financial statements made available to the public. The amount of cost of goods sold is reported as a single line item on the income statement in exactly the same manner as demonstrated for the perpetual inventory. Indeed, the financial statements in Exhibit 5–6 (page 203) will be the same regardless of whether JPS used the perpetual or periodic method to account for inventory transactions.

Lost, Damaged, or Stolen Merchandise

In the *periodic inventory method*, lost, damaged, or stolen merchandise is included in the cost of goods sold as part of the computational process. Since lost, damaged, or stolen merchandise would not be included in the year-end physical count, these goods are assumed to have been sold when the cost of goods sold is computed by subtracting ending inventory from cost of goods available for sale. From a managerial perspective, this is a major disadvantage of the periodic method. Since the periodic method does not separate the cost of lost, damaged, or stolen merchandise

Exhibit 5–10 *General Journal Entries*

Event No.	Account Title	Debit	Credit
1	Purchases	8,000	
	Accounts Payable		8,000
2	Transportation-in	300	
	Cash		300
3	Accounts payable	1,000	
	Purchase Returns and Allowances		1,000
4	Accounts Payable	140	
	Purchase Discounts		140
5	Accounts Payable	6,860	
	Cash		6,860
6	Cash	5,000	
	Note Payable		5,000
7	Cash	24,750	
	Sales Revenue		24,750
8	Transportation-out	450	
	Cash		450
9	Purchases	14,000	
	Accounts Payable		14,000
10	Interest Expense	250	
	Cash		250
11	Note Payable	5,000	
	Cash		5,000
12	Accounts Receivable	16,800	
	Sales Revenue		16,800
13	Accounts Payable	7,000	
	Cash		7,000
14	Selling and Administrative Expenses	8,000	
	Cash		8,000
ADJ	Cost of Goods Sold	20,160	
	Inventory	1,000	
	Purchase Returns and Allowances	1,000	
	Purchase Discounts	140	
	Purchases		22,000
	Transportation-in		300
CL	Sales Revenue	41,550	
	Cost of Goods Sold		20,160
	Transportation-out		450
	Selling and Administrative Expenses		8,000
	Interest Expense		250
	Retained Earnings		12,690

Exhibit 5–11 *Schedule of Cost of Goods Sold*

Beginning Inventory	$ 6,000
Purchases	22,000
Purchase Returns and Allowances	(1,000)
Purchase Discounts	(140)
Transportation-in	300
Cost of Goods Available for Sale	27,160
Ending Inventory	(7,000)
Cost of Goods Sold	$20,160

from the cost of goods sold, the amount of the inventory loss is unknown. Without knowing the amount of the inventory loss, management cannot make informed decisions on the cost/benefit trade-offs of various security systems.

Advantages and Disadvantages of the Periodic Method versus the Perpetual Method

The chief advantage of the periodic method is recording efficiency. Recording inventory transactions occasionally (periodically) requires less work than recording them on a continuous basis (perpetually). The impracticality of a fast-food restaurant's use of a perpetual inventory system would be even greater for a typical grocery store. Think of the number of transactions the grocery store would have to record every business day under the perpetual method. The recording advantage of the periodic method must be weighed against the control advantage inherent in the perpetual method. Since the perpetual method increases and decreases the Inventory account balance when purchases and sales are made, the book balance of inventory should agree with the amount of inventory in stock at any given time. The amount of lost, damaged, destroyed, or stolen inventory can be determined by checking the book balance against a physical count of inventory. Also, the availability of immediate feedback simplifies reorder decisions and profitability assessments.

SELF-STUDY REVIEW PROBLEMS

Academy Sales Company (ASC) started the 2004 accounting period with the balances given in the following financial statements model. During 2004 ASC experienced the following business events:

1. Purchased $16,000 of merchandise inventory on account, terms 2/10, n/30.
2. The goods that were purchased in Event 1 were delivered FOB shipping point. Freight costs of $600 were paid in cash by the responsible party.
3. Returned $500 of goods purchased in Event 1.

4a. Recorded the cash discount on the goods purchased in Event 1.
4b. Paid the balance due on the account payable within the discount period.
5a. Recognized $21,000 of cash revenue from the sale of merchandise.
5b. Recognized $13,000 of cost of goods sold.

6. The merchandise in Event 5a was sold to customers FOB destination. Freight costs of $950 were paid in cash by the responsible party.
7. Paid cash of $4,000 for selling and administrative expenses.

Required

a. Record these transactions in a financial statements model like the following one:

Event No.	Cash	+	Merch. Inv.	=	Accts. Pay.	+	Com. Sh.	+	Ret. Earn.	Rev.	−	Exp.	=	Net Inc.	Cash Flow Statement
Bal.	25,000	+	3,000	=	0	+	18,000	+	10,000	NA	−	NA	=	NA	NA

b. Calculate the gross profit percentage. Based on ASC's gross profit percentage and the information shown in Exhibit 5–8, classify ASC as an upscale department store or a retail discount store.

Solution to Requirement a

Event No.	Cash	+	Merch. Inv.	=	Accts. Pay.	+	Com. Sh.	+	Ret. Earn.	Rev.	−	Exp.	=	Net Inc.	Cash Flow Statement
Bal.	25,000	+	3,000	=	0	+	18,000	+	10,000	NA	−	NA	=	NA	NA
1	16,000	+	16,000	=		+		+			−		=		
2	(600)	+	600	=		+		+			−		=		(600) OA
3		+	(500)	=	(500)	+		+			−		=		
4a		+	(310)	=	(310)	+		+			−		=		
4b	(15,190)	+		=	(15,190)	+		+			−		=		(15,190) OA
5a	21,000	+		=		+		+	21,000	21,000	−		=	21,000	(21,000) OA
5b		+	(13,000)	=		+		+	(13,000)		−	13,000	=	13,000	
6	(950)	+		=		+		+	(950)		−	950	=	(950)	(950) OA
7	(4,000)	+		=		+		+	(4,000)		−	4,000	=	(4,000)	(4,000) OA
Bal.	25,260	+	5,790	=	0	+	18,000	+	13,050	21,000	−	17,950	=	3,050	260 NC

Solution to Requirement b

Gross profit equals sales minus cost of goods sold. In this case, the gross profit is \$8,000 (\$21,000 − \$13,000). The gross profit percentage is computed by dividing gross profit by sales. In this case, the gross profit percentage is 38 percent (\$8,000 ÷ \$21,000). Since this percentage is closest to the percentage shown for the upscale store, Tommy Hilfiger, the data suggest ASC is also an upscale store.

KEY TERMS

allowance *197*
cash discount *197*
common size financial statements *206*
cost of goods available for sale *190*
cost of goods sold *190*
delivery expense *198*
FOB (free on board) destination point *196*
FOB (free on board) shipping point *196*
gross profit *190*
gross profit percentage *206*
inventory *189*
merchandise inventory *189*
merchandising businesses *189*
multistep income statements *202*
net income percentage *207*
opportunity cost *208*
period costs *190*
periodic inventory method *191*
perpetual inventory method *191*
product cost *190*
purchase discount *197*
retail companies *189*
return on sales *207*
schedule of cost of goods sold *210*
selling and administrative costs *190*
single-step income statement *202*
transportation-in (freight-in) *196*
transportation-out (freight-out) *198*
2/10, n/30 *197*
wholesale companies *189*

QUESTIONS

1. Define *inventory*. What items might be included in inventory?
2. Define *merchandise inventory*. Distinguish between inventory and merchandise inventory. What types of costs are included in the Merchandise Inventory account?
3. What is the difference between a product cost and a selling and administrative cost?
4. How is the cost of goods available for sale determined?
5. What portion of cost of goods available for sale is shown on the balance sheet? What portion is shown on the income statement?
6. When are period costs expensed? When are product costs expensed?
7. If PetCo had net sales of \$600,000, goods available for sale of \$450,000, and cost of goods sold of \$375,000, what is its gross profit? What amount of inventory will be shown on its balance sheet?

8. Explain the difference between a perpetual inventory method and a periodic inventory method. Discuss the advantages of each. Must a physical inventory be taken with both methods? Why or why not?
9. What are the effects of the following types of transactions on the accounting equation? Also, identify the financial statements that are affected. (Assume that the perpetual inventory method is used.)
   a. Acquisition of cash from the issue of common shares.
   b. Contribution of inventory by an owner of a company.
   c. Purchase of inventory with cash by a company.
   d. Sale of inventory for cash.
10. Northern Merchandising Company sold inventory that cost $12,000 for $20,000 cash. How does this event affect the accounting equation? What financial statements and accounts are affected? (Assume that the perpetual inventory method is used.)
11. If goods are shipped FOB shipping point, which party (buyer or seller) is responsible for the shipping costs?
12. Define *transportation-in*. Is it a product or a period cost?
13. Quality Cellular Co. paid $80 for freight on merchandise that it had purchased for resale to customers (transportation-in) and paid $135 for freight on merchandise delivered to customers (transportation-out). What account is debited for the $80 payment? What account is debited for the $135 payment?
14. Why would a seller grant an allowance to a buyer of the seller's merchandise?
15. Dyer Department Store purchased goods with the terms 2/10, n/30. What do these terms mean?
16. Eastern Discount Stores incurred a $5,000 cash cost. How does the accounting treatment of this cost differ if the cash were paid for inventory versus commissions to sales personnel?
17. What is the purpose of giving a cash discount to credit customers?
18. Define *transportation-out*. Is it a product cost or a period cost for the seller?
19. Explain the difference between purchase returns and sales returns. How do purchase returns affect the financial statements of both buyer and seller? How do sales returns affect the financial statements of both buyer and seller?
20. How is net sales determined?
21. What is the difference between a multistep income statement and a single-step income statement?
22. What is the purpose of preparing a schedule of cost of goods sold?
23. What is the advantage of using common size statements to present financial information for several accounting periods?
24. What information is provided by the return on sales ratio?

EXERCISES

When the instructions for any exercise or problem call for the preparation of an income statement, use the *multistep format* unless otherwise indicated.

L.O. 1, 3, 5 EXERCISE 5–1 *Comparing a Merchandising Company with a Service Company*

The following information is available for two different types of businesses for the accounting period. Darwin Consulting Co. is a service business that provides consulting services to small businesses. Book Mart Inc. is a merchandising business that sells books to college students.

Data for Darwin Consulting Co.

1. Borrowed $10,000 from the bank to start the business.
2. Provided $12,000 of services to customers and collected $12,000 cash.
3. Paid salary expense of $7,200.

Data for Book Mart Inc.

1. Borrowed $10,000 from the bank to start the business.
2. Purchased $8,250 of inventory for cash.
3. Inventory costing $6,500 was sold for $12,000 cash.
4. Paid $700 cash for operating expenses.

Required

a. Prepare an income statement, balance sheet, and cash flow statement for each of the companies.
b. What is different about the income statements of the two businesses?
c. What is different about the balance sheets of the two businesses?
d. How are the cash flow statements different for the two businesses?

EXERCISE 5–2 *Effect of Inventory Transactions on Journals, Ledgers, and Financial Statements: Perpetual Method* **L.O. 3, 5**

Hope Jackson Corp. started a small merchandising business in 2006. The business experienced the following events during its first year of operation. Assume that the company uses the perpetual inventory method.

1. Acquired $25,000 cash from the issue of common shares.
2. Purchased inventory for $22,000 cash.
3. Sold inventory costing $17,000 for $24,000 cash.

Required

a. Record the events in general journal format.
b. Post the entries to T-accounts.
c. Prepare an income statement for 2006.
d. What is the amount of total assets at the end of the period?

EXERCISE 5–3 *Effect of Inventory Transactions on the Income Statement and Cash Flow Statement: Perpetual Method* **L.O. 3, 5**

During 2007, Stonebrook Merchandising Company purchased $50,000 of inventory on account. The company sold inventory on account that cost $36,000 for $56,000. Cash payments on accounts payable were $30,000. There was $40,000 cash collected from accounts receivable. Stonebrook also paid $8,000 cash for operating expenses. Assume that Stonebrook started the accounting period with $48,000 in cash and common shares.

Required

a. Identify the events described in the preceding paragraph and record them in a horizontal statements model like the following one:

Assets						=	Liab.	+	Equity								Cash Flow Statement
Cash	+	Accts. Rec.	+	Inv.		=	A. Pay	+	C. Sh.	+	Ret. Ear.	Rev.	−	Exp.	=	Net Inc.	
48,000	+	NA	+	NA		=	NA	+	48,000	+	NA	NA	−	NA	=	NA	NA

b. What is the balance of accounts receivable at the end of 2007?
c. What is the balance of accounts payable at the end of 2007?
d. What are the amounts of gross profit and net income for 2007?
e. Determine the amount of net cash flow from operating activities.
f. Explain any differences between net income and net cash flow from operating activities.

EXERCISE 5–4 *Recording Inventory Transactions in the General Journal and Posting Entries to T-Accounts: Perpetual Method* **L.O. 5**

Mary's Beauty Supply experienced the following events during 2006:

1. Acquired $10,000 cash from the issue of common shares.
2. Purchased inventory for $7,000 cash.
3. Sold inventory costing $5,200 for $7,800 cash.
4. Paid $600 for advertising expense.

Required

a. Record the general journal entries for the preceding transactions.
b. Post each of the entries to T-accounts.
c. Prepare a trial balance to prove the equality of debits and credits.

L.O. 6 EXERCISE 5–5 *Determining Which Party Is Responsible for Freight Cost*

Required

Determine which party, buyer or seller, is responsible for freight charges in each of the following situations:

a. Sold merchandise, freight terms FOB shipping point.
b. Sold merchandise, freight terms FOB destination point.
c. Purchased merchandise, freight terms FOB shipping point.
d. Purchased merchandise, freight terms FOB destination point.

L.O. 3 EXERCISE 5–6 *Effect of Purchase Returns and Allowances and Freight Costs on the Journal, Ledger, and Financial Statements: Perpetual Method*

The trial balance for The Gift Shop Inc. as of January 1, 2003, was as follows:

Account Titles	Debit	Credit
Cash	$ 8,000	
Inventory	3,000	
Common Shares		$10,000
Retained Earnings		1,000
Total	$11,000	$11,000

The following events affected the company during the 2003 accounting period:

1. Purchased merchandise on account that cost $5,500.
2. Purchased goods FOB shipping point with freight cost of $250 cash.
3. Returned $800 of damaged merchandise for credit on account.
4. Agreed to keep other damaged merchandise for which the company received a $350 allowance.
5. Sold merchandise that cost $4,000 for $7,750 cash.
6. Delivered merchandise to customers under terms FOB destination point with freight costs amounting to $200 cash.
7. Paid $4,000 on the merchandise purchased in Event 1.

Required

a. Record the transactions in general journal format.
b. Open general ledger T-accounts with the appropriate beginning balances, and post the journal entries to the T-accounts.
c. Prepare an income statement and cash flow statement.
d. Explain why a difference does or does not exist between net income and net cash flow from operating activities.

L.O. 2, 5 EXERCISE 5–7 *Accounting for Product Costs: Perpetual Inventory Method*

Which of the following would be debited to the Inventory account for a merchandising business using the perpetual inventory method?

Required

a. Purchase of inventory.
b. Allowance received for damaged inventory.
c. Transportation-out.
d. Purchase discount.
e. Transportation-in.
f. Purchase of a new computer to be used by the business.

EXERCISE 5–8 *Effect of Product Cost and Period Cost: Horizontal Statements Model* **L.O. 2, 5**

Turner Co. experienced the following events for the 2008 accounting period:

1. Acquired $2,500 cash from the issue of common shares.
2. Purchased $14,000 of inventory on account.
3. Received goods purchased in Event 2 FOB shipping point. Freight cost of $150 paid in cash.
4. Returned $600 of goods purchased in Event 2 because of poor quality.
5. Sold inventory on account that cost $8,250 for $14,350.
6. Paid freight cost on the goods sold in Event 5 of $60. The goods were shipped FOB destination point. Cash was paid for the freight cost.
7. Collected $11,750 cash from accounts receivable.
8. Paid $10,000 cash on accounts payable.
9. Paid $275 for advertising expense.
10. Paid $500 cash for insurance expense.

Required

a. Which of these transactions result in period (selling and administrative) costs? Which result in product costs? If neither, label the transaction NA.

b. Record each event in a horizontal statements model like the following one. The first event is recorded as an example.

Assets					=	Liab.	+	Equity								Cash Flow Statement
Cash	+	Accts. Rec.	+	Inv.	=	A. Pay	+	C. Sh.	+	Ret. Ear.	Rev.	−	Exp.	=	Net Inc.	
2,500	+	NA	+	NA	=	NA	+	2,500	+	NA	NA	−	NA	=	NA	2,500 FA

EXERCISE 5–9 *Cash Discounts and Purchase Returns* **L.O. 3, 6**

On March 6, 2004, Rue's Imports Ltd. purchased $12,400 of merchandise from The Glass Exchange, terms 2/10, n/45. On March 10, Rue returned $2,400 of the merchandise to The Glass Exchange for credit. Rue paid cash for the merchandise on March 15, 2004.

Required

a. What is the amount of the cheque that Rue must write to The Glass Exchange on March 15?

b. Prepare the journal entries for these transactions.

c. How much must Rue pay for the merchandise purchased if the payment is not made until March 20, 2004?

d. Why would The Glass Exchange sell merchandise with the terms 2/10, n/45?

EXERCISE 5–10 *Effect of Sales Returns and Allowances and Freight Costs on the Journal, Ledger, and Financial Statements: Perpetual Method* **L.O. 3, 5**

Upton Company began the 2006 accounting period with $13,000 cash, $70,000 inventory, $40,000 common shares, and $43,000 retained earnings. During the 2006 accounting period, Upton experienced the following events:

1. Sold merchandise costing $60,400 for $90,800 on account to Jones General Store.
2. Delivered the goods to Jones under terms FOB destination. Freight costs were $2,600 cash.
3. Received goods returned by Jones. The goods cost Upton $5,600 and were sold to Jones for $8,800.
4. Granted Jones a $3,400 allowance for other damaged goods that Jones agreed to keep.
5. Collected partial payment of $56,000 cash from accounts receivable.

Required

a. Record the transactions in general journal format.

b. Open general ledger T-accounts with the appropriate beginning balances and post the journal entries to the T-accounts.

c. Prepare an income statement, balance sheet, and cash flow statement.

d. Why would Upton grant the $3,400 allowance to Jones? Who benefits more?

L.O. 5, 6

EXERCISE 5–11 *Effect of Cash Discounts on the Journal, Ledger, and Financial Statements: Perpetual Method*

Stone Sales Inc. was started in 2005. The company experienced the following accounting events during its first year of operation:

1. Started business when it acquired $60,000 cash from the issue of common shares.
2. Purchased merchandise costing $36,000 on account, terms 2/10, n/30.
3. Paid off the account payable within the discount period.
4. Sold inventory on account that cost $20,000 for $30,000. Credit terms were 1/20, n/30.
5. Collected cash from the account receivable within the discount period.
6. Paid $7,600 cash for operating expenses.

Required

a. Record the transactions in general journal format.
b. Open general ledger T-accounts, and post the journal entries to the T-accounts.
c. Record the events in a horizontal statements model like the following one.

Assets					=	Liab.	+	Equity			Rev.	−	Exp.	=	Net Inc.	Cash Flow Statement
Cash	+	Accts. Rec.	+	Inv.	=	A. Pay	+	C. Sh.	+	Ret. Ear.						

d. What is the amount of gross profit for the period? What is the net income for the period?
e. Why would Stone sell merchandise with the terms 1/20, n/30?
f. What do the terms 2/10, n/30 in Event 2 mean to Stone?

L.O. 5, 6

EXERCISE 5–12 *Effect of Inventory Transactions on the Financial Statements: Comprehensive Exercise with Sales and Purchase Returns and Discounts*

Retail Sales Company had the following balances in its accounts on January 1, 2004:

Cash	$15,000
Merchandise Inventory	10,000
Common Shares	20,000
Retained Earnings	5,000

Retail experienced the following events during 2004:

1. Purchased merchandise inventory on account for $30,000, terms 1/10, n/30.
2. Paid freight of $500 on the merchandise purchased.
3. Sold merchandise inventory that cost $17,000 for $26,000 on account, terms 2/10, n/45.
4. Returned $1,000 of damaged merchandise purchased in Event 1.
5. Agreed to keep other merchandise that was slightly damaged and was granted an allowance of $200.
6. Received return of $4,000 of merchandise that had a cost of $2,400 from customer in Event 3.
7. Collected the balance of accounts receivable within the discount period.
8. Paid for one-half of the merchandise in Event 1 within the discount period.
9. Paid $3,200 cash for selling and administrative expenses.
10. Paid the balance of accounts payable (not within the discount period).

Required

a. Record each of these events in general journal format.
b. Open general ledger T-accounts. Post the beginning balances and the events to the accounts.
c. Prepare a trial balance.
d. Prepare an income statement, balance sheet (assume closing entries have been made), and a cash flow statement.

EXERCISE 5–13 *Effect of Inventory Losses: Perpetual Method* **L.O. 3, 5**

Burk Merchandising experienced the following events during 2006, its first year of operation:

1. Started the business when it acquired $80,000 cash from the issue of common shares.
2. Paid $56,000 cash to purchase inventory.
3. Sold inventory costing $43,000 for $68,400 cash.
4. Physically counted inventory, showing $11,600 inventory was on hand at the end of the accounting period.

Required

a. Open appropriate ledger T-accounts, and record the events in the accounts.
b. Prepare an income statement and balance sheet for 2006.
c. Explain how differences between the book balance and the physical count of inventory could arise. Why is being able to determine whether differences exist useful to management?

EXERCISE 5–14 *Determining the Effect of Inventory Transactions on the Horizontal Statements Model: Perpetual Method* **L.O. 3, 5**

Lobo Sales Company experienced the following events:

1. Purchased merchandise inventory for cash.
2. Purchased merchandise inventory on account.
3. Sold merchandise inventory for cash. Label the revenue recognition 3a and the expense recognition 3b.
4. Sold merchandise inventory on account. Label the revenue recognition 4a and the expense recognition 4b.
5. Returned merchandise purchased on account.
6. Paid cash for selling and administrative expenses.
7. Paid cash on accounts payable within the discount period.
8. Paid cash for transportation-in.
9. Collected cash from accounts receivable.
10. Paid cash for transportation-out.

Required

Identify each event as asset source (AS), asset use (AU), asset exchange (AE), or claims exchange (CE). Also explain how each event affects the financial statements by placing a + for increase, – for decrease, or NA for not affected under each of the components in the following statements model. Assume the use of the perpetual inventory method. The first event is recorded as an example.

Event No.	Event Type	Assets	=	Liab.	+	Equity	Rev.	–	Exp.	=	Net Inc.	Cash Flow Statement
1	AE	+ –	=	NA	+	NA	NA	–	NA	=	NA	– OA

EXERCISE 5–15 *Effect of Inventory Transactions on the Income Statement and Balance Sheet: Periodic Method* **L.O. 12**

Bob Ott is the owner of The Sports Store Ltd. At the beginning of the year, Ott had $1,050 in inventory. During the year, Ott purchased inventory that cost $5,250. At the end of the year, inventory on hand amounted to $2,200.

Required

Calculate the following:

a. Cost of goods available for sale during the year.
b. Cost of goods sold for the year.
c. Inventory amount The Sports Store would report on its year-end balance sheet.

EXERCISE 5–16 *Multistep Income Statement* **L.O. 7**

The following information was taken from the accounts of Quick Foods, a delicatessen. The accounts are listed in alphabetical order, and each has a normal balance.

Accounts Payable	$150
Accounts Receivable	175
Accumulated Amortization	50
Advertising Expense	100
Cash	205
Common Shares	100
Cost of Goods Sold	225
Interest Expense	35
Merchandise Inventory	75
Prepaid Rent	20
Retained Earnings	255
Sales Revenue	400
Salaries Expense	65
Supplies Expense	28

Required
Prepare an income statement using the multistep approach.

L.O. 12 EXERCISE 5–17 *Determining Cost of Goods Sold: Periodic Method (Appendix)*

Valley Retailers Ltd. uses the periodic inventory method to account for its inventory transactions. The following account titles and balances were drawn from Valley's records: beginning balance in inventory, $24,900; purchases, $306,400; purchase returns and allowances, $9,600; sales, $680,000; sales returns and allowances, $6,370; freight-in, $2,160; and operating expenses, $51,400. A physical count indicated that $29,300 of merchandise was on hand at the end of the accounting period.

Required
a. Prepare a schedule of cost of goods sold.
b. Prepare a multistep income statement.

L.O. 12 EXERCISE 5–18 *Basic Transactions: Periodic Method, Single Cycle (Appendix)*

The following events apply to Joy Gift Shop Co. for 2007:

1. Acquired $33,500 cash from the issue of common shares.
2. Acquired $2,500 of gift merchandise and issue common shares to Kayla Taylor, one of the owners, who had acquired the merchandise prior to opening the shop. (*Hint*: Debit Merchandise Inventory since this will represent the beginning inventory balance in the company.)
3. Purchased $43,500 of inventory on account.
4. Paid $2,750 for advertising expense.
5. Sold inventory for $77,500.
6. Paid $8,000 in salary to a part-time salesperson.
7. Paid $35,000 on accounts payable (see Event 3).
8. Physically counted inventory, which indicated that $7,000 of inventory was on hand at the end of the accounting period.

Required
a. Record each of these events in general journal form. Joy Gift Shop uses the periodic system.
b. Post each of the events to ledger T-accounts.
c. Prepare an income statement, statement of shareholders' equity, balance sheet, and cash flow statement for 2007.
d. Prepare the necessary closing entries at the end of 2007, and post them to the appropriate T-accounts.
e. Prepare a post-closing trial balance.
f. Discuss an advantage of using the periodic method instead of the perpetual method.
g. Why is the common shares balance on the statement of shareholders' equity different from the common shares issued in the cash flow from financing activities section of the cash flow statement?

L.O. 3, 5, 11 EXERCISE 5–19 *Determining Cost of Financing Inventory*

On January 1, 2008, Al Smith started a small sailboat merchandising business that he named Al's Sails Inc. The company experienced the following events during the first year of operation:

1. Started the business when Smith borrowed $25,000 from his parents. He issued them a one-year note dated January 1, 2008. The note had a 7 percent annual rate of interest.
2. Paid $20,000 cash to purchase inventory.
3. Sold a sailboat that cost $9,000 for $17,000 on account.
4. Collected $7,000 cash from accounts receivable.
5. Paid $2,500 for operating expenses.
6. Recognized accrued interest on the note payable on December 31.

Required

a. Record the events in general journal format, using the perpetual method.
b. Open general ledger T-accounts, and post the journal entries to the T-accounts.
c. Prepare an income statement, balance sheet, and cash flow statement. (Assume that year-end closing entries have been made.)
d. "Since Al sold inventory for $17,000, he will be able to repay more than half of the $25,000 loan from his parents when it comes due on January 1, 2009." Do you agree with this statement? Why or why not?

EXERCISE 5–20 *Financing Inventory and Cash Discounts* **L.O. 6, 11**

Kay Haynes came to you for advice. She has just purchased a large amount of inventory with the terms 2/10, n/60. The amount of the invoice is $260,000. She is currently short on cash but has good credit. She can borrow the money at the appropriate time to take advantage of the discount. The annual interest rate is 7 percent if she decides to borrow the money. Haynes is sure she will have the necessary cash by the due date of the invoice (but not by the discount date).

Required

a. For how long would Haynes need to borrow the money to take advantage of the discount?
b. How much money would Haynes need to borrow?
c. Write a memo to Haynes outlining the most cost-effective strategy for her to follow. Include in your memo the amount of savings from the alternative you suggest.

PROBLEMS—SERIES A

PROBLEM 5–1A *Basic Transactions for Three Accounting Cycles: Perpetual Method* **L.O. 3, 5**

Mackey Company was started in 2007 when it acquired $20,000 from the issue of common shares. The following data summarize the company's first three years' operating activities. Assume that all transactions were cash transactions.

	2007	2008	2009
Purchases of Inventory	$ 9,800	$12,000	$18,500
Sales	14,100	17,500	26,000
Cost of Goods Sold	7,150	9,500	15,000
Selling and Administrative Expenses	4,600	6,200	7,400

Required

Prepare an income statement and balance sheet for each fiscal year. (*Hint:* Record the transaction data for each accounting period in T-accounts before preparing the statements for that year.)

PROBLEM 5–2A *Identifying Product and Period Costs* **L.O. 2**

Required

Indicate whether each of the following costs is a product cost or a period cost:

a. Cleaning supplies for the office.
b. Freight on goods purchased for resale.
c. Salary of the marketing director.
d. Freight on goods sold to customer with terms FOB destination.

e. Utilities expense incurred for office building.
f. Amortization on office equipment.
g. Insurance on vans used to deliver goods to customers.
h. Salaries of sales supervisors.
i. Monthly maintenance expense for a copier.
j. Goods purchased for resale.

L.O. 2 PROBLEM 5–3A *Identifying Freight Cost*

Required

For each of the following events, determine the amount of freight paid by Rick's Garage Co. Also indicate whether the freight is classified as a product or period cost.

a. Purchased inventory with freight costs of $550, FOB destination.
b. Sold merchandise to a customer. Freight costs were $200, FOB shipping point.
c. Purchased additional merchandise with costs of $190, FOB shipping point.
d. Shipped merchandise to customers with freight costs of $100, FOB destination.

L.O. 3, 5 PROBLEM 5–4A *Effect of Purchase Returns and Allowances and Purchase Discounts on the Financial Statements: Perpetual Method*

The following events were completed by Doss Heater Company in September 2009:

Sept. 1 Acquired $30,000 cash from the issue of common shares.
1 Purchased $18,000 of merchandise on account with terms 2/10, n/30.
5 Paid $800 cash for freight to obtain merchandise purchased on September 1.
8 Sold merchandise that cost $4,500 to customers for $8,800 on account.
8 Returned $900 of defective merchandise from the September 1 purchase to the supplier.
10 Paid cash for one-half of the balance due on the merchandise purchased on September 1.
15 Received cash from customers of September 8 sale in settlement of the account balances.
30 Paid the balance due on the merchandise purchased on September 1.
30 Paid $1,720 cash for selling expenses.

Required

a. Record each event in a statements model like the following one. The first event is recorded as an example.

Assets					=	Liab.	+	Equity								Cash Flow Statement
Cash	+	Accts. Rec.	+	Inv.	=	A. Pay	+	C. Sh.	+	Ret. Ear.	Rev.	−	Exp.	=	Net Inc.	
30,000	+	NA	+	NA	=	NA	+	30,000	+	NA	NA	−	NA	=	NA	30,000 FA

b. Record each of these transactions in general journal form.
c. Post each of the transactions to general ledger T-accounts.
d. Prepare an income statement for the month ending September 30.
e. Prepare a cash flow statement for the month ending September 30.
f. Explain why there is a difference between net income and cash flow from operating activities.

L.O. 3, 5, 8 PROBLEM 5–5A *Comprehensive Cycle Problem: Perpetual Method*

At the beginning of 2005, the W. Coyle Company had the following balances in its accounts:

Cash	$ 4,300
Merchandise Inventory	9,000
Common Shares	10,000
Retained Earnings	3,300

During 2005, the company experienced the following events:

1. Purchased inventory that cost $2,200 on account from Blue Company under terms 1/10, n/30. The merchandise was delivered FOB shipping point. Freight costs of $110 were paid in cash.
2. Returned $200 of the inventory that it had purchased because the inventory was damaged in transit. The freight company agreed to pay the return freight cost.
3. Paid the amount due on its account payable to Blue Company within the cash discount period.
4. Sold inventory that had cost $3,000 for $5,500 on account, under terms 2/10, n/45.
5. Received returned merchandise from a customer. The merchandise originally cost $400 and was sold to the customer for $710 cash. The customer was paid $710 cash for the returned merchandise.
6. Delivered goods FOB destination. Freight costs of $60 were paid in cash.
7. Collected the amount due on the account receivable within the discount period.
8. Took a physical count indicating that $7,970 of inventory was on hand at the end of the accounting period.

Required

a. Identify each of these events as asset source (AS), asset use (AU), asset exchange (AE), or claims exchange (CE). Also explain how each event would affect the financial statements by placing a + for increase, − for decrease, or NA for not affected under each of the components in the following statements model. Assume that the perpetual inventory method is used. When an event has more than one part, use letters to distinguish the effects of each part. The first event is recorded as an example.

Event No.	Event Type	Assets	=	Liab.	+	Equity	Rev.	−	Exp.	=	Net Inc.	Cash Flow Statement
1a	AS	+	=	+	+	NA	NA	−	NA	=	NA	NA
1b	AE	+−	=	NA	+	NA	NA	−	NA	=	NA	− OA

b. Record the events in general journal format.
c. Open ledger T-accounts, and post the beginning balances and the events to the accounts.
d. Prepare an income statement, a statement of shareholders' equity, a balance sheet, and a cash flow statement.
e. Record and post the closing entries, and prepare a post-closing trial balance.

PROBLEM 5–6A ***Preparing a Schedule of Cost of Goods Sold and Multistep and Single-Step Income Statements: Periodic Method (Appendix)*** **L.O. 7, 12**

The following account titles and balances were taken from the adjusted trial balance of Pittman Sales Co. at December 31, 2004. The company uses the periodic inventory method.

Account Title	Balance
Advertising Expense	$12,800
Amortization Expense	3,000
Income Tax Expense	10,700
Interest Expense	5,000
Merchandise Inventory, January 1	18,000
Merchandise Inventory, December 31	20,100
Miscellaneous Expense	800
Purchases	130,000
Purchase Returns and Allowances	2,700
Rent Expense	14,000
Salaries Expense	53,000
Sales	290,000
Sales Discounts	13,500
Sales Returns and Allowances	8,000
Transportation-in	5,500
Transportation-out	10,800

Required

a. Prepare a schedule to determine the amount of cost of goods sold.
b. Prepare a multistep income statement.
c. Prepare a single-step income statement.

L.O. 12 PROBLEM 5–7A *Comprehensive Cycle Problem: Periodic Method (Appendix)*

The following trial balance pertains to Horner Home Products Inc. as of January 1, 2005:

Account Title	Debit	Credit
Cash	$14,000	
Accounts Receivable	9,000	
Merchandise Inventory	60,000	
Accounts Payable		$ 5,000
Notes Payable		20,000
Common Shares		50,000
Retained Earnings		8,000
Total	$83,000	$83,000

The following events occurred in 2005. Assume that Horner Home Products Inc. uses the periodic inventory method.

1. Purchased land for $8,000 cash and a building for $45,000 by paying $5,000 cash and issuing a 20-year note with an annual interest rate of 8 percent. The building has a 40-year estimated life with no residual value.
2. Purchased merchandise on account for $23,000, terms 2/10, n/30.
3. The merchandise purchased was shipped FOB shipping point for $230 cash.
4. Returned $2,000 of defective merchandise purchased in Event 2.
5. Sold merchandise for $27,000 cash.
6. Sold merchandise on account for $50,000, terms 1/20, n/30.
7. Paid cash within the discount period on accounts payable due on merchandise purchased in Event 2.
8. Paid $1,200 cash for selling expenses.
9. Collected part of the balance due from accounts receivable. Collections were made after the discount period on $12,000 of the receivables. Collections were made during the discount period on $35,000 of the receivables.
10. Paid cash to the bank for one full year's interest on the note issued in Event 1.
11. Paid $2,000 on the principal of the note issued in Event 1.
12. Recorded one full year's amortization on the building purchased in Event 1.
13. Performed a physical count indicating that $30,000 of inventory was on hand at the end of the accounting period.

Required

a. Record these transactions in a general journal.
b. Post the transactions to ledger T-accounts.
c. Prepare an income statement, a statement of shareholders' equity, a balance sheet, and a cash flow statement for 2005.

L.O. 9 PROBLEM 5–8A *Using Common Size Income Statements to Make Comparisons*

The following income statements were drawn from the annual reports of Marcy Company:

	2004*	2005*
Net Sales	$ 302,900	$ 370,500
Cost of Goods Sold	(217,400)	(264,700)
Gross Profit	85,500	105,800
Less: Operating Expense		
Selling and Administrative Expenses	(40,800)	(58,210)
Net Income	$ 44,700	$ 47,590

* All dollar amounts are reported in thousands.

The president's message in the company's annual report stated that the company had implemented a strategy to increase market share by spending more on advertising. The president indicated that prices held steady and sales grew as expected. Write a memo indicating whether you agree with the president's statements. How has the strategy affected profitability? Support your answer by measuring growth in sales and selling expenses. Also prepare common size income statements and make appropriate references to the differences between 2004 and 2005.

PROBLEMS—SERIES B

PROBLEM 5–1B *Basic Transactions for Three Accounting Cycles: Perpetual Method* L.O. 3, 5

Flower Company was started in 2007 when it acquired $80,000 cash from the issue of common shares. The following data summarize the company's first three years' operating activities. Assume that all transactions were cash transactions.

	2007	2008	2009
Purchases of Inventory	$ 60,000	$ 90,000	$130,000
Sales	102,000	146,000	220,000
Cost of Goods Sold	54,000	78,000	140,000
Selling and Administrative Expenses	40,000	52,000	72,000

Required

Prepare an income statement and balance sheet for each fiscal year. (*Hint:* Record the transaction data for each accounting period in T-accounts before preparing the statements for that year.)

PROBLEM 5–2B *Identifying Product and Period Costs* L.O. 2

Required

Indicate whether each of the following costs is a product cost or a period (selling and administrative) cost.

a. Transportation-in.
b. Insurance on the office building.
c. Office supplies.
d. Costs incurred to improve the quality of goods available for sale.
e. Goods purchased for resale.
f. Salaries of salespersons.
g. Advertising costs.
h. Transportation-out.
i. Interest on a note payable.
j. Salary of the company president.

PROBLEM 5–3B *Identifying Freight Costs*

Required

For each of the following events, determine the amount of freight paid by The Book Shop Company. Also indicate whether the freight cost would be classified as a product or period (selling and administrative) cost.

a. Purchased additional merchandise with freight costs of $300. The merchandise was shipped FOB shipping point.
b. Shipped merchandise to customers, freight terms FOB shipping point. The freight costs were $100.
c. Purchased inventory with freight costs of $1,000. The goods were shipped FOB destination point.
d. Sold merchandise to a customer. Freight costs were $500. The goods were shipped FOB destination point.

L.O. 3, 5 PROBLEM 5–4B *Effect of Purchase Returns and Allowances and Purchase Discounts on the Financial Statements: Perpetual Method*

The following transactions were completed by The Jewel Shop Ltd. in May 2008:

May 1 Acquired $100,000 cash from the issue of common shares.
1 Purchased $60,000 of merchandise on account with terms 2/10, n/30.
2 Paid $1,200 cash for freight to obtain merchandise purchased on May 1.
4 Sold merchandise that cost $44,000 for $74,000 to customers on account.
4 Returned $5,000 of defective merchandise from the May 1 purchase for credit on account.
10 Paid cash for one-half of the balance due on the merchandise purchased on May 1.
13 Received cash from customers of May 4 sale in settlement of the account balance.
31 Paid the balance due on the merchandise purchased on May 1.
31 Paid selling expenses of $7,800.

Required

a. Record each event in a horizontal statements model like the following one. The first event is recorded as an example.

Assets					=	Liab.	+	Equity			Rev.	−	Exp.	=	Net Inc.	Cash Flow Statement
Cash	+	Accts. Rec.	+	Inv.	=	A. Pay	+	C. Sh.	+	Ret. Ear.						
100,000	+	NA	+	NA	=	NA	+	100,000	+	NA	NA	−	NA	=	NA	100,000 FA

b. Record each of the transactions in general journal form.
c. Post each of the transactions to general ledger T-accounts.
d. Prepare an income statement for the month ending May 31.
e. Prepare a cash flow statement for the month ending May 31.
f. Explain why there is a difference between net income and cash flow from operating activities.

L.O. 3, 5, 8 PROBLEM 5–5B *Comprehensive Cycle Problem: Perpetual Method*

At the beginning of 2006, M & M Enterprises Ltd. had the following balances in its accounts:

Cash	$ 8,400
Merchandise Inventory	2,000
Common Shares	8,000
Retained Earnings	2,400

During 2006, M & M Enterprises experienced the following events:

1. Purchased inventory costing $5,600 on account from Smoot Company under terms 2/10, n/30. The merchandise was delivered FOB shipping point. Freight costs of $500 were paid in cash.
2. Returned $400 of the inventory that it had purchased because the inventory was damaged in transit. The freight company agreed to pay the return freight cost.
3. Paid the amount due on its account payable to Smoot Company within the cash discount period.
4. Sold inventory that had cost $6,000 for $9,000. The sale was on account under terms 2/10, n/45.
5. Received returned merchandise from a customer. The merchandise had originally cost $520 and had been sold to the customer for $840 cash. The customer was paid $840 cash for the returned merchandise.
6. Delivered goods FOB destination point. Freight costs of $600 were paid in cash.
7. Collected the amount due on accounts receivable within the discount period.
8. Took a physical count indicating that $1,800 of inventory was on hand at the end of the accounting period.

Required

a. Identify each of these events as asset source (AS), asset use (AU), asset exchange (AE), or claims exchange (CE). Also explain how each event affects the financial statements by placing a + for increase, − for decrease, or NA for not affected under each of the components in the following statements model. Assume that the perpetual inventory method is used. When an event has more than one part, use letters to distinguish the effects of each part. The first event is recorded as an example.

Event No.	Event Type	Assets	=	Liab.	+	Equity	Rev.	−	Exp.	=	Net Inc.	Cash Flow Statement
1a	AS	+	=	+	+	NA	NA	−	NA	=	NA	NA
1b	AE	+−	=	NA	+	NA	NA	−	NA	=	NA	− OA

b. Record the events in general journal format.
c. Open ledger T-accounts and post the beginning balances and the events to the accounts.
d. Prepare an income statement, statement of shareholders' equity, balance sheet, and cash flow statement.
e. Record and post the closing entries, and prepare a post-closing trial balance.

PROBLEM 5–6B *Preparing Schedule of Cost of Goods Sold and Multistep and Single-Step Income Statements: Periodic Method (Appendix)* **L.O. 7, 12**

The following account titles and balances were taken from the adjusted trial balance of Martin Farm Co. for 2006. The company uses the periodic inventory method.

Account Title	Balance
Sales Returns and Allowances	$ 2,250
Income Tax Expense	3,700
Miscellaneous Expense	400
Transportation-out	600
Sales	69,750
Advertising Expense	2,750
Salaries Expense	7,900
Transportation-in	1,725
Purchases	40,000
Interest Expense	360
Merchandise Inventory, January 1	5,075
Sales Discounts	405
Rent Expense	5,000
Merchandise Inventory, December 31	4,050
Purchase Returns and Allowances	1,450
Amortization Expense	710

Required

a. Prepare a schedule to determine the amount of cost of goods sold.
b. Prepare a multistep income statement.
c. Prepare a single-step income statement.

PROBLEM 5–7B *Comprehensive Cycle Problem: Periodic Method (Appendix)* **L.O. 12**

The following trial balance pertains to John's Jungle Co. as of January 1, 2008:

Account Titles	Debit	Credit
Cash	$26,000	
Accounts Receivable	4,000	
Merchandise Inventory	50,000	
Accounts Payable		$ 4,000
Notes Payable		6,000
Common Shares		37,000
Retained Earnings		33,000
Totals	$80,000	$80,000

The following events occurred in 2008. Assume that John uses the periodic inventory method.

1. Purchased land for $20,000 cash and a building for $90,000 by paying $10,000 cash and issuing a 20-year note for $8,000 with an annual interest rate of 8 percent. The building has a 40-year estimated life with no residual value.
2. Purchased merchandise on account for $126,000, terms 1/10, n/45.
3. Paid freight of $1,000 cash on merchandise shipped FOB shipping point.
4. Returned $3,600 of defective merchandise purchased in Event 2.
5. Sold merchandise for $86,000 cash.
6. Sold merchandise on account for $120,000, terms 2/10, n/30.
7. Paid cash within the discount period on accounts payable due on merchandise purchased in Event 2.
8. Paid $11,600 cash for selling expenses.
9. Collected part of the balance due from accounts receivable. Collections were made after the discount period on $60,000 of the receivables. Collections were made during the discount period on $50,000 of the receivables.
10. Paid cash to the bank for one full year's interest on the note issued in Event 1.
11. Paid $10,000 on the principal of the note issued in Event 1.
12. Recorded one full year's amortization on the building purchased in Event 1.
13. A physical count indicated that $27,600 of inventory was on hand at the end of the accounting period.

Required

a. Record these transactions in a general journal.
b. Post the transactions to ledger T-accounts.
c. Prepare an income statement, statement of shareholders' equity, balance sheet, and cash flow statement for 2008.

L.O. 9 PROBLEM 5–8B *Using Common Size Income Statements to Make Comparisons*

The following income statements were drawn from the annual reports of Madison Company:

	2007*	2008*
Net Sales	$74,507	$ 80,000
Cost of Goods Sold	(28,317)	(34,400)
Gross Profit	46,190	45,600
Less: Operating Expenses		
Selling and Administrative Expenses	(43,210)	(40,800)
Net Income	$ 2,980	$ 4,800

* All figures are reported in thousands of dollars.

Required

The president's message in the company's annual report stated that the company increased profitability by decreasing prices and controlling operating expenses. Write a memorandum indicating whether you agree with the president's statement. Support your answer by preparing common size income statements and making appropriate references to the differences between 2007 and 2008.

ANALYZE, THINK, COMMUNICATE

ATC 5–1 BUSINESS APPLICATIONS CASE *Bombardier's Annual Report*

Required

Using the Bombardier financial statements in Appendix B, answer the following questions:

a. What is Bombardier's gross profit percentage for 2001 and 2002?
b. What was Bombardier's return on sales for 2001 and 2002?
c. Bombardier's gross profit percentage was lower for 2002 than for 2001. Ignoring taxes, how much higher would its 2002 net income have been if the gross profit percentage for 2002 had been the same as for 2001?

GROUP EXERCISE *Multistep Income Statement* ATC 5–2

The following quarterly information is given for Mark's Work Wearhouse Ltd. for the year ended 2001 (amounts shown are in thousands).

	First Quarter	Second Quarter	Third Quarter	Fourth Quarter
Sales	$88,077	$136,574	$74,523	$81,658
Gross Profit	36,510	55,586	31,782	33,274
Net Income (Loss)	1,426	782	(907)	(448)

Required

a. Divide the class into groups and organize the groups into sections. Assign each section one quarter of the financial information.
   (1) Each group should compute the gross profit percentage and cost of goods sold percentage for their spe-cific quarter.
   (2) Have a representative of each group put that quarter's sales, cost of goods percentage, and gross profit percentage on the board.

Class Discussion

b. Have the class discuss the change in each of these items from quarter to quarter and provide some logical explanation as to why the change might have occurred. Which was the best quarter and why?

REAL-WORLD CASE *Identifying Companies Based on Financial Statement Information* ATC 5–3

The following is selected information from the annual reports of four companies. This information is for the 2000/2001 fiscal years. The four companies, in alphabetical order, are Bell Canada Enterprises, a telephone company; Caterpillar, Inc., a manufacturer of heavy machinery; Chapters On-Line Inc., an e-commerce book store; and Danier Leather Inc., the second largest specialty apparel retailer in the world. The data for the companies, presented in the order of the amount of their sales in thousands of dollars, are as follows:

	A	B	C	D
Sales	$ 20,175,000	$ 18,094,000	$ 165,418	$ 51,091
Cost of Goods Sold	14,497,000	N/A	82,818	40,997
Net Earnings	1,053,000	4,861,000	12,078	(38,786)
Inventory	2,692,000	N/A	39,227	1,333
Accounts Receivable	8,079,000	4,334,000	664	716
Total Assets	28,464,000	51,383,000	68,438	18,836

Required

Based on these financial data and your knowledge and assumptions about the nature of the businesses that the companies operate, determine which data relate to which companies. Write a memorandum explaining your decisions. Include a discussion of which ratios you used in your analysis, and show the computations of these ratios in your memorandum.

ATC 5–4 BUSINESS APPLICATIONS CASE *Using Ratios to Make Comparisons*

The following income statements were drawn from the annual reports of Richard Company and Jennifer Company.

	Richard*	Jennifer*
Net Sales	$32,600	$86,200
Cost of Goods Sold	17,930	64,650
Gross Profit	14,670	21,550
Less: Selling and Admin. Expenses	13,040	18,960
Net Income	$ 1,630	$ 2,590

* All figures are reported in thousands of dollars.

Required

a. One of the companies is a high-end retailer that operates in exclusive shopping malls. The other operates discount stores located in low-cost stand-alone buildings. Identify the high-end retailer and the discounter. Support your answer with appropriate ratios.

b. If Richard and Jennifer have equity of $16,200 and $20,400, respectively, which company is the more profitable?

ATC 5–5 BUSINESS APPLICATIONS CASE *Using Common Size Statements and Ratios to Make Comparisons*

At the end of 2007, the following information is available for Karen and Patrick companies:

	Karen	Patrick
Sales	$1,000,000	$1,000,000
Cost of Goods Sold	650,000	550,000
Operating Expenses	250,000	375,000
Total Assets	1,200,000	1,200,000
Shareholders' Equity	450,000	300,000

Required

a. Prepare common size income statements for each company.

b. Compute the return on assets and return on equity for each company.

c. Which company is more profitable from the shareholders' perspective?

d. One company is a high-end retailer, and the other operates a discount store. Which is the discounter? Support your selection by referring to appropriate ratios.

ATC 5–6 WRITTEN ASSIGNMENT, CRITICAL THINKING *Effect of Sales Returns on Financial Statements*

Bell Farm and Garden Equipment reported the following sales information for 2005:

Net Sales of Equipment	$2,450,567
Other Income	6,786
Cost of Goods Sold	1,425,990
Selling, General, and Administrative Expense	325,965
Amortization	3,987
Net Operating Income	$ 701,411

Selected information from the balance sheet as of December 31, 2005, follows:

Cash and Marketable Securities	$113,545
Inventory	248,600
Accounts Receivable	82,462
Property, Plant, and Equipment—net	335,890
Other Assets	5,410
Total Assets	$785,907

Assume that a major customer returned a large order to Bell on December 31, 2005. The amount of the sale had been $146,800 with a cost of sales of $94,623. The return was recorded in the books on January 1, 2006. The company president does not want to correct the books. He argues that it makes no difference as to whether the return is recorded in 2005 or 2006. Either way, the return has been duly recognized.

Required

a. Assume that you are the CFO for Bell Farm and Garden Equipment Co. Write a memo to the president explaining how omitting the entry on December 31, 2005, could cause the financial statements to be misleading to investors and creditors. Explain how net income and the balance sheet would be affected.
b. Why might the president want to record the return on January 1, 2006, instead of December 31, 2005?
c. If the president of the company refuses to correct the financial statements, what action should you take?

ETHICAL DILEMMA *Wait Until I Get Mine*

ATC 5–7

Ada Fontanez is the president of a large company that owns a chain of athletic shoe stores. The company was in poor financial condition when she was hired three years ago. In an effort to motivate Fontanez, the board of directors included a bonus plan as part of her compensation package. According to her employment contract, on January 15 of each year, Fontanez is paid a cash bonus equal to 5 percent of the amount of net income reported on the preceding December 31 income statement. Fontanez was sufficiently motivated. Through her leadership, the company prospered. Her efforts were recognized throughout the industry, and she received numerous attractive offers to leave the company. One offer was so enticing that she decided to change jobs. Her decision was made in late December 2005. However, she decided to resign effective February 1, 2006, to ensure the receipt of her January bonus. On December 31, 2005, the chief accountant, Walter Smith, advised Fontanez that the company had a sizable quantity of damaged inventory. A warehouse fire had resulted in smoke and water damage to approximately $600,000 of inventory. The warehouse was not insured, and the accountant recommended that the loss be recognized immediately. After examining the inventory, Fontanez argued that it could be sold as *damaged goods* to customers at reduced prices. She refused to allow the write-off the accountant recommended. She stated that so long as she is president, the inventory stays on the books at cost. She told the accountant that he could take up the matter with the new president in February.

Required

a. How would an immediate write-off of the damaged inventory affect the December 31, 2005, income statement, balance sheet, and cash flow statement?
b. How would the write-off affect Fontanez's bonus?
c. If the new president is given the same bonus plan, how will Fontanez's refusal to recognize the loss affect his or her bonus?
d. Assuming that the damaged inventory is truly worthless, comment on the ethical implications of Fontanez's refusal to recognize the loss in the 2005 accounting period.
e. Assume that the damaged inventory is truly worthless and that you are Smith. How would you react to Fontanez's refusal to recognize the loss?

ATC 5–8 SEDAR DATABASE *Analyzing Dofasco's Profit Margins*

Instructions for using SEDAR are in Appendix A. Using the most current annual report available on SEDAR, answer the following questions about Dofasco:

Required

a. What was Dofasco's gross profit percentage for the most current year?
b. What was Dofasco's gross profit percentage for the previous year? Has it changed significantly?
c. What was Dofasco's return on sales percentage for the most current year?
d. What percentage of Dofasco's total sales for the most current year was from operations in Canada? In the United States?
e. Comment on the appropriateness of comparing Dofasco's gross profit with that of Ford Motor Company. If one company has a higher gross profit, does it mean that company is a better managed company?

ATC 5–9 SPREADSHEET ANALYSIS *Using Excel*

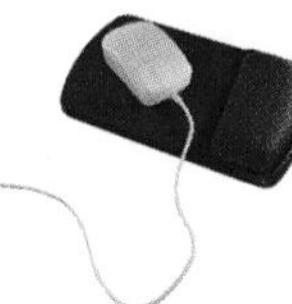

The following accounts, balances, and other financial information are drawn from the records of Vong Company for the year 2004:

Net Sales Revenue	$18,800	Beginning Common Shares	$ 9,000
Unearned Revenue	2,600	Land	8,000
Accounts Receivable	6,000	Term Deposit	10,000
Cost of Goods Sold	6,000	Interest Revenue	100
Inventory	5,000	Interest Receivable	100
Accounts Payable	5,800	Dividends	1,500
Notes Payable	6,000	Beginning Retained Earnings	8,500
Interest Expense	550	Cash from Shares Issued	3,000
Accrued Interest Payable	550	Cash	7,200
Supplies	50	Gain on Sale of Land	1,050
Supplies Expense	750	Loss on Sale of Property	50
Office Equipment	3,500	Salaries Expense	1,400
Amortization Expense	500	Accrued Salaries Payable	400
Accumulated Amortization	1,000	Rent Expense	1,100
Transportation-out Expense	500	Prepaid Rent	100
Miscellaneous Operating Expense	4,500		

The Cash account revealed the following cash flows:

Received cash from advances from customers	$ 2,600
Purchased office equipment	(3,500)
Received cash from issuing shares	3,000
Collected cash from accounts receivable	3,800
Purchased land	(8,000)
Received cash from borrowing funds	6,000
Paid cash for rent	(1,200)
Sold land	10,000
Paid cash for dividends	(1,500)
Paid cash for operating expenses	(1,000)
Purchased term deposit	(10,000)

Required

Build an Excel spreadsheet to construct a multistep income statement, statement of shareholders' equity, balance sheet, and cash flow statement for the year 2004.

SPREADSHEET ANALYSIS *Mastering Excel* **ATC 5–10**

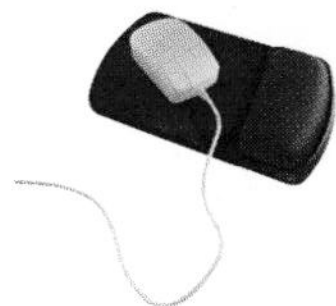

At the end of 2004, the following information is available for Short and Wise Companies:

Microsoft Excel - ch5-2.xls

File Edit View Insert Format Tools Data Window Help

Arial 10 B I U

C3 = =B3/$B$3

	A	B	C	D	E	F	G
1		Short			Wise		
2		Actual	% Sales		Actual	% Sales	
3	Sales	1,500,000	100.00%		1,500,000		
4	Cost of Goods Sold	1,050,000			900,000		
5	Gross Profit						
6	Operating Expenses	375,000			450,000		
7	Net Income						
8							
9		Actual	Return		Actual	Return	
10	Total Assets	1,800,000			1,800,000		
11	Shareholders' Equity	540,000			540,000		
12							
13							
14							
15							

Required

a. Set up the spreadsheet shown here. Complete the income statements by using Excel formulas.
b. Prepare a common size income statement for each company by completing the % Sales columns.
c. One company is a high-end retailer, and the other operates a discount store. Which is the discounter? Support your selection by referring to the common size statements.
d. Compute the return on assets and return on equity for each company.
e. Which company is more profitable from the shareholders' perspective?
f. Assume that a shortage of goods from suppliers is causing cost of goods sold to increase 10 percent for each company. Change the respective cost of goods sold balances in the Actual income statement column for each company. Note the new calculated amounts on the income statement and in the ratios. Which company's profits and returns are more sensitive to inventory price hikes?

Spreadsheet Tip

Cell C3 (% Sales) can be copied down the income statement if the formula in cell C3 designates Sales (cell B3) as a fixed number. Designate a number as fixed by positioning $ signs within the cell address. Notice that the formula for C3 is = B3/$B$3.

Chapter 6

Internal Control and Accounting for Cash

Learning Objectives

After completing this chapter, you should be able to:

1 Explain the types and purposes of internal controls.

2 Identify the key elements of a strong system of internal control.

3 Identify special internal controls for computer systems.

4 Identify special internal controls for cash.

5 Prepare a bank reconciliation.

6 Explain the use of a petty cash fund.

7 Prepare a classified balance sheet.

8 Identify the length of an operating cycle.

9 Use the current ratio to assess the level of liquidity.

the *curious* accountant

In January 2001, Air Canada and Canadian Airlines were amalgamated to form one company, known as Air Canada. The financing of this merger plus existing debt (totalling $11 billion) requires the company to pay almost $1 million in interest per day. The terrorist attacks of September 11, 2001, have placed further stresses on the company's financial position. Before September 2001, the airline had expected to achieve its financial targets. In late September 2001, the company issued a news release stating that it would need to substantially reduce its earnings projections for the next quarter. The price of the stock declined from $20 per share in mid-2000 to under $3 per share by October 2001. To help it through this difficult time, the company has hired a financial advisor (BMO Nesbitt Burns) to identify alternatives. If you were the advisor, what kind of advice would you give?

The successful operation of a business enterprise requires control. How can upper management of a major retailer such as Wal-Mart know that all its stores will open at a certain time? How can the president of General Motors rest assured that the numbers in the company's financial reports accurately reflect the company's operating activities? How can the owner of a small restaurant be confident that the wait staff are not giving food to friends and relatives? The answer to each of these questions is: by exercising effective control over the enterprise. The policies and procedures used to provide reasonable assurance that the objectives of an enterprise will be accomplished are called ***internal controls****.*

Internal controls can be divided into two categories: accounting and administrative. ***Accounting controls*** *include procedures designed to safeguard the assets and ensure that the accounting records contain reliable information.* ***Administrative controls*** *involve evaluating performance and assessing the degree of compliance with company policies and public laws.*

Key Features of Internal Control Systems

LO1 Explain the types and purposes of internal control.

LO2 Identify the key elements of a strong system of internal control.

The mechanics of internal control systems vary from company to company. That being said, most systems reflect a common set of general policies and procedures that have proven effective in accounting practice. The typical features of a strong system of internal control are now discussed.

Separation of Duties

There should be a clear **separation of duties**. The likelihood of fraud or theft is reduced if it becomes necessary for the wrongdoer to collude with others. For example, a person selling seats to a movie may be tempted to pocket some of the money received from customers who enter the theatre. This temptation is reduced if the person staffing the box office is required to issue tickets that a different employee then collects as people enter the theatre. The ticket stubs collected by a different employee could be compared with the cash receipts; then any cash shortages would become apparent. Furthermore, friends and relatives of the ticket agent could not enter the theatre without paying. Theft or unauthorized entry would require collusion between the ticket agent and the usher who collects the tickets. Both individuals would have to be dishonest enough to agree to steal from the theatre's owner, yet trustworthy enough to convince each other that they could keep the embezzlement secret. Clearly, the opportunity for crime is less than it would be if a single individual were permitted to sell the tickets and allow access to the theatre.

Whenever possible, the functions of *authorization*, *recording*, and *custody* should be carried out by separate individuals. For example, one person should authorize the purchase of inventory, a second person should keep the inventory records, and a third person should manage the warehouse in which the goods are stored. With this design, each person acts as a check on the other two. If the purchasing agent agreed to permit a supplier to deliver fewer goods than were ordered, the accountant would notice that the quantities on the purchase order were larger than the quantities shown on the receiving report prepared by the warehouse supervisor. Clearly, the likelihood of errors and embezzlement is minimized when duties are separated.

Quality of Employees

Employees should be competent. A business is only as good as the people who run it. Cheap labour is not a bargain if the quality of output is so poor as to require rework. A job done once at a cost of $6 per performance is less expensive than one that has to be done twice at a cost of $4 per performance. Employees should be trained to perform a variety of tasks. The ability of employees to substitute for one another prevents disruptions that occur when co-workers are absent due to illnesses, vacations, or other commitments. The capacity to rotate jobs also relieves boredom and increases respect for the work of other employees. Every business should strive to maximize the productivity of each and every employee. Ongoing training programs are essential to a strong system of internal controls.

Bonded Employees

The adage "the best defence is a good offence" is especially true when it comes to hiring employees. The best way to ensure honesty is to hire employees with *high personal integrity*. Employers should screen job applicants through interviews, background checks, and references from past employers. Even the best screening programs may fail to identify character weaknesses. Indeed, many frauds are committed by employees who have had long records of exemplary service prior to committing the crime. In other words, some employees with impeccable records at the time they are hired can change after they have been hired. Employees in positions of trust should be bonded. A **fidelity bond** is insurance that the company buys to protect itself from loss due to employee dishonesty. Before a firm bonds an employee, the bonding company runs a check on the employee. This check is another review of the employee in addition to the verification performed by the hiring firm. The insurance company will cover losses if the firm can prove that the losses occurred due to the illegal actions of a bonded employee.

Periods of Absence

Employees should be required to take extended vacations and should be rotated from time to time. Employees may be able to cover up illegal or unscrupulous activities when present in the work environment. However, such activities are likely to be discovered in their absence. Consider the case of a collection agent for a city's parking meter division. If the same agent always covers the same area, there is no basis for comparing that employee's collection pattern with patterns of other individuals. However, if the routes are altered, or if someone else covers the route while the regular agent is on vacation, improprieties may be discovered when the replacement agent reports different levels of cash receipts. In one case, an embezzlement was discovered when a meter reader who had covered the same route for several years with no vacation became sick. When the substitute reported more money each day than the regular reader usually reported, management checked past records. It found that the sick meter reader had been understating the cash receipts and pocketing the difference between the actual and reported collections. If management had required vacations or rotated the routes, the embezzlement would have been discovered much earlier.

Procedures Manual

There should be proper procedures for processing transactions. These procedures should be carefully designed to promote accuracy and to ensure reasonable control. For example, a clerk should be instructed to prepare a cheque only after receiving a copy of the invoice and notification from the receiving department that the goods involved in the payment have arrived in acceptable condition. Also, the cheque signer should not sign the cheque unless it is accompanied by adequate supporting documents. In this way, the cheque signer ensures that the clerk has followed the proper procedures in preparing the cheque. These and other appropriate accounting procedures should be set down in a **procedures manual**. The manual should be constantly updated, and reviews should be conducted to ensure that employees are following the procedures outlined in the manual.

Authority and Responsibility

Clear lines of authority and responsibility should be established. Motivation is maximized when individuals are given authority to act on their own judgment. Reasonable caution is exercised when employees are held accountable for their actions. Individuals often disagree on which course of action is most likely to accomplish an organization's objectives. Businesses operate more effectively when clear lines of authority are established before disputes arise. Businesses should prepare a manual that establishes a clear *chain of command*. The manual should provide guidance for both specific and general authorizations. **Specific authorizations** outline the limitations that apply to different levels of management. For example, a production supervisor may authorize overtime, and the plant manager may authorize the purchase of production equipment. These authorizations apply to specific positions within the organization. In contrast, **general authority** applies across different levels of management. It includes making decisions regarding items such as credit limits for customers, the class (coach or first class) of employees' flights on business trips, the price ranges for purchases, and the names of vendors from which goods and services may be acquired.

Prenumbered Documents

You have probably seen signs in stores that offer rewards to customers for reporting clerks who do not provide sales receipts. The signs read something like this: "If you fail to receive a valid sales receipt, your purchase is free." Without a record of sales transactions, management has no means of knowing how much money should be in the cash register. Clerks could sell merchandise and keep the proceeds for themselves. Likewise, if management does not control the supply of unused sales receipts, clerks could give customers receipts but fail to report the fact that a receipt had been used. Again, management would be left in the dark, and the clerk could steal the proceeds from the unrecorded sales transaction. If clerks are required to use prenumbered sales receipts, the number of sales transactions can be determined by identifying the number of missing receipts. The use of *prenumbered documents* can diminish the likelihood of embezzlement.

Prenumbered forms should be used for all important documents such as purchase orders, receiving reports, invoices, and cheques. To reduce errors, the forms should be easy to use. Also, the documents should allow for a signature by authorized personnel. For example, credit sales slips should be signed by the customer making the purchase. These procedures leave no doubt as to who made the purchase, and thereby reduce the likelihood of unauthorized transactions.

Physical Control

There should be adequate physical control over assets. Most people would not think of leaving cash lying around; they are often more careless with respect to other valuable assets. Employees walk away with billions of dollars of business assets each year. To limit losses, inventory should be kept in a storeroom and not released without proper authorization. Serial numbers on equipment should be recorded along with the name of the individual to whom the equipment was assigned. Unannounced physical counts should be conducted to ensure that the equipment remains in the business. Term deposits and marketable securities should be kept in fireproof vaults. Access to these vaults should be limited to authorized personnel. These procedures protect the documents from fire and limit access to only those who have proper security clearance.

In addition to safeguarding assets, there should be physical control over the accounting records. The accounting journals, ledgers, and supporting documents should be kept in a fireproof safe. Only personnel responsible for recording transactions into the journals should have access to them. With limited access, there is less chance that someone will change the records to hide fraud or embezzlement.

Performance Evaluations

There must be independent verification of performance because few people can evaluate their own performance objectively. For example, someone other than the person who has control over the inventory should take a physical count of inventory. This count should be compared with the accounting records. Discrepancies could alert management that inventory is being lost, stolen, or damaged. Internal and external audits independently verify performance. These auditors should appraise the effectiveness of the internal control system as well as verify the accuracy of the accounting records. External auditors also attest that GAAP are being applied to the reporting process.

A system of internal controls is designed to prevent errors and fraud. However, no system is perfect or foolproof. Internal controls can be circumvented by collusion among employees. Two or more employees working together can hide embezzlement by covering for each other. For example, if an embezzler goes on vacation, illegal activity will not be reported by a replacement who is in collusion with the embezzler. No system can prevent all fraud. However, a good system of internal controls minimizes illegal or unethical activities by reducing temptation and increasing the likelihood of early detection.

What are nine features of an internal control system?

Answer The nine features follow.

1. Separating duties so that fraud or theft requires collusion.
2. Hiring and training competent employees.
3. Bonding employees to recover losses through insurance.
4. Requiring employees to be absent from their jobs so that their replacements can discover errors or fraudulent activity that might have occurred.
5. Establishing proper procedures for processing transactions.
6. Establishing clear lines of authority and responsibility.
7. Using prenumbered documents.
8. Implementing physical controls such as locking cash in a safe.
9. Conducting performance evaluations through independent internal and external audits.

Internal Control in Computer Systems

LO3 Identify special internal controls for computer systems.

The basic internal control features discussed earlier apply to both manual and computer systems. The use of computers does not reduce the need to hire competent employees with high personal integrity. People in positions of trust should still be bonded. The segregation and rotation of duties remain important, and the physical control of assets is still a high priority. Indeed, computers often require special environmental features such as climate control and sophisticated electric circuitry. Thus, computers actually increase the need for internal controls. Some of the additional control requirements follow:

1. Computers do not think on their own. They are neutral to the size of numbers. They would treat a \$1,000,000 sales order in exactly the same way as a \$100 sales order. Thus, *tests of reasonableness* must be built into the operating programs. For example, programs could be designed to require a coded access number prior to initiating delivery orders for sales transactions over \$10,000. Similar controls should be put in place to ensure that human logic remains an active component of business operations.
2. Significant technical expertise may be required to design and run the automated accounting system. Therefore, the computer programmers may be more knowledgeable than the auditors assigned. Background checks and fidelity bonding for the programmers may be important under these circumstances.
3. There may be less documentary evidence in computer-based accounting systems. Information is usually stored on magnetic disks, where it is unobservable to the human eye. These data can be easily destroyed or manipulated without the traditional traces that facilitate detection. To test the system, auditors may have to **audit around the computer**, that is, test procedures by providing input that is expected to result in a designated output. The system is tested by comparing the actual output with the expected output. If actual output is consistent with expectations, that is evidence of accurate processing. Differences signal the need for further investigation. For example, instead of analyzing a computer program to determine whether it was designed to compute payroll tax correctly, the auditor could input the gross salary of a test case and analyze the tax figures generated by the program to see if it is operating correctly.
4. In automated accounting systems, it may be more difficult to control access to sensitive data. Hackers have the ability to gain unauthorized access to highly sophisticated computer systems. Large quantities of data can be transferred across phone lines, which permits thieves to commit their crimes without leaving the security of their own work environment. Care must be taken to control access to the system. Passwords and other screening devices should be employed to reduce the risk of unauthorized access to computer programs and data files.

answer to the *curious* accountant

Air Canada is struggling under its current debt load. The company needs to obtain additional cash flows to remain financially viable. Cash can be generated through increased revenues. However, since September 11, 2001, revenues have drastically fallen off. The projected revenue picture is for a marked decline in air travel, and this is not expected to change in the near future. Therefore, revenue generation probably won't be an answer to Air Canada's cash flow problems. Cost control is the next consideration. The events have already forced layoffs of personnel from all areas of the company, a reduction in the number of flights (which saves costs but also decreases revenues), and the sale of airplanes. This will allow for a reduction of operating costs and will reduce cash outlays, thus providing more cash. However, it won't provide enough to meet the company's cash needs. A further option may be to replace some of the debt with equity financing. This would reduce the interest charges for the company and allow the generation of more positive cash flow. Finally, the government may decide to provide cash on a temporary basis, but discussions to date indicate that Air Canada will have to restructure the company first and show the government that this downturn is only temporary in nature. Air Canada has received financial support from the government in prior years, and the government cannot afford to keep providing additional cash resources if the company does not show that its financial position will be turned around.

5. It is important to maintain proper documentation regarding the development and operation of the computer programs used in the business. Without proper documentation, the system comes to depend on the knowledge base of a particular programmer. If the programmer becomes ill or otherwise incapacitated, the operating system can collapse. Many small businesses find the use of standard commercial programs a cost-effective alternative to writing their own programs. You do not have to build a car to benefit from riding in one; you simply buy, lease, or rent an automobile. Likewise, you do not have to write a computer program to obtain the benefits of an automated accounting system. Many existing commercial programs meet the needs of most small businesses. These programs provide proper documentation and technical support at affordable prices.
6. Finally, it is vital to safeguard the programs and databases. Programs and databases are easily destroyed or sabotaged. Backup files should be maintained in a fireproof vault in a separate location to minimize the dangers associated with lost or damaged programs and data files.

Accounting for Cash

LO4 Identify special internal controls for cash.

Cash is broadly defined for financial statement purposes. Generally, **cash** includes currency and other items that are payable *on demand*, such as cheques, money orders, bank drafts, and certain savings accounts. Savings accounts that require substantial penalties for early withdrawal should be classified as *investments* rather than as cash. Also, post-dated cheques and IOUs represent receivables and should not be accounted for as cash. In practice, most companies use captions that highlight that items other than currency are included in the cash classification, such as *cash* and *cash equivalents*.

The amount of cash on hand must be closely monitored to ensure the viability of the business. There must be enough cash available to pay employees, suppliers, and creditors as amounts become due. When a company fails to pay legal debts, the creditors can force the business into bankruptcy. While the availability of cash is critical, management should avoid accumulating excess idle cash. The failure to invest excess cash in earning assets adversely affects profitability. Cash inflows and outflows must be properly managed to prevent a shortage or surplus of cash.

Controlling Cash

More than any other asset, cash requires strict adherence to internal control procedures. Cash has universal appeal. Relatively small amounts of high-denomination currency can be used to represent significant amounts of value. Aslo, it is difficult to prove who owns currency. In most cases, possession equals ownership. Because of these qualities, cash is highly susceptible to theft and must be kept under close scrutiny. Cash is most susceptible to embezzlement at the points of receipt and disbursement. The following procedures should be employed to reduce the likelihood of theft.

Cash Receipts

A record of all cash receipts should be prepared immediately. If cash receipts are recorded in a timely and accurate manner, missing amounts of money can be detected by comparing the actual balances of cash with the book balances. Customers should be given written copies of the receipts that evidence payment. This practice results in a control on the receipts clerk by the customer. A customer usually reviews the receipt to ensure that she or he has been given credit for the amount paid and calls any errors to the clerk's attention.

Cash receipts should be deposited in a bank or other financial institution on a timely basis. Cash collected late in the day should be deposited in a night depository. Every effort should be made to minimize the amount of cash on hand. Large amounts of cash place the business at risk of loss from theft; they also place the employees in danger of being harmed by criminals who attempt to rob the company.

Cash Payments

To control cash, a company should make all disbursements by cheque; this provides a record of cash payments. All cheques should be prenumbered and kept under lock. When cheques are prenumbered, lost or stolen cheques are easily identifiable by comparing the supply of unwritten and cancelled cheques with the list of prenumbered cheques. If cheques are kept locked and under the care of a responsible person, there is less opportunity for unauthorized disbursements.

The duties of approving disbursements, signing cheques, and recording transactions should be separated. If one person is authorized to approve, sign, and record cheques, it is easy for that person to falsify supporting documents, write a cheque, and record it in the records. When these duties are separated, the cheque signer reviews the documentation provided by the approving agent before signing the cheque. Likewise, the recording clerk reviews the work of both the approval agent and the signer when information is input to the accounting records. Again, collusion is required to circumvent the system of controls created by the separation of these duties.

Supporting documents with authorized approval signatures should be required when cheques are presented to the cheque signer. Supporting documents prove an actual need for payment. Before the payment is approved, invoice amounts should be checked and the payee verified as a legitimate vendor. Thus, the authorized approval signature acts as a check on the documents submitted by the payables clerk. Both the supporting documents and an authorized approval help deter the payables clerk from creating fake documents, with the disbursement being made to a friend or fictitious business. Also, the approver serves as a check on the accuracy of the work of the payables clerk.

Supporting documents should be marked *Paid* when the cheque is signed. If the documents are not indelibly marked, they could be retrieved from the file and resubmitted for a second payment. A payables clerk could work with the payee to share in any extra cash paid out by submitting the same supporting invoices for a second payment.

All spoiled and voided cheques should be defaced and retained. An employee may claim that a certain cheque was written for an incorrect amount and therefore thrown away. Unless there is physical proof of the existence of the cheque, the firm has no way of knowing whether the clerk is telling the truth. To prevent this uncertainty, all spoiled and voided cheques should be kept.

The Cost of Protecting Cash

Could you afford to buy a safe like the one shown here? The vault is only one of many expensive security devices used by banks to safeguard cash. By using chequing accounts, companies are able to avoid many of the costs associated with keeping cash safe. Besides providing physical control, chequing accounts enable companies to maintain a written audit trail regarding cash receipts and payments. Indeed, chequing accounts are the most widely used internal control device in modern society. It is difficult to imagine a business operating without the use of chequing accounts.

Chequing Account Documents

The previous section established the need for businesses and individuals to use chequing accounts. The following are the four main types of forms associated with a bank chequing account.

Signature Card

A bank **signature card** contains the bank account number and the signatures of the people authorized to write cheques on the account. The form is retained in the bank's files. If a bank employee is unfamiliar with the signature on a cheque that is presented to the bank for payment, she or he can refer to the signature card to verify the signature for that particular account.

Deposit Ticket

Each deposit of cash or cheques is accompanied by a **deposit ticket**, which normally contains the account number and the name of the account. The depositor fills in the amount of currency, coins, and cheques deposited. The total of all currency, coins, and cheques deposited is noted on the deposit ticket.

Bank Cheque

A written cheque involves three parties: (1) the person or business writing the cheque (the *payer*), (2) the bank on which the cheque is drawn, and (3) the person or business to whom the cheque is made payable (the *payee*). **Cheques** are often multicopy, prenumbered forms, with the name of the business issuing them preprinted on the face. A remittance notice is usually attached to the cheque. This portion of the cheque gives the payer space in which to establish a record that identifies why the cheque is being written (what invoices are being paid), the amount being disbursed, and the date of payment. When signed by the person whose signature is on the signature card, the cheque authorizes the bank to transfer the face amount of the cheque from the payer's account to the payee.

Bank Statement

Periodically, the bank sends the depositor a **bank statement**. It is important to note that the bank statement is presented from the bank's point of view. Since the bank is obligated to pay back the money that customers have deposited in their accounts, a chequing account is a liability to the bank. Therefore, the chequing account carries a credit balance on the bank's books. **Bank statement debit memos** describe transactions that reduce the balance of the bank's liability (the customer's account). **Bank statement credit memos** describe activities that increase the bank's liability (the customer's account balance). To avoid confusion, remember that the chequing account is an asset (Cash) to the depositor. Therefore, a *debit memo* listed in the bank statement requires a *credit entry* to the Cash account on the depositor's books.

The information contained in the bank statement normally includes (a) the balance of the account at the beginning of the period, (b) additions created by customer deposits made during the period, (c) other additions described in credit memos (e.g., earned interest), (d) subtractions made for the payment of cheques drawn on the account during the period, (e) other subtractions described in debit memos (e.g., service charges), (f) a running balance of the account, and (g) the balance of the account at the end of the period. In Exhibit 6–1, examples of these items are referenced with the letters in parentheses. Normally, the cancelled cheques or copies of them are enclosed with the bank statement.

Exhibit 6–1 *A Bank Statement*

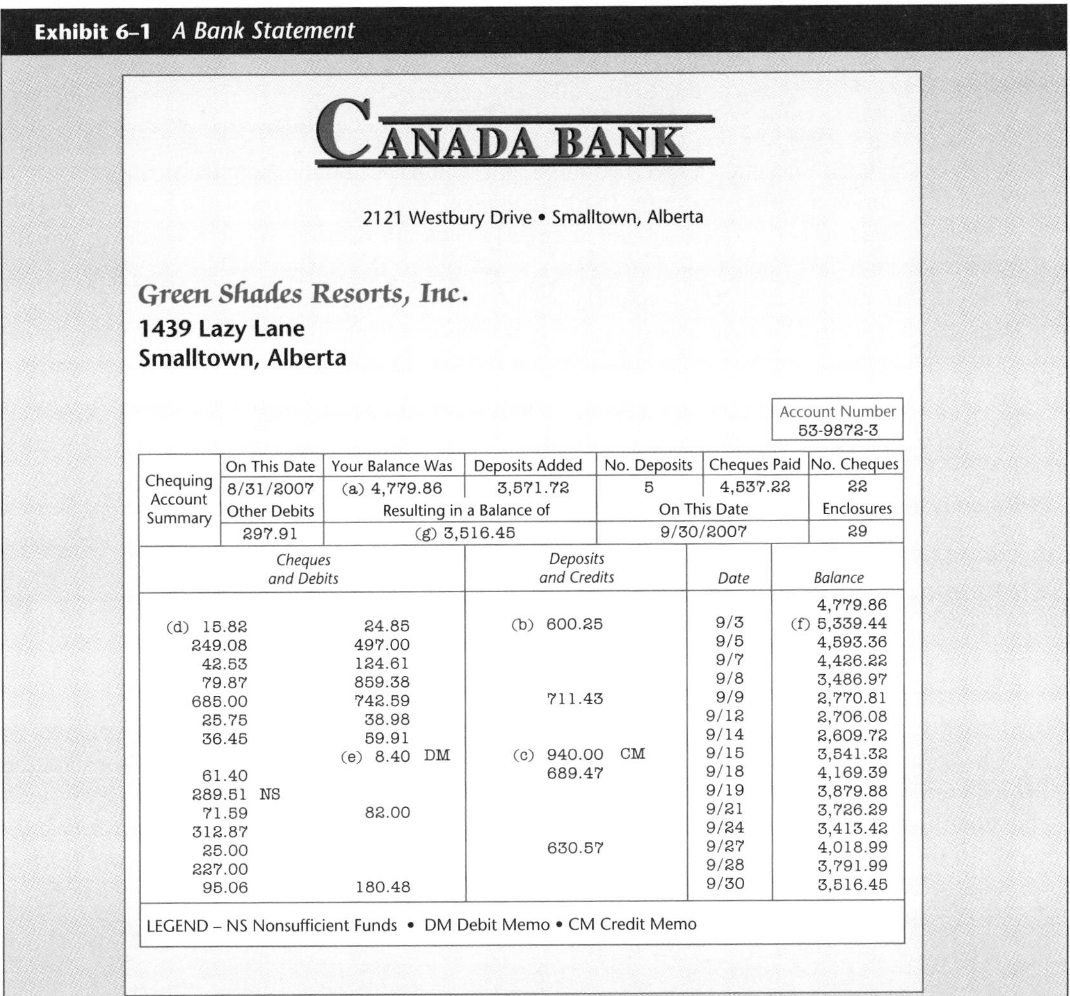

CANADA BANK

2121 Westbury Drive • Smalltown, Alberta

Green Shades Resorts, Inc.
1439 Lazy Lane
Smalltown, Alberta

Account Number
53-9872-3

Chequing Account Summary	On This Date	Your Balance Was	Deposits Added	No. Deposits	Cheques Paid	No. Cheques
	8/31/2007	(a) 4,779.86	3,571.72	5	4,537.22	22
	Other Debits	Resulting in a Balance of		On This Date		Enclosures
	297.91	(g) 3,516.45		9/30/2007		29

Cheques and Debits		Deposits and Credits	Date	Balance
				4,779.86
(d) 15.82	24.85	(b) 600.25	9/3	(f) 5,339.44
249.08	497.00		9/5	4,593.36
42.53	124.61		9/7	4,426.22
79.87	859.38		9/8	3,486.97
685.00	742.59	711.43	9/9	2,770.81
25.75	38.98		9/12	2,706.08
36.45	59.91		9/14	2,609.72
	(e) 8.40 DM	(c) 940.00 CM	9/15	3,541.32
61.40		689.47	9/18	4,169.39
289.51 NS			9/19	3,879.88
71.59	82.00		9/21	3,726.29
312.87			9/24	3,413.42
25.00		630.57	9/27	4,018.99
227.00			9/28	3,791.99
95.06	180.48		9/30	3,516.45

LEGEND – NS Nonsufficient Funds • DM Debit Memo • CM Credit Memo

Reconciling the Bank Statement

LO5

Prepare a bank reconciliation.

Usually the balance shown on the bank statement differs from the balance shown in the Cash account on the depositor's books. The difference is normally a result of timing. For example, a depositor deducts the amount of a cheque from the account immediately after writing the cheque. However, the bank has no knowledge of the cheque until the payee presents it for payment, which may occur several weeks or even months after the cheque is written. Similarly, there may be a delay between the time a bank adjusts a depositor's account and the time the customer becomes aware that the adjustment was made. For example, a customer may not be aware that the bank deposited interest in or subtracted service charges from his or her account until the customer receives and reads the bank statement. Therefore, the bank statement may reflect a balance larger or smaller than the balance recorded in the depositor's books. The following items cause the balance on the bank statement to be larger than the balance shown in the depositor's cash account:

1. Outstanding cheques. These are disbursements that have been properly recorded as cash deductions on the payer's books. However, the amounts have not been deducted from the payer's bank account because the cheques have not yet been presented by the payee to the bank for payment; that is, the cheques have not "cleared" the bank.
2. Deposits made by the bank. These are additions to the depositor's account made directly by the bank. They may be the result of collections made by the bank on behalf of the depositor or of interest paid to the depositor by the bank.

Alternatively, the balance reported on the bank statement may be less than the balance recorded in the depositor's books. This may be due to the following causes:

1. **Service charges**. These are fees charged by the bank for services performed or as a penalty for the depositor's failing to maintain a specified minimum cash balance throughout the period.
2. Deductions for **non-sufficient-funds (NSF) cheques**. These are cheques that were deposited. However, when the cheques were submitted for payment to the bank on which they were drawn, the accounts did not have enough funds to cover the amount of the cheques. When such cheques are returned, they must be deducted from the depositor's bank account.
3. **Deposits in transit**. These are deposits that have been recorded by the depositor in the accounting records but have not yet been recorded by the bank. They are also known as *outstanding deposits*.

Also, there may be differences between the bank statement's cash balance and the depositor's cash balance due to errors by either the bank or the depositor. For example, the bank may pay a cheque written by a customer named *Turpen* from the account of a customer named *Turpin*. In this case, both the Turpen and Turpin bank statements would be incorrect. All errors should be corrected immediately.

Determining the Adjusted (True) Cash Balance

A schedule is prepared to reconcile the differences between the cash balance shown on the bank statement and the cash balance recorded in the depositor's accounting records. This schedule is called a **bank reconciliation**. It begins with the cash balance reported by the bank as of the statement date (the **unadjusted bank balance**). The schedule then lists the adjustments necessary to determine the amount of cash that the depositor actually has as of the date of the bank statement. The balance is called the **adjusted cash balance**. The adjusted cash balance is determined a second time by making adjustments to the **unadjusted book balance**. The bank statement is reconciled when the adjusted cash balance determined from the perspective of the unadjusted *bank* balance agrees with the adjusted cash balance determined from the perspective of the unadjusted *book* balance. The procedures necessary to arrive at the *adjusted cash balance* from the two different perspectives are outlined here.

Adjustments to the Bank Balance

Step 1 in determining the adjusted bank balance from the perspective of the bank statement is to compare the deposit tickets with deposits shown in the depositor's records. Any deposits recorded in the depositor's books but not yet recorded by the bank are, as noted, deposits in transit. Since deposits are often made in the night depository or on the day following the receipt of cash, this is a frequent occurrence. Deposits in transit have not been recorded by the bank, so they are added to the unadjusted bank balance to arrive at the true cash balance.

Step 2 is to sort the cheques returned with the bank statement into numerical sequence. These cheques are then compared with cheques listed in the depositor's cash records, and the amounts are verified. After verification of all the cheques returned with the bank statement, there may be some cheques that were issued by the depositor but not presented to the bank for payment. These **outstanding cheques** must be deducted from the unadjusted bank balance to determine the adjusted bank balance. Some banks do not return paid cheques. In this case outstanding cheques are identified by comparing the company's cheque register with the cheque numbers listed on the bank statement. A **certified cheque** is a cheque guaranteed by a bank to be a cheque drawn on an account having sufficient funds. Whereas a regular cheque is deducted from the customer's account when it is presented for payment, a certified cheque is deducted from the customer's account when the bank certifies that the cheque is good. Therefore, all certified cheques have been deducted by the bank in the determination of the unadjusted bank balance, whether they have cleared the bank or remain outstanding as of the date of the bank statement. For this reason, it is not necessary to deduct *outstanding certified cheques* from the unadjusted bank balance to determine the true balance of cash.

Adjustments to the Book Balance

The unadjusted book balance must be adjusted to reflect the credit and debit memos shown in the bank statement. Credit memo items such as earned interest are added to the unadjusted book balance, and debit memo items such as service charges are subtracted from it. NSF cheques must be subtracted from the unadjusted book balance to determine the adjusted bank balance.

Correction of Errors

Errors can affect the determination of the adjusted balance from the perspective of either the bank statement or the depositor's books. If an error is found on the bank statement, the bank should be notified immediately, and an adjustment is made to the unadjusted bank balance to determine the adjusted bank balance. In contrast, errors made by the depositor require adjustments to the book balance to arrive at the adjusted book balance.

Illustrating the Bank Reconciliation

The following example illustrates the process of preparing the bank reconciliation for Green Shades Resorts, Inc. (GSRI). Recall that Exhibit 6–1 is the bank statement for GSRI. Exhibit 6–2 represents the completed bank reconciliation statement. The items included in the reconciliation statement are now described.

Adjustments to Bank Balance

As of September 30, 2007, the bank statement shows an unadjusted balance of $3,516.45. Assume that a review of the bank statement discloses two adjustments that must be added to this amount. First, assume that a review of the deposit tickets indicated there was $724.11 of deposits in transit. Second, assume that an examination of the returned cheques disclosed that a $25 cheque written by

Exhibit 6–2 *A Bank Reconciliation Statement*

GREEN SHADES RESORTS, INC.
Bank Reconciliation Statement
as at September 30, 2007

Unadjusted Bank Balance, September 30, 2007			$3,516.45
Add: Deposits in Transit			724.11
Bank Error: Cheque drawn on Green Valley Resorts Charged to GSRI			25.00
Less: Outstanding Cheques			
Cheque No.	**Date**	**Amount**	
639	Sept. 18	$ 13.75	
646	Sept. 20	29.00	
672	Sept. 27	192.50	
Total Outstanding Cheques			(235.25)
Adjusted Bank Balance, Sept 30, 2007			$4,030.31
Unadjusted Book Balance, September 30, 2007			$3,361.22
Add: Receivable Collected by Bank			940.00
Error Made by Accountant (Cheque no. 633 recorded as $63.45 instead of $36.45)			27.00
Less: Bank Service Charges			(8.40)
NSF Cheque			(289.51)
Adjusted Book Balance, September 30, 2007			$4,030.31

Must be equal

Green Valley Resorts had been deducted from GSRI's bank account. Since the bank by mistake deducted this amount from GSRI's account, the amount must be added back to the unadjusted bank balance to arrive at the adjusted balance.

Finally, assume that the returned cheques included in the bank statement were sorted and compared to the cash records and that three cheques were outstanding. Since these cheques have not yet been deducted from GSRI's bank account, the unadjusted bank balance must be reduced. Exhibit 6–2 assumes that the amount of the outstanding cheques was $235.25. After this deduction is made, the adjusted bank balance is $4,030.31.

Adjustments to Book Balance

As indicated in Exhibit 6–2, GSRI's unadjusted book balance as of September 30, 2007, amounted to $3,361.22. This balance does not accurately reflect GSRI's adjusted book balance because of four unrecorded accounting events: (1) The bank collected a $940 account receivable for GSRI, (2) GSRI's accountant made a $27 recording error, (3) the bank charged GSRI an $8.40 service fee, and (4) GSRI accepted a $289.51 cheque from a customer who did not have sufficient funds to cover the cheque. Each event requires an adjustment to GSRI's accounting records. The adjustments and their effects on the financial statements are now explained.

Adjustment 1 Recording the $940 receivables collection increases Cash and reduces Accounts Receivables.

The event is an asset exchange transaction. The effect of the collection on GSRI's financial statements follows:

Assets			=	Liab.	+	Equity	Rev.	−	Exp.	=	Net Inc.	Cash Flow Statement	
Cash	+	Accts. Rec.											
940	+	(940)	=	NA	+	NA	NA	−	NA	=	NA	940	OA

Adjustment 2

Assume that the $27 recording error occurred because GSRI's accountant made a transposition error when recording cheque no. 633.

The cheque was written to pay utilities expense in the amount of $36.45 but was recorded as a $63.45 disbursement. Since cash payments are overstated by $27.00 ($63.45 − $36.45), this amount must be added back to GSRI's cash balance and deducted from the Utilities Expense account. Since the deduction causes the Utilities Expense account to decline, the net income increases. The effects on the financial statements are shown next:

Assets	=	Liab.	+	Equity	Rev.	−	Exp.	=	Net Inc.	Cash Flow Statement	
27	=	NA	+	27	NA	−	(27)	=	27	27	OA

Adjustment 3

The $8.40 service charge is a typical expense item that reduces assets, equity, income, and cash flow.

The effects are shown here:

Assets	=	Liab.	+	Equity	Rev.	−	Exp.	=	Net Inc.	Cash Flow Statement	
(8.40)	=	NA	+	(8.40)	NA	−	8.40	=	(8.40)	(8.40)	OA

Adjustment 4

The $289.51 NSF cheque reduces GSRI's cash balance.

GSRI increased its Cash account when it accepted the customer's cheque. Now GSRI must reduce its Cash account because there is not enough money in the customer's bank account to pay the cheque. GSRI will try to collect the money directly from the customer. In the meantime, it will show the amount due as an account receivable. Therefore, the adjusting entry required to record the NSF cheque is an asset exchange transaction. The Cash account decreases, and the Accounts Receivable account increases. The effect on GSRI's financial statements is as follows:

Assets			=	Liab.	+	Equity	Rev.	−	Exp.	=	Net Inc.	Cash Flow Statement	
Cash	+	Accts. Rec.											
(289.51)	+	289.51	=	NA	+	NA	NA	−	NA	=	NA	(289.51)	OA

Determination of the Adjusted Cash Balance

Two of the adjustments increase the unadjusted cash balance. The other two adjustments decrease the unadjusted balance. After the adjustments have been recorded, the Cash account reflects the adjusted cash balance of $4,030.31 ($3,361.22 unadjusted cash balance + $940.00 receivable collection + $27.00 recording error − $8.40 service charge − $289.51 NSF cheque). Since the adjusted balance determined from the perspective of the bank account agrees with the adjusted balance determined from the perspective of GSRI's books, the bank statement has been successfully reconciled with the accounting records.

Cash Balance Updated

The journal entries required for the four adjustments described are as follows:

Account Title	Debit	Credit
Cash	940.00	
Accounts Receivable		940.00
To record the account receivable collected by the bank		
Cash	27.00	
Utilities Expense		27.00
To correct error on recording cheque no. 633		
Bank Service Charge Expense	8.40	
Cash		8.40
To record service charge expense		
Accounts Receivable	289.51	
Cash		289.51
To establish receivable due from customer who wrote the bad cheque		

Cash Short and Over

Sometimes errors are made when employees are collecting cash or making change to customers. If these errors occur, the amount of money in the cash register will not agree with the amount of cash receipts recorded on the cash register tape. For example, suppose that when a customer paid for $17.95 of merchandise with a $20 bill, the sales clerk returned $3.05 in change instead of the correct amount of $2.05. If, at the end of the day, the cash register tape shows total receipts of $487.50, the cash drawer contains only $486.50. The actual cash balance is less than the expected cash balance by $1. Any shortage of cash or excess of cash is recorded in a special account named **Cash Short and Over**. In this example, the shortage is recorded in the following journal entry:

Account Title	Debit	Credit
Cash	486.50	
Cash Short and Over	1.00	
Sales		487.50

A debit to the Cash Short and Over account indicates a cash shortage that represents an expense. An overage of cash is considered revenue and is recorded by crediting the Cash Short and Over account. As with other expense and revenue items, the balance of the Cash Short and Over account is closed to the Retained Earnings account at the end of the accounting period.

The following information was drawn from Reliance Company's October bank statement. The unadjusted bank balance on October 31 was $2,300. The statement showed that the bank had collected a $200 account receivable for Reliance. The statement also included $20 of bank service charges for October and a $100 cheque payable to Reliance that was returned NSF. A comparison of the bank statement with company accounting records indicates that there was a $500 deposit in transit and $1,800 of cheques outstanding at the end of the month. Based on this information, determine the adjusted cash balance on October 31.

Answer Since the unadjusted book balance is not given, start with the unadjusted bank balance to determine the true cash balance. The collection of the receivable, the bank service charges, and the NSF cheque are already recognized in the unadjusted bank balance, so these items are not used to determine the adjusted cash balance. Determine the adjusted cash balance by adding the deposit in transit to and subtracting the outstanding cheques from the unadjusted bank balance. The adjusted cash balance is $1,000 ($2,300 unadjusted bank balance + $500 deposit in transit − $1,800 outstanding cheques).

Using Petty Cash Funds

LO6 Explain the use of a petty cash fund.

It is best to make all disbursements by cheque, but it may be more practical and convenient to make certain small payments in cash. Payments for postage, delivery charges, taxi fares, employees' supper money, and other small items are often made with cash. To allow for these small payments and still keep effective control over cash disbursements, a company may establish a **petty cash fund**. The fund is established for some specified dollar amount, such as $300, and is controlled by one employee, called the *petty cash custodian*.

Petty cash funds are usually maintained on an **imprest basis**, which means that the cash disbursed is replenished on a periodic basis. The fund is created by drawing a cheque on the regular chequing account, cashing it, and giving the currency to a petty cash custodian. The custodian normally keeps the cash under lock and key. In other words, the establishment of a petty cash fund merely transfers cash from a bank account to a safety box inside the company offices. As such, the event is an asset exchange. The Cash account decreases, and the Petty Cash account increases. The effect on the financial statements and the journal entry required to record the event are as follows:

Assets			=	Liab.	+	Equity						Cash Flow Statement
Cash	+	Petty Cash					Rev.	−	Exp.	=	Net Inc.	
(300)	+	300	=	NA	+	NA	NA	−	NA	=	NA	NA

Account Title	Debit	Credit
Petty Cash	300.00	
Cash		300.00

The amount of the petty cash fund depends on what it is used for, how often it is used, and how often it is replenished. It should be large enough to handle disbursements for a reasonable time, such as a week or a month.

When money is disbursed from the petty cash fund, the custodian should fill out a petty cash **voucher**, such as the one in Exhibit 6–3. Any supporting documents, such as an invoice, restaurant bill, or parking fee receipt, should be attached to the petty cash voucher. The person who receives the cash should always sign the voucher as evidence of the receipt. At any time, the total of the amounts recorded on the petty cash vouchers plus the remaining coin and currency should equal the balance of the petty cash ledger account. *There is no journal entry made in the accounting records when petty cash funds are disbursed.* The effect on the financial statements is recorded at the time when the petty cash fund is topped up (when additional cash is put into the petty cash safety box).

When the amount of cash in the petty cash fund is relatively low, the fund should be replenished. To accomplish the replenishment, the petty cash vouchers are totalled, the amount of any cash short or over is determined, and a cheque is issued to the bank to obtain the currency needed to return the fund to its

Exhibit 6–3 *A Petty Cash Voucher*

Petty cash voucher no. ______

To: ____________________ Date ________, 20__

Explanation: Account No. ________ Amount ________

Approved by ____________ Received by ____________

full balance. For example, suppose the petty cash fund is replenished when the total amount of petty cash vouchers equals $216. The vouchers can be classified according to different types of expenses or listed in total as miscellaneous expense. Assuming that the Miscellaneous Expense account is used in this example, the journal entries to record the replenishment of the funds are as follows:

Account Title	Debit	Credit
Miscellaneous Expense	216.00	
Petty Cash		216.00
To record expenses paid from the petty cash fund		
Petty Cash	216.00	
Cash		216.00
To replenish the petty cash fund		

Note that the effect of the entries could have been recorded more efficiently. Since the debit to the Petty Cash account is offset by the credit, a single entry debiting Miscellaneous Expense and crediting Cash would have the same effect on the accounts. Indeed, the entry more often used in practice to record the replenishment of petty cash appears as follows:

Account Title	Debit	Credit
Miscellaneous Expense	216.00	
Cash		216.00

The replenishment affects the financial statements in the same manner as any other cash expense. It reduces assets, equity, income, and cash flow. The effects are shown here:

Assets	=	Liab.	+	Equity	Rev.	−	Exp.	=	Net Inc.	Cash Flow Statement
(216)	=	NA	+	(216)	NA	−	216	=	(216)	(216) OA

If the vouchers and their amounts are separated as postage, $66; delivery charges, $78.40; taxi fares, $28; and supper money, $43.60, the journal entry to replenish the fund could be recorded as follows:

Account Title	Debit	Credit
Postage Expense	66.00	
Delivery Expense	78.40	
Taxi Fares Expense	28.00	
Employee Meal Expense	43.60	
Cash		216.00

Once the vouchers are checked, the fund replenished, and the journal entry recorded, the vouchers should be indelibly marked *Paid* so that they cannot be reused.

Sometimes, cash shortages and overages are discovered when a physical count is taken of the money in the petty cash fund. Suppose that a physical count reveals $212.30 in petty cash vouchers and only $87 in cash. Assuming a normal petty cash balance of $300, the journal entry necessary to record the replenishment is as follows:

Account Title	Debit	Credit
Miscellaneous Expense	212.30	
Cash Short and Over	.70	
Cash		213.00
To record expenses paid and replenish the petty cash fund		

If a cash shortage or overage does not occur often and it is an insignificant amount, the shortage or overage may be included in miscellaneous expense.

Cornerstone Corporation established a $400 petty cash fund that was replenished when it contained $30 of currency and coins and $378 of receipts for miscellaneous expenses. Based on this information, determine the amount of cash short or over to be recognized. Explain how the shortage or overage would be reported in the financial statements. Also determine the amount of petty cash expenses that were recognized when the fund was replenished.

Answer The fund contained $408 of currency and receipts ($30 currency + $378 of receipts), resulting in a cash overage of $8 ($408 − $400). The overage would be reported as miscellaneous revenue on the income statement. The amount of petty cash expenses recognized would equal the amount of the expense receipts, which is $378.

Assessment of the Level of Liquidity

Current versus Noncurrent

LO7 Prepare a classified balance sheet.

Assets have been defined as items that have probable future economic benefits to a business, and *liabilities* as the creditors' claim on some of those assets. However, not all assets and liabilities are the same; a significant distinguishing feature relates to their liquidity. The more quickly an asset is converted to cash, the more *liquid* it is. This is important because companies usually pay their bills with cash. Land and buildings are valuable assets, but they cannot be used to pay this month's electric bill.

Why not keep all assets in cash or liquid investments? Because investments in liquid assets usually do not earn as much money as investments in other assets. Thus, a company must try to maintain a proper balance between liquid assets (so it can pay its bills) and nonliquid assets (so it can earn a good return).

This distinction is so important that accountants organize items on the balance sheet according to liquidity. There are two major classes of assets: *current* and *noncurrent*. Current items are also referred to as *short term* and noncurrent items as *long term*. A **current (short-term) asset** is one that will be converted to cash or consumed within one year or an operating cycle, whichever is longer. For example, accounts receivable are usually expected to be collected (converted to cash) within one year. Therefore, they are classified as current.

LO8 Identify the length of an operating cycle.

An **operating cycle** is defined as the average time it takes a business to convert cash to inventory, inventory to accounts receivable, and accounts receivable back to cash. Graphically, it can be shown as follows:

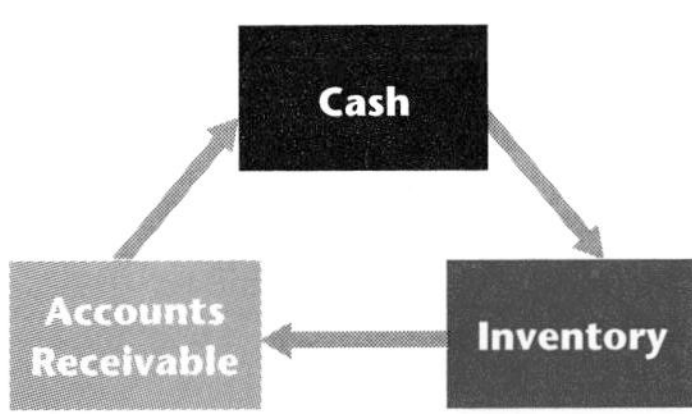

Operating cycles for most businesses are less than one year, but they can be longer. Consider the time it takes a construction company to build and sell a house—this time could easily exceed one year. Ratios that help measure the length of a company's operating cycle are introduced in Chapters 7 and 8. However, unless there is strong evidence to the contrary, assume that operating cycles are less than one year. The one-year rule usually prevails with respect to the classification of current assets.

Based on the definition of *current* as explained here, the typical current assets section of a balance sheet includes the following items:

Current Assets
Cash
Marketable Securities
Accounts Receivable
Short-Term Notes Receivable
Interest Receivable
Inventory
Supplies
Prepaids

Given the definition of current assets, it seems logical that a **current (short-term) liability** would be one that must be repaid within one year or an operating cycle, whichever is longer. This is almost always correct. However, this definition places some surprising accounts in the category of current liabilities. If a company issues bonds[1] that are to be repaid in 20 years, the bonds are included in long-term liabilities (until they have been outstanding for 19 years). After 19 years, the 20-year bonds become due within one year and are classified as a current liability on the balance sheet.

There is an exception to the general rule for determining which liabilities should be listed as short term. If a business does not plan to use any of its current assets to repay a debt, that debt is listed as long term even if it is due within one year. How can debt be repaid without using current assets? Assume that the 20-year bonds referred to are now due within the next year. The company may plan to issue new 20-year bonds (long-term debt) and use the proceeds from those bonds to repay the old bonds. In this case, the currently maturing debt is classified as long term. This situation is referred to as *refinancing short-term debt on a long-term basis.*

Liabilities typically found in the current section of a balance sheet include the following:

Current Liabilities
Accounts Payable
Short-Term Notes Payable
Wages Payable
Taxes Payable
Interest Payable

Balance sheets that distinguish between current and noncurrent items are called **classified balance sheets**. To enhance the usefulness of accounting information, most real-world balance sheets are classified. However, there is no requirement to present information in this fashion. Exhibit 6–4 is an example of a classified balance sheet.

Liquidity versus Solvency

Liquidity, as explained, deals with the ability to generate short-term cash flows. **Solvency** is the ability to repay liabilities in the long run. Liquidity and solvency are both important to the survival of a

[1] *Bonds* are certificates issued to creditors that evidence a company's obligation to pay interest and return of principal on borrowed funds. They are normally issued to the general public in exchange for the receipt of borrowed money. Bonds usually carry long terms to maturity, with 20 years being typical.

Exhibit 6–4 *Balance Sheet*

LIMBAUGH COMPANY
Balance Sheet
December 31, 2006

Assets			
Current Assets			
Cash		$ 20,000	
Accounts Receivable		35,000	
Inventory		230,000	
Prepaid Rent		3,600	
Total Current Assets			$288,600
Capital Assets			
Office Equipment	$ 80,000		
Less: Accumulated Amortization	(25,000)	55,000	
Building	340,000		
Less: Accumulated Amortization	(40,000)	300,000	
Land		120,000	
Total Capital Assets			475,000
Total Assets			$763,600
Liabilities and Shareholders' Equity			
Current Liabilities			
Accounts Payable		$ 32,000	
Notes Payable		120,000	
Salaries Payable		32,000	
Unearned Revenue		9,800	
Total Current Liabilities			$193,800
Long-Term Liabilities			
Note Payable			100,000
Total Liabilities			293,800
Shareholders' Equity			
Common Shares		200,000	
Retained Earnings		269,800	469,800
Total Liabilities and Shareholders' Equity			$763,600

business, but one may be more important to a particular user than the other. If a bank is considering loaning a company money that must be repaid in six months, obviously the bank is concerned more with the company's liquidity. An investor thinking of purchasing the company's 20-year bonds is interested in the company's solvency as well as its liquidity because a company that cannot pay its bills in the short term will not be around to repay the bonds 20 years from now.

Current Ratio

Financial statement users calculate several ratios when making the comparisons needed to evaluate a company's liquidity and solvency. The debt to assets ratio introduced in Chapter 3 is one tool for examining solvency. The main ratio used to evaluate liquidity is the **current ratio**, defined as

LO9 Use the current ratio to assess the level of liquidity.

$$\frac{\text{Current assets}}{\text{Current liabilities}}$$

Since current assets normally exceed current liabilities, this ratio usually produces a result larger than 100 percent. Many individuals find large percentages difficult to interpret. Therefore, the current ratio is often expressed as a decimal rather than as a percentage. For example, a company with $250 in current assets and $100 in current liabilities has a current ratio of 2.5 to 1 ($250 ÷ $100 = $2.50 in current assets for every $1 in current liabilities). This is, of course, the same as saying that current assets are 250 percent of current liabilities. However, as stated earlier, traditional practice tends to favour the decimal expression. Therefore, this book uses that format when making reference to the current ratio.

Real-World Data

The current ratio is one of the most commonly used ratios to analyze accounting information. Current ratios can be too high, suggesting that the company has more assets available to pay current liabilities than are needed. This result would suggest that earnings could probably be improved by converting some of the short-term assets to longer-term investments that yield a higher return. Indeed, given the desire for profit maximization, you are likely to find more real-world companies with ratios that are too low than companies with those that are too high.

Exhibit 6–5 presents the current ratios and debt to assets ratios expressed in decimal format for six real-world companies from three different industries.

Which of these companies faces the highest level of financial risk? Notice that the banks have higher debt to assets ratios than those of the companies in the building supplies business. Does this mean that banks are riskier investments? Not necessarily. Since the companies are in different industries, one must be careful when comparing ratios. Banks traditionally have high debt to asset ratios, so those of CIBC and the Royal Bank are not unusual. Remember that financial leverage can increase profitability if the return on invested funds exceeds the cost of interest, so high debt levels can be productive if a company operates in a relatively stable industry. The Building Box is showing a low current ratio, probably because it is a fairly new entry into the Canadian building supplies industry, opening 15 new stores across Canada over the past few years.

Finally, note that the ratios for the companies tend to be "grouped by industry." Current ratios do vary somewhat among different industries, but they probably do not vary as much as the debt to asset ratios. Why? Because all companies, regardless of how they finance their total assets, must keep sufficient current assets on hand to repay current liabilities.

Exhibit 6–5

Industry	Company	Current Ratio	Debt to Assets Ratio
Banks	CIBC (Oct. 2000)	1.26	0.96
	Royal Bank (Oct. 2000)	1.28	0.95
Grocery stores	Sobeys (May 2001)	0.93	0.63
	Loblaws (Dec. 2000)	0.91	0.63
Building supplies	Home Depot (Jan. 2001)	1.77	0.30
	The Building Box (Jan. 2001)	0.87	0.59

The policies and procedures used to provide reasonable assurance that the objectives of an enterprise will be accomplished are called *internal controls*. These can be subdivided into two categories: accounting controls and administrative controls. *Accounting controls* include procedures designed to safeguard the assets and ensure that the accounting records contain reliable information. *Administrative controls* are designed to evaluate performance and the degree of compliance with company policies and public laws. While the mechanics of internal control systems vary from company to company, the more prevalent features include the following:

1. *Separation of duties.* Whenever possible, the functions of authorization, recording, and custody should be exercised by different individuals.
2. *Quality of employees.* Employees should be qualified to competently perform the duties that are assigned to them. The enterprise must establish hiring practices to screen out unqualified candidates. Also, procedures should be established to ensure that employees receive the training they need to maintain competence.
3. *Bonded employees.* Employees in sensitive positions should be covered by a fidelity bond that provides insurance to reimburse losses that are due to illegal actions committed by employees.
4. *Periods of absence.* Employees should be required to take extended absences from their jobs so that they are not always present to hide unscrupulous or illegal activities.
5. *Procedures manual.* To promote compliance, the procedures for processing transactions should be clearly described in a manual.
6. *Authority and responsibility.* To motivate employees and promote effective control, clear lines of authority and responsibility should be established.
7. *Prenumbered documents.* Numbered documents minimize the likelihood of missing or duplicate documents. Accordingly, prenumbered forms should be used for all important documents such as purchase orders, receiving reports, invoices, and cheques.
8. *Physical control.* Locks, fences, security personnel, and other physical devices should be employed to safeguard assets.
9. *Performance evaluation.* Because few people can evaluate their own performance objectively, independent performance evaluations should be performed. Substandard performance will likely persist unless employees are encouraged to take corrective action.
10. *Internal control in computer systems.* The basic internal control features discussed are applicable to computer systems as well as manual systems.

Because cash is so important to businesses and because some people find it tempting to steal, much of the discussion of internal controls in this chapter related specifically to cash controls. Special procedures should be employed to control the receipts and payments of cash. One of the most common control devices is the use of *chequing accounts.*

Bank statements should be compared with internal accounting records through a procedure known as a *bank reconciliation.* One common way to accomplish a reconciliation is to determine the adjusted cash balance based on both bank and book records. Typical items shown on a bank reconciliation include the following:

Unadjusted Bank Balance	xxx	Unadjusted Book Balance	xxx
Add:		Add:	
Deposits in Transit	xxx	Interest Revenue	xxx
		Collection of Receivables	xxx
Less:		Less:	
Outstanding Cheques	xxx	Bank Service Charges	xxx
		NSF Cheques	xxx
Adusted Bank Balance	xxx	Adjusted Book Balance	xxx

Attaining equality between the two adjusted cash balances provides evidence of accuracy in the accounting for cash transactions.

Another commonly used internal control device for protecting cash is a *petty cash* fund. Normally, an employee who is designated as the petty cash custodian is entrusted with a small amount of cash. The custodian reimburses employees for small expenditures made on behalf of the organization and collects receipts from the employees at the time of the reimbursement. At any point in time, the receipts plus the remaining cash should equal the amount of funds entrusted to the custodian. Journal entries to recognize the expenses incurred are made at the time the fund is replenished.

Finally, the chapter discussed the assessment of organizational *liquidity.* The *current ratio* is determined by dividing current assets by current liabilities. The higher the ratio, the more liquid the organization.

a look forward

The material in Chapters 6 through 11 is organized mainly in the order of the arrangement of a classified balance sheet, which was discussed in this chapter. This chapter presented several issues related to accounting for cash; Chapter 7 addresses issues related to accounting for accounts receivable, and so on, until Chapter 11, which addresses issues related to accounting for equity. Shareholders' equity is the final section of a classified balance sheet.

SELF-STUDY REVIEW PROBLEM

The following information pertains to Terry's Pest Control Company (TPCC) for July:

1. The unadjusted bank balance at July 31 was $870.
2. The bank statement included the following items:
   a. A $60 credit memo for interest earned by TPCC.
   b. A $200 NSF cheque made payable to TPCC.
   c. A $110 debit memo for bank service charges.
3. The unadjusted book balance at July 31 was $1,400.
4. A comparison of the bank statement with company accounting records disclosed the following:
   a. A $400 deposit in transit at July 31.
   b. Outstanding cheques totalling $120 at the end of the month.

Required

a. Prepare a bank reconciliation statement.
b. Prepare in general journal format the entries necessary to adjust TPCC's cash account to its true balance.

Solution to Requirement a

TERRY'S PEST CONTROL COMPANY
Bank Reconciliation
as of July 31

Unadjusted bank balance	$ 870
Add: Deposits in transit	400
Less: Outstanding cheques	(120)
Adjusted bank balance	$1,150
Unadjusted book balance	$1,400
Add: Interest revenue	60
Less: NSF cheque	(200)
Less: Bank service charges	(110)
Adjusted book balance	$1,150

Solution to Requirement b

Ref.	Account Title	Debit	Credit
1.	Cash	60	
	Interest Revenue		60
2.	Accounts Receivable	200	
	Cash		200
3.	Service Charge Expense	110	
	Cash		110

KEY TERMS

accounting controls *235*
adjusted cash balance *244*
administrative controls *235*
audit around the computer *239*
bank reconciliation *244*
bank statement *243*
bank statement credit memo *243*
bank statement debit memo *243*
cash *240*
cash short and over *248*
certified cheque *245*
cheques *242*
classified balance sheet *252*
current (short-term) asset *251*
current (short-term) liability *252*
current ratio *253*
deposit ticket *242*
deposits in transit *244*
fidelity bond *236*
general authority *237*
imprest basis *249*
internal controls *235*
liquidity *252*
non-sufficient-funds (NSF) cheque *244*
operating cycle *251*
outstanding cheques *245*
petty cash fund *249*
procedures manual *237*
separation of duties *236*
service charges *244*
signature card *242*
solvency *252*
specific authorizations *237*
unadjusted bank balance *244*
unadjusted book balance *244*
voucher *249*

QUESTIONS

1. What are the policies and procedures called that are used to provide reasonable assurance that the objectives of an enterprise will be accomplished?
2. What is the difference between accounting controls and administrative controls?
3. What are several features of a strong internal control system?
4. What is meant by *separation of duties*? Give an illustration.
5. What are the attributes of a high-quality employee?
6. What is a fidelity bond? Explain its purpose.
7. Why is it important that every employee periodically take a leave of absence or vacation?
8. What are the purpose and importance of a procedures manual?
9. What is the difference between specific and general authorizations?
10. Why should documents (cheques, invoices, receipts) be prenumbered?
11. What procedures are important in the physical control of assets and accounting records?
12. What is the purpose of independent verification of performance?
13. What are the six control requirements for computer systems discussed in this chapter? Explain each.
14. What items are considered cash?
15. Why is cash more susceptible to theft or embezzlement than other assets?
16. Giving written copies of receipts to customers can help prevent what type of illegal acts?
17. What procedures can help to protect cash receipts?
18. What procedures can help protect cash disbursements?
19. What effect does a debit memo in a bank statement have on the Cash account? What effect does a credit memo in a bank statement have on the Cash account?
20. What information is normally included in a bank statement?
21. Why might a bank statement reflect a balance that is larger than the balance recorded in the depositor's books? What could cause the bank balance to be smaller than the book balance?
22. What is the purpose of a bank reconciliation?
23. What is an outstanding cheque?
24. What is a deposit in transit?
25. What is a certified cheque?
26. How is an NSF cheque accounted for in the accounting records?
27. What is the purpose of the Cash Short and Over account?
28. What is the purpose of a petty cash fund?
29. What types of expenditures are usually made from a petty cash fund?
30. What is the difference between a current asset and a noncurrent asset?
31. What are some common current assets?
32. What does *operating cycle* mean?
33. What are some common current liabilities?
34. What is a classified balance sheet?
35. What is the difference between the liquidity and the solvency of a business?
36. The higher the current ratio, the better the company's financial condition. Do you agree or disagree with this statement? Explain.
37. Does a high (80 to 95 percent) debt to assets ratio mean that a business is in financial difficulty? What types of businesses traditionally operate with high debt to assets ratios?

EXERCISES

L.O. 2 EXERCISE 6–1 *Features of a Strong Internal Control System*

Required
List and describe nine features of a strong internal control system described in this chapter.

L.O. 3 EXERCISE 6–2 *Internal Controls for a Computer System*

Required
Basic internal control features apply to computer systems, but additional controls are necessary. List and explain the six control requirements for computers discussed in this chapter.

L.O. 4 EXERCISE 6–3 *Features of Internal Control Procedures for Cash*

Required
List and discuss effective internal control procedures that apply to cash.

L.O. 1, 2 EXERCISE 6–4 *Internal Control Procedures*

Dick Haney is opening a new business that will sell sporting goods. It will initially be a small operation, and he is concerned about the security of his assets. He will not be able to be at the business all of the time and will have to rely on his employees and internal control procedures to ensure that transactions are properly accounted for and assets are safeguarded. He will have a store manager and two other employees who will be sales personnel and stock personnel and who will also perform any other duties necessary. Dick will be in the business on a regular basis. He has come to you for advice.

Required
Write a memo to Dick outlining the procedures that he should implement to ensure that his store assets are protected and that the financial transactions are properly recorded.

L.O. 2 EXERCISE 6–5 *Internal Controls to Prevent Theft*

Rhonda Cox worked as the parts manager for First Line Automobiles, a local automobile dealership. Rhonda was very dedicated and never missed a day of work. Since First Line was a small operation, she was the only employee in the parts department. Her duties consisted of ordering parts for stock and as needed for repairs, receiving the parts and checking them in, distributing them as needed to the shop or to customers for purchase, and keeping track of and taking the year-end inventory of parts. First Line decided to expand and needed to secure additional financing. The local bank agreed to a loan contingent on an audit of the dealership. One requirement of the audit was to oversee the inventory count of both automobiles and parts on hand. Rhonda was clearly nervous, explaining that she had just inventoried all parts in the parts department and supplied the auditors with a detailed list. The inventory showed parts on hand worth $225,000. This seemed a little excessive, and the accountants decided they needed to verify at least a substantial part of the inventory. When the auditors began their counts, a pattern began to develop. Each type of part seemed to be one or two items short when the actual count was taken. This raised more concern. Although Rhonda assured the auditors the parts were just misplaced, the auditors continued the count. After completing the count of parts on hand, the auditors could document only $155,000 of actual parts. Suddenly, Rhonda quit her job and moved to another province.

Required
a. What do you suppose caused the discrepancy between the actual count and the count that Rhonda had supplied?
b. What procedures could be put into place to prevent this type of problem?

EXERCISE 6–6 *Treatment of an NSF Cheque* L.O. 5

The bank statement of Best Supplies Co. included a $125 NSF cheque that one of Best's customers had written to pay for supplies purchased.

Required

a. Show the effects of recognizing the NSF cheque on the financial statements by recording the appropriate amounts in a horizontal statements model like the following one.

Assets			=	Liab.	+	Equity	Rev.	−	Exp.	=	Net Inc.	Cash Flow Statement
Cash	+	Accts. Rec.										

b. Is the recognition of the NSF cheque on Best's books an asset source, use, or exchange transaction?

c. Suppose the customer redeems the cheque by giving Best $150 cash in exchange for the bad cheque. The additional $25 paid a service fee charged by Best. Show the effects on the financial statements in the horizontal statements model in Requirement *a*.

d. Is the receipt of cash referred to in Requirement *c* an asset source, use, or exchange transaction?

EXERCISE 6–7 *Adjustments to the Balance per Books* L.O. 5

Required

Identify which of the following items are added to or subtracted from the unadjusted book balance to arrive at the adjusted book balance. Distinguish the additions from the subtractions by placing a + beside the items that are added to the unadjusted book balance and a − beside those that are subtracted from it. Use NA if the item is neither added nor subtracted from the book balance. The first item is recorded as an example.

Reconciling Items	Book Balance Adjusted?	Added or Subtracted?
Charge for cheques	Yes	—
NSF cheque from customer		
ATM fee		
Outstanding cheques		
Interest revenue earned on the account		
Deposits in transit		
Service charge		
Automatic debit for utility bill		

EXERCISE 6–8 *Adjustments to the Balance per Bank* L.O. 5

Required

Identify which of the following items are added to or subtracted from the unadjusted bank balance to arrive at the adjusted bank balance. Distinguish the additions from the subtractions by placing a + beside the items that are added to the unadjusted bank balance and a − beside those that are subtracted from it. Use NA if the item is neither added nor subtracted from the bank balance. The first item is recorded as an example.

Reconciling Items	Bank Balance Adjusted?	Added or Subtracted?
NSF cheque from customer	No	NA
Interest revenue		
Bank service charge		
Outstanding cheques		
Deposits in transit		
Debit memo		
Credit memo		
ATM fee		
Petty cash voucher		

L.O. 5 EXERCISE 6–9 *Adjusting the Cash Account*

As of May 31, 2004, the bank statement showed an ending balance of $14,625. The unadjusted Cash account balance was $14,330. The following information is available:

1. Deposit in transit, $1,590.
2. Credit memo in bank statement for interest earned in May, $20.
3. Outstanding cheque, $1,873.
4. Debit memo for service charge, $8.

Required

a. Determine the adjusted cash balance by preparing a bank reconciliation as of May 31, 2004, using the preceding information.
b. Record in general journal format the adjusting entries necessary to correct the unadjusted book balance.

L.O. 5 EXERCISE 6–10 *Determining the Adjusted Cash Balance, Starting with the Unadjusted Bank Balance*

The following information is available for Hill Company for the month of August:

1. The unadjusted balance per the bank statement on August 31 was $75,925.
2. Deposits in transit on August 31 were $2,600.
3. A debit memo was included with the bank statement for a service charge of $20.
4. A $4,925 cheque written in August had not been paid by the bank.
5. The bank statement included a $1,000 credit memo for the collection of a note. The principal of the note was $950, and the interest collected was $50.

Required

Determine the adjusted cash balance as of August 31. (*Hint:* It is not necessary to use all of the preceding items to determine the adjusted balance.)

L.O. 5 EXERCISE 6–11 *Determining the Adjusted Cash Balance, Starting with the Unadjusted Book Balance*

Peery Company had an unadjusted cash balance of $5,600 as of April 30. The company's bank statement, also dated April 30, included a $75 NSF cheque written by one of Peery's customers. There were $625 in outstanding cheques and $250 in deposits in transit as of April 30. According to the bank statement, service charges were $50, and the bank collected a $500 note receivable for Peery. The bank statement also showed $15 of interest revenue earned by Peery.

Required

Determine the adjusted cash balance as of April 30. (*Hint*: It is not necessary to use all of the preceding items to determine the adjusted balance.)

L.O. 6 EXERCISE 6–12 *Effect of Establishing a Petty Cash Account*

Belcher Transfer Company established a $200 petty cash fund on January 1, 2007.

Required

a. Is the establishment of the petty cash fund an asset source, use, or exchange transaction?
b. Record the establishment of the petty cash fund in a horizontal statements model like the following one:

Assets			=	Liab.	+	Equity	Rev.	−	Exp.	=	Net Inc.	Cash Flow Statement
Cash	+	Petty Cash										

c. Record the establishment of the fund in general journal format.

EXERCISE 6–13 *Effect of Petty Cash Events on the Financial Statements* L.O. 6

Xterra, Inc., established a petty cash fund of $300 on January 2. On January 31, the fund contained cash of $52.50 and vouchers for the following cash payments:

Postage	$65.00
Office supplies	80.75
Printing expense	10.50
Entertainment expense	88.25

The distinct accounting events affecting the petty cash fund for the period were (1) establishment of the fund, and (2) recognition of expenses and replenishment of the fund.

Required

a. Record each of the events in a horizontal statements model like the following one. In the Cash Flow Statement column, indicate whether the item is an operating activity (OA), investing activity (IA), or a financing activity (FA). Use NA to indicate that an account was not affected by the event.

Assets			=	Liab.	+	Equity	Rev.	−	Exp.	=	Net Inc.	Cash Flow Statement
Cash	+	Petty Cash										

b. Record the events in general journal format.

EXERCISE 6–14 *Determining the Amount of Petty Cash Expense* L.O. 6

Consider the following events:

1. A petty cash fund of $150 was established on April 1, 2006.
2. Employees were reimbursed when they presented petty cash vouchers to the petty cash custodian.
3. On April 30, 2006, the petty cash fund contained vouchers totalling $125.20 plus $26.80 of currency.

Required

Answer the following questions:

a. How did the establishment of the petty cash fund affect (increase, decrease, or have no effect on) total assets?
b. What is the amount of total petty cash expenses to be recognized during April?
c. When are petty cash expenses recognized (at the time of establishment, reimbursement, or replenishment)?

EXERCISE 6–15 *Preparing a Classified Balance Sheet* L.O. 7

Required

Use the following information to prepare a classified balance sheet for Borg Co. at June 30, 2005.

Office Equipment, net	$26,500
Accounts Receivable	42,500
Accounts Payable	11,000
Cash	15,260
Common Shares	40,000
Long-Term Notes Payable	23,000
Merchandise Inventory	32,000
Retained Earnings	45,460
Prepaid Insurance	3,200

L.O. 8 EXERCISE 6–16 *Operating Cycle*

Portland Co. sells gifts and novelty items mostly on account. It takes an average of 90 days to sell its inventory and an average of 35 days to collect the accounts receivable.

Required

a. Draw a diagram of the operating cycle for Portland Co.
b. Compute the length of the operating cycle based on the information given.

PROBLEMS—SERIES A

L.O. 1, 2, 4 PROBLEM 6–1A *Using Internal Control to Restrict Illegal or Unethical Behaviour*

Required

For each of the following fraudulent acts, describe one or more internal control procedures that could have prevented (or helped prevent) the problems.

a. Paula Wissel, the administrative assistant in charge of payroll, created a fictional employee, wrote weekly cheques to the fictional employee, and then personally cashed the cheques for her own benefit.
b. Larry Kent, the receiving manager of Southern Lumber, created a fictitious supplier named F&M Building Supply. F&M regularly billed Southern Lumber for supplies purchased. Kent had printed shipping slips and billing invoices with the name of the fictitious company and opened a post office box as the mailing address. Kent simply prepared a receiving report and submitted it for payment to the accounts payable department. The accounts payable clerk then paid the invoice when it was received because Kent acknowledged receipt of the supplies.
c. Holly Baker works at a local hobby shop and usually operates the cash register. She has developed a way to give discounts to her friends. When they come by, she rings a lower price or does not charge the friend for some of the material purchased. At first, Baker thought she would get caught, but no one seemed to notice. Indeed, she has become so sure that there is no way for the owner to find out that she has started taking home some supplies for her own personal use.

L.O. 5 PROBLEM 6–2A *Preparing a Bank Reconciliation*

Kevin Long owns a construction business, Long Builders Inc. The following cash information is available for the month of October 2007.

As of October 31, the bank statement shows a balance of $8,000. The October 31 unadjusted balance in the Cash account of Long Builders Inc. is $8,580. A review of the bank statement revealed the following information:

1. A deposit of $2,000 on October 31, 2007, does not appear on the October 31 bank statement.
2. A debit memo for $50 was included in the bank statement for the purchase of a new supply of cheques.
3. When cheques written during the month were compared with those paid by the bank, three cheques amounting to $1,200 were found to be outstanding.
4. It was discovered that a cheque to pay for equipment was correctly written and paid by the bank for $3,030 but was recorded on the books as $3,300.

Required

a. Prepare a bank reconciliation at the end of October showing the adjusted cash balance.
b. Prepare any necessary journal entries to adjust the books to the adjusted cash balance.

L.O. 5 PROBLEM 6–3A *Missing Information in a Bank Reconciliation*

The following data apply to Barkley Flying Service for April 2007:

1. Balance per the bank on April 30, $10,000.
2. Deposits in transit not recorded by the bank, $1,000.
3. Bank error; cheque written by Barkley Office Supply was drawn on Barkley Flying Service's account, $800.
4. The following cheques written and recorded by Barkley Flying Service were not included in the bank statement: Cheque #2012 for $220; Cheque #2052 for $380; and Cheque #2055 for $1,700.
5. Note collected by the bank, $450.
6. Service charge for collection of note, $15.

7. The bookkeeper recorded a cheque written for $548 to pay for April's repair expense as $845 in the cash disbursements journal.
8. Bank service charge in addition to the note collection fee, $40.
9. NSF cheques returned by the bank, $250.

Required
Determine the amount of the unadjusted cash balance per Barkley Flying Service's books.

PROBLEM 6–4A *Adjustments to the Cash Account Based on the Bank Reconciliation*

L.O. 5

Required
Determine whether the following items in Home Imports' bank reconciliation require adjusting or correcting entries on Home Imports' books. When an entry is required, record it in general journal format. When an entry is not required write "no entry."

a. Home Imports wrote an $880 certified cheque that was still outstanding as of the closing date of the bank statement.
b. The bank collected $8,000 of Home Imports' accounts receivable. Home Imports had instructed its customers to send their payments directly to the bank.
c. The bank mistakenly gave Imports, Inc., credit for a $500 deposit made by Home Imports.
d. Deposits in transit were $4,550.
e. Home Imports' bank statement contained a $375 NSF cheque. Home Imports had received the cheque from a customer and had included it in one of its bank deposits.
f. The bank statement indicated that Home Imports earned $75 of interest revenue.
g. Home Imports' accountant mistakenly recorded a $156 cheque that was written to purchase supplies as $651.
h. Bank service charges for the month were $40.
i. The bank reconciliation disclosed the fact that $1,000 had been stolen from Home Imports' business.
j. Outstanding cheques amounted to $1,500.

PROBLEM 6-5A *Bank Reconciliation and Adjustments to the Cash Account*

L.O. 5

The following information is available for Oceanside Hotel for October 2005:

Bank Statement

CANADA BANK

Oceanside Hotel 10 Main Street Victoria, B.C.	Account number 12-4567 October 31, 2005

Beginning balance 9/30/2005	$ 8,831
Total deposits and other credits	29,075
Total cheques and other debits	23,906
Ending balance 10/31/2005	14,000

Cheques and Debits		Deposits and Credits	
Cheque No.	Amount	Date	Amount
2350	$3,761	October 1	$1,102
2351	1,643	October 10	6,498
2352	8,000	October 15	4,929
2354	2,894	October 21	6,174
2355	1,401	October 26	5,963
2357	6,187	October 30	2,084
DM	20	CM	2,325

The following is a list of cheques and deposits recorded on the books of the Oceanside Hotel for October 2005:

Date	Cheque No.	Amount of Cheque	Date	Amount of Deposit
October 2	2351	$1,643	October 8	$6,498
October 4	2352	8,000	October 14	4,929
October 10	2353	1,500	October 21	6,174
October 10	2354	2,894	October 26	5,963
October 15	2355	1,401	October 29	2,084
October 20	2356	745	October 30	3,550
October 22	2357	6,187		

Other Information

1. Cheque no. 2350 was outstanding from September.
2. Credit memo was for collection of notes receivable.
3. All cheques were paid at the correct amount.
4. Debit memo was for printed cheques.
5. The September 30 bank reconciliation showed a deposit in transit of $1,102.
6. The unadjusted Cash account balance at October 31 was $13,000.

Required

a. Prepare the bank reconciliation for Oceanside Hotel at the end of October.
b. Record in general journal form any necessary entries to the Cash account.

L.O. 5 PROBLEM 6–6A *Effect of Adjustments to Cash on the Accounting Equation*

After reconciling its bank account, Putt Equipment Company made the following adjusting entries:

Entry No.	Account Title	Debit	Credit
1	Rent Expense	35	
	Cash		35
	To correct understatement of expense		
2	Service Charge Expense	15	
	Cash		15
	To record bank service charge		
3	Cash	175	
	Accounts Receivable		175
	To record bank collection		
4	Cash	40	
	Interest Revenue		40
	To record interest revenue		
5	Accounts Receivable, K. Wilson	250	
	Cash		250
	To record NSF cheque from Wilson		

Required

Identify the event depicted in each journal entry as asset source (AS), asset use (AU), asset exchange (AE), or claims exchange (CE). Also explain how each entry affects the accounting equation by placing a + for increase, − for decrease, or NA for not affected under the following components of the accounting equation. The first event is recorded as an example.

Event No.	Type of Event	Assets	=	Liabilities	+	Equity: Common Shares	+	Equity: Retained Earnings
1	AU	−		NA		NA		−

PROBLEM 6–7A *Bank Reconciliation and Internal Control*

L.O. 2, 3, 4

Following is a bank reconciliation for Pete's Sandwich Shop for May 31, 2006:

	Cash Account	Bank Statement
Balance as of 5/31/06	$25,000	$22,000
Deposit in transit		4,250
Outstanding cheques		(465)
Note collected by bank	1,815	
Bank service charge	(30)	
Automatic payment on loan	(1,000)	
Adjusted cash balance as of 5/31/06	$25,785	$25,785

Because of limited funds, Pete's employed only one accountant who was responsible for receiving cash, recording receipts and disbursements, preparing deposits, and preparing the bank reconciliation. The accountant left the company on June 8, 2006, after preparing the preceding statement. His replacement compared the cheques returned with the bank statement to the cash disbursements journal and found the total of outstanding cheques to be $5,000.

Required

a. Prepare a corrected bank reconciliation statement.
b. What is the total amount of cash missing, and how was the difference between the "true cash" per the bank and the "true cash" per the books hidden on the reconciliation prepared by the former employee?
c. What could Pete's do to avoid cash theft in the future?

PROBLEM 6–8A *Petty Cash Fund*

L.O. 6

The following data pertain to the petty cash fund of Crain Company:

1. The petty cash fund was created on an imprest basis at $100 on March 1.
2. On March 31, a physical count of the fund disclosed $8 in currency and coins, vouchers authorizing meal allowances totalling $42, vouchers authorizing purchase of postage stamps of $32, and vouchers for payment of delivery charges of $20.

Required

a. Prepare all general journal entries necessary to (1) establish the fund and (2) recognize expenses and replenish the fund as of March 31. (*Hint:* Journal entries may not be required for all three events.)
b. Explain how the Cash Short and Over account required in this case affects the income statement.
c. Identify the event depicted in each journal entry recorded in Requirement *a* as asset source (AS), asset use (AU), asset exchange (AE), or claims exchange (CE).
d. Record the effects on the financial statements of the events in Requirement *a* using a horizontal statements model like the following one. In the Cash Flow Statement column, indicate whether the item is an operating activity (OA), investing activity (IA), or financing activity (FA). Use NA to indicate that an account was not affected by the event.

Assets			=	Liab.	+	Equity	Rev.	−	Exp.	=	Net Inc.	Cash Flow Statement
Cash	+	Petty Cash										

L.O. 7 **PROBLEM 6–9A** *Classified Balance Sheet and Multistep Income Statement*

Required

Use the following information to prepare a classified balance sheet and a multistep income statement for Trudeau Enterprises for the year end of December 31, 2005.

Accounts Receivable	$ 4,000
Common Shares	41,000
Salaries Expense	118,000
Interest Expense	12,200
Cash	3,600
Accounts Payable	1,000
Retained Earnings	42,000
Accumulated Amortization	4,800
Unearned Revenue	9,600
Land	50,000
Salaries Payable	1,800
Cost of Goods Sold	174,000
Supplies	500
Note Receivable (short term)	6,000
Inventory	9,000
Office Equipment	58,000
Gain on Sale of Equipment	6,400
Interest Receivable (short term)	240
Operating Expenses	19,000
Sales Revenue	340,000
Prepaid Rent	9,600
Interest Payable (short term)	740
Interest Revenue	420
Notes Payable (long term)	40,000

PROBLEMS—SERIES B

L.O. 1, 3, 4 **PROBLEM 6–1B** *Using Internal Control to Restrict Illegal or Unethical Behaviour*

Required

For each of the following fraudulent acts, describe one or more internal control procedures that could have prevented (or helped prevent) the problems.

a. Everyone in the office has noticed what a dedicated employee Jennifer Reidel is. She never misses work, not even for a vacation. Reidel is in charge of the petty cash fund. She transfers funds from the company's bank account to the petty cash account on an as-needed basis. During a surprise audit, the petty cash fund was found to contain fictitious receipts. Over a three-year period, Reidel had used more than $4,000 of petty cash to pay for personal expenses.

b. Bill Bruton was hired as the vice president of the manufacturing division of a corporation. His impressive résumé listed a master's degree in business administration from a large university and numerous awards and activities, when in fact Bruton had only a high school diploma. In a short time, the company was in poor financial condition because of his inadequate knowledge and bad decisions.

c. Havolene Manufacturing has good internal control over its manufacturing materials inventory. However, office supplies are kept on open shelves in the employee break room. The office supervisor has noticed that he is having to order paper, tape, staplers, and pens on an increasingly frequent basis.

L.O. 5 **PROBLEM 6–2B** *Preparing a Bank Reconciliation*

Bob Carson owns a card shop, We Trade. The following cash information is available for the month of August 2006. As of August 31, the bank statement shows a balance of $17,000. The August 31 unadjusted balance in the Cash account of We Trade is $16,000. A review of the bank statement revealed the following information:

1. A deposit of $2,260 on August 31, 2006, does not appear on the August bank statement.
2. It was discovered that a cheque to pay for baseball cards was correctly written and paid by the bank for $4,040 but was recorded on the books as $4,400.
3. When cheques written during the month were compared with those paid by the bank, three cheques amounting to $3,000 were found to be outstanding.
4. A debit memo for $100 was included in the bank statement for the purchase of a new supply of cheques.

Required

a. Prepare a bank reconciliation at the end of August showing the adjusted cash balance.
b. Prepare any necessary journal entries to adjust the books to the adjusted cash balance.

PROBLEM 6–3B *Missing Information in a Bank Reconciliation* **L.O. 5**

The following data apply to Best Auto Supply, Inc., for May 2007:

1. Balance per the bank on May 31, $8,000.
2. Deposits in transit not recorded by the bank, $975.
3. Bank error; cheque written by Allen Auto Supply was drawn on Best Auto Supply's account, $650.
4. The following cheques written and recorded by Best Auto Supply were not included in the bank statement: Cheque #3013 for $385; Cheque #3054 for $735; and Cheque #3056 for $1,900.
5. Note collected by the bank, $500.
6. Service charge for collection of note, $10.
7. The bookkeeper recorded a cheque written for $188 to pay for the May utilities expense as $888 in the cash disbursements journal.
8. Bank service charge in addition to the note collection fee, $25.
9. Customer cheques returned by the bank as NSF, $125.

Required

Determine the amount of the unadjusted cash balance per Best Auto Supply's books.

PROBLEM 6–4B *Adjustments to the Cash Account Based on the Bank Reconciliation* **L.O. 5**

Required

Determine whether the following items included in Curtis Company's bank reconciliation will require adjusting or correcting entries on Curtis's books. When an entry is required, record it in general journal format. If no entry is required, write "no entry."

a. An $877 deposit was recorded by the bank as $778.
b. Four cheques totalling $450 written during the month of January were not included with the January bank statement.
c. A $54 cheque written to Office Max for office supplies was recorded in the general journal as $45.
d. The bank statement indicated that the bank had collected a $330 note for Curtis.
e. Curtis recorded $500 of receipts on January 31, 2006, which was deposited in the night depository of the bank. These deposits were not included in the bank statement.
f. Service charges of $22 for the month of January were listed on the bank statement.
g. The bank charged a $297 cheque drawn on Cave Restaurant to Curtis's account. The cheque was included in Curtis's bank statement.
h. A cheque of $31 was returned to the bank because of insufficient funds and was noted on the bank statement. Curtis received the cheque from a customer and thought that it was good when it was deposited into the account.

PROBLEM 6–5B *Bank Reconciliation and Adjustments to the Cash Account* **L.O. 5**

The following information is available for Bob's Garage for March 2006:

Bob's Garage			Account number
629 Main Street			62-00062
Victoria, B.C.			March 31, 2006

Beginning balance 3/1/2006	$15,000.00
Total deposits and other credits	7,000.00
Total cheque and other debits	6,000.00
Ending balance 3/31/2006	16,000.00

Cheque and Debits		Deposits and Credits	
Cheque No.	Amount	Date	Amount
1462	$ 1,163.00	March 1	$ 1,000.00
1463	62.00	March 2	1,340.00
1464	1,235.00	March 6	210.00
1465	750.00	March 12	1,940.00
1466	1,111.00	March 17	855.00
1467	964.00	March 22	1,480.00
DM	15.00	CM	175.00
1468	700.00		

The following is a list of cheques and deposits recorded on the books of Bob's Garage for March 2006:

Date	Cheque No.	Amount of Cheque	Date	Amount of Deposit
March 1	1463	$ 62.00	March 1	$1,340.00
March 5	1464	1,235.00	March 5	210.00
March 6	1465	750.00		
March 9	1466	1,111.00	March 10	1,940.00
March 10	1467	964.00		
March 14	1468	70.00	March 16	855.00
March 19	1469	1,500.00	March 19	1,480.00
March 28	1470	102.00	March 29	2,000.00

Other Information

1. Cheque no. 1462 was outstanding from February.
2. A credit memo for collection of accounts receivable was included in the bank statement.
3. All cheques were paid at the correct amount.
4. The bank statement included a debit memo for service charges.
5. The February 28 bank reconciliation showed a deposit in transit of $1,000.
6. Cheque no. 1468 was for the purchase of equipment.
7. The unadjusted Cash account balance at March 31 was $16,868.

Required

a. Prepare the bank reconciliation for Bob's Garage at the end of March.
b. Record in general journal form any necessary entries to the Cash account.

L.O. 5 PROBLEM 6–6B *Effect of Adjustments to Cash on the Accounting Equation*

After reconciling its bank account, Monroe Company made the following adjusting entries:

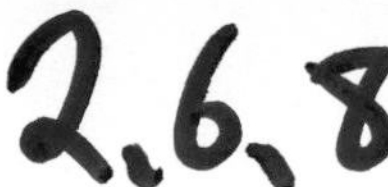

Entry No.	Account Title	Debit	Credit
1	Cash	845	
	Accounts Receivable		845
	To record bank collection		
2	Cash	44	
	Interest Revenue		44
	To record interest revenue		
3	Service Charge Expense	35	
	Cash		35
	To record bank service charge		
4	Accounts Receivable, D. Beat	174	
	Cash		174
	To record NSF cheque from Beat		
5	Cash	20	
	Supplies Expense		20
	To correct overstatement of expense		

Required

Identify the event depicted in each journal entry as asset source (AS), asset use (AU), asset exchange (AE), or claims exchange (CE). Also explain how each entry affects the accounting equation by placing a + for increase, − for decrease, or NA for not affected under the following components of the accounting equation. The first event is recorded as an example.

						Equity		
Event No.	Type of Event	Assets	=	Liabilities	+	Common Shares	+	Retained Earnings
1	AE	+ −		NA		NA		NA

PROBLEM 6–7B *Bank Reconciliation and Internal Control*

L.O. 2, 4, 5

Following is a bank reconciliation for Park Company for June 30, 2005:

	Cash Account	Bank Statement
Balance as of 6/30/05	$1,618	$3,000
Deposit in transit		600
Outstanding cheques		(1,507)
Note collected by bank	2,000	
Bank service charge	(25)	
NSF cheque	(1,500)	
Adjusted cash balance as of 6/30/05	$2,093	$2,093

When reviewing the bank reconciliation, Park's auditor was unable to locate any reference to the NSF cheque on the bank statement. Furthermore, the clerk who reconciles the bank account and records the adjusting entries could not find the actual NSF cheque that should have been included in the bank statement. Finally, there was no specific reference in the accounts receivable subsidiary account identifying a party who had written a bad cheque.

Required

a. Prepare the adjusting entry that the clerk would have made to record the NSF cheque.
b. Assume that the clerk who prepares the bank reconciliation and records the adjusting entries also makes bank deposits. Explain how the clerk could use a fictitious NSF cheque to hide the theft of cash.
c. How could Park Company avoid the theft of cash that is concealed by the use of fictitious NSF cheques?

L.O. 6 PROBLEM 6–8B *Petty Cash Fund*

Hayes Co. established a petty cash fund by issuing a cheque for $250 and appointing Bob Potts as petty cash custodian. Potts had vouchers for the following petty cash payments during the month:

Stamps	$ 14.00
Miscellaneous items	25.00
Taxi fare	80.00
Window-washing service	22.00
Cleaners	75.00

There was $32 of currency in the petty cash box at the time it was replenished.

Required

a. Prepare all general journal entries necessary to (1) establish the fund, (2) recognize expenses, and (3) replenish the fund. (*Hint:* Journal entries may not be required for all the events.)

b. Explain how the Cash Short and Over account required in this case will affect the income statement.

c. Identify the event depicted in each journal entry recorded in Requirement *a* as asset source (AS), asset use (AU), asset exchange (AE), or claims exchange (CE).

d. Record the effects of the events in Requirement *a* on the financial statements using a horizontal statements model like the following one. In the Cash Flow Statement column, indicate whether the item is an operating activity (OA), investing activity (IA), or financing activity (FA). Use NA to indicate that an account was not affected by the event.

Assets			=	Liab.	+	Equity	Rev.	−	Exp.	=	Net Inc.	Cash Flow Statement
Cash	+	Petty Cash										

L.O. 7 PROBLEM 6–9B *Classified Balance Sheet and Multistep Income Statement*

Required

Use the following information to prepare a classified balance sheet as of December 31, 2004, and a multistep income statement for the year ending December 31, 2004.

Accounts Receivable	$ 6,000
Common Shares	68,000
Salaries Expense	154,000
Interest Expense	5,000
Cash	20,000
Accounts Payable	1,800
Retained Earnings 12/31	76,000
Accumulated Amortization	10,000
Unearned Revenue	16,000
Land	90,000
Salaries Payable	3,400
Cost of Goods Sold	175,000
Supplies	900
Note Receivable (long term)	10,000
Inventory	16,000
Office Equipment	52,000
Gain on Sale of Equipment	10,000
Interest Receivable (short term)	400
Operating Expenses	34,000
Sales Revenue	400,000
Prepaid Rent	8,000
Interest Payable (short term)	1,200
Notes Payable (long term)	26,900
Interest Revenue	800

ANALYZE, THINK, COMMUNICATE

BUSINESS APPLICATIONS CASE *Bombardier's Annual Report*

ATC 6–1

Required

Using Bombardier's financial statements in Appendix B, answer the following questions:

a. What is Bombardier's current ratio as of January 31, 2002?
b. Which of Bombardier's current assets had the largest balance at January 31, 2002?
c. What percentage of Bombardier's total assets consisted of current assets?
d. Does Bombardier have any restrictions placed on it by its creditors?

GROUP ASSIGNMENT *Analyzing Financial Statements*

ATC 6–2

The following selected information was taken from the annual reports of three companies. Amounts are given in thousands of dollars.

	Company 1	Company 2	Company 3
Accounts Receivable	$ 76,530	$ 4,128	$ 66,755
Accounts Payable	160,891	105,541	107,157
Other Current Liabilities	707,622	4,845	105,457
Accumulated Amortization	1,375,631	138,179	537,910
Cash	623,343	32,280	234,262
Property, Plant, and Equipment	4,811,324	355,015	1,803,410
Inventories	0	220,013	35,633
Retained Earnings	1,632,115	118,721	839,215
Common Shares	376,903	204,327	345,019
Other Current Assets	108,543	29,057	44,904
Other Long-Term Assets	4,051	67,954	294,626
Long-Term Liabilities	1,370,629	136,834	544,832

Required

a. Organize the class into three sections and divide each section into three groups of three to five students. Assign Company 1 to groups in section 1, Company 2 to groups in section 2, and Company 3 to groups in section 3.

Group Tasks

1. Prepare a classified balance sheet for the company assigned to your group.
2. Select a representative from a group in each section and put the balance sheet on the board.

REAL-WORLD CASE *Whose Numbers Are They Anyway?*

ATC 6–3

The following excerpt, sometimes referred to as *management's responsibility for financial statements*, was taken from Danier Leather Inc.'s report for the fiscal year ended June 30, 2001.

Company Statement on Financial Information (partial)

The accompanying financial statements and other financial information contained in this annual report are the responsibility of management. The financial statements have been prepared in conformity with Canadian generally accepted accounting principles using management's best estimates and judgments based on currently available information, where appropriate. The financial information contained elsewhere in this annual report has been reviewed to ensure consistency with that in the financial statements. Management is also responsible for a system of internal controls which is *designed to provide reasonable assurance* that (1) assets are safeguarded, (2) liabilities are recognized, and (3) financial records are properly maintained *to provide timely and accurate* financial reports.

The Board of Directors is responsible for ensuring that management fulfills its responsibility in respect of financial reporting and internal control. The (4) Audit Committee of the Board, which is comprised solely of unrelated and outside directors, meets regularly to review significant accounting and auditing matters with management and the independent auditors and to review the interim and annual financial statements.

Required

Assume that a colleague, who has never taken an accounting course, asks you to explain Danier Leather's "company statement on financial information." Write a memorandum to your colleague that explains each of the numbered portions of the above material. When appropriate, include examples to explain these concepts of internal control to your colleague.

ATC 6–4 BUSINESS APPLICATIONS CASE *Using the Current Ratio*

	Code-Breakers	Cipher-Tec
Current assets	$40,000	$70,000
Current liabilities	25,000	55,000

Required

a. Compute the current ratio for each company.
b. Which company has the greater likelihood of being able to pay its bills?
c. Assuming that both companies have the same amount of total assets, speculate as to which company would produce the higher return on assets ratio.

ATC 6–5 BUSINESS APPLICATIONS CASE *Using Current Ratios to Make Comparisons*

The following accounting information pertains to Stillman and Tsay companies at the end of 2006:

Account Title	Stillman	Tsay
Cash	$ 15,000	$ 25,000
Wages Payable	20,000	25,000
Merchandise Inventory	30,000	55,000
Building	80,000	80,000
Accounts Receivable	35,000	30,000
Long-Term Notes Payable	90,000	120,000
Land	45,000	50,000
Accounts Payable	40,000	45,000
Sales Revenue	220,000	270,000
Expenses	190,000	245,000

Required

a. Identify the current assets and current liabilities, and compute the current ratio for each company.
b. Assuming that all assets and liabilities are listed here, compute the debt to assets ratio for each company.
c. Determine which company has the greater financial risk in both the short term and the long term.

WRITING ASSIGNMENT *Internal Control Procedures* **ATC 6–6**

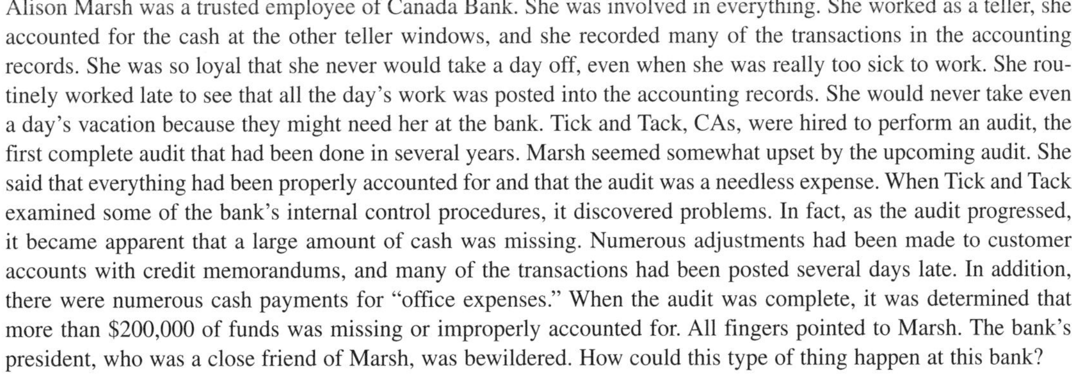

Alison Marsh was a trusted employee of Canada Bank. She was involved in everything. She worked as a teller, she accounted for the cash at the other teller windows, and she recorded many of the transactions in the accounting records. She was so loyal that she never would take a day off, even when she was really too sick to work. She routinely worked late to see that all the day's work was posted into the accounting records. She would never take even a day's vacation because they might need her at the bank. Tick and Tack, CAs, were hired to perform an audit, the first complete audit that had been done in several years. Marsh seemed somewhat upset by the upcoming audit. She said that everything had been properly accounted for and that the audit was a needless expense. When Tick and Tack examined some of the bank's internal control procedures, it discovered problems. In fact, as the audit progressed, it became apparent that a large amount of cash was missing. Numerous adjustments had been made to customer accounts with credit memorandums, and many of the transactions had been posted several days late. In addition, there were numerous cash payments for "office expenses." When the audit was complete, it was determined that more than $200,000 of funds was missing or improperly accounted for. All fingers pointed to Marsh. The bank's president, who was a close friend of Marsh, was bewildered. How could this type of thing happen at this bank?

Required

Prepare a written memo to the bank president, outlining the procedures that should be followed to prevent this type of problem in the future.

ETHICAL DILEMMA *See No Evil, Hear No Evil, Report No Evil* **ATC 6–7**

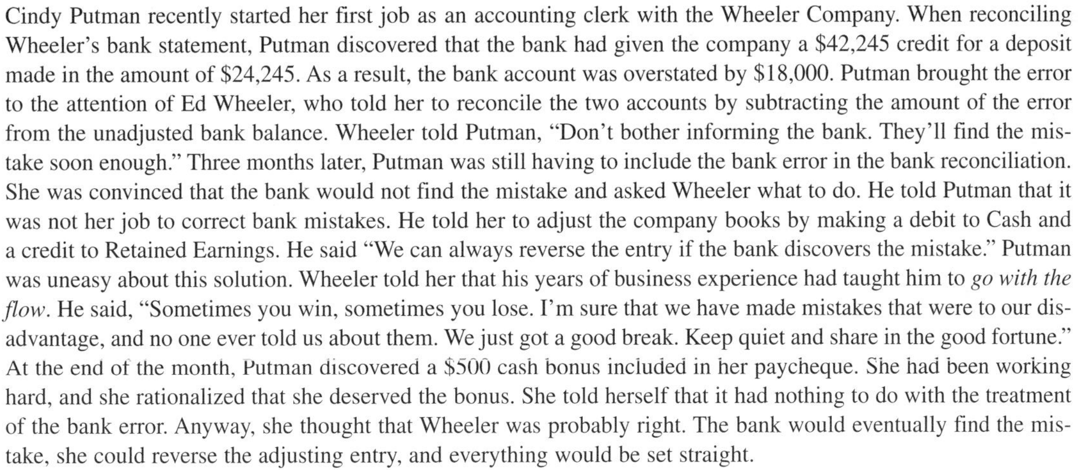

Cindy Putman recently started her first job as an accounting clerk with the Wheeler Company. When reconciling Wheeler's bank statement, Putman discovered that the bank had given the company a $42,245 credit for a deposit made in the amount of $24,245. As a result, the bank account was overstated by $18,000. Putman brought the error to the attention of Ed Wheeler, who told her to reconcile the two accounts by subtracting the amount of the error from the unadjusted bank balance. Wheeler told Putman, "Don't bother informing the bank. They'll find the mistake soon enough." Three months later, Putman was still having to include the bank error in the bank reconciliation. She was convinced that the bank would not find the mistake and asked Wheeler what to do. He told Putman that it was not her job to correct bank mistakes. He told her to adjust the company books by making a debit to Cash and a credit to Retained Earnings. He said "We can always reverse the entry if the bank discovers the mistake." Putman was uneasy about this solution. Wheeler told her that his years of business experience had taught him to *go with the flow*. He said, "Sometimes you win, sometimes you lose. I'm sure that we have made mistakes that were to our disadvantage, and no one ever told us about them. We just got a good break. Keep quiet and share in the good fortune." At the end of the month, Putman discovered a $500 cash bonus included in her paycheque. She had been working hard, and she rationalized that she deserved the bonus. She told herself that it had nothing to do with the treatment of the bank error. Anyway, she thought that Wheeler was probably right. The bank would eventually find the mistake, she could reverse the adjusting entry, and everything would be set straight.

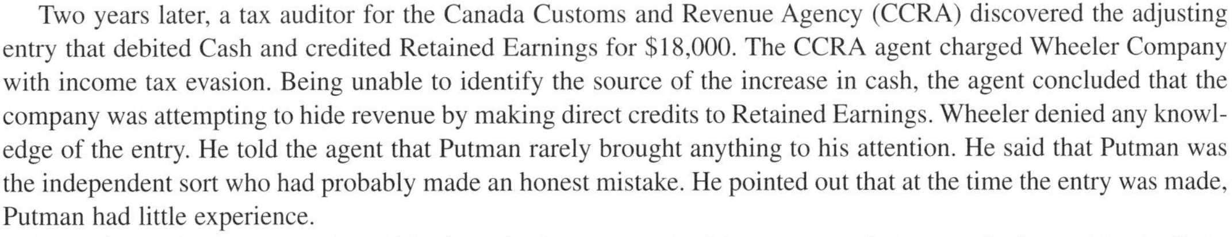

Two years later, a tax auditor for the Canada Customs and Revenue Agency (CCRA) discovered the adjusting entry that debited Cash and credited Retained Earnings for $18,000. The CCRA agent charged Wheeler Company with income tax evasion. Being unable to identify the source of the increase in cash, the agent concluded that the company was attempting to hide revenue by making direct credits to Retained Earnings. Wheeler denied any knowledge of the entry. He told the agent that Putman rarely brought anything to his attention. He said that Putman was the independent sort who had probably made an honest mistake. He pointed out that at the time the entry was made, Putman had little experience.

Later in a private conversation, Wheeler told Putman to plead ignorance and that they both would get off the hook. He said that if she did not keep quiet, they would go down together. He reminded her of the $500 bonus. Wheeler told Putman that accepting payment to defraud the CCRA constituted a crime that would land her in jail. Putman was shocked that Wheeler would not tell the truth. She had expected some loyalty from him, and it was clear that she was not going to get it.

Required

Answer the following questions:

a. Explain how the direct credit to retained earnings understated net income.
b. What course of action would you advise Putman to take?
c. Why was Putman foolish to expect loyalty from Wheeler?

d. Suppose Putman had credited Miscellaneous Revenue instead of Retained Earnings and the company had paid income taxes on the $18,000. Under these circumstances, the bank error would never have been discovered. Is it OK to hide the error from the bank if it is reported on the tax return?

ATC 6–8 SEDAR DATABASE *Analyzing Magna's Liquidity*

Required

Using the most current annual report available on SEDAR, answer the following questions about Magna International, Inc., for the most recent year reported. Instructions for using SEDAR are in Appendix A.

a. What is Magna's current ratio?
b. Which of Magna's current assets had the largest balance?
c. What percentage of Magna's total assets consisted of current assets?
d. Did Magna have any "currently maturing" long-term debt included in current liabilities on its balance sheet?

ATC 6–9 SPREADSHEET ASSIGNMENT *Using Excel*

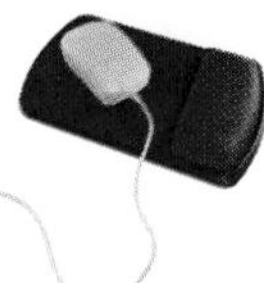

At the end of 2005, the following accounting information is available for Bainbridge and Crist Companies.

Microsoft Excel - ch6-3.xls

B8 = =SUM(B5:B7)

	A	B	C	D	E	F	G
1	**Classified Balance Sheet**	**Bainbridge**	**Crist**		**Multistep Income Statement**	**Bainbridge**	**Crist**
2	**Assets**						
3					Sales	500,000	575,000
4	**Current Assets**				Cost of Goods Sold	170,000	200,000
5	Cash	18,000	22,500		Gross Profit	330,000	375,000
6	Accounts Receivable	19,000	19,500		Operating Expenses	285,000	345,000
7	Inventory	14,000	18,000		Net Income	45,000	30,000
8	Total Current Assets	51,000	60,000				
9							
10	**Capital Assets**				**RATIOS**		
11	Land	52,500	50,000		Current Ratio	1.46	0.85
12	Building	135,000	120,000		Debt to Total Assets	46.12%	82.83%
13	Total Capital Assets	187,500	170,000		Equity to Total Assets	53.88%	17.17%
14					Gross Profit Percentage	66.00%	65.22%
15	Total Assets	238,500	230,000		Return on Sales	9.00%	5.22%
16					Return on Assets	18.87%	13.04%
17	**Liabilities**				Return on Equity	35.02%	75.95%
18	**Current Liabilities**						
19	Accounts Payable	20,000	52,500				
20	Wages Payable	15,000	18,000				
21	Total Current Liabilities	35,000	70,500				
22							
23	**Long-Term Liabilities**						
24	Notes Payable	75,000	120,000				
25							
26	Total Liabilities	110,000	190,500				
27							
28	**Shareholders' Equity**						
29	Common Shares	30,000	9,500				
30	Retained Earnings	98,500	30,000				
31							
32	Total Shareholders' Equity	128,500	39,500				
33							
34	Total Liabilities and Shareholders' Equity	238,500	230,000				
35							

problem | Problem(2) | Problem 6-3 solution | Problem 6-3 Solu

Required

a. Set up the preceding spreadsheet. Complete the balance sheet and income statement. Use Excel formulas for rows that "total" on the balance sheet and for gross margin and net income on the income statement.
b. Calculate the designated ratios using Excel formulas.
c. Which company is more likely to be able to pay its current liabilities?
d. Which company carries a greater financial risk?
e. Which company is more profitable from the shareholders' perspective?
f. Based on profitability alone, which company performed better?

g. Assume that sales increased 10 percent and that the additional sales were made on account. Adjust the balance sheet and income statement for the effects. Notice that Retained Earnings will also need to be adjusted to keep the balance sheet in balance. What is the resultant effect on the ratios?
h. Return the financial statements to the original data. Assume that operating expenses increased 10 percent and that the additional expenses were acquired on credit. Adjust the financial statements for the effects. Notice that Retained Earnings must be adjusted to keep in balance. What is the resultant effect on the ratios?

SPREADSHEET ANALYSIS *Mastering Excel*

ATC 6–10

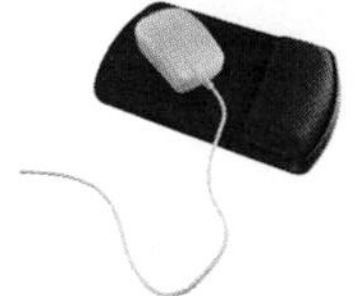

Refer to Problem 6–9B.

Required

Complete the classified balance sheet and multistep income statement on an Excel spreadsheet.

Chapter 7

Accounting for Accruals—Advanced Topics *Receivables and Payables*

Learning Objectives

After completing this chapter, you should be able to:

1. State why credit terms are offered to customers.
2. Explain how the allowance method of accounting for bad debts affects financial statements.
3. Show how the direct write-off method of accounting for bad debts affects financial statements.
4. Explain how accounting for credit card sales affects financial statements.
5. Explain how accounting for warranty obligations affects financial statements.
6. Show how discount notes and related interest charges affect financial statements.
7. Show how payroll accounting affects financial statements.
8. Explain the cost of financing credit sales.
9. Show the effects of sales taxes on financial statements.

the *curious* accountant

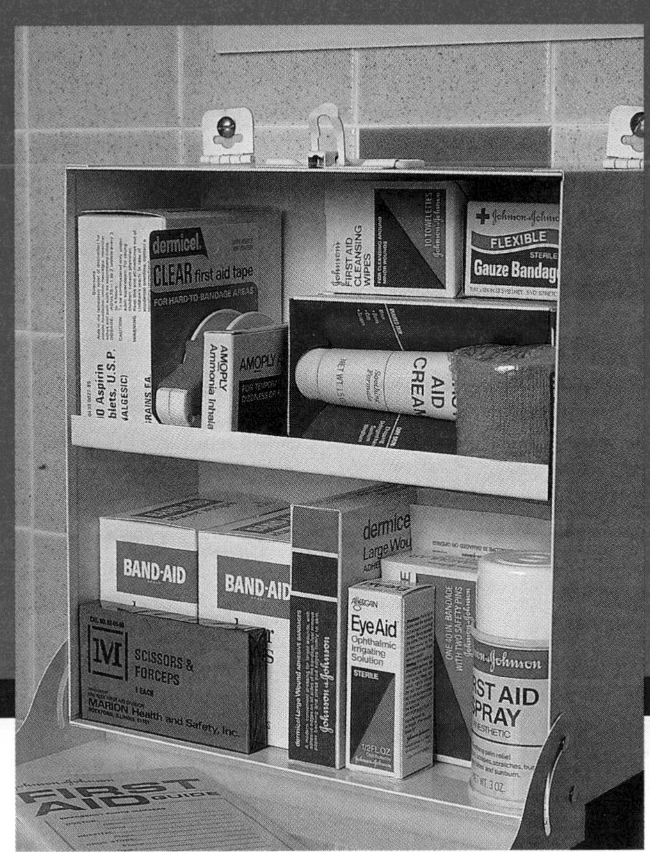

Suppose that Shoppers Drug Mart orders goods from Johnson & Johnson, Inc. Assume that Shoppers offers to pay for the goods on the day it receives them from Johnson & Johnson (a cash purchase) or 60 days later (a purchase on account). Assume that Johnson & Johnson is certain Shoppers will pay its account when due. Why should Johnson & Johnson care whether it makes the sale to Shoppers for cash or on account? See page 279 for an answer.

Many people are impulse buyers. A particular mix of environment and emotion sparks an immediate urge to purchase. If people are forced to wait, because of a lack of funds, that mix shifts and the desire to buy may be reduced. Recognizing this phenomenon, merchants offer credit terms that permit customers to "buy now and pay later." By offering credit, businesses can increase their sales. The disadvantage of this strategy arises when some customers can't or won't pay their bills. However, the widespread availability of credit shows that the advantages of increased sales generally outweigh the disadvantages associated with bad debts.

When a company permits a customer to buy now and pay later, the expected future receipt is called an ***account receivable****. Accounts receivable are usually quite small, and the terms to maturity are short. Collection on most accounts receivable occurs in 30 to 60 days. When a longer credit term is required or when the amount of the receivable is large, a note evidencing a credit agreement between the parties is usually exchanged. The note specifies the maturity date, rate of interest, and other credit terms. Receivables evidenced by such notes are called* ***notes receivable****. Accounts and notes receivable are shown as assets on the balance sheet. For every receivable listed on one company's books, there is a corresponding obligation listed on another company's books. In other words,* *if one company expects to collect, another company expects to pay. Current obligations to make future economic sacrifices such as cash payments are often called* **payables**. *Accounts and notes payable*[1] *are shown as liabilities on the balance sheet.*

LO1
State why credit terms are offered to customers.

Receivables and payables represent future expected cash receipts or payments. However, most companies do not expect to receive the full face value of their receivables because they know that some of their customers will be unable or unwilling to pay the amounts due. Companies recognize this fact by reporting receivables at face value less an allowance for accounts whose collection is doubtful. The **net realizable value** (amount actually expected to be collected) is the amount included in the computation of total assets. In contrast, payables are normally carried at face value because companies operate under the **going concern assumption**. Since companies believe they will continue to operate (they are going concerns), they assume they will be responsible for paying the full balance of their obligations. Therefore, it is customary to carry receivables at net realizable value and payables at face value on the balance sheet.

The practice of reporting the net realizable value of receivables in the financial statements is commonly called the **allowance method of accounting for bad debts**. Below we demonstrate the application of the allowance method for Allen's Tutoring Services.

LO2
Explain how the allowance method of accounting for bad debts affects financial statements.

Accounting Events Affecting the 2005 Period

Allen's Tutoring Services was started as a part-time venture by Mark Allen. Allen is a bright, young university student who started the tutoring service during his second year. Three accounting events that affected Allen's Tutoring Services during its first year of operation follow. As you read, try to anticipate the effect of each event on the financial statements. Then check your accuracy by looking at the statements model that follows the transaction. You will learn more quickly if you think about the possible effects of each transaction *before* you read the results. To simplify the illustration, we have assigned a number to each event.

Event 1 Revenue Recognition

Allen's Tutoring Services recognized $14,000 of service revenue earrned on account during 2005.

By now, you should be familiar with this type of event. It is an *asset source* transaction. Allen's Tutoring Services obtains assets (Accounts Receivable) by providing services to its customers. Therefore, both assets and equity (Retained Earnings) increase. The event increases revenue and net income. Cash flow is not affected. These effects are shown in the following horizontal statements model:

Event No.	Assets	=	Liab.	+	Equity	Rev.	−	Exp.	=	Net Inc.	Cash Flow Statement
1	14,000	=	NA	+	14,000	14,000	−	NA	=	14,000	NA

Event 2 Collection of Receivables

Allen's Tutoring Services collected $12,500 cash from accounts receivable in 2005.

This event is an *asset exchange* transaction. One asset, Cash, increases; and another asset, Accounts Receivable, decreases. The total amount of assets is unchanged. Net income is not affected because the revenue was recognized in the previous transaction. The cash inflow is shown in the operating activities section of the cash flow statement.

[1] Notes can be classified as short term or long term, depending on the time to maturity. Short-term notes mature within one year or the operating cycle, whichever is longer. Notes with longer maturities are classified as long-term notes. This chapter focuses on accounting for short-term notes; accounting for long-term notes is discussed in Chapter 10.

answers to the *curious* accountant

Johnson & Johnson would definitely prefer to make the sale to Shoppers Drug Mart in cash rather than on account. Even though it may be certain to collect its accounts receivable from Shoppers, the sooner Johnson & Johnson gets its cash, the sooner the cash can be reinvested.

The interest cost related to a small account receivable of $50 that takes 60 days to collect may seem minor; at 6.5 percent, the lost interest amounts to less than $1. However, when one considers that Johnson & Johnson had approximately $4.5 billion of accounts receivable on December 31, 2000, the cost of financing receivables for a real-world company becomes apparent. At 6.5 percent, the cost of waiting 60 days to collect $4.5 billion of cash is $48 million ($4.5 billion × 0.065 × [60 ÷ 365]). For one full year, the cost to Johnson & Johnson would be more than $290 million ($4.5 billion × 0.065). In 2000 it took Johnson & Johnson approximately 55 days to collect its accounts receivable, and the weighted-average interest rate on its debt was approximately 6.4 percent.

Event No.	Assets			=	Liab.	+	Equity	Rev.	−	Exp.	=	Net Inc.	Cash Flow Statement	
	Cash	+	Accts. Rec.											
2	12,500	+	(12,500)	=	NA	+	NA	NA	−	NA	=	NA	12,500	OA

Allen's Tutoring Services recognized bad debts expense for accounts expected to be uncollectible in the future.

Event 3
Recognizing Bad Debts Expense

The ending balance in the receivable account is $1,500 ($14,000 of revenue on account, $12,500 of collections). Although Allen's Tutoring Services hopes to collect the full $1,500 in 2006, the company is not likely to do so because some of its customers may not pay the amounts due. Therefore, the $1,500 receivables balance does not represent the amount of cash truly expected to be collected. Allen's Tutoring Services is quite sure that some of its customers will not pay, but the actual amount of uncollectible accounts cannot be known until the future period, when the customers default (refuse to pay). Even so, the company can make a reasonable *estimate* of the amount of receivables that will be uncollectible. The estimated amount is used to match possible bad debts expense against the period when the revenues were earned (matching principle).

Suppose that Allen's Tutoring Services believes that $75 of the receivables is uncollectible. To improve accuracy, the company can recognize the anticipated future write-down of receivables in the current accounting period. Specifically, the company records a year-end adjusting entry that recognizes **bad debts expense**, thereby reducing the book value of total assets and equity (Retained Earnings). Like any other expense recognition transaction, the adjusting entry for bad debts expense reduces the amount of reported net income. The cash flow statement is not affected. The effects of the recognition of bad debts expense are shown in the following horizontal statements model:

Event No.	Assets	=	Liab.	+	Equity	Rev.	−	Exp.	=	Net Inc.	Cash Flow Statement
3	(75)	=	NA	+	(75)	NA	−	75	=	(75)	NA

The amount of receivables expected to be uncollectible ($75) is accumulated in a contra asset account called **Allowance for Doubtful Accounts**. The difference between the amount in accounts receivable and the contra allowance account is called the *net realizable value of receivables*. The net realizable value of receivables represents the amount of receivables the company believes it will actually collect. In this case, the net realizable value of receivables is:

Accounts Receivable	$1,500
Less: Allowance for Doubtful Accounts	(75)
Net Realizable Value of Receivables	$1,425

General Journal Entries and Ledger T-Accounts

Exhibit 7–1 shows the journal entries and ledger T-accounts for the business events experienced by Allen's Tutoring Services. The exhibit includes the entry used to close the revenue and expense accounts at the end of the 2005 accounting period. The closing entry is a *claims exchange* transaction, with some equity accounts decreasing while others increase. The amount of total equity is not affected by the closing entry. Also, the income statement and the cash flow statement are not affected by the closing entry. The ledger account balances are used to prepare the financial statements shown in Exhibit 7–2. To confirm your understanding of the accounting treatment for bad debts, trace the transactions to the ledger accounts and the account balances to the financial statements. The relevant accounting events are summarized here for your convenience:

1. Earned $14,000 of revenue on account.
2. Collected $12,500 cash from accounts receivable.
3. Adjusted the accounts to reflect management's estimate that bad debts expense would be $75.
4. Closed the revenue and expense accounts. The letters "*cl*" are used as a posting reference for the closing entries.

Exhibit 7–1 *General Journal Entries and General Ledger T-Accounts*

Event No.	Account Title	Debit	Credit
1	Account Receivable	14,000	
	Service Revenue		14,000
2	Cash	12,500	
	Accounts Receivable		12,500
3	Bad Debt Expense	75	
	Allowance for Doubtful Accounts		75
cl	Service Revenue	14,000	
	Bad Debt Expense		75
	Retained Earnings		13,925

Cash = **Liabilities** + **Retained Earnings**

Cash				=	Liabilities				+	Retained Earnings			
(2)	12,500						0	Bal.				13,925	(cl)
Bal.	12,500											13,925	Bal.

Accounts Receivable

	Debit	Credit	
(1)	14,000	12,500	(2)
Bal.	1,500		

Service Revenue

	Debit	Credit	
(cl)	14,000	14,000	(1)
		0	Bal.

Allowance for Doubtful Accounts

	Debit	Credit	
		75	(3)
		75	Bal.

Bad Debts Expense

	Debit	Credit	
(3)	75	75	(cl)
Bal.	0		

Exhibit 7–2 *Financial Statements for 2005*

Income Statement

Service Revenue	$14,000
Bad Debts Expense	(75)
Net Income	$13,925

Balance Sheet

Assets		
Cash		$12,500
Accounts Receivable	$1,500	
Less: Allowance	(75)	
Net Realizable Value		1,425
Total Assets		$13,925
Shareholders' Equity		
Retained Earnings		$13,925

Cash Flow Statement

Operating Activities	
Inflow from Customers	$12,500
Investing Activities	0
Financing Activities	0
Net Change in Cash	12,500
Plus: Beginning Cash Balance	0
Ending Cash Balance	$12,500

Financial Statements

Estimating bad debts improves the accuracy of the 2005 financial statements in two important ways. First, the net realizable value of accounts receivable is shown on the balance sheet. This lets the statement users see not only the gross amount of receivables but also the amount that Allen's Tutoring Services actually expects to collect ($1,500 − $75 = $1,425). As well, the amount of bad debts expense ($75) is shown in the 2005 income statement along with the revenue that was recognized when receivables were recorded. Since the associated revenues and expenses are shown on the same income statement, the allowance method improves matching and provides a better measure of managerial performance. As you continue to review the statements in Exhibit 7–2, observe carefully that the amount of cash flow from operations ($12,500) is different from the amount of net income ($13,925) because only cash collections are reported on the cash flow statement. In contrast, the income statement includes revenues earned on account less the estimated amount of bad debts expense.

Estimation of Bad Debts Expense

In the case of Allen's Tutoring, we simply provided the estimated amount of bad debts expense. How do real-world accountants make such estimates? Most accountants start by reviewing the company's credit history. They ask, "How much of the company's credit sales (sales on account) could not be collected in the past?" A convenient way to express the answer to this question is to state the estimated amount of bad debts expense as a percentage of credit sales. To illustrate, assume that in the previous accounting period, Tannon Company was unable to collect $10,000 of $1,000,000 sales on account. Therefore, Tannon's bad debts expense amounted to 1 percent of the credit sales ($10,000 ÷ $1,000,000).

Before the historical percentage is applied to the current sales on account, it is normally adjusted for anticipated future circumstances. For example, the percentage could be lowered if the company plans to apply more rigorous approval standards to new credit applicants. Alternatively, the percentage may be increased if economic forecasts signal a downturn in the economy that would make future defaults more likely. To illustrate, assume that Tannon Company decides to relax its credit standards to expand sales in a recessionary economy. Specifically, the company decides to increase the estimated bad debts percentage from 1 to 1.5 percent of credit sales. Assuming current sales on account of $1,200,000, the estimated bad debts expense is $18,000 ($1,200,000 × 0.015). This method of estimating bad debt expense is often referred to as the income statement (or percentage of sales) method.

An alternative approach is referred to as the balance sheet (percentage of accounts receivable) method. This method estimates the balance required in the allowance account based on a percentage of accounts receivable outstanding at the end of the period. Assume Kramer Company has $100,000 in accounts receivable and a $1,000 balance in the allowance account at the end of the year. The company has estimated that 5 percent of its accounts receivable balance will not be collected. This method requires a two-step approach. Step 1 multiplies the accounts receivable balance by an estimated uncollectible percentage. The result of this calculation determines the balance that is required in the allowance account. For Kramer Company, the allowance account requires a balance of $5,000 ($100,000 × 5 percent). The second step then compares the balance in the allowance before any adjustment is made with this required balance to determine the amount of the adjustment that is required, as follows:

Required balance	$5,000
Current balance before adjustment	1,000
Required adjustment	$4,000

Determining the estimated bad debts percentage may be particularly difficult when a company is in its first year of operation because it has no credit history on which to base the estimate. In this case, it must consult with trade associations or business associates (other people in the same industry who do have experience) to develop a reasonable estimate of the expected losses.

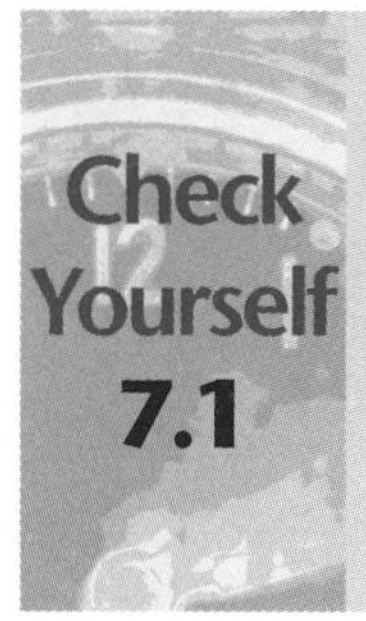

Pamlico, Inc., began operations on January 1, 2006. During 2006, it earned $400,000 of revenue on account. The company collected $370,000 of accounts receivable. At the end of the year, Pamlico estimates bad debts expense will be 1 percent of sales. Based on this information alone, what is the net realizable value of accounts receivable as of December 31, 2006?

Answer Accounts receivable at year end are $30,000 ($400,000 sales on account − $370,000 collection of receivables). The amount in the allowance for doubtful accounts would be $4,000 ($400,000 credit sales × 0.01). The net realizable value of accounts receivable is therefore $26,000 ($30,000 − $4,000).

LO2 Explain how the allowance method of accounting for bad debts affects financial statements.

Accounting Events Affecting the 2006 Period

Now we discuss eight accounting events that occurred during the 2006 accounting cycle. As before, you should anticipate the effect of each event on the financial statements before reviewing the appropriate statements model. An accounting textbook should not be merely read; it should be worked. Read the book with pencil in hand. Anticipate the results, trace the transactions, and verify the numbers. You will learn more by *doing* accounting than by *reading* about it. So do the accounting as you read the text.

Event 1 Write-Off of an Uncollectible Account Receivable

Allen's Tutoring Services wrote off an uncollectible account receivable.

Since the impact of recognizing bad debts was shown in the 2005 financial statements, the actual *write-off of uncollectible accounts* does not affect the balance sheet. When a specific account is determined to be uncollectible, the balance of the account is removed from the Receivables account and from the Allowance for Bad Debts account. Therefore, the event constitutes an *asset exchange* transaction. Total assets, liabilities, and equity are the same immediately after the write-off in 2006. Likewise, the income statement and the cash flow statement are not affected by a write-off of an uncollectible account. To illustrate, assume that one of Allen's Tutoring Services' customers refuses to pay a $70 receivable balance. Allen's Tutoring Services has tried in every way to collect the amount due and has determined that regardless of further efforts, the funds are not collectible now or in the future. Allen has decided to write off the account. The effect on the financial statements is shown in the following horizontal statements model:

Event No.	Assets			=	Liab.	+	Equity	Rev.	−	Exp.	=	Net Inc.	Cash Flow Statement
	Accts. Rec.	−	Allow.										
1	(70)	−	(70)	=	NA	+	NA	NA	−	NA	=	NA	NA

Clearly, the write-off is an asset exchange transaction. The decrease in Accounts Receivable is offset by a reduction in the balance of the Allowance account. Note that while the balances in Accounts Receivable and the Allowance accounts decrease, the net realizable value of receivables—and therefore total assets—remains unchanged.

	Before Write-Off	After Write-Off
Accounts Receivable	$1,500	$1,430
Allowance for Doubtful Accounts	(75)	(5)
Net Realizable Value	$1,425	$1,425

Event 2
Investment in Note Receivable

Allen's Tutoring Services invested in a note receivable.

After taking an accounting course, Mark Allen becomes concerned about the growing balance in his company's Cash account. He realizes that he could improve his company's profitability by investing some of the idle cash. Therefore, on May 1, 2006, Allen's Tutoring Service loans $12,000 cash to another student who is starting a business of her own. The borrower issues a 9 percent interest-bearing note to Allen's. The note carries a one-year term. The loan represents an investment by Allen's Tutoring Services. One asset account, *Cash*, decreases; another asset account, *Notes Receivable*, increases. Total assets are unchanged. The income statement is unaffected by the event. The cash outflow is shown in the investing activities section of the cash flow statement. These effects are reflected in the following statements model:

Event No.	Assets			=	Liab.	+	Equity	Rev.	−	Exp.	=	Net Inc.	Cash Flow Statement
	Cash	+	Note Rec.										
2	(12,000)	+	12,000	=	NA	+	NA	NA	−	NA	=	NA	(12,000) IA

Event 3
Revenue Recognition

Allen's Tutoring Services provided $10,000 of tutoring services on account during the 2006 accounting period.

Assets (Accounts Receivable) and equity (Revenue) increase. The recognition of revenue increases net income. Cash flow is not affected. The effects on the financial statements are shown here:

Event No.	Assets	=	Liab.	+	Equity	Rev.	−	Exp.	=	Net Inc.	Cash Flow Statement
3	10,000	=	NA	+	10,000	10,000	−	NA	=	10,000	NA

Event 4
Collection of Accounts Receivable

Allen's Tutoring Services collected $8,430 cash from accounts receivable.

The balance in the Cash account increases, and the balance in the Receivables account decreases. Total assets are unaffected. Net income is not affected because revenue was recognized earlier. The cash inflow is shown in the operating activities section of the cash flow statement.

Event No.	Assets			=	Liab.	+	Equity	Rev.	−	Exp.	=	Net Inc.	Cash Flow Statement
	Cash	+	Accts. Rec.										
4	8,430	+	(8,430)	=	NA	+	NA	NA	−	NA	=	NA	8,430 OA

Event 5
Recovery of Bad Debt: Reestablishment of Receivable

Allen's Tutoring Services recovered a bad debt that was previously written off.

Sometimes, a company receives payment from a customer whose account was previously written off. When this occurs, the customer's account should be reestablished and then the collection should be recorded as usual. This practice provides a complete record of activity that may be useful in the event the customer requests additional credit at some future date or in case the company is asked to provide a credit history of the customer to a credit bureau, bank, or some other interested party. To illustrate, assume that Allen's Tutoring Services receives a $10 cash payment from a customer whose account had previously been written off. The first step is to reestablish the Receivable and Allowance accounts that were written off. The effect is simply the reverse of a write-off. Accounts Receivable increases, and the

Allowance account increases. Since the Allowance is a contra asset account, the increase in this account offsets the increase in the Receivables account, and total assets are unchanged. Net income and cash flow are unaffected. These effects are shown here:

Event No.	Assets			=	Liab.	+	Equity	Rev.	−	Exp.	=	Net Inc.	Cash Flow Statement
	Accts. Rec.	−	Allow.										
5	10	−	10	=	NA	+	NA	NA	−	NA	=	NA	NA

Event 6 Recovery of Bad Debt: Collection of Receivable

Allen's Tutoring Services collected the reestablished receivable.

The collection of the $10 is treated as any other collection of a receivable account. The Cash account increases, and the Receivables account decreases.

Event No.	Assets			=	Liab.	+	Equity	Rev.	−	Exp.	=	Net Inc.	Cash Flow Statement
	Cash	+	Accts. Rec.										
6	10	+	(10)	=	NA	+	NA	NA	−	NA	=	NA	10 OA

Event 7 Adjustment for Recognition of Bad Debts Expense

Allen's Tutoring Services recognized bad debts expense for 2006.

Assume that Allen's estimates bad debts expense to be 1.35 percent of credit sales. Here, the amount of bad debts expense to recognize would be $135 ($10,000 × 0.0135). The recognition of the $135 bad debts expense decreases assets (net realizable value of receivables) and equity (Retained Earnings). The recognition of the expense decreases the amount of net income. The cash flow statement is not affected. The effects on the financial statements follow:

Event No.	Assets			=	Liab.	+	Equity	Rev.	−	Exp.	=	Net Inc.	Cash Flow Statement
	Accts. Rec.	−	Allow.				Ret. Earn.						
7	NA	−	135	=	NA	+	(135)	NA	−	135	=	(135)	NA

Event 8 Recognition of Interest Revenue

Allen's Tutoring Services recognized interest revenue on the note receivable.

Recall that on May 1, 2006, Allen's Tutoring Services invested $12,000 in a note receivable with a one-year term and a 9 percent annual rate of interest. By December 31, 2006, the note will have earned $720 ($12,000 × 0.09 × [8 ÷ 12]). The recognition of the earned interest increases assets (Interest Receivable) and equity (Retained Earnings). The recognition of revenue increases net income. Cash flow is not affected. The effects on the financial statements are shown here:

Event No.	Assets	=	Liab.	+	Equity	Rev.	−	Exp.	=	Net Inc.	Cash Flow Statement
8	720	=	NA	+	720	720	−	NA	=	720	NA

General Journal Entries and Ledger T-Accounts

Exhibit 7–3 shows the journal entries and ledger T-accounts for the 2006 business events experienced by Allen's Tutoring Services. The exhibit includes the entry used to close the revenue and expense accounts at the end of the 2006 accounting period. The ledger account balances are used to prepare the financial statements shown in Exhibit 7–4 (page 286). The relevant accounting events are summarized here for your convenience:

Exhibit 7–3 *General Journal Entries and Ledger T-Accounts*

Event No.	Account Title	Debit	Credit
1	Allowance for Doubtful Accounts	70	
	Accounts Receivable		70
2	Note Receivable	12,000	
	Cash		12,000
3	Accounts Receivable	10,000	
	Service Revenue		10,000
4	Cash	8,430	
	Accounts Receivable		8,430
5	Accounts Receivable	10	
	Allowance for Doubtful Accounts		10
6	Cash	10	
	Accounts Receivable		10
7	Bad Debt Expense	135	
	Allowance for Doubtful Accounts		135
8	Interest Receivable	720	
	Interest Revenue		720
cl	Service Revenue	10,000	
	Interest Revenue	720	
	Bad Debt Expense		135
	Retained Earnings		10,585

Assets = Liabilities + Equity

Cash = Liabilities + Retained Earnings

Cash

	Debit	Credit	
Bal.	12,500	12,000	(2)
(4)	8,430		
(6)	10		
Bal.	8,940		

Liabilities

	Debit	Credit	
		0	Bal.

Retained Earnings

	Debit	Credit	
		13,925	Bal.
		10,585	(cl)
		24,510	Bal.

Accounts Receivable

	Debit	Credit	
Bal.	1,500	70	(1)
(3)	10,000	8,430	(4)
(5)	10	10	(6)
Bal.	3,000		

Service Revenue

	Debit	Credit	
(cl)	10,000	10,000	(3)
		0	Bal.

Interest Revenue

	Debit	Credit	
(cl)	720	720	(8)
		0	Bal.

Allowance for Doubtful Accounts

	Debit	Credit	
(1)	70	75	Bal.
		10	(5)
		135	(7)
		150	Bal.

Bad Debts Expense

	Debit	Credit	
(7)	135	135	(cl)
Bal.	0		

Notes Receivable

	Debit	Credit
(2)	12,000	

Interest Receivable

	Debit	Credit
(8)	720	

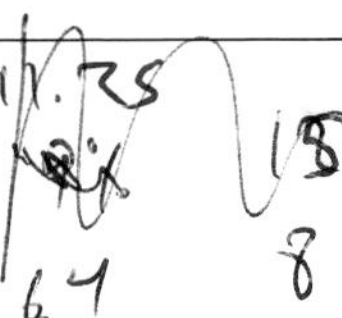

1. Wrote off a $70 account receivable as uncollectible.
2. Invested $12,000 in a note receivable.
3. Earned $10,000 of tutoring service revenue on account.
4. Collected $8,430 cash from accounts receivable.
5. Reestablished a $10 account receivable that had previously been written off.

6. Collected $10 from the reestablished receivable.
7. Adjusted accounts to recognize $135 of estimated bad debts expense.
8. Adjusted accounts to recognize $720 of accrued interest revenue.
9. Closed the revenue and expense accounts. The letters *cl* are used as a posting reference for the closing entries.

Analysis of Financial Statements

Exhibit 7–4 shows the relevant financial statements. Note that the amount of bad debts expense ($135) is different from the ending balance of the Allowance account ($150). Recall that the Allowance account had a $15 balance just before the 2006 adjusting entry for bad debts expense was made. This balance existed because the estimate for uncollectible accounts in 2005 was overstated. In 2005, Allen's Tutoring Services estimated that there would be $75 of uncollectible accounts when, in fact, only $70 of accounts was written off and $10 of those accounts was recovered, resulting in a net loss of uncollectible accounts of only $60. Therefore, the expense for 2005 was overstated by $15. However, if no estimate had been made, the amount of bad debts expense would have been understated by $60. Remember that bad debts expense is an estimated amount. In some accounting periods the amount may be overstated; in others it may be understated. The allowance method does not result in perfection but does improve the accuracy of the financial statements. Since there were no dividends, ending retained earnings are computed as last year's retained earnings plus this year's net income ($13,925 + $10,585 = $24,510). Once again, the cash flow from operations ($8,440) is different from the amount of net income ($10,585) because the cash flow statement does not include the effects of revenues earned on account or the recognition of bad debts expense.

Exhibit 7–4 *Financial Statements for 2006*

Income Statement

Service Revenue	$10,000
Bad Debts Expense	(135)
Operating Income	9,865
Interest Revenue	720
Net Income	$10,585

Balance Sheet

Assets		
Cash		$ 8,940
Accounts Receivable	$3,000	
Less: Allowance	(150)	
Net Realizable Value		2,850
Note Receivable		12,000
Interest Receivable		720
Total Assets		$24,510
Shareholders' Equity		
Retained Earnings		$24,510

Cash Flow Statement

Operating Activities	
Inflow from Customers	$ 8,440
Investing Activities	
Outflow from Note Receivable	(12,000)
Financing Activities	0
Net Change in Cash	(3,560)
Plus: Beginning Cash Balance	12,500
Ending Cash Balance	$ 8,940

Maher Company had beginning balances in Accounts Receivable and Allowance for Doubtful Accounts of $24,200 and $2,000, respectively. During the accounting period Maher earned $230,000 of revenue on account and collected $232,500 of cash from receivables. The company also wrote off $1,950 of uncollectible accounts during the period. Maher estimates bad debts expense will be 1 percent of credit sales. Based on this information, what is the net realizable value of receivables at the end of the period?

Answer The balance in the Accounts Receivable account is $19,750 ($24,200 + $230,000 − $232,500 − $1,950). The amount of bad debts expense for the period is $2,300 ($230,000 × 0.01). The balance in the Allowance for Doubtful Accounts is $2,350 ($2,000 − $1,950 + $2,300). The net realizable value of receivables is therefore $17,400 ($19,750 − $2,350).

Recognition of Bad Debts under the Direct Write-Off Method

LO3 Show how the direct write-off method of accounting for bad debts affects financial statements.

If the amount of uncollectible accounts is immaterial, bad debts expense can be recognized when accounts are determined to be uncollectible. This method is called the **direct write-off method** of accounting for bad debts. Since the direct write-off method does not make an allowance for uncollectible accounts, it overstates the net realizable value of receivables on the balance sheet. Therefore, the method does not comply with generally accepted accounting principles (GAAP). However, if the amount of uncollectible accounts is insignificant, the overstatement is tolerated as a fair trade-off for the recording convenience offered by the direct write-off method. This is an example of applying the **materiality** concept. The reporting of immaterial items does not have to conform to GAAP.

No estimates, allowance account, or adjusting entries are needed under the direct write-off method. Simply record the bad debts as they occur. Sales or services on account are recognized in the customary fashion in the period in which goods or services are provided. Bad debts expense is then recognized in the period in which a particular account is judged to be uncollectible. To illustrate, assume that the following events apply to Dr. Price's optical services company.

Event 1 Recognition of Revenue on Account

During 2005, the company provides $50,000 of services on account.

The effects of this event on the financial statements are shown here:

Event No.	Assets	=	Liab.	+	Equity	Rev.	−	Exp.	=	Net Inc.	Cash Flow Statement
1	50,000	=	NA	+	50,000	50,000	−	NA	=	50,000	NA

The following entry is used to record the transaction in the general journal:

Account Title	Debit	Credit
Accounts Receivable	50,000	
Service Revenue		50,000

Event 2 Recognition of Bad Debts Expense

Assume that Price determines in 2006 that one of his customers who owes $200 for services delivered in 2005 is unable to pay the amount due.

The write-off of the account results in the recognition of bad debts expense in 2006, even though the associated revenue was recognized in 2005. In other words, the expense is recognized in the year in which an account is determined to be uncollectible. Accuracy is compromised because revenues are not matched with related expenses. As noted earlier, such inaccuracies are tolerated only to the extent that they are deemed to be immaterial. The effect of the write-off of the uncollectible account on the financial statements follows:

Event No.	Assets	=	Liab.	+	Equity	Rev.	−	Exp.	=	Net Inc.	Cash Flow Statement
2	(200)	=	NA	+	(200)	NA	−	200	=	(200)	NA

The only entry required to recognize bad debts is made in 2006. This entry is shown here in general journal format.

Account Title	Debit	Credit
Bad Debts Expense	200	
Accounts Receivable		200

Accounting for Credit Card Sales

LO4 Explain how accounting for credit card sales affects financial statements.

The effective management of credit is a complex task that can be very expensive in terms of time and money. Every company incurs bad debts expense, and the clerical costs of keeping track of it are high. Creditworthiness must be established for each customer, and detailed records of each transaction must be maintained. Many businesses pass these costs on to financial institutions that service the merchant's credit sales for a fee of between 2 and 8 percent of gross sales.

The financial institution (credit card company)[2] provides the customer a plastic card that permits the cardholder to charge purchases at various retail outlets. When a sale is made, the seller records the transaction on an invoice the customer signs. The invoice is forwarded to the credit card company, which immediately pays the merchant. The service charge is deducted from the gross amount of the invoice, and the merchant is paid the net balance (gross invoice less credit card discount) in cash. The credit card company collects the amount of the gross sales directly from the customer. In this way, the merchant avoids the risk of bad debts as well as the cost of maintaining credit records. To illustrate, assume that the following events apply to Joan Wilson's consulting practice.

Event 1 Recognition of Revenue and Expense on Credit Card Sales

Wilson accepts a credit card as payment for $1,000 of services rendered to one of her customers.

Assume that the credit card company charges a 5 percent fee for handling the credit ($1,000 × 0.05 = $50). Income increases by the amount of revenue ($1,000) and decreases by the amount of the credit card expense ($50). Therefore, net income increases by $950. The event increases assets (Accounts Receivable due from the credit card company) and equity (Retained Earnings) by $950. Cash flow is not affected. The effect of the event on the financial statements is as follows:

Event No.	Assets	=	Liab.	+	Equity	Rev.	−	Exp.	=	Net Inc.	Cash Flow Statement
1	950	=	NA	+	950	1,000	−	50	=	950	NA

The following entry is used to record the transaction in the general journal:

Account Title	Debit	Credit
Accounts Receivable—Credit Card Company	950	
Credit Card Expense	50	
Service Revenue		1,000

Event 2 Collection of Credit Card Receivable

The collection of the receivable due from the credit card company is treated as any other collection of a receivable.

When Wilson collects the net amount of $950 ($1,000 − $50) from the credit card company, one asset account (Cash) increases and another asset account (Accounts Receivable) decreases. Total assets are not affected. The income statement is not affected by the transaction. There is a $950 cash inflow shown in the operating activities section of the cash flow statement. The effect of the collection on the financial statement elements is shown here:

Event No.	Assets			=	Liab.	+	Equity	Rev.	−	Exp.	=	Net Inc.	Cash Flow Statement	
	Cash	+	Accts. Rec.											
2	950	+	(950)	=	NA	+	NA	NA	−	NA	=	NA	950	OA

[2] A merchant will record the receipt of cash at a different point in time depending on the type of credit card used by the customer. Visa and MasterCard transactions are treated as if those transactions were cash sales. American Express and other nonbank credit cards are treated as a sale on account. Therefore, the merchant would receive cash from these transactions at a later date.

The following entry is used to record the transaction in the general journal:

Account Title	Debit	Credit
Cash	950	
Accounts Receivable		950

Warranty Obligations

LO5 Explain how accounting for warranty obligations affects financial statements.

Global competition has forced most companies to guarantee customer satisfaction. A promise to correct a deficiency or dissatisfaction in quality, quantity, or performance is called a **warranty**. Warranties take many forms. Usually, they provide a guarantee that extends over some specified period after the point of sale. Within this period, the seller promises to replace or repair defective products without charge. Many companies promise satisfaction or "your money back." Some even offer double or triple money-back guarantees. The obligations stemming from warranties may be uncertain as to amount, timing, or customer. That said, they usually represent legal liabilities that must be recognized in the accounts.

Next we demonstrate the accounting treatment for warranty obligations. Assume that Perfect Picture Frame (PPF) Company had cash of $2,000, inventory of $6,000, common shares of $5,000, and retained earnings of $3,000 on January 1, 2005. The 2005 accounting period is affected by three accounting events: (1) sale of merchandise, (2) recognition of warranty obligations to customers who purchased the merchandise, and (3) settlement of a warranty claim made by a customer.

Event 1 Sale of Merchandise

PPF sold merchandise that cost $4,000 for $7,000 cash.

In the statements model shown here, the sale is referenced with the notation 1(a) and the cost of the sale as 1(b). The recognition of sales revenue increases assets and equity. Net income also increases. The cash flow statement includes a $7,000 cash inflow in the operating activities section. The recognition of expense (cost of goods sold) decreases assets and equity. Net income also decreases. Cash flow is not affected by the expense recognition. The effects on the financial statements are indicated here:

Event No.	Assets			=	Liab.	+	Equity	Rev.	−	Exp.	=	Net Inc.	Cash Flow Statement	
	Cash	+	Inventory											
1(a)	7,000	+	NA	=	NA	+	7,000	7,000	−	NA	=	7,000	7,000	OA
1(b)	NA	+	(4,000)	=	NA	+	(4,000)	NA	−	4,000	=	(4,000)	NA	

Event 2 Recognition of Warranty Expense

PPF guaranteed the merchandise sold in Event 1 to be free from defects for a one-year period following the date of sale.

Although the exact amount of future warranty claims is unknown, PPF must inform financial statement users of the obligation that the company has incurred. So it must estimate the amount of the liability and include that estimate in the current period's financial statements. Assume that the warranty obligation is estimated to be $100. Recognizing this obligation increases liabilities (Warranties Payable) and reduces equity (Retained Earnings). The recognition of the warranty expense reduces net income. The cash flow statement is not affected by the recognition of the obligation and corresponding expense. The effects on the financial statements are shown here:

Event No.	Assets	=	Liab.	+	Equity	Rev.	−	Exp.	=	Net Inc.	Cash Flow Statement
2	NA	=	100	+	(100)	NA	−	100	=	(100)	NA

reality bytes

Most electrical appliances come with a manufacturer's warranty that obligates the manufacturer to pay for defects that occur during some designated period of time after the point of sale. Why would Circuit City issue warranties that obligate it to pay for defects that occur after the manufacturer's warranty has expired? Warranties are in fact insurance policies that generate profits. Indeed, the Circuit City Group reported that the gross dollar sales from extended warranty programs were 5.1 percent of its total sales in fiscal year 2001. Even more important, Circuit City notes that gross profit margins on products sold with extended warranties are higher than the gross profit margins on products sold without extended warranties. It should be noted that warranties produce revenues for manufacturers as well as retailers. The only difference is that the revenues generated from manufacturer's warranties are embedded in the sales price. Indeed, products with longer, more comprehensive warranties usually sell at higher prices than products with shorter, less extensive warranties.

Event 3
Settlement of Warranty Obligation

PPF paid $40 cash to repair defective merchandise returned by customers.

Note that the payment for the repair is not an expense. The expense was recognized in the period in which the sale was made (when the Warranties Payable account was created). Thus, rather than being an expense, the cash payment reduces the Warranties Payable account. Therefore, the payment reduces the assets (Cash) and liabilities (Warranties Payable). The income statement is not affected by the repairs payment. However, there is a $40 cash outflow shown in the operating activities section of the cash flow statement.

Event No.	Assets	=	Liab.	+	Equity	Rev.	−	Exp.	=	Net Inc.	Cash Flow Statement	
3	(40)	=	(40)	+	NA	NA	−	NA	=	NA	(40)	OA

General Journal Entries, Ledger T-Accounts, and Financial Statements

Exhibit 7–5 presents the journal entries and ledger T-accounts for the business events experienced by PPF. The exhibit includes the entry used to close the revenue and expense accounts at the end of the 2005 accounting period. The ledger account balances are used to prepare the financial statements shown in Exhibit 7–6. The relevant accounting events are summarized here for your convenience:

Transactions for 2005

1. Sold merchandise that cost $4,000 for $7,000 cash.
2. Recognized a $100 warranty obligation and the corresponding expense.
3. Paid $40 to satisfy a warranty claim.
4. Closed the revenue and expense accounts. The letters *cl* are used as a posting reference for the closing entries.

Exhibit 7–5 *General Journal Entries*

Event No.	Account Title	Debit	Credit
1(a)	Cash	7,000	
	Sales Revenue		7,000
1(b)	Cost of Goods Sold	4,000	
	Inventory		4,000
2	Warranty Expense	100	
	Warranties Payable		100
3	Warranties Payable	40	
	Cash		40
cl	Sales Revenue	7,000	
	Cost of Goods Sold		4,000
	Warranty Expense		100
	Retained Earnings		2,900

Assets = Liabilities + Equity

Cash

	Debit	Credit	
Bal.	2,000	40	(3)
(1a)	7,000		
Bal.	8,960		

Inventory

	Debit	Credit	
Bal.	6,000	4,000	(1b)
Bal.	2,000		

Warranties Payable

	Debit	Credit	
(3)	40	100	(2)
		60	Bal.

Common Shares

	Debit	Credit	
		5,000	Bal.

Retained Earnings

	Debit	Credit	
		3,000	Bal.
		2,900	(cl)
		5,900	Bal.

Sales Revenue

	Debit	Credit	
(cl)	7,000	7,000	(1a)
		0	Bal.

Cost of Goods Sold

	Debit	Credit	
(1b)	4,000	4,000	(cl)
Bal.	0		

Warranty Expense

	Debit	Credit	
(2)	100	100	(cl)
Bal.	0		

Exhibit 7–6 *Financial Statements for 2005*

Income Statement

Sales Revenue	$7,000
Cost of Goods Sold	(4,000)
Gross Profit	3,000
Warranties Exp.	(100)
Net Income	$2,900

Balance Sheet

Assets	
Cash	$ 8,960
Inventory	2,000
Total Assets	$10,960
Liabilities	
Warranties Payable	$ 60
Shareholders' Equity	
Common Shares	5,000
Retained Earnings	5,900
Total Liab. and Shareholders' Equity	$10,960

Cash Flow Statement

Operating Activities	
Inflow from Customers	$7,000
Outflow for Warranty	(40)
Net Inflow from Oper.	6,960
Investing Activities	0
Financing Activities	0
Net Change in Cash	6,960
Plus: Beginning Cash Balance	2,000
Ending Cash Balance	$8,960

LO6 Show how discount notes and related interest charges affect financial statements.

Accounting for Discount Notes

Up to this point, all notes payable have been assumed to be **interest-bearing notes**. At maturity, the amount due is the *face value* of the note *plus accrued interest*. In contrast, **discount notes** have the interest included in the face value of the note. Therefore, a $5,000 face value discount note is repaid with a $5,000 cash payment at maturity. This payment includes principal and accrued interest. To illustrate, assume that the following four events apply to Beacon Management Services Ltd.

Event 1 Borrowing by Issuing a Discount Note

Beacon Management Services was started by issuing a $10,000 face value discount note to a local bank on March 1, 2005.

The note carried a 9 percent *discount rate* and a one-year term to maturity. As with interest-bearing notes, the **issuer of the note** gives the promissory note in exchange for the receipt of cash. The first step in accounting for the discount note is to divide the face amount between the discount and the principal (amount borrowed). The discount is calculated by multiplying the face value of the note by the interest rate by the time period. In this case, the discount is $900 ($10,000 × 0.09). The amount borrowed is determined by subtracting the discount from the face value of the note ($10,000 − $900 = $9,100). In this case, the **principal** (the amount of cash borrowed) is $9,100, and the **discount** (the amount of interest to be incurred over the term of the loan) is $900. In summary, *on the issue date*, assets and total liabilities increase by the amount borrowed (the $9,100 principal). The *income statement* is not affected by the borrowing transaction on the issue date. There is a $9,100 cash inflow shown in the financing activities section of the *cash flow statement*. These effects are shown here:

Event No.	Assets	=	Liab.	+	Equity	Rev.	−	Exp.	=	Net Inc.	Cash Flow Statement	
1	9,100	=	9,100	+	NA	NA	−	NA	=	NA	9,100	FA

For internal record-keeping purposes, the amount of the discount is normally contained in a separate account titled **Discount on Notes Payable**. This account is a **contra liability account**. It is subtracted from the Notes Payable account to determine the *carrying value* of the liability. The carrying value, also known as the *book value*, gets its name from the fact that it is the amount at which the liability is shown (carried) on the books. In this case, Beacon's ledger contains the Notes Payable account with a $10,000 credit balance and the Discount on Notes Payable account with a $900 debit balance. The carrying value is computed as follows:

Notes Payable	$10,000
Discount on Notes Payable	(900)
Carrying Value of Liability	$ 9,100

Event 2 Recognition of Operating Expenses

Beacon incurred $8,000 of cash operating expenses.

The payment for these expenses reduces assets and equity. The effect of the event on the income statement is to increase expenses and decrease net income. The cash outflow is shown in the operating activities section of the cash flow statement. These effects are shown here:

Event No.	Assets	=	Liab.	+	Equity	Rev.	−	Exp.	=	Net Inc.	Cash Flow Statement	
2	(8,000)	=	NA	+	(8,000)	NA	−	8,000	=	(8,000)	(8,000)	OA

Beacon recognized $12,000 of cash revenue.

Event 3
Recognition of Revenue

The recognition of the revenue increases assets and equity. The amount of net income increases. The cash inflow is shown in the operating activities section of the cash flow statement. These effects follow:

Event No.	Assets	=	Liab.	+	Equity	Rev.	−	Exp.	=	Net Inc.	Cash Flow Statement	
3	12,000	=	NA	+	12,000	12,000	−	NA	=	12,000	12,000	OA

Beacon recognized accrued interest expense.

Event 4
Adjustment for Accrued Interest

On December 31, 2005, Beacon must adjust the accounting records to reflect the accrual of 10 months of interest for the 2005 accounting period. Interest expense accrues at the rate of $75 per month ($900 ÷ discount = 12). Therefore, $750 ($75 × 10) of interest is accrued as of December 31. The reduction in equity caused by recognition of interest expense is balanced by an increase in liabilities. The increase in liabilities occurs by reducing the contra liability account, *Discount on Notes Payable.* Recall that the carrying value of the liability was $9,100 ($10,000 face value less $900 discount) on the day the note was issued. The entry to record the accrued interest expense removes $750 from the discount account, leaving a $150 balance ($900 − $750) after the adjusting entry is posted. The practice of converting the discount to interest expense over a designated period is referred to as the **amortization** of the discount. After 10 months of amortization, the carrying value of the liability shown on the December 31, 2005, balance sheet in Exhibit 7–8 is $9,850 ($10,000 face value − the $150 discount). The effect of recognizing the interest on the income statement is to increase expenses and decrease net income by $750. The cash flow statement is not affected by the accrual. Cash is paid for the interest at the maturity date. The effects of the adjusting entry for accrued interest expense are shown here:

Event No.	Assets	=	Liab.	+	Equity	Rev.	−	Exp.	=	Net Inc.	Cash Flow Statement
4	NA	=	750	+	(750)	NA	−	750	=	(750)	NA

General Journal Entries, Ledger T-Accounts, and Financial Statements

Exhibit 7–7 shows the journal entries and ledger T-accounts for the business events experienced by Beacon Management Services. The exhibit includes the entry used to close the revenue and expense accounts at the end of the 2005 accounting period. The ledger account balances are used to prepare the financial statements shown in Exhibit 7–8. The relevant accounting events are summarized here for your convenience:

1. Issued a $10,000 face value discount note with a 9 percent discount rate.
2. Paid $8,000 cash for operating expenses.
3. Earned $12,000 cash revenue.
4. Recognized $750 of accrued interest expense.
5. Closed the revenue and expense accounts. The letters *cl* are used as a posting reference for the closing entries.

Exhibit 7–7 *General Journal Entries and General Ledger*

Event No.	Account Title	Debit	Credit
1	Cash	9,100	
	Discount on Note Payable	900	
	Note Payable		10,000
2	Operating Expense	8,000	
	Cash		8,000
3	Cash	12,000	
	Service Revenue		12,000
4	Interest Expense	750	
	Discount on Note Payable		750
cl	Service Revenue	12,000	
	Operating Expense		8,000
	Interest Expense		750
	Retained Earnings		3,250

Assets = Liabilities + Equity

Cash

	Debit	Credit	
(1)	9,100	8,000	(2)
(3)	12,000		
Bal.	13,100		

Notes Payable

	Debit	Credit	
		10,000	(1)

Discount on Notes Payable

	Debit	Credit	
(1)	900	750	(4)
Bal.	150		

Retained Earnings

	Debit	Credit	
		3,250	(cl)
		3,250	Bal.

Service Revenue

	Debit	Credit	
(cl)	12,000	12,000	(3)
		0	Bal.

Operating Expenses

	Debit	Credit	
(2)	8,000	8,000	(cl)
Bal.	0		

Interest Expense

	Debit	Credit	
(4)	750	750	(cl)
Bal.	0		

Exhibit 7–8 *Financial Statements for 2005*

Income Statement

Service Revenue	$12,000
Operating Exp.	(8,000)
Operating Income	4,000
Interest Exp.	(750)
Net Income	$ 3,250

Balance Sheet

Assets		
Cash		$13,100
Liabilities		
Notes Payable	$10,000	
Less: Disc. on Notes Pay.	(150)	
Total Liabilities		$ 9,850
Shareholders' Equity		
Retained Earnings		3,250
Total Liab. and Shareholders' Equity		$13,100

Cash Flow Statement

Operating Activities	
Inflow from Customers	$12,000
Outflow for Expenses	(8,000)
Net Inflow from Oper.	4,000
Investing Activities	0
Financing Activities	
Inflow from Creditors	9,100
Net Change in Cash	13,100
Plus: Beginning Cash Balance	0
Ending Cash Balance	$13,100

Accounting Events Affecting the 2006 Period

This section introduces four accounting events that apply to Beacon's 2006 accounting cycle.

Beacon recognized 2 months of accrued interest.

Event 1
Accrual of Interest for 2006

Since the note carried a one-year term, two months of interest must be accrued at the maturity date on February 28, 2006. Since interest expense accrues at the rate of $75 per month ($900 discount ÷ 12 = 75), there is $150 ($75 × 2) of interest expense accrued in 2006. The recognition of the interest increases liabilities (reduces the discount account to zero) and decreases equity. Recognition on the income statement increases expenses and decreases net income by $150. The cash flow statement is not affected by the transaction. These effects are shown here:

LO6
Show how discount notes and related interest charges affect financial statements.

Event No.	Assets	=	Liab.	+	Equity	Rev.	−	Exp.	=	Net Inc.	Cash Flow Statement
1	NA	=	150	+	(150)	NA	−	150	=	(150)	NA

Beacon repaid face value on the discount note payable.

Event 2
Payment of Face Value

The face value ($10,000) of the note is due on the maturity date. The repayment of the note is an asset use transaction causing assets and liabilities to decrease. The income statement is not affected by the event. The $10,000 cash payment includes $900 for interest and $9,100 for principal. There is a $900 outflow shown in the operating activities section and a $9,100 outflow shown in the financing activities section of the cash flow statement. These effects are shown here:

Event No.	Assets	=	Liab.	+	Equity	Rev.	−	Exp.	=	Net Inc.	Cash Flow Statement	
2	(10,000)	=	(10,000)	+	NA	NA	−	NA	=	NA	(900)	OA
											(9,100)	FA

Beacon recognized $13,000 of cash revenue.

Event 3
Revenue Recognition

Assets and equity increase as a result of the recognition. Net income also increases. The cash inflow is shown in the operating activities section of the cash flow statement. These effects are shown here:

Event No.	Assets	=	Liab.	+	Equity	Rev.	−	Exp.	=	Net Inc.	Cash Flow Statement	
3	13,000	=	NA	+	13,000	13,000	−	NA	=	13,000	13,000	OA

Beacon incurred $8,500 of cash operating expenses.

Event 4
Recognition of Operating Expenses

This event causes assets and equity to decrease. Also, net income decreases. The cash outflow is shown in the operating activities section of the cash flow statement. These effects follow:

Event No.	Assets	=	Liab.	+	Equity	Rev.	−	Exp.	=	Net Inc.	Cash Flow Statement	
4	(8,500)	=	NA	+	(8,500)	NA	−	8,500	=	(8,500)	8,500	OA

General Journal Entries, Ledger T-Accounts, and Financial Statements

Exhibits 7–9 and 7–10 present the journal entries, relevant ledger T-accounts, and financial statements, respectively. Notice in Exhibit 7–10 that the balance in liabilities is zero because both interest and principal have been paid, leaving Beacon with no obligations as of the 2006 fiscal closing date. Retained earnings includes the total of net income for 2005 and 2006. This result occurs because all income was retained in the business since no dividends were paid to shareholders in 2005 and 2006. The relevant accounting events are summarized here for your convenience:

1. Recognized $150 of accrued interest expense.
2. Repaid the note payable plus accrued interest.
3. Earned $13,000 cash revenue.
4. Paid $8,500 of cash operating expenses.

Exhibit 7–9 *General Journal Entries and General Ledger*

Event No.	Account Title	Debit	Credit
1	Interest Expense	150	
	Discount on Notes Payable		150
2	Notes Payable	10,000	
	Cash		10,000
3	Cash	13,000	
	Service Revenue		13,000
4	Operating Expense	8,500	
	Cash		8,500
cl	Service Revenue	13,000	
	Operating Expense		8,500
	Interest Expense		150
	Retained Earnings		4,350

Assets = Liabilities + Equity

Cash

	Debit	Credit	
Bal.	13,100	10,000	(2)
(3)	13,000	8,500	(4)
Bal.	7,600		

Notes Payable

	Debit	Credit	
(2)	10,000	10,000	Bal.
0	Bal.		

Discount on Notes Payable

	Debit	Credit	
Bal.	150	150	(1)
Bal.	0		

Retained Earnings

	Debit	Credit	
		3,250	Bal.
		4,350	(cl)
		7,600	Bal.

Service Revenue

	Debit	Credit	
(cl)	13,000	13,000	(3)
0	Bal.		

Operating Expense

	Debit	Credit	
(4)	8,500	8,500	(cl)
Bal.	0		

Interest Expense

	Debit	Credit	
(1)	150	150	(cl)
Bal.	0		

Exhibit 7-10 *Financial Statements for 2006*

Income Statement	
Service Revenue	$13,000
Operating Expenses	(8,500)
Operating Income	4,500
Interest Exp.	(150)
Net Income	$ 4,350

Balance Sheet	
Assets	
Cash	$7,600
Liabilities	$ 0
Shareholders' Equity	
Retained Earnings	7,600
Total Liab. & Shareholders' Equity	$7,600

Cash Flow Statement	
Operating Activities	
Inflow from Customers	$13,000
Outflow for Expenses	(8,500)
Outflow for Interest	(900)
Net Inflow from Oper.	3,600
Investing Activities	0
Financing Activities	
Outflow to Creditors	(9,100)
Net Change in Cash	(5,500)
Plus: Beginning Cash Balance	13,100
Ending Cash Balance	$ 7,600

Payroll Accounting

LO7 Show how payroll accounting affects financial statements.

Basic payroll accounting is an important part of any introductory accounting course. Nearly every student will be receiving a paycheque from an employer at some point in their working years. As well, payroll costs are a huge investment in many corporations.

Payroll is often broken into categories based on how an employee's pay is calculated. When the employee is hired on a **salary** basis, an annualized lump sum amount is negotiated (e.g., $52,000 per year). When an employee is hired on a **wage** basis, a constant unit price is determined (e.g., $10 per hour). Wages are often paid on a per diem basis using hours worked or units produced as the factor.

Gross Pay

Gross pay is calculated as the amount an employee earns before any deductions. For example, assume that Debbie worked 45 hours this week. Her normal wage is $10 per hour, but she receives time-and-a-half for hours worked in excess of 40 hours. The following calculations are required to compute gross pay for the week:

Regular hours	40 hours @ $10 per hour =	$400
Overtime hours	5 hours @ $15 per hour =	75
Gross pay		$475

Statutory Deductions

When Debbie receives her first paycheque, she is surprised to see the cheque has been made out for substantially less than the $475 she expected to collect. Where did all the money go? Unfortunately for Debbie, an employer must withhold certain amounts from an employee's cheque. These **statutory deductions** are set by the federal and provincial governments to help ensure that government-sponsored programs continue to exist. There are three main statutory deductions that must be understood regarding payroll: Canada Pension Plan, Employment Insurance, and income tax. The amounts to be contributed by an employee are based on specific regulations set by the government. To determine the required contributions, employers can use payroll tables supplied by the government, software programs that automatically perform the calculations, or payroll services from a bank or other financial institution. All numbers provided in the sections below are based on the 2001 payroll deduction requirements.

Canada Pension Plan (CPP)

Almost all employees must contribute to the **Canada Pension Plan (CPP)** during their working years. The federal government adjusts the amount of contributions required by employees annually to maximize the funds available after retirement. CPP is deducted from an employee up to a maximum of \$38,300 per year. Contributors who earn more than the \$38,300 ceiling on pensionable earnings (in the year 2001) are not required or allowed to contribute more to the CPP. As well, the basic exemption is \$3,500. This means that for employees who earn less than \$3,500, no CPP contributions are required. For weekly payroll, this means that an exemption of \$67.31 (\$3,500 divided by 52 weeks) would be allowed. The employee's gross earnings less the exemption are then multiplied by 4.3 percent to determine the required contribution. For 2001, the maximum employee contribution to the plan would be \$1,496.40 [(\$38,300 − \$3,500) × 4.3 percent]. Debbie's CPP contribution is calculated as:

$$(\$475 - \$67.31) \times 4.3\% = \$17.53$$

Employment Insurance (EI)

Employment Insurance (EI) was created to fund employees through difficult times when they became unemployed. Most employees have to contribute to the EI fund. The calculation multiplies an employee's earnings up to a stated maximum of \$39,000 by a given percentage (2.25 percent in 2001). The maximum EI contribution for employees for the year 2001 is \$878 (\$39,000 × 2.25 percent). Debbie's EI contribution is calculated as:

$$\$475 \times 2.25\% = \$10.69$$

Income Tax

The government originally set up the Income Tax Act as a mechanism to help fund the war effort. Later, they found that the money collected was hard to give up, with the result that what was supposed to be a temporary measure continues to exist. An employee's paycheque includes deductions for both federal and provincial taxes. The system is set up on a graduated rate system and varies by province. The calculation of the taxes owing is simplified by the use of tax tables provided by the government. Let's assume Debbie's tax rate is 20 percent. Her income tax deduction is then calculated as:

$$\$475 \times 20\% = \$95$$

Voluntary Deductions

The statutory deductions discussed above are required by government regulations. However, employees are also allowed to make what are referred to as **voluntary deductions**. Voluntary deductions include donations made to charities, registered retirement savings plan (RRSP) contributions, union dues payments, and medical plan payments. The employer then passes these contributions on to the appropriate recipient (the charity, RRSP provider, union, etc.). Debbie supports her union with a weekly payment of \$10. She also gives \$5 per pay to the United Way.

Net Pay

The amount received by Debbie on her paycheque is referred to as her **net pay**. It is calculated as her gross pay less statutory deductions less voluntary deductions. Debbie's net pay was calculated as follows:

Gross pay	$475.00
CPP	17.53
EI	10.69
Income tax	95.00
Union dues	10.00
United Way donation	5.00
Net pay	$336.78

Record the net pay for our employee, Debbie. **Event 1**

The recording of Debbie's net pay for the period increases liabilities and reduces equity. On the income statement, the event increases expenses and decreases net income. The cash flow is not affected because the amount has not yet been paid to Debbie. The effect of this transaction on the horizontal statement model follows:

Event No.	Assets	=	Liab.	+	Equity	Rev.	−	Exp.	=	Net Inc.	Cash Flow Statement
1	NA	=	475	+	(475)	NA	−	475	=	(475)	NA

The only item that affects the income statement is the gross pay, as this would increase Wages Expense. The remaining items are all liabilities because the amounts are owed to (1) the government, (2) various organizations, and (3) the employee.

Employer Costs

As noted earlier, employers spend a lot of time and money satisfying the requirements of payroll accounting. As well, employers face other costs associated with payroll. When payrolls are large, the additional costs associated with employer benefits can be quite onerous.

Canada Pension Plan

With respect to CPP, employers are required to make a contribution equal to the employees' contributions. This means that for every dollar collected from an employee, the government also collects a dollar from the employer.

Employment Insurance

A similar requirement exists with the EI contribution. Here, however, the employer must contribute 140 percent of the employee's contributions. This means that for every dollar collected from an employee for EI, the employer must contribute a further $1.40.

Compute and record the employer costs associated with Debbie's pay. **Event 2**

For Debbie's pay, the employer costs would be calculated as follows:

CPP	= $17.53 × 1	=	$17.53
EI	= $10.69 × 1.4	=	14.96
Total		=	$32.49

These amounts affect the income statement as part of the employer's expense, as well as the balance sheet from the creation of a liability to the government offset by a reduction in equity. Cash flow is not affected until the amount is paid to the government. The effect of this transaction on the horizontal statement model follows:

Event No.	Assets	=	Liab.	+	Equity	Rev.	−	Exp.	=	Net Inc.	Cash Flow Statement
2	NA	=	32.49	+	(32.49)	NA	−	32.49	=	(32.49)	NA

The final stage of payroll accounting requires the payment of the liabilities created. These entries reduce assets and liabilities. They don't affect the income statement. The cash outflow is shown in the operating activities section of the cash flow statement. The events related to this are recorded in the statements model below:

Event No.	Assets	=	Liab.	+	Equity	Rev.	−	Exp.	=	Net Inc.	Cash Flow Statement	
3	(336.78)	=	(336.78)	+	NA	NA	−	NA	=	NA	(336.78)	OA
4	(155.71)	=	(155.71)	+	NA	NA	−	NA	=	NA	(155.71)	OA
5	(15.00)	=	(15.00)	+	NA	NA	−	NA	=	NA	(15.00)	OA

General Journal Entries and Ledger T-Accounts

Exhibit 7–11 presents the journal entries and ledger T-accounts for the business events related to payroll. The relevant accounting events are summarized below for your convenience:

Transactions for Payroll

1. Record the employee's payroll costs.
2. Record the employer's payroll costs.
3. Pay the employee.
4. Pay the CPP, EI, and income tax to the government.
5. Pay other amounts withheld to appropriate entities.

Real-World Credit Costs

Costs of Managing Accounts Receivable

LO8 Explain the cost of financing credit sales.

Why do companies sell goods on credit or *on account*? Why not simply require all customers to pay cash for the goods and services they receive? There are two good reasons why a business might allow customers to buy now and pay later. First, as explained earlier, people buy more goods if credit sales are available. Second, if a business sells goods to other companies, the selling company may have to give the buying company time to generate the cash needed to pay for the goods purchased.

To illustrate, assume that Mattel sells toys to Toys R Us. If the goods are delivered (sold) to Toys R Us on September 1, they may not be resold to retail customers until October or November. If Mattel gives Toys R Us 60 days to pay for the goods, Toys R Us can use the money it receives from selling the

Exhibit 7–11 *General Journal Entries and General Ledger*

Event No.	Account Title	Debit	Credit
1	Wages Expense	475.00	
	CPP Payable		17.53
	EI Payable		10.69
	Income Taxes Payable		95.00
	Union Dues Payable		10.00
	United Way Payable		5.00
	Wages Payable		336.78
2	CPP Expense	17.53	
	EI Expense	14.96	
	CPP Payable		17.53
	EI Payable		14.96
3	Wages Payable	336.78	
	Cash		336.78
4	CPP Payable ($17.53 + 17.53)	35.06	
	EI Payable ($10.69 + 14.96)	25.65	
	Income Taxes Payable	95.00	
	Cash		155.71
5	Union Dues Payable	10.00	
	United Way Payable	5.00	
	Cash		15.00

Assets = Liabilities + Equity

Cash

	Debit	Credit	
(Bal.)	5,000	336.78	(3)
		155.71	(4)
		15.00	(5)

Wages Payable

	Debit	Credit	
(3)	336.78	336.78	(1)

CPP Payable

	Debit	Credit	
		17.53	(1)
(4)	35.06	17.53	(2)

EI Payable

	Debit	Credit	
		10.69	(1)
(4)	25.65	14.96	(2)

Income Tax Payable

	Debit	Credit	
(4)	95.00	95.00	(1)

Union Dues Payable

	Debit	Credit	
(5)	10.00	10.00	(1)

United Way Payable

	Debit	Credit	
(5)	5.00	5.00	(1)

Common Shares

	Debit	Credit	
		5,000	(Bal.)

Wages Expense

	Debit	Credit
(1)	475.00	

CPP Expense

	Debit	Credit
(2)	17.53	

EI Expense

	Debit	Credit
(2)	14.96	

goods to its customers to pay Mattel. For many small companies that do not have the cash to pay up front, buying on credit is the only way to obtain necessary inventory. If a manufacturer or wholesaler wants to sell to these customers, it has to offer *sales on account*.

Costs of Making Credit Sales

The policy of allowing customers to buy goods on account may generate more sales, and more gross profit, but it is not without additional costs. One such cost is obvious. Some customers may never pay their bills. Bad debts constitute a major cost of extending credit. Other costs are more subtle. As mentioned earlier, there is the cost of keeping the records related to accounts receivable. These costs can be significant. Large companies have entire departments devoted to managing their accounts receivable. For these companies, it may cost literally millions of dollars to buy the equipment and pay the staff necessary to operate their accounts receivable departments. Finally, there is an implicit interest charge associated with the extension of credit. When a customer is allowed to delay payment, the creditor loses the opportunity to use the amount due. Indeed, many real-world companies sell their receivables for less than the full amount due in order to obtain cash. The difference between the face value of the receivables and the amount of cash collected from the sale of the receivables is equivalent to the discount interest.

Average Number of Days to Collect Accounts Receivable

The longer it takes a company to collect accounts receivable, the higher the cost to the company. As explained earlier, when a company extends credit, it loses the opportunity to invest funds elsewhere, and the longer the funds are not available, the greater the lost income. Also, the older an account receivable becomes, the less likely it is to be collected. Finally, taking longer to collect an account typically means that more money is spent on salaries, equipment, and supplies used in trying to collect it. Therefore, businesses are very interested in knowing the time it takes to collect their receivables. They want to know if they are taking more or less time to collect receivables than they took in past periods, and how their collection period compares to the collection periods of their competitors. Ratio analysis can help managers convert absolute dollar values to common units of measure that enable them to make such comparisons.

Two ratios are available to help a company's management, or other users, express the collection period in common measurement units. The first is the **accounts receivable turnover ratio**. It is defined as[3]

$$\frac{\text{Net sales}}{\text{Accounts receivable}}$$

Dividing a company's sales by its accounts receivable tells how many times the accounts receivable balance is "turned over" (turned into cash) each year. The more rapid the turnover, the shorter the collection period. The problem with this ratio is that it is difficult to interpret because it does not provide a measure in units of time. Therefore, the accounts receivable turnover ratio is often taken one step further to determine the **average number of days to collect accounts receivable**, sometimes called the *average collection period.* This is computed as

$$\frac{\text{365 days}}{\text{Accounts receivable turnover ratio}}$$

This ratio tells the user how many days, on average, it takes a company to collect its accounts receivable. Since longer collection periods equate to higher costs, shorter periods are obviously more desirable. To illustrate the computation of the *average number of days to collect accounts receivable* ratio for Allen's Tutoring Services, refer to the 2006 financial statements in Exhibit 7–4 (page 286). On average, the company takes 104 days to collect its receivables. This collection period can be computed in two steps:

1. Accounts receivable turnover is 3.509 times ($10,000 ÷ $2,850).
2. Average number of days to collect receivables is 104 days (365 ÷ 3.509).

In the preceding computations, the net realizable value of accounts receivable is used because that is the amount typically shown in published financial statements. The results would not have been materially different had total accounts receivable been used.

[3] To be more correct, technically, the ratio should be computed using only credit sales and average accounts receivable. Often, however, credit sales alone are not given in published financial statements. Average accounts receivable, if desired, is easily computed as ([beginning receivables + ending receivables] ÷ 2). For the purposes of this course, use the simpler ratio defined here (sales ÷ accounts receivable).

Real-World Data

What is the collection period for real-world companies? The answer depends on the industry in which the company operates. Exhibit 7–12 shows the average number of days to collect receivables for seven companies in three different industries.

Exhibit 7–12

Industry	Company	Average Number of Days to Collect Receivables
Fast Food	McDonald's	13
	Wendy's	11
	Starbucks	9
Retail	Wal-Mart	4
	Mark's Work Wearhouse	17
Alcohol	Seagram	63
	Molson	13

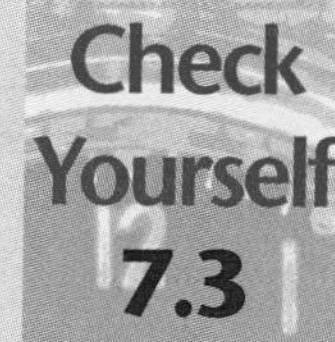

Randolph Corporation had sales for the year of $535,333 and an Accounts Receivable balance at year end of $22,000. Determine Randolph's average number of days to collect accounts receivable.

Answer The accounts receivable turnover is 24.33 times ($535,333 ÷ $22,000) per year. The average number of days to collect accounts receivable is 15 days (365 ÷ 24.33).

Note that there is significant variation in the collection periods among different industries. Also note that the fast-food companies do have accounts receivable, which may seem odd to some readers because these restaurants require customers to pay cash when purchasing hamburgers or coffee. The accounts receivable for McDonalds's, Wendy's, and Starbucks exist because these companies sell goods to restaurants that are independent franchisees, so the money is owed by individual restaurants, not by the individual who purchases a Happy Meal.

Is the collection period for Seagram too long? The answer depends on its credit policies. If Seagram is selling goods to customers for net 30-day terms, there may be reason for concern, but if it allows customers 60 days to pay and the cost of this policy has been built into the pricing structure, there is less need for concern.

In Chapter 6, the operating cycle was defined as the average time it takes a company to go from cash to inventory to accounts receivable and back to cash. The *average number of days to collect accounts receivable* is a measure of the time necessary to complete part of this cycle. A method for computing the remainder of the cycle is explained in Chapter 8.

a look back

Accounting for receivables and payables was introduced first in Chapter 2. This chapter presented several more challenging issues related to short-term receivables and payables. More specifically, the chapter discussed the *allowance method of accounting for bad debts*. The allowance method seeks to match expenses with revenues. The *percent of sales* method of estimating bad debts expense was also discussed in this chapter. Under this method bad debts expense is estimated to be a certain percentage of credit sales. For example, if credit sales amounted to $500,000 and bad debts were estimated to be 1 percent of credit sales, then bad debts expenses would be $5,000 ($500,000 × .01). Recall that this is an estimated amount of the actual expense that will be incurred in the future. The estimated amount of bad debts expense is recognized in the current period (the same period in which the associated revenue is recognized), thereby meeting the matching objective. Bad debts expense decreases equity, net income, and the net realizable value of receivables (Accounts Receivable − Allowance for Doubtful Accounts).

The allowance method of accounting for bad debts is compared to the *direct write-off method*, which recognizes bad debts expense when an account is determined to be uncollectible. The method is conceptually invalid because it overstates the value of accounts receivable shown on the balance sheet and it fails to properly match revenue and expense. However, the method is simple to apply. It is used when the amount of bad debts is considered to be insignificant. When the amount of bad debts is immaterial, the benefits derived from recording convenience are considered more important than conceptual accuracy.

This chapter also discussed accounting for *warranty obligations*. The amount of warranty expense is recognized in the period in which the sale is made or service provided. The associated warranty obligation is shown as a liability on the balance sheet until the future period in which the obligation is settled.

The chapter also introduced a new method of measuring interest. *Discount notes* include the interest at their face value. The borrower is given an amount of cash that is less than the face value of the note. For example, a borrower signing a $5,000, 8 percent note would receive $4,600 ($5,000 − [$5,000 × 0.08]). The $400 difference between the amount borrowed ($4,600) and the amount repaid ($5,000) is interest.

Payroll accounting is not just paying employee wages or salaries. Therefore, we included a brief introduction to payroll in this chapter. It looked at gross pay and net pay calculations, and provided the required journal entries.

Finally, the chapter discussed the costs of making credit sales. Along with bad debts, interest is a major cost of financing receivables. Determining the length of the collection period provides a measure of the quality of receivables. Short collection periods usually indicate low amounts of uncollectible accounts and interest cost. Long collection periods imply higher costs. The collection period can be measured in two steps. First, determine the *accounts receivable turnover ratio* by dividing sales by the accounts receivable balance. Next, determine the *average number of days to collect accounts receivable* by dividing the number of days in the year (365) by the accounts receivable turnover ratio.

a look forward

It is especially important that you understand how to account for discount notes. Chapter 10 presents topics related to long-term debt that are very similar to accounting issues related to discount notes. It is essential for you to understand how to account for discount notes if you are to understand the topics covered in Chapter 10.

This chapter also discussed the costs associated with collecting accounts receivable. Specifically, the longer it takes to collect receivables, the higher the cost of financing those receivables. Chapter 8 presents several topics associated with accounting for inventory. One of these topics concerns the costs associated with holding inventory, which are similar to the financing costs associated with the collection of receivables.

APPENDIX

LO9 Show the effects of sales taxes on financial statements.

Sales Taxes[4]

Sales taxes affect almost every accounting transaction in Canada. Sales taxes take many forms, including provincial sales tax (PST), the goods and services tax (GST), and the harmonized sales tax (HST).

Provincial Sales Tax (PST)

Most provinces (except Alberta and the three territories) charge a retail sales tax. This tax is generally charged to all end users of products. Companies that purchase goods with the intent of reselling the goods are therefore exempt from the sales tax. The provincial sales tax rates vary by province. The treatment of the provincial sales tax varies

[4] Sales taxes are a very specialized area of accounting. This introductory textbook summarizes the rules for only the simplest of applications. As well, only the goods and services tax's effects will be demonstrated.

depending on whether goods are being purchased or sold. The provincial sales tax paid on purchases increases the cost of the goods purchased. The provincial sales tax collected from sales is remitted on a monthly basis to the provincial government.

Goods and Services Tax (GST)

In the early 1990s, the federal government created the goods and services tax. This 7 percent tax is applied to most goods and services provided in Canada. The GST collected from sales represents a liability for the company, as the amount collected is owed to the federal government. However, the GST paid on purchases can be used to offset (reduce) the balance that would otherwise be paid. The net amount due is, therefore, based on the additional value attached to the goods sold or services provided to customers. This is why the GST is often referred to as a **value added tax**.

Event 1 Purchase of Goods

Stone Company purchased goods with a cost of $600 on account. The goods are subject to a 7 percent GST.

The GST paid on the purchase is $600 × 7 percent = $42. Therefore, the total cost of the goods purchased will be $600 + 42 = $642. The GST paid of $42 is recorded in an account called GST Recoverable. As previously indicated, this account is used to offset the GST collected from sales and is a contra liability account. On the balance sheet, the asset (Inventory) account will be increased by $600, and the net liabilities will be increased by $600. This is because the increase in the liability (Accounts Payable) account of $642 is offset by the decrease created by the contra liability (GST Recoverable) of $42. The income statement is not affected until the goods are sold. The cash flow statement is not affected until the goods are paid for.

Event 2a Sale of Goods

Stone will resell these goods for $1,000 cash. GST of 7 percent will be charged on the sale.

The GST collected from the sale is $70 ($1,000 × 7 percent) and the total owed by the customer is $1,070 ($1,000 + $70). The total of $1,070 will increase assets (Cash). The $70 of GST will be set up in a liability account and is owed to the federal government. The remaining amount will increase equity (Retained Earnings). The income statement will show an increase in revenues and net income. Cash flow is not affected until the customer pays the account.

Event 2b Record Cost of Goods Sold

Recording the cost of goods sold causes a decrease in assets (Inventory) and equity (Retained Earnings). The Cost of Goods Sold increases the income statement expenses and causes income to decrease. The cash flow statement is not affected.

The three events are shown in the following horizontal financial statements model:

Event No.	Assets	=	Liab.	+	Equity	Rev.	−	Exp.	=	Net Inc.	Cash Flow Statement
1	600	=	600*	+	NA	NA	−	NA	=	NA	NA
2a	1,070	=	70	+	1,000	1,000	−	NA	=	1,000	NA
2b	(600)	=	NA	+	(600)	NA	−	600	=	(600)	NA

* Recall that this amount includes the original accounts payable of $642 less GST Recoverable of $42.

The net change in income is $400 ($1,000 − $600) and the net balance of GST owed to the government is $28 ($70 − $42). So we can see the GST is a value added tax because only the net increase in value of $400 is taxed at 7 percent.

Harmonized Sales Tax (HST)

In some areas of the country, especially in eastern Canada, the federal and provincial sales taxes are combined into one tax called the harmonized sales tax (HST). The HST rate is generally 15 percent.

SELF-STUDY REVIEW PROBLEM

During 2007 Calico Company experienced the following accounting events:

1. Provided $120,000 of services on account.
2. Collected $85,000 cash from accounts receivable.
3. Issued a $12,000 face value discount note with a 10 percent discount rate and a one-year term to maturity.
4. Wrote off $1,800 of accounts receivable that were uncollectible.
5. Paid $90,500 cash for operating expenses.
6. Estimated that bad debts expense would be 2 percent of credit sales. Recorded the adjusting entry.
7. Recorded seven months of accrued interest on the discount note.
8. Estimated warranty expense would be $900. Recorded the adjusting entry.

The following ledger accounts present the balances in Calico Company's records on January 1, 2007:

	Assets					=	Liabilities					+	Equity		
Event No.	Cash	+	Accts. Rec.	−	Allow.	=	Note Pay.	+	Disc. on Note Pay	+	War. Pay	+	Com. Shares	+	Ret. Earn.
1	2,000	+	18,000	−	2,200	=		+		+		+	10,000	+	7,800

Required

a. Record the 2007 accounting events in the ledger accounts.
b. Determine net income for 2007.
c. Determine net cash flow from operating activities for 2007.
d. Determine the net realizable value of accounts receivable at December 31, 2007.

Solution to Requirement a.

	Assets					=	Liabilities					+	Equity		
Event No.	Cash	+	Accts. Rec.	−	Allow.	=	Note Pay.	+	Disc. on Note Pay	+	War. Pay	+	Com. Shares	+	Ret. Earn.
Bal.	2,000	+	18,000	−	2,200	=		+		+		+	10,000	+	7,800
1		+	120,000	−		=		+		+		+		+	120,000
2	85,000	+	(85,000)	−		=		+		+		+		+	
3	10,800	+		−		=	12,000	+	1,200	+		+		+	
4		+	(1,800)	−	(1,800)	=		+		+		+		+	
5	(90,500)	+		−		=		+		+		+		+	(90,500)
6		+		−	2,400	=		+		+		+		+	(2,400)
7		+		−		=		+	(700)	+		+		+	(700)
8		+		−		=		+		+	900	+		+	(900)
Totals	7,300	+	51,200	−	2,800	=	12,000	+	500	+	900	+	10,000	+	33,300

Solution to Requirements b–d.

b. Net income is $25,500 ($120,000 − $90,500 − $2,400 − $700 − $900).
c. Net cash flow from operating activities is an outflow of $5,500 ($85,000 − $90,500).
d. The net realizable value of accounts receivable is $48,400 ($51,200 − $2,800).

KEY TERMS

account receivable *277*
accounts receivable turnover ratio *302*
allowance for doubtful accounts *279*
allowance method of accounting for bad debts *278*
amortization *293*
average number of days to collect accounts receivable *302*
bad debts expense *279*
Canada Pension Plan (CPP) *298*
contra liability account *292*
direct write-off method *287*
discount *292*
discount notes *292*
discount on notes payable *292*
Employment Insurance (EI) *298*
going concern assumption *278*
gross pay *297*
interest-bearing notes *292*
issuer of the note *292*
materiality *287*
net pay *298*
net realizable value *278*
notes receivable *277*
payables *278*
principal *292*
salary *297*
statutory deductions *297*
value added tax *305*
voluntary deductions *298*
wage *297*
warranty *289*

QUESTIONS

1. What is the difference between accounts receivable and notes receivable?
2. What is the *net realizable value* of receivables?
3. Explain the *going concern* assumption. How does it affect the way accounts receivable versus accounts payable are reported in financial statements?
4. What is the difference between the allowance method and the direct write-off method of accounting for bad debts?
5. What is the most common format for reporting accounts receivable on the balance sheet? What information does this method provide beyond showing only the net amount?
6. What are two ways in which estimating bad debts improves the usefulness of the financial statements?
7. Why is it necessary to make an entry to reinstate a previously written-off account receivable before the collection is recorded?
8. What are some factors considered in estimating the amount of uncollectible accounts receivable?
9. What is the effect on the accounting equation of recognizing bad debts expense?
10. What is the effect on the accounting equation of writing off an uncollectible account receivable when the allowance method is used? When the direct write-off method is used?
11. How does the recovery of a bad debt affect the income statement when the allowance method is used? How does the recovery of a bad debt affect the cash flow statement when the allowance method is used?
12. What is the advantage of using the allowance method of accounting for bad debts? What is the advantage of using the direct write-off method?
13. When is it acceptable to use the direct write-off method of accounting for bad debts?
14. Why is it generally beneficial for a business to accept credit cards as payment for goods and services even when the fee charged by the credit card company is substantial?
15. What types of costs do businesses avoid when they accept major credit cards as compared with handling credit sales themselves?
16. What does the term *warranty* mean?
17. What effect does recognizing warranty expense have on the balance sheet? On the income statement?
18. When is warranty cost reported on the cash flow statement?
19. What is the difference between an interest-bearing note and a discount note?
20. How is the carrying value of a discount note computed?
21. Will the effective rate of interest be the same on a $10,000 face value, 12 percent interest-bearing note and a $10,000 face value, 12 percent discount note? Is the amount of cash received upon making these two loans the same? Why or why not?
22. How does the *amortization* of a discount affect the income statement, balance sheet, and cash flow statement?
23. What is the effect on the accounting equation of borrowing $8,000 by issuing a discount note that has a 10 percent discount rate and a one-year term to maturity? What is the effect on the accounting equation of the periodic amortization of the discount? What is the effect on the accounting equation of the payment of the face value of the note at maturity?
24. What type of account is *Discount on Notes Payable*?
25. Explain the difference between gross pay and net pay.
26. How is the employer's contribution for CPP and EI determined?
27. What payroll amounts appear as expenses on the income statement?
28. How is the accounts receivable turnover ratio computed? What information does the ratio provide?
29. How is the average number of days to collect accounts receivable computed? What information does the ratio provide?

EXERCISES

L.O. 2 EXERCISE 7–1 *Effect of Recognizing Bad Debts Expense on Financial Statements: Allowance Method*

Stateline Auto Service was started on January 1, 2004. The company experienced the following events during its first year of operation:

Events Affecting 2004

1. Provided $20,000 of repair services on account.
2. Collected $18,000 cash from accounts receivable.
3. Adjusted the accounting records to reflect the estimate that bad debt expense would be 1 percent of the service revenue on account.

Events Affecting 2005

1. Wrote off a $160 account receivable that was determined to be uncollectible.
2. Provided $22,000 of repair services on account.
3. Collected $19,000 cash from accounts receivable.
4. Adjusted the accounting records to reflect the estimate that bad debt expense would be 1 percent of the service revenue on account.

Required

a. Write an accounting equation and record the events for 2004 in T-accounts under the appropriate categories.
b. Determine the following amounts:
   (1) Net income for 2004.
   (2) Net cash flow from operating activities for 2004.
   (3) Balance of accounts receivable at the end of 2004.
   (4) Net realizable value of accounts receivable at the end of 2004.
c. Repeat the requirements in Requirements *a* and *b* for the 2005 accounting period.

L.O. 2 EXERCISE 7–2 *Analyzing Financial Statement Effects of Accounting for Bad Debts Using the Allowance Method*

Businesses using the allowance method to account for bad debts expense routinely experience four accounting events:

1. Recognition of revenue on account.
2. Collection of cash from accounts receivable.
3. Recognition of bad debts expense through a year-end adjusting entry.
4. Write-off of uncollectible accounts.

Required

Show the effect of each event on the elements of the financial statements, using a horizontal statements model like the one shown here. Use + for increase, − for decrease, and NA for not affected. In the Cash Flow Statement column, indicate whether the item is an operating activity (OA), investing activity (IA), or financing activity (FA). The first transaction is entered as an example.

Event No.	Assets	=	Liab.	+	Equity	Rev.	−	Exp.	=	Net Inc.	Cash Flow Statement
1	+		NA		+	+		NA		+	NA

L.O. 2 EXERCISE 7–3 *Analyzing Account Balances for a Company Using the Allowance Method of Accounting for Bad Debts*

The following account balances come from the records of Hawk Company:

	Beginning Balance	Ending Balance
Accounts Receivable	$2,000	$2,200
Allowance for Bad Debts	100	170

During the accounting period, Hawk recorded $9,000 of service revenue on account. The company also wrote off a $110 account receivable.

Required

a. Determine the amount of cash collected from receivables.
b. Determine the amount of bad debts expense recognized during the period.

EXERCISE 7–4 *Effect of Recovering a Receivable Previously Written Off* — L.O. 2

The accounts receivable balance for Sports Shoes at December 31, 2006, was $97,000. Also on that date, the balance in Allowance for Doubtful Accounts was $3,200. During 2007, $3,400 of accounts receivable were written off as uncollectible. Also, Sports Shoes unexpectedly collected $920 of receivables that had been written off in a previous accounting period. Sales on account during 2007 were $204,000, and cash collections from receivables were $197,000. Bad debts expense was estimated to be 2 percent of the sales on account for the period.

Required

(*Hint:* Post the transactions to T-accounts under the accounting equation before completing the requirements.)

a. Based on the preceding information, compute (after year-end adjustment):
   (1) Balance of Allowance for Doubtful Accounts at December 31, 2007.
   (2) Balance of Accounts Receivable at December 31, 2007.
   (3) Net realizable value of Accounts Receivable at December 31, 2007.
b. What amount of bad debts expense will Sports Shoes report for 2007?
c. Explain how the recovery of the $920 receivables affected the accounting equation.

EXERCISE 7–5 *Accounting for Bad Debts: Allowance versus Direct Write-Off Method* — L.O. 2, 3

C & E Auto Parts sells new and used auto parts. Although most of its sales are cash sales, it makes a significant amount of credit sales. During 2008, its first year of operations, C & E Auto Parts experienced the following:

Credit sales	$352,000
Cash sales	625,000
Collections of accounts receivable	320,000
Uncollectible accounts charged off during the year	320

Required

a. Assume that C & E Auto Parts uses the allowance method of accounting for bad debts and estimates that 1 percent of its sales on account will not be collected. Answer the following questions:
   (1) What is the Accounts Receivable balance at December 31, 2008?
   (2) What is the ending balance of Allowance for Doubtful Accounts at December 31, 2008, after all entries and adjusting entries are posted?
   (3) What is the amount of bad debts expense for 2008?
   (4) What is the net realizable value of accounts receivable at December 31, 2008?
b. Assume that C & E Auto Parts uses the direct write-off method of accounting for bad debts. Answer the following questions:
   (1) What is the Accounts Receivable balance at December 31, 2008?
   (2) What is the amount of bad debts expense for 2008?
   (3) What is the net realizable value of accounts receivable at December 31, 2008?

L.O. 3 EXERCISE 7–6 *Accounting for Bad Debts: Direct Write-Off Method*

Ben's Repair Shop has mostly a cash business but does have a small number of sales on account. Consequently, it uses the direct write-off method to account for bad debts. During 2006 Ben's Repair Shop earned $12,000 of cash revenue and $1,500 of revenue on account. Cash operating expenses were $8,200. After many attempts to collect a $50 account receivable from Larry Raines, the account was determined to be uncollectible in 2007.

Required

a. Record the effects of (1) cash revenue, (2) revenue on account, (3) cash expenses, and (4) write-off of the uncollectible account on the financial statements using a horizontal statements model like the one shown here. In the Cash Flow Statement column, indicate whether the item is an operating activity (OA), investing activity (IA), or financing activity (FA). Use NA to indicate that an element is not affected by the event.

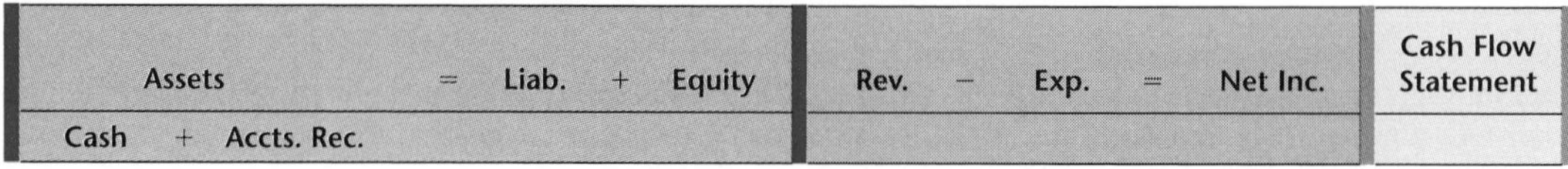

Assets			=	Liab.	+	Equity	Rev.	−	Exp.	=	Net Inc.	Cash Flow Statement
Cash	+	Accts. Rec.										

b. What amount of net income did Ben's Repair Shop report on the 2006 income statement?
c. Prepare the general journal entries for the four accounting events listed in Requirement *a*.

L.O. 4 EXERCISE 7–7 *Effect of Credit Card Sales on Financial Statements*

Big Elk Hunting Lodge provided $80,000 of services during 2006. All customers paid for the services with credit cards. Big Elk turned the credit card receipts over to the credit card company immediately. The credit card company paid Big Elk cash in the amount of face value less a 4 percent service charge.

Required

a. Record the credit card sales and the subsequent collection of accounts receivable in a horizontal statements model like the one shown here. In the Cash Flow Statement column, indicate whether the item is an operating activity (OA), investing activity (IA), or financing activity (FA). Use NA to indicate that an element is not affected by the event.

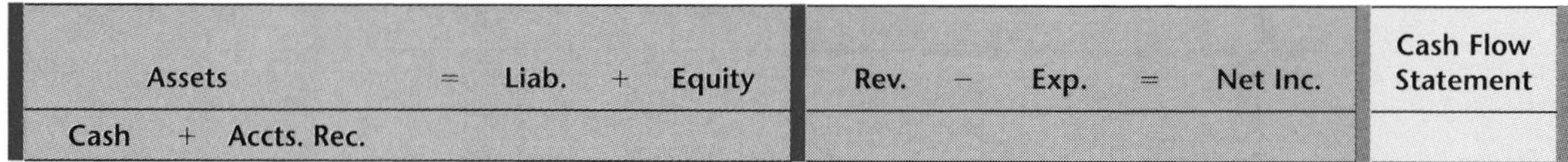

Assets			=	Liab.	+	Equity	Rev.	−	Exp.	=	Net Inc.	Cash Flow Statement
Cash	+	Accts. Rec.										

b. Answer the following questions:
   (1) What is the amount of total assets at the end of the accounting period?
   (2) What is the amount of revenue reported on the income statement?
   (3) What is the amount of cash flow from operating activities reported on the cash flow statement?
   (4) Why would Big Elk Hunting Lodge accept credit cards instead of providing credit directly to its customers? In other words, why would Big Elk be willing to pay 4 percent of sales to have the credit card company handle its sales on account?

L.O. 4 EXERCISE 7–8 *Recording Credit Card Sales*

Biggers Company accepted credit cards in payment for $3,450 of merchandise sold during March 2006. The credit card company charged Biggers a 3 percent service fee. The credit card company paid Biggers as soon as it received the invoices.

Required

a. Prepare the general journal entry to record the merchandise sale.
b. Prepare the general journal entry for the collection of the receivable from the credit card company.
c. Based on this information alone, what is the amount of net income earned during the month of March?

EXERCISE 7–9 *Effect of Warranties on Income and Cash Flow* **L.O. 5**

To support herself while attending school, Sara Taylor sold computers to other students. During her first year of operation, she sold computers that had cost her $75,000 cash for $110,000 cash. She provided her customers with a one-year warranty against defects in parts and labour. Based on industry standards, she estimated that warranty claims would amount to 5 percent of sales. During the year she paid $320 cash to replace a defective keyboard.

Required
Prepare an income statement and cash flow statement for Taylor's first year of operation. Explain the difference between net income and the amount of cash flow from operating activities.

EXERCISE 7–10 *Effect of Warranty Obligations and Payments on Financial Statements* **L.O. 5**

The Hurt Appliance Co. provides a 120-day parts-and-labour warranty on all merchandise it sells. Hurt estimates the warranty expense for the current period to be $900. During the period a customer returned a product that cost $315 to repair.

Required

a. Show the effects of these transactions on the financial statements using a horizontal statements model like the example shown here. Use a + to indicate increase, a − for decrease, and NA for not affected. Also in the Cash Flow Statement column, indicate whether the item is an operating activity (OA), investing activity (IA), or financing activity (FA).

Assets	=	Liab.	+	Equity	Rev.	−	Exp.	=	Net Inc.	Cash Flow Statement

b. Prepare the journal entry to record the warranty expense for the period.
c. Prepare the journal entry to record payment for the actual repair costs.
d. Discuss the advantage of estimating the amount of warranty expense.

EXERCISE 7–11 *Effect of a Discount Note on Financial Statements* **L.O. 6**

George Barnes started a moving company on January 1, 2006. On March 1, 2006, Barnes borrowed cash from a local bank by issuing a one-year $50,000 face value note with annual interest based on a 12 percent discount. During 2006, Barnes provided services for $36,800 cash.

Required
Answer the following questions. Record the events in T-accounts prior to answering the questions.

a. What is the amount of total liabilities on the December 31, 2006, balance sheet?
b. What is the amount of net income on the 2006 income statement?
c. What is the amount of cash flow from operating activities on the 2006 cash flow statement?
d. Provide the general journal entries necessary to record issuing the note on March 1, 2006; recognizing accrued interest on December 31, 2006; and repaying the loan on February 28, 2007.

EXERCISE 7–12 *Comparing Effective Interest Rates on Discount versus Interest-Bearing Notes* **L.O. 6**

Glen Pounds borrowed money by issuing two notes on January 1, 2006. The financing transactions are described here:

1. Borrowed funds by issuing a $20,000 face value discount note to a local bank. The note had a 12 percent discount rate, a one-year term to maturity, and was paid off on January 1, 2007.
2. Borrowed funds by issuing a $20,000 face value, interest-bearing note to a local bank. The note had a 12 percent stated rate of interest, a one-year term to maturity, and was paid off on January 1, 2007.

Required

a. Show the effects of issuing the two notes on the financial statements using separate horizontal financial statement models like the ones here. Record the transaction amounts under the appropriate categories. Also in the

Cash Flow Statement column, indicate whether the item is an operating activity (OA), investing activity (IA), or financing activity (FA). Record only the events occurring on the date of issue. Do not record accrued interest or the repayment at maturity.

Discount Note

Assets	=	Liabilities			+	Equity	Rev.	−	Exp.	=	Net Inc.	Cash Flow Statement
Cash	=	Notes Pay.	−	Disc. on Notes Pay.	+	Ret. Ear.						

Interest-Bearing Note

Assets	=	Liabilities	+	Equity	Rev.	−	Exp.	=	Net Inc.	Cash Flow Statement
Cash	=	Notes Pay.	+	Ret. Ear.						

b. What is the total amount of interest to be paid on each note?
c. What amount of cash was received from each note?
d. Which note has the higher effective interest rate? Support your answer with appropriate computations.

L.O. 6 EXERCISE 7–13 *Recording Accounting Events for a Discount Note*

Ray Co issued a $30,000 face value discount note to a local bank on June 1, 2006. The note had a 10 percent discount rate and a one-year term to maturity.

Required
Prepare general journal entries for the following:
a. The issuance of the note on June 1, 2006.
b. The adjustment for accrued interest at the end of the year, December 31, 2006.
c. Recording interest expense for 2007 and repaying the principal on May 31, 2007.

L.O. 7 EXERCISE 7–14 *Recording Payroll Entries*

The payroll register for the pay period ended March 1 showed the following totals: gross earnings, $5,872.30; CPP contributions, $113.19; EI premiums, $63.80; income tax, $1,172.24; union dues, $152.50.

Required
Prepare the journal entries to record the following:
a. The payroll.
b. The employer's share of the CPP contributions and the EI premiums.

L.O. 7 EXERCISE 7–15 *Calculate and Record Payroll*

Presented below is information from the May 17 payroll register of REMO Company:

Gross earnings	$13,672
CPP contributions	757
EI premiums	634
Income tax	(a)
Charitable donations	175
Total deductions	(b)
Net pay	9,127
Accounts Debited	
Office salaries	8,775
Shop wages	(c)

Required

a. Calculate the missing amounts.
b. Calculate REMO company's share of CPP and EI.
c. Prepare the journal entry to record the payroll.
d. Prepare the journal entry to record the company's share of EI and CPP.
e. Prepare the journal entry to pay the employees on May 24.

EXERCISE 7–16 *Comprehensive Single-Cycle Problem*

L.O. 2, 5, 6

The following post-closing trial balance was drawn from the accounts of A-1 Steel Co. as of December 31, 2006.

	Debit	Credit
Cash	$ 3,000	
Accounts Receivable	15,000	
Allowance for Doubtful Accounts		$ 800
Inventory	21,000	
Accounts Payable		7,500
Common Shares		12,000
Retained Earnings		18,700
Totals	$39,000	$39,000

Transactions for 2007

1. A-1 acquired an additional $5,000 cash from the issue of common shares.
2. A-1 purchased $47,000 of inventory on account.
3. A-1 sold inventory that cost $46,000 for $82,000. Sales were made on account.
4. The products sold were warranted, and A-1 estimated future warranty costs would amount to 4 percent of sales.
5. The company wrote off $600 of uncollectible accounts.
6. On September 1, A-1 issued an $8,000 face value, 9 percent discount note. The note had a one-year term.
7. A-1 paid $1,100 cash to satisfy warranty claims.
8. A-1 paid $9,600 cash for salaries expense.
9. The company collected $75,000 cash from accounts receivable.
10. A cash payment of $52,000 was paid on accounts payable.
11. The company paid a $2,000 cash dividend to the shareholders.
12. Bad debts are estimated to be 1 percent of sales on accounts.
13. Recorded the accrued interest at December 31, 2006.

Required

a. Open T-accounts and record the beginning balances and the effects of the accounting events described.
b. Prepare an income statement, statement of shareholders' equity, balance sheet, and cash flow statement for 2007.

EXERCISE 7–17 *Effect of GST on Financial Statements (Appendix)*

L.O. 9

On March 1, the local office supply store had 10 packages of computer paper on hand. Each package originally cost $6.00. The following transactions occurred during the first 15 days in March:

March 3 Purchased 50 more packages of computer paper at $6.00 each from a supplier on account, terms net 30.
8 Sold 15 packages of the computer paper to a customer for $9.00 each.
11 Sold 10 more packages of computer paper to a local law firm for $9.00 each, terms, 2/10, net 30.
15 Returned 3 packages to the supplier for credit.

Required

Using a financial statement model like the one shown below, record the appropriate amounts for the above four events, including GST of 7 percent:

Event No.	Assets	=	Liab.	+	Equity	Rev.	−	Exp.	=	Net. Inc.	Cash Flow Statement
1											

PROBLEMS—SERIES A

L.O. 2 PROBLEM 7–1A *Accounting for Bad Debts—Two Cycles Using the Allowance Method*

The following transactions apply to Durm's Consulting for 2006, the first year of operation:

1. Recognized $40,000 of service revenue earned on account.
2. Collected $34,000 from accounts receivable.
3. Adjusted accounts to recognize bad debts expense. Durm uses the allowance method of accounting for bad debts and estimates that bad debts expense will be 2 percent of sales on account.

The following transactions apply to Durm's Consulting for 2007:

1. Recognized $51,500 of service revenue on account.
2. Collected $47,500 from accounts receivable.
3. Determined that $150 of the accounts receivable were uncollectible and wrote them off.
4. Collected $12 of an account that had been written off previously.
5. Paid $36,500 cash for operating expenses.
6. Adjusted accounts to recognize bad debts expense for 2007. Durm estimates that bad debts expense will be 1 percent of sales on account.

Required

Complete all the following requirements for 2006 and 2007. Complete all requirements for 2006 prior to beginning the requirements for 2007.

a. Identify the type of each transaction (asset source, asset use, asset exchange, or claims exchange).
b. Show the effect of each transaction on the elements of the financial statements, using a horizontal statements model like the one shown here. Use + for increase, − for decrease, and NA for not affected. Also, in the Cash Flow Statement column, indicate whether the item is an operating activity (OA), investing activity (IA), or financing activity (FA). The first transaction is entered as an example. (*Hint:* Closing entries do not affect the statements model.)

Event No.	Assets	=	Liab.	+	Equity	Rev.	−	Exp.	=	Net Inc.	Cash Flow Statement
1	+		NA		+	+		NA		+	NA

c. Record the transactions in general journal form, and post them to T-accounts (begin 2007 with the ending T-account balances from 2006).
d. Prepare the income statement, statement of shareholders' equity, balance sheet, and cash flow statement.
e. Prepare closing entries and a post-closing trial balance. Post the closing entries to the T-accounts.

L.O. 2 PROBLEM 7–2A *Determining Account Balances and Preparing Journal Entries: Allowance Method of Accounting for Bad Debts*

The following information pertains to Hill Cabinet Company's sales on account and accounts receivable:

Accounts Receivable Balance, January 1, 2007	$ 172,800
Allowance for Doubtful Accounts, January 1, 2007	5,184
Sales on Account, 2007	1,269,800
Cost of Goods Sold	800,000
Collections of Accounts Receivable, 2007	1,284,860

After several collection attempts, Hill Cabinet Company wrote off $4,500 of accounts that could not be collected. Hill estimates that bad debts expense will be 0.5 percent of sales on account.

Required

a. Compute the following amounts:
   (1) Using the allowance method, the amount of bad debts expense for 2007.
   (2) Net realizable value of receivables at the end of 2007.
b. Prepare the general journal entries to:
   (1) Record sales on account for 2007 and the corresponding cost of goods sold.
   (2) Record cash collections from accounts receivable for 2007.
   (3) Write off the accounts that are not collectible.
   (4) Record the estimated bad debts expense for 2007.
c. Explain why the bad debts expense amount is different from the amount that was written off as uncollectible.

PROBLEM 7–3A *Accounting for Credit Card Sales, Warranties, and Bad Debts: Direct Write-Off Method*

L.O. 3–5

Brigg's Supply Company had the following transactions in 2004:

1. Acquired $70,000 cash from the issue of common shares.
2. Purchased $240,000 of merchandise for cash in 2004.
3. Sold merchandise that cost $190,000 for $370,000 during the year under the following terms:

$100,000	Cash Sales
250,000	Credit Card Sales (The credit card company charges a 3 percent service fee.)
20,000	Sales on Account

4. Collected all the amount receivable from the credit card company.
5. Collected $16,000 of accounts receivable.
6. Used the direct write-off method to account for bad debts expense and wrote off $240 of accounts receivable that were uncollectible.
7. Brigg's gives a one-year warranty on equipment it sells. It estimated that warranty expense for 2004 would be $650.
8. Paid selling and administrative expenses of $53,000.

Required

a. Show the effects of each of the transactions on the elements of the financial statements, using a horizontal statements model like the one shown here. Use + for increase, − for decrease, and NA for not affected. The first transaction is entered as an example. (*Hint*: Closing entries do not affect the statements model.)

Event No.	Assets	=	Liab.	+	Equity	Rev.	−	Exp.	=	Net Inc.	Cash Flow Statement
1	+		NA		+	NA		NA		NA	+ FA

b. Prepare general journal entries for each of the transactions, and post them to T-accounts.
c. Prepare an income statement, statement of shareholders' equity, balance sheet, and cash flow statement for 2004.

PROBLEM 7–4A *Accounting for a Discount Note—Two Accounting Cycles*

L.O. 6

City Corp. was started in 2006. The following summarizes transactions that occurred during 2006:

1. Issued a $40,000 face value discount note to a local bank on April 1, 2006. The note had a 9 percent discount rate and a one-year term to maturity.
2. Incurred and paid $118,000 cash for selling and administrative expenses.
3. Recognized revenue from services performed for cash, $176,000.
4. Amortized the discount at the end of the year, December 31, 2006.
5. Prepared the necessary closing entries at December 31, 2006.

The following summarizes transactions that occurred in 2007:

1. Recognized $292,000 of service revenue in cash.
2. Incurred and paid for $198,000 for selling and administrative expenses.
3. Amortized the remainder of the discount for 2007 and paid the face value of the note.
4. Prepared the necessary closing entries at December 31, 2007.

Required

a. Show the effects of each of the transactions on the elements of the financial statements, using a horizontal statements model like the one shown here. Use + for increase, − for decrease, and NA for not affected. The first transaction is entered as an example. (*Hint:* Closing entries do not affect the statements model.)

Event No.	Assets	=	Liab.	+	Equity	Rev.	−	Exp.	=	Net Inc.	Cash Flow Statement
1	+		+		NA	NA		NA		NA	+ FA

b. Prepare the entries in general journal form for the transactions for 2006 and 2007, and post them to T-accounts.

c. Prepare an income statement, statement of shareholders' equity, balance sheet, and cash flow statement for 2006 and 2007.

L.O. 3–5 PROBLEM 7–5A *Effect of Transactions on the Elements of Financial Statements*

Required

Identify each of the following independent transactions as asset source (AS), asset use (AU), asset exchange (AE), or claims exchange (CE). Also explain how each event affects assets, liabilities, shareholders' equity, net income, and cash flow by placing a + for increase, − for decrease, or NA for not affected under each of the categories. The first event is recorded as an example.

Event	Type of Event	Assets	Liabilities	Common Shares	Retained Earnings	Net Income	Cash Flow Statement
a	AS	+	NA	NA	+	+	+

a. Provided services for cash.
b. Paid cash for salaries expense.
c. Provided services on account.
d. Wrote off an uncollectible account (use direct write-off method).
e. Collected cash from customers paying their accounts.
f. Recovered a bad debt that was previously written off (assume direct write-off method was used).
g. Paid cash for equipment.
h. Recognized warranty expense.
i. Sold merchandise at a price above cost. Accepted payment by credit card. The credit card company charges a service fee. The receipts have not yet been forwarded to the credit card company for collection.
j. Realized a gain when equipment was sold for cash.
k. Paid cash to satisfy warranty obligations.
l. Submitted receipts to the credit card company in Requirement *i* above and collected cash.
m. Issued a discount note to a local bank.
n. Paid cash to creditors on accounts payable.
o. Amortized three months of the discount on a discount note payable.

L.O. 2, 5, 6 PROBLEM 7–6A *Classified Balance Sheet and Multistep Income Statement*

Required

Use the following information to prepare a classified balance sheet and a multistep income statement for Belmont Equipment Co. for 2003. (*Hint:* Some of the items will *not* appear on either statement, and ending retained earnings must be calculated.)

Salaries Expense	$ 96,000	Interest Receivable (short term)	$ 500
Common Shares	40,000	Beginning Retained Earnings	10,400
Notes Receivable (short term)	12,000	Warranties Payable (short term)	1,300
Allowance for Doubtful Accounts	4,000	Gain on Sale of Equipment	6,400
Accumulated Amortization	30,000	Other Operating Expenses	70,000
Discount on Note Payable	2,400	Cash Flow from Investing Activities	80,000
Notes Payable (long term)	106,000	Prepaid Rent	9,600
Residual Value of Equipment	4,000	Land	36,000
Interest Payable (short term)	1,800	Cash	17,800
Bad Debts Expense	10,800	Inventory	122,800
Supplies	1,600	Accounts Payable	46,000
Equipment	60,000	Interest Expense	24,000
Interest Revenue	4,200	Salaries Payable	9,200
Sales Revenue	396,000	Unearned Revenue	52,600
Dividends	8,000	Cost of Goods Sold	143,000
Warranty Expense	3,400	Accounts Receivable	90,000

PROBLEM 7–7A *Missing Information* **L.O. 2, 5, 6**

The following information comes from the accounts of Breedlove Company:

Account Title	Beginning Balance	Ending Balance
Accounts Receivable	$30,000	$28,000
Allowance for Doubtful Accounts	2,000	1,800
Warranties Payable	3,600	3,000
Notes Payable	40,000	40,000
Discount on Notes Payable	2,400	1,600

Required

a. There were $240,000 in sales on account during the accounting period. Write-offs of uncollectible accounts were $1,600. What was the amount of cash collected from accounts receivable? What amount of bad debts expense was reported on the income statement? What was the net realizable value of receivables at the end of the accounting period?

b. Warranty expense for the period was $1,100. How much cash was paid to settle warranty claims?

c. What amount of interest expense was recognized during the period? How much cash was paid for interest? What book value was reported for the discount note on the year-end balance sheet?

PROBLEM 7–8A *Comprehensive Accounting Cycle Problem (Uses Direct Write-Off Method)* **L.O. 3–6**

The following trial balance was prepared for Water Way Sales and Service on December 31, 2006, after the closing entries were posted.

Account Title	Debit	Credit
Cash	87,100	
Accounts Receivable	17,800	
Inventory	94,600	
Accounts Payable		$ 44,000
Common Shares		90,000
Retained Earnings		65,500
Totals	$199,500	$199,500

Water Way had the following transactions in 2007:

1. Purchased merchandise on account for $390,000.
2. Sold merchandise that cost $364,000 on account for $522,000.
3. Performed $44,000 of services for cash.
4. Sold merchandise for $26,400 to credit card customers. The merchandise cost $18,600. The credit card company charges a 5 percent fee.
5. Collected $504,000 cash from accounts receivable.
6. Paid $396,000 cash on accounts payable.
7. Paid $150,000 cash for selling and administrative expenses.
8. Collected cash for the full amount due from the credit card company.
9. Issued a $60,000 face value discount note with an 8 percent discount rate and a one-year term to maturity.
10. Wrote off $450 of accounts as uncollectible (use the direct write-off method).
11. The December 31 payroll register showed the following totals: gross earnings, $23,482; income tax, $4,379; CPP contributions, $781; EI premiums, $693; health insurance, $275; RRSP contributions, $1,200.
12. Made the following adjusting entries:
    a. Recorded three months' interest on the discount note at December 31, 2007.
    b. Estimated warranty expense to be $3,090.

Required

Prepare general journal entries for these transactions; post the entries to T-accounts; and prepare an income statement, a statement of shareholders' equity, a balance sheet, and a cash flow statement for 2007.

L.O. 9 PROBLEM 7–9A *Effect of GST on Financial Statements (Appendix)*

A local department store had the following items available in the luggage section: 10 briefcases, cost $56 each; 6 overnight bags, cost $85 each; 4 carry-on bags, cost $79 each; 3 large suitcases, cost $110 each.

During the month of June, the following transactions occurred:

June	2	Sold 5 briefcases for $69.00 each.
	5	Purchased 4 briefcases for $56.00 each on account.
	8	Sold 2 carry-on bags for $92.00 each.
	11	Sold 1 large suitcase for $149.00.
	15	Purchased 2 large suitcases for $110.00 each on account.
	19	Customer returned 1 briefcase from the June 2 sale.
	24	Sold 3 overnight bags for $109.00 each.
	29	Purchased 4 overnight bags for $85.00 each on account.

Required

Using a financial statement model like the one shown below, record the appropriate amounts for the above events, including GST of 7 percent.

Event No.	Assets	=	Liab.	+	Equity	Rev.	−	Exp.	=	Net Inc.	Cash Flow Statement
1											

PROBLEMS—SERIES B

L.O. 2 PROBLEM 7–1B *Accounting for Bad Debts: Two Cycles Using the Allowance Method*

The following transactions apply to J & J Company for 2005, the first year of operation:

1. Recognized $255,000 of service revenue earned on account.
2. Collected $159,000 from accounts receivable.
3. Paid $150,000 cash for operating expense.
4. Adjusted the accounts to recognize bad debts expense. J & J uses the allowance method of accounting for bad debts and estimates that bad debts expense will be 1 percent of sales on account.

The following transactions apply to J & J for 2006:

1. Recognized $408,000 of service revenue on account.
2. Collected $411,000 from accounts receivable.
3. Determined that $1,800 of the accounts receivable were uncollectible and wrote them off.
4. Collected $600 of an account that had previously been written off.
5. Paid $126,000 cash for operating expenses.
6. Adjusted the accounts to recognize bad debts expense for 2006. J & J estimates bad debts expense will be 0.5 percent of sales on account.

Required

Complete the following requirements for 2005 and 2006. Complete all requirements for 2005 prior to beginning the requirements for 2006.

a. Identify the type of each transaction (asset source, asset use, asset exchange, or claims exchange).
b. Show the effect of each transaction on the elements of the financial statements, using a horizontal statements model like the one shown here. Use + for increase, − for decrease, and NA for not affected. Also, in the Cash Flow Statement column, indicate whether the item is an operating activity (OA), investing activity (IA), or financing activity (FA). The first transaction is entered as an example. (*Hint*: Closing entries do not affect the statements model.)

Event No.	Assets	=	Liab.	+	Equity	Rev.	−	Exp.	=	Net Inc.	Cash Flow Statement
1	+		NA		+	+		NA		+	NA

c. Record the transactions in general journal form, and post them to T-accounts (begin 2006 with the ending T-account balances from 2005).
d. Prepare the income statement, statement of shareholders' equity, balance sheet, and cash flow statement.
e. Prepare closing entries and a post-closing trial balance. Post the closing entries to the T-accounts.

PROBLEM 7–2B *Determining Account Balances and Preparing Journal Entries: Allowance Method of Accounting for Bad Debts* **L.O. 2**

During the first year of operation, 2006, ACE Appliance recognized $300,000 of service revenue on account. At the end of 2006, the accounts receivable balance was $58,000. For this first year in business, the owner believes bad debts expense will be about 1 percent of sales on account.

Required

a. What amount of cash did ACE collect during 2006?
b. Assuming ACE uses the allowance method to account for bad debts, what amount should ACE record as bad debts expense for 2006?
c. Prepare the journal entries to:
   (1) Record service revenue on account.
   (2) Record collection from accounts receivable.
   (3) Record the entry to recognize bad debts expense.
d. What is the net realizable value of receivables at the end of 2006?
e. Show the effects of the transactions in Requirement *c* on the financial statements by recording the appropriate amounts in a horizontal statements model like the one shown here. In the Cash Flow Statement column, indicate whether the item is an operating activity (OA), investing activity (IA), or financing activity (FA). Use NA for not affected.

Assets					=	Liab.	+	Equity	Rev.	−	Exp.	=	Net Inc.	Cash Flow Statement
Cash	+	Accts. Rec.	−	Allow.										

L.O. 3, 4, 5 PROBLEM 7–3B *Accounting for Credit Card Sales, Warranties, and Bad Debts: Direct Write-Off Method*

Byrd Company had the following transactions in 2005:

1. The business was started when it acquired $500,000 cash from the issue of common shares.
2. Byrd purchased $1,200,000 of merchandise for cash in 2005.
3. During the year, the company sold merchandise for $1,600,000. The merchandise cost $900,000. Sales were made under the following terms:

$600,000	Cash sales
500,000	Credit card sales (The credit card company charges a 4 percent service fee.)
500,000	Sales on account

4. The company collected all the amount receivable from the credit card company.
5. The company collected $400,000 of accounts receivable.
6. Byrd used the direct write-off method to account for bad debts expense and wrote off $5,000 of accounts receivable that were uncollectible.
7. Byrd gives a one-year warranty on equipment it sells. It estimated that warranty expense for 2005 would be $4,500.
8. The company paid $100,000 cash for selling and administrative expenses.

Required

a. Show the effects of each of the transactions on the elements of the financial statements, using a horizontal statements model like the one shown here. Use + for increase, − for decrease, and NA for not affected. The first transaction is entered as an example. (*Hint*: Closing entries do not affect the statements model.)

Event No.	Assets	=	Liab.	+	Equity	Rev.	−	Exp.	=	Net Inc.	Cash Flow Statement
1	+		NA		+	NA		NA		NA	+ FA

b. Prepare general journal entries for each of the transactions, and post them to T-accounts.

c. Prepare an income statement, statement of shareholders' equity, balance sheet, and cash flow statement for 2005.

L.O. 6 PROBLEM 7–4B *Accounting for a Discount Note across Two Accounting Cycles*

Laura White opened White & Company, an accounting practice, in 2006. The following summarizes transactions that occurred during 2006:

1. Issued a $200,000 face value discount note to Canada Bank on July 1, 2006. The note had a 10 percent discount rate and a one-year term to maturity.
2. Recognized cash revenue of $336,000.
3. Incurred and paid $132,000 of operating expenses.
4. Adjusted the books to recognize interest expense at December 31, 2006.
5. Prepared the necessary closing entries at December 31, 2006.

The following summarizes transactions that occurred in 2007:

1. Recognized $984,000 of cash revenue.
2. Incurred and paid $416,000 of operating expenses.
3. Recognized the interest expense for 2007 and paid the fair value of the note.
4. Prepared the necessary closing entries at December 31, 2007.

Required

a. Show the effects of each of the transactions on the elements of the financial statements, using a horizontal statements model like the one shown here. Use + for increase, − for decrease, and NA for not affected. The first transaction is entered as an example. (*Hint*: Closing entries do not affect the statements model.)

Event No.	Assets	=	Liab.	+	Equity	Rev.	−	Exp.	=	Net Inc.	Cash Flow Statement
1	+		+		NA	NA		NA		NA	+ FA

b. Prepare entries in general journal form for the transactions for 2006 and 2007, and post them to T-accounts.
c. Prepare an income statement, statement of shareholders' equity, balance sheet, and cash flow statement for 2006 and 2007.

PROBLEM 7–5B *Effect of Transactions on the Elements of Financial Statements* L.O. 3–6

Required
Identify each of the following independent transactions as asset source (AS), asset use (AU), asset exchange (AE), or claims exchange (CE). Also explain how each event affects assets, liabilities, shareholders' equity, net income, and cash flow by placing a + for increase, − for decrease, or NA for not affected under each of the categories. The first two events are recorded as examples.

Event	Type of Event	Assets	Liabilities	Common Shares	Retained Earnings	Net Income	Cash Flow Statement
a	AE	+ −	NA	NA	NA	NA	−
b	AS	+	NA	NA	+	+	NA

a. Paid cash for equipment.
b. Sold merchandise at a price above cost. Accepted payment by credit card. The credit card company charges a service fee. The receipts have not yet been forwarded to the credit card company for collection.
c. Submitted receipts to the credit card company and collected cash.
d. Realized a gain when equipment was sold for cash.
e. Provided services for cash.
f. Paid cash to satisfy warranty obligations.
g. Paid cash for salaries expense.
h. Recovered a bad debt that had been previously written off (assume the direct write-off method is used to account for bad debts).
i. Paid cash to creditors on accounts payable.
j. Issued a discount note to a local bank.
k. Provided services on account.
l. Wrote off an uncollectible account (use the direct write-off method).
m. Amortized three months of the discount on a discount note payable.
n. Collected cash from customers paying their accounts.
o. Recognized warranty expense.

PROBLEM 7–6B *Classified Balance Sheet and Multistep Income Statement* L.O. 2, 5, 6

Required
Use the following information to prepare a classified balance sheet and a multistep income statement for Daniels Company for 2004. (*Hint*: Some of the items will not appear on either statement, and ending retained earnings must be calculated.)

Other Operating Expenses	$ 90,000	Cash	$ 23,000
Land	50,000	Interest Receivable (short term)	800
Accumulated Amortization	38,000	Cash Flow from Investing Activities	102,000
Accounts Payable	60,000	Allowance for Doubtful Accounts	7,000
Unearned Revenue	58,000	Interest Payable (short term)	3,000
Warranties Payable (short term)	2,000	Discount on Notes Payable	4,000
Equipment	77,000	Sales Revenue	500,000
Notes Payable (long term)	133,000	Bad Debts Expense	14,000
Residual Value of Equipment	7,000	Interest Expense	32,000
Dividends	12,000	Accounts Receivable	113,000
Warranty Expense	5,000	Salaries Payable	12,000
Beginning Retained Earnings	28,800	Supplies	3,000
Interest Revenue	6,000	Prepaid Rent	14,000
Gain on Sale of Equipment	10,000	Common Shares	52,000
Inventory	154,000	Cost of Goods Sold	179,000
Notes Receivable (short term)	17,000	Salaries Expense	122,000

L.O. 2, 5, 6 PROBLEM 7–7B *Missing Information*

The following information comes from the accounts of Jersey Company:

Account Title	Beginning Balance	Ending Balance
Accounts Receivable	$30,000	$34,000
Allowance for Doubtful Accounts	1,800	1,700
Warranties Payable	4,000	3,000
Notes Payable	40,000	40,000
Discount on Note Payable	1,200	800

Required

a. There were $170,000 in sales on account during the accounting period. Write-offs of uncollectible accounts were $1,400. What was the amount of cash collected from accounts receivable? What amount of bad debts expense was reported on the income statement? What was the net realizable value of receivables at the end of the accounting period?
b. Warranty expense for the period was $3,600. How much cash was paid to settle warranty claims?
c. What amount of interest expense was recognized during the period? How much cash was paid for interest? What book value was reported for the discount note on the year-end balance sheet?

L.O. 2–6 PROBLEM 7–8B *Comprehensive Accounting Cycle Problem (Uses Allowance Method)*

The following trial balance was prepared for The Sport Shop Inc. on December 31, 2006, after the closing entries were posted.

Account Title	Debit	Credit
Cash	$118,000	
Accounts Receivable	172,000	
Allowance for Doubtful Accounts		$ 10,000
Inventory	690,000	
Accounts Payable		142,000
Common Shares		720,000
Retained Earnings		108,000
Totals	$980,000	$980,000

The Sport Shop Inc. had the following transactions in 2007:

1. Purchased merchandise on account for $420,000.
2. Sold merchandise that cost $288,000 for $480,000 on account.
3. Sold for $240,000 cash merchandise that had cost $144,000.
4. Sold merchandise for $180,000 to credit card customers. The merchandise had cost $108,000. The credit card company charges a 4 percent fee.
5. Collected $526,000 cash from accounts receivable.
6. Paid $540,000 cash on accounts payable.
7. Paid $134,000 cash for selling and administrative expenses.
8. Collected cash for the full amount due from the credit card company.
9. Issued a $48,000 face value discount note with a 10 percent discount rate and a one-year term to maturity.
10. Wrote off $7,200 of accounts as uncollectible.
11. The following data were obtained from the company's December 31 payroll register: gross earnings, $31,700; income tax, $6,210; CPP contributions, $932; EI premiums, $842; United Way contributions, $350; and Canada Savings Bonds, $600.
12. Made the following adjusting entries:
    a. Recorded bad debts expense estimated at 1 percent of sales on account.
    b. Recorded seven months of interest on the discount note at December 31, 2007.
    c. Estimated warranty expense to be $1,800.

Required

a. Prepare general journal entries for these transactions; post the entries to T-accounts; and prepare an income statement, a statement of shareholders' equity, a balance sheet, and a cash flow statement for 2007.
b. Compute the net realizable value of accounts receivable at December 31, 2007.
c. If The Sport Shop Inc. used the direct write-off method, what amount of bad debts expense would it report on the income statement?

PROBLEM 7–9B *Effect of GST on Financial Statements (Appendix)*

L.O. 9

Goods and services tax of 7 percent is applied to purchases and sales. Credit terms are net 30 for purchases and sales. The following transactions for Bowman Company occurred during September:

Sept. 2 Purchased merchandise on account from Remo Industries, $4,200.
5 Sold merchandise for cash, $750. Original cost was $575.
9 Returned merchandise for credit of $1,100 from the Sept. 2 transaction.
16 Purchased merchandise on account from Aero Company, $2,700.
27 Sold merchandise on account, $475. Original cost of $295.

Required

Using a financial statement model like the one shown below, record the appropriate amounts for the above events, including GST of 7 percent.

Event No.	Assets	=	Liab.	+	Equity	Rev.	−	Exp.	=	Net Inc.	Cash Flow Statement
1											

ANALYZE, THINK, COMMUNICATE

BUSINESS APPLICATIONS CASE *Bombardier's Annual Report*

ATC 7–1

Required

Using the Bombardier financial statements in Appendix B, answer the following questions:

a. What was the average number of days to collect accounts receivable for the year ended January 31, 2002?
b. Approximately what percentage of Bombardier's accounts receivable as of January 31, 2002, does the company think will not be collected?
c. What percentage of Bombardier's current assets at January 31, 2002, was represented by accounts receivable?

GROUP ASSIGNMENT *Missing Information*

ATC 7–2

The following selected financial information is available for three companies:

	Bell	Card	Zore
Total sales	$125,000	$210,000	?
Cash sales	?	26,000	$120,000
Credit sales	40,000	?	75,000
Accounts receivable, January 1, 2008	6,200	42,000	?
Accounts receivable, December 31, 2008	5,600	48,000	7,500
Allowance for doubtful accounts, January 1, 2008	?	?	405
Allowance for doubtful accounts, December 31, 2008	224	1,680	?
Bad debts expense, 2008	242	1,200	395
Uncollectible accounts charged off	204	1,360	365
Collections of accounts receivable, 2008	?	?	75,235

Required

a. Divide the class into three sections and divide each section into groups of three to five students. Assign one of the companies to each of the sections.

Group Tasks

(1) Determine the missing amounts for your company.
(2) Determine the percentage of accounts receivable estimated to be uncollectible at the end of 2007 and 2008 for your company.
(3) Determine the percentage of total sales that are credit sales for your company.
(4) Determine the accounts receivable turnover for your company.

Class Discussion

b. Have a representative of each section put the missing information on the board and explain how it was determined.
c. Which company has the highest percentage of sales that are credit sales?
d. Which company is doing the best job of collecting its accounts receivable? What procedures and policies can a company use to better collect its accounts receivable?

ATC 7–3 REAL-WORLD CASE *Time Needed to Collect Accounts Receivable*

Presented here are the average days to collect accounts receivable ratios for four companies in different industries. The data are for 2000.

Company	Days
Boeing (aircraft manufacturer)	35 days
Chrysler (automobile manufacturer)	18
Leon's (furniture retailer)	13
Coca-Cola (soft-drink producer)	32

Required

Write a brief memorandum that provides possible explanations to each of the following questions:

a. Why would a company that manufactures cars (Chrysler) collect its accounts receivable faster than a company that sells soft drinks (Coca-Cola)?
b. Why would a company that manufactures and sells large airplanes (Boeing) collect its accounts receivable slower than a company that sells furniture (Leon's)?

ATC 7–4 BUSINESS APPLICATIONS CASE *Using Average Number of Days to Collect Accounts Receivable to Make Comparisons*

The following information was drawn from the accounting records of Shafer and Burgess.

Account Title	Shafer	Burgess
Accounts Receivable (year end)	$ 80,000	$ 50,000
Sales	920,000	450,000

Required

a. Determine the average number of days to collect accounts receivable for each company.
b. Which company is likely to incur more costs associated with extending credit?
c. Identify and discuss some of the costs associated with extending credit.
d. Explain why a company would be willing to accept the costs of extending credit to its customers.

BUSINESS APPLICATIONS CASE *Using Ratios to Make Comparisons*

ATC 7–5

The following accounting information exists for Playfair and Pigpen companies at the end of 2007.

	Playfair	Pigpen
Cash	$ 25,000	$ 70,000
Accounts receivable	105,000	260,000
Allowance for doubtful accounts	5,000	10,000
Merchandise inventory	75,000	150,000
Accounts payable	80,000	200,000
Cost of goods sold	475,000	630,000
Building	125,000	200,000
Sales	650,000	1,000,000

Required

a. For each company, compute the gross profit percentage and the average number of days to collect accounts receivable (use the net realizable value of receivables to compute the average days to collect accounts receivable).
b. In relation to cost, which company is charging more for its merchandise?
c. Which company is likely to incur higher financial costs associated with the granting of credit to customers? Explain.
d. Which company appears to have more restrictive credit standards when authorizing credit to its customers? (*Hint*: There is no specific answer to this question. Use your judgment and general knowledge of ratios to answer.)

WRITING ASSIGNMENT *Elements of Financial Statements*

ATC 7–6

Paul South is opening a men's clothing store in University City. He has some of the necessary funds to lease the building and purchase the inventory but will need to borrow between $45,000 and $50,000. He has talked with two financial institutions that have offered the money according to the following terms:

1. South can borrow the money from Bank 1 by issuing a $50,000, one-year note with an interest rate of 10 percent.
2. South can borrow the money from Bank 2 by issuing a $50,000 face value discount note. The note will have a 9.5 percent discount rate and a one-year term to maturity.

South does not understand much about financial matters but wants the best alternative. He has come to you for advice.

Required

Write a memo to South explaining the difference in the two types of notes. Also advise him regarding the best alternative and why. Include in your explanation the true cost of each of the loans.

ETHICAL DILEMMA *What They Don't Know Won't Hurt Them, Right?*

ATC 7–7

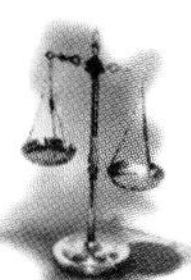

Alonzo Saunders owns a small training services company that is experiencing growing pains. The company has grown rapidly by offering liberal credit terms to its customers. While his competitors require payment for services provided within 30 days, Saunders permits his customers to delay payment for up to 90 days. This extended delay allows his customers time to fully evaluate the training that employees receive before being required to pay for that training. Saunders guarantees satisfaction. If the customer is unhappy, the customer does not have to pay. Saunders works with reputable companies, provides top-quality training, and rarely encounters dissatisfied customers. However, the long collection period has left Saunders with a cash flow problem. He has a large accounts receivable balance, but needs cash to pay the current bills. He has recently negotiated a loan agreement with a local bank that should solve his cash flow problems. A condition of the loan is that the accounts receivable be pledged as collateral for the loan. The bank agreed to loan Saunders 70 percent of the value of his receivables balance. The current balance in the receivables account is roughly $100,000, thereby giving him access to $70,000 cash. Saunders feels very comfortable with this arrangement because he estimates that he needs approximately $60,000, which is well within the range permitted by the bank.

Unfortunately, on the day Saunders was scheduled to execute the loan agreement, he heard a rumour that his largest customer was experiencing financial problems and was considering the declaration of bankruptcy. The customer owed Saunders $45,000. Saunders immediately called the company's chief accountant and was told "off the record" that the rumour was true. The accountant advised Saunders that the company had a substantial negative net worth and that most of the valuable assets were collateralized against bank loans. He said that, in his opinion, Saunders was unlikely to be able to collect the balance due. Saunders's immediate concern was the impact that the situation would have on his loan agreement with the bank. Removing the receivable from the collateral pool would leave only $55,000 in the pool and thereby reduce his available credit to $38,500 ($55,000 × 0.70). Even worse, the recognition of the bad debts expense would so adversely affect his income statement that the bank might decide to reduce the available credit by lowering the percentage of receivables allowed under the current loan agreement.

As Saunders heads for the bank, he wonders how he will make ends meet. If he cannot obtain the cash he needs, he will soon be declaring bankruptcy himself. He wonders whether he should even tell the bank about the bad debt or just let the bank discover the situation after the fact. He knows that he will have to sign an agreement attesting to the quality of the receivables at the date of the loan. However, he reasons that the information he received is off the record and that therefore he may not be legally bound to advise the bank of the condition of the receivables balance. He wishes that he had gone to the bank before he called to confirm the rumour.

Required

a. Assuming that Saunders uses the direct write-off method of accounting for bad debts, explain how the $45,000 write-off of the uncollectible account affects his financial statements.
b. Should Saunders advise the bank of the condition of the receivables? What are the ethical implications associated with telling or not telling the bank about the uncollectible account?

ATC 7–8 SEDAR DATABASE *Analyzing Coca-Cola's Accounts Receivable*

Required

Using the most current annual report available on SEDAR, answer the following questions about Coca-Cola Enterprises Inc. for the most recent year reported. Instructions for using SEDAR are in Appendix A.

a. What was Coca-Cola's average days to collect accounts receivable?
b. What percentage of accounts receivable did Coca-Cola estimate would not be collected?
c. Did Coca-Cola provide any information about bad debts relating to customers? If so, what information was provided?

ATC 7–9 SPREADSHEET ANALYSIS *Using Excel*

Set up the spreadsheet comparing Vong and Crist Companies as shown on page 327.

Required

a. For each company, compute gross profit, gross profit percentage, net realizable value, accounts receivable turnover, and average days to collect.
b. In relation to cost, which company is charging more for its merchandise?
c. Which company is likely to incur higher financial costs associated with granting credit to customers? Explain the reasons for your answer.
d. Which company appears to have more restrictive credit standards when authorizing credit to customers? How do you know?

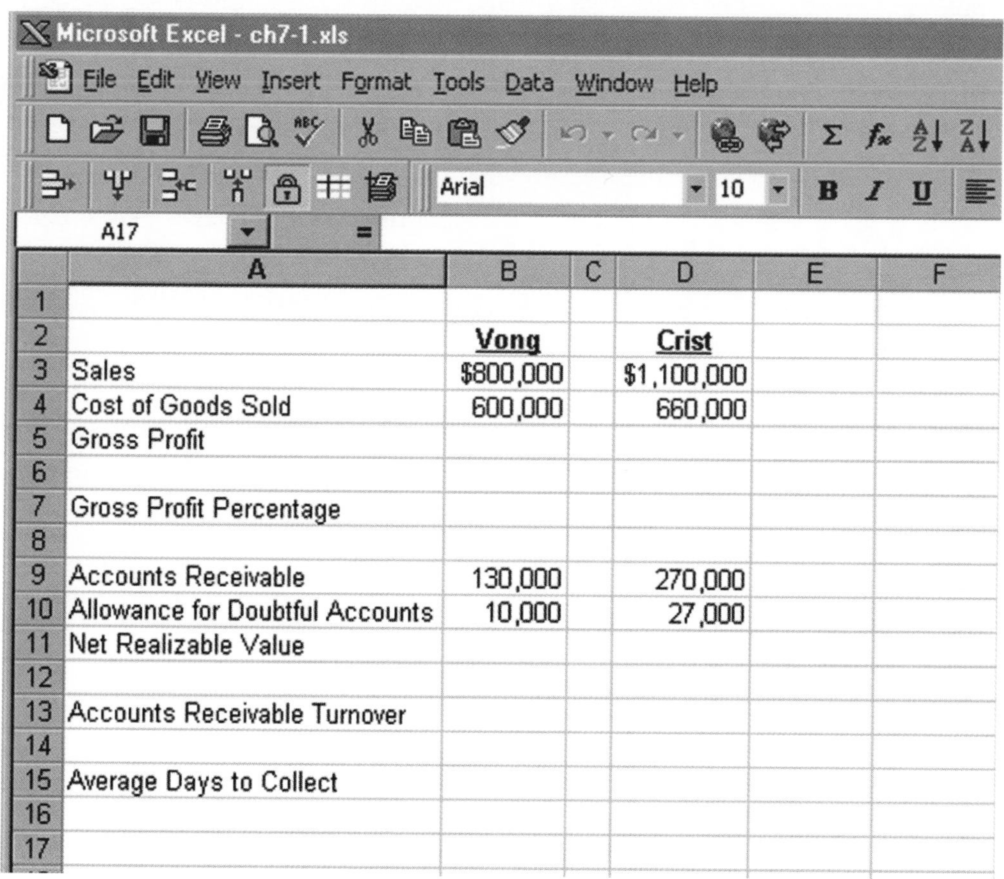

	A	B	C	D	E	F
1						
2		**Vong**		**Crist**		
3	Sales	$800,000		$1,100,000		
4	Cost of Goods Sold	600,000		660,000		
5	Gross Profit					
6						
7	Gross Profit Percentage					
8						
9	Accounts Receivable	130,000		270,000		
10	Allowance for Doubtful Accounts	10,000		27,000		
11	Net Realizable Value					
12						
13	Accounts Receivable Turnover					
14						
15	Average Days to Collect					
16						
17						

SPREADSHEET ANALYSIS *Mastering Excel*

ATC 7–10

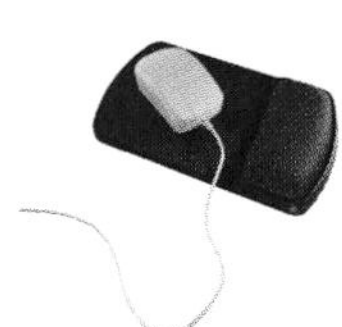

Refer to Problem 7–6B.

Required

Prepare the financial statements using an Excel spreadsheet.

Chapter 8

Asset Valuation
Accounting for Inventories

Learning Objectives

After completing this chapter, you should be able to:

1 Explain how different inventory cost flow methods (specific identification, FIFO, LIFO, and weighted average) affect financial statements.

2 Show the computations for FIFO, LIFO, and weighted average.

3 Apply the lower-of-cost-or-market rule to inventory valuation.

4 Show how to make inventory estimates.

5 Explain the effect of inventory errors on financial statements.

6 Explain the importance of inventory turnover to a company's profitability.

7 Show how to compute a company's operating cycle.

8 Explain inventory cost flow in a periodic system.

the *curious* accountant

A few years ago, workers at a metal stamping plant went on strike. This plant manufactured parts used in a number of automobile assembly plants. Within four days, the strike at this plant caused several automobile assembly plants to close due to a shortage of parts. Within two weeks after the beginning of the strike, most of the automobile assembly plants had closed down. Considering the enormous costs of having to stop production at its assembly plants, why does a company not keep a larger inventory of parts available so that a strike at one plant will not cause most assembly plants to stop production within two weeks? See page 341 for an answer.

The process of determining the cost of inventory was simplified in our introduction to inventory concepts in Chapter 5 by the assumption that the cost per unit remained constant. In practice, different prices may be paid for identical inventory items, thereby requiring a decision as to which costs to allocate to cost of goods sold versus ending inventory. For example, assume that Baker Company paid cash to purchase two inventory items. The first item was purchased at a cost of $100; the second was purchased sometime later for $110. Except for cost, both items are identical. Suppose that the items are mixed together so that Baker cannot determine which item was purchased first. If Baker sells one of the inventory items, which cost should be removed from the Inventory account and charged to Cost of Goods Sold? There are several ***inventory cost flow methods*** *that offer alternative solutions to this problem. These cost flow methods are discussed in the following section of this chapter.*

Inventory Cost Flow Methods

LO1 Explain how different inventory cost flow methods (specific identification, FIFO, LIFO, and weighted average) affect financial statements.

The four common methods for assigning product costs to the income statement are (1) specific identification; (2) first-in, first-out (FIFO); (3) last-in, first-out (LIFO); and (4) weighted average. Each cost flow method is explained in the following discussion.

Specific Identification

If the two inventory items Baker Company purchased were tagged when they were purchased so that the specific cost of each item could be identified, then the actual cost of the item sold could be charged to cost of goods sold. When the inventory consists of low-priced, high-turnover goods such as food items, the record-keeping necessary for **specific identification** can become burdensome. Think of the work required to maintain a record of the specific cost of each food item in a grocery store. Another potential disadvantage of the specific identification method is that it provides the opportunity to manipulate the income statement. By selecting which items to deliver to customers, management can control the cost of goods sold expense and thereby manipulate the amount of net income reported in the financial statements. Even so, specific identification is often used for high-priced, low-turnover items such as automobiles. Here the record keeping is minimal, and customer demands for specific products limit management's ability to select the merchandise being sold.

First-In, First-Out (FIFO)

The **first-in, first-out (FIFO) cost flow method** assumes that the cost of the items purchased *first* should be assigned to Cost of Goods Sold. Under FIFO, the cost of goods sold by Baker Company is $100.

Last-In, First-Out (LIFO)

The **last-in, first-out (LIFO) cost flow method** requires that the cost of the *last* items purchased be charged to Cost of Goods Sold. Under this method, the cost of goods sold for Baker Company is $110.

Weighted Average

Under the **weighted-average cost flow method**, the average unit cost of the inventory is determined by totalling the costs incurred and dividing by the number of units ([100 + 110] ÷ 2 = 105). The average unit cost is then multiplied by the number of units sold, and the result is charged to Cost of Goods Sold. In the Baker Company case, $105 is assigned to the cost of goods sold.

Physical Flow

It is important to note that the preceding discussion referred to the *flow of costs* through the accounting records. The **physical flow of goods** is an entirely separate consideration. Goods are usually moved physically on a FIFO basis, which means that the first merchandise in (the oldest merchandise) is the first merchandise to be delivered to customers. The last items in (the newest goods) are retained by the business. Obviously, this procedure is necessary to keep inventories from becoming filled with dated merchandise. However, note that while the *physical flow* of goods is being conducted on a FIFO basis, the *flow of costs* can have an entirely different basis, such as LIFO or weighted average.

Effect of Cost Flow on Financial Statements

Effect on Income Statement

The cost flow method a company uses can have a strong effect on the amount of gross profit reported in the income statement. To demonstrate this point, assume that Baker Company sold the inventory item under discussion for $120. The amounts of gross profit under the FIFO, LIFO, and weighted-average cost flow assumptions are shown in the following table:

	FIFO	LIFO	Weighted Average
Sales	$120	$120	$120
Cost of goods sold	100	110	105
Gross profit	$ 20	$ 10	$ 15

Note that the amount of gross profit reported under FIFO is double the amount reported under LIFO. This result occurs even though the accounting events described by each cost flow method are identical. In each case, the same inventory items were bought and sold. *Companies experiencing identical economic events with respect to the purchase and sale of inventories can report significantly different results in their financial statements*. Financial analysis requires an understanding of reporting practices as well as economic relationships.

Effect on Balance Sheet

Since total product costs are allocated between costs of goods sold and ending inventory, the type of cost flow method used affects the balance sheet as well as the income statement. For example, since FIFO transfers the first cost to the income statement, it leaves the last costs on the balance sheet. Similarly, by transferring the last cost to the income statement, LIFO leaves the first costs in ending inventory. The weighted-average method uses the average cost per unit to determine the amount of both cost of goods sold and ending inventory. The amount of ending inventory reported on the balance sheet for each of the three cost flow methods is shown in the following table:

	FIFO	LIFO	Weighted Average
Ending inventory	$110	$100	$105

All three methods are used extensively in business. Indeed, the same company may use one cost flow method for some of its products and different cost flow methods for other products.

Nash Office Supply (NOS) purchased two Model 303 copiers at different times. The first copier purchased cost $400 and the second copier purchased cost $450. NOS sold one of the copiers for $600. Determine the gross profit on the sale and the ending inventory balance assuming NOS accounts for inventory using (1) FIFO, (2) LIFO, and (3) weighted average.

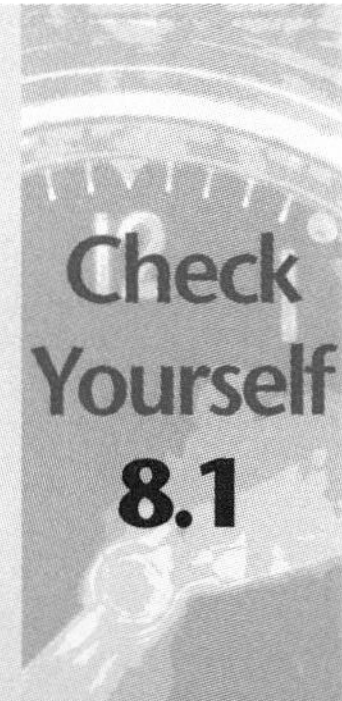

Answer

	FIFO	LIFO	Weighted Average
Sales	$600	$600	$600
Cost of goods sold	(400)	(450)	(425)
Gross profit	$200	$150	$175
Ending inventory	$450	$400	$425

Inventory Cost Flow under a Perpetual System

Multiple Layers with Multiple Quantities

LO2 Show the computations for FIFO, LIFO, and weighted average.

To make it easier to understand the different cost flow methods, the preceding example used a simplified case that included only two cost layers ($100 and $110), with one inventory item in each layer. The following information is used to demonstrate a more interesting situation that includes multiple layers, with different quantities in each layer. The underlying allocation concepts remain unchanged and should help you understand the more complex situation.

Suppose that the accounting records of The Mountain Bike Company (TMBC) contained the following account balances as of January 1, 2006: Cash, $12,000; Inventory, $2,000; Common Shares, $6,000; and Retained Earnings, $8,000. During 2006, TMBC made two cash purchases of inventory. The following table shows the detailed records of the beginning inventory balance and the two purchases:

Jan. 1	Beginning inventory	10 units @ $200	=	$ 2,000
Mar. 18	First purchase	20 units @ $220	=	4,400
Aug. 21	Second purchase	25 units @ $250	=	6,250
Total cost of the 55 bikes available for sale				$12,650

Assume that in October 2006, TMBC sold 43 bikes at $350 per bike. Also assume that TMBC incurred $2,600 of cash operating expenses during 2006. Finally, assume that the company paid cash for income taxes at a rate of 30 percent of net income. There are five events that affected the company in the 2006 accounting period: (1 and 2) the cash purchases of inventory, (3) the cash sale of inventory, (4) the cash payment of operating expenses, and (5) the cash payment of taxes. Exhibit 8–1 shows the effect of each event on the financial statements under three different inventory cost flow assumptions: FIFO, LIFO, and weighted average. The exhibit also assumes that TMCB uses a *perpetual inventory system*.

Events 1 and 2 Purchase of Inventory

As shown in Exhibit 8–1, purchases of inventory are treated exactly the same under FIFO, LIFO, and weighted-average assumptions. In each case, the purchase constitutes an asset exchange. The asset *Inventory* increases, and the asset *Cash* decreases. Total assets are unaffected. The income statement is not affected; the cash outflow is shown in the operating activities section of the cash flow statement.

Event 3a Sale of Inventory

As with purchases, the treatment of sales revenue is not affected by the flow of inventory cost. Note that under all three cost flow methods, sales amounted to $15,050 (43 bikes × $350 per bike). The sale represents a source of assets. The effect of recognizing the sales revenue increases assets (Cash) and equity (Revenue). Recognition of the sales revenue increases net income. The cash inflow from the sale is shown in the operating activities section of the cash flow statement.

FIFO Inventory Cost Flow

Event 3b Cost of Sale

When goods are sold, the cost of those goods is transferred from the Inventory account to the Cost of Goods Sold account. Therefore, assets (Inventory) and equity decrease. The decrease in equity results from the increase in the expense account *Cost of Goods Sold*, which reduces net income and ultimately retained earnings. The amount to be transferred from Inventory to Cost of Goods Sold is determined by the type of cost flow method that is applied. The FIFO method transfers the cost of the *first 43 bikes* that came into TMBC to the Cost of Goods Sold account. This allocation occurs no matter which bikes were actually sold. Remember, physical flow and cost flow are totally separate events. The first 43 bikes acquired by TMBC include the 10 bikes that were in the beginning inventory (these were left over from purchases made in the prior period) plus the 20 bikes that were purchased in March and 13 of the bikes

Exhibit 8–1 *Effect of Events on Financial Statements*

Panel 1

Event No.	Balance Sheet							Income Statement					Cash Flow Statement	
	Assets			=	Equity									
	Cash	+	Inventory	=	C. Sh.	+	Ret. Earn.	Rev.	−	Exp.	=	Net Inc.		
Bal.	12,000	+	2,000	=	6,000	+	8,000	0	−	0	=	0	0	
1	(4,400)	+	4,400	=	NA	+	NA	NA	−	NA	=	NA	(4,400)	OA
2	(6,250)	+	6,250	=	NA	+	NA	NA	−	NA	=	NA	(6,250)	OA
3(a)	15,050	+	NA	=	NA	+	15,050	15,050	−	NA	=	15,050	15,050	OA
3(b)	NA	+	(9,650)	=	NA	+	(9,650)	NA	−	9,650	=	(9,650)	NA	
4	(2,600)	+	NA	=	NA	+	(2,600)	NA	−	2,600	=	(2,600)	(2,600)	OA
5	(840)	+	NA	=	NA	+	(840)	NA	−	840	=	(840)	(840)	OA
Bal.	12,960	+	3,000	=	6,000	+	9,960	15,050	−	13,090	=	1,960	960	NC

Panel 2

Event No.	Balance Sheet							Income Statement					Cash Flow Statement	
	Assets			=	Equity									
	Cash	+	Inventory	=	C. Sh.	+	Ret. Earn.	Rev.	−	Exp.	=	Net Inc.		
Bal.	12,000	+	2,000	=	6,000	+	8,000	0	−	0	=	0	0	
1	(4,400)	+	4,400	=	NA	+	NA	NA	−	NA	=	NA	(4,400)	OA
2	(6,250)	+	6,250	=	NA	+	NA	NA	−	NA	=	NA	(6,250)	OA
3(a)	15,050	+	NA	=	NA	+	15,050	15,050	−	NA	=	15,050	15,050	OA
3(b)	NA	+	(10,210)	=	NA	+	(10,210)	NA	−	10,210	=	(10,210)	NA	
4	(2,600)	+	NA	=	NA	+	(2,600)	NA	−	2,600	=	(2,600)	(2,600)	OA
5	(672)	+	NA	=	NA	+	(672)	NA	−	672	=	(672)	(672)	OA
Bal.	13,128	+	2,440	=	6,000	+	9,568	15,050	−	13,482	=	1,568	1,128	NC

Panel 3

Event No.	Balance Sheet							Income Statement					Cash Flow Statement	
	Assets			=	Equity									
	Cash	+	Inventory	=	C. Sh.	+	Ret. Earn.	Rev.	−	Exp.	=	Net Inc.		
Bal.	12,000	+	2,000	=	6,000	+	8,000	0	−	0	=	0	0	
1	(4,400)	+	4,400	=	NA	+	NA	NA	−	NA	=	NA	(4,400)	OA
2	(6,250)	+	6,250	=	NA	+	NA	NA	−	NA	=	NA	(6,250)	OA
3(a)	15,050	+	NA	=	NA	+	15,050	15,050	−	NA	=	15,050	15,050	OA
3(b)	NA	+	(9,890)	=	NA	+	(9,890)	NA	−	9,890	=	(9,890)	NA	
4	(2,600)	+	NA	=	NA	+	(2,600)	NA	−	2,600	=	(2,600)	(2,600)	OA
5	(768)	+	NA	=	NA	+	(768)	NA	−	768	=	(768)	(768)	OA
Bal.	13,032	+	2,760	=	6,000	+	9,792	15,050	−	13,258	=	1,792	1,032	NC

purchased in August. Panel 1 of Exhibit 8–1 shows the cost of goods sold expense recognition. The expense recognition decreases net income. There is no effect on cash flow at this time. The effect on cash flow occurred at the time the inventory was purchased. The amount of the Cost of Goods Sold ($9,650) is computed as follows:

Jan. 1	Beginning inventory	10 units @ $200	=	$2,000
Mar. 18	First purchase	20 units @ $220	=	4,400
Aug. 21	Second purchase	13 units @ $250	=	3,250
	Total cost of the 43 bikes sold			$9,650

LIFO Inventory Cost Flow

As shown in Panel 2 of Exhibit 8–1, the amount of cost transferred from Inventory to Cost of Goods Sold under a LIFO system is $10,210. This amount is determined by computing the cost of the *last 43 bikes* acquired by TMBC as shown:

Aug. 21	Second purchase	25 units @ $250	=	$ 6,250
Mar. 18	First purchase	18 units @ $220	=	3,960
	Total cost of the 43 bikes sold			$10,210

Weighted-Average Cost Flow

To compute the amount of cost of goods sold under the weighted-average method, we must begin by calculating the weighted-average cost per unit. This is determined by dividing the *total cost of goods available for sale* by the *total number of goods available for sale*. In the case of TMBC, the weighted-average cost per unit is $230 ($12,650 ÷ 55). The weighted-average cost of goods sold is then determined by multiplying the cost per unit by the number of units sold ($230 × 43 = $9,890). Panel 3 of Exhibit 8–1 shows the cost of goods sold expense recognition.

Event 4 Operating Expenses Paid

The payment of operating expenses is not affected by the inventory cost flow method. In all cases, the $2,600 of operating expenses reduce assets (Cash) and equity (Retained Earnings). The expense recognition decreases net income. The cash outflow is shown in the operating activities section of the cash flow statement.

Event 5 Income Taxes Paid

Since the inventory cost flow method affects the amount of cost of goods sold, it will also affect the amount of net income and, therefore, the amount of income tax expense. While the *amount* of the tax due (net income before tax × tax rate) will vary depending on which cost flow method is applied, the *effect* of the tax expense on the financial statements will be the same under all three methods. In each case, the tax expense will reduce assets (Cash) and equity (Retained Earnings). The expense recognition decreases net income. The cash outflow is shown in the operating activities section of the cash flow statement.

Effect of Cost Flow on Financial Statements

LO1 Explain how different inventory cost flow methods (specific identification, FIFO, LIFO, and weighted average) affect financial statements.

Exhibit 8–2 contains an income statement, balance sheet, and cash flow statement for each of the three cost flow assumptions. Look at these financial statements and decide which cost flow method you would recommend TMBC use in its published financial statements. The initial recommendation that most people make is FIFO. Indeed, FIFO produces the highest amount of net income as well as the largest balance in the ending inventory. Therefore, assets and income look better under FIFO. However, a closer look reveals that net cash inflow is lower under FIFO because more income taxes must be paid on the higher amount of reported net income. Recall that except for taxes, the economic circumstances are identical under all three methods. In other words, the only real economic difference between FIFO and LIFO is that FIFO requires the payment of more taxes. In these circumstances, TMBC would prefer to use the LIFO method.

Exhibit 8–2

TMBC COMPANY
Comparative Financial Statements

Income Statements

	FIFO	LIFO	Weighted Average
Sales	$15,050	$15,050	$15,050
Cost of Goods Sold	(9,650)	(10,210)	(9,890)
Gross Profit	5,400	4,840	5,160
Operating Expenses	(2,600)	(2,600)	(2,600)
Income before Taxes (IBT)	2,800	2,240	2,560
Income Tax Expense (IBT × 0.30)	(840)	(672)	(768)
Net Income	$ 1,960	$ 1,568	$ 1,792

Balance Sheets

	FIFO	LIFO	Weighted Average
Assets			
Cash	$12,960	$13,128	$13,032
Inventory	3,000	2,440	2,760
Total Assets	$15,960	$15,568	$15,792
Shareholders' Equity			
Common Shares	$ 6,000	$ 6,000	$ 6,000
Retained Earnings	9,960	9,568	9,792
Total Shareholders' Equity	$15,960	$15,568	$15,792

Cash Flow Statements

	FIFO	LIFO	Weighted Average
Operating Activities			
Cash Inflow from Customers	$15,050	$15,050	$15,050
Cash Outflow for Inventory	(10,650)	(10,650)	(10,650)
Cash Outflow for Operating Expenses	(2,600)	(2,600)	(2,600)
Cash Outflow for Tax Expense	(840)	(672)	(768)
Net Cash Inflow from Operations	960	1,128	1,032
Investing Activities	0	0	0
Financing Activities	0	0	0
Net Increase in Cash	960	1,128	1,032
Beginning Cash Balance	12,000	12,000	12,000
Ending Cash Balance	$12,960	$13,128	$13,032

However, the LIFO method is not allowed for tax purposes in Canada. As well, calculations of LIFO under a perpetual system can become very complex. Therefore, this text will only cover simplified calculations where sales are assumed to take place at the end of the period. More in-depth coverage of this topic is left to a more advanced accounting course.

You may wonder if the advantages of reporting the more positive financial image under FIFO outweigh the disadvantage of having to pay more taxes. Given an optimistic report of more assets and higher income, would investors not be more interested in the company even if TMBC had to pay more income taxes? Research suggests that investors are not deceived by reporting procedures. They make investment decisions on the basis of economic substance regardless of how it is presented in financial statements.

Note that FIFO produces higher reported income and assets than LIFO only in an environment of rising prices (inflationary conditions). In an inflationary environment, the most recent prices are the highest prices. The oldest prices (first-in prices) are the lowest prices. Since FIFO assigns the oldest prices to the income statement, expenses (Cost of Goods Sold) are lower and net income is higher. Also, the newest (highest) prices are retained in ending inventory, which results in a higher amount of reported assets. Notice that this condition reverses in times of falling prices (deflationary conditions), such as those facing firms in the computer industry. Under conditions of deflation, the oldest prices are the highest prices, and the newest prices are the lowest prices. Therefore, FIFO assigns the first-in (oldest and highest) costs to the income statement and the newest (lowest) to the balance sheet, which means that in a deflationary economy, FIFO results in the reporting of lower amounts of income and assets.

Check Yourself 8.2

The following information was drawn from the inventory records of Fields, Inc.

Beginning inventory	200 units @ $20
First purchase	400 units @ $22
Second purchase	600 units @ $24

Assume that Fields sold 900 units of inventory.

1. Determine the amount of cost of goods sold using FIFO.
2. Would using LIFO produce a higher or lower amount of cost of goods sold? Why?

Answer

1. Cost of goods sold using FIFO:

Beginning inventory	200 units @ $20	=	$ 4,000
First purchase	400 units @ $22	=	8,800
Second purchase	300 units @ $24	=	7,200
Total cost of goods sold			$20,000

2. The inventory records reflect an inflationary environment of steadily rising prices. Since LIFO charges the latest costs (in this case the highest costs) to the income statement, using LIFO would produce a higher amount of cost of goods sold than would using FIFO.

Inventory Cost Flow When Sales and Purchases Occur Intermittently

LO2 Show the computations for FIFO, LIFO, and weighted average.

In the previous sections, all purchases were made before any of the goods were sold. This section addresses sales transactions that occur intermittently with purchases. To illustrate, assume that the following table describes the beginning inventory, purchases, and sales transactions for Sharon Sales Company (SSC) during 2008:

Date	Transaction	Description
Jan. 1	Beginning inventory	100 units @ $20.00
Feb. 14	Purchased	200 units @ $21.50
Apr. 5	Sold	220 units @ $30.00
June 21	Purchased	160 units @ $22.50
Aug. 18	Sold	100 units @ $30.00
Sept. 2	Purchased	280 units @ $23.50
Nov. 10	Sold	330 units @ $30.00

FIFO Cost Flow

Exhibit 8–3 contains the supporting computations for determining the amounts of cost of goods sold and inventory, assuming that SSC uses a FIFO cost flow. Note that the inventory is maintained in layers. Each time a sales transaction occurs, the unit cost contained in the first layer is applied to the number of goods sold. If there are not enough items in the first layer to cover the total number of units sold, the unit cost of the next layer is applied to the remaining number of goods sold. For example, the cost of 220 units of inventory sold on April 5 is determined by adding the cost of 100 units of inventory in the first layer (beginning inventory) to the cost of 120 units of inventory contained in the second layer. The cost of goods sold for this transaction is $4,580 (100 units @ $20.00 + 120 units @ $21.50). As shown in Exhibit 8–3, the cost of goods sold for subsequent sales transactions is computed in a similar fashion.

Exhibit 8–3 *Sales and Transactions under FIFO Cost Flow*

	Purchase			Cost of Goods			Sold Inventory		
Date	Units	Cost	Total	Units	Cost	Total	Units	Cost	Total
Jan. 1							100	@ $20.00	= $2,000
Feb. 14	200	@ $21.50	= $4,300				200	@ $21.50	= $4,300
Apr. 5				100	@ $20.00	= $ 2,000			
				120	@ $21.50	= $ 2,580	80	@ $21.50	= $1,720
June 21	160	@ $22.50	= $3,600				160	@ $22.50	= $3,600
Aug. 18				80	@ $21.50	= $ 1,720			
				20	@ $22.50	= $ 450	140	@ $22.50	= $3,150
Sept. 2	280	@ $23.50	= $6,580				280	@ $23.50	= $6,580
Nov. 10				140	@ $22.50	= $ 3,150			
				190	@ $23.50	= $ 4,465	90	@ $23.50	= $2,115
				Total COGS		= $14,365	Ending Bal.		= $2,115

The computation of gross profit for the 2008 accounting period under a FIFO cost flow is shown here:

Sales (650 units @ $30 each)	$19,500
Cost of goods sold	14,365
Gross profit	$ 5,135

Weighted-Average and LIFO Cost Flows

When we attempt to apply LIFO or the weighted-average cost flow methods to intermittent sales and purchase transactions, a problem emerges at the point of the first sales event. For example, LIFO requires that the cost of the *last items* purchased *during the period* be charged to cost of goods sold. This is not possible because the period is not over and the last items have not been purchased at the time the first sale is made. Accountants often solve this problem by recording only the quantities of sales and purchases on a perpetual basis; this enables them to obtain many of the benefits of a perpetual inventory system even when cost data are unavailable. For example, management can identify the quantity of lost, damaged, or stolen goods, and it can determine when it is time to reorder merchandise. At the end of the accounting period, when complete information about purchases and sales is available, costs are assigned to the quantity data that have been maintained perpetually. Although a complete discussion of weighted-average and LIFO cost flow approaches is beyond the scope of this text, be aware that the potential problems associated with intermittent sales are manageable. Indeed, weighted average and LIFO are used by many companies that experience intermittent sales and purchase transactions.

reality bytes

To avoid spoilage, most companies use a first-in, first-out (FIFO) approach for the flow of physical goods. The older goods (first units purchased) are sold before the newer goods are sold. For example, Loblaw's and other food stores stack older merchandise at the front of the shelf where customers are more likely to pick it up first. As a result, merchandise is sold before it becomes spoiled. However, when spoilage is not an issue, convenience may dictate the use of the last-in, first-out (LIFO) method. Examples of products that often move on a LIFO basis include rock, gravel, dirt, and other nonwasting assets. Indeed, rock, gravel, and dirt are normally stored in piles that are unprotected from weather. New inventory is simply piled on top of the old. Inventory that is sold is taken from the top of the pile because it is convenient to do so. Accordingly, the last inventory purchased is the first inventory sold. Regardless of whether the flow of physical goods is accomplished on a LIFO or FIFO basis, costs can flow differently. The flow of inventory through the physical facility is a separate issue from the flow of costs through the accounting system.

Lower-of-Cost-or-Market Rule

LO3 Apply the lower-of-cost-or-market rule to inventory valuation.

To this point, the discussion has been directed toward the flow of inventory costs. Once the cost of ending inventory has been determined, accounting practice requires that it be compared with the current market value and that the inventories be carried at the *lower-of-cost-or-market value (LCM)*. For the purposes of this comparison, *market* is defined as the amount that would have to be paid to replace the merchandise. Regardless of whether a decline in market value to a point below cost is due to physical damage, deterioration, obsolescence, or a general decline in the level of prices, the resultant loss must be recognized in the current period.

The **lower-of-cost-or-market rule** can be applied to (1) each individual inventory item, (2) major classes or categories of inventory, or (3) the entire stock of inventory in aggregate. The most common practice is to apply LCM to total inventory. To illustrate the application to individual inventory items, assume that Wilson Office Supply Company purchased 100 calculators at a cost of $14 each. If the current replacement cost of the calculators is above $14, then the ending inventory is carried at cost (100 × $14 = $1,400). However, if some form of technological advance permits the manufacturer to reduce the unit price of the calculators to $11, then the replacement cost to Wilson will fall below the historical cost, and the carrying value of the inventory will be written down to $1,100 (100 × $11). Exhibit 8–4 demonstrates the computation of ending inventory for a company that has four different inventory items.

In the case presented in Exhibit 8–4, the company must reduce the $30,020 historical cost of its ending inventory to $28,410. This $1,610 reduction causes a decline in the amount of the company's gross profit for the period. The procedure used to reflect the inventory write-down in the accounts will depend on whether the company uses the perpetual or periodic inventory system. If the perpetual system is used, the effect of the write-down and the journal entry necessary to record it are as follows:

Assets	=	Liab.	+	Equity	Rev.	−	Exp.	=	Net Inc.	Cash Flow Statement
(1,610)	=	NA	+	(1,610)	NA	−	1,610	=	(1,610)	NA

Account Title	Debit	Credit
Cost of Goods Sold (Inventory Loss)	1,610	
Inventory		1,610

Exhibit 8–4 ***Determination of Ending Inventory at Lower of Cost or Market***

Item	Quantity (a)	Unit Cost (b)	Unit Market (c)	Total Cost (a × b)	Total Market (a × c)	Lower of Cost or Market
A	320	$21.50	$22.00	$ 6,880	$ 7,040	$ 6,880
B	460	18.00	16.00	8,280	7,360	7,360
C	690	15.00	14.00	10,350	9,660	9,660
D	220	20.50	23.00	4,510	5,060	4,510
				$30,020	$29,120	$28,410

Conceptually, the loss should be shown as an operating expense on the income statement. However, if the amount is immaterial, it can be included in the cost of goods sold.

When ending inventory is shown at the lower of cost or market, any loss is automatically included in the cost of goods sold. When we increase the cost of goods sold, we reduce net income and ultimately equity, which balances against the reduction in assets (Inventory). Cash flow is not affected by the write-down.

Estimating the Ending Inventory Balance

LO4 Show how to make inventory estimates.

Under the *perpetual inventory system*, the best estimate of the amount of inventory on hand at any time is the book balance in the Inventory account. Recall that the book balance is increased when purchases are made and is decreased when goods are sold. As a result, if records are maintained accurately, the balance in the Inventory account should be equal to the amount of goods on hand except for unrecorded items such as lost, damaged, or stolen goods.

Effect of Inventory Errors on Financial Statements

LO5 Explain the effect of inventory errors on financial statements.

Inventory is one of the largest assets on the balance sheets of most merchandising businesses. It constitutes the lifeblood of a business. If it sells, the business thrives; if it does not, the business dies. It is often used to collateralize loans. Therefore, both investors and creditors are keenly interested in the character and content of a company's inventory. In conditions of adversity, managers may be tempted to misrepresent the financial condition of their companies by manipulating the balance of the Inventory account. Indeed, some of the most significant frauds in the history of business have involved the falsification of inventory records. It is critically important that business students become aware of the effects of inventory errors (legitimate or otherwise) on financial statements.

Errors under a Perpetual System

Large inventory errors are more likely to be discovered under the perpetual system because the book balance can be compared to the physical count. Since the two balances should be the same except for differences caused by lost, damaged, or stolen goods, major differences would be investigated and their cause identified. Even so, mistakes can still occur. For example, suppose a company failed to count $5,000 of inventory on hand at the end of the accounting period. Since the inventory was not counted, it would be assumed to be lost or stolen, and the company would record an inventory loss. As a result, expenses (Cost of Goods Sold or Inventory Loss) would be overstated. The ending balance in the Inventory account would be understated, as would net income and Retained Earnings. The Inventory and Retained Earnings would continue to be understated until such time as the error was discovered and corrected.

Understanding How the Length of the Operating Cycle Affects Profitability

LO6 Explain the importance of inventory turnover to a company's profitability.

The importance of the gross profit percentage to the management of merchandising companies was discussed in Chapter 5. While it is certainly important to know the difference between what a product costs and its selling price, more information is needed to assess the desirability of selling individual inventory items. To illustrate, assume that a grocery store sells two brands of kitchen cleansers, Zjax and Cosmos. Zjax costs $1 and sells for $1.25, resulting in a gross profit of $0.25 ($1.25 − $1.00). Cosmos costs $1.20 and sells for $1.60, resulting in a gross profit of $0.40 ($1.60 − $1.20). Accordingly, Zjax has a 20 percent gross profit percentage ($0.25 ÷ $1.25), while Cosmos has a 25 percent gross profit ($0.40 ÷ $1.60). Does this mean that it is more desirable to stock Cosmos than Zjax? Not if you can sell significantly more cans of Zjax than Cosmos. Suppose the lower price results in higher customer demand for Zjax. Indeed, the manager of the grocery store expects that in the coming year, the store can sell 7,000 units of Zjax but only 3,000 units of Cosmos. In these circumstances, Zjax will return a total gross profit of $1,750 (7,000 units × $0.25 per unit), while Cosmos will return only $1,200 (3,000 units × $0.40 per unit). So, it is important to consider how rapidly inventory sells as well as the spread between cost and selling price.

Average Number of Days to Sell Inventory

The measure of how fast inventory sells is called **inventory turnover**, and it is defined as follows:

$$\frac{\text{Cost of goods sold}}{\text{Inventory}}$$

LO7 Show how to compute a company's operating cycle.

The result of this computation is the number of times the balance in the Inventory account is turned over (sold) each year. As with the accounts receivable turnover ratio, the inventory turnover ratio may be somewhat difficult to interpret because it does not provide a measure in units of time. To alleviate this problem, the inventory turnover ratio is often taken one step further to determine the average number of days required to sell inventory. The **average days in inventory ratio** (sometimes called **average number of days to sell inventory ratio**) is computed as

$$\frac{365}{\text{Inventory turnover}}$$

an answer for the *curious* accountant

As explained, the cost of carrying inventory can be very high. Many other companies have decided that the costs of closing plants due to potential strikes are lower than the costs of carrying excessive inventory at all times. The strategy of carrying as little inventory as possible is referred to as a just-in-time (JIT) inventory system. As indicated by its name, JIT systems attempt to obtain inventory just in time for it to be used or sold, thereby eliminating the need for large stockpiles of parts and products.

As indicated, a retailer's success from selling inventory depends on a combination of two factors: gross profit and inventory turnover. The most desirable scenario is an inventory system with a high profit margin that turns over rapidly. However, due to competition, companies often focus on one of these elements more than on the other. For example, *discount merchandisers* offer lower prices in the hope that they can stimulate rapid sales. In contrast, *specialty stores* often require larger gross profits to compensate for the fact that their goods sell more slowly. Specialty stores often offer something such as better service to persuade customers that the higher prices are justified.

Will a person buy a high-quality camera at Zellers or at a local camera shop? It depends on whether price or service is more important to that individual. A person needing considerable advice about which model to choose may be willing to pay the camera shop's higher price to get more professional help. So, although decisions about pricing, advertising, service, and so on, are often thought of as marketing decisions, they cannot be made properly without understanding the interaction between the gross profit percentage and **inventory turnover**.

Real-World Data

The discussion of operating cycles that began in Chapter 6 and continued in Chapter 7 can now be completed. The length of a company's operating cycle is the sum of its average number of days to sell inventory plus its average number of days to collect accounts receivable.

Exhibit 8–5 shows operating cycles for seven real-world companies. These numbers are for 2000.

Exhibit 8–5

Industry	Company	Average Days in Inventory	Average Days to Collect Receivables	Length of Operating Cycle
Fast-Food	McDonald's	10	13	23
	Wendy's	13	11	24
	Starbucks	61	9	70
Retail	Wal-Mart	52	4	56
	Mark's Work Wearhouse	166	17	183
Alcohol	Segram	99	63	162
	Molson	30	13	43

What is the significance of operating cycles of different lengths? Recall from Chapter 6 that the operating cycle for a business is the time required for the business to get back the cash it invested in inventory. As explained earlier, the longer this takes, the more it costs the company. Notice from Exhibit 8–5 that Mark's operating cycle was 114 days longer than Wal-Mart's. All other things being equal, roughly how much did this extra time increase Mark's costs compared to Wal-Mart's? Assume that Mark's could invest excess cash at 8 percent (or alternatively, assume that it pays 8 percent to finance its inventory and accounts receivable). Using accounting information provided in Mark's 2000 financial statements, we can determine the solution as follows:

Mark's Investment in Inventory	×	Interest Rate	×	Time	=	Cost
$76,982,000		8%		114/365		$1,924,000

Based on the assumed 8 percent cost of money, the extra time it takes Mark's to get back its investment in inventory costs the company almost $2 million per operating cycle. Based on approximately two cycles per year (365 ÷ 183), the extended operating cycle costs Mark's almost $4 million annually. The preceding certainly is a rough estimate, but it clearly demonstrates that it is important for businesses to monitor the length of their operating cycles.

There are other costs of having excess inventory besides the financing cost explained in the preceding paragraphs. The more inventory a company maintains, the more expense it will incur for storage and insurance and the more likely its inventory will be damaged or stolen during storage. Of course, carrying too little inventory can result in lost sales, so constant monitoring is necessary to ensure that the proper level of inventory is on hand.

Returning to the data in Exhibit 8–5, why do Seagram's and Molson's operating cycles differ so greatly? Beer has a relatively short shelf life, while liquor can age in the bottle. Therefore, their average days in inventory appear as would be expected.

Finally, why does Starbucks hold its inventory so much longer than the other two fast-food businesses? Starbucks' main inventory is coffee. Before being roasted, coffee, unlike hamburgers or fresh vegetables, can be held for long periods without its quality deteriorating. Coffee is not grown in Canada. Therefore, Starbucks cannot wait until the last minute to order its inventory. This problem is further complicated by the fact that coffee is harvested during only one season of the year. Cattle can be processed into hamburgers year-round.

Once again, to understand a company, you must understand the industry in which that company operates. Understanding the accounting procedures used to prepare its financial statements is only part of the task.

Effects of Cost Flow on Ratio Analysis

As demonstrated earlier in the chapter, the inventory cost flow assumption that a company uses affects its cost of goods sold and thereby its gross profit, net income, and retained earnings. The method selected also affects the cost assigned to ending inventory, which in turn affects current assets and total assets. Financial statement analysis is also affected if it is based on ratios that use any of the items mentioned in their computation. Therefore, almost every ratio discussed in this book is affected. Previously defined ratios that are affected include the following:

- Current ratio
- Debt to assets ratio
- Return on assets ratio
- Return on equity ratio
- Return on sales ratio
- Gross profit percentage
- Average days to sell inventory

a look back

Chapter 5 introduced the basic issues associated with accounting for inventory and cost of goods sold. This chapter expanded the subject to include a discussion of inventory cost flow methods including first-in, first-out (FIFO), last-in, first-out (LIFO), weighted average, and specific identification. Under *FIFO*, the cost of the items purchased first is shown on the income statement, and the cost of the items purchased last is shown on the balance sheet. Under *LIFO*, the cost of the items purchased last is shown on the income statement, and the cost of the items purchased first is shown on the balance sheet. Under the *weighted-average method*, the average cost of inventory is shown on the income statement and the balance sheet. Finally, under specific identification the actual cost of the goods is shown on the income statement and the balance sheet.

Generally accepted accounting principles often allow companies to account for the same types of events in different ways. The different cost flow assumptions presented in this chapter—FIFO, LIFO, weighted average, specific identification—are excellent examples of alternative accounting procedures allowed by GAAP. People who use financial information must be aware of the accounting alternatives available for a given event and the effects that choosing one method over another have on companies' financial statements and ratios.

This chapter also completed the discussion of the operating cycle, which began in Chapter 6. The measure of how fast inventory sells is called *inventory turnover*; it is computed by dividing cost of goods sold by inventory. The result of this computation is the number of times the balance in the Inventory account is turned over each year. The *average number of days in inventory ratio* can be determined by dividing the number of days in a year (365) by the inventory turnover ratio.

a look forward

Chapter 9 discusses accounting for long-term assets such as buildings and equipment. Although this topic is very different from accounting for inventory that a company purchases to sell to customers, it is similar in that GAAP allows different companies to use different accounting methods to account for the same types of events. The lives of accounting students would be easier if all companies had to use the same accounting methods. However, accounting methods used by different companies in the real world are probably becoming even more diverse. Thus, it is important that users of financial information consider these differences when making decisions.

SELF-STUDY REVIEW PROBLEM

Erie Jewellers sells gold earrings. Its beginning inventory of Model 407 gold earrings consisted of 100 pairs of earrings at $50 per pair. Erie purchased two batches of Model 407 earrings during the year. The first batch purchased consisted of 150 pairs at $53 per pair; the second batch consisted of 200 pairs at $56 per pair. During the year, Erie sold 375 pairs of Model 407 earrings.

Required

Determine the amount of product cost Erie would allocate to cost of goods sold and ending inventory assuming that Erie uses (a) FIFO, (b) LIFO, and (c) weighted average.

Solution to Requirements a–c

Goods Available for Sale					
Beginning inventory	100	@	$50	=	$ 5,000
First purchase	150	@	53	=	$ 7,950
Second purchase	200	@	56	=	$11,200
Goods available for sale	450				$24,150

a. FIFO

	Pairs		Cost per Pair		Cost of Goods Sold
From beginning inventory	100	@	$50	=	$ 5,000
From first purchase	150	@	53	=	$ 7,950
From second purchase	125	@	56	=	$ 7,000
Total pairs sold	375				$19,950

Ending inventory = Goods available for sale − Cost of goods sold
Ending inventory = $24,150 − $19,950 = $4,200

b. LIFO

	Pairs		Cost per Pair		Cost of Goods Sold
From second purchase	200	@	$56	=	$11,200
From first purchase	150	@	$53	=	$ 7,950
From beginning inventory	25	@	$50	=	$ 1,250
Total pairs sold	375				$20,400

Ending inventory = Goods available for sale − Cost of goods sold
Ending inventory = $24,150 − $20,400 = $3,750

c. Weighted average

Goods available for sale ÷ Total pairs = Cost per pair
$24,150 ÷ 450 = $53.6667

Cost of goods sold: 375 units @ $53.6667 = $20,125
Ending inventory: 75 units @ $53.6667 = $ 4,025

APPENDIX

LO8 Explain inventory cost flow in a periodic system.

Inventory Cost Flow in a Periodic System

Recall that under the *periodic inventory system*, inventory records are not changed when goods are purchased or sold. The amount of ending inventory is determined by taking a physical count of goods on hand at the end of the accounting period. As well, the amount of *cost of goods sold* is computed by subtracting the amount of *ending inventory* from *cost of goods available for sale*. Therefore, the assignment of cost focuses on the measurement of ending inventory. To illustrate, assume the same facts as those used for Sharon Sales Company in the previous section. For your convenience, these data are repeated in Exhibit 8–6. Although the facts are the same, the data have been arranged in a different order to reflect the use of a periodic as opposed to a perpetual inventory system.

LO2 Show the computations for LIFO, FIFO, and weighted average.

Exhibit 8–6 *Sales and Purchase Transactions for Sharon Sales Company*

Date	Transaction		Description		Cost of Goods Available for Sale	Sales
Jan. 1	Beg. inventory		100 units @ $20.00	=	$ 2,000	
Feb. 14	Purchased		200 units @ $21.50	=	$ 4,300	
Apr. 5	Sold	220	units @ $30.00	=		$ 6,600
June 21	Purchased		160 units @ $22.50	=	$ 3,600	
Aug. 18	Sold	100	units @ $30.00	=		$ 3,000
Sept. 2	Purchased		280 units @ $23.50	=	$ 6,580	
Nov. 10	Sold	330	units @ $30.00	=		$ 9,900
	Totals	650	740		$16,480	$19,500

Exhibit 8–7 shows the computations for the allocation of the *cost of goods available for sale* between *ending inventory* and *cost of goods sold* under the FIFO, LIFO, and weighted-average cost flow methods. All three methods are shown because the periodic method does not involve the computational problems associated with the perpetual method. According to the data in Exhibit 8–6, 740 inventory items were available for sale (beginning inventory of 100 units + purchases of 640 units). Since 650 items were sold, ending inventory contains 90 units. FIFO transfers the *first* costs (older) to cost of good sold and thereby leaves the *last costs* (newest) in ending inventory. Therefore, ending inventory under FIFO is $2,115.00 (90 × $23.50). LIFO allocates the last costs to cost of goods sold, leaving the *first* costs in ending inventory. Ending inventory under LIFO is $1,800.00 (90 × $20.00). Finally, the weighted-average unit cost of $22.27 ($16,480.00 ÷ 740) times 90 units of inventory yields an ending Inventory balance of $2,004 (rounded to the nearest dollar). Remember that the perpetual and periodic accounting procedures represent two different approaches for arriving at the same end result; only the method of computation differs. This fact can be verified by comparing the cost of goods sold and the balance in ending inventory in Exhibit 8–3 (page 337) with the amounts under the FIFO column in Exhibit 8–7.

Exhibit 8–7 *Allocation of Cost of Goods Available for Sale under a Periodic Inventory System*

	FIFO	LIFO	Weighted Average
Cost of goods available for sale	$16,480	$16,480	$16,480
Less: Ending inventory	(2,115)	(1,800)	(2,004)
Cost of goods sold	$14,365	$14,680	$14,476

Lower-of-Cost-or-Market Rule

LO3 Apply the lower-of-cost-or-market rule to inventory valuation.

Under the periodic method, the amount of ending inventory is shown at the lower of cost or market in the schedule of cost of goods sold. By lowering the ending inventory, we increase cost of goods. These relationships are shown in the following schedule of cost of goods sold:

Schedule of Cost of Goods Sold

Beginning Inventory	xxx	
Plus: Purchases	xxx	
Cost of Goods Available for Sale	xxx	
Less: Ending Inventory	(xxx)	Lower amount reported here results in a
Cost of Goods Sold	xxx	higher amount reported here

Estimating the Ending Inventory Balance

LO4 Show how to make inventory estimates.

The Inventory account is not altered when goods are purchased or sold under the periodic system. It may be necessary to estimate the amount of inventory on hand at various times when a company is using the periodic inventory system.

Estimates of the amount of inventory are necessary when a company wants to prepare monthly or quarterly financial statements but does not want to incur the expense of undertaking a physical count of goods on hand. Also, estimates may be needed to support insurance claims when inventory has been destroyed by fire, storms, or other natural disasters. Finally, estimates of inventory can be used to evaluate the accuracy of a physical count of goods. One common method used to estimate the amount of inventory is called the *gross profit method.*

The **gross profit method** assumes that the percentage of gross profit to sales remains relatively stable from one accounting period to the next. Information regarding the amount of sales and the cost of goods available for sale is drawn from the general ledger. As well, the percentage of gross profit to sales is determined on the basis of the historical relationship between these two accounts (the average of the last five years' sales is divided into the average gross profit for the same five-year period). The percentage is then multiplied by the amount of sales for the current period to estimate the current period's gross profit. The estimated gross profit is subtracted from sales in order to compute the amount of estimated cost of goods sold. The estimated cost of goods sold is then subtracted from the cost of goods available for sale to arrive at the estimated ending inventory.

To illustrate, assume that the information in Exhibit 8–8 is drawn from the accounting records of the T-Shirt Company.

Exhibit 8–8

The T-Shirt Company
Schedule for Estimating the Ending Inventory Balance
For the Period Ending June 30, 2002

Beginning Inventory	$ 5,100	
Purchases	18,500	
Goods Available for Sale		$23,600
Sales through June 30, 2002	22,000	
Less: Estimated Gross Profit*	?	
Estimated Cost of Goods Sold		?
Estimated Ending Inventory		$?

*Historically, gross profit has amounted to approximately 25 percent of sales.

The cost of the estimated ending inventory can be computed as follows:

1. Estimate the amount of gross profit by multiplying the gross profit percentage by the sales ($22,000 × 0.25 = $5,500).
2. Estimate the amount of the cost of goods sold by subtracting the estimated gross profit from sales ($22,000 − $5,500 = $16,500).
3. Estimate the amount of ending inventory by subtracting the estimated cost of goods sold from the amount of goods available for sale ($23,600 − $16,500 = $7,100).

Cantrell, Inc., recently lost its inventory in a fire. The accounting records indicate that its beginning inventory had been $20,000. During the period prior to the fire, Cantrell had purchased $70,000 of inventory and had recognized $140,000 of sales revenue. Cantrell's gross profit percentage is normally 40 percent of sales. Estimate the amount of inventory lost in the fire.

Answer Goods available for sale was $90,000 ($20,000 beginning inventory + $70,000 purchases). Estimated cost of goods sold was $84,000 ($140,000 sales − [$140,000 × 0.40] gross profit). Estimated inventory lost would be $6,000 ($90,000 goods available for sale − $84,000 cost of goods sold).

Errors under a Periodic System

The financial condition of a company can be severely misrepresented by merely overstating the amount of ending inventory in the year-end physical count under a periodic system. The overstatement of ending inventory causes an understatement of cost of goods sold and thereby a corresponding overstatement of net income. The overstatement of net income causes an overstatement of retained earnings, which creates the increase in equity that balances with the overstated value of the inventory. To illustrate, assume that McCrary Merchandising overstates its year-end inventory balance by $1,000. As indicated in the following schedule, this overstatement causes the understatement of cost of goods sold:

	Ending Inventory Is Accurate	Ending Inventory Is Overstated	
Beginning inventory	$ 4,000	$ 4,000	
Purchases	6,000	6,000	
Cost of goods available for sale	10,000	10,000	
Ending inventory	(3,000)	(4,000)	$1,000 Overstated
Cost of goods sold	$ 7,000	$ 6,000	$1,000 Understated

The understatement of cost of goods sold results in the overstatement of gross profit, as indicated in the following income statement:

	Ending Inventory Is Accurate	Ending Inventory Is Overstated	Effect on Cost of Goods Sold
Sales	$11,000	$11,000	
Cost of goods sold	(7,000)	(6,000)	$1,000 Understated
Gross profit	$ 4,000	$ 5,000	$1,000 Overstated

On the balance sheet, assets (Inventory) and equity (Retained Earnings) are overstated as follows:

	Ending Inventory Is Accurate	Ending Inventory Is Overstated	
Assets			
Cash	$ 1,000	$ 1,000	
Inventory	3,000	4,000	$1,000 Overstated
Other assets	5,000	5,000	
Total assets	$ 9,000	$10,000	
Shareholders' equity			
Common shares	$ 5,000	$ 5,000	
Retained earnings	4,000	5,000	$1,000 Overstated
Total Shareholders' equity	$ 9,000	$10,000	

Since the current period's ending inventory becomes the next period's beginning inventory, the error in the current period reverses itself in the next period. Net income for the current period is overstated, and net income of the next period is understated. The retained earnings at the end of the second period are stated correctly as a result of the counterbalancing errors shown on the following income statements:

McCRARY MERCHANDISING
Schedule of Cost of Goods
Second Accounting Period

Beginning Inventory	$ 4,000	$1,000 Overstated
Purchases	xxx	
Cost of Goods Available for Sale	xxx	$1,000 Overstated
Ending Inventory	(xxx)	
Cost of Goods Sold	$ xxx	$1,000 Overstated
Income Statement		
Sales	$ xxx	
Cost of Goods Sold	(xxx)	$1,000 Overstated
Gross Profit	$ xxx	$1,000 Understated

According to this, the first period's overstatement of net income is offset by the second period's understatement. Therefore, the balance sheet reported at the end of the second period is not affected by the error made in the first period.

KEY TERMS

average days in inventory ratio (or average number of days to sell inventory ratio) *340*

first-in, first-out (FIFO) cost flow method *330*

gross profit method *345*

inventory cost flow methods *329*

inventory turnover *340*

last-in, first-out (LIFO) cost flow method *330*

lower-of-cost-or-market rule *338*

physical flow of goods *330*

specific identification *330*

weighted-average cost flow method *330*

QUESTIONS

1. Why are historical costs generally used in financial statements?
2. Name and discuss the four cost flow methods discussed in this chapter.
3. What are some advantages and disadvantages of the specific identification method of accounting for inventory?
4. What are some advantages and disadvantages of using the FIFO method of inventory valuation?
5. What are some advantages and disadvantages of using the LIFO method of inventory valuation?
6. In an inflationary period, which inventory cost flow method will produce the largest net income? Explain.
7. In an inflationary period, which inventory cost flow method will produce the largest amount of total assets on the balance sheet? Explain.
8. What is the difference between the flow of costs and the physical flow of goods?
9. Does the choice of cost flow method (FIFO, LIFO, or weighted average) affect the cash flow statement? Explain.
10. Assume that Key Co. purchased 1,000 units of merchandise in its first year of operations for $25 per unit. The company sold 850 units for $40. What is the amount of cost of goods sold using FIFO? LIFO? Weighted average?
11. Assume that Key Co. purchased 1,500 units of merchandise in its second year of operation for $27 per unit. Its beginning inventory was determined in Question 10. Assuming that 1,500 units are sold, what is the amount of cost of goods sold using FIFO? LIFO? Weighted average?
12. Refer to Questions 10 and 11. Which method might be preferable for financial statements? For income tax reporting? Explain.
13. In an inflationary period, which cost flow method, FIFO or LIFO, produces the larger cash flow? Explain.
14. Which inventory cost flow method produces the largest net income in a deflationary period?
15. How is the weighted-average cost per unit computed by using a moving-average cost flow?
16. What is the difference between a periodic inventory system and a perpetual inventory system?
17. How does the phrase *lower-of-cost-or-market* value apply to inventory valuation?
18. If some merchandise declined in value because of damage or obsolescence, what effect will the lower-of-cost-or-market rule have on the income statement? Explain.
19. What are three situations in which estimates of the amount of inventory may be useful or even necessary?
20. Under which inventory system, periodic or perpetual, is it easier for management to manipulate net income if tempted to do so?
21. If the amount of goods available for sale is $123,000, the amount of sales is $130,000, and the gross profit is 25 percent of sales, what is the amount of ending inventory?
22. Assume that inventory is overstated by $1,500 at the end of 2004. What effect will this have on the 2004 income statement? The 2004 balance sheet? The 2005 income statement? The 2005 balance sheet? (Assume that the periodic inventory method is used.)
23. What information does inventory turnover provide?
24. What is an example of a business that would have a high inventory turnover? A low inventory turnover?
25. How is a company's operating cycle calculated?

EXERCISES

L.O. 1 EXERCISE 8–1 *Effect of Inventory Cost Flow Assumption on Financial Statements*

Required

For each of the following situations, fill in the blank with *FIFO*, *LIFO*, or *weighted average*.

a. ______ would produce the highest amount of net income in an inflationary environment.
b. ______ would produce the highest amount of assets in an inflationary environment.
c. ______ would produce the lowest amount of net income in a deflationary environment.
d. ______ would produce the same unit cost for assets and cost of goods sold in an inflationary environment.
e. ______ would produce the lowest amount of net income in an inflationary environment.
f. ______ would produce an asset value that was the same regardless of whether the environment was inflationary or deflationary.
g. ______ would produce the lowest amount of assets in an inflationary environment.
h. ______ would produce the highest amount of assets in a deflationary environment.

L.O. 1, 2 EXERCISE 8–2 *Allocating Product Cost between Cost of Goods Sold and Ending Inventory: Single Purchase*

Tyler Co. started the year with no inventory. During the year, it purchased two identical inventory items. The inventory was purchased at different times. The first purchase cost $3,000 and the other, $4,000. One of the items was sold during the year.

Required

Based on this information, how much product cost would be allocated to cost of goods sold and ending inventory on the year-end financial statements, assuming use of

a. FIFO?
b. LIFO?
c. weighted average?

EXERCISE 8–3 *Allocating Product Cost between Cost of Goods Sold and Ending Inventory: Multiple Purchases* **L.O. 1, 2**

Breckin Company sells coffee makers used in business offices. Its beginning inventory of coffee makers was 100 units at $40 per unit. During the year, Breckin made two batch purchases of coffee makers. The first was a 150-unit purchase at $60 per unit; the second was a 200-unit purchase at $68 per unit. During the period, Breckin sold 260 coffee makers.

Required

Determine the amount of product costs that would be allocated to cost of goods sold and ending inventory, assuming that Breckin uses

a. FIFO.
b. LIFO.
c. weighted average.

EXERCISE 8–4 *Effect of Inventory Cost Flow (FIFO, LIFO, and Weighted Average) on Gross Profit* **L.O. 1, 2**

The following information pertains to Porter Company for 2005:

Beginning inventory	50 units @ $10
Units purchased	275 units @ $15

Ending inventory consisted of five units. Porter sold 320 units at $30 each. All purchases and sales were made with cash.

Required

a. Compute the gross profit for Porter Company using the following cost flow assumptions: (1) FIFO, (2) LIFO, and (3) weighted average.
b. What is the dollar amount of difference in net income between using FIFO versus LIFO? (Ignore income tax considerations.)
c. Determine the cash flow from operating activities, using each of the three cost flow assumptions listed in Requirement *a*. Ignore the effect of income taxes. Explain why these cash flows have no differences.

EXERCISE 8–5 *Effect of Inventory Cost Flow on Ending Inventory Balance* **L.O. 2**

McKee Sales had the following transactions for cameras for 2004, its first year of operations:

Jan. 20	Purchased 450 units @ $20	=	$9,000
Apr. 21	Purchased 200 units @ $24	=	4,800
July 25	Purchased 100 units @ $30	=	3,000
Sept. 19	Purchased 75 units @ $18	=	1,350

During the year, McKee Sales sold 725 cameras for $50 each.

Required

a. Compute the amount of ending inventory McKee would report on the balance sheet, assuming the following cost flow assumptions: (1) FIFO, (2) LIFO, and (3) weighted average.
b. Compute the difference in gross profit between the FIFO and LIFO cost flow assumptions.

L.O. 1, 2 EXERCISE 8–6 *Income Tax Effect of Shifting from FIFO to LIFO*

The following information pertains to the inventory of the Foley Company:

Jan. 1	Beginning Inventory	500 units @ $10
Apr. 1	Purchased	2,500 units @ $11
Oct. 1	Purchased	800 units @ $14

During the year, Foley sold 3,400 units of inventory at $20 per unit and incurred $17,000 of operating expenses. Foley currently uses the FIFO method but is considering a change to LIFO. All transactions are cash transactions. Assume a 30 percent income tax rate.

Required

a. Prepare income statements using FIFO and LIFO.
b. Determine the amount of income taxes Foley would save if it changed cost flow methods.
c. Determine the cash flow from operating activities under FIFO and LIFO.
d. Explain why cash flow from operating activities is lower under FIFO when that cost flow method produced the higher gross profit.

L.O. 1, 2 EXERCISE 8–7 *Effect of FIFO versus LIFO on Income Tax Expense*

Tiny Tots Company had sales of $125,000 for 2006, its first year of operation. On April 2, the company purchased 200 units of inventory at $175 per unit. On September 1, an additional 150 units were purchased for $190 per unit. The company had 100 units on hand at the end of the year. The company's income tax rate is 40 percent. All transactions are cash transactions.

Required

a. The preceding paragraph describes five accounting events: (1) a sales transaction, (2) the first purchase of inventory, (3) a second purchase of inventory, (4) the recognition of cost of goods sold expense, and (5) the payment of income tax expense. Record the amounts of each event in horizontal statements models like the following ones, assuming first a FIFO and then a LIFO cost flow.

Effects of Events on Financial Statements

Panel 1: FIFO Cost Flow

Event No.	Balance Sheet							Income Statement					Cash Flow Statement
	Cash	+	Inventory	=	C. Sh.	+	Ret. Earn.	Rev.	−	Exp.	=	Net Inc.	

Panel 2: LIFO Cost Flow

Event No.	Balance Sheet							Income Statement					Cash Flow Statement
	Cash	+	Inventory	=	C. Sh.	+	Ret. Earn.	Rev.	−	Exp.	=	Net Inc.	

b. Compute net income using FIFO.
c. Compute net income using LIFO.
d. Explain the difference, if any, in the amount of income tax expense incurred using the two cost flow assumptions.
e. How does the use of the FIFO versus the LIFO cost flow assumption affect the cash flow statement?

EXERCISE 8–8 *Recording Inventory Transactions Using the Perpetual Method: Intermittent Sales and Purchases*

L.O. 2

The following inventory transactions apply to Nikols Company for 2004:

Jan. 1	Purchased	250 units @ $10
Apr. 1	Sold	125 units @ $18
Aug. 1	Purchased	400 units @ $11
Dec. 1	Sold	500 units @ $19

The beginning inventory consisted of 175 units at $11 per unit. All transactions are cash transactions.

Required

a. Record these transactions in general journal format, assuming that Nikols uses the FIFO cost flow assumption and keeps perpetual records.
b. Compute the ending balance in the Inventory account.

EXERCISE 8–9 *Effect of Cost Flow on Ending Inventory: Intermittent Sales and Purchases*

L.O. 2

Spring Hill, Inc., had the following series of transactions for 2007:

Date	Transaction	Description
Jan. 1	Beginning inventory	50 units @ $20
Mar. 15	Purchased	200 units @ $24
May 30	Sold	170 units @ $40
Aug. 10	Purchased	275 units @ $25
Nov. 20	Sold	340 units @ $40

Required

a. Determine the quantity and dollar amount of inventory at the end of the year, assuming Spring Hill uses the FIFO cost flow assumption and keeps perpetual records.
b. Write a memo explaining why Spring Hill, Inc., would have difficulty applying the LIFO method on a perpetual basis. Include a discussion of how to overcome these difficulties.

EXERCISE 8–10 *Lower-of-Cost-or-Market Rule: Perpetual System*

L.O. 3

The following information pertains to Auto Parts Co.'s ending inventory for the current year:

Item	Quantity	Unit Cost	Unit Market Value
P	100	$4	$3
D	50	5	4
S	20	6	7
J	15	5	4

Required

a. Determine the value of the ending inventory using the lower-of-cost-or-market rule applied to (1) each individual inventory item and (2) the total inventory in aggregate.
b. Prepare any necessary journal entries, using (1) the individual method and (2) the aggregrate method. Auto Parts Co. uses the perpetual inventory system.

L.O. 3 **EXERCISE 8–11** *Lower-of-Cost-or-Market Rule: Periodic System (Appendix)*

Moore Company carries three inventory items. The following information pertains to the ending inventory:

Item	Quantity	Unit Cost	Unit Market Value
O	200	$10	$ 9
J	250	15	14
R	175	5	8

Required

a. Determine the ending inventory that will be reported on the balance sheet, assuming that Moore applies the lower-of-cost-or-market rule to individual inventory items.
b. Explain how the write-down would be recorded under the periodic inventory system.

L.O. 4 **EXERCISE 8–12** *Estimating Ending Inventory: Periodic System (Appendix)*

A substantial portion of inventory owned by Rick's Fishing Supplies was recently destroyed when the roof collapsed during a rainstorm. The accountant must estimate the loss from the storm for insurance reporting and financial statement purposes. Rick's uses the periodic inventory system. The following pertains to Rick's books:

Beginning inventory	$100,000
Purchases to date of storm	400,000
Sales to date of storm	550,000

The value of undamaged inventory counted was $8,000. Historically Rick's gross profit percentage has been approximately 20 percent of sales.

Required

Estimate the following:
a. Gross profit in dollars
b. Cost of goods sold
c. Ending inventory
d. Amount of lost inventory

L.O. 4 **EXERCISE 8–13** *Estimating Ending Inventory: Perpetual System*

Steve Li owned a small company that sold boating equipment. The equipment was expensive, and a perpetual system was maintained for control purposes. Even so, lost, damaged, and stolen merchandise normally amounted to 5 percent of the inventory balance. On June 14, Li's warehouse was destroyed by fire. Just prior to the fire, the accounting records contained a $164,000 balance in the Inventory account. However, inventory costing $21,000 had been sold and delivered to customers but had not been recorded in the books at the time of the fire. The fire did not affect the showroom, which contained inventory that cost $37,500.

Required

Estimate the amount of inventory destroyed by fire.

L.O. 5 **EXERCISE 8–14** *Effect of Inventory Error on Financial Statements: Perpetual System*

Marshall Company failed to count $12,000 of inventory in its 2007 year-end physical count.

Required

Explain how this error will affect Marshall's 2007 financial statements, assuming that Marshall uses the perpetual inventory system.

EXERCISE 8–15 *Effect of Inventory Error on Elements of Financial Statements: Periodic System (Appendix)* **L.O. 5**

The ending inventory for Tedall Co. was understated by $5,200 at the end of 2005.

Required
Was each of the following amounts overstated, understated, or not affected by the error?

Item No.	Year	Amount
1	2005	Beginning inventory
2	2005	Purchases
3	2005	Goods available for sale
4	2005	Cost of goods sold
5	2005	Gross profit
6	2005	Net income
7	2006	Beginning inventory
8	2006	Purchases
9	2006	Goods available for sale
10	2006	Cost of goods sold
11	2006	Gross profit
12	2006	Net income

PROBLEMS—SERIES A

PROBLEM 8–1A *Effect of Different Inventory Cost Flow Methods on Financial Statements* **L.O. 1, 2**

The accounting records of Sharp Photography, Inc., reflected the following balances as of January 1, 2007:

Cash	$22,000	
Beginning Inventory	16,500	(150 units @ $110)
Common Shares	14,300	
Retained Earnings	24,200	

The following five transactions occurred in 2007:

1. First purchase (cash) 120 units @ $85
2. Second purchase (cash) 200 units @ $100
3. Sales (all cash) 300 units @ $185
4. Paid $12,000 cash for operating expenses.
5. Paid cash for income tax at the rate of 40 percent of income before taxes.

Required

a. Compute the cost of goods sold and ending inventory, assuming (1) FIFO cost flow, (2) LIFO cost flow, and (3) weighted-average cost flow.

b. Use a vertical model to prepare the 2007 income statement, balance sheet, and cash flow statement under FIFO, LIFO, and weighted average. (*Hint:* Record the events under an accounting equation before preparing the statements.)

PROBLEM 8–2A *Allocating Product Costs between Cost of Goods Sold and Ending Inventory: Intermittent Purchases and Sales of Merchandise* **L.O. 2**

Milan, Inc., had the following sales and purchase transactions during 2006. Beginning inventory consisted of 80 items at $120 each. Milan uses the FIFO cost flow assumption and keeps perpetual inventory records.

Date	Transaction	Description
Mar. 5	Purchased	80 items @ $125
Apr. 10	Sold	60 items @ $245
June 19	Sold	70 items @ $245
Sept. 16	Purchased	60 items @ $130
Nov. 28	Sold	55 items @ $255

Required

a. Record the inventory transactions in general journal format.
b. Calculate the gross profit Milan would report on the 2006 income statement.
c. Determine the ending inventory balance Milan would report on the December 31, 2006, balance sheet.

L.O. 3

PROBLEM 8–3A *Inventory Valuation Based on the Lower-of-Cost-or-Market Rule: Perpetual System*

At the end of the year, Dot Computer Repair had the following items in inventory:

Item	Quantity	Unit Cost	Unit Market Value
D1	60	$30	$35
D2	30	55	50
D3	44	40	55
D4	40	50	35

Required

a. Determine the amount of ending inventory using the lower-of-cost-or-market rule applied to each individual inventory item.
b. Provide the general journal entry necessary to write down the inventory based on Requirement *a*. Assume that Dot Computer Repair uses the perpetual inventory system.
c. Determine the amount of ending inventory, assuming that the lower-of-cost-or-market rule is applied to the total inventory in aggregate.
d. Provide the general journal entry necessary to write down the inventory based on Requirement *c*. Assume that Dot Computer Repair uses the perpetual inventory system.

L.O. 4 PROBLEM 8–4A *Estimating Ending Inventory: Perpetual System*

Fran's Fun House had its inventory destroyed by a tornado on July 16 of the current year. Fortunately, the accounting records were at the home of one of the owners and were not damaged. Lost, damaged, or stolen merchandise normally amounts to 4 percent of the inventory balance. Just before the tornado, the accounting records contained a $340,000 balance in the Inventory account. However, inventory costing $65,000 had been sold and delivered to customers but had not been recorded in the books at the time of the tornado. Fran's Fun House also had inventory of $45,000 in another location that was not affected by the tornado.

Required

Estimate the amount of inventory destroyed by the tornado so an insurance claim can be processed.

L.O. 4 PROBLEM 8–5A *Estimating Ending Inventory: Gross Profit Method—Periodic System (Appendix)*

Beach Supplies had its inventory destroyed by a hurricane on September 21 of the current year. Back-up copies of the accounting records were stored in an off-site location and were not damaged. The following information was available for the period of January 1 through September 21:

Beginning inventory, January 1	$ 68,000
Purchases through September 21	350,000
Sales through September 21	520,000

The gross profit for Beach Supplies has traditionally been 25 percent of sales.

Required

a. For the period ending September 21, compute the following:
   (1) Estimated gross profit.
   (2) Estimated cost of goods sold.
   (3) Estimated inventory at September 21.
b. Assume that $8,000 of the inventory was not damaged. What is the amount of the loss from the hurricane?
c. If Beach Supplies had used the perpetual inventory system, how would it have determined the amount of the inventory loss?

PROBLEM 8–6A *Estimating Ending Inventory: Gross Profit Method—Periodic System (Appendix)* **L.O. 4**

Lexington Company wants to produce quarterly financial statements but takes a physical count of inventory only at year end. The following historical data were taken from the 2004 and 2005 accounting records:

	2004	2005
Net sales	$140,000	$200,000
Cost of goods sold	62,000	90,000

At the end of the first quarter of 2006, Lexington Company's ledger had the following account balances:

Sales	$240,000
Sales Discounts	10,000
Purchases	160,000
Transportation-in	4,000
Transportation-out	6,000
Beginning Inventory	60,000

Required

Using the information provided, estimate the following for the first quarter of 2006:

a. Gross profit
b. Ending inventory at March 31

PROBLEM 8–7A *Effect of Inventory Errors on Financial Statements* **L.O. 5**

The following income statement was prepared for ROC Company for the year 2006:

ROC COMPANY Income Statement For the Year Ended December 31, 2006	
Sales	$69,000
Cost of Goods Sold	(38,640)
Gross Profit	30,360
Operating Expenses	(9,100)
Net Income	$21,260

During the year-end audit, the following errors were discovered:

1. A $1,400 payment for repairs was erroneously charged to the Cost of Goods Sold account. (Assume that the perpetual inventory system is used.)
2. Sales to customers for $2,400 at December 31, 2006, were not recorded in the books for 2006. Also, the $1,344 cost of selling these goods was not recorded. The error was not discovered in the physical count because the goods had not been delivered.
3. A mathematical error was made in determining ending inventory. Ending inventory was understated by $1,200. (The Inventory account was written down in error.)

Required

Determine the effect, if any, of each of the errors on the following items. Give the dollar amount of the effect and whether it would overstate (+), understate (−), or not affect (NA) the account. The effect on sales is recorded as an example.

Error No. 1	Amount of Error	Effect
Sales 2006	NA	NA
Ending inventory, December 31, 2006		
Gross profit, 2006		
Beginning inventory, January 1, 2007		
Cost of goods sold, 2006		
Net income, 2006		
Retained earnings, December 31, 2006		
Total assets, December 31, 2006		

Error No. 2	Amount of Error	Effect
Sales 2006	$2,400	−
Ending inventory, December 31, 2006		
Gross profit, 2006		
Beginning inventory, January 1, 2007		
Cost of goods sold, 2006		
Net income, 2006		
Retained earnings, December 31, 2006		
Total assets, December 31, 2006		

Error No. 3	Amount of Error	Effect
Sales 2006	NA	NA
Ending inventory, December 31, 2006		
Gross profit, 2006		
Beginning inventory, January 1, 2007		
Cost of goods sold, 2006		
Net income, 2006		
Retained earnings, December 31, 2006		
Total assets, December 31, 2006		

PROBLEMS—SERIES B

L.O. 1, 2 PROBLEM 8–1B *Effect of Different Inventory Cost Flow Methods on Financial Statements*

The accounting records of Paul's Bicycle Shop reflected the following balances as of January 1, 2007:

Cash	$50,800	
Beginning Inventory	56,000	(200 units @ $280)
Common Shares	43,000	
Retained Earnings	63,800	

The following five transactions occurred in 2007:

1. First purchase (cash) 120 units @ $300
2. Second purchase (cash) 140 units @ $330
3. Sales (all cash) 400 units @ $450
4. Paid $30,000 cash for salaries expense.
5. Paid cash for income tax at the rate of 25 percent of income before taxes.

Required

a. Compute the cost of goods sold and ending inventory, assuming (1) FIFO cost flow, (2) LIFO cost flow, and (3) weighted-average cost flow.
b. Compute the amount of net income and income tax paid, assuming (1) FIFO cost flow, (2) LIFO cost flow, and (3) weighted-average cost flow.
c. Use a vertical model to prepare the 2007 income statement, balance sheet, and cash flow statement under FIFO, LIFO, and weighted average. (*Hint:* Record the events under an accounting equation before preparing the statements.)

PROBLEM 8–2B *Allocating Product Costs between Cost of Goods Sold and Ending Inventory: Intermittent Purchases and Sales of Merchandise* L.O. 2

Fred's Fireplaces had the following sales and purchase transactions during 2008. Beginning inventory consisted of 60 items at $350 each. The company uses the FIFO cost flow assumption and keeps perpetual inventory records.

Date	Transaction	Description
Mar. 5	Purchased	50 items @ $370
Apr. 10	Sold	40 items @ $450
June 19	Sold	50 items @ $450
Sept. 16	Purchased	50 items @ $390
Nov. 28	Sold	35 items @ $470

Required

a. Record the inventory transactions in general journal format.
b. Calculate the gross profit Fred's would report on the 2008 income statement.
c. Determine the ending inventory balance Fred's would report on the December 31, 2008, balance sheet.

PROBLEM 8–3B *Inventory Valuation Based on the Lower-of-Cost-or-Market Rule: Perpetual System* L.O. 3

At the end of the year, Ed's Repair Service had the following items in inventory:

Item	Quantity	Unit Cost	Unit Market Value
P1	80	$ 80	$ 90
P2	60	60	66
P3	100	140	130
P4	50	130	140

Required

a. Determine the amount of ending inventory using the lower-of-cost-or-market rule applied to each individual inventory item.
b. Provide the general journal entry necessary to write down the inventory based on Requirement *a.* Assume that Ed's Repair Service uses the perpetual inventory system.
c. Determine the amount of ending inventory, assuming that the lower-of-cost-or-market rule is applied to the total inventory in aggregate.
d. Provide the general journal entry necessary to write down the inventory based on Requirement *c.* Assume that Ed's Repair Service uses the perpetual inventory system.

PROBLEM 8–4B *Estimating Ending Inventory: Perpetual System* L.O. 4

Jolly Mermaid had its inventory destroyed by a hurricane on October 21 of the current year. Fortunately, the accounting records were stored off-site and were not damaged. Lost, damaged, or stolen merchandise normally amounts to 5 percent of the inventory balance. Just prior to the hurricane, the accounting records contained a $520,000 balance in the Inventory account. However, inventory costing $165,000 had been sold and delivered to customers but had not been recorded in the books at the time of the hurricane. Jolly Mermaid also had inventory of $72,000 in another location that was not affected by the hurricane.

Required
Estimate the amount of inventory destroyed by the hurricane so an insurance claim can be processed.

L.O. 4 PROBLEM 8–5B *Estimating Ending Inventory: Gross Profit Method (Appendix)*

Hank's Fun House had its inventory destroyed by a tornado on October 6 of the current year. Fortunately, back-up copies of the accounting records were at the home of one of the owners and were not damaged. The following information was available for the period of January 1 through October 6:

Beginning inventory, January 1	$ 162,000
Purchases through October 6	680,000
Sales through October 6	1,140,000

Gross profit for Hank's Fun House has traditionally been 30 percent of sales.

Required

a. For the period ending October 6, compute the following:
   (1) Estimated gross profit.
   (2) Estimated cost of goods sold.
   (3) Estimated inventory at October 6.
b. Assume that $20,000 of the inventory was not damaged. What is the amount of the loss from the tornado?
c. If Hank's Fun House had used the perpetual inventory system, how would it have determined the amount of the inventory loss?

L.O. 4 PROBLEM 8–6B *Estimating Ending Inventory: Gross Profit Method (Appendix)*

Elle's Eatery wishes to produce quarterly financial statements, but it takes a physical count of inventory only at year end. The following historical data were taken from the 2006 and 2007 accounting records:

	2006	2007
Net sales	$60,000	$70,000
Cost of goods sold	31,000	36,500

At the end of the first quarter of 2008, Elle's ledger had the following account balances:

Sales	$56,500
Sale Discounts	2,500
Purchases	41,000
Transportation-in	2,000
Transportation-out	5,000
Beginning Inventory	12,500

Required
Using the information provided, estimate the following for the first quarter of 2008:
a. Gross profit
b. Ending inventory at March 31

PROBLEM 8–7B *Effect of Inventory Errors on Financial Statements* **L.O. 5**

The following income statement was prepared for Eddie's Fireworks for the year 2006:

EDDIE'S FIREWORKS Income Statement For the Year Ended December 31, 2006	
Sales	$140,000
Cost of Goods Sold	(77,200)
Gross Profit	62,800
Operating Expenses	(40,900)
Net Income	$ 21,900

During the year-end audit, the following errors were discovered:

1. A $2,000 payment for repairs was erroneously charged to the Cost of Goods Sold account. (Assume that the perpetual inventory system is used.)
2. Sales to customers for $500 at December 31, 2006, were not recorded in the books for 2006. Also, the $300 cost of selling these goods was not recorded. The error was not discovered in the physical count because the goods had not been delivered.
3. A mathematical error was made in determining ending inventory. Ending inventory was understated by $1,800. (The Inventory account was written down in error.)

Required

Determine the effect, if any, of each of the errors on the following items. Give the dollar amount of the effect and whether it would overstate (+), understate (−), or not affect (NA) the account. The first item is recorded as an example.

Error No. 1	Amount of Error	Effect
Sales 2006	NA	NA
Ending inventory, December 31, 2006		
Gross profit, 2006		
Beginning inventory, January 1, 2007		
Cost of goods sold, 2006		
Net income, 2006		
Retained earnings, December 31, 2006		
Total assets, December 31, 2006		

Error No. 2	Amount of Error	Effect
Sales 2006	$500	−
Ending inventory, December 31, 2006		
Gross profit, 2006		
Beginning inventory, January 1, 2007		
Cost of goods sold, 2006		
Net income, 2006		
Retained earnings, December 31, 2006		
Total assets, December 31, 2006		

Error No. 3	Amount of Error	Effect
Sales 2006	NA	NA
Ending inventory, December 31, 2006		
Gross profit, 2006		
Beginning inventory, January 1, 2007		
Cost of goods sold, 2006		
Net income, 2006		
Retained earnings, December 31, 2006		
Total assets, December 31, 2006		

L.O. 5 PROBLEM 8–8B *Effect of Inventory Error on Elements of Financial Statements: Periodic System (Appendix)*

The ending inventory for Caldwell Co. was understated by $5,200 for the year 2004.

Required
Was each of the following amounts overstated, understated, or not affected by the error?

Item No.	Year	Amount
1	2004	Beginning inventory
2	2004	Purchases
3	2004	Goods available for sale
4	2004	Cost of goods sold
5	2004	Gross profit
6	2004	Net income
7	2005	Beginning inventory
8	2005	Purchases
9	2005	Goods available for sale
10	2005	Cost of goods sold
11	2005	Gross profit
12	2005	Net income

ANALYZE, THINK, COMMUNICATE

ATC 8–1 BUSINESS APPLICATIONS CASE *Bombardier's Annual Report*

Required
Using the Bombardier financial statements in Appendix B, answer the following questions:

a. What are the inventory classes used by Bombardier? Calculate the percentage each is of total inventory for the year ended January 31, 2002.
b. What cost flow method(s) did Bombardier use to account for inventory?
c. For 2002, calculate Bombardier's total inventory as a percentage of its total current assets and total assets.

ATC 8–2 GROUP ASSIGNMENT *Inventory Cost Flow*

The accounting records of Blue Bird Co. showed the following balances at January 1, 2008:

Cash	$30,000
Beginning Inventory (100 units @ $50, 70 units @ $55)	8,850
Common Shares	20,000
Retained Earnings	18,850

Transactions for 2008 were as follows:

Purchased 100 units @ $54 per unit.
Sold 220 units @ $80 per unit.
Purchased 250 units @ $58 per unit.
Sold 200 units @ $90 per unit.
Paid operating expenses of $3,200.
Paid income tax expense. The income tax rate is 30%.

Required

a. Organize the class into three sections, and divide each section into groups of three to five students. Assign each section one of the cost flow methods, FIFO, LIFO, or weighted average.

Group Tasks

Determine the amount of ending inventory, cost of goods sold, gross profit, and net income after income tax for the cost flow method assigned to your section. Also prepare an income statement using that cost flow assumption.

Class Discussion

b. Have a representative of each section put its income statement on the board. Discuss the effect that each cost flow method has on assets (ending inventory), net income, and cash flows. Which method is preferred for tax reporting? For financial reporting? What restrictions are placed on the use of LIFO for tax reporting?

REAL-WORLD CASE *Evaluating the Cost Savings from Managing Inventory More Efficiently* ATC 8–3

This chapter reported earlier that in its 1999 fiscal year, Starbucks Coffee took 61 days to sell its inventory. This is a significant improvement over its 1995 fiscal year, when it held inventory an average of 126 days before it was sold. Additional information about Starbucks for 1999 and 1995 is presented here (all dollar amounts are in thousands):

	1995	1999
Average Number of Days to Sell Inventory	126	61
Average Inventory on Hand	n/a	$180,886
Sales	$465,213	$1,680,145
Cost of Goods Sold	$360,064	$739,364
Net Income	$26,102	$101,693
Approximate Number of Stores	800	2,038
Income Tax Rate	39.5%	38.0%

Required

a. Assume that Starbucks paid an average of 6 percent interest on money that it borrowed during 1999. Determine how much the company saved in inventory financing costs, *after taxes*, in 1999 by selling its inventory in 61 days versus the 126 days it was holding inventory during 1995. In other words, how much lower would Starbucks' 1999 net income have been if it had maintained 126 days of sales in inventory rather than 61? Show your computations in good form. (*Hint:* You may want to refer to the discussion of Mark's Work Wearhouse versus Wal-Mart in the chapter to help with this analysis.)

b. Using your answer for Requirement *a* and based on the *average profit generated per store at Starbucks in 1995* (which must be computed), answer the following question. The increase in net income resulting from the more efficient management of inventory produced the same increase in income as if Starbucks had opened what number of new stores?

WRITING ASSIGNMENT *Using the Average Days to Sell Inventory Ratio to Make a Lending Decision* ATC 8–4

Bradford's Wholesale Fruits has applied for a loan and has agreed to use its inventory to collateralize the loan. The company currently has an inventory balance of $289,000. The cost of goods sold for the past year was $7,518,000. The average shelf life for the fruit that Bradford's sells is 10 days, after which time it begins to spoil and must be sold at drastically reduced prices to dispose of it rapidly. The company had maintained steady sales over the past three years and expects to continue at current levels for the foreseeable future.

Required

Based on your knowledge of inventory turnover, write a memo that describes the quality of the inventory as collateral for the loan.

ATC 8–5 BUSINESS APPLICATIONS CASE *Using Ratios to Make Comparisons*

The following accounting information pertains to Cosmos Comics and Fantasy Funnies at the end of 2008. The only difference between the two companies is that Cosmos uses FIFO while Fantasy uses LIFO.

	Cosmos Comics	Fantasy Funnies
Cash	$ 80,000	$ 80,000
Accounts Receivable	320,000	320,000
Merchandise Inventory	240,000	180,000
Accounts Payable	220,000	220,000
Cost of Goods Sold	1,200,000	1,260,000
Building	400,000	400,000
Sales	2,000,000	2,000,000

Required

a. Compute the gross profit percentage for each company, and identify the company that appears to be charging the higher prices in relation to its costs.
b. For each company, compute the inventory turnover ratio and the average number of days to sell inventory. Identify the company that *appears* to be incurring the higher inventory financing cost.
c. Explain why the company with the lower gross profit percentage has the higher inventory turnover ratio.
d. Compute the length of the operating cycle for each company. Explain why short operating cycles are more desirable than long operating cycles.

ATC 8–6 ETHICAL DILEMMA *Show Them Only What You Want Them to See*

Clair Coolage is the chief accountant for a sales company called Far Eastern Imports. The company has been highly successful and is trying to increase its capital base by attracting new investors. The company operates in an inflationary environment and has been using the LIFO inventory cost flow method to minimize its net earnings and thereby reduce its income taxes. Katie Bailey, the vice president of finance, asked Coolage to estimate the change in net earnings that would occur if the company switched to FIFO. After reviewing the company's books, Coolage estimated that pretax income would increase by $1,200,000 if the company adopted the FIFO cost flow method. However, the switch would result in approximately $400,000 of additional taxes. The overall effect would result in an increase of $800,000 in net earnings. Bailey told Coolage to avoid the additional taxes by preparing the tax return on a LIFO basis but to prepare a set of statements on a FIFO basis to be distributed to potential investors.

Required

a. Comment on the implications of Bailey's decision.
b. How will the switch to FIFO affect Far Eastern's balance sheet?

ATC 8–7 SEDAR DATABASE *Analyzing Inventory at Gap Inc.*

Required

Using the most current annual report available on SEDAR, answer the following questions about Gap Inc. The company's Web site can be found at www.gapinc.com.

a. What was the average amount of inventory per store? Use all stores operated by Gap, not just those called *The Gap*. (*Hint:* The answer to this question must be computed. The number of stores in operation at the end of the most recent year can be found in the MD&A section of the annual report.)
b. How many *new* stores did Gap open during the year?
c. Using the quarterly financial information contained in the annual report, complete the following chart.

Quarter	Sales During Each Quarter
1	$
2	
3	
4	

d. Referring to the chart in Requirement *c*, explain why Gap's sales vary so widely throughout its fiscal year. Do you believe that Gap's inventory level varies throughout the year in relation to sales?

SPREADSHEET ANALYSIS *Using Excel*

ATC 8–8

At January 1, 2005, the accounting records of Bronco Boutique had the following balances:

Cash	$1,000	
Beginning Inventory	2,250	(150 units @ $15)
Common Shares	2,000	
Retained Earnings	1,250	

During January, Bronco Boutique entered into five cash transactions:

1. Purchased 120 units of inventory @ $16 each.
2. Purchased 160 units of inventory @ $17 each.
3. Sold 330 units of inventory @ $30 each.
4. Incurred $1,700 of operating expenses.
5. Paid income tax at the rate of 30 percent of income before taxes.

Required

a. Set up rows 1 through 10 of the following spreadsheet to compute cost of goods sold and ending inventory, assuming (1) FIFO, (2) LIFO, and (3) weighted-average cost flows. Notice that the FIFO cost flow has already been completed for you. Use columns O through W to complete the LIFO and weighted-average cost flow computations. Be sure to use formulas for all calculations.

Microsoft Excel - ch8-1.xls

B16 = =K7

	A	B	C	D	E	F	G	H	I	J	K	L	M	N
1	Cost of Goods Available For Sale					FIFO Ending Inventory			FIFO Cost of Goods Sold			LIFO Ending Inventory		
2			Unit	Total			Unit	Total		Unit	Total		Unit	Total
3		Units	Price	Cost		Units	Price	Cost	Units	Price	Cost	Units	Price	Cost
4	Beginning Inventory	150	$15	$2,250					150	$15	$2,250			
5	First Purchase (cash)	120	$16	$1,920					120	$16	$1,920			
6	Second Purchase (cash)	160	$17	$2,720		100	$17	$1,700	60	$17	$1,020			
7	Total Cost of Goods Available for Sale	430		$6,890		100		$1,700	330		$5,190			
8														
9	Average Cost		$16.02				Check:	EI + CGS	430	Units				
10								EI + CGS	$6,890	Total Cost				

	A	B	C	D
13				WEIGHTED
14	Income Statements	FIFO	LIFO	AVERAGE
15	Sales (330 units @ $30 each) (cash)	$9,900		
16	Cost of Goods Sold	5,190		
17	Gross Profit	4,710		
18	Operating Expenses (cash)	1,700		
19	Income Before Taxes	3,010		
20	Income Tax Expense (30%) (cash)	903		
21	Net Income	$2,107		
22				
23	Cash Flow Statement	FIFO		
24	Cash from Operating Activities:			
25	Cash received from Customers	$9,900		
26	Cash paid for Inventory Purchased	(4,640)		
27	Cash paid for Operating Expenses	(1,700)		
28	Cash paid for Income Taxes	(903)		
29	Net Cash Flow from Operating Activities	2,657		
30	Beginning Cash	1,000		
31	Ending Cash	$3,657		

Problem 8-1 Answer Key | Problem | Sheet2 | Sheet3

b. In rows 13 through 31, compute the amount of net income and net cash flow from operations under FIFO, LIFO, and weighted average. The FIFO column has been provided as an example.

SPREADSHEET ASSIGNMENT *Mastering Excel*

ATC 8–9

Required

Complete ATC 8–5 using an Excel spreadsheet. Use Excel problem ATC 7–9 as a resource for structuring the spreadsheet.

Chapter 9

Long-Term Operational Assets

Learning Objectives

After completing this chapter, you should be able to:

1 Distinguish between tangible and intangible assets.

2 Identify different types of long-term operational assets.

3 Determine the cost of long-term operational assets.

4 Explain how expense recognition affects financial statements throughout the life cycle of a tangible asset.

5 Determine how a gain or loss from the disposal of long-term operational assets affects financial statements.

6 Determine how different amortization methods affect the amount of expense recognized in a particular accounting period.

7 Identify tax issues related to long-term operational assets.

8 Explain how revising estimates affects financial statements.

9 Explain how continuing expenditures for operational assets affect financial statements.

10 Explain how expense recognition for natural resources affects financial statements.

11 Explain how expense recognition for intangible assets affects financial statements.

12 Describe how expense recognition choices and industry characteristics affect financial performance measures.

13 Describe why some businesses generate high revenue with few operational assets.

the *curious* accountant

In the normal course of operations, most companies acquire long-term assets each year. The way a company hopes to make money with these assets varies according to the type of business and the asset acquired.

During 2000, Weyerhaeuser Company made cash acquisitions of property and equipment of US$848 million and cash acquisitions of timber and timberlands of US$81 million. How does Weyerhaeuser plan to use each type of asset to produce earnings for the company? Should the accounting treatment for trees differ from the accounting treatment for trucks? For an answer, see page 369.

Long-term operational assets *are the resources businesses use to produce revenue. The size of a company's operational assets relative to the income it generates by using them will depend on the nature of its operating activity. For example, a trucking company requires substantial investments in physical equipment to move freight from one destination to another. In contrast, a firm of lawyers uses intellectual rather than physical assets to meet the needs of its clients. Therefore, law offices tend to generate significantly more revenue per dollar invested in operational assets than do trucking companies.*

How long is long term*? There is no definitive time limit. However, as noted earlier, assets that are used in more than one accounting period are usually considered long term. The cost of long-term assets is normally recognized as an expense in the accounting periods in which the asset is used. In other words, you do not expense the total cost of long-term assets in a single year; instead, you spread the expense recognition over the life of the assets (matching principle). This chapter teaches you how to classify costs into long-term asset categories and explains how to account for the utilization of these assets from the date of purchase to their final disposal.*

Classifications of Long-Term Operational Assets

LO1 Distinguish between tangible and intangible assets.

Long-term assets are either tangible or intangible. **Tangible assets** can be "touched" and include equipment, machinery, natural resources, and land. **Intangible assets** may be represented by pieces of paper or contracts that seem tangible; however, the true value of an intangible asset lies in the rights and privileges extended to its owners. For example, a *patent* is a legal right granting its owner an exclusive privilege to produce and sell a commodity that has one or more unique features. Therefore, inventors who own intangible patent rights can protect their inventions by seeking legal recourse against anyone who attempts to profit by copying their innovations.

Tangible Long-Term Assets

Property, Plant, and Equipment

LO2 Identify different types of long-term operational assets.

Property, plant, and equipment is a category whose assets are sometimes called *plant assets* or *capital assets*. Examples of property, plant, and equipment include furniture, cash registers, machinery, delivery trucks, computers, mechanical robots, and buildings. Rather than recording all of these assets in a single account, each company uses subcategories to satisfy its particular needs for information. One company may include all office machinery in one account, whereas another company might divide office equipment into computers, desks, chairs, and so on. As indicated in earlier chapters, the process of recognizing expense for property, plant, and equipment is called **amortization.**[1]

Natural Resources

Mineral deposits, oil and gas reserves, and reserves of timber, mines, and quarries are known as **natural resources**. They are sometimes called *wasting assets* because their value "wastes away" as the resources are removed. The balance sheet classification for natural resources as long-term assets sometimes conflicts with how these assets are expensed. Conceptually, natural resources are inventories. Indeed, these assets are often expensed through the cost of goods sold. However, they are classified as long-term assets because (1) the resource deposits generally have long lives, (2) the accounting treatment is very similar to that for other long-term assets, and (3) practice and convention have made this the acceptable treatment. The process of expense recognition for natural resources is also called *amortization*.

Land

Land is classified in a separate category from other property for one major reason: Land is not subject to amortization. It is considered to have an infinite life. In other words, land is not destroyed through the process of its use. When buildings or natural resources are purchased simultaneously with land, the amount paid must be carefully divided between the land and the other assets because of the nonamortizable nature of the land.

[1] In the past, capital assets were *depreciated*, intangible assets were *amortized*, and natural resources were *depleted*. These terms have now been replaced with one term, *amortization*, which is now used to describe the allocation of cost over useful life for *all* types of operational assets.

Intangible Assets

Intangible assets may be classified into two groups: those that are specifically identifiable and can be acquired individually, and those that arise from the purchase of a group of assets and cannot be attributed to any one asset.

Specifically Identifiable Intangible Assets

This category includes patents, trademarks, franchises, copyrights, and other privileges extended by government agencies. The costs of acquiring these assets range from relatively insignificant legal fees to huge sums paid for fast-food franchises. Later in this chapter we look at several of these intangibles on an individual basis, but the accounting treatment is basically the same for each. The process of recognizing expense for the cost of intangible assets is called *amortization*.

Goodwill

Goodwill refers to the benefits resulting from purchasing a company with a good reputation, an established clientele, a favourable business location, or other features that provide an above-average profit potential. For example, a fast-food restaurant with the name *McDonald's* will likely produce higher revenues than another restaurant named *Joe's*, even if both have the same physical asset base. An investor will have to pay more to acquire a business with above-average profit potential than to acquire an identical set of assets that are separated from the favourable business conditions. Like other intangible assets, this extra amount, or goodwill, is amortized (expensed) over its useful life.

Determining the Cost of Long-Term Assets

LO3 Determine the cost of long-term operational assets.

The **historical cost concept** requires that assets be recorded at the amount paid for them. This amount includes the purchase price plus whatever costs are necessary to obtain the asset and prepare it for its intended use. As years go by, the historical cost may begin to bear little relation to the current value of the asset for several reasons: (1) amortization may not approximate the use of the asset, (2) inflation may change the value of the dollar, or (3) the value of the asset itself may increase or decrease. Because of these factors, many critics have suggested that companies be allowed to revalue their assets periodically to reflect the assets' current values. However, due to a lack of objective measurement techniques, most long-term assets are still reported at historical cost in the primary financial statements.

Sheridan Construction Company purchased a new bulldozer that had a $260,000 list price. The seller agreed to allow a 4 percent cash discount in exchange for immediate payment. The bulldozer was delivered FOB shipping point at a cost of $1,200. Sheridan hired a new employee to operate the dozer for an annual salary of $36,000. The employee was trained to operate the dozer for a one-time training fee of $800. The cost of the company's theft insurance policy increased by $300 per year as a result of adding the dozer to the policy. The dozer had a five-year useful life and an expected residual value of $26,000. Determine the asset's cost.

Answer

List price	$260,000
Less: Cash discount ($260,000 × 0.04)	(10,400)
Shipping cost	1,200
Training cost	800
Total asset cost (amount capitalized)	$251,600

The cost of an asset includes all expenditures that are normally necessary to obtain it and prepare it for its intended use. However, *payments for fines, damages, and so on, are not considered normal costs of acquiring an asset* and are therefore not included. Some of the more common costs associated with particular types of assets include the following:

- *Purchase of buildings*: (1) purchase price, (2) sales taxes, (3) title search and transfer documents, (4) real estate fees and legal fees, and (5) remodelling costs.
- *Purchase of land*: (1) purchase price, (2) sales taxes, (3) title search and transfer documents, (4) realtor's and legal fees, and (5) removal of old buildings (less proceeds received from salvageable materials), and (6) grading.
- *Purchase of equipment*: (1) purchase price (less discounts), (2) sales taxes, (3) delivery costs, (4) installation, and (5) costs to adapt to intended use.

Basket Purchase Allocation

LO3 Determine the cost of long-term operational assets.

A **basket purchase** is the acquisition of several assets in a single transaction. Often a single price is assigned to that purchase, and the acquiring company must determine how much of that price should be assigned to each asset. This can be done by using the **relative fair market value method**.

Assume that Beatty Company purchased a building and plot of land for $240,000 cash. A real estate appraiser was called in and determined the fair market value of each to be as follows:

Building	$270,000
Land	90,000
Total	$360,000

Beatty paid less than the appraised values but can still use these values to determine a reasonable basis for assigning the total cost to the two assets. The appraisal indicated that the land is worth 25 percent ($90,000 ÷ $360,000) of the total value, and the building, 75 percent ($270,000 ÷ $360,000). Applying these percentages to the actual purchase price results in the following cost allocation:

Building	0.75 × $240,000 =	$180,000
Land	0.25 × $240,000 =	60,000
Total		$240,000

Life Cycle of Operational Assets

The life cycle of an operational asset begins with the effort to obtain the financing necessary to acquire it. The next step is to acquire the asset (invest the funds). The asset is then used to produce revenue. The final step is to retire the asset. The use and retirement of the asset should generate enough funds to replace the asset and to provide a reasonable return on the invested funds. Exhibit 9–1 depicts the life cycle of an operational asset.

Exhibit 9–1 *Life Cycle of an Operational Asset*

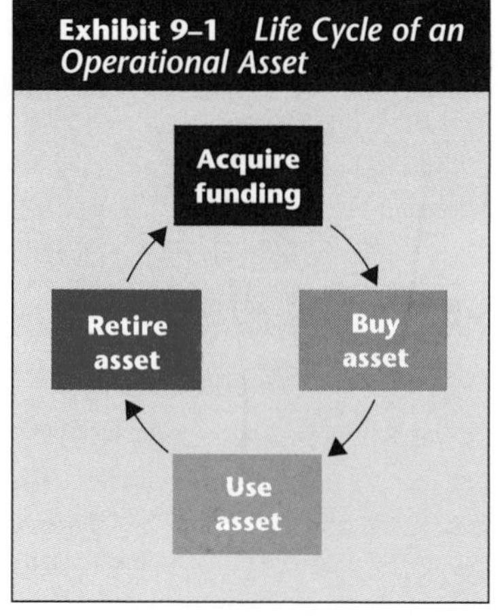

answers to the *curious* accountant

Equipment is a long-term asset used to produce revenue. The portion of the equipment used each accounting period is recognized as amortization expense. Therefore, the expense recognition for the cost of equipment is spread over the useful life of the asset. Timber, however, is not used until the trees are grown. Conceptually, the cost of the trees should be treated as inventories and expensed as cost of goods sold at the time the products made from trees are sold. Even so, some timber companies recognize a periodic charge in a manner similar to that used for equipment.

Accounting for unusual long-term assets such as timber requires an understanding of specialized "industry practice" accounting rules that are beyond the scope of this course. Be aware that many industries have unique accounting problems, and business managers in such industries must make the effort to understand specialized accounting rules that relate to their companies.

Accounting for Operational Assets Throughout the Life Cycle

LO4 Explain how expense recognition affects financial statements throughout the life cycle of a tangible asset.

The acquisition of capital results in an increase in assets and equity. Once the financing has been acquired, the funds are invested in an asset. The cost of the asset is then systematically expensed over its useful life. In prior chapters, the expense recognition phase for tangible assets was spread evenly over the life of the asset. This method of amortizing an asset is called **straight-line amortization**. Straight-line amortization is appropriate when an asset is used evenly over its life. However, not all assets are used evenly. Some assets may be used much more rapidly when they are new and gradually less as they grow older. These assets require **accelerated amortization methods**, which charge more of the cost of the asset to expense in the early years of the asset's useful life. Other assets may be used extensively in one accounting period, infrequently in the next, and extensively again in another accounting period. In other words, their use varies from one accounting period to the next. This means that methods other than straight-line are needed to accurately reflect the use of many assets. The next section of this chapter reviews straight-line amortization and introduces two new methods, the *double-declining-balance* and *units-of-activity (production) methods*.

Methods of Amortization

LO4 Explain how expense recognition affects financial statements throughout the life cycle of a tangible asset.

Three things must be established before a capital asset can be amortized:

1. The *cost* to be capitalized. The cost of the asset was covered on page 367.
2. The **residual value** of the asset. Residual (or salvage) value represents the estimate of the value of the asset at the end of its useful life.
3. The **estimated useful life** of the asset. The estimated useful life of the asset is an estimate of the length of time the asset will be in service.

It is important to notice that both the residual value and the estimated life of the asset are based on estimates made by management at the time an asset is purchased and are, therefore, subject to adjustment as new information or better estimates become available. This will be discussed further later in this chapter.

To demonstrate how the different amortization methods affect expense recognition over the life cycle, we trace the events of Dryden Enterprises for a five-year time span. Dryden was started on January 1, 2004, when it issued $25,000 of common shares. Immediately after acquiring capital, Dryden purchased a van. The van had a list price of $23,500. Dryden was able to obtain a 10 percent cash discount from the dealer. However, the van was delivered FOB shipping point, and Dryden agreed to pay an additional $250 for transportation costs. Dryden also paid $2,600 to have the van customized to make it more appealing as a rental vehicle. Therefore, the amount to be capitalized in the Van account is computed as follows:

List price	$23,500	
Less: Cash discounts	(2,350)	$23,500 × 0.10
Plus: Transportation costs	250	
Plus: Cost of customization	2,600	
Total	$24,000	

The van has an estimated residual value of $4,000 and an estimated useful life of four years. The revenue stream is expected to be distributed evenly over the van's useful life at a rate of $8,000 per year. Next we discuss the effects of the accounting treatment during the four phases of the life cycle.

Straight-Line Amortization

Given that the revenue is expected to flow smoothly over the asset's useful life, it is logical to assume that the asset will be used evenly over its life. Therefore, straight-line amortization is appropriate.

Life Cycle Phase 1

The first phase of the life cycle is the acquisition of capital. Here, Dryden acquired $25,000 cash by issuing common shares. The effect of this share issue on the financial statements is shown here:

Assets					=	Equity			Rev.	−	Exp.	=	Net Inc.	Cash Flow Statement	
Cash	+	Van	−	Acc. Amort.	=	Com. Sh.	+	Ret. Earn.							
25,000	+	NA	−	NA	=	25,000	+	NA	NA	−	NA	=	NA	25,000	FA

Clearly, the share issue affects the balance sheet and cash flow statement but not the income statement. Trace these effects to the financial statements in Exhibit 9–2. Notice that the financing activities section of the cash flow statement shows a cash inflow from the share issue amounting to $25,000. Also, the balance sheet shows a $25,000 balance in the equity section under the Common Shares account. Since the balance sheet accounts reflect the cumulative effect of events that have occurred from a company's inception, the $25,000 in common shares appears in the statements throughout the life cycle. In contrast, the cash flow statement reflects activities for a particular accounting period. The inflow from the share issue appears only once during the 2004 accounting period. The cash balance shown in the balance sheet is not equal to $25,000 because the Cash account is affected by other events during 2004.

Life Cycle Phase 2

The second phase of the life cycle is the investment in the operational asset (purchase of the van). The purchase price was computed earlier as $24,000 cash. The effect of the investment on the financial statements is shown here:

Assets					=	Equity			Rev.	−	Exp.	=	Net Inc.	Cash Flow Statement	
Cash	+	Van	−	Acc. Amort.	=	Com. Sh.	+	Ret. Earn.							
(24,000)	+	24,000	−	NA	=	NA	+	NA	NA	−	NA	=	NA	(24,000)	IA

Exhibit 9–2 *Financial Statements under Straight-Line Amortization*

DRYDEN ENTERPRISES
Financial Statements

	2004	2005	2006	2007	2008
Income Statements					
Rent Revenue	$ 8,000	$ 8,000	$ 8,000	$ 8,000	$ 0
Amortization Expense	(5,000)	(5,000)	(5,000)	(5,000)	0
Operating Income	3,000	3,000	3,000	3,000	0
Gain	0	0	0	0	500
Net Income	$ 3,000	$ 3,000	$ 3,000	$ 3,000	$ 500
Balance Sheets					
Assets					
Cash	$ 9,000	$17,000	$25,000	$33,000	$37,500
Van	24,000	24,000	24,000	24,000	0
Accumulated Amortization	(5,000)	(10,000)	(15,000)	(20,000)	0
Total Assets	$28,000	$31,000	$34,000	$37,000	$37,500
Shareholders' Equity					
Common Shares	$25,000	$25,000	$25,000	$25,000	$25,000
Retained Earnings	3,000	6,000	9,000	12,000	12,500
Total Shareholders' Equity	$28,000	$31,000	$34,000	$37,000	$37,500
Cash Flow Statements					
Operational Activities					
Inflow from Customers	$ 8,000	$ 8,000	$ 8,000	$ 8,000	$ 0
Investing Activities					
Outflow to Purchase Van	(24,000)	0	0	0	0
Inflow from Sale of Van	0	0	0	0	4,500
Financing Activities					
Inflow from Share Issue	25,000	0	0	0	0
Net Change in Cash	9,000	8,000	8,000	8,000	4,500
Beginning Cash Balance	0	9,000	17,000	25,000	33,000
Ending Cash Balance	$ 9,000	$17,000	$25,000	$33,000	$37,500

The investment is an asset exchange transaction involving a cash payment. As such, it affects the balance sheet and the cash flow statement. Refer to Exhibit 9–2 to see how this is reflected on the financial statements. Note that the cash outflow is shown one time in 2004 under the investing activities section of the cash flow statement. However, the cost of the asset is shown on the balance sheet as $24,000 throughout the entire life cycle (2004–2007). The historical cost is removed from the asset account when the van is retired in 2008.

Life Cycle Phase 3

The asset generates $8,000 of revenue per year. The wear and tear on the asset are reflected in the amortization expense. The amount of the amortization expense calculated on a straight-line basis is determined by subtracting the residual value from the original cost and dividing the result by the useful life. This computation results in the recognition of $5,000 ([$24,000 − $4,000] ÷ 4) of amortization expense each year. The expense recognition is shown in a **contra asset account** titled **Accumulated Amortization**. The effects of the revenue and expense recognition on the financial statements are shown here. To save space, we show the events only once. In fact, they would occur four times—once for each year the asset is in use.

Assets			=	Equity		Rev. − Exp. = Net Inc.			Cash Flow Statement	
Cash +	Van −	Acc. Amort.	=	Com. Sh. +	Ret. Earn.					
8,000 +	NA −	NA	=	NA +	8,000	8,000 −	NA =	8,000	8,000	OA
NA +	NA −	5,000	=	NA +	(5,000)	NA −	5,000 =	(5,000)	NA	

The revenue event affects all three statements. Amortization expense affects the balance sheet and the income statement but not the cash flow statement. Recall that the cash paid for the van was spent on January 1, 2004. The total cash outflow is shown in the investing section of the cash flow statement. Therefore, the cash flow consequences have already been recognized and so are not affected by the recognition of amortization expense. This is the meaning of the statement "amortization is a noncash expenditure." Amortization represents the use of the physical asset rather than the expenditure of cash.

Again, trace the events to the financial statements in Exhibit 9–2. As shown in the cash flow statement, the revenue stream produces $8,000 of cash per year for four years (2004–2007). The use (rental) of the van provided $32,000 of cash ($8,000 × 4) over its life cycle. Note that the amortization expense is shown in the income statement but does not affect the cash flow statement. (The reason for this effect was explained in the previous paragraph.) Observe here that the effects of amortization occur throughout the life cycle of the asset. Indeed, it is interesting that the amortization expense stays at $5,000 each year, whereas the Accumulated Amortization account grows from $5,000 to $10,000 to $15,000 and finally to $20,000 between 2004 and 2007.

LO5

Determine how a gain or loss from the disposal of operational assets affects financial statements.

Life Cycle Phase 4

The final stage in the life cycle of an operational asset is its retirement and removal from the company's records. This occurs on January 1, 2008, when Dryden sells the van for $4,500 cash. The effect of this event on the financial statements is shown below. Since the net book value at the time of the sale was only $4,000, Dryden recognizes a $500 gain ($4,500 − $4,000).

Assets			=	Equity		Rev. − Exp. = Net Inc.			Cash Flow Statement	
Cash +	Van −	Acc. Amort.	=	Com. Sh. +	Ret. Earn.					
4,500 +	(24,000) −	(20,000)	=	0 +	500	500 −	0 =	500	4,500	IA

Tracing the effects of these events to the financial statements in Exhibit 9–2 provides interesting insights as to how businesses recover their invested funds. Although the gain shown on the income statement is only $500, the amount of cash inflow is $4,500. This amount is shown as an inflow in the investing activities section of the cash flow statement. The gain is not shown separately on the cash flow statement but instead is included in the $4,500 shown in the investing section. The total cash inflow from using and retiring the van amounts to $36,500 ([$8,000 revenue × 4 years] + $4,500 actual residual value), which means that Dryden not only recovered the cost of the asset ($24,000) but also generated a $12,500 return on its investment. In other words, over its life cycle, the operational asset generated $12,500 more than it cost ($36,500 − $24,000). This is consistent with the total amount of net income that was earned over the life cycle. The difference between income and cash flow is a matter of timing. Other interesting insights include the fact that the amount of the ending balance in the Retained Earnings account is equal to the sum of the amounts of net income that appear on the 2004 through 2008 income statements. This result occurs because all earnings were retained in the business. No dividends were paid to the shareholders.

Exhibit 9–3 *General Journal Entries*

Life Cycle	Account Title	Debit	Credit
Phase 1	Cash	25,000	
	Common Shares		25,000
	Entry on January 1, 2004, to record capital acquisition		
Phase 2	Van	24,000	
	Cash		24,000
	Entry on January 1, 2004, to record investment in van		
Phase 3 (each year for 4 years)	Cash	8,000	
	Revenue		8,000
	Revenue recognition entries on December 31, 2004–2007		
	Amortization Expense	5,000	
	Accumulated Amortization		5,000
	Expense recognition entries on December 31, 2004–2007		
	Cash	4,500	
	Accumulated Amortization	20,000	
	Van		24,000
	Gain on Sale of Van		500
	Entry on January 1, 2008, to record asset disposal		

Recording Procedures

Exhibit 9–3 shows the general journal entries required to record the transactions over the life cycle of the van.

Double-Declining-Balance Amortization

LO4 Explain how expense recognition affects financial statements throughout the life cycle of a tangible asset.

Assume the same set of facts as those just presented, with one exception. Suppose that Dryden believes that customer demand for the van will diminish over time. When the van is new, it looks more attractive, drives better, and is less susceptible to breakdowns. Therefore, more people will want to use the van when it is new. As it ages, fewer and fewer people will be willing to rent the vehicle. As a result, the van will be used less often as time goes by. Since the purpose of amortization is to reflect asset use, the amount of amortization expense should be higher when the van is new and should decline as the van ages. A method of amortization known as **double-declining-balance amortization** is specifically designed to recognize larger amounts of amortization in the earlier stages of an asset's life and progressively lower levels of expense as the asset ages. Since the double-declining-balance method recognizes amortization expense more rapidly than the straight-line method does, it is sometimes referred to as an *accelerated amortization method*. The amount of amortization to recognize under the double-declining-balance method can be determined by performing three simple computations:

1. *Determine the straight-line rate.* If the asset is amortized evenly over its useful life, you can determine the portion amortized each year by dividing the full use (100 percent) by the expected useful life of the asset. For example, since Dryden's van was expected to have a four-year useful life, the straight-line rate is 25 percent (100 percent ÷ 4 years) per year.
2. *Determine the double-declining-balance rate.* Multiply the straight-line rate by 2 (*double* the rate). The double-declining-balance rate for the van is 50 percent (25 percent × 2).
3. *Apply the double-declining-balance rate to the net book value.* Multiply the double-declining-balance rate by the net book value of the asset *at the beginning of the period* (**net book value** being historical cost less the amount of *accumulated amortization*).

Applying the computations to Dryden's van will produce the following schedule of charges for the years 2004 through 2007:

Year	Book Value at Beginning of Period	×	Double the Straight-Line Rate	=	Annual Amortization Expense	Accumulated Amortization
2004	($24,000 − $0)	×	50%	=	$12,000	$12,000
2005	($24,000 − 12,000)	×	50%	=	6,000	18,000
2006	($24,000 − 18,000)	×	50%	=	2,000	20,000
2007	($24,000 − 20,000)	×	50%	=	0	20,000

Computations for the third year are complicated by the fact that *the net book value of an asset cannot be amortized below its residual value*. Since the van cost $24,000 and had a $4,000 residual value, the total amount of cost to be amortized is $20,000 ($24,000 − $4,000). Since $18,000 ($12,000 + $6,000) of the cost is amortized in the first two years, only $2,000 ($20,000 − $18,000) more can be amortized. The $3,000 formula value is ignored in year 3 because it exceeds the $2,000 maximum. Similarly, the formula value for 2007 is ignored because the maximum allowable amortization was charged in the first three years.

Exhibit 9–4 is a full set of financial statements prepared under the assumption that Dryden is using double-declining-balance amortization. Trace the amortization charges shown in the exhibit to the financial statements. Observe how the amount of amortization expense is larger in the earlier years and smaller in the later years of the asset's life. Since the van is used more during the early years, it is logical to assume higher amounts of revenue during those years. We presume a revenue stream of $15,000, $9,000, $5,000, and $3,000 for the four years respectively.

Since the use of the asset is directly related to the production of revenue, the double-declining-balance method smooths the amount of net income reported on the income statement. The high revenues produced by the extensive use of the asset in the first years are offset by high expenses that reflect the corresponding level of asset use. Similarly, declining levels of use produce lower levels of expense as well as revenue. As a result, net income remains constant at a level of $3,000 per year.

How does accelerated amortization improve financial reporting? Compare the income figures in Exhibit 9–4 with the outcome that would have occurred had Dryden used the straight-line method. Given the revenue stream in Exhibit 9–4, a constant $5,000 per year amortization charge would have resulted in reported net income of $10,000, $4,000, $0, and ($2,000) for the four years respectively. These figures suggest a state of steadily declining economic viability, though in fact the company is performing as expected. As a result, use of straight-line amortization would have provided a false impression of managerial performance. As this discussion implies, financial reporting provides a more accurate representation of business activity when expense recognition is closely aligned with asset use.

Olds Company purchased an asset that cost $36,000 on January 1, 2006. The asset had an expected useful life of five years and an estimated residual value of $5,000. Assuming Olds uses the double-declining-balance method, determine the amount of amortization expense and the amount of accumulated amortization Olds would report on the 2008 financial statements.

Answer

Year	Book Value at the Beginning of the Period	×	Double the Straight-Line Rate*	=	Annual Amortization Expense
2006	($36,000 − $ 0)	×	40%	=	$14,400
2007	($36,000 − 14,400)	×	40%	=	8,640
2008	($36,000 − 23,040)	×	40%	=	5,184
Total accumulated amortization at December 31, 2008					$28,224

*Double-declining-balance rate = 2 × Straight-line rate = 2 × (100% ÷ 5 years) = 40%

Exhibit 9–4 *Financial Statements under Double-Declining-Balance Amortization*

DRYDEN ENTERPRISES Financial Statements	2004	2005	2006	2007	2008
Income Statements					
Rent Revenue	$15,000	$ 9,000	$ 5,000	$ 3,000	$ 0
Amortization Expense	(12,000)	(6,000)	(2,000)	0	0
Operating Income	3,000	3,000	3,000	3,000	0
Gain	0	0	0	0	500
Net Income	$ 3,000	$ 3,000	$ 3,000	$ 3,000	$ 500
Balance Sheets					
Assets					
Cash	$16,000	$25,000	$30,000	$33,000	$37,500
Van	24,000	24,000	24,000	24,000	0
Accumulated Amortization	(12,000)	(18,000)	(20,000)	(20,000)	0
Total Assets	$28,000	$31,000	$34,000	$37,000	$37,500
Shareholders' Equity					
Common Shares	$25,000	$25,000	$25,000	$25,000	$25,000
Retained Earnings	3,000	6,000	9,000	12,000	12,500
Total Shareholders' Equity	$28,000	$31,000	$34,000	$37,000	$37,500
Cash Flow Statements					
Operating Activities					
Inflow from Customers	$15,000	$ 9,000	$ 5,000	$ 3,000	$ 0
Investing Activities					
Outflow to Purchase Van	(24,000)	0	0	0	0
Inflow from Sale of Van	0	0	0	0	4,500
Financing Activities					
Inflow from Share Issue	25,000	0	0	0	0
Net Change in Cash	16,000	9,000	5,000	3,000	4,500
Beginning Cash Balance	0	16,000	25,000	30,000	33,000
Ending Cash Balance	$16,000	$25,000	$30,000	$33,000	$37,500

Effects During Other Phases of the Life Cycle

The effects of acquiring the financing, investing the funds, and retiring the asset are not changed by the method of amortization. Therefore, descriptions of the effects of the accounting events in these life cycle phases are the same as under the straight-line approach. If you need reinforcement in this area, review the appropriate earlier sections. Similarly, the recording procedures are not affected by the amortization method. Different amortization methods affect only the amounts of the transactions, not the accounts included in the entries. To avoid redundancy, the general journal entries are not shown for the double-declining-balance or the units-of-production amortization methods.

Units-of-Activity Amortization

LO4 Explain how expense recognition affects financial statements throughout the life cycle of a tangible asset.

Given the need to match expense recognition with asset use, a third amortization method has been developed to reflect asset use that fluctuates from one accounting period to another. For example, suppose that Dryden experiences a demand for rentals that depends on general economic conditions. In a robust economy, travel increases, and the demand for renting the van is high. In a stagnant economy, demand for van rentals declines. This means that the pattern of asset use varies from one accounting period to the next, depending on the state of the economy. In these circumstances, it is more reasonable to use some measure of total production, rather than time, as the basis for determining the amount of amortization. For a van, the number of kilometres driven may represent a reasonable measure of total activity. If the asset to be amortized were a saw used to cut pieces of wood into baseball bats, an appropriate measure of total production would be the number of bats the saw was expected to produce during its useful life. In other words, the basis for measuring production depends on the nature of the asset being amortized.

To illustrate the computation of amortization under the **units-of-activity amortization** method, assume that Dryden measures asset use according to the number of kilometres the van is driven each year. Also, assume that Dryden expects the van to have a useful life of 100,000 km. The first step in determining the amount of amortization expense is to compute the cost per unit of production. In the case of the van, we can determine the amount by dividing the total amortizable cost (historical cost − residual value) by the number of units of total expected productive capacity (100,000 km). Therefore, the cost per kilometre is \$0.20 ([\$24,000 cost − \$4,000 residual] ÷ 100,000 km). The amortization expense is computed by multiplying the cost per kilometre by the number of kilometres driven. Based on mileage records that show the van was driven 40,000 km, 20,000 km, 30,000 km, and 15,000 km in 2004, 2005, 2006, and 2007, respectively, Dryden developed the following schedule of amortization charges.

Year	Cost per Km (a)	Km Driven (b)	Amortization Expense (a × b)
2004	\$0.20	40,000	\$8,000
2005	0.20	20,000	4,000
2006	0.20	30,000	6,000
2007	0.20	15,000	2,000

As with the double-declining-balance method, the asset's book value cannot be amortized below the residual value. Since \$18,000 of cost is amortized in the first three years of operation, and since total amortizable cost is \$20,000 (\$24,000 cost − \$4,000 residual), only \$2,000 (\$20,000 − \$18,000) of cost is charged to amortization in year 4, even though the application of the computational formula suggests a \$3,000 charge. As the preceding table indicates, the general formula for determining the amount of units-of-production amortization is as follows:

$$\frac{\text{Cost} - \text{Residual value}}{\text{Total estimated units of acitvity}} \times \begin{array}{c}\text{Units of activity}\\ \text{in current}\\ \text{accounting period}\end{array} = \begin{array}{c}\text{Annual}\\ \text{amortization}\\ \text{expense}\end{array}$$

Exhibit 9–5 provides a full set of financial statements that assumes that Dryden uses units-of-activity amortization. Again, it is logical to assume that revenue will fluctuate with asset use. The exhibit assumes that Dryden collected cash revenue of \$11,000, \$7,000, \$9,000, and \$5,000 for 2004, 2005, 2006, and 2007, respectively. Notice that the revenue pattern fluctuates with the amortization charges. The result is a constant amount of \$3,000 per year of reported net income.

LO6
Determine how different amortization methods affect the amount of expense recognized in a particular accounting period.

Comparing the Methods

Note that the total amount of amortization expense recognized under all three methods was \$20,000. The different amortization methods affect the timing of recognition but not the total amount of cost to be recognized. The different methods simply assign the \$20,000 to different accounting periods. Exhibit 9–6 depicts all three methods. Each method offers unique opportunities to match expense recognition with asset use. As noted earlier, matching asset use with expense recognition is desirable because it improves the capacity of financial reports to describe managerial performance.

Exhibit 9–5 *Financial Statements under Units-of-Activity Amortization*

DRYDEN ENTERPRISES
Financial Statements

	2004	2005	2006	2007	2008
Income Statements					
Rent Revenue	$11,000	$7,000	$9,000	$ 5,000	$ 0
Amortization Expense	(8,000)	(4,000)	(6,000)	(2,000)	0
Operating Income	3,000	3,000	3,000	3,000	0
Gain	0	0	0	0	500
Net Income	$ 3,000	$ 3,000	$ 3,000	$ 3,000	$ 500
Balance Sheets					
Assets					
Cash	$12,000	$19,000	$28,000	$33,000	$37,500
Van	24,000	24,000	24,000	24,000	0
Accumulated Amortization	(8,000)	(12,000)	(18,000)	(20,000)	0
Total Assets	$28,000	$31,000	$34,000	$37,000	$37,500
Shareholders' Equity					
Common Shares	$25,000	$25,000	$25,000	$25,000	$25,000
Retained Earnings	3,000	6,000	9,000	12,000	12,500
Total Shareholders' Equity	$28,000	$31,000	$34,000	$37,000	$37,500
Cash Flow Statements					
Operating Activities					
Inflow from Customers	$11,000	$ 7,000	$ 9,000	$ 5,000	$ 0
Investing Activities					
Outflow to Purchase Van	(24,000)	0	0	0	0
Inflow from Sale of Van	0	0	0	0	4,500
Financing Activities					
Inflow from Common Shares	25,000	0	0	0	0
Net Change in Cash	12,000	7,000	9,000	5,000	4,500
Beginning Cash Balance	0	12,000	19,000	28,000	33,000
Ending Cash Balance	$12,000	$19,000	$28,000	$33,000	$37,500

Exhibit 9–6 *Amortization Expense under Different Amortization Methods*

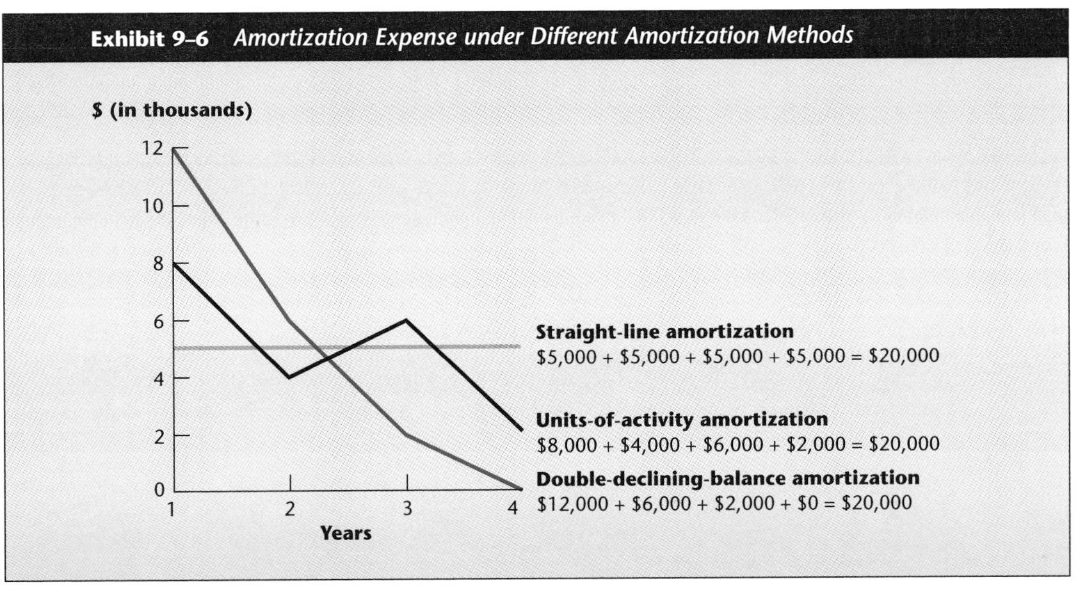

Income Tax Considerations

LO7

Identify tax issues related to long-term operational assets.

Although matching asset use with revenue recognition is important in assessing managerial performance, it is not a meaningful consideration for the payment of income taxes. In Canada, for tax reporting purposes, the Income Tax Act requires a declining balance method of amortization, known as the **capital cost allowance (CCA) method**. The maximum amortization currently allowed under tax law is computed using the CCA percentage factors specified in the Income Tax Act. The balance remaining to be amortized is called the **undepreciated capital cost (UCC)**. This balance represents the net book value of the asset for tax purposes. As well, a special rule exists for tax purposes, called the **half-year rule**. This rule allows only one-half of the first year's amortization to be claimed, regardless of when the asset was purchased. Because CCA is a declining balance method, taxable income is reduced in the early years of an asset's life. In essence, a company is "deferring" or delaying tax payments for future periods.

To illustrate the computation of CCA, let's assume equipment was purchased for $200,000 cash, the CCA rate is 20 percent, and the company follows the half-year rule. CCA for Year 1 is $20,000 ($200,000 × 0.20 × 1/2). To calculate future years, the UCC at the beginning of the year is multiplied by the CCA rate of 20 percent. A schedule similar to the one presented below is often prepared.

Year*	UCC (beg. of year)	CCA Rate	CCA	UCC (end of year)
1	$200,000	20% × 1/2	$20,000	$180,000
2	180,000	20%	36,000	144,000
3	144,000	20%	28,800	115,200

*Note that only the first three years are shown.

Revision of Estimates

LO8

Determine how revising estimates affects financial statements.

When an estimate of residual value, life, or total production is revised during the use of the asset, nothing is done to correct the previously reported figures. There are so many estimates used in accounting that revisions are considered a normal part of business. The new information is simply folded into any present and future calculations.

To illustrate, assume that McGraw Company purchased an asset on January 1, 2006, for $50,000. The machine was estimated to have a useful life of 8 years and a residual value of $3,000. McGraw used the straight-line amortization method and determined the annual amortization charge according to the following formula:

($50,000 − $3,000) ÷ 8 years = $5,875 per year

Using these assumptions, consider the possibility of two different revisions occurring in the fifth year. At the beginning of the fifth year, the amount in accumulated amortization is $23,500 ($5,875 × 4), making the net book value $26,500 ($50,000 − $23,500). Each revision should be considered separately from the other.

Revision of Life

If McGraw revised the expected life to 14 years rather than 8 years, the asset would now be expected to last 10 more years rather than 4 more years. Residual remains at $3,000, so computation of each remaining year's amortization is

($26,500 net book value − $3,000 residual) ÷ 10-year remaining life = $2,350

Revision of Residual

If the original expected life remained the same but the residual value were revised to $6,000, the amortization charge for each of the remaining four years would be

($26,500 net book value − $6,000 residual) ÷ 4-year remaining life = $5,125

Notice that it was not important when the company revised its estimates during the year. The entire year's amortization was considered changed.

Continuing Expenditures for Plant Assets

Over the life of an asset, it is often necessary or advisable to make expenditures to maintain or improve the asset's productivity. These expenditures fall into two classifications: expensed and capitalized.

LO9 Explain how continuing expenditures for operational assets affect financial statements.

Costs That Are Expensed (Revenue Expenditures)

When an expenditure that is necessary to keep the asset in good working order is made, it is expensed in the period in which it is incurred. These costs consist of such things as routine maintenance and minor repairs. Extending the example for the machine owned by McGraw Company, we assume that $500 was spent to lubricate the machine and replace minor parts. The effect of the expenditure on the financial statements and the journal entry necessary to record it are as follows:

Assets	=	Equity			Rev.	−	Exp.	=	Net Inc.	Cash Flow Statement	
Cash	=	C. Sh.	+	Ret. Earn.							
(500)	=	NA	+	(500)	NA	−	500	=	(500)	(500)	OA

Account Title	Debit	Credit
Repairs Expense	500	
Cash		500

Costs That Are Capitalized (Capital Expenditures)

Capital expenditures are usually substantial amounts spent to improve the quality or extend the life of an asset. As such, these expenses affect the remainder of the asset's life and should not be treated as an expense of the current accounting period. Capital expenditures *improve the quality* or *extend the life* of the asset.

When an expenditure is deemed to have improved the quality of an asset or extended the life of an asset, the cost is added to the asset's historical cost, and this extra amount ends up being expensed over the remainder of the asset's life through the process of amortization. Continuing with the McGraw Company example, we assume that a major expenditure costing $4,000 is made in the fifth year. The expenditure improves the productive capacity of the company's machine. Recall that the asset originally cost $50,000, had an estimated residual value of $3,000, and had a predicted useful life of 8 years. If we assume straight-line amortization, the amount in accumulated amortization at the beginning of the fifth year is $23,500 ($5,875 × 4), making the net book value $26,500 ($50,000 − $23,500). The effect of the $4,000 expenditure on the financial statements and the journal entry necessary to record it are as follows:

Assets			=	Equity		Rev. − Exp. = Net Inc.	Cash Flow Statement	
Cash +	Mach. −	A. Amort.	=	C. Sh. +	Ret. Earn.			
(4,000) +	4,000 −	NA	=	NA +	NA	NA − NA = NA	(4,000)	IA

Account Title	Debit	Credit
Machine	4,000	
Cash		4,000

After we recognize the effects of the expenditure, the machine contains a $54,000 balance, resulting in a net book value of $30,500 ($54,000 − $23,500). The amortization charges for the remaining four years are calculated as follows:

($30,500 net book value − $3,000 residual) ÷ 4-year remaining life = $6,875

Extending Life

When a company undertakes a capital expenditure that extends the life of the asset but not its quality, it is theoretically objectionable to increase the cost of the asset. Instead, the expenditure is looked on as cancelling some of the amortization that has already been charged to expense. The event is still an asset exchange. Cash decreases, and the net book value of the machine increases. The net book value of the machine is increased by reducing the amount in the contra asset account, Accumulated Amortization. To illustrate, assume that instead of increasing productive capacity, McGraw's $4,000 expenditure had merely extended the useful life of the machine by two years. The effect of the event on the financial statements and the journal entry necessary to record it are as follows:

Assets			=	Equity		Rev. − Exp. = Net Inc.	Cash Flow Statement	
Cash +	Mach. −	A. Amort.	=	C. Sh. +	Ret. Earn.			
(4,000) +	NA −	(4,000)	=	NA +	NA	NA − NA = NA	(4,000)	IA

Account Title	Debit	Credit
Accumulated Amortization—Machine	4,000	
Cash		4,000

Notice that the net book value is now the same as if the $4,000 had been added to the Machine account ($50,000 cost − $19,500 adjusted balance in accumulated amortization = $30,500). Amortization expense for each of the remaining six years is calculated as follows:

($30,500 net book value − $3,000 residual) ÷ 6-year remaining life = $4,583.33

LO10 Explain how expense recognition for natural resources affects financial statements.

Natural Resources

Natural resources are recorded in the books at the cost of acquisition. Other costs often capitalized in natural resource accounts include the cost of exploration necessary to locate resources and payments for corresponding geographic surveys and estimates.

Amortization is a process of expense recognition that systematically allocates the cost of natural resources to expense. The units-of-activity method is the most common method for calculating amortization. The cost of the natural resource is divided by the total estimated number of units to be extracted to produce a charge per unit. If Apex Coal Mining paid $4,000,000 cash to purchase a mine with an

Check Yourself 9.3

On January 1, 2006, Dager, Inc., purchased an asset that cost $18,000. It had a five-year useful life and a $3,000 residual value. Dager uses straight-line amortization. On January 1, 2008, it incurred a $1,200 cost related to the asset. With respect to this asset, determine the amount of expense and accumulated amortization Dager would report in the 2008 financial statements under each of the following assumptions:

1. The $1,200 cost was incurred to repair damage resulting from an accident.
2. The $1,200 cost improved the operating capacity of the equipment. The total useful life and residual value remained unchanged.
3. The $1,200 cost extended the useful life of the asset by one year. The residual value remained unchanged.

Answer

1. Dager would report the $1,200 repair cost as an expense. Dager would also report amortization expense of $3,000 ([$15,000 − $3,000] ÷ 4). Total expenses related to this asset in 2008 would be $4,200 ($1,200 repair expense + $3,000 amortization expense). Accumulated amortization at the end of 2008 would be $9,000 ($3,000 amortization expense × 3 years).
2. The $1,200 cost would be capitalized in the asset account, increasing both the net book value of the asset and the annual amortization expense.

	After Effects of Capital Improvement
Amount in asset account ($18,000 + $1,200)	$19,200
Less: Residual value	(3,000)
Accumulated amortization on January 1, 2008	(6,000)
Remaining amortizable cost before recording 2008 amortization	$10,200
Amortization for 2008 ($10,200 ÷ 3 years)	$ 3,400
Accumulated amortization at December 31, 2008 ($6,000 + $3,400)	$ 9,400

3. The $1,200 cost would be subtracted from the accumulated amortization account, increasing the net book value of the asset. The remaining useful life would increase to four years, which would decrease the amortization expense.

	After Effects of Capital Improvement
Amount in asset account	$18,000
Less: Residual value	(3,000)
Accumulated amortization on January 1, 2008 ($6,000 − $1,200)	(4,800)
Remaining amortizable cost before recording 2008 amortization	$10,200
Amortization for 2008 ($10,200 ÷ 4 years)	$2,550
Accumulated amortization at December 31, 2008 ($4,800 + $2,550)	$7,350

estimated 16,000,000 tonnes of coal, the unit charge is $0.25 per tonne ($4,000,000 ÷ 16,000,000). If Apex mines 360,000 tonnes of coal in the first year, the amortization charge is $90,000 (360,000 × $0.25). The amortization of a natural resource has the same effect on the accounting equation as other expense recognition events. Assets (in this case, a *coal mine*) decrease and equity decreases because the amortization expense reduces net income and ultimately retained earnings. The effect on the financial statements and the journal entries necessary to record the acquisition and amortization of the coal mine are as follows:

Assets			=	Equity			Rev.	−	Exp.	=	Net Inc.	Cash Flow Statement	
Cash	+	Coal Mine	=	C. Sh.	+	Ret. Earn.							
(4,000,000)	+	4,000,000	=	NA	+	NA	NA	−	NA	=	NA	(4,000)	IA
NA	+	(90,000)	=	NA	+	(90,000)	NA	−	NA	=	NA	NA	

Account Title	Debit	Credit
Coal Mine	4,000,000	
Cash		4,000,000
Amortization Expense	90,000	
Coal Mine		90,000

The decrease in the asset Coal Mine could have been shown in a contra account titled *Accumulated Amortization*, as was shown with property, plant, and equipment. However, most companies deduct the amount of amortization directly from the natural resource account. That is why this book emphasizes the direct deduction approach.

Intangible Assets

LO11

Explain how expense recognition for intangible assets affects financial statements.

Intangible assets provide rights, privileges, and special opportunities to businesses. Some of the more common intangible assets include trademarks, patents, copyrights, franchises, and goodwill. Intangible assets have different characteristics and purposes. Some of the unique features of the more common ones are described in the following sections.

Trademarks

A **trademark** is a name or symbol that identifies a company or an individual product. Some trademarks that you may be familiar with are the Polo emblem, the name *Coca-Cola*, and the slogan "I AM Canadian." Trademarks are registered with the Canadian Intellectual Property Office and have an indefinite legal lifetime.

The costs to be capitalized include those required to develop the trademark and those incurred to defend it. When trademarks are purchased, the amount of the purchase price is capitalized in the Trademark account. Companies want their trademarks to become familiar but fear the situation in which the trademark begins to be treated as the generic name for a product. Companies in this predicament expend large amounts to protect the trademark, including legal fees and extensive advertising programs to educate consumers. Some well-known trademarks that have been subject to this problem are Coke, Xerox, Kleenex, and Vaseline.

Patents

As noted earlier, a **patent** is an exclusive right to produce and sell a commodity that has one or more unique features. Patents granted by the Canadian Intellectual Property Office have a legal life of 20 years. Patents may be purchased, leased, or developed within the company. When a company develops a patent, the question arises as to what costs should be capitalized in the Patent account. Clearly, the legal costs associated with obtaining and defending the patent are capitalized. What about the research and development costs incurred to make the product that is being patented? Product research and development is often unsuccessful; companies spend hundreds of millions of dollars on research projects that lead nowhere. Because it is difficult to determine which research and development costs will produce future revenues, GAAP requires that these costs be expensed in the period in which they are incurred. Thus, the costs capitalized in the Patent account are usually limited to a purchase price and/or legal fees.

Copyrights

A **copyright** protects writings, musical compositions, and other works of art for the exclusive benefit of the creator or persons assigned the right by the creator. The cost of a copyright includes the purchase price and the legal costs associated with obtaining and defending the copyright. Copyrights are granted by the Canadian Intellectual Property Office for a period defined as the life of the creator plus 50 years. A radio commercial could use a Bach composition as background music with no legal ramifications; however, if "Ironic" were desired instead, royalties would have to be paid to Alanis Morrisette or to the assigned owner of the copyright. Often the cost of a copyright is expensed very early because future royalties may be uncertain.

Franchises

Franchises are exclusive rights to sell products or perform services in certain geographic areas. Fast-food restaurant chains, private labels such as President's Choice, and real estate offices are examples of private business franchises. Franchises can cost hundreds of thousands and even millions of dollars. The legal and useful lives of a franchise are often difficult to define. This is why judgment is often crucial to the establishment of the appropriate accounting treatment for franchises.

Goodwill

Goodwill is the added value of a business that is attributable to favourable factors such as reputation, location, and superior products. To better understand goodwill, consider the most popular restaurant in your town. If the owner sold the restaurant, do you think the purchase price would simply be the total value of the chairs, tables, kitchen equipment, and building? Certainly not, because much of the restaurant's value lies in its popularity, in other words, its ability to generate a high return.

Calculation of goodwill can be very complex; here we present a very simple example to illustrate how it is determined. Suppose the accounting records of a restaurant named Bendigo's show assets of $200,000, liabilities of $50,000, and equity of $150,000. A food services company that wants to acquire the restaurant agrees to purchase it by assuming the liabilities and paying the owner $300,000 cash. The amount of goodwill acquired can be determined by subtracting the fair market value of the assets on the day of purchase from the amount paid to acquire them. In this case, the amount paid includes $50,000 of liabilities that were assumed plus $300,000 cash. Assume that an independent appraiser assessed the fair market value of the assets as $280,000 on the date of purchase. In these circumstances, the amount of goodwill purchased is $70,000 ([$50,000 + $300,000] − $280,000). The effect of the purchase on the financial statements of the buyer is shown here:

Assets					=	Liab.	+	Equity	Rev.	−	Exp.	=	Net Inc.	Cash Flow Statement	
Cash	+	Rest. Assets	+	Goodwill											
(300,000)	+	280,000	+	70,000	=	50,000	+	NA	NA	−	NA	=	NA	(300,000)	IA

reality bytes

Corporations use their own discretion in determining the estimated useful life of their amortizable capital assets. Even within industries, these estimates can vary considerably. In the 2000 annual report for Wendy's International, property and equipment are amortized using the straight-line method over the following useful lives: building, up to 40 years; leasehold improvements, the lesser of useful lives of assets or lease terms including option periods; and equipment, 3 to 12 years. McDonald's also uses the straight-line method; however, their useful lives are estimated as follows: buildings, up to 40 years; leasehold improvements, up to 25 years; restaurant equipment, up to 15 years; and other equipment, up to 10 years. It is management's responsibility to review these estimated lives for appropriateness on a regular basis.

Companies are required to disclose information concerning the amortization methods and rates used. This disclosure is made in the notes that accompany the financial statements. Users should review this information when evaluating or comparing companies to determine the potential effect on income.

The journal entry required to record the acquisition of the restaurant follows:

Account Title	Debit	Credit
Restaurant Assets	280,000	
Goodwill	70,000	
Cash		300,000
Liabilities		50,000

Note that the fair market value of the restaurant assets represents the historical cost to the new owner. Therefore, it becomes the basis for future amortization charges.

Expensing Intangible Assets

As with other long-term operational assets, intangibles with identifiable useful lives are capitalized in asset accounts at historical cost and are systematically expensed over their useful lives.

Intangible assets are normally amortized (expensed) on a straight-line basis. In determining how much to expense each year, the company must consider two possible lifetimes of the intangible: (1) its legal life and (2) its useful life. An intangible asset should be amortized over the shortest of these two possible lives.

To illustrate, assume that Flowers Industries pays $44,000 cash to purchase a patent. Although the patent has a legal life of 20 years, Flowers estimates that it will be useful for only 11 years. In this case, the annual charge is $4,000 ($44,000 ÷ 11 years). The effect of the purchase of the patent and its amortization on the financial statements and the journal entries necessary to record the events are as follows:

Assets				Equity			Rev.	−	Exp.	=	Net Inc.	Cash Flow Statement	
Cash	+	Patent	=	C. Sh.	+	Ret. Earn.							
(44,000)	+	44,000	=	NA	+	NA	NA	−	NA	=	NA	(44,000)	IA
NA	+	(4,000)	=	NA	+	(4,000)	NA	−	4,000	=	(4,000)	NA	

Account Title	Debit	Credit
Patent	44,000	
Cash		44,000
Amortization Expense, Patent	4,000	
Patent		4,000

Balance Sheet Presentation

In this chapter, you learned about the acquisition, expense allocation, and disposal of a wide range of long-term assets. Exhibit 9–7 shows a typical balance sheet that exemplifies many of the assets discussed.

Exhibit 9–7 *Balance Sheet Presentation of Operational Assets*

Balance Sheets			
Capital Assets			
Plant and Equipment			
Buildings	$4,000,000		
Less: Accumulated Amortization	(2,500,000)	$1,500,000	
Equipment	1,750,000		
Less: Accumulated Amortization	(1,200,000)	550,000	
Total Plant and Equipment			$2,050,000
Land	850,000		
Natural Resources			
Mineral Deposits, net		2,100,000	
Oil Reserves, net		890,000	
Total Natural Resources			2,990,000
Intangibles			
Patents (Less: Amortization)		38,000	
Goodwill		175,000	
Total Intangible Assets			213,000
Total Capital Assets			$6,103,000

Understanding How Expense Recognition Affects Financial Performance Measures

LO12 Describe how expense recognition choices and industry characteristics affect financial performance measures.

Clearly, the amount of expense recognized in any particular accounting period depends on which allocation method (straight-line, accelerated, or units-of-activity) a company uses. Ideally, a company should use the method that best matches the pattern of asset use. More expense should be recognized in periods in which the assets are used extensively. Smaller amounts should be recognized in periods in which assets are used less often. Unfortunately, the pattern of asset use may be uncertain when the expense recognition method is selected. Since asset use occurs in the future, different managers may have different opinions about how assets will be used. As a result, managers of different companies may use different expense recognition methods for similar assets. In other words, companies affected by an identical set of economic circumstances could produce significantly different financial statements.

Effect of Judgment and Estimation

As a simple example, assume that two companies, Alpha and Zeta, are affected by the same economic events in 2005 and 2006. Both generate revenue of $50,000 and incur cost of goods sold of $30,000 during each year. In 2005, each company pays $20,000 for an asset with an expected useful life of five years and no residual value. How will the companies' financial statements differ if one uses the straight-line method and the other uses the double-declining-balance method? To answer this question, begin by computing the amortization expense for both companies for 2005 and 2006.

If Alpha Company uses straight-line amortization, the amount of amortization for 2005 and 2006 is computed as follows:

(Cost − Residual)	÷	Useful life in years	=	Amortization expense per year
($20,000 − $0)	÷	5	=	$4,000

In contrast, if Zeta Company uses the double-declining-balance method, Zeta recognizes the following amounts of amortization expense for 2005 and 2006:

	(Cost − Accumulated Amortization)	× 2 ×	(Straight-Line Rate)	=	Amortization Expense
2005	($20,000 − $0)	×	(2 × [1 ÷ 5])	=	$8,000
2006	($20,000 − $8,000)	×	(2 × [1 ÷ 5])	=	$4,800

Based on these computations, the income statements for the two companies appear as follows:

Income Statements

	2005		2006	
	Alpha Co.	Zeta Co.	Alpha Co.	Zeta Co.
Sales	$50,000	$50,000	$50,000	$50,000
Cost of Goods Sold	(30,000)	(30,000)	(30,000)	(30,000)
Gross Profit	20,000	20,000	20,000	20,000
Amortization Expense	(4,000)	(8,000)	(4,000)	(4,800)
Net Income	$16,000	$12,000	$16,000	$15,200

The relevant sections of the balance sheets are as follows:

Plant Assets

	2005		2006	
	Alpha Co.	Zeta Co.	Alpha Co.	Zeta Co.
Asset	$20,000	$20,000	$20,000	$20,000
Accumulated Amortization	(4,000)	(8,000)	(8,000)	(12,800)
Net Book Value	$16,000	$12,000	$12,000	$7,200

Clearly, the amortization method selected by each company affects its expenses and thus its net income and retained earnings. The method used also affects the accumulated amortization, which in turn affects the net book value of plant assets and total assets. Financial statement analysis is affected if it is based on ratios whose computations use any of the items mentioned. Previously defined ratios that are affected include the (1) debt to assets ratio, (2) return on assets ratio, (3) return on equity ratio, and (4) return on sales ratio.

The amortization method is not the only aspect of expense recognition that can vary for two companies. The companies may also make different assumptions about the useful lives and residual values of plant assets. Thus, even if the same amortization method is used, amortization expense may still differ. To illustrate, assume that both Air Canada and WestJet buy an airplane that costs $40 million and that both decide to use straight-line amortization. Air Canada might choose to amortizate the plane over

15 years while WestJet may choose 20 years. If residual value is expected to be negligible, the amortization expense per year for each airplane is

	(Cost − Residual)	÷	Estimated Life	=	Amortizaton Expense
Air Canada	($40 million − $0)	÷	15	=	$2.67 million
WestJet	($40 million − $0)	÷	20	=	$2.00 million

Based on these numbers, Air Canada's amortization expense is 35 percent higher than WestJet's for the next 15 years. This difference could have a significant impact on the companies' financial statements and the ratios used to evaluate financial performance. Although the performance measures are affected, the real economic substance as measured by cash flow is not affected. Thus, an uninformed user may conclude that performance differences exist when in fact they do not.

Users of accounting information must be aware of all accounting policies a company uses before analyzing that company's financial statements and financial ratios. For this reason, companies that wish to have their statements audited are required to disclose all significant accounting policies such as amortization and inventory cost flow methods used. This disclosure is usually provided in the notes that accompany the financial statements.

Effect of Industry Characteristics

LO13 Describe why some businesses generate high revenue with few operational assets.

Financial performance measures can also be affected by industry characteristics. Some businesses use more amortizable assets than other businesses. For example, companies in manufacturing industries rely on heavy machinery while insurance companies use human capital. Therefore, manufacturing companies can be expected to have relatively higher amortization charges than insurance companies. The ability to evaluate a company's financial performance requires an understanding of the industry in which it operates. To illustrate how the type of industry can affect financial reporting, review the information in Exhibit 9–8. This exhibit compares the ratio of sales to property, plant, and equipment for two companies for each of three different industries. These data are for 2000.

The table indicates that for every $1.00 invested in property, plant, and equipment, Investors Group produced $12.20 of sales. In contrast, WestJet produced only $1.40 in sales for each $1.00 it invested in operational assets. In other words, the higher the investment in operational assets, the lower the ratio.

Given the investment in airplanes, we would expect that airline companies would have an even smaller ratio. Passengers flying on an airline tend to underestimate the investment in human capital because they see only the crew plus a few employees inside the air terminal. Airlines have many employees, such as reservation agents, schedulers, baggage handlers, and mechanics, whom most passengers do not see.

A failure to understand that financial statements reflect industry characteristics can lead to a misinterpretation of managerial performance. For example, the fact that a stock brokerage company uses fewer operational assets than a fast-food company is not an indication that stock brokerage companies are better managed. Rather, it means that the two companies operate in different business environments. When you use financial ratios for performance evaluation, it is critically important that you compare ratios of companies from the same industry. Also, do not forget that even within the same industry, companies may use different expense recognition methods and may reach different conclusions regarding the estimated useful lives and residual values of their operational assets. Financial statement analysis requires not only an understanding of the technical aspects of accounting but also the ability to assess the reasonableness of management's judgments.

Exhibit 9–8 *Industry Data Reflecting the Use of Operational Assets*

Industry	Company	Sales ÷ Property, Plant, and Equipment
Stock Brokerage	Investors Group	12.2 times
	Merrill Lynch	7.8
Airlines	Air Canada	2.2
	WestJet	1.4
Fast-Food	McDonald's	2.4
	Wendy's	1.5

a look back

In Chapter 3 you learned that the main objective of amortization is to match the cost of a long-term operational asset with the revenues that the asset is expected to generate. This chapter showed how this basic concept can be extended to natural resources, and to intangible assets. This chapter also explained how different methods can be used to account for the same event (straight-line versus double-declining-balance). Companies experiencing exactly the same business events could produce different financial statements. The alternative accounting methods for amortizing assets include the (1) straight-line, (2) double-declining-balance, and (3) units-of-activity methods.

The *straight-line method* recognizes the same amount of expense during each accounting period. The amount of the expense to recognize is determined by the formula ([cost − residual] ÷ number of years of useful life). The *double-declining-balance method* recognizes proportionately larger amounts of expense in the early years of an asset's useful life and increasingly smaller amounts of expense in the later years of the asset's useful life. The formula for calculating expense based on the double-declining-balance method is (net book value at beginning of period × double the straight-line rate). The *units-of-activity method* recognizes expense in direct proportion to the number of units produced during an accounting period. The amount of expense to recognize each period is computed by the formula ([cost − residual] ÷ total estimated units of activity = allocation rate × units of activity in current accounting period).

The chapter also discussed *capital cost allowance (CCA)*, which is a tax treatment. A company may use CCA for tax purposes and straight-line or one of the other methods for public reporting. As a result, differences may exist in the amount of tax expense and the amount of tax liability. Such differences are called *deferred taxes*.

This chapter covered the accounting treatment for *changes in estimates* such as the useful life or the residual value. Under these circumstances, the amount of amortization recognized previous to the change in estimate is not affected. Instead, the remaining net book value of the asset is expensed over its remaining useful life.

Three types of costs occur after an asset has been placed into service. These costs include maintenance, quality improvement, and extensions of useful life. *Maintenance costs* are expensed in the period in which they are incurred. *Costs that improve the quality* or *that extend the useful life* of an asset are added to the cost of the asset, thereby increasing the net book value and the amount of future amortization charges.

a look forward

In Chapter 10 we leave the assets section of the balance sheet and investigate some issues related to accounting for long-term liabilities. As you will learn, tax issues are also important when considering the consequences of borrowing money.

SELF-STUDY REVIEW PROBLEM

The following information pertains to a machine purchased by Bakersfield Company on January 1, 2006.

Purchase price	$ 63,000
Delivery cost	$ 2,000
Installation charge	$ 3,000
Estimated useful life	8 years
Estimated units the machine will produce	130,000
Estimated residual value	$ 3,000

The machine produced 14,400 units during 2006 and 17,000 units during 2007.

Required

Determine the amortization expense Bakersfield would report for 2006 and 2007 using each of the following methods.

a. Straight line.
b. Double-declining-balance.
c. Units of activity.
d. CCA assuming a rate of 20 percent and using the half-year rule.

Solution to Requirements a–d.

a. Straight Line

Purchase price	$ 63,000	
Delivery cost	2,000	
Installation charge	3,000	
Total cost of machine	$ 68,000	
Less: Residual value	(3,000)	
	$ 65,000	÷ 8 = $8,125 amortization per year
2006	$ 8,125	
2007	$ 8,125	

b. Double-Declining-Balance

Year	Cost	−	Accumulated Amortization at Beginning of Year	×	2 × S-L Rate	=	Annual Amortization
2006	$68,000	−	$ 0	×	(2 × 0.125)	=	$17,000
2007	68,000	−	17,000	×	(2 × 0.125)	=	12,750

c. Units of Activity

(1) (Cost − Residual value) ÷ Estimated units of production = Amortization cost per unit produced

$$\frac{(\$68{,}000 - \$3{,}000)}{130{,}000} = \$0.50 \text{ per unit}$$

(2) Cost per unit × Annual units produced = Annual amortization expense

2006	$0.50 × 14,400 = $7,200
2007	0.50 × 17,000 = 8,500

d. CCA

UCC × CCA rate = Annual amortization
2006 20% = $13,600 × 1/2 = $6,800
2007 ($68,000 − $6,800) × 20% = $12,240

KEY TERMS

accelerated amortization methods *369*
accumulated amortization *371*
amortization *366*
basket purchase *368*
capital cost allowance (CCA) method *378*
capital expenditures *379*
contra asset account *371*
copyright *383*
double-declining-balance amortization *373*
estimated useful life *369*
franchise *383*
goodwill *367*
half-year rule *378*
historical cost concept *367*
intangible assets *366*
long-term operational assets *365*
natural resources *366*
net book value *373*
patent *382*
property, plant, and equipment *366*
relative fair market value method *368*
residual value *369*
straight-line amortization *369*
tangible assets *366*
trademark *382*
undepreciated capital cost (UCC) *378*
units-of-activity amortization *376*

QUESTIONS

1. What is the difference in the functions of long-term operational assets and investments?
2. What is the difference between tangible and intangible assets? Give an example of each.
3. What is the difference between goodwill and specifically identifiable intangible assets?
4. Define *amortization*. What kind of asset is amortized?
5. Why are natural resources called *wasting assets*?
6. Is land amortized? Why or why not?
7. Explain the historical cost concept as it applies to long-term operational assets. Why is the net book value of an asset likely to be different from the current market value of the asset?
8. What different kinds of expenditures might be included in the recorded cost of a building?
9. What is a basket purchase of assets? When a basket purchase is made, how is cost assigned to individual assets?
10. What is the life cycle of a long-term operational asset?
11. Explain straight-line, units-of-activity, and double-declining-balance methods. When is it appropriate to use each of these methods?
12. What effect does the recognition of amortization expense have on total assets? On total equity?
13. Does the recognition of amortization expense affect cash flows? Why or why not?
14. MalMax purchased an amortizable asset. What would be the difference in total assets at the end of the first year if MalMax chooses the straight-line versus the double-declining-balance method?
15. John Smith mistakenly expensed the cost of a long-term tangible fixed asset. Specifically, he charged the cost of a truck to a delivery expense account. How will this error affect the income statement and the balance sheet in the year in which the mistake is made?
16. What is *residual value*?
17. What type of account (classification) is accumulated amortization?
18. Why is amortization that has been recognized over the life of an asset shown in a contra account? Why not just reduce the asset account?
19. Assume that a piece of equipment cost $5,000 and had accumulated amortization recorded of $3,000. What is the net book value of the equipment? Is the net book value equal to the fair market value of the equipment? Explain.
20. Why would a company choose to amortize one piece of equipment using the double-declining-balance method and another piece of equipment using the straight-line method?
21. Explain capital cost allowance (CCA).
22. Why may it be necessary to revise the estimated life of a plant asset? When the estimated life is revised, does it affect the amount of amortization per year? Why or why not?
23. How are capital expenditures made to improve the quality of a capital asset accounted for? Would the answer change if the expenditure extended the life of the asset but did not improve quality? Explain.
24. When a long-term operational asset is sold at a gain, how is the balance sheet affected? Is the cash flow statement affected? If so, how?
25. List several of the most common intangible assets. How is the life determined that is to be used to compute amortization?
26. How do differences in expense recognition and industry characteristics affect financial performance measures?

EXERCISES

Unless specifically included, income tax considerations should be ignored in all exercises and problems.

EXERCISE 9–1 *Long-Term Operational Assets Used in a Business* L.O. 2

Required

Give some examples of long-term operational assets that each of the following companies is likely to own: (a) Greyhound Bus Co., (b) Esso, (c) Molly Maid, and (d) McDonald's.

EXERCISE 9–2 *Identifying Long-Term Operational Assets* L.O. 2

Required

Which of the following items should be classified as long-term operational assets?

a. Inventory
b. Patent
c. Tract of timber
d. Land
e. Computer
f. Goodwill
g. Cash
h. Buildings
i. Production machinery
j. Accounts receivable
k. Term deposit (6 months)
l. Franchise

EXERCISE 9–3 *Classifying Tangible and Intangible Assets* L.O. 1

Required

Identify each of the following long-term operational assets as either tangible (T) or intangible (I).

a. Delivery van
b. Land
c. Franchise
d. Computer
e. Copyright
f. Copper mine
g. Plant warehouse
h. Drill press
i. Patent
j. Oil well
k. Desk
l. Goodwill

EXERCISE 9–4 *Determining the Cost of an Asset* L.O. 3

B.C. Lumber Co. purchased an electronic saw to cut various types and sizes of logs. The saw had a list price of $90,000. The seller agreed to allow a 5 percent discount because B.C. Lumber paid cash. Delivery terms were FOB shipping point. Freight cost amounted to $1,000. B.C. Lumber had to hire an individual to operate the saw. The operator was trained to run the saw for a one-time training fee of $900. The operator was paid an annual salary of $25,000. The cost of the company's theft insurance policy increased by $1,100 per year as a result of the acquisition of the saw. The saw had a four-year useful life and an expected residual value of $6,000.

Required

Determine the amount to be capitalized in an asset account for the purchase of the saw.

EXERCISE 9–5 *Allocating Costs on the Basis of Relative Market Values* L.O. 3

Western Company purchased a building and the land on which the building is situated for a total cost of $600,000 cash. The land was appraised at $140,000 and the building at $560,000.

Required

a. What is the accounting term for this type of acquisition?
b. Determine the amount of the purchase cost to allocate to the land and the amount to allocate to the building.
c. Would the company recognize a gain on the purchase? Why or why not?
d. Record the purchase in a statements model like the following one.

Assets					=	Liab.	+	Equity	Rev.	−	Exp.	=	Net Inc.	Cash Flow Statement
Cash	+	Land	+	Building										

L.O. 3 **EXERCISE 9–6** *Allocating Costs for a Basket Purchase*

Deeds Company purchased a restaurant building, land, and equipment for $500,000. Deeds paid $100,000 in cash and issued a 20-year, 8 percent note to a local bank for the balance. The appraised value of the assets was as follows:

Land	$120,000
Building	300,000
Equipment	180,000
Total	$600,000

Required

a. Compute the amount to be recorded on the books for each of the assets.
b. Record the purchase in a horizontal statements model like the following one.

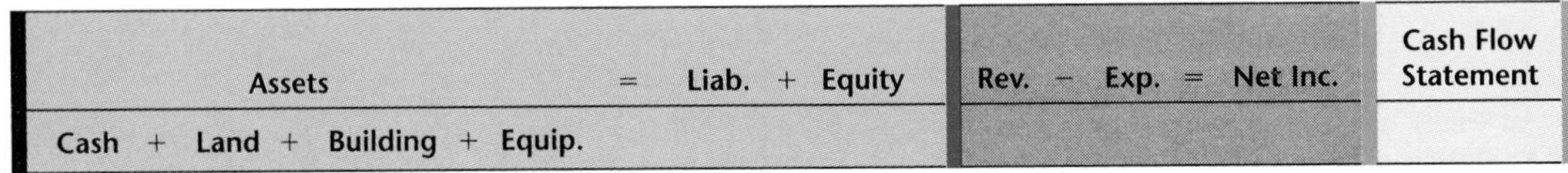

Assets	=	Liab. + Equity	Rev. − Exp. = Net Inc.	Cash Flow Statement
Cash + Land + Building + Equip.				

c. Prepare the general journal entry to record the purchase.

L.O. 4 **EXERCISE 9–7** *Effect of Double-Declining-Balance Method on Financial Statements*

Swift Company started by acquiring $160,000 cash from the issue of common shares. The company purchased an asset that cost $160,000 cash on January 1, 2005. The asset had an expected useful life of five years and an estimated residual value of $20,000. Swift Company earned $92,000 and $65,000 of cash revenue during 2005 and 2006, respectively. Swift Company uses double-declining-balance amortization.

Required

Prepare income statements, balance sheets, and cash flow statement for 2005 and 2006. Use a vertical statements format. (*Hint:* Record the events in T-accounts prior to preparing the statements.)

L.O. 4, 5 **EXERCISE 9–8** *Events Related to the Acquisition, Use, and Disposal of a Tangible Plant Asset: Straight-Line Method*

Mario's Pizza purchased a delivery van on January 1, 2005, for $30,000. In addition, Mario's had to pay sales tax and title fees of $1,000. The van is expected to have a five-year life and a residual value of $6,000.

Required

a. Using the straight-line method, compute the amortization expense for 2005 and 2006.
b. Prepare the general journal entry to record the 2005 amortization.
c. Assume the van was sold on January 1, 2008, for $20,000. Prepare the journal entry for the sale of the van in 2008.

L.O. 6 **EXERCISE 9–9** *Computing and Recording Straight-Line versus Double-Declining-Balance Method*

At the beginning of 2007, Expert Manufacturing purchased a new computerized drill press for $40,000. It is expected to have a five-year life and a $4,000 residual value.

Required

a. Compute the amortization for each of the five years, assuming that the company uses
   (1) Straight-line amortization.
   (2) Double-declining-balance amortization.
b. Record the purchase of the drill press and the amortization expense for the first year under the straight-line and double-declining-balance methods in a financial statements model like the following one:

Assets					=	Shareholders' Equity	Rev. − Exp. = Net Inc.	Cash Flow Statement
Cash	+	Drill Press	+	Acc. Amort.	=	Ret. Ear.		

c. Prepare the journal entries to recognize amortization for each of the five years, assuming that the company uses the
   (1) Straight-line method.
   (2) Double-declining-balance method.

EXERCISE 9–10 *Effect of the Disposal of Plant Assets on the Financial Statements* L.O. 5

A plant asset with a cost of $20,000 and accumulated amortization of $15,000 is sold for $6,000.

Required
a. What is the net book value of the asset at the time of sale?
b. What is the amount of gain or loss on the disposal?
c. How would the sale affect net income (increase, decrease, no effect) and by how much?
d. How would the sale affect the amount of total assets shown on the balance sheet (increase, decrease, no effect) and by how much?
e. How would the event affect the cash flow statement (inflow, outflow, no effect) and in what section?

EXERCISE 9–11 *Double-Declining-Balance and Units-of-Activity: Gain or Loss on Disposal* L.O. 5, 6

Copy Service Co. purchased a new colour copier at the beginning of 2005 for $40,000. The copier is expected to have a five-year useful life and a $4,000 residual value. The expected copy production was estimated at 2,000,000 copies. Actual copy production for the five years was as follows:

2005	550,000
2006	480,000
2007	380,000
2008	390,000
2009	240,000
Total	2,040,000

The copier was sold at the end of 2009 for $5,200.

Required
a. Compute the amortization expense for each of the five years, using the double-declining-balance method.
b. Compute the amortization expense for each of the five years, using the units-of-activity method. (Round cost per unit to three decimal places.)
c. Calculate the amount of gain or loss from the sale of the asset under each of the amortization methods.

EXERCISE 9–12 *Computing Amortization for Tax Purposes* L.O. 7

Quality Computer Company purchased $120,000 of equipment on September 1, 2008.

Required
Compute the amount of CCA for 2008 and 2009, assuming that the equipment has a CCA rate of 20 percent. The company follows the half-year rule.

EXERCISE 9–13 *Revision of Estimated Useful Life* L.O. 8

On January 1, 2007, Davis Milling Co. purchased a compressor and related installation equipment for $48,000. The equipment had a three-year estimated life with a $6,000 residual value. Straight-line amortization was used. At the beginning of 2009, Davis revised the expected life of the asset to four years rather than three years. The residual value was revised to $4,000.

Required
Compute the amortization expense for each of the four years.

L.O. 9 EXERCISE 9–14 *Distinguishing between Maintenance Costs and Capital Expenditures*

Chung's Cleaning Service has just completed a minor repair on a service truck. The repair cost was $700, and the net book value prior to the repair was $5,000. In addition, the company spent $6,000 to replace the roof on a building. The new roof extended the life of the building by five years. Prior to the roof replacement, the general ledger reflected the Building account at $90,000 and related Accumulated Amortization account at $40,000.

Required
After the work was completed, what net book value should Chung's report on the balance sheet for the service truck and the building?

L.O. 9 EXERCISE 9–15 *Effect of Maintenance Costs versus Capital Expenditures on Financial Statements*

Yukon Construction Company purchased a forklift for $106,000 cash. It had an estimated useful life of four years and a $6,000 residual value. At the beginning of the third year of use, the company spent an additional $10,000 that was related to the forklift. The company's financial condition just prior to this expenditure is shown in the following statements model:

Assets						=	Shareholders' Equity			Rev.	−	Exp.	=	Net Inc.	Cash Flow Statement
Cash	+	Forklift	−	Acc. Amort.		=	C. Sh.	+	Ret. Earn.						
17,000	+	106,000	−	(50,000)		=	24,000	+	44,000	NA	−	NA	=	NA	NA

Required
Record the $10,000 expenditure in the statements model under each of the following independent assumptions:

a. The expenditure was for routine maintenance.
b. The expenditure extended the forklift's life.
c. The expenditure improved the forklift's operating capacity.

L.O. 9 EXERCISE 9–16 *Effect of Maintenance Costs versus Capital Expenditures on Financial Statements*

On January 1, 2005, Mountain Power Company overhauled four turbine engines that generate power for customers. The overhaul resulted in a slight increase in the capacity of the engines to produce power. Such overhauls occur regularly at two-year intervals and have been treated as maintenance expense in the past. Management is considering whether to capitalize this year's $30,000 cash cost in the engine asset account or to expense it as a maintenance expense. Assume that the engines have a remaining useful life of two years and no expected residual value. Assume the straight-line method is used.

Required

a. Determine the amount of additional amortization expense Mountain would recognize in 2005 and 2006 if the cost were capitalized in the engine account.
b. Determine the amount of expense Mountain would recognize in 2005 and 2006 if the cost were recognized as maintenance expense.
c. Determine the effect of the overhaul on cash flow from operating activities for 2005 and 2006 if the cost were capitalized and expensed through amortization charges.
d. Determine the effect of the overhaul on cash flow from operating activities for 2005 and 2006 if the cost were recognized as maintenance expense.

L.O. 10 EXERCISE 9–17 *Computing and Recording Amortization Expense*

Valley Sand and Gravel paid $500,000 to acquire 800,000 cubic metres of sand reserves. The following statements model reflects Valley's financial condition just prior to purchasing the sand reserves. The company extracted 350,000 cubic metres of sand in year 1 and 380,000 cubic metres in year 2.

Assets			=	Equity			Rev. − Exp. = Net Inc.	Cash Flow Statement
Cash	+	Sand. Res.	=	C. Sh.	+	Ret. Earn.		
750,000	+	NA	=	750,000	+	NA	NA − NA = NA	NA

Required

a. Compute the amortization charge per unit.
b. Record the acquisition of the sand reserves and the amortization expense for years 1 and 2 in a financial statements model like the preceding one.
c. Prepare the general journal entries to record the amortization expense for years 1 and 2.

EXERCISE 9–18 *Computing and Recording the Amortization of Intangibles* L.O. 11

Moncton Manufacturing paid cash to purchase the assets of an existing company. Among the assets purchased were the following items:

Patent with 5 remaining years of legal life	$28,000
Goodwill	60,000

Moncton's financial condition just prior to the purchase of these assets is shown in the following statements model:

Assets					=	Liab.	+	Equity	Rev. − Exp. = Net Inc.	Cash Flow Statement
Cash	+	Patent	+	Goodwill						
94,000	+	NA	+	NA	=	NA	+	94,000	NA − NA = NA	NA

Required

a. Compute the annual amortization expense for these items if applicable.
b. Record the purchase of the intangible assets and the related amortization expense for year 1 in a horizontal statements model like the preceding one.
c. Prepare the journal entries to record the purchase of the intangible assets and the related amortization for year 1, assuming goodwill at the end of year 1 has an estimated value of $52,500.

EXERCISE 9–19 *Computing and Recording Goodwill* L.O. 12

Fran Wallace purchased the business Alpha Peripherals for $300,000 cash and assumption of all liabilities at the date of purchase. Alpha's books showed assets of $250,000, liabilities of $30,000, and equity of $220,000. An appraiser assessed the fair market value of the tangible assets at $270,000 at the date of purchase. Wallace's financial condition just prior to the purchase is shown in the following statements model:

Assets					=	Liab.	+	Equity	Rev. − Exp. = Net Inc.	Cash Flow Statement
Cash	+	Assets	+	Goodwill						
400,000	+	NA	+	NA	=	NA	+	400,000	NA − NA = NA	NA

Required

a. Compute the amount of goodwill purchased.
b. Record the purchase in a financial statements model like the preceding one.

PROBLEMS—SERIES A

L.O. 3 PROBLEM 9–1A *Accounting for Acquisition of Assets Including a Basket Purchase*

May Company made several purchases of long-term assets in 2009. The details of each purchase are presented here.

New Office Equipment
1. List price: $25,000; terms: 1/10, n/30; paid within the discount period.
2. Transportation-in: $900.
3. Installation: $650.
4. Cost to repair damage during unloading: $450.
5. Routine maintenance cost after eight months: $90.

Basket Purchase of Office Furniture, Copier, Computers, and Laser Printers for $40,000 with fair market values of
1. Office furniture, $6,000.
2. Copier, $6,000.
3. Computers, $28,000.
4. Laser printers, $10,000.

Land for new headquarters with old barn torn down
1. Purchase price, $60,000.
2. Demolition of barn, $3,000.
3. Lumber sold from old barn, $2,000.
4. Grading in preparation for new building, $6,000.
5. Construction of new building, $180,000.

Required
In each of these cases, determine the amount of cost to be capitalized in the asset account.

L.O. 4, 5 PROBLEM 9–2A *Accounting for Amortization over Multiple Accounting Cycles*

Astro Company began operations when it acquired $25,000 cash from the issue of common shares on January 1, 2005. The cash acquired was immediately used to purchase a $25,000 asset that had a $3,000 residual value and an expected useful life of four years. The asset was used to produce the following revenue stream (assume all revenue transactions are for cash). At the beginning of the fifth year, the asset was sold for $2,500 cash. Astro uses the straight-line method.

	2005	2006	2007	2008	2009
Revenue	$6,000	$6,200	$6,500	$7,000	$0

Required
Prepare income statements, statements of shareholders' equity, balance sheets, and cash flow statements for each of the five years.

L.O. 3, 4, 8, 9 PROBLEM 9–3A *Purchase and Use of Tangible Asset: Three Accounting Cycles, Double-Declining-Balance Method*

The following transactions pertain to Business Solutions Services Inc. Assume the transactions for the purchase of the computer and any capital improvements occur on January 1 each year.

2007
1. Acquired $50,000 cash from the issue of common shares.
2. Purchased a computer system for $15,000. It has an estimated useful life of five years and a $3,000 residual value.
3. Paid $500 sales tax on the computer system.
4. Collected $20,000 in data entry fees from clients.
5. Paid $800 in fees to service the computers.

6. Recorded double-declining-balance amortization on the computer system for the year.
7. Closed the revenue and expense accounts to Retained Earnings at the end of 2007.

2008

1. Paid $550 for repairs to the computer system.
2. Bought a case of toner cartridges for the printers that are part of the computer system, $600.
3. Collected $30,000 in data entry fees from clients.
4. Paid $900 in fees to service the computers.
5. Recorded double-declining-balance amortization for the year.
6. Closed the revenue and expense accounts to Retained Earnings at the end of 2008.

2009

1. Paid $2,500 to upgrade the computer system, which extended the total life of the system to six years.
2. Paid $800 in fees to service the computers.
3. Collected $35,000 in data entry fees from clients.
4. Recorded double-declining-balance amortization for the year.
5. Closed the revenue and expense accounts at the end of 2009.

Required

a. Use a horizontal statements model like the following one to show the effect of these transactions on the elements of financial statements. Use + for increase, − for decrease, and NA for not affected. The first event is recorded as an example.

2007 Event No.	Assets	=	Liabilities	+	Equity	Net Inc.	Cash Flow Statement
1	+		NA		+	NA	+ FA

b. Use a vertical model to present financial statements for 2007, 2008, and 2009. (Record the transactions in T-accounts before attempting to prepare the financial statements.)

PROBLEM 9–4A *Calculating Amortization Expense Using Three Different Methods* L.O. 6, 7

O'Brian Service Company purchased a copier on January 1, 2008, for $5,000 and paid an additional $200 for delivery charges. The copier was estimated to have a life of four years or 1,000,000 copies. Residual value was estimated at $1,200. The copier produced 230,000 copies in 2008 and 250,000 copies in 2009.

Required

Compute the amount of amortization expense for the copier for calendar years 2008 and 2009, using these methods:

a. Straight-line.
b. Double-declining-balance.
c. Units-of-activity.
d. Capital cost allowance using a 20 percent rate.

PROBLEM 9–5A *Effect of Straight-Line versus Double-Declining-Balance Method on the Recognition of Expense and Gains or Losses* L.O. 4, 6

Same Day Laundry Services purchased a new steam press machine in 2007 for $38,000. It is expected to have a five-year useful life and a $3,000 residual value. Same Day expects to use the equipment more extensively in the early years.

Required

a. Calculate the amortization expense for each of the five years, using the straight-line method.
b. Calculate the amortization expense for each of the five years, using the of double-declining-balance method.
c. Would the choice of one amortization method over another produce a different amount of annual cash flow for any year? Why or why not?
d. Assume that Same Day Laundry Services sold the steam press machine at the end of the third year for $20,000. Compute the amount of gain or loss using each amortization method.

L.O. 4, 5 PROBLEM 9–6A *Computing and Recording Units-of-Activity Amortization*

Stubbs Corporation purchased a delivery van for $35,000 in 2007. The firm's financial condition immediately prior to the purchase is shown in the following horizontal statements model:

Assets					=	Shareholders' Equity			Rev.	–	Exp.	=	Net Inc.	Cash Flow Statement
Cash	+	Van	–	Acc. Amort.	=	C. Sh.	+	Ret. Earn.						
50,000	+	NA	–	NA	=	50,000	+	NA	NA	–	NA	=	NA	NA

The van was expected to have a useful life of 150,000 kilometres and a residual value of $5,000. Actual mileage was as follows:

2007	50,000 km
2008	70,000
2009	58,000

Required

a. Compute the amortization for each of the three years, assuming the use of the units-of-activity method.

b. Assume that Stubbs earns $21,000 of cash revenue during 2007. Record the purchase of the van and the recognition of the revenue and the amortization expense for the first year in a financial statements model like the preceding one.

c. Assume that Stubbs sold the van at the end of the third year for $4,000. Record the general journal entry for the sale.

L.O. 6 PROBLEM 9–7A *Determining the Effect of Amortization Expense on Financial Statements*

Three different companies each purchased a machine on January 1, 2005, for $60,000. Each machine was expected to last five years or 200,000 hours. Residual value was estimated to be $4,000. All three machines were operated for 50,000 hours in 2005, 55,000 hours in 2006, 40,000 hours in 2007, 44,000 hours in 2008, and 31,000 hours in 2009. Each of the three companies earned $30,000 of cash revenue during each of the five years. Company A uses straight-line amortization, company B uses double-declining-balance amortization, and company C uses units-of-activity amortization.

Required

Answer each of the following questions. Ignore the effects of income taxes.

a. Which company will report the highest amount of net income for 2005?

b. Which company will report the lowest amount of net income for 2007?

c. Which company will report the highest net book value on the December 31, 2007, balance sheet?

d. Which company will report the highest amount of retained earnings on the December 31, 2008, balance sheet?

e. Which company will report the lowest amount of cash flow from operating activities on the 2007 cash flow statement?

L.O. 8, 10 PROBLEM 9–8A *Accounting for Natural Resources*

Northwest Exploration Corporation engages in the exploration and development of many types of natural resources. In the last two years, the company has engaged in the following activities:

Jan. 1, 2007	Purchased a coal mine estimated to contain 200,000 tonnes of coal for $720,000.
July 1, 2007	Purchased for $1,800,000 a tract of timber estimated to yield 3,000,000 board feet of lumber and to have a residual land value of $150,000.
Feb. 1, 2008	Purchased a silver mine estimated to contain 30,000 tonnes of silver for $900,000.
Aug. 1, 2008	Purchased for $880,000 oil reserves estimated to contain 250,000 barrels of oil, of which 30,000 would be unprofitable to pump.

Required

a. Prepare the journal entries to account for the following:
   (1) The 2007 purchases.
   (2) Amortization on the 2007 purchases, assuming that 80,000 tonnes of coal were mined and 1,100,000 board feet of lumber were cut.
   (3) The 2008 purchases.
   (4) Amortization on the four reserves, assuming that 62,000 tonnes of coal, 1,450,000 board feet of lumber, 9,000 tonnes of silver, and 78,000 barrels of oil were extracted.

b. Prepare the portion of the December 31, 2008, balance sheet that reports natural resources.

c. Assume that in 2009 the estimates changed to reflect only 50,000 tonnes of coal remaining. Prepare the amortization entry for 2009 to account for the extraction of 35,000 tonnes of coal.

PROBLEM 9–9A *Recording Continuing Expenditures for Plant Assets*

L.O. 4, 5, 8, 9

Summit, Inc., recorded the following transactions over the life of a piece of equipment purchased in 2008:

Jan. 1, 2008	Purchased equipment for $24,000 cash. The equipment is estimated to have a five-year life and $4,000 residual value and was to be amortized using the straight-line method.
Dec. 31, 2008	Recorded amortization expense for 2008.
May 5, 2009	Undertook routine repairs costing $350.
Dec. 31, 2009	Recorded amortization expense for 2009.
Jan. 1, 2010	Made an adjustment costing $3,000 to the equipment. It improved the quality of the output but did not affect the life estimate.
Dec. 31, 2010	Recorded amortization expense for 2010.
Mar. 1, 2011	Incurred $250 cost to oil and clean the equipment.
Dec. 31, 2011	Recorded amortization expense for 2011.
Jan. 1, 2012	Had the equipment completely overhauled at a cost of $5,600. The overhaul was estimated to extend the total life to seven years.
Dec. 31, 2012	Recorded amortization expense for 2012.
July 1, 2013	Received and accepted an offer of $9,500 for the equipment.

Required

a. Use a horizontal statements model like the following one to show the effects of these transactions on the elements of the financial statements. Use + for increase, − for decrease, and NA for not affected. The first event is recorded as an example.

Date	Assets	=	Liabilities	+	Equity	Net Inc.	Cash Flow Statement	
Jan, 1 2002	+−		NA		NA	NA	−	IA

b. Determine the amount of amortization expense Summit will report on the income statements for the years 2008 through 2012.

c. Determine the net book value (cost − accumulated amortization) Summit will report on the balance sheets at the end of the years 2008 through 2012.

d. Determine the amount of the gain or loss Summit will report on the disposal of the equipment on July 1, 2013.

PROBLEM 9–10A *Accounting for Continuing Expenditures*

L.O. 8, 9

Kaye Manufacturing Co. paid $26,000 to purchase a computerized assembly machine on January 1, 2005. The machine had an estimated life of eight years and a $4,000 residual value. Kaye's financial condition as of January 1, 2009, is shown in the following financial statements model. Kaye uses the straight-line method for amortization.

Assets						=	Shareholders' Equity			Rev.	−	Exp.	=	Net Inc.	Cash Flow Statement
Cash	+	Mach.	−	Acc. Amort.		=	C. Sh.	+	Ret. Earn.						
15,000	+	26,000	−	11,000		=	8,000	+	22,000	NA	−	NA	=	NA	NA

Kaye Manufacturing made the following expenditures on the computerized assembly machine in 2009:

Jan. 2	Added an overdrive mechanism for $6,000 that would improve the overall quality of the performance of the machine but would not extend its life. The residual value was revised to $3,000.
Aug. 1	Performed routine maintenance, $920.
Oct. 2	Replaced some computer chips (considered routine), $620.
Dec. 31	Recognized 2009 amortization expense.

Required

a. Record the 2009 transactions in a statements model like the preceding one.
b. Prepare journal entries for the 2009 transactions.

L.O. 11 PROBLEM 9–11A *Accounting for Intangible Assets*

Wallace Company purchased a fast-food restaurant for $1,395,000. The fair market values of the assets purchased were as follows. No liabilities were assumed.

Equipment	$600,000
Land	250,000
Building	155,000
Franchise (5-year life)	150,000

Required

a. Calculate the amount of goodwill purchased.
b. Prepare the journal entry to record the amortization of the franchise fee at the end of year 1.

L.O. 11 PROBLEM 9–12A *Accounting for Goodwill*

Branson Inc. purchased the assets of Crayton Co. for $1,200,000 in 2003. The estimated fair market value of the assets at the purchase date was $1,100,000. Goodwill of $100,000 was recorded at purchase. In 2006, because of negative publicity, one-half of the goodwill purchased from Crayton Co. was judged to be permanently impaired.

Required

a. How will Branson account for the impairment of the goodwill?
b. Prepare the journal entry to record the permanent impairment of goodwill.

PROBLEMS—SERIES B

L.O. 3 PROBLEM 9–1B *Accounting for Acquisition of Assets Including a Basket Purchase*

Sun Co., Inc., made several purchases of long-term assets in 2009. The details of each purchase are presented here.

New Office Equipment

1. List price: $60,000; terms: 2/10, n/30; paid within discount period.
2. Transportation-in: $1,600.
3. Installation: $2,200.
4. Cost to repair damage during unloading: $1,000.
5. Routine maintenance cost after six months: $300.

Basket Purchase of Copier, Computer, and Scanner for $15,000 with fair market values of

1. Copier, $10,000.
2. Computer, $6,000.
3. Scanner, $4,000.

Land for new warehouse with an old building torn down

1. Purchase price, $200,000.
2. Demolition of building, $10,000.
3. Lumber sold from old building, $7,000.

4. Grading in preparation for new building, $14,000.
5. Construction of new building, $500,000.

Required

In each of these cases, determine the amount of cost to be capitalized in the asset account.

PROBLEM 9–2B *Accounting for Amortization over Multiple Accounting Cycles: Straight-Line Method* L.O. 4, 5

Hobart Company started business by acquiring $60,000 cash from the issue of common shares on January 1, 2004. The cash acquired was immediately used to purchase a $60,000 asset that had a $12,000 residual value and an expected useful life of four years. The asset was used to produce the following revenue stream (assume that all revenue transactions are for cash). At the beginning of the fifth year, the asset was sold for $6,800 cash. Hobart uses straight-line amortization.

	2004	2005	2006	2007	2008
Revenue	$15,200	$14,400	$13,000	$12,000	$0

Required

Prepare income statements, statements of shareholders' equity, balance sheets, and cash flow statement for each of the five years. Present the statements in the form of a vertical statements model.

PROBLEM 9–3B *Purchase and Use of Tangible Asset: Three Accounting Cycles, Straight-Line Method* L.O. 4, 8, 9

The following transactions relate to Jim's Towing Service Co. Assume the transactions for the purchase of the wrecker and any capital improvements occur on January 1 of each year.

2007

1. Acquired $40,000 cash from the issue of common shares.
2. Purchased a used wrecker for $26,000. It has an estimated useful life of three years and a $2,000 residual value.
3. Paid sales tax on the wrecker of $1,800.
4. Collected $17,600 in towing fees.
5. Paid $3,000 for gasoline and oil.
6. Recorded straight-line amortization on the wrecker for the year.
7. Closed the revenue and expense accounts to Retained Earnings at the end of 2007.

2008

1. Paid for a tune-up for the wrecker's engine, $400.
2. Bought four new tires, $600.
3. Collected $18,000 in towing fees.
4. Paid $4,200 for gasoline and oil.
5. Recorded straight-line amortization for the year.
6. Closed the revenue and expense accounts to Retained Earnings at the end of 2008.

2009

1. Paid to overhaul the wrecker's engine, $1,400, which extended the life of the wrecker to a total of four years.
2. Paid for gasoline and oil, $3,600.
3. Collected $30,000 in towing fees.
4. Recorded straight-line amortization for the year.
5. Closed the revenue and expense accounts at the end of 2009.

Required

a. Use a horizontal statements model like the following one to show the effect of these transactions on the elements of financial statements. Use + for increase, − for decrease, and NA for not affected. The first event is recorded as an example.

2007 Event No.	Assets	=	Liabilities	+	Equity	Net Inc.	Cash Flow Statement
1	+		NA		+	NA	+ FA

b. Use a vertical model to present financial statements for 2007, 2008, and 2009. (*Hint*: Record the transactions in T-accounts before attempting to prepare the financial statements.)

L.O. 5, 6 PROBLEM 9–4B *Calculating Amortization Expense Using Four Different Methods*

Action, Inc., manufactures sporting goods. The following information applies to a machine purchased on January 1, 2005:

Purchase price	$70,000
Delivery cost	$2,000
Installation charge	$1,000
Estimated life	5 years
Estimated units	140,000
Residual estimate	$3,000

During 2005 the machine produced 26,000 units, and during 2006 it produced 21,000 units.

Required

Determine the amount of amortization expense for 2005 and 2006 using each of the following methods:

a. Straight-line.
b. Double-declining-balance.
c. Units-of-activity.
d. CCA using a 20 percent rate.

L.O. 4, 5, 6 PROBLEM 9–5B *Effect of Straight-Line versus Double-Declining-Balance Method on the Recognition of Expense and Gains or Losses*

Graves Office Service Ltd. purchased a new computer system in 2008 for $60,000. It is expected to have a five-year useful life and a $5,000 residual value. The company expects to use the equipment more extensively in the early years.

Required

a. Calculate the amortization expense for each of the five years, using the straight-line method.
b. Calculate the amortization expense for each of the five years, using the double-declining-balance method.
c. Would the choice of one amortization method over another produce a different amount of cash flow for any year? Why or why not?
d. Assume that Graves Office Service sold the computer system at the end of the fourth year for $15,000. Compute the amount of gain or loss using each amortization method.
e. Explain any differences in gain or loss due to using the different methods.

L.O. 4, 5 PROBLEM 9–6B *Computing and Recording Units-of-Activity Amortization*

Telcom purchased assembly equipment for $700,000 on January 1, 2007. Telcom's financial condition immediately prior to the purchase is shown in the following horizontal statements model:

Assets					=	Shareholders' Equity			Rev.	−	Exp.	=	Net Inc.	Cash Flow Statement
Cash	+	Equip.	−	Acc. Amort.	=	C. Sh.	+	Ret. Earn.						
800,000	+	NA	−	NA	=	800,000	+	NA	NA	−	NA	=	NA	NA

The equipment is expected to have a useful life of 100,000 machine hours and a residual value of $20,000. Actual machine-hour use was as follows:

2007	32,000
2008	33,000
2009	35,000
2010	28,000
2011	12,000

Required

a. Compute the amortization for each of the five years, using the units-of-activity method.
b. Assume that Telcom earns $320,000 of cash revenue during 2007. Record the purchase of the equipment and the recognition of the revenue and the amortization expense for the first year in a financial statements model like the preceding one.
c. Assume that Telcom sold the equipment at the end of the fifth year for $18,000. Record the general journal entry for the sale.

PROBLEM 9–7B *Determining the Effect of Amortization Expense on Financial Statements* L.O. 6

Three different companies each purchased trucks on January 1, 2006, for $40,000. Each truck was expected to last four years or 200,000 km. Residual value was estimated to be $5,000. All three trucks were driven 66,000 km in 2006, 42,000 km in 2007, 40,000 km in 2008, and 60,000 km in 2009. Each of the three companies earned $30,000 of cash revenue during each of the four years. Company A uses straight-line amortization, Company B uses double-declining-balance amortization and Company C uses units-of-activity amortization.

Required

Answer each of the following questions. Ignore the effects of income taxes.

a. Which company will report the highest amount of net income for 2006?
b. Which company will report the lowest amount of net income for 2009?
c. Which company will report the highest net book value on the December 31, 2008, balance sheet?
d. Which company will report the highest amount of retained earnings on the December 31, 2009, balance sheet?
e. Which company will report the lowest amount of cash flow from operating activities on the 2008 cash flow statement?

PROBLEM 9–8B *Accounting for Natural Resources* L.O. 8, 10

Lakeland Company engages in the exploration and development of many types of natural resources. In the last two years, the company has engaged in the following activities:

Jan. 1, 2006	Purchased for $1,600,000 a silver mine estimated to contain 100,000 tonnes of silver ore.
July 1, 2006	Purchased for $1,500,000 a tract of timber estimated to yield 1,000,000 board feet of lumber and the residual value of the land was estimated at $100,000.
Feb. 1, 2007	Purchased for $1,800,000 a gold mine estimated to yield 30,000 tonnes of gold-veined ore.
Sept. 1, 2007	Purchased oil reserves for $1,360,000. The reserves were estimated to contain 282,000 barrels of oil, of which 10,000 would be unprofitable to pump.

Required

a. Prepare the journal entries to account for the following:
   (1) The 2006 purchases.
   (2) Amortization on the 2006 purchases, assuming that 12,000 tonnes of silver were mined and 500,000 board feet of lumber were cut.
   (3) The 2007 purchases.
   (4) Amortization on the four natural resource assets, assuming that 20,000 tonnes of silver ore, 300,000 board feet of lumber, 4,000 tonnes of gold ore, and 50,000 barrels of oil were extracted.
b. Prepare the portion of the December 31, 2007, balance sheet that reports natural resources.
c. Assume that in 2008 the estimates changed to reflect only 20,000 tonnes of gold ore remaining. Prepare the amortization entry in 2008 to account for the extraction of 6,000 tonnes of gold ore.

L.O. 4, 5, 8, 9 PROBLEM 9–9B *Recording Continuing Expenditures for Plant Assets*

Cain, Inc., recorded the following transactions over the life of a piece of equipment purchased in 2004:

Jan. 1, 2004	Purchased equipment for $80,000 cash. The equipment was estimated to have a five-year life and $5,000 residual value and was to be amortized using the straight-line method.
Dec. 31, 2004	Recorded amortization expense for 2004.
Sept. 30, 2005	Undertook routine repairs costing $750.
Dec. 31, 2005	Recorded amortization expense for 2005.
Jan. 1, 2006	Made an adjustment costing $3,000 to the equipment. It improved the quality of the output but did not affect the life estimate.
Dec. 31, 2006	Recorded amortization expense for 2006.
June 1, 2007	Incurred $620 cost to oil and clean the equipment.
Dec. 31, 2007	Recorded amortization expense for 2007.
Jan. 1, 2008	Had the equipment completely overhauled at a cost of $8,000. The overhaul was estimated to extend the total life to seven years.
Dec. 31, 2008	Recorded amortization expense for 2008.
Oct. 1, 2009	Received and accepted an offer of $18,000 for the equipment.

Required

a. Use a horizontal statements model like the following one to show the effects of these transactions on the elements of the financial statements. Use + for increase, − for decrease, and NA for not affected. The first event is recorded as an example.

Date	Assets	=	Liabilities	+	Equity	Net Inc.	Cash Flow Statement	
Jan, 1 2004	+−		NA		NA	NA	−	IA

b. Determine the amount of amortization expense to be reported on the income statements for the years 2004 through 2008.

c. Determine the net book value (cost − accumulated amortization) Cain will report on the balance sheets at the end of the years 2004 through 2008.

d. Determine the amount of the gain or loss Cain will report on the disposal of the equipment on October 1, 2009.

L.O. 8, 9 PROBLEM 9–10B *Continuing Expenditures with Statements Model*

Mercury Company owned a service truck that was purchased at the beginning of 2007 for $20,000. It had an estimated life of three years and an estimated residual value of $2,000. Mercury uses straight-line amortization. Its financial condition as of January 1, 2009, is shown in the following financial statements model:

Assets					=	Shareholders' Equity			Rev.	−	Exp.	=	Net Inc.	Cash Flow Statement
Cash	+	Truck	−	Acc. Amort.	=	C. Sh.	+	Ret. Earn.						
14,000	+	20,000	−	12,000	=	4,000	+	18,000	NA	−	NA	=	NA	NA

In 2009, Mercury spent the following amounts on the truck:

Jan.	4	Overhauled the engine for $4,000. The estimated life was extended one additional year, and the residual value was revised to $3,000.
July	6	Obtained oil change and transmission service, $160.
Aug.	7	Replaced the fan belt and battery, $360.
Dec.	31	Purchased gasoline for the year, $5,000.
	31	Recognized 2009 amortization expense.

Required

a. Record the 2009 transactions in a statements model like the preceding one.
b. Prepare journal entries for the 2009 transactions.

PROBLEM 9–11B *Accounting for Intangible Assets* L.O. 11

Green Vision purchased Atlantic Transportations Co. for $1,200,000. The fair market values of the assets purchased were as follows. No liabilities were assumed.

Equipment	$400,000
Land	100,000
Building	400,000
Franchise (10-year life)	20,000

Required

a. Calculate the amount of goodwill purchased.
b. Prepare the journal entry to record the amortization of the franchise fee at the end of year 1.

PROBLEM 9–12B *Accounting for Goodwill* L.O. 11

Sulley Equipment Manufacturing Co. purchased the assets of Malcom Inc., a competitor, in 2006. It recorded goodwill of $50,000 at purchase. Because of defective machinery Malcom had produced prior to the purchase, it has been determined that all of the purchased goodwill has been permanently impaired.

Required

Prepare the journal entry to record the permanent impairment of the goodwill.

ANALYZE, THINK, COMMUNICATE

BUSINESS APPLICATIONS CASE *Bombardier's Annual Report* ATC 9–1

Required

Using the Bombardier financial statements in Appendix B, answer the following questions:

a. What method of amortization was used?
b. What types of capital assets does Bombardier have?
c. What does Bombardier estimate the useful lives of its capital assets to be?

GROUP ASSIGNMENT *Different Amortization Methods* ATC 9–2

Sweet's Bakery makes cakes, pies, and other pastries that it sells to local grocery stores. The company experienced the following transactions during 2008.

1. Started business by acquiring $60,000 cash from the issue of common shares.
2. Purchased bakery equipment for $46,000.
3. Had sales in 2008 amounting to $42,000.
4. Paid $8,200 of cash for supplies expense used to make baked goods.
5. Incurred other operating expenses of $12,000 for 2008.
6. Recorded amortization assuming the equipment had a four-year life and a $6,000 residual value. The CCA rate is 20 percent.
7. Paid income tax. The tax rate is 30 percent.

Required

a. Organize the class into three sections and divide each section into groups of three to five students. Assign each section a method: straight-line, double-declining-balance, or CCA.

Group Task

Prepare an income statement and balance sheet using the preceding information and the amortization method assigned to your group.

Class Discussion

b. Have a representative of each section put its income statement on the board. Are there differences in net income? In the amount of income tax paid? How will these differences in the amount of amortization expense change over the life of the equipment?

ATC 9–3 REAL-WORLD CASE *Different Numbers for Different Industries*

The following ratios are for four companies in different industries. Some of these ratios have been discussed in the textbook; others have not, but their names explain how the ratio was computed. The four sets of ratios, presented randomly, are as follows:

Ratio	Company 1	Company 2	Company 3	Company 4
Current assets ÷ total assets	77%	18%	15%	13%
Operating cycle	138 days	311 days	24 days	49 days
Return on assets	(0.3%)	5.6%	8.9%	4.1%
Gross profit	30.0%	78.9%	28.3%	39.4%
Sales ÷ property, plant, and equipment	6.5 times	2.6 times	2.3 times	2.7 times
Sales ÷ current assets	0.8 times	1.5 times	12.3 times	5.7 times
Sales ÷ number of full-time employees	$304,187	$16,708	$31,195	$653,526

These are the four companies to which these ratios relate, listed in alphabetical order:

Darden Restaurants, Inc., operates restaurants, including Red Lobster and The Olive Garden. Its fiscal year-end was May 31, 2001.

Deere & Company manufactures heavy equipment for construction and farming. Its fiscal year-end was October 31, 2001.

GlaxoSmithKline is a pharmaceutical company. Its fiscal year-end was December 31, 2000.

Molson, Inc., produces beer and related products. Its fiscal year-end was March 31, 2001.

Required

Match each company with a set of the ratios. Write a memorandum explaining your decisions.

ATC 9–4 BUSINESS APPLICATIONS CASE *Effect of Amortization on the Return on Assets Ratio*

Greentree Publishing Company was started on January 1, 2005, when it acquired $80,000 cash from the issue of common shares. The company immediately purchased a printing press that cost $80,000 cash. The asset had an estimated residual value of $8,000 and an expected useful life of eight years. Greentree used the asset during 2005 to produce $25,000 of cash revenue. Assume that these were the only events affecting Greentree Publishing Company during 2005.

Required

(*Hint*: Prepare an income statement and a balance sheet prior to completing the following requirements.)

a. Compute the return on assets ratio as of December 31, 2005, assuming Greentree Publishing Company uses the straight-line amortization method.
b. Recompute the ratio assuming Greentree uses the double-declining-balance method.
c. Which amortization method makes it *appear* that Greentree is utilizing its assets more effectively?

ATC 9–5 BUSINESS APPLICATIONS CASE *Effect of Amortization on Financial Statement Analysis: Straight-Line versus Double-Declining-Balance*

Qin Company and Roche Company experienced the exact same set of economic events during 2005. Both companies purchased machines on January 1, 2005. Except for the effects of this purchase, the accounting records of both companies had the following accounts and balances.

As of January 1, 2005:	
Total Assets	$200,000
Total Liabilities	$ 80,000
Total Shareholders' Equity	$120,000
During 2005:	
Total Sales Revenue	$100,000
Total Expenses (not including amortization)	$ 60,000
Liabilities were not affected by transactions in 2005.	

The machines purchased by the companies each cost $40,000 cash. The machines had expected useful lives of five years and estimated residual values of $4,000. Qin uses straight-line amortization. Roche uses double-declining-balance amortization.

Required

a. For both companies, calculate the balances in the preceding accounts on December 31, 2005, after the effects of the purchase and amortization of the machines have been applied. (*Hint*: The purchases of the machines are asset exchange transactions that do not affect total assets. However, the effect of amortizing the machine changes the amounts in total assets, expense, and equity [Retained Earnings]).

b. Based on the revised account balances determined in Requirement *a*, calculate the following ratios for both companies:
   (1) Debt to assets ratio.
   (2) Return on assets ratio.
   (3) Return on equity ratio.

c. Disregarding the effects of income taxes, which company produced the higher increase in real economic wealth during 2005?

WRITING ASSIGNMENT *Impact of Historical Cost on Asset Presentation on the Balance Sheet* **ATC 9–6**

Assume that you are examining the balance sheets of two companies and note the following information:

	Company A	Company B
Equipment	$1,130,000	$ 900,000
Accumulated Amortization	(730,000)	(500,000)
Net Book Value	$ 400,000	$ 400,000

Maxie Smith, a student who has had no accounting courses, remarks that Company A and Company B have the same amount of equipment.

Required

In a short paragraph, explain to Maxie that the two companies do not have equal amounts of equipment. You may want to include in your discussion comments regarding the possible age of each company's equipment, the impact of the historical cost concept on balance sheet information, and the impact of different amortization methods on book value.

ETHICAL DILEMMA *Good Standards/Bad People or Just Plain Bad Standards?* **ATC 9–7**

Eleanor Posey has been reading the financial statements of her fiercest competitor, Barron Bailey, who like herself owns a regionally based heating and cooling services company. The statements were given to her by a potential investor, Jim Featherson, who told her that the statements convinced him to put his investment money in Bailey's business instead of Posey's. Bailey's statements show a net income figure 10 percent higher than that reported by Posey's company. When analyzing the notes to the financial statements, Posey noticed that Bailey amortizes all property, plant, and equipment on a straight-line basis. In contrast, she amortizes only her building on a straight-line basis. All her equipment is amortized by the double-declining-balance method, which she believes matches the pattern of use of equipment in the heating and cooling services business.

Posey arranges a meeting with Featherson in which she attempts to inform him of the effects of amortization on financial statements. She explains that Bailey's reporting practices are deceptive. While Bailey's income figure is higher now, the situation will reverse in the near future because her amortization charges will decline whereas Bailey's will stay constant. She explains that Bailey may even have to report losses because declines in the use of equipment also translate to lower revenues. Featherson tells Posey that Bailey's financial statements were reviewed by a very respectable CGA firm. He tells her that nobody can predict the future and that he makes his decisions on the basis of current facts.

After Featherson leaves, Posey becomes somewhat resentful of the rules of accounting. Reporting amortization in the way that she and her accountant believe to be consistent with actual use has caused her to lose an investor with a significant base of capital. She writes a letter to the chairperson of the Canadian Institute of Chartered Accountants in which she suggests that the Board establish a single amortization method that is required to be used by all companies. She argues that this approach would be better for investors who know little about accounting alternatives. If all companies were required to use the same accounting rules, comparability would be significantly improved.

Required

Answer the following questions under the assumption that actual use is, in fact, greater in the earlier part of the life of equipment in the heating and cooling services business.

a. Are Posey's predictions regarding Bailey's future profitability accurate? Explain.
b. Comment on the ethical implications associated with Bailey's decision to amortize his equipment using the straight-line method.
c. Comment on Posey's recommendation that the CICA eliminate alternative amortization methods to improve comparability.
d. Comment on Featherson's use of accounting information.

ATC 9–8 SEDAR DATABASE *Comparing Microsoft and Intel*

Required

a. Using the SEDAR database, fill in the missing data in the following table, drawing on the most current annual reports available for Microsoft Corporation and Intel Corporation. The percentages must be computed; they are not included in the reports. See Appendix A for instructions on using SEDAR. (*Note:* The percentages for current assets and property, plant, and equipment will not sum to 100.)

	Current Assets	Property, Plant, and Equipment	Total Assets
Microsoft			
Dollar Amount	$ ______	$ ______	$ ______
% of Total Assets	______ %	______ %	100%
Intel			
Dollar Amount	$ ______	$ ______	$ ______
% of Total Assets	______ %	______ %	100%

b. Briefly explain why these two companies have different percentages of their assets in current assets versus property, plant, and equipment.

ATC 9–9 SPREADSHEET ASSIGNMENT *Amortization Schedules Using Excel*

Required

Using the data from Problem 9–4A, prepare the amortization schedules for each of the five years using an Excel spreadsheet under each of the following methods:

a. Straight-line.
b. Units-of-activity
c. Double-declining-balance.
d. Capital cost allowance using a 20 percent rate.

SPREADSHEET ASSIGNMENT *Alternative Methods of Amortization*

ATC 9–10

Short Company purchased a computer on January 1, 2005, for $5,000. An additional $100 was paid for delivery charges. The computer was estimated to have a life of five years or 10,000 hours. Residual value was estimated at $300. During the five years, the computer was used as follows:

2005	2,500 hours
2006	2,400 hours
2007	2,000 hours
2008	1,700 hours
2009	1,400 hours

Required

a. Prepare a five-year amortization schedule for the computer using the straight-line amortization method. Be sure to use formulas for all computations including amortization expense. Set up the following headings for your schedule:

	Beginning				Ending		
Year	Cost	Accumulated Amortization	Net Book Value	Amortization Expense	Cost	Accumulated Amortization	Net Book Value

b. Prepare another five-year amortization schedule for the computer using the units-of-activity method. Use (copy) the headings used in Requirement *a*.

c. Prepare another five-year amortization schedule for the computer using the double-declining-balance method. Use (copy) the headings used in Requirement *a*.

Spreadsheet Tip

After the year 2005, enter subsequent dates automatically. Position the mouse in the lower right-hand corner of the highlighted cell "2005" until a thin cross appears. Click and drag down four additional rows.

Chapter

10

Accounting for Long-Term Debt

Learning Objectives

After completing this chapter, you should be able to:

1. Explain the need for long-term debt financing.
2. Describe how the amortization of long-term notes affects financial statements.
3. Describe how a line of credit affects financial statements.
4. Describe the different types of bonds that companies issue.
5. Explain why bonds are issued at face value, a discount, or a premium.
6. Explain how to account for bonds and their related interest costs.
7. Describe how bond liabilities and their related interest costs affect financial statements.
8. Explain the advantages and disadvantages of debt financing.
9. Explain the time value of money.
10. Account for bonds using the straight-line method.
11. Compare the effective interest rate method with the straight-line method.

the *curious* accountant

Laidlaw Inc. is a holding company for North America's largest providers of school and inter-city bus transportation, public transit, patient transportation, and emergency department management services. Laidlaw Inc. had a net loss of $114 million for the nine months ended May 31, 2001. During the same period, Laidlaw had an interest expense of $210.6 million. Does the fact that Laidlaw had a net loss indicate that it probably was not able to pay the interest owed to its creditors? See page 415 for the answer.

Most businesses spend large sums of cash in the course of daily operations. They use cash to replace inventories, pay employees, settle liabilities, purchase supplies, obtain advertising, buy insurance, and so on. For most firms, expenditures for short-term operating activities consume only a portion of the funds needed to keep the business running. Expenditures for long-term operational assets, such as newer, more technologically advanced machinery and improved buildings and plant facilities, require even larger amounts of cash. The need for cash is so exhaustive that most companies are forced to borrow some of the funds they need to meet their goals and objectives.

A number of options are available for the interest and principal payments associated with borrowed funds. Interest may be paid annually, semiannually, or monthly or may be added to the principal balance of the debt and paid at maturity. Interest rates may remain the same over the term of the loan or may fluctuate with market conditions. Rates that do not change over the life of a loan are called ***fixed interest rates****; those that fluctuate are called* ***variable interest rates****. The principal (amount borrowed) may be repaid in one lump sum at the maturity date of the debt. Alternatively, the* ***amortization of the loan***[1] *can*

[1] The term *amortization* was used in Chapter 9 to describe the process of expense recognition by systematically allocating the *cost of capital assets* over their useful lives. It will become apparent in this chapter that the word has a broader meaning that applies to a variety of allocation processes. Here the word is used to describe the systematic process of allocating the *principal repayment* over the life of a loan.

occur over the life of the loan (paid systematically). This chapter covers the major forms of debt refinancing and the options available for paying principal and interest.

Long-Term Notes Payable

LO1 Expalin the need for long-term debt financing.

LO2 Describe how the amortization of long-term notes affects financial statements.

Notes payable can be classified as short term or long term, depending on the time to maturity. As discussed in Chapter 7, short-term notes mature within one year or the operating cycle, whichever is longer. In contrast, **long-term notes payable** are used to satisfy financing needs for periods of two or more years. Most long-term loans are obtained from banks or other financial institutions, and they often require periodic payments of principal as well as interest. To illustrate, assume that Bill Blair obtained the cash needed to start a small business by issuing a $100,000 face value note to National Bank on January 1, 2005. As with other debt-financing activities, the issue of a long-term note payable increases assets (Cash) and liabilities (Notes Payable). The income statement is not affected when the note is issued. The cash inflow is shown in the financing activities section of the cash flow statement. The effects on the financial statements are shown here:

Assets	=	Liab.	+	Equity	Rev.	−	Exp.	=	Net Inc.	Cash Flow Statement	
100,000	=	100,000	+	NA	NA	−	NA	=	NA	100,000	FA

The note carried a 9 percent annual rate of interest and a five-year term. Principal and interest are to be paid through a single $25,709 payment[2] made on December 31 of each year from 2005 through 2009. Exhibit 10–1 shows the allocation[3] of this payment to principal and interest. The amount of interest paid each year is determined by multiplying the outstanding principal balance of the loan by the 9 percent interest rate. The portion of the payment that is not used for interest reduces the principal balance of the loan. For example, the first interest payment made on December 31, 2005, amounts to $9,000 ($100,000 × 0.09). Therefore, $16,709 ($25,709 − $9,000) is applied to reducing the principal balance of the loan. The second interest payment is computed by multiplying the new principal balance of $83,291 ($100,000 − $16,709) by the 9 percent interest rate. As a result, the payments for interest and principal reduction on December 31, 2006, are $7,496 ($83,291 × 0.09) and $18,213 ($25,709 − $7,496), respectively. Allocations for the final three payments are computed in a similar way. Check your understanding of the amortization schedule by doing the computations required to extend the table for the 2007 payment.

Exhibit 10–1 *Amortization Schedule for Note Issued by Bill Blair*

Accounting Period	Principal Balance on Jan. 1	Cash Payment Dec. 31	Applied to Interest	Applied to Principal
2005	$100,000	$25,709	$9,000	$16,709
2006	83,291	25,709	7,496	18,213
2007	65,078	25,709	5,857	19,852
2008	45,226	25,709	4,070	21,639
2009	23,587	25,710	2,123	23,587

[2] The determination of the annual payment is based on the present value concepts presented in the appendix to this chapter.

[3] All computations are rounded to the nearest dollar. Rounding differences resulted in the necessity to add an additional dollar to the final payment in order to fully liquidate the liability.

Notice that the amount allotted to interest declines each period while the amount allotted to principal increases because the amount borrowed declines as a portion of the principal is repaid each year. Since the amount borrowed declines, the amount of interest due on the debt also declines.

The amounts allotted to principal and interest are different for each accounting period; however, the effects of the annual payment on the financial statements are the same for each accounting period. With respect to the balance sheet, assets (Cash) decrease. Liabilities decrease by the amount of the principal repayment (see Exhibit 10–1, the column Applied to Principal). Similarly, the recognition of interest expense (see Exhibit 10–1, the column Applied to Interest) reduces equity (Retained Earnings). Net income decreases as a result of the recognition of interest. The portion of the cash payment applied to principal should be shown in the financing activities section of the cash flow statement. The portion of the cash payment applied to interest should be shown in the operating activities section. The effects on the 2005 financial statements are shown here:

Assets	=	Liab.	+	Equity	Rev.	−	Exp.	=	Net Inc.	Cash Flow Statement	
(25,709)	=	(16,709)	+	(9,000)	NA	−	9,000	=	(9,000)	(9,000)	OA
										(16,709)	FA

Exhibit 10–2 shows income statements, balance sheets, and cash flow statements for Blair's company for the accounting periods 2005 through 2009. Note the differences between Blair's income statements and its cash flow statements. First, the $100,000 of borrowed funds is shown under the financing activities section of the cash flow statement but is not shown on the income statement. Also, only the interest portion of the annual $25,709 payment is shown on the income statement. In contrast, the whole

Exhibit 10–2

BLAIR COMPANY
Financial Statements

	2005	2006	2007	2008	2009
Income Statements					
Rent Revenue	$12,000	$12,000	$12,000	$12,000	$12,000
Interest Expense	(9,000)	(7,496)	(5,857)	(4,070)	(2,123)
Net Income	$3,000	$ 4,504	$ 6,143	$ 7,930	$ 9,877
Balance Sheets					
Assets					
Cash	$86,291	$72,582	$58,873	$45,164	$31,454
Liabilities					
Note Payable	$83,291	$65,078	$45,226	$23,587	$ 0
Shareholders' Equity					
Retained Earnings	3,000	7,504	13,647	21,577	31,454
Total Liabilities and Shareholders' Equity	$86,291	$72,582	$58,873	$45,164	$31,454
Cash Flow Statements					
Operating Activities					
Inflow from Customers	$12,000	$12,000	$12,000	$12,000	$12,000
Outflow for Interest	(9,000)	(7,496)	(5,857)	(4,070)	(2,123)
Investing Activities	0	0	0	0	0
Financing Activities					
Inflow from Note Issue	100,000	0	0	0	0
Outflow to Repay Note	(16,709)	(18,213)	(19,852)	(21,639)	(23,587)
Net Change in Cash	86,291	(13,709)	(13,709)	(13,709)	(13,710)
Plus: Beginning Cash Balance	0	86,291	72,582	58,873	45,164
Ending Cash Balance	$86,291	$72,582	$58,873	$45,164	$31,454

payment is shown on the cash flow statement (part in operating activities for interest expense and part in financing activities to reflect the principal payment).

With respect to the balance sheet, the amount in the Cash account decreases each year from 2006 through 2009 because the amount of cash paid for principal and interest ($25,709) is higher than the amount of cash collected from revenue ($12,000). The annual $13,709 net cash outflow ($12,000 − $25,709) causes the steady decline in the cash balance. Also note that the liability declines as time passes because the annual payment includes a principal reduction as well as an interest component. In other words, some of the debt is being paid off each year. Finally, note that the Retained Earnings account increases by the amount of net income each year. Since the company pays no dividends, it retains all income in the business.

Security for Bank Loan Agreements

Bankers are interested in securing the collection of principal and interest. To ensure collection, they often require debtors to pledge designated assets as **collateral for loans**. For example, a bank usually holds legal title to automobiles that are purchased with the proceeds of its loans. If the debtor cannot make principal and interest payments, the bank repossesses the car. The car is then sold to another individual, and the proceeds from the sale are used to pay the debt. Besides collateral, bankers often include **restrictive covenants** in loan agreements. For example, a bank may restrict additional borrowing by requiring debtors to maintain a minimal debt to assets ratio. If the ratio rises above the designated level, the loan is considered in default and is due immediately. Other common restrictions include limits on the payment of dividends to owners and salaries to management. Finally, banks often ask key personnel to provide copies of their personal tax returns and financial statements. The financial condition of key executives is important because they may be asked to pledge personal property as collateral for business loans.

On January 1, 2004, Krueger Company issued a $50,000 note to a local bank. The note had a 10-year term and an 8 percent interest rate. Krueger agreed to repay the principal and interest in 10 annual payments of $7,451.47 at the end of each year. Determine the amount of principal and interest Krueger paid during the first and second year that the note was outstanding.

Answer

Accounting Period	Principal Balance January 1 A	Cash Payment December 31 B	Applied to Interest C = A × 0.08	Applied to Principal B − C
2004	$50,000.00	$7,451.47	$4,000.00	$3,451.47
2005	46,548.53	7,451.47	3,723.88	3,727.59

Line of Credit

LO3

Describe how a line of credit affects financial statements.

Another form of short- and intermediate-term credit many companies use is the **line of credit**. A line of credit enables companies to borrow a limited amount of funds on an as-needed basis. As long as the company stays within the preapproved boundaries, funds can be obtained and repaid at will. The interest rate usually fluctuates in proportion to the bank's prime rate (the publicly announced rate that banks charge their best customers). The typical term of a line of credit is one year. In other words, the funds borrowed are due for repayment within one year. However, most lines of credit are renewable and for all practical purposes represent a relatively permanent source of financing. So, although they are classified on the balance sheet as short-term liabilities, often they are paid off, year after year, by simply renewing the credit agreement.

answers to the *curious* accountant

Laidlaw Inc. was able to make its interest payments for two reasons. First, remember that interest is paid with cash, not accrual earnings. Many of the expenses on the company's income statement did not require the use of cash. Indeed the company's cash flow statement shows a net cash flow from operating activities of $277.4 million. Second, the net loss the company incurred was after the interest expense had been deducted. The capacity of operations to support interest payments is measured by the amount of earnings before interest deductions. For example, look at the 2007 income statement for Blair Company in Exhibit 10–2. This statement shows only $3,000 of net income, but there was $12,000 of revenue available for the payment of interest. Similarly, Laidlaw's net loss is not an indication of the company's ability to pay interest.

To illustrate the use of a line of credit, assume that Terry Parker owns a wholesale jet ski distributorship. Parker borrows money through a line of credit to build up inventory levels in the spring. The funds are repaid in the summer months when sales generate cash inflow. Parker's line of credit carries a variable interest rate adjusted monthly to remain 2 percentage points above the bank's prime rate. The following table shows Parker's borrowing activity and interest charges for the current accounting period:

Date	Amount Borrowed (Repaid)	Loan Balance at End of Month	Effective Interest Rate per Month (%)	Interest Expense (rounded to nearest $1)
Mar. 1	$20,000	$20,000	0.09 ÷ 12	$150
Apr. 1	30,000	50,000	0.09 ÷ 12	375
May 1	50,000	100,000	0.105 ÷ 12	875
June 1	(10,000)	90,000	0.10 ÷ 12	750
July 1	(40,000)	50,000	0.09 ÷ 12	375
Aug. 1	(50,000)	0	0.09 ÷ 12	0

Each borrowing event (March 1, April 1, and May 1) is an asset source transaction. The asset account Cash increases, and the line-of-credit liability increases. Each repayment (June 1, July 1, and August 1) is an asset use transaction, with the assets and liabilities decreasing. The expense recognition for the payment of monthly interest is an asset use transaction. Cash decreases, and the corresponding increase in interest expense causes equity (Retained Earnings) to decrease. The effects of borrowing, repayment, and interest recognition on the financial statements follow:

Date	Assets	=	Liabilities	+	Equity	Rev.	−	Exp.	=	Net Inc.	Cash Flow Statement	
Mar. 1	20,000	=	20,000	+	NA	NA	−	NA	=	NA	20,000	FA
31	(150)	=	NA	+	(150)	NA	−	150	=	(150)	(150)	OA
Apr. 1	30,000	=	30,000	+	NA	NA	−	NA	=	NA	30,000	FA
30	(375)	=	NA	+	(375)	NA	−	375	=	(375)	(375)	OA
May 1	50,000	=	50,000	+	NA	NA	−	NA	=	NA	50,000	FA
31	(875)	=	NA	+	(875)	NA	−	875	=	(875)	(875)	OA
June 1	(10,000)	=	(10,000)	+	NA	NA	−	NA	=	NA	(10,000)	FA
30	(750)	=	NA	+	(750)	NA	−	750	=	(750)	(750)	OA
July 1	(40,000)	=	(40,000)	+	NA	NA	−	NA	=	NA	(40,000)	FA
31	(375)	=	NA	+	(375)	NA	−	375	=	(375)	(375)	OA
Aug. 1	(50,000)	=	(50,000)	+	NA	NA	−	NA	=	NA	(50,000)	FA
31	NA	=	NA	+	NA	NA	−	NA	=	NA	NA	

Bond Liabilities

LO4 Describe the different types of bonds that companies issue.

One of the most common methods of obtaining long-term financing is by issuing bonds. An example of a bond certificate is shown at the bottom of this page. The company that borrows money issues (gives) a *bond*, which describes the company's responsibilities to pay interest and repay the principal. *Since the borrower issues the bond, the borrower is called the* **issuer of a bond**.

Obtaining funds through bond issues has advantages and disadvantages. An advantage is that companies can usually obtain longer-term commitments from bondholders than they can obtain from financial institutions. The typical term of a bond is 20 years, whereas term loans from banks are normally limited to a maximum of 5 years. Second, the amount of interest may be lower than the amount that banks or other financial institutions charge. Banks obtain much of the money that they use for making loans from their depositors. In other words, banks use the money that the public deposits in savings and chequing accounts to make loans to their customers. Banks profit by charging a higher rate of interest on loans than they pay for deposits. For example, banks may pay 4 percent interest on a term deposit and charge 9 percent for an auto loan. The 5 percent **spread** (9 percent − 4 percent) is used to pay the expenses of operating the bank and to provide a return to the owners of the bank. The spread can be avoided if a company can borrow directly from the public through a bond issue. Since bonds are not insured by the federal government, as bank deposits are, businesses have to pay more than the bank rate of interest to encourage the public to accept the risk of default (the failure to pay principal or interest). However, the huge sums of money that pass through the bond markets indicate that the public is willing to accept a higher level of risk to obtain higher interest. Thus, companies can often borrow money by issuing bonds at lower rates of interest than they would have to pay to borrow money from banks or other financial institutions.

Whether interest is paid to banks or to bondholders, it is deductible when determining income for tax purposes. Thus, although interest reduces income, part of the effect is offset by the lower taxes the company pays. Also, as discussed in earlier chapters, borrowing activities may even lead to earnings

increases. When a firm can generate earnings of 14 percent on assets and can borrow money at only 10 percent interest, the 4 percent differential actually increases the firm's profitability. As noted in Chapter 3, the concept of increasing earnings through debt financing is referred to as **financial leverage**. The concept has been a key element in generating wealth for many individuals and corporations. Finally, as with other forms of borrowing, inflation has an advantageous effect in that the debt is repaid with dollars that have less purchasing power than the dollars borrowed.

Some very real disadvantages often negate the advantages just listed. A firm is legally bound to pay the specified interest. Also, it has a legal liability to repay the principal. Failure to satisfy these obligations can force companies into bankruptcy. If the company is forced to liquidate, the bondholders, like other creditors, have claims on the firm's assets that have priority over the claims of the owners. Even in financially sound companies, bondholders may impose conditions that restrict managers from taking actions that increase the risk of default. So, the freedom to run the business *any way you wish* may be diminished by the incurrence of debt.

Characteristics of Bonds

As stated earlier, a **bond** is a written promise to pay a sum of money in the future to the bondholder. The amount to be paid at maturity is called the **face value** of the bond. The issuer must pay the bondholder the face value of the bond at maturity. As well, most bonds include a commitment to pay a **stated interest rate** at specified intervals over the life of the bond. The face value and stated rate of interest are set forth in a contract called a **bond indenture**. The bond indenture also specifies any special characteristics, such as forms of collateral (property pledged as security for a loan), the manner of payment, the timing of maturity, and *restrictive covenants*, which are designed to prohibit management from taking certain actions that place the bondholders at risk.

Security of Bonds

Bonds can be classified as either secured or unsecured; within each category, there are different forms of indebtedness.

1. **Secured bonds** contain a clause that guarantees the bondholders will be given certain identifiable assets in case of default. A common type of secured bond is a **mortgage bond**, which conditionally transfers title of a designated piece of property to the bondholder until the bond is paid.
2. **Unsecured bonds**, also known as **debentures**, are simply issued on the general credit of the organization. The holders of debentures share claims against the total assets of the company with other creditors. Often the bond indenture specifies the priority of debenture holders in relation to other creditors. **Subordinated debentures** have lower priority than other creditors, whereas **unsubordinated debentures** have equal claims.

The security of a bond is an important factor to potential investors. There is a trade-off between the risk of default and the magnitude of the return that a bondholder demands for lending money. To entice investors to purchase a bond with considerable risk, an organization must offer very high interest rates. To reduce risk and thereby lower interest rates, companies often include *restrictive covenants* in the bond indenture agreement. These covenants provide assurances to creditors regarding the payment of principal and interest. Like the covenants included in bank notes, restrictive covenants in bond indentures may limit the payment of dividends to owners or the salaries of key employees. Debt restrictions measured by financial ratios are also often included in bond covenants.

Manner of Interest Payment

Bonds also differ in the manner in which the issuer pays interest. They may be either *registered* or *unregistered.*

1. **Registered bonds** are those issued by most corporations. The firm keeps a record of the names and addresses of the bondholders and sends interest and maturity payments directly to the individuals on file. When these bonds are transferred, the bond certificate must be endorsed, and notification of the change must be sent to the issuing corporation.
2. **Unregistered bonds**, also known as **bearer** or **coupon bonds**, are often issued by municipalities. Interest payments are made to any individual who redeems the coupon attached to the bond. Because no record of the purchaser is kept, coupon bonds are much like cash in that they are vulnerable to theft.

Timing of Maturity

The maturity date of bonds can be established in a number of ways. Even bonds sold in a single issuance may mature in different ways.

1. **Term bonds** mature on a specified date in the future.
2. **Serial bonds** mature at specified intervals throughout the life of the total issuance. For example, bonds with a total face value of $1,000,000 may mature in increments of $100,000 every year for 10 years.

Often the bond indenture calls for the issuing corporation to annually set aside funds to ensure the availability of cash for the payment of the face value at the maturity date. The company makes payments into what is known as a **sinking fund**. This fund is usually managed by an independent trustee, often a bank, charged with the responsibility of investing the funds until the bonds mature. At maturity, the funds and the proceeds from the investments are used to repay the debt.

Special Features

Many bonds have special features that make them more attractive to investors or that allow the issuing corporation more flexibility in its financing activities.

1. **Convertible bonds** may be exchanged by the bondholder for an ownership interest in the corporation. The bond indenture sets forth the conditions under which this exchange may take place. Usually, an investor agrees to accept a lower interest rate in the hope that the value of the ownership interest will increase.
2. **Callable bonds** allow the corporation to pay off the bonds before their maturity dates. This feature is desirable if interest rates decline. In these circumstances, the company would borrow money at lower rates and use the proceeds to pay off the more expensive bonds. Obviously, the call feature is undesirable from the perspective of the bondholders, who do not want to give up their high-yield investment. To encourage investors to buy this type of bond, the bond indenture generally specifies a call price that exceeds the face value of the bonds. The difference between the call price and the face value is commonly referred to as a **call premium**.

Bond Rating

Many features affect the security of a bond. Several financial services, such as Moody's, analyze the risk of default and publish their ratings as guides to bond investors. The highest possible rating is AAA, the next highest AA, and so forth. Companies and governments that issue bonds try to maintain high credit ratings because lower ratings force them to pay higher interest rates.

On November 8, 2001, Enron Corporation announced that it would have to reduce is shareholders' equity by approximately US$1.2 billion. On December 2, 2001, the company filed for bankruptcy protection.

When covering this story, most of the media focused on the overstatement of earnings that resulted from Enron's improper use of a form of partnerships called "special purpose entities." However, these entities were also used to improperly keep as much as US$1 billion of debt off Enron's balance sheet. Why did this matter to Enron? Enron was a very rapidly growing company and it used lots of debt to finance this growth. From 1999 to 2000 its assets grew from US$33.4 billion to US$65.5 billion, but its debt grew from US$23.8 billion to US$54.0 billion. This caused its debt to assets ratio to rise from 71.3 percent to 82.4 percent. The higher debt burden put Enron at risk of having to pay higher interest rates—a very unattractive option for a company with this much debt.

Bonds Issued at Face Value

Fixed-Rate, Fixed-Term, Annual Interest Bonds

LO5 Explain why bonds are issued at face value, a discount, or a premium.

To illustrate the effects of a bond issue on the books of the borrower, assume that Marsha Mason needs cash in order to seize a business opportunity. Mason is aware of a company that needs a plot of land on which to store its inventory of crushed stone. The company has agreed to pay Mason $12,000 per year to lease the land it needs. Mason knows of a suitable tract of land that could be purchased for $100,000. The only problem facing Mason is a lack of funds for making the acquisition.

When Mason heard some of her friends complaining about the low interest rates that banks pay on term deposits (TDs), she suggested that they invest in bonds instead of TDs. She then offered to sell her friends bonds carrying a 9 percent stated rate of interest payable in cash on December 31 of each year. To make the bonds an attractive alternative for her friends, Mason constructed a bond indenture that called for a five-year term and provided the security of having the land pledged as collateral for the bonds.[4] Her friends were favourably impressed, and Mason issued the bonds to them on January 1, 2005.

Mason used the funds to purchase the land and immediately entered into a contract to lease the land. The arrangement proceeded according to plan for the five-year term of the bonds. At the maturity date of the bond (December 31, 2009), Mason was able to sell the land for its $100,000 net book value. She used the proceeds from the sale to repay the bond liability.

[4] In practice, bonds are usually issued for large sums of money that often amount to hundreds of millions of dollars. Also, terms to maturity are normally long periods, with 20 years being common. Demonstrating issues of such magnitude is impractical for instructional purposes. The effects of bond issues can be illustrated more efficiently by using smaller amounts of debt with shorter maturities, such as that assumed in the case of Marsha Mason.

Effect of Events on Financial Statements

Six distinct accounting events are associated with Mason's business venture. These events are summarized here:

1. Received $100,000 cash from the issue of bonds at face value.
2. Invested proceeds from bond issue to purchase land costing $100,000 cash.
3. Earned $12,000 annual cash revenue from land lease.
4. Paid $9,000 annual interest on December 31 of each year.
5. Sold land for $100,000 cash.
6. Repaid bond principal to bondholders.

The effects of these events on Mason's financial statements are now discussed.

Event 1 Bond Issue

The bond issue is an asset source transaction.

Assets (Cash) and liabilities (Bonds Payable) increase. The income statement is not affected. The $100,000 cash inflow is shown in the financing activities section of the cash flow statement. The effect is shown here:

Assets	=	Liab.	+	Equity	Rev.	−	Exp.	=	Net Inc.	Cash Flow Statement	
100,000	=	100,000	+	NA	NA	−	NA	=	NA	100,000	FA

Event 2 Investment in Land

Event 2 involves the $100,000 cash purchase of land, which is an asset exchange transaction.

The asset account Cash decreases, and the asset account Land increases. The income statement is not affected. The cash outflow is shown in the investing activities section of the cash flow statement. These effects are shown here:

Assets			=	Liab.	+	Equity	Rev.	−	Exp.	=	Net Inc.	Cash Flow Statement	
Cash	+	Land	=										
(100,000)	+	100,000	=	NA	+	NA	NA	−	NA	=	NA	(100,000)	IA

Event 3 Revenue Recognition

Event 3 recognizes the $12,000 cash revenue generated from the rental of the property.

This event is repeated each year from 2005 through 2009. The event is an asset source transaction that increases assets and equity. The revenue recognition causes net income to increase. The cash inflow is shown in the operating activities section of the cash flow statement. These effects are shown here:

Assets	=	Liab.	+	Equity	Rev.	−	Exp.	=	Net Inc.	Cash Flow Statement	
12,000	=	NA	+	12,000	12,000	−	NA	=	12,000	12,000	OA

Event 4 Expense Recognition

Event 4 applies to the $9,000 ($100,000 × 0.09) cash payment of interest expense.

This event is also repeated each year from 2005 through 2009. The interest payment is an asset use transaction. The Cash account decreases, and the recognition of interest expense causes a decrease in equity (Retained Earnings). The expense recognition causes net income to decrease. The cash outflow is shown in the operating activities section of the cash flow statement. These effects are shown here:

Assets	=	Liab.	+	Equity	Rev.	−	Exp.	=	Net Inc.	Cash Flow Statement	
(9,000)	=	NA	+	(9,000)	NA	−	9,000	=	(9,000)	(9,000)	OA

Event 5 occurs when the land is sold for $100,000 cash.

Event 5
Sale of Investment in Land

The sale is an asset exchange transaction. The Cash account increases and the Land account decreases. Since there was no gain or loss on the sale, the income statement is not affected. The cash inflow is shown in the investing activities section of the cash flow statement. These effects are shown here:

Assets			=	Liab.	+	Equity	Rev.	−	Exp.	=	Net Inc.	Cash Flow Statement	
Cash	+	Land	=										
100,000	+	(100,000)	=	NA	+	NA	NA	−	NA	=	NA	100,000	IA

Finally, Event 6 concerns the repayment of the face value of the bond liability.

Event 6
Payoff of Bond Liability

This is an asset use transaction. The Cash and Bonds Payable accounts decrease. The income statement is not affected. The cash outflow is shown in the financing activities section of the cash flow statement:

Assets	=	Liab.	+	Equity	Rev.	−	Exp.	=	Net Inc.	Cash Flow Statement	
(100,000)	=	(100,000)	+	NA	NA	−	NA	=	NA	(100,000)	FA

Recording Procedures

LO6
Explain how to account for bonds and their related interest costs.

Exhibit 10–3 summarizes the general journal entries for recording the six events that Mason Company experienced.

Exhibit 10–3 *General Journal Entries*

Event No.	Account Title	Debit	Credit
1	Cash	100,000	
	Bonds Payable		100,000
	Entry on January 1, 2005, to record bond issue		
2	Land	100,000	
	Cash		100,000
	Entry on January 1, 2005, to record investment in land		
3	Cash	12,000	
	Revenue		12,000
	Revenue recognition entries on December 31, 2005–2009		
4	Interest Expense	9,000	
	Cash		9,000
	Expense recognition entries on December 31, 2005–2009		
5	Cash	100,000	
	Land		100,000
	Entry on December 31, 2009, to record sale of land		
6	Bonds Payable	100,000	
	Cash		100,000
	Entry on December 31, 2009, to record bond payment		

Financial Statements

LO7
Describe how bond liabilities and their related interest costs affect financial statements.

Exhibit 10–4 shows the financial statements of Mason Company. Rent revenue and interest expense are constant across all accounting periods, resulting in the recognition of $3,000 of net income in each accounting period. With respect to the balance sheet, the Cash account increases by $3,000 each year because cash revenue exceeds cash paid for interest. The Land account stays at $100,000 from the date of purchase in 2005 until the land is sold in 2009. Similarly, Bonds Payable remains at $100,000 from the date of issue in 2005 until the liability is paid off on December 31, 2009.

Exhibit 10–4 *Financial Statements*

Under the Assumption That Bonds Are Issued at Face Value

	2005	2006	2007	2008	2009
Income Statements					
Rent Revenue	$ 12,000	$ 12,000	$ 12,000	$ 12,000	$ 12,000
Interest Expense	(9,000)	(9,000)	(9,000)	(9,000)	(9,000)
Net Income	$ 3,000	$ 3,000	$ 3,000	$ 3,000	$ 3,000
Balance Sheets					
Assets					
Cash	$ 3,000	$ 6,000	$ 9,000	$ 12,000	$ 15,000
Land	100,000	100,000	100,000	100,000	0
Total Assets	$103,000	$106,000	$109,000	$112,000	$ 15,000
Liabilities					
Bonds Payable	$100,000	$100,000	$100,000	$100,000	$ 0
Shareholders' Equity					
Retained Earnings	3,000	6,000	9,000	12,000	15,000
Total Liabilities and Shareholders' Equity	$103,000	$106,000	$109,000	$112,000	$ 15,000
Cash Flow Statements					
Operating Activities					
Inflow from Customers	$ 12,000	$ 12,000	$ 12,000	$ 12,000	$ 12,000
Outflow for Interest	(9,000)	(9,000)	(9,000)	(9,000)	(9,000)
Investing Activities					
Outflow to Purchase Land	(100,000)	0	0	0	0
Inflow from Sale of Land	0	0	0	0	100,000
Financing Activities					
Inflow from Bond Issue	100,000	0	0	0	0
Outflow to Repay Bond Liab.	0	0	0	0	(100,000)
Net Change in Cash	3,000	3,000	3,000	3,000	3,000
Beginning Cash Balance	0	3,000	6,000	9,000	12,000
Ending Cash Balance	$ 3,000	$ 6,000	$ 9,000	$ 12,000	$ 15,000

Compare the income statements for Bill Blair shown in Exhibit 10–2 with those of Mason Company shown in Exhibit 10–4. In both cases, a face value of $100,000 cash was borrowed at a stated interest rate of 9 percent. Both companies also earned $12,000 revenue per year, yet Blair produced a total net income of $31,454 while Mason's net earnings for the same period were only $15,000. The difference is attributable solely to the additional interest that Mason had to pay because no payment of principal was made until the maturity date. By repaying the loan more rapidly, Blair was able to lower its liabilities and thereby the amount of interest expense.

Bonds Issued at a Discount

Effective Interest Rate

LO5 Explain why bonds are issued at face value, a discount, or a premium.

At the time bonds are issued, market conditions may force a company to pay more interest than the *stated rate* of interest. In other words, if the *stated rate* of interest is too low, no one will buy the bonds. The rate of interest the issuer must pay to sell the bonds is called the *effective interest rate*. The **effective interest rate** reflects the true cost of borrowing. The amount of the effective rate is dictated by the availability of other investment opportunities. For example, if an investor can purchase a low-risk government bond that yields 8 percent, she or he will be willing to invest in a higher-risk corporate bond only if the return is higher than 8 percent. The rate that is available on a wide range of alternative investments is referred to as the **market interest rate**. Theoretically, the *effective rate* and the *market rate* for investments with similar levels of risk are equal at the time the bonds are issued. However, once the bonds have been sold, the *effective rate* becomes fixed by the price paid for the bonds, whereas the *market rate* continues to vary with the changing economic conditions.

The bond indenture requires that the cash payment for interest be determined by multiplying the *stated rate of interest by the face value* of the bond. In other words, the periodic cash payments for interest are fixed, which means that companies cannot adjust the effective interest rate by changing the periodic cash payments for interest. If a company wishes to adjust the effective rate of interest upward (pay more than the stated rate), it must do so by lowering the purchase price of the bonds. For example, a $1,000 face value bond may be issued for $900. At maturity, the investor who purchased the bond will receive $1,000 even though he or she paid only $900 to obtain the bond. The $100 differential represents an additional interest payment. In other words, the creditor (bond investor) will receive the regular cash payments for interest (stated rate times face value) plus the $100 difference between the face value ($1,000) and the price paid for the bond ($900).

When bonds are sold at an amount below their face value, the difference between the purchase price and the face value is called a **bond discount**. As indicated, bonds sell at a discount when the market rate of interest is higher than the stated rate on the issue date. To demonstrate the accounting treatment for bonds issued at a discount, assume the same facts as those presented in the preceding example involving Mason Company. One more factor will be considered. Suppose that Mason's friends receive an offer to buy bonds from another entrepreneur willing to pay a rate of interest higher than the 9 percent stated rate contained in Mason's indenture. Although they feel some sense of commitment to Mason, they conclude that business decisions cannot be made on the basis of friendship. Mason is understanding and wants to provide a counteroffer. There is no time to change the bond indenture, so she states that she is willing to accept $95,000 for the bonds today and will still repay the full face value of $100,000 at the maturity date. The $5,000 differential makes her offer competitive, and the transaction for the bond issue is consummated immediately.

Bond Prices

In accounting terms, the bonds were sold *at a discount for a price of 95*. As this statement implies, *bond prices are normally expressed as a percentage of the face value* that is received when the bonds are sold. Amounts of less than 1 percentage point are usually expressed as a fraction. Therefore, a bond selling for 98¾ sells for 98.75 percent of the face value of the bond.

Tax Advantage Associated with Debt Financing

LO8 Explain the advantages and disadvantages of debt financing.

Two important concepts must be understood when comparing debt financing with equity financing. The first is the concept of financial leverage, explained in Chapter 3. The second is the tax advantage of debt financing. Debt financing has a tax advantage over equity financing because interest payments are deductible in computing taxable income. In contrast, dividends are not deductible in determining taxable income. The effect of this difference is now described.

Suppose that $100,000 is needed to start Maduro Company. Assume that the company can be started by issuing $100,000 of common shares (equity financing). Alternatively, it can be started by borrowing $100,000 (debt financing). In the first year of operation, the company earns $60,000 of revenue and incurs $40,000 of expenses, not including interest. If shares are issued, the shareholders are paid an $8,000 dividend. Alternatively, if the business is financed with debt, it must pay 8 percent annual interest (interest expense is $8,000). Assuming a 30 percent tax rate, which form of financing will produce the larger addition to retained earnings for the business? The answer can be computed as follows:

Computation of Addition to Retained Earnings

	Equity Financing	Debt Financing
Revenue	$60,000	$60,000
Expense (excluding interest)	(40,000)	(40,000)
Earnings before Interest and Taxes	20,000	20,000
Interest (100,000 × 8%)	0	(8,000)
Pretax Income	20,000	12,000
Income Tax (30%)	(6,000)	(3,600)
Net Income	14,000	8,400
Dividend	(8,000)	0
Addition to Retained Earnings	$ 6,000	$ 8,400

Note that if the company is financed with debt, it produces $2,400 more retained earnings than if it is financed with equity because the interest expense is tax deductible. If equity financing is used, the company pays $6,000 of income taxes, whereas debt financing requires only $3,600 of income taxes. Therefore, debt financing saved $2,400 of income tax expense. In other words, the effective cost (after-tax cost) of the debt is only $5,600 ($8,000 interest expense − $2,400 tax savings). In contrast, the $8,000 dividend is not tax deductible. As a result, it removes a full $8,000 from the amount of earnings to be retained in the business. In both cases, the investors or creditors receive $8,000. The difference lies in the fact that under debt financing, the Canada Customs and Revenue Agency receives $2,400 less.

In general terms, the after-tax interest cost of debt can be computed as

$$\text{Total interest expense} \times (1.0 - \text{Tax rate})$$

In the case of Maduro Company, this formula confirms the previous analysis. The after-tax cost of debt is computed to be

$$\$8{,}000 \times (1.0 - 0.30) = \$5{,}600$$

We can compute the after-tax interest rate that Maduro is paying by applying the same logic. It is 5.6 percent (8 percent × 0.70). In contrast, there is no difference in the before-tax and after-tax effects of an 8 percent dividend. This means that $1 of dividends cost the company a full $1 of retained earnings, while $1 of interest has an after-tax cost of only $0.70 (assuming a 30 percent tax rate). All else being equal, debt financing results in higher profitability than equity financing because it lowers the amount of taxes that must be paid. This conclusion assumes that the business is operating profitably. There can be no tax savings if there is no income because businesses that produce consistent losses pay no taxes.

EBIT and Ratio Analysis

Several ratios presented in this book use net income in their computations. In practice, some of these ratios are computed by using *earnings before interest and taxes* (EBIT) rather than net income. One such ratio is the *return on assets* (ROA) ratio, explained in Chapter 3. The purpose of the ROA ratio is to measure how efficiently a business is using its assets. If net income is used in its computation rather than EBIT, the ratio may be distorted by the nature of the company's financing activities.

To illustrate, we return to the example of Maduro Company. Recall that Maduro plans to invest the $100,000 it receives in exactly the same manner regardless of whether it obtains the funds from equity or debt financing. Even so, the ROA ratio with net income as the numerator is 14 percent ($14,000 ÷ $100,000) under equity financing but only 8.4 percent ($8,400 ÷ $100,000) under debt financing. Since the assets are used in exactly the same manner regardless of how they are obtained, the difference between the 14 percent ROA and the 8.4 percent ROA ratios is due to financing strategy rather than asset management. The use of EBIT avoids this discrepancy and thereby provides a better measure of asset utilization. In the case of Maduro Company, the ROA ratio computed on the basis of EBIT is 20 percent ($20,000 ÷ $100,000) whether debt or equity financing is used. Since the assets are used in the same manner regardless of how they are financed, the measure of asset utilization should be the same regardless of the method of financing. Thus, the use of EBIT for computing the ROA ratio provides a better measure of asset use. However, for simplicity, continue to use net income when you compute ratios unless instructed otherwise.

Times Interest Earned Ratio

Debt financing has some disadvantages. The increased risk to a business that uses more debt versus less debt has been noted. Financial statement users have ratios that help assess this risk. One is the debt to assets ratio, explained in Chapter 3. Another is the **times interest earned ratio**, defined as

$$\frac{\text{EBIT}}{\text{Interest expense}}$$

Because the amount of earnings before interest and taxes is available for paying interest, the times interest earned ratio must be based on EBIT, not on net income. This ratio tells *how many times* a company would be able to pay its interest by using the amount of earnings available to make interest payments. The higher the ratio, the less likely a company is to be unable to make its interest payments. Since the failure to pay interest can lead to bankruptcy, higher times interest earned ratios suggest lower levels of risk. Shown here are the times interest earned ratios and debt to assets ratios for six real-world companies. These numbers are for 2000.

Industry	Company	Times Interest Earned	Debt to Assets
Breakfast Cereal	Kellogg's	7.31 times	0.82
	Quaker Oats	11.21	0.84
Tools	Black & Decker	3.73	0.83
	Stanley Works	11.84	0.61
Hotel	Hilton Hotels	3.38	0.85
	Marriott	8.57	0.60

Sometimes companies have times interest earned ratios that are negative numbers, yet these companies can still to make the required interest payments to their creditors. Remember that bills are paid with cash, not net income. The fact that a company has no EBIT does not mean that it does not have cash provided by operations. This case demonstrates that effective financial statement analysis cannot be done on the basis of any single ratio or, for that matter, any set of ratios. Ratios must be used in

Selected financial data pertaining to Shaver and Goode Companies follow (amounts are in thousands):

	Shaver Company	Goode Company
Earnings before interest and taxes	$750,720	$2,970,680
Interest expense	234,600	645,800

Based on this information, which company is more likely to be able to make its interest payments?

Answer The times interest earned ratio for Shaver Company is 3.2 ($750,720 ÷ $234,600) times. The times interest earned ratio for Goode Company is 4.6 ($2,970,680 ÷ $645,800) times. Based on this data, Goode Company is more likely to be able to make its interest payments.

conjunction with one another and with other information to make rational business decisions. A company with terrible ratios and a patent on a newly discovered drug that cures cancer may be a far better investment than a company with great ratios and a patent on a chemotherapy product that will soon be out of date. Remember that ratios are based on historical facts. They are useful only to the extent that history is likely to repeat itself.

a look back

This chapter addressed the basic issues related to accounting for long-term debt. *Long-term notes* have a maturity period of two to five years and usually require payments that include a return of principal plus interest. A *line of credit* enables companies to borrow a limited amount of funds on an as-needed basis. Although a line of credit normally carries a term of one year, companies often refinance, thereby extending the effective maturity date to the intermediate range of five or more years. Interest for a line of credit is normally paid on a monthly basis.

Long-term debt financing with terms exceeding 10 years is usually accomplished through the issue of *bonds*. Bond agreements normally commit a company to *semiannual interest* at an amount that is equal to a fixed percentage of the face value. The amount of interest required by the bond agreement is called the *stated interest rate*. If bonds are sold when the *market interest rate* is different from the stated interest rate, companies are required to issue the bonds at a price above or below the face value. They must do this to achieve an effective rate of interest that is consistent with market conditions. Selling bonds at a *discount* (below face value) increases the effective interest rate above the stated rate. Selling bonds at a *premium* decreases the effective rate of interest.

This chapter explained the tax advantages of using debt financing versus equity financing. Basically, interest is a *tax-deductible* expense that is subtracted before taxable income is determined. In contrast, distributions to owners such as dividends are not deductible in the determination of taxable income.

a look forward

A company that needs long-term financing might choose to use debt, such as the types of bonds or term loans that were discussed in this chapter. Equity is another source of long-term financing. Several equity alternatives are available, depending on the type of business organization the owners choose to establish. For example, a company could be organized as a sole proprietorship, a partnership, or a corporation. Chapter 11 presents some accounting issues related to equity transactions of each of these types of business structures.

SELF-STUDY REVIEW PROBLEM

During 2004 and 2005, Herring Corp. completed the following selected transactions relating to its bond issue. The corporation's fiscal year ends on December 31.

2004

Jan. 1 Sold $400,000 of 10–year, 9 percent bonds at face value. Interest is payable in cash on December 31 each year.

Dec. 31 Paid the bond interest.

2005

Dec. 31 Paid the bond interest.

Required

a. Show how these events would affect Herring's financial statements by recording them in a financial statements model like the following one:

	Assets	=	Liabilities	+	Equity	Rev.	−	Exp.	=	Net Inc.	Cash Flow Statement
	Cash	=	Bond Pay.	+	Ret. Ear.						
1/1/04											
12/31/04											
12/31/05											

b. Assuming Herring had earnings before interest and taxes of $198,360 in 2005, calculate the times interest earned ratio.

Solution to Requirements a–c

a.

	Assets	=	Liabilities	+	Equity	Rev.	−	Exp.	=	Net Inc.	Cash Flow Statement	
	Cash	=	Bond Pay.	+	Ret. Ear.							
1/1/04	400,000	=	400,000	+	NA	NA	−	NA	=	NA	388,000	FA
12/31/04	(36,000)	=	NA	+	(36,000)	NA	−	36,000	=	(36,000)	(36,000)	OA
12/31/05	(36,000)	=	NA	+	(36,000)	NA	−	36,000	=	(36,000)	(36,000)	OA

b. The times interest earned ratio is 5.51 times ($198,360 ÷ $36,000).

APPENDIX

Time Value of Money

LO9 Explain the time value of money.

Future Value

Suppose you recently won a $10,000 cash prize in a local lottery. You decide to save the money to have funds available to obtain a masters of business administration (MBA) degree. You plan to enter the program three years from today. Assuming that you invest the money in an account that earns 8 percent annual interest, how much money will you have available in three years? The answer depends on whether your investment will earn *simple* or *compound* interest.

To determine the amount of funds available assuming that you earn 8 percent **simple interest**, multiply the principal balance by the interest rate to determine the amount of interest earned per year ($10,000 × 0.08 = $800). Next, multiply the amount of annual interest by the number of years for which the funds will be invested ($800 × 3 = $2,400). Finally, add the interest earned to the principal balance to determine the total amount of funds available at the end of the three-year term ($10,000 principal + $2,400 interest = $12,400 cash available at the end of three years).

Most investors can increase their returns by reinvesting the income earned from their investments. For example, at the beginning of the second year, you will have available for investment not only the original $10,000 principal balance but also $800 of interest earned during the first year. In other words, you will be able to earn interest on the interest that you previously earned. The practice of earning interest on interest is called **compounding**. Assuming that you are able to earn 8 percent compound interest, the amount of funds available to you at the end of three years can be computed, as shown in Exhibit 10–5.

Obviously, you earn more with compound interest ($2,597.12 compound versus $2,400 simple). The number of computations required for **compound interest** can become cumbersome when the investment term is long. Fortunately, there are mathematical formulas, interest tables, and computer programs that reduce the computational burden. For example, a compound interest factor can be developed from the formula

$$(1 + i)^n$$

where i = interest

n = number of periods

Exhibit 10–5

Year	Amount Invested	×	Interest Rate	=	Interest Earned	+	Amount Invested	=	New Balance
1	$10,000.00	×	0.08	=	$ 800.00	+	$10,000.00	=	$10,800.00
2	10,800.00	×	0.08	=	864.00	+	10,800.00	=	11,664.00
3	11,664.00	×	0.08	=	933.12	+	11,664.00	=	12,597.12
	Total interest earned				$2,597.12				

The value of the investment is determined by multiplying the compound-interest factor by the principal balance. The compound-interest factor for a three-year term and an 8 percent interest rate is 1.259712 (1.08 × 1.08 × 1.08 = 1.259712). Assuming a $10,000 original investment, the value of the investment at the end of three years is $12,597.12 ($10,000 × 1.259712). This is, of course, the same amount that was computed in the previous illustration (see final figure in the New Balance column of Exhibit 10–5).

The mathematical formulas have been used to develop tables containing interest factors that can be used to determine the **future value** of an investment under a variety of interest rates and time periods. For example, Table I on page 437 contains the interest factor for an investment with a three-year term earning 8 percent compound interest. To confirm this point, move down the column marked *n* to the third period. Next move across to the column marked 8%, where you will find the value 1.259712. This is identical to the amount computed by using the mathematical formula in the preceding paragraph. Here also, the value of the investment at the end of three years can be determined by multiplying the principal balance by the compound interest factor ($10,000 × 1.259712 = $12,597.12). These same factors and amounts can be determined through the use of computer programs contained in calculators and spreadsheet software.

Clearly, there are a variety of ways to determine the future value of an investment, given a principal balance, interest rate, and term to maturity. In our case, we showed that your original investment of $10,000 would be worth $12,597 in three years, assuming an 8 percent compound interest rate. Suppose that you determine that this amount is insufficient to get you through the MBA program you want to complete. Indeed, assume that you believe you will need $18,000 three years from today to sustain yourself while you finish the degree. Suppose your parents agree to cover the shortfall. They ask how much money you need today in order to have $18,000 three years from now.

Present Value

The mathematical formula required to convert the future value of a dollar to its **present value** equivalent is

$$\frac{1}{(1 + i)^n}$$

where i = interest
n = number of periods

For easy conversion, the formula has been used to develop Table II (page 437), titled Present Value of $1. At an 8 percent annual compound interest rate, the present value equivalent of $18,000 to be received three years from today is computed as follows: Move down the far-left column to the spot where $n = 3$. Next, move right to the column marked 8%. At this point, you should see the interest factor 0.793832. Multiplying this factor by the desired future value of $18,000 yields the present value result of $14,288.98 ($18,000 × 0.793832). This means that if you invest $14,288.98 (present value) today at an annual compound-interest rate of 8 percent, you will have the $18,000 (future value) you need to enter the MBA program three years from now.

If you currently have $10,000, you will need an additional $4,288.98 from your parents to make the required $14,288.98 investment that will yield the future value of $18,000 you need to enter the MBA program. In other words, having $14,288.98 today is the same thing as having $18,000 three years from today, assuming you can earn 8 percent compound interest. To validate this conclusion, use Table I to determine the future value of $14,288.98, given a three-year term and an 8 percent annual compound interest. As previously indicated, the future-value conversion factor under these conditions is 1.259712. Multiplying this factor by the $14,288.98 present value produces the expected future value of $18,000 ($14,288.98 × 1.259712 = $18,000). The factors in Table I can be used to convert present values to future values, and the corresponding factors in Table II are used to convert future values to present values.

Future Value Annuities

The previous examples described present and future values associated with a single lump-sum payment. Many financial transactions involve a series of payments. To illustrate, we return to the example in which you want to have $18,000 available three years from today. We continue the assumption that you can earn 8 percent compound interest. However, now we assume that you do not have $14,288.98 to invest today. Instead, you decide to save part of the money during each of the next three years. How much money must you save each year to have $18,000 at the end of three years? *The series of equal payments made over a number of periods in order to acquire a future value is called an* **annuity**. The factors contained in Table III (page 438), Future Value of an Annuity of $1, can be used to determine the amount of the annuity needed to produce the desired $18,000 future value. The table is constructed so that future values can be determined by multiplying the conversion factor by the amount of the annuity. These relationships can be expressed algebraically as follows:

Amount of annuity payment × Table conversion factor = Future value

To determine the amount of the required annuity payment in our example, first locate the future value conversion factor. In Table III, move down the first column on the left-hand side until you locate period 3. Next move to the right until you locate the 8% column. At this location you will see a conversion factor of 3.2464. This factor can be used to determine the amount of the annuity payment as indicated here:

Amount of annuity payment × Table conversion factor = Future value
Amount of annuity payment = Future value ÷ Table conversion factor
Amount of annuity payment = $18,000.00 ÷ 3.2464
Amount of annuity payment = $5,544.60

If you deposit $5,544.60 in an investment account at the end of each of the next three years,[5] the investment account balance will be $18,000, assuming your investment earns 8 percent interest compounded annually. This conclusion is validated by the following schedule:

End of Year	Beg. Acct. Bal.	+	Interest Computation	+	Payment	=	End. Acct. Bal.
1	0	+	0	+	$5,544.60	=	$5,544.60
2	$5,544.60	+	$5,544.60 × 0.08 = $443.57	+	5,544.60	=	11,532.77
3	11,532.77	+	11,532.77 × 0.08 = 922.62	+	5,544.60	=	18,000.00*

*Total does not add exactly due to rounding.

Present Value Annuities

We previously demonstrated that a future value of $18,000 is equivalent to a present value of $14,288.98, given annual compound interest of 8 percent for a three-year period. Therefore, if the future value of a $5,544.60 annuity is for three years equivalent to $18,000, that same annuity should have a present value of $14,288.98. We can test this conclusion by using the conversion factors shown in Table IV (page 438), Present Value of an Annuity of $1. The present value annuity table is constructed so that present values can be determined by multiplying the conversion factor by the amount of the annuity. These relationships can be expressed algebraically as follows:

Amount of annuity payment × Table conversion factor = Present value

To determine the present value of the annuity payment in our example, first locate the present value conversion factor. In Table IV, move down the first column on the left-hand side until you locate period 3. Next move to the right until you locate the column for the 8% interest rate. At this location you will see a conversion factor of 2.577097. This factor can be used to determine the amount of the present value of the annuity payment, as indicated:

Amount of annuity payment × Table conversion factor = Present value
$5,544.60 × 2.577097 = $14,288.97*

In summary, Tables III and IV can be used to convert annuities to future or present values for a variety of different assumptions regarding interest rates and time periods.

[5] A payment made at the end of a period is known as an *ordinary annuity*. A payment made at the beginning of a period is called an *annuity due*. Tables are generally set up to assume ordinary annuities. Minor adjustments must be made when dealing with an annuity due. For the purposes of this text, we consider all annuities to be ordinary.

* The 1 cent difference between this value and the expected value of $14,288.98 is due to rounding.

Business Applications

Long-Term Notes Payable

In the early part of this chapter, we considered a case in which Bill Blair borrowed $100,000 from a local bank. We indicated that Blair agreed to repay the bank through a series of annual payments (an *annuity*) of $25,709 each. How was this amount determined? Recall that Blair agreed to pay the bank 9 percent interest over a five-year term. Under these circumstances, we are trying to find the annuity equivalent to the $100,000 present value that the bank is loaning Blair. The first step in determining the annuity (annual payment) is to locate the appropriate present value conversion factor from Table IV. At the fifth row under the 9% column, you will find the value 3.889651. This factor can be used to determine the amount of the annuity payment as indicated here:

$$\text{Amount of annuity payment} \times \text{Table conversion factor} = \text{Present value}$$
$$\text{Amount of annuity payment} = \text{Present value} \div \text{Table conversion factor}$$
$$\text{Amount of annuity payment} = \$100{,}000 \div 3.889651$$
$$\text{Amount of annuity payment} = \$25{,}709$$

There are many applications in which debt repayment is accomplished through annuities. Common examples with which you are probably familiar include auto loans and home mortgages. Payment schedules for such loans may be determined from the interest tables, as demonstrated here. However, most real-world businesses have further refined the computational process by using sophisticated computer programs. The software program prompts the user to provide the relevant information regarding the present value of the amount borrowed, number of payments, and interest rate. Given this information and a few simple keystrokes, the computer program produces the amount of the amortization payment along with an amortization schedule showing the amounts of principal and interest payments over the life of the loan. Similar results can be accomplished with spreadsheet software applications such as Excel and Lotus. Even many handheld calculators have present and future value functions that enable users to quickly compute annuity payments for an infinite number of interest rate and time period assumptions.

LO10 Account for bonds using the straight-line method.

Mason Company Revisited

The next section revisits the Mason Company illustration. The same six events are examined under a new assumption: The bonds are issued at a discount. This assumption changes the amounts appearing on the financial statements. For example, Event 1 in year 2005 reflects the fact that only $95,000 cash was obtained from the bond issue. Likewise, since there was only $95,000 available to invest in land, the illustration assumes that a less desirable piece of property was acquired. This property generated only $11,400 of rent revenue per year.

Event 1 Issue of Bond Liability

When bonds are issued at a discount, the amount of the discount is recorded in a contra liability account titled **Discount on Bonds Payable**.

Here, the $100,000 face value of the bonds is recorded in the Bonds Payable account. The $5,000 discount is shown in a separate contra account. As indicated in the following discussion, the contra account is subtracted from the face value to determine the **carrying value** (net book value) of the bonds.

Bonds Payable	$100,000
Less: Discount on Bonds Payable	(5,000)
Carrying Value	$ 95,000

From Mason's perspective, her company borrowed only $95,000. When the $100,000 is paid at maturity, it will include a return of the $95,000 principal borrowed plus a $5,000 cash payment for interest. Mason will have to continue to make the annual $9,000 ($100,000 face value × 0.09 stated interest rate) cash payment for interest. The extra $5,000 of interest paid at maturity will cause the effective interest rate to be higher than the stated rate.

The bond issue is an asset source transaction with assets and total liabilities both increasing by $95,000. Net income is not affected. The cash inflow is shown in the financing activities section of the cash flow statement. The effect of the bond issue on the financial statements and the journal entry required to record it are shown here:

Assets	=	Liabilities			+	Equity	Rev.	−	Exp.	=	Net Inc.	Cash Flow Statement	
Cash	=	Bonds Pay.	−	Discount	+	Equity							
95,000	=	100,000	−	5,000	+	NA	NA	−	NA	=	NA	95,000	FA

Account Title	Debit	Credit
Cash	95,000	
Discount on Bonds Payable	5,000	
Bonds Payable		100,000

In the financial statements, the $5,000 debit to the Discount account is offset by the $100,000 credit to the Bonds Payable account. The remaining $95,000 credit balance represents the carrying value of the bond liability.

Event 2
Investment in Land

Event 2 involves the $95,000 cash purchase of land, which is an asset exchange transaction.

The asset account Cash decreases, and the asset account Land increases. The income statement is not affected. The cash outflow is shown in the investing activities section of the cash flow statement. These effects are shown here:

Assets			=	Liab.	+	Equity	Rev.	−	Exp.	=	Net Inc.	Cash Flow Statement	
Cash	+	Land	=										
(95,000)	+	95,000	=	NA	+	NA	NA	−	NA	=	NA	(95,000)	IA

Event 3
Revenue Recognition

Event 3 recognizes the $11,400 cash revenue generated from the rental of the property.

This event is repeated each year from 2005 through 2009. The event is an asset source transaction that results in an increase in assets and equity. The revenue recognition causes net income to increase. The cash inflow is shown in the operating activities section of the cash flow statement. These effects are shown here:

Assets	=	Liab.	+	Equity	Rev.	−	Exp.	=	Net Inc.	Cash Flow Statement	
11,400	=	NA	+	11,400	11,400	−	NA	=	11,400	11,400	OA

Event 4
Expense Recognition

Although the interest associated with the $5,000 discount will be paid in one lump sum at maturity, it is systematically allocated to the Interest Expense account over the life of the bond.

Under **straight-line amortization**, the amount of the discount recognized as expense in each accounting period is $1,000 ($5,000 discount ÷ 5 years). As a result, there is $10,000 of interest expense recognized in each accounting period. This figure is composed of $9,000 of stated interest plus $1,000 amortization of this bond discount. Compare this amount with the $9,000 charge for interest expense shown in the previous illustration when the bonds were sold at face value (no discount).

Recall that an expense is either a decrease in assets or an increase in liabilities. The $9,000 cash payment for interest is an asset use transaction. The $1,000 portion of interest expense recognition through the amortization of the discount is a claims exchange transaction. This transaction increases liabilities. More specifically, amounts are removed from the Discount account and placed into the Interest Expense account. Since the Discount account is a contra liability account, reducing it increases the carrying value of the bond liability. In summary, $10,000 of interest expense is recognized. The recognition of the interest expense causes equity (Retained Earnings) to decrease. The $10,000 decrease in Retained Earnings is offset by a $9,000 decrease in the Cash account and a $1,000 increase in the carrying value of the bond liability (a decrease in the Discount account). The effect of the interest expense recognition on the financial statements and the journal entry necessary to record it for each accounting period are as follows:

Assets	=	Liabilities			+	Equity	Rev.	−	Exp.	=	Net Inc.	Cash Flow Statement	
Cash	=	Bonds Pay.	−	Discount									
(9,000)	=	NA	−	(1,000)	+	(10,000)	NA	−	10,000	=	(10,000)	(9,000)	OA

Account Title	Debit	Credit
Interest Expense	10,000	
Cash		9,000
Discount on Bonds Payable		1,000

Event 5 Sale of Investment in Land

Event 5 occurs when the land is sold for $95,000 cash.

The sale is an asset exchange transaction. The Cash account increases and the Land account decreases. Since there was no gain or loss on the sale, the income statement is not affected. The cash inflow is shown in the investing activities section of the cash flow statement. These effects are shown here:

Assets			=	Liab.	+	Equity	Rev.	−	Exp.	=	Net Inc.	Cash Flow Statement	
Cash	+	Land	=										
95,000	+	(95,000)	=	NA	+	NA	NA	−	NA	=	NA	95,000	IA

Event 6 Payoff of Bond Liability

Finally, Event 6 concerns the repayment of the face value of the bond liability.

This is an asset use transaction. The Cash and Bonds Payable accounts decrease. The income statement is not affected. The cash outflow is shown in the financing activities section of the cash flow statement. The outflow associated with the repayment of the principal is $95,000. The remaining $5,000 represents an interest charge associated with the discount. In practice, the amount of the discount is often immaterial and is included in the financing activities section along with the principal payment:

Assets	=	Liabilities	+	Equity	Rev.	−	Exp.	=	Net Inc.	Cash Flow Statement	
(100,000)	=	(100,000)	+	NA	NA	−	NA	=	NA	(95,000)	FA
										(5,000)	OA

LO7

Describe how bond liabilities and their related interest costs affect financial statements.

Effect on Financial Statements

Exhibit 10–6 contains the financial statements that reflect Mason's business venture under the assumption that the bonds were issued at a discount. Note that the amount of net income is significantly lower than the amount reported in Exhibit 10–4 (page 422), where it was assumed that the bonds were sold at face value. The lower income results from two factors. First, since the bonds were sold at a discount, there was less money to invest in land, and the lower investment (less desirable property was purchased) produced lower revenues. Second, the effective interest rate was higher than the stated rate, resulting in higher expenses. Lower revenues coupled with higher expenses result in less profitability.

With respect to the balance sheet, note that the carrying value of the bond liability increases each year until the liability is equal to the face value of the bond on the December 31, 2009, year-end closing date. This is logical because Mason is obligated to pay the full $100,000 at maturity. Also note that the amount of retained earnings ($7,000) on December 31, 2009, is equal to the total amount of net income reported over the 5-year life of the business ($1,400 × 5). Again, this is logical because no dividends were made during the 5-year period; all earnings were retained in the business.

The differences between net income and cash flow are a result of several factors. First, although $10,000 of interest expense is shown on the 2005 income statement, only $9,000 of cash was paid for interest. The $1,000 differential is a result of the amortization of the bond discount. The cash outflow for the amortization of the discount is included in the $100,000 payment made at maturity. This payment is composed of $95,000 repayment of principal and $5,000 payment for interest.[6] Since there is a $9,000 cash payment for the interest expense in 2009, the total cash paid for interest is $14,000 ($9,000 based on the stated rate + $5,000 for discount). Even though $14,000 of cash is paid for interest in 2009, only $10,000 is recognized as interest expense on the income statement. Although the total net cash inflow over the five-year life of the business ($7,000) is equal to the total amount of net income reported for the same period, there are significant differences in the timing of the recognition of the interest expense and the cash outflows associated with it.

Effect of Semiannual Interest Payments

So far, our examples assumed that interest payments were made on an annual basis. In practice, most bond indentures call for the payment of interest on a semiannual basis, which means that interest is paid in cash twice each

[6] In practice, many companies do not separate the discount from the principal for the presentation of information on the cash flow statement. In other words, the entire face value of the bond liability is shown in the financing section of the cash flow statement. While this practice is conceptually invalid, it is acceptable as long as the amounts are considered immaterial.

Exhibit 10–6 *Financial Statements*

Under the Assumption That Bonds Are Issued at a Discount

	2005	2006	2007	2008	2009
Income Statements					
Rent Revenue	$ 11,400	$ 11,400	$ 11,400	$ 11,400	$11,400
Interest Expense	(10,000)	(10,000)	(10,000)	(10,000)	(10,000)
Net Income	$ 1,400	$ 1,400	$ 1,400	$ 1,400	$ 1,400
Balance Sheets					
Assets					
Cash	$ 2,400	$ 4,800	$ 7,200	$ 9,600	$ 7,000
Land	95,000	95,000	95,000	95,000	0
Total Assets	$ 97,400	$ 99,800	$102,200	$104,600	$ 7,000
Liabilities					
Bonds Payable	$100,000	$100,000	$100,000	$100,000	$ 0
Discount on Bonds Payable	(4,000)	(3,000)	(2,000)	(1,000)	0
Carrying Value of Bond Liab.	96,000	97,000	98,000	99,000	0
Shareholders' Equity					
Retained Earnings	1,400	2,800	4,200	5,600	7,000
Total Liabilities and Shareholders' Equity	$ 97,400	$ 99,800	$102,200	$104,600	$ 7,000
Cash Flow Statements					
Operating Activities					
Inflow from Customers	$ 11,400	$ 11,400	$ 11,400	$ 11,400	$11,400
Outflow for Interest	(9,000)	(9,000)	(9,000)	(9,000)	(14,000)
Investing Activities					
Outflow to Purchase Land	(95,000)	0	0	0	0
Inflow for Sale of Land	0	0	0	0	95,000
Financing Activities					
Inflow from Bond Issue	95,000	0	0	0	0
Outflow to Repay Bond Liab.	0	0	0	0	(95,000)
Net Change in Cash	2,400	2,400	2,400	2,400	(2,600)
Beginning Cash Balance	0	2,400	4,800	7,200	9,600
Ending Cash Balance	$ 2,400	$ 4,800	$ 7,200	$ 9,600	$ 7,000

On January 1, 2004, Moffett Company issued bonds with a $600,000 face value at 98. The bonds had a 9 percent annual interest rate and a 10-year term. Interest is payable in cash on December 31 of each year. What amount of interest expense will Moffett report on the 2006 income statement? What carrying value for bonds payable will Moffett report on the December 31, 2006, balance sheet?

Answer The bonds were issued at a $12,000 ($600,000 × 0.02) discount. The discount will be amortized over the 10-year life at the rate of $1,200 ($12,000 ÷ 10 years) per year. The amount of interest expense for 2006 is $55,200 ([$600,000 × 0.09] = $54,000 annual cash interest + $1,200 discount amortization).

The carrying value of the bond liability is equal to the face value less the unamortized discount. By the end of 2006, $3,600 of the discount will have been amortized ($1,200 × 3 years = $3,600). The unamortized discount as of December 31, 2006, will be $8,400 ($12,000 − $3,600). The carrying value of the bond liability as of December 31, 2006, will be $591,600 ($600,000 − $8,400).

year. If Marsha Mason's bond indenture required semiannual interest payments, her company would have had to make a $4,500 ($100,000 × 0.09 = $9,000 ÷ 2 = $4,500) cash payment for interest on June 30, 2005, and December 31 of each year. The journal entries necessary to record interest for each year are as follows (the entries apply to the bonds issued at a discount):

Date	Account Title	Debit	Credit
June 30	Interest Expense	5,000	
	Discount on Bonds Payable		500
	Cash		4,500
Dec. 31	Interest Expense	5,000	
	Discount on Bonds Payable		500
	Cash		4,500

The same total amount of expense is recognized and paid over the life of the bond. The difference centres on the timing of the cash payments. If the interest is paid semiannually, then cash outflow for interest is made earlier and more often. This is a disadvantage from the issuer's point of view because the capacity to use the cash is transferred to the investor earlier. Considering the financial advantages associated with delaying the cash payments, the issuer prefers to make payments annually. However, since investors have become accustomed to receiving semiannual interest collections, bonds that pay interest annually are more difficult to sell. Most bonds in Canadian markets pay semiannual interest.

LO5 Explain why bonds are issued at face value, a discount, or a premium.

Bonds Issued at a Premium

When bonds are sold at an amount above their face value, the differential between the two amounts is called a **bond premium**. Bonds sell at a premium when the market rate of interest is below the stated rate. Bond premiums act to lower the effective interest rate to the market rate. Thus, they lower interest expense. For example, assume that Marsha Mason sold her bonds for 105. Mason would receive $105,000 cash when the bonds were issued. Even so, she must repay only the $100,000 face value of the bonds at the maturity date. The $5,000 difference between the amount received and the amount paid reduces the amount of interest expense. The Premium on Bonds Payable account is shown on the balance sheet as an adjunct liability account (it adds to the carrying value of the bond liability). The bond liability would be shown on the balance sheet as indicated here:

Bonds Payable	$100,000
Plus: Premium on Bonds Payable	5,000
Carrying Value	$105,000

The effect of issuing the bonds at a premium on the financial statements is as follows:

Assets	=	Liabilities			+	Equity	Rev.	−	Exp.	=	Net Inc.	Cash Flow Statement	
Cash	=	Bond Pay.	+	Premium									
105,000	=	100,000	+	5,000	+	NA	NA	−	NA	=	NA	105,000	FA

Note that the entire $105,000 cash inflow is shown under the financing activities section of the cash flow statement even though the $5,000 premium pertains to interest. Conceptually, the premium is related to operating activities. But, in practice, the amounts associated with premiums are usually so small that they are considered immaterial. So, the entire cash inflow is normally classified as a financing activity.

The journal entries necessary to record the bond issue at a premium and the first interest payment are as follows (the entries assume an annual interest payment):

Date	Account Title	Debit	Credit
Jan. 1	Cash	105,000	
	Bonds Payable		100,000
	Premium on Bonds Payable		5,000
Dec. 31	Interest Expense	8,000	
	Premium on Bonds Payable	1,000	
	Cash		9,000

Bond Redemptions

The previous exhibits for the bonds issued by Marsha Mason assumed that the bonds were redeemed on the maturity date. The bondholders were paid the face value of the bonds, and the bond liability was removed from the books. The discount or premium was fully amortized so these accounts no longer existed at the time the bonds were redeemed.

Often bonds with a *call provision* are redeemed before the maturity date. When they are, the company must pay the bondholders the **call price**, which is an amount that is normally higher than the maturity value. For example, suppose that Mason's bond indenture includes a provision that enables her to call the bonds at a price of 103. Assume that her client refuses to renew the contract to rent the land at the end of 2007. Mason is forced to sell the land and pay off the bonds. Using the data that assumes the bonds were sold for a discount, there is a $2,000 balance in the Discount on Bonds Payable account on January 1, 2008 (see Exhibit 10–6 for details).

Mason must pay the bondholders $103,000 ($100,000 face value × 103 call price) to redeem the bonds. Since the book value of the bond liability is $98,000 ($100,000 face value − $2,000 remaining discount), she experiences a $5,000 loss ($103,000 redemption price − $98,000 book value) when the bonds are paid off. Therefore, cash, the carrying value of the bond liability, and equity all decrease as a result of the redemption. The effect of the redemption on the financial statements is as follows:

Assets	=	Liabilities			+	Equity	Rev.	−	Exp.	=	Net Inc.	Cash Flow Statement	
Cash	=	Bond Pay.	−	Discount									
(103,000)	=	(100,000)	−	(2,000)	+	(5,000)	NA	−	5,000	=	(5,000)	(103,000)	FA

Note that the entire $103,000 cash outflow is shown under the financing activities section of the cash flow statement. Conceptually, some of this amount is attributable to activities other than financing. But, in practice, the amounts not associated with financing are usually so small that they are considered immaterial. Therefore, the entire cash outflow is classified as a financing activity.

The general journal entry necessary for recording the bond redemption is shown here:

Account Title	Debit	Credit
Loss on Bond Redemption	5,000	
Bonds Payable	100,000	
Discount on Bonds Payable		2,000
Cash		103,000

The loss on redemption of bonds, if material, appears on Mason's income statement as an **extraordinary item**. Extraordinary items are set apart from operating income to highlight unusual items that are not likely to recur.

Bond Liabilities Determine Price

We discussed the use of discounts and premiums as means of producing an effective rate of interest that is higher or lower than the stated rate of interest. For example, if the stated rate of interest is lower than the market rate of interest at the time the bonds are issued, the issuer can increase the effective interest rate by selling the bonds for a price lower than their face value. At maturity, the issuer will settle the obligation by paying the face value of the bond. The difference between the discounted bond price and the face value of the bond is additional interest. To illustrate, assume that Tower Company issues $100,000 face value bonds with a 20-year term and a 9 percent stated rate of annual interest. At the time the bonds are issued, the market rate of interest for bonds of comparable risk is 10 percent annual interest. For what amount would Tower Company be required to sell the bonds in order to move its 9 percent stated rate of interest to an effective rate of 10 percent?

Information from present value Tables II (page 437) and IV (page 438) is required to determine the amount of the discount required to produce a 10% effective rate of interest. First, we define the future cash flows that will be generated by the bonds. Based on the stated interest rate, the bonds will pay $9,000 ($100,000 face value × 0.09 interest) interest per year. This constitutes a 20-year annuity that should be discounted back to its present value equivalent. Also, at the end of 20 years, the bonds will require a single $100,000 lump-sum payment to settle the principal obligation. This amount must also be discounted back to its present value in order to determine the bond price. The computations required to determine the discounted bond price are shown here:

Present value of principal	$100,000 × 0.148644	=	$14,864.40
	(Table II, n = 20, i = 10%)		
Present value of interest	$9,000 × 8.513564	=	76,622.08
	(Table IV, n = 20, i = 10%)		
Bond Price			$91,486.48

Tower Company bonds sell at an $8,513.52 discount ($100,000 − $91,486.48) to produce a 10 percent effective interest rate. Note carefully that in these computations, the stated rate of interest was used to determine the amount of cash flow, and the effective rate of interest was used to determine the table conversion factor.

LO11 Compare the effective interest rate method with the straight-line method.

Bond Liabilities: Effective Interest Method of Amortization

To this point, the straight-line method has been used to amortize bond discounts or premiums. This method is commonly used in practice because it is simple to apply and easy to understand. However, the method is theoretically deficient because it results in the recognition of a constant amount of interest expense while the carrying value of the bond liability fluctuates. Consider the discount on Tower Company bonds just discussed as an example. In this case, the amount of interest expense recognized each period is computed as follows:

Stated rate of interest	$100,000.00 × 0.09	=	$9,000.00
Amortization of discount	$8,513.52 ÷ 20	=	425.68
Interest expense recognized each accounting period		=	$9,425.68

As shown earlier, the amortization of the bond discount increases the carrying value of the bond liability. Thus, under the straight-line method, the bond liability increases while the amount of interest expense recognized remains constant. Logically, the amount of interest expense should increase as the amount of liability increases. This rational relationship can be accomplished by applying the **effective interest rate method** to the amortization of bond discounts and premiums. The effective interest rate method is required when the result of its application will cause a material effect on the financial statements.

Under the effective interest rate method, the amount of interest expense recognized in the financial statements is determined by multiplying the effective rate of interest by the carrying value of the bond liability. The amount of the discount to be amortized is determined by the difference between the interest expense and the cash outflow, as defined by the stated rate of interest. The following schedule demonstrates the application of the effective interest rate method for recognizing interest expense during the first three years that Tower Company bonds were outstanding.

End of Year	Cash Payment	Interest Expense	Discount Amortization	Carrying Value
1	$9,000*	$9,148.65†	$148.65‡	$91,635.13§
2	9,000	9,163.51	163.51	91,798.64
3	9,000	9,179.86	179.86	91,978.50

*Cash outflow based on the stated rate of interest ($100,000 × 0.09).

†Effective interest rate times the carrying value (10 × $91,486.48).

‡Interest expense minus cash outflow ($9,148.65 − $9,000.00).

§Previous carrying value plus portion of discount amortized ($91,486.48 + $148.65).

Notice that the effective interest rate method results in larger and larger amounts of expense recognition as the carrying value of the bond liability increases. The effect of the expense recognition on the financial statements and the journal entry necessary to record it for the first accounting period are as follows:

Cash	=	Bond Liab.	+	Equity	Rev.	−	Exp.	=	Net Inc.	Cash Flow Statement	
(9,000)	=	148.65*	+	(9,148.65)	NA	−	9,148.65	=	(9,148.65)	(9,000)	OA

*The decrease in the amount of the discount acts to increase the bond liability.

Account Title	Debit	Credit
Interest Expense	9,148.65	
Cash		9,000.00
Discount on Bonds Payable		148.65

Table I *Future Value of $1*

n	4%	5%	6%	7%	8%	9%	10%	12%	14%	16%	20%
1	1.040000	1.050000	1.060000	1.070000	1.080000	1.090000	1.100000	1.120000	1.140000	1.160000	1.200000
2	1.081600	1.102500	1.123600	1.144900	1.166400	1.188100	1.210000	1.254400	1.299600	1.345600	1.440000
3	1.124864	1.157625	1.191016	1.225043	1.259712	1.295029	1.331000	1.404928	1.481544	1.560896	1.728000
4	1.169859	1.215506	1.262477	1.310796	1.360489	1.411582	1.464100	1.573519	1.688960	1.810639	2.073600
5	1.216653	1.276282	1.338226	1.402552	1.469328	1.538624	1.610510	1.762342	1.925415	2.100342	2.488320
6	1.265319	1.340096	1.418519	1.500730	1.586874	1.677100	1.771561	1.973823	2.194973	2.436396	2.985984
7	1.315932	1.407100	1.503630	1.605781	1.713824	1.828039	1.948717	2.210681	2.502269	2.826220	3.583181
8	1.368569	1.477455	1.593848	1.718186	1.850930	1.992563	2.143589	2.475963	2.852586	3.278415	4.299817
9	1.423312	1.551328	1.689479	1.838459	1.999005	2.171893	2.357948	2.773079	3.251949	3.802961	5.159780
10	1.480244	1.628895	1.790848	1.967151	2.158925	2.367364	2.593742	3.105848	3.707221	4.411435	6.191736
11	1.539454	1.710339	1.898299	2.104852	2.331639	2.580426	2.853117	3.478550	4.226232	5.117265	7.430084
12	1.601032	1.795856	2.012196	2.252192	2.518170	2.812665	3.138428	3.895976	4.817905	5.936027	8.916100
13	1.665074	1.885649	2.132928	2.409845	2.719624	3.065805	3.452271	4.363493	5.492411	6.885791	10.699321
14	1.731676	1.979932	2.260904	2.578534	2.937194	3.341727	3.797498	4.887112	6.261349	7.987518	12.839185
15	1.800944	2.078928	2.396558	2.759032	3.172169	3.642482	4.177248	5.473566	7.137938	9.265521	15.407022
16	1.872981	2.182875	2.540352	2.952164	3.425943	3.970306	4.594973	6.130394	8.137249	10.748004	18.488426
17	1.947900	2.292018	2.692773	3.158815	3.700018	4.327633	5.054470	6.866041	9.276464	12.467685	22.186111
18	2.025817	2.406619	2.854339	3.379932	3.996019	4.717120	5.559917	7.689966	10.575169	14.462514	26.623333
19	2.106849	2.526950	3.025600	3.616528	4.315701	5.141661	6.115909	8.612762	12.055693	16.776517	31.948000
20	2.191123	2.653298	3.207135	3.869684	4.660957	5.604411	6.727500	9.646293	13.743490	19.460759	38.337600

Table II *Present Value of $1*

n	4%	5%	6%	7%	8%	9%	10%	12%	14%	16%	20%
1	0.961538	0.952381	0.943396	0.934579	0.925926	0.917431	0.909091	0.892857	0.877193	0.862069	0.833333
2	0.924556	0.907029	0.889996	0.873439	0.857339	0.841680	0.826446	0.797194	0.769468	0.743163	0.694444
3	0.888996	0.863838	0.839619	0.816298	0.793832	0.772183	0.751315	0.711780	0.674972	0.640658	0.578704
4	0.854804	0.822702	0.792094	0.762895	0.735030	0.708425	0.683013	0.635518	0.592080	0.552291	0.482253
5	0.821927	0.783526	0.747258	0.712986	0.680583	0.649931	0.620921	0.567427	0.519369	0.476113	0.401878
6	0.790315	0.746215	0.704961	0.666342	0.630170	0.596267	0.564474	0.506631	0.455587	0.410442	0.334898
7	0.759918	0.710681	0.665057	0.622750	0.583490	0.547034	0.513158	0.452349	0.399637	0.353830	0.279082
8	0.730690	0.676839	0.627412	0.582009	0.540269	0.501866	0.466507	0.403883	0.350559	0.305025	0.232568
9	0.702587	0.644609	0.591898	0.543934	0.500249	0.460428	0.424098	0.360610	0.307508	0.262953	0.193807
10	0.675564	0.613913	0.558395	0.508349	0.463193	0.422411	0.385543	0.321973	0.269744	0.226684	0.161506
11	0.649581	0.584679	0.526788	0.475093	0.428883	0.387533	0.350494	0.287476	0.236617	0.195417	0.134588
12	0.624597	0.556837	0.496969	0.444012	0.397114	0.355535	0.318631	0.256675	0.207559	0.168463	0.112157
13	0.600574	0.530321	0.468839	0.414964	0.367698	0.326179	0.289664	0.229174	0.182069	0.145227	0.093464
14	0.577475	0.505068	0.442301	0.387817	0.340461	0.299246	0.263331	0.204620	0.159710	0.125195	0.077887
15	0.555265	0.481017	0.417265	0.362446	0.315242	0.274538	0.239392	0.182696	0.140096	0.107927	0.064905
16	0.533908	0.458112	0.393646	0.338735	0.291890	0.251870	0.217629	0.163122	0.122892	0.093041	0.054088
17	0.513373	0.436297	0.371364	0.316574	0.270269	0.231073	0.197845	0.145644	0.107800	0.080207	0.045073
18	0.493628	0.415521	0.350344	0.295864	0.250249	0.211994	0.179859	0.130040	0.094561	0.069144	0.037561
19	0.474642	0.395734	0.330513	0.276508	0.231712	0.194490	0.163508	0.116107	0.082948	0.059607	0.031301
20	0.456387	0.376889	0.311805	0.258419	0.214548	0.178431	0.148644	0.103667	0.072762	0.051385	0.026084

Table III *Future Value of an Annuity of $1*

n	4%	5%	6%	7%	8%	9%	10%	12%	14%	16%	20%
1	1.000000	1.000000	1.000000	1.000000	1.000000	1.000000	1.000000	1.000000	1.000000	1.000000	1.000000
2	2.040000	2.050000	2.060000	2.070000	2.080000	2.090000	2.100000	2.120000	2.140000	2.160000	2.200000
3	3.121600	3.152500	3.183600	3.214900	3.246400	3.278100	3.310000	3.374400	3.439600	3.505600	3.640000
4	4.246464	4.310125	4.374616	4.439943	4.506112	4.573129	4.641000	4.779328	4.921144	5.066496	5.368000
5	5.416323	5.525631	5.637093	5.750739	5.866601	5.984711	6.105100	6.352847	6.610104	6.877135	7.441600
6	6.632975	6.801913	6.975319	7.153291	7.335929	7.523335	7.715610	8.115189	8.535519	8.977477	9.929920
7	7.898294	8.142008	8.393838	8.654021	8.922803	9.200435	9.487171	10.089012	10.730491	11.413873	12.915904
8	9.214226	9.549109	9.897468	10.259803	10.636628	11.028474	11.435888	12.299693	13.232760	14.240093	16.499085
9	10.582795	11.026564	11.491316	11.977989	12.487558	13.021036	13.579477	14.775656	16.085347	17.518508	20.798902
10	12.006107	12.577893	13.180795	13.816448	14.486562	15.192930	15.937425	17.548735	19.337295	21.321469	25.958682
11	13.486351	14.206787	14.971643	15.783599	16.645487	17.560293	18.531167	20.654583	23.044516	25.732904	32.150419
12	15.025805	15.917127	16.869941	17.888451	18.977126	20.140720	21.384284	24.133133	27.270749	30.850169	39.580502
13	16.626838	17.712983	18.882138	20.140643	21.495297	22.953385	24.522712	28.029109	32.088654	36.786196	48.496603
14	18.291911	19.598632	21.015066	22.550488	24.214920	26.019189	27.974983	32.392602	37.581065	43.671987	59.195923
15	20.023588	21.578564	23.275970	25.129022	27.152114	29.360916	31.772482	37.279715	43.842414	51.659505	72.035108
16	21.824531	23.657492	25.672528	27.888054	30.324283	33.003399	35.949730	42.753280	50.980352	60.925026	87.442129
17	23.697512	25.840366	28.212880	30.840217	33.750226	36.973705	40.544703	48.883674	59.117601	71.673030	105.930555
18	25.645413	28.132385	30.905653	33.999033	37.450244	41.301338	45.599173	55.749715	68.394066	84.140715	128.116666
19	27.671229	30.539004	33.759992	37.378965	41.446263	46.018458	51.159090	63.439681	78.969235	98.603230	154.740000
20	29.778079	33.065954	36.785591	40.995492	45.761964	51.160120	57.274999	72.052442	91.024928	115.379747	186.688000

Table IV *Present Value of an Annuity of $1*

n	4%	5%	6%	7%	8%	9%	10%	12%	14%	16%	20%
1	0.961538	0.952381	0.943396	0.934579	0.925926	0.917431	0.909091	0.892857	0.877193	0.862069	0.833333
2	1.886095	1.859410	1.833393	1.808018	1.783265	1.759111	1.735537	1.690051	1.646661	1.605232	1.527778
3	2.775091	2.723248	2.673012	2.624316	2.577097	2.531295	2.486852	2.401831	2.321632	2.245890	2.106481
4	3.629895	3.545951	3.465106	3.387211	3.312127	3.239720	3.169865	3.037349	2.913712	2.798181	2.588735
5	4.451822	4.329477	4.212364	4.100197	3.992710	3.889651	3.790787	3.604776	3.433081	3.274294	2.990612
6	5.242137	5.075692	4.917324	4.766540	4.622880	4.485919	4.355261	4.111407	3.888668	3.684736	3.325510
7	6.002055	5.786373	5.582381	5.389289	5.206370	5.032953	4.868419	4.563757	4.288305	4.038565	3.604592
8	6.732745	6.463213	6.209794	5.971299	5.746639	5.534819	5.334926	4.967640	4.638864	4.343591	3.837160
9	7.435332	7.107822	6.801692	6.515232	6.246888	5.995247	5.759024	5.328250	4.946372	4.606544	4.030967
10	8.110896	7.721735	7.360087	7.023582	6.710081	6.417658	6.144567	5.650223	5.216116	4.833227	4.192472
11	8.760477	8.306414	7.886875	7.498674	7.138964	6.805191	6.495061	5.937699	5.452733	5.028644	4.327060
12	9.385074	8.863252	8.383844	7.942686	7.536078	7.160725	6.813692	6.194374	5.660292	5.197107	4.439217
13	9.985648	9.393573	8.852683	8.357651	7.903776	7.486904	7.103356	6.423548	5.842362	5.342334	4.532681
14	10.563123	9.898641	9.294984	8.745468	8.244237	7.786150	7.366687	6.628168	6.002072	5.467529	4.610567
15	11.118387	10.379658	9.712249	9.107914	8.559479	8.060688	7.606080	6.810864	6.142168	5.575456	4.675473
16	11.652296	10.837770	10.105895	9.446649	8.851369	8.312558	7.823709	6.973986	6.265060	5.668497	4.729561
17	12.165669	11.274066	10.477260	9.763223	9.121638	8.543631	8.021553	7.119630	6.372859	5.748704	4.774634
18	12.659297	11.689587	10.827603	10.059087	9.371887	8.755625	8.201412	7.249670	6.467420	5.817848	4.812195
19	13.133939	12.085321	11.158116	10.335595	9.603599	8.905115	8.364920	7.365777	6.550369	5.877455	4.843496
20	13.590326	12.462210	11.469921	10.594014	9.818147	9.128546	8.513564	7.469444	6.623131	5.928841	4.869580

KEY TERMS

amortization of loan *411*
annuity 429
bearer or coupon bonds *418*
bond *417*
bond discount *423*
bond indenture *417*
bond premium *434*
call premium *418*
call price *435*
callable bonds *418*
carrying value *430*
collateral for loans *414*
compound interest *427*
compounding *427*
convertible bonds *418*
debenture *417*
discount on bonds payable *430*
effective interest rate *422*
effective interest rate method *436*
extraordinary items *435*
face value *417*
financial leverage *417*
fixed interest rate *411*
future value *428*
issuer of a bond *416*
line of credit *414*
long-term notes payable *412*
market interest rate *423*
mortgage bonds *417*
present value *428*
registered bonds *418*
restrictive covenants *414*
secured bonds *417*
serial bonds *418*
simple interest *427*
sinking fund *418*
spread *416*
stated interest rate *417*
straight-line amortization *431*
subordinated debentures *417*
term bonds *418*
times interest earned ratio *425*
unregistered bonds *418*
unsecured bonds *417*
unsubordinated debentures *417*
variable interest rate *411*

QUESTIONS

1. What is the difference between classification of a note as short term or long term?
2. At the beginning of year 1, B Co. has a note payable of $72,000 that calls for an annual payment of $16,246, which includes both principal and interest. If the interest rate is 8 percent, what is the amount of interest expense in year 1 and in year 2? What is the balance of the note at the end of year 2?
3. What is the purpose of a line of credit for a business? Why would a company choose to obtain a line of credit instead of issuing bonds?
4. What are the main sources of debt financing for most large companies?
5. What are some advantages of issuing bonds versus borrowing from a bank?
6. What are some disadvantages of issuing bonds?
7. Why can a company usually issue bonds at a lower interest rate than the company would pay if the funds were borrowed from a bank?
8. What effect does income tax have on the cost of borrowing funds for a business?
9. What is the concept of financial leverage?
10. Which type of bond, secured or unsecured, is likely to have a lower interest rate? Explain.
11. What is the function of restrictive covenants attached to bond issues?
12. Why are unregistered bonds (bearer or coupon bonds) more vulnerable to theft than registered bonds?
13. What is the difference between term bonds and serial bonds?
14. What is the purpose of establishing a sinking fund?
15. What is the call price of a bond? Is it usually higher or lower than the face amount of the bond? Explain.
16. If Roc Co. issued $100,000 of 5 percent, 10-year bonds at the face amount, what is the effect of the issuance of the bonds on the financial statements? What amount of interest expense will Roc Co. recognize each year?
17. What mechanism is used to adjust the stated interest rate to the market rate of interest?
18. When the effective interest rate is higher than the stated interest rate on a bond issue, will the bond sell at a discount or premium? Why?
19. What type of transaction is the issuance of bonds by a company?
20. What factors may cause the effective interest rate and the stated interest rate to be different?
21. If a bond is selling at 97.5, how much cash will the company receive from the sale of a $1,000 bond?
22. How is the carrying value of a bond computed?
23. Gay Co. has a balance in the Bonds Payable account of $25,000 and a balance in the Discount on Bonds Payable account of $5,200. What is the carrying value of the bonds? What is the total amount of the liability?
24. When the effective interest rate is higher than the stated interest rate, will interest expense be higher or lower than the amount of interest paid?
25. Assuming that the selling price of the bond and the face value are the same, would the issuer of a bond rather make annual or semiannual interest payments? Why?
26. Rato Co. called some bonds and had a loss on the redemption of the bonds of $2,850. How is this amount reported on the income statement?
27. Which method of financing, debt or equity, is generally more advantageous from a tax standpoint? Why?
28. If a company has a tax rate of 30 percent and interest expense was $10,000, what is the after-tax cost of the debt?

29. Which type of financing, debt or equity, increases the risk factor of a business? Why?
30. What information does the times interest earned ratio provide?
31. What is the difference between simple and compound interest?
32. What is meant by the future value of an investment? How is it determined?
33. If you have $10,000 to invest at the beginning of year 1 at an interest rate of 8 percent, what is the future value of the investment at the end of year 4?
34. What is meant by the present value of an investment? How is it determined?
35. Assume that your favourite aunt gave you $25,000, but you will not receive the gift until you are 25 years old. You are presently 22 years old. What is the current value of the gift, assuming an interest rate of 8 percent?
36. What is the present value of four payments of $4,000 each to be received at the end of each of the next four years, assuming an interest rate of 8 percent?
37. How does the effective interest rate method of bond amortization differ from the straight-line method of bond amortization? Which method is conceptually more correct?

EXERCISES

L.O. 2 EXERCISE 10–1 *How Credit Terms Affect Financial Statements*

Weston Co. is planning to finance an expansion of its operations by borrowing $100,000. A local bank has agreed to loan Weston the funds. Weston has two repayment options: (1) to issue a note with the principal due in 10 years and with interest payable annually or (2) to issue a note to repay $10,000 of the principal each year along with the annual interest based on the unpaid principal balance. Assume the interest rate is 9 percent for each option.

Required

a. What amount of interest will Weston pay in year 1
   (1) Under option 1?
   (2) Under option 2?
b. What amount of interest will Weston pay in year 2
   (1) Under option 1?
   (2) Under option 2?
c. Explain the advantage of each option.

L.O. 2 EXERCISE 10–2 *Accounting for a Long-Term Note Payable with Annual Payments That Include Interest and Principal*

On January 1, 2004, Wallace Co. borrowed $80,000 cash from a local bank by issuing a four-year, 9 percent note. The principal and interest are to be paid by making annual payments in the amount of $24,693. Payments are to be made December 31 of each year, beginning December 31, 2004.

Required

Prepare an amortization schedule for the interest and principal payments for the four-year period.

L.O. 1, 2 EXERCISE 10–3 *Long-Term Installment Note Payable*

Jim Yang started a business by issuing a $100,000 face value note to a local bank on January 1, 2004. The note had an 8 percent annual rate of interest and a 10-year term. Payments of $14,903 are to be made each December 31 for 10 years.

Required

a. What portion of the December 31, 2004, payment is applied to
   (1) Interest expense?
   (2) Principal?
b. What is the principal balance on January 1, 2005?
c. What portion of the December 31, 2005, payment is applied to
   (1) Interest expense?
   (2) Principal?

EXERCISE 10–4 *Amortization of a Long-Term Loan* L.O. 1, 2

Apartial amortization schedule for a five-year note payable that Bragg Co. issued on January 1, 2006, is shown here:

Accounting Period	Principal Balance January 1	Cash Payment	Applied to Interest	Applied to Principal
2006	$150,000	$38,563	$13,500	$25,063
2007	124,937	38,563	11,244	27,319

Required

a. What rate of interest is Bragg Co. paying on the note?

b. Using a financial statements model like the one shown here, record the appropriate amounts for the following two events:

(1) January 1, 2006, issue of the note payable.

(2) December 31, 2006, payment on the note payable.

Event No.	Assets	=	Liabilities	+	Equity	Rev.	−	Exp.	=	Net Inc.	Cash Flow Statement
1											

c. If the company earned $100,000 cash revenue and paid $50,000 in cash expenses in addition to the interest in 2006, what is the amount of each of the following?

(1) Net income for 2006.

(2) Cash flow from operating activities for 2006.

(3) Cash flow from financing activities for 2006.

d. What is the amount of interest expense on this loan for 2008?

EXERCISE 10–5 *Accounting for a Line of Credit* L.O. 3

Max Company has a line of credit with a local bank. Max can borrow up to $400,000 at any time over the course of the 2004 calendar year. The following table shows the prime rate expressed as an annual percentage along with the amounts borrowed and repaid during the first four months of 2004. Max agreed to pay interest at an annual rate equal to 2 percent above the bank's prime rate. Funds are borrowed or repaid on the first day of each month. Interest is payable in cash on the last day of the month. The interest rate is applied to the outstanding monthly balance. For example, Max pays 8 percent (6 percent + 2 percent) annual interest on $100,000 for the month of January.

Month	Amount Borrowed or (Repaid)	Prime Rate for the Month, %
January	$100,000	6.0
February	50,000	5.0
March	(60,000)	5.5
April	10,000	5.0

Required

Provide all journal entries pertaining to Max's line of credit for the first four months of 2004.

EXERCISE 10–6 *Annual versus Semiannual Interest Payments* L.O. 7

Huggins Co. issued bonds with a face value of $50,000 on January 1, 2004. The bonds had a 9 percent stated rate of interest and a five-year term. The bonds were issued at face value.

Required

a. What total amount of interest will Huggins pay in 2004 if bond interest is paid annually each December 31?

b. What total amount of interest will Huggins pay in 2004 if bond interest is paid semiannually each June 30 and December 31?

c. Write a memo explaining which option Huggins would prefer.

L.O. 5, 6 EXERCISE 10–7 *Determining Cash Receipts from Bond Issues*

Required

Compute the cash proceeds from bond issues under the following terms. For each case, indicate whether the bonds sold at a premium or discount.

a. Kay, Inc., issued $100,000 of 8-year, 10 percent bonds at 101.
b. Sam Co. issued $150,000 of 4-year, 8 percent bonds at 98.
c. Bill Co. issued $200,000 of 10-year, 7 percent bonds at 102 1/4.
d. Jay, Inc., issued $40,000 of 5-year, 6 percent bonds at 97 1/2.

L.O. 5 EXERCISE 10–8 *Identifying the Relationship between the Stated Rate of Interest and the Market Rate of Interest*

Required

Indicate whether a bond will sell at a premium (P), discount (D), or face value (F) for each of the following conditions:

a. _______ The stated rate of interest is higher than the market rate.
b. _______ The market rate of interest is higher than the stated rate.
c. _______ The stated rate of interest is less than the market rate.
d. _______ The market rate of interest is less than the stated rate.
e. _______ The market rate of interest is equal to the stated rate.

L.O. 5 EXERCISE 10–9 *Identifying Bond Premiums and Discounts*

Required

In each of the following situations, state whether the bonds will sell at a premium or discount.

a. Marshall issued $100,000 of bonds with a stated interest rate of 9.0 percent. At the time of issue, the market rate of interest for similar investments was 9.5 percent.
b. Telco issued $150,000 of bonds with a stated interest rate of 7 percent. At the time of issue, the market rate of interest for similar investments was 8 percent.
c. Lee Inc. issued callable bonds with a stated interest rate of 10.0 percent. The bonds were callable at 102. At the date of issue, the market rate of interest was 9.5 percent for similar investments.

L.O. 5 EXERCISE 10–10 *Determining the Amount of Bond Premiums and Discounts*

Required

For each of the following situations, calculate the amount of bond discount or premium, if any.

a. Smart Co. issued $60,000 of 7 percent bonds at 104.
b. Swift, Inc., issued $90,000 of 10-year, 8 percent bonds at 101 1/2.
c. Ray, Inc., issued $200,000 of 20-year, 10 percent bonds at 98 1/4.
d. Gray Co. issued $150,000 of 15-year, 6 percent bonds at 96.

L.O. 10 EXERCISE 10–11 *Effect of a Bond Discount on Financial Statements: Annual Interest (Appendix)*

Heeley Company issued $200,000 face value of bonds on January 1, 2005. The bonds had a 10 percent stated rate of interest and a 10-year term. Interest is paid in cash annually, beginning December 31, 2005. The bonds were issued at 98.

Required

a. Show the effect of (1) the bond issue, (2) amortization of the discount on December 31, 2005, and (3) the December 31, 2005, interest payment on the financial statements using a horizontal statements model like the following one. Use + for increase, − for decrease, and NA for not affected.

Event No.	Assets	=	Liabilities	+	Equity	Rev.	−	Exp.	=	Net Inc.	Cash Flow Statement
1											

b. Determine the carrying value (face value less discount or plus premium) of the bond liability as of December 31, 2005.
c. Determine the amount of interest expense reported on the 2005 income statement.
d. Determine the carrying value (face value less discount or plus premium) of the bond liability as of December 31, 2006.
e. Determine the amount of interest expense reported on the 2006 income statement.

EXERCISE 10–12 *Effect of a Bond Premium on Financial Statements: Annual Interest (Appendix)* **L.O. 10**

Strauss Company issued $200,000 face value of bonds on January 1, 2006. The bonds had a 10 percent stated rate of interest and a 10-year term. Interest is paid in cash annually, beginning December 31, 2006. The bonds were issued at 102.

Required

a. Show the effect of (1) the bond issue, (2) amortization of the premium on December 31, 2006, and (3) the December 31, 2006, interest payment on the financial statements using a horizontal statements model like the following one. Use + for increase, for − decrease, and NA for not affected.

Event No.	Assets	=	Liabilities	+	Equity	Rev.	−	Exp.	=	Net Inc.	Cash Flow Statement
1											

b. Determine the carrying value (face value less discount or plus premium) of the bond liability as of December 31, 2006.
c. Determine the amount of interest expense reported on the 2006 income statement.
d. Determine the carrying value of the bond liability as of December 31, 2007.
e. Determine the amount of interest expense reported on the 2007 income statement.

EXERCISE 10–13 *Effect of Bonds Issued at a Discount on Financial Statements: Semiannual Interest (Appendix)* **L.O. 10**

Home Supplies, Inc., issued $100,000 of 10-year, 6 percent bonds on July 1, 2005, at 95. Interest is payable in cash semiannually on June 30 and December 31.

Required

a. Prepare the journal entries to record issuing the bonds and any necessary journal entries for 2005 and 2006. Post the journal entries to T-accounts.
b. Prepare the liabilities section of the balance sheet at the end of 2005 and 2006.
c. What amount of interest expense will Home report on the financial statements for 2005 and 2006?
d. What amount of cash will Home pay for interest in 2005 and 2006?

EXERCISE 10–14 *Recording Bonds Issued at Face Value and Associated Interest for Two Accounting Cycles: Annual Interest* **L.O. 6, 7**

On January 1, 2008, Hammond Corp. issued $200,000 of 10-year, 8 percent bonds at their face amount. Interest is payable on December 31 of each year with the first payment due December 31, 2008.

Required

Prepare all the general journal entries related to these bonds for 2008 and 2009.

EXERCISE 10–15 *Recording Bonds Issued at a Discount: Annual Interest (Appendix)* **L.O. 10**

On January 1, 2004, Macy Co. issued $200,000 of five-year, 8 percent bonds at 96. Interest is payable annually on December 31. The discount is amortized using the straight-line method.

Required

Prepare the journal entries to record the bond transactions for 2004 and 2005. Include any required year-end adjusting entries.

L.O. 10 EXERCISE 10–16 *Recording Bonds Issued at a Premium: Annual Interest (Appendix)*

On January 1, 2004, Bay Company issued $200,000 of five-year, 8 percent bonds at 102. Interest is payable annually on December 31. The premium is amortized using the straight-line method.

Required

Prepare the journal entries to record the bond transactions for 2004 and 2005. Include any required year-end adjusting entries.

L.O. 6, 7 EXERCISE 10–17 *Two Complete Accounting Cycles: Bonds Issued at Face Value with Annual Interest*

Goode Company issued $500,000 of 20-year, 8 percent bonds on January 1, 2004. The bonds were issued at face value. Interest is payable in cash on December 31 of each year. Goode immediately invested the proceeds from the bond issue in land. The land was leased for an annual $60,000 of cash revenue, which was collected on December 31 of each year, beginning December 31, 2004.

Required

a. Prepare the journal entries for these events, and post them to T-accounts for 2004 and 2005.
b. Prepare the income statement, balance sheet, and cash flow statement for 2004 and 2005.

L.O. 6, 7 EXERCISE 10–18 *Recording Callable Bonds*

Boark Co. issued $400,000 of 10 percent, 10-year, callable bonds on January 1, 2004, for their face value. The call premium was 2 percent (bonds are callable at 102). Interest was payable annually on December 31. The bonds were called on December 31, 2007.

Required

Prepare the journal entries to record the bond issue on January 1, 2004, and the bond redemption on December 31, 2007. Assume that all entries to accrue and pay interest were recorded correctly.

L.O. 8 EXERCISE 10–19 *Determining the After-Tax Cost of Debt*

The following 2004 information is available for three companies:

	Ames Co.	Cox Co.	Douglas Co.
Face value of bonds payable	$200,000	$500,000	$800,000
Interest rate	8%	7%	6%
Income tax rate	35%	20%	25%

Required

a. Determine the annual before-tax interest cost for each company *in dollars*.
b. Determine the annual after-tax interest cost for each company *in dollars*.
c. Determine the annual after-tax interest cost for each company as *a percentage* of the face value of the bonds.

L.O. 9 EXERCISE 10–20 *Future Value and Present Value (Appendix)*

Required

Using Tables I, II, III, or IV in the appendix, calculate the following:

a. The future value of $25,000 invested at 5 percent for 10 years.
b. The future value of eight annual payments of $1,500 at 8 percent interest.
c. The amount that must be deposited today (present value) at 6 percent to accumulate $100,000 in five years.
d. The annual payment on a 10-year, 7 percent, $80,000 note payable.

L.O. 9 EXERCISE 10–21 *Computing the Payment Amount (Appendix)*

Betty Carnes is a business major at university. She will be graduating this year and is planning to start a consulting business. She will need to purchase computer equipment that costs $25,000. She can borrow the money from the local bank but will have to make annual payments of principal and interest.

Required

a. Compute the annual payment Betty will be required to make on a $25,000, four-year, 8 percent loan.
b. If Betty can afford to make annual payments of only $6,000, how much can she borrow?

EXERCISE 10–22 *Saving for a Future Value (Appendix)*

L.O. 9

Billy Bob and Betty Sue were recently married and want to start saving for their dream home. They expect the house they want will cost approximately $225,000. They hope to be able to purchase the house for cash in 10 years.

Required

a. How much will Billy Bob and Betty Sue have to invest each year to purchase their dream home at the end of 10 years? Assume an interest rate of 8 percent.
b. Billy Bob's parents want to give the couple a substantial wedding gift for the purchase of their future home. How much must Billy Bob's parents give them now if they are to have the desired amount of $225,000 in 10 years? Assume an interest rate of 8 percent?

EXERCISE 10–23 *Sale of Bonds at a Discount Using Present Value (Appendix)*

L.O. 9

Moss Corporation issued $50,000 of 8.0 percent, 10-year bonds on January 1, 2003, for a price that reflected a 7 percent market rate of interest. Interest is payable annually on December 31.

Required

a. What was the selling price of the bonds?
b. Prepare the journal entry to record issuing the bonds.
c. Prepare the journal entry for the first interest payment on December 31, 2003, using the effective interest rate method.

EXERCISE 10–24 *Comparing the Effective Interest Rate Method with the Straight-Line Method (Appendix)*

L.O. 11

Required

Write a short memo explaining why the effective interest rate method produces a different amount of interest expense from the straight-line method in any given year.

PROBLEMS—SERIES A

PROBLEM 10–1A *Effect of a Term Loan on Financial Statements*

L.O. 2

On January 1, 2007, Jones Co. borrowed cash from a local bank by issuing an $80,000 face value, three-year term note that had an 8 percent annual interest rate. The note is to be repaid by making annual payments of $31,043 that include both interest and principal on December 31. Jones invested the proceeds from the loan in land that generated lease revenues of $36,000 cash per year.

Required

a. Prepare an amortization schedule for the three-year period.
b. Prepare an income statement, balance sheet, and cash flow statement for each of the three years. (*Hint*: Record the transactions for each year in T-accounts before preparing the financial statements.)
c. Does cash outflow from operating activities remain constant or change each year? Explain.

PROBLEM 10–2A *Effect of a Line of Credit on Financial Statements*

L.O. 3

Powell Company has a line of credit with a local bank. Powell can borrow up to $150,000 at any time over the course of the 2008 calendar year. The following table shows the prime rate expressed as an annual percentage along with the amounts borrowed and repaid during 2008. Powell agreed to pay interest at an annual rate equal to 3 percent above the bank's prime rate. Funds are borrowed or repaid on the first day of each month. Interest is payable in cash on the last day of the month. The interest rate is applied to the outstanding monthly balance. For example, Powell pays 7 percent (4 percent + 3 percent) annual interest on $80,000 for the month of January.

Month	Amount Borrowed or (Repaid)	Prime Rate for the Month %
January	$80,000	4
February	50,000	4
March	(30,000)	5
April through October	No change	No change
November	(60,000)	5
December	(40,000)	4

Powell earned $18,000 of cash revenue during 2008.

Required

a. Prepare an income statement, balance sheet, and cash flow statement for 2008.
b. Write a memo discussing the advantages of arranging a line of credit to a business.

L.O. 10 PROBLEM 10–3A *Accounting for a Bond Premium over Multiple Accounting Cycles (Appendix)*

Maywood Company was started when it issued bonds with $150,000 face value on January 1, 2004. The bonds were issued for cash at 105. They had a 15-year term to maturity and a 10 percent annual interest rate. Interest was payable annually. Maywood immediately purchased land with the proceeds (cash received) from the bond issue. Maywood leased the land for $17,500 cash per year. On January 1, 2007, the company sold the land for $160,000 cash. Immediately after the sale, Maywood repurchased its bonds (repaid the bond liability) at 106. Assume that no other accounting events occurred in 2007.

Required

Prepare an income statement, statement of shareholders' equity, balance sheet and cash flow statement for each of the 2004, 2005, 2006, and 2007 accounting periods. Assume that the company closes its books on December 31 of each year. Prepare the statements using a vertical statements format. (*Hint*: Record each year's transactions in T-accounts prior to preparing the financial statements.)

L.O. 10 PROBLEM 10–4A *Recording and Reporting a Bond Discount over Two Cycles: Semiannual Interest (Appendix)*

During 2007 and 2008, Adams Co. completed the following transactions relating to its bond issue. The company's fiscal year ends on December 31.

2007

Mar. 1 Issued $50,000 of eight-year, 9 percent bonds for $48,000. Interest is payable on March 1 and September 1, beginning September 1, 2007.
Sept. 1 Paid the semiannual interest on the bonds.
Dec. 31 Recorded the accrued interest on the bonds.
31 Recorded the bond discount amortization using the straight-line method.
31 Closed the interest expense account.

2008

Mar. 1 Paid the semiannual interest on the bonds.
Sept. 1 Paid the semiannual interest on the bonds.
Dec. 31 Recorded the accrued interest on the bonds.
31 Recorded the bond discount amortization using the straight-line method.
31 Closed the interest expense account.

Required

a. When the bonds were issued, was the market rate of interest more or less than the stated rate of interest? If the bonds had sold at face value, what amount of cash would Adams Co. have received?
b. Prepare the general journal entries for these transactions.
c. Prepare the liabilities section of the balance sheet at December 31, 2007 and 2008.
d. Determine the amount of interest expense Adams would report on the income statements for 2007 and 2008.
e. Determine the amounts of interest Adams would pay to the bondholders in 2007 and 2008.

PROBLEM 10–5A *Effect of a Bond Premium on the Elements of Financial Statements (Appendix)* L.O. 10

Western Land Co. was formed when it acquired cash from the issue of common shares. The company then issued bonds at a premium on January 1, 2004. Interest is payable annually on December 31 of each year, beginning December 31, 2004. On January 2, 2004, Western Land Co. purchased a piece of land and leased it for an annual rental fee. The rent is received annually on December 31, beginning December 31, 2004. At the end of the eight-year period (December 31, 2011), the land was sold at a gain, and the bonds were paid off. A summary of the transactions for each year follows:

2004

1. Acquired cash from the issue of common shares.
2. Issued eight-year bonds.
3. Purchased land.
4. Received lease revenue.
5. Amortized bond premium at December 31.
6. Paid cash for interest expense at the stated rate on December 31.
7. Prepared the December 31 entry to close for Rent Revenue.
8. Prepared the December 31 entry to close Interest Expense.

2005–2010

9. Received lease revenue.
10. Amortized bond premium at December 31.
11. Paid cash for interest expense at the stated rate on December 31.
12. Prepared the December 31 entry to close Rent Revenue.
13. Prepared the December 31 entry to close Interest Expense.

2011

14. Sold land at a gain.
15. Retired bonds at face value.

Required

Identify each of these 15 transactions as asset source (AS), asset use (AU), asset exchange (AE), or claims exchange (CE). Explain how each event affects assets, liabilities, equity, net income, and cash flow by placing a + for increase, − for decrease, or NA for not affected under each category. In the Cash Flow column, indicate whether the item is an operating activity (OA), investing activity (IA), or financing activity (FA). The first event is recorded as an example.

Event No.	Type of Event	Assets	Liabilities	Common Shares	Retained Earnings	Net Income	Cash Flow
1	AS	+	NA	+	NA	NA	+ FA

PROBLEM 10–6A *Recording Transactions for Callable Bonds* L.O. 6, 7

Simpson Co. issued $100,000 of 10-year, 10 percent, callable bonds on January 1, 2005, with interest payable annually on December 31. The bonds were issued at their face amount. The bonds are callable at 101 1/2. The fiscal year of the corporation is the calendar year.

Required

a. Show the effect of the following events on the financial statements by recording the appropriate amounts in a horizontal statements model like the following one. In the Cash Flow Statement column, indicate whether the item is an operating activity (OA), investing activity (IA), or financing activity (FA). Use NA if an element was not affected by the event.
   (1) Issued the bonds on January 1, 2005.
   (2) Paid interest due to bondholders on December 31, 2005.
   (3) On January 1, 2013, Simpson Co. called the bonds. Assume that all interim entries were correctly recorded.

Event No.	Assets = Liabilities + Equity	Rev. − Exp. = Net Inc.	Cash Flow Statement
1			

b. Prepare journal entries for the three events listed in Requirement *a*.

L.O. 8 PROBLEM 10–7A *Effect of Debt Transactions on Financial Statements*

Required

Show the effect of each of the following independent accounting events on the financial statements using a horizontal statements model like the following one. Use + for increase, − for decrease, and NA for not affected. The first event is recorded as an example.

Event No.	Assets	=	Liabilities	+	Equity	Rev.	−	Exp.	=	Net Inc.	Cash Flow Statement
1	+		+		NA	NA	−	NA	=	NA	+ FA

a. Borrowed funds using a line of credit.
b. Made an interest payment for funds that had been borrowed against a line of credit.
c. Made a cash payment on a note payable, including interest.
d. Issued a bond at face value.
e. Made an interest payment on a bond that had been issued at face value.
f. Issued a bond at a discount.
g. Made an interest payment on a bond that had been issued at a discount.
h. Amortized bond discount.
i. Issued a bond at a premium.
j. Made an interest payment on a bond that had been issued at a premium.
k. Amortized bond premium.

L.O. 6, 9 PROBLEM 10–8A *Sale of Bonds at a Premium and Amortization Using the Effective Interest Rate Method (Appendix)*

On January 1, 2005, Knight Corp. sold $200,000 of its own 8 percent, 10-year bonds. Interest is payable annually on December 31. The bonds were sold to yield an effective interest rate of 7 percent. Knight Corp. uses the effective interest rate method.

Required

a. Using the data in the appendix, calculate the selling price of the bonds.
b. Prepare the journal entry for the issuance of the bonds.
c. Prepare the journal entry for the amortization of the bond premium and the payment of the interest on December 31, 2007.
d. Calculate the amount of interest expense for 2008.

PROBLEMS—SERIES B

L.O. 2 PROBLEM 10–1B *Effect of a Long-Term Note Payable on Financial Statements*

On January 1, 2005, Mixon Co. borrowed cash from a local bank by issuing a $100,000 face value, four-year term note that had a 10 percent annual interest rate. The note is to be repaid by making annual cash payments of $31,547 that include both interest and principal on December 31 of each year. Mixon used the proceeds from the loan to purchase land that generated rental revenues of $40,000 cash per year.

Required

a. Prepare an amortization schedule for the four-year period.
b. Prepare an income statement, balance sheet, and cash flow statement for each of the four years. (*Hint*: Record the transactions for each year in T-accounts before preparing the financial statements.)
c. Given that revenue is the same for each period, explain why net income increases each year.

L.O. 3 PROBLEM 10–2B *Effect of a Line of Credit on Financial Statements*

Libby Company has a line of credit with a local bank. Libby can borrow up to $200,000 at any time over the course of the 2006 calendar year. The following table shows the prime rate expressed as an annual percentage along with the amounts borrowed and repaid during 2006. Libby agreed to pay interest at an annual rate equal to 2 percent above the bank's prime rate. Funds are borrowed or repaid on the first day of each month. Interest is payable in cash on the last day of the month. The interest rate is applied to the outstanding monthly balance. For example, Libby pays 7 percent (5 percent + 2 percent) annual interest on $100,000 for the month of January.

Month	Amount Borrowed or (Repaid)	Prime Rate for the Month %
January	$100,000	5
February	50,000	6
March	(40,000)	7
April through October	No change	No change
November	(80,000)	6
December	(20,000)	5

Libby earned $30,000 of cash revenue during 2006.

Required

a. Prepare an income statement, balance sheet, and cash flow statement for 2006. (*Note*: Round computations to the nearest dollar.)
b. Write a memo to explain how the business was able to generate retained earnings when the owner contributed no assets to the business.

PROBLEM 10–3B *Accounting for a Bond Discount over Multiple Accounting Cycles (Appendix)* L.O. 10

Box Company was started when it issued bonds with a $400,000 face value on January 1, 2005. The bonds were issued for cash at 96. They had a 20-year term to maturity and an 8 percent annual interest rate. Interest was payable on December 31 of each year. Box Company immediately purchased land with the proceeds (cash received) from the bond issue. Box leased the land for $50,000 cash per year. On January 1, 2008, the company sold the land for $400,000 cash. Immediately after the sale of the land, Box redeemed the bonds at 98. Assume that no other accounting events occurred during 2008.

Required

Prepare an income statement, statement of shareholders' equity, balance sheet, and cash flow statement for the 2005, 2006, 2007, and 2008 accounting periods. Assume that the company closes its books on December 31 of each year. Prepare the statements using a vertical statements format. (*Hint*: Record each year's transactions in T-accounts prior to preparing the financial statements.)

PROBLEM 10–4B *Recording and Reporting Bond Discount over Two Cycles (Appendix)* L.O. 5, 10

During 2006 and 2007, Joy Corp. completed the following transactions relating to its bond issue. The corporation's fiscal year is the calendar year.

2006

Jan. 1 Issued $100,000 of 10-year, 10 percent bonds for $96,000. Interest is payable annually on December 31.
Dec. 31 Paid the interest on the bonds.
31 Recorded the bond discount amortization using the straight-line method.
31 Closed the interest expense account.

2007

Dec. 31 Paid the interest on the bonds.
31 Recorded the bond discount amortization using the straight-line method.
31 Closed the interest expense account.

Required

a. When the bonds were issued, was the market rate of interest more or less than the stated rate of interest? If Joy had sold the bonds at their face amount, what amount of cash would Joy have received?
b. Prepare the general journal entries for these transactions.
c. Prepare the liabilities section of the balance sheet at December 31, 2006 and 2007.
d. Determine the amount of interest expense that will be reported on the income statements for 2006 and 2007.
e. Determine the amounts of interest that will be paid in cash to the bondholder in 2006 and 2007.

L.O. 10 **PROBLEM 10–5B** ***Effect of a Bond Discount on the Elements of Financial Statements (Appendix)***

Stafford Co. was formed when it acquired cash from the issue of common shares. The company then issued bonds at a discount on January 1, 2008. Interest is payable on December 31 with the first payment made December 31, 2008. On January 2, 2008, Stafford Co. purchased a piece of land that produced rent revenue annually. The rent is collected on December 31 of each year, beginning December 31, 2008. At the end of the six-year period (January 1, 2014), the land was sold at a gain, and the bonds were paid off at face value. A summary of the transactions for each year follows:

2008
1. Acquired cash from the issue of common shares.
2. Issued six-year bonds.
3. Purchased land.
4. Received lease revenue.
5. Amortized bond discount at December 31.
6. Paid cash for interest expense at the stated rate on December 31.
7. Prepared December 31 entry to close Rent Revenue.
8. Prepared December 31 entry to close Interest Expense.

2009–2013

9. Received lease revenue.
10. Amortized bond discount at December 31.
11. Paid cash for interest expense at the stated rate on December 31.
12. Prepared December 31 entry to close Rent Revenue.
13. Prepared December 31 entry to close Interest Expense.

2014

14. Sold the land at a gain.
15. Retired the bonds at face value.

Required

Identify each of these 15 transactions as asset source (AS), asset use (AU), asset exchange (AE), or claims exchange (CE). Explain how each event affects assets, liabilities, equity, net income, and cash flow by placing a + for increase, − for decrease, or NA for not affected under each of the categories. In the Cash Flow column, indicate whether the item is an operating activity (OA), investing activity (IA), or financing activity (FA). The first event is recorded as an example.

Event No.	Type of Event	Assets	Liabilities	Common Shares	Retained Earnings	Net Income	Cash Flow
1	AS	+	NA	+	NA	NA	+ FA

L.O. 6, 7 **PROBLEM 10–6B** ***Recording Transactions for Callable Bonds***

IHL Corp. issued $300,000 of 20-year, 10 percent, callable bonds on January 1, 2004, with interest payable annually on December 31. The bonds were issued at their face amount. The bonds are callable at 105. The fiscal year of the corporation ends December 31.

Required

a. Show the effect of the following events on the financial statements by recording the appropriate amounts in a horizontal statements model like the following one. In the Cash Flow Statement column, indicate whether the item is an operating activity (OA), investing activity (IA), or financing activity (FA). Use NA if an element was not affected by the event.
   (1) Issued the bonds on January 1, 2004.
   (2) Paid interest due to bondholders on December 31, 2004.
   (3) On January 1, 2009, IHL Corp. called the bonds. Assume that all interim entries were correctly recorded.

Event No.	Assets	=	Liabilities	+	Equity	Rev.	−	Exp.	=	Net Inc.	Cash Flow Statement
1											

b. Prepare journal entries for the three events listed in Requirement *a*.

PROBLEM 10–7B *Effect of Debt Transactions on Financial Statements* L.O. 6

The three typical accounting events associated with borrowing money through a bond issue are:
1. Exchanging the bonds for cash on the day of issue.
2. Making cash payments for interest expense and recording amortization when applicable.
3. Repaying the principal at maturity.

Required
a. Assuming the bonds are issued at face value, show the effect of each of the three events on the financial statements, using a horizontal statements model like the following one. Use + for increase, − for decrease, and NA for not affected.

Event No.	Assets	=	Liabilities	+	Equity	Rev.	−	Exp.	=	Net Inc.	Cash Flow Statement
1											

b. Repeat the requirements in Requirement *a*, but assume instead that the bonds are issued at a discount.
c. Repeat the requirements in Requirement *a*, but assume instead that the bonds are issued at a premium.

PROBLEM 10–8B *Sale of Bonds at a Discount and Amortization Using the Effective Interest Method (Appendix)* L.O. 9, 11

On January 1, 2004, Pond Corp. sold $500,000 of its own 8 percent, 10-year bonds. Interest is payable annually on December 31. The bonds were sold to yield an effective interest rate of 9 percent. Pond uses the effective interest rate method.

Required
a. Using the information in the appendix, calculate the selling price of the bonds.
b. Prepare the journal entry for the issuance of the bonds.
c. Prepare the journal entry for the amortization of the bond discount and the payment of the interest at December 31, 2004.
d. Calculate the amount of interest expense for 2005.

ANALYZE, THINK, COMMUNICATE

BUSINESS APPLICATIONS CASE *Bombardier's Annual Report* ATC 10–1

Required
Using the Bombardier financial statements in Appendix B, answer the following questions:
a. What was the primary type of long-term debt that Bombardier had in 2002?
b. What was the maximum length to maturity of Bombardier's long-term debt?
c. What was the maximum amount available to Bombardier through its line of credit?

GROUP ASSIGNMENT *Missing Information (Appendix)* ATC 10–2

The following three companies issued the following bonds:
1. Lot, Inc., issued $100,000 of 8 percent, five-year bonds at 102 1/4 on January 1, 2006. Interest is payable annually on December 31.
2. Max, Inc., issued $100,000 of 8 percent, five-year bonds at 98 on January 1, 2006. Interest is payable annually on December 31.
3. Par, Inc., issued $100,000 of 8 percent, five-year bonds at 104 on January 1, 2006. Interest is payable annually on December 31.

Required

a. Organize the class into three sections and divide each section into groups of three to five students. Assign each of the sections one of the companies.

Group Tasks

(1) Compute the following amounts for your company:
  (a) Cash proceeds from the bond issue.
  (b) Interest expense for 2006.
  (c) Interest paid in 2006.

(2) Prepare the liabilities section of the balance sheet as of December 31, 2006.

Class Discussion

b. Have a representative of each section put the liabilities section for its company on the board.
c. Is the amount of interest expense different for the three companies? Why or why not?
d. Is the amount of interest paid different for each of the companies? Why or why not?
e. Is the amount of total liabilities different for each of the companies? Why or why not?

ATC 10–3 REAL-WORLD CASE *Using Accounting Numbers to Assess Creditworthiness*

Dominion Bond Rating Service (DBRS) evaluates the creditworthiness of various companies. The DBRS grading scheme works as follows: AAA is the highest rating, followed by AA, A, BBB, and so on.

The following are selected financial data for four companies whose overall, long-term creditworthiness was rated by DBRS. The date the company was rated by DBRS is shown in parentheses. The companies, listed alphabetically, are as follows: Dupont Canada Inc., GE Canada Enterprises Company, Laurentian Bank of Canada, and Molson Canada.

Dollar amounts are in millions.

	Net Income	Cash Flow from Operating Activities	Current Ratio	Debt to Assets Ratio	Times Interest Earned	Return on Assets Ratio
Dupont (1/16/02)						
2000	$ 270	$ 257	3.3	0.3	NA	13%
1999	253	253	3.1	0.3	NA	13
GE Canada (9/7/01)						
2000	12,735	22,690	1.9	0.9	2.6	3
1999	10,717	24,593	1.7	0.9	2.6	3
Laurentian Bank (7/5/01)						
2001	91	41	0.2	1.0	1.2	5
2000	82	39	0.1	1.0	1.2	6
Molson (4/16/01)						
2001	134	228	0.8	0.8	5.1	4
2000	(44)	156	0.7	0.7	1.3	(1)

Each company received a different credit rating from DBRS. The grades awarded, in descending order, were AAA, AA, A, and BBB.

Required

Determine which grade was assigned to each company. Explain the reason for your decisions.

ATC 10–4 BUSINESS APPLICATIONS CASE *Using Ratios to Make Comparisons*

The following accounting information pertains to Quality Landscaping Co. and Super Lawn Care, Inc., at the end of 2005.

	Quality Landscaping Co.	Super Lawn Care, Inc.
Current assets	$ 20,000	$ 20,000
Total assets	350,000	350,000
Current liabilities	35,000	25,000
Total liabilities	300,000	220,000
Shareholders' equity	50,000	130,000
Interest expense	27,500	20,000
Income tax expense	31,000	34,000
Net income	46,500	51,000

Required

a. Compute the following ratios for each company: debt to assets, current, and times interest earned (EBIT must be computed). Identify the company with the greater financial risk.

b. For each company, compute the return on equity and return on assets ratios. Use EBIT instead of net income to compute the return on assets ratio. Identify the company that is managing its assets more effectively. Identify the company that is producing the higher return from the shareholders' perspective. Explain how one company was able to produce a higher return on equity than the other.

BUSINESS APPLICATIONS CASE *Determining the Effects of Financing Alternatives on Ratios* ATC 10–5

Tipstaff Industries has the following account balances:

Current Assets	$100,000	Current Liabilities	$ 65,000
Noncurrent Assets	225,000	Noncurrent Liabilities	160,000
		Shareholders' Equity	100,000

The company wishes to raise $100,000 in cash and is considering two financing options. Either it can sell $100,000 of bonds payable, or it can issue additional common shares for $100,000. To help in the decision process, Tipstaff's management wants to determine the effects of each alternative on its current ratio and debt to assets ratio.

Required

a. Help Tipstaff's management by completing the following chart:

Ratio	Currently	If Bonds Are Issued	If Shares Are Issued
Current ratio			
Debt to assets ratio			

b. Assume that after the funds are invested, EBIT amounts to $50,000. Also assume that Tipstaff pays $10,000 in dividends or $10,000 in interest, depending on which source of financing is used. Based on a 30 percent tax rate, determine the amount of the increase in retained earnings under each financing option.

WRITING ASSIGNMENT *Debt versus Equity Financing* ATC 10–6

Mack Company plans to invest $50,000 in land that will produce annual rent revenue equal to 15 percent of the investment starting on January 1, 2008. The revenue will be collected in cash at the end of each year, starting December 31, 2008. Mack can obtain the cash necessary to purchase the land from two sources. Funds can be obtained by issuing $50,000 of 10 percent, five-year bonds at their face amount. Interest due on the bonds is payable on December 31 of each year with the first payment due on December 31, 2008. Alternatively, the $50,000 needed to invest in land can be obtained from equity financing. In this case, the shareholders will be paid a $5,000 annual dividend. Mack Company is in a 30 percent income tax bracket.

Required

a. Compute the amount of net income for 2008 and 2009 under the two alternative financing proposals.
b. Write a short memorandum explaining why one financing alternative provides more net income but less cash flow than the other.

ATC 10–7 ETHICAL DILEMMA *I Don't Want to Pay Taxes*

Dana Harbert recently started a very successful small business. Indeed, the business had grown so rapidly that she was no longer able to finance its operations by investing her own resources in the business. She needed additional capital but had no more of her own money to put into the business. A friend, Gene Watson, was willing to invest $100,000 in the business. Harbert estimated that with Watson's investment, the company would be able to increase revenue by $40,000. Furthermore, she believed that operating expenses would increase by only 10 percent. Harbert and Watson agree that Watson's investment should entitle him to receive a cash dividend equal to 20 percent of net income. A set of forecasted statements with and without Watson's investment is presented here. (Assume that all transactions involving revenue, expense, and dividends are cash transactions.)

Financial Statements	Forecast 1 Without Watson's Investment	Forecast 2 With Watson's Investment
Income Statements		
Revenue	$120,000	$160,000
Operating Expenses	(70,000)	(77,000)
Income before Interest and Taxes	50,000	83,000
Income Tax Expense (effective tax rate is 30%)	(15,000)	(24,900)
Net Income	$ 35,000	$ 58,100
Statement of Shareholders' Equity		
Beginning Retained Earnings	$ 15,000	$ 15,000
Plus: Net Income	35,000	58,100
Less: Dividend to Watson (20% of $58,100)	0	(11,620)
Ending Retained Earnings	$ 50,000	$ 61,480
Balance Sheets		
Assets (computations explained in following paragraph)	$400,000	$511,480
Liabilities	$ 0	$ 0
Shareholders' Equity		
Common Shares	350,000	450,000
Retained Earnings	50,000	61,480
Total Liabilities and Shareholders' Equity	$400,000	$511,480

The balance for assets in forecast 1 is computed as the beginning balance of $365,000 plus net income of $35,000. The balance for assets in forecast 2 is computed as the beginning balance of $365,000, plus the $100,000 cash investment, plus net income of $58,100, less the $11,620 distribution. Alternatively, total assets can be computed by determining the amount of total claims (total assets = total claims).

Harbert tells Watson that there would be a $3,486 tax advantage associated with debt financing. She says that if Watson is willing to become a creditor instead of an owner, she could pay him an additional $697.20 (20 percent of the tax advantage). Watson tells Harbert that he has no interest in participating in the management of the business, but Watson wants an ownership interest to guarantee that he will always receive 20 percent of the profits of the business. Harbert suggests that they execute a formal agreement in which Watson is paid 11.62 percent interest on his $100,000 loan to the business. This agreement will be used for income tax reporting. In addition, Harbert says that she is willing to establish a private agreement to write Watson a personal cheque for any additional amount necessary to make Watson's total return equal to 20 percent of all profits plus a $697.20 bonus for his part of the tax advantage. She tells Watson, "It's just like ownership. The only difference is that we call it debt for the CCRA. If they want to have some silly rule that says if you call it debt, you get a tax break, then we are foolish if we don't call it debt. I will call it anything they want, just as long as I don't have to pay taxes on it."

Required

a. Construct a third set of forecasted financial statements (forecast 3) at 11.62 percent annual interest, assuming that Watson is treated as creditor (he loans the business $100,000).
b. Verify the tax advantage of debt financing by comparing the balances of the Retained Earnings account in forecast 2 and forecast 3.
c. If you were Watson, would you permit Harbert to classify the equity transaction as debt to provide a higher return to the business and to you?
d. Comment on the ethical implications of misnaming a financing activity for the sole purpose of reducing income taxes.

SEDAR DATABASE *Analyzing Long-Term Debt at Air Canada*

ATC 10–8

Many companies have a form of debt called *capital leases*. A capital lease is created when a company agrees to rent an asset, such as equipment or a building, for such a long time that GAAP treats this lease as if the asset were purchased by using borrowed funds. Thus, a capital lease creates a liability for the company that acquired the leased asset because the company has promised to make payments to another company for several years in the future. If a company has any capital leases, it must disclose them in the notes to the financial statements and sometimes disclose them on a separate line in the liabilities section of the balance sheet.

Required

Using the most current annual report available on SEDAR, answer the following questions about Air Canada. Instructions for using SEDAR are in Appendix A.

a. What was Air Canada's debt to assets ratio?
b. How much interest expense did Air Canada incur?
c. What amount of liabilities did Air Canada have as a result of capital leases?
d. What percentage of Air Canada's long-term liabilities was the result of capital leases?

SPREADSHEET ASSIGNMENT *Using Excel*

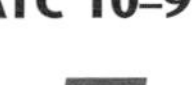

ATC 10–9

On January 1, 2005, Bainbridge Company borrowed $100,000 cash from a bank by issuing a 10-year, 9 percent note. The principal and interest are to be paid by making annual payments in the amount of $15,582. Payments are to be made December 31 of each year beginning December 31, 2005.

Required

a. Set up the spreadsheet shown on page 456. Notice that Excel can be set up to calculate the loan payment. If you're unfamiliar with this, see the following Spreadsheet Tips section. The Beginning Principal Balance (B12) and Cash Payment (C12) can be referenced from the Loan Information section. The interest rate used to calculate Interest Expense (D12) can also be referenced from the Loan Information section.
b. Complete the spreadsheet for the 10 periods.
c. In Row 23, calculate totals for cash payments, interest expense, and applied to principal.
d. Consider how the amounts would differ if Bainbridge were to borrow the $100,000 at different interest rates and time periods. The results of the original data (option 1) have been entered in the following schedule. In the spreadsheet, delete 9 percent and 10 from cells B4 and B5. Enter the data for the second option (8 percent and 10 years) in cells B4 and B5. Enter in the payment and total interest in the schedule for the second option. Continue the same process for options 3 through 9 by deleting the prior rate and number of periods in the spreadsheet and entering in the next option's data. The number of years scheduled (rows 12 through 21) will have to be shortened for the 7-year options and lengthened for the 13-year options.

Microsoft Excel - dch10-1.xls

File Edit View Insert Format Tools Data Window Help

B6 = =PMT(B4,B5,B3)

	A	B	C	D	E	F
1						
2	Loan Information					
3	Principal	100,000				
4	Interest Rate	9%				
5	Periods	10				
6	Payments	(15,582)				
7						
8			December 31			
9		Beginning			Applied	Ending
10		Principal	Cash	Interest	To	Principal
11	Year	Balance	Payment	Expense	Principal	Balance
12	2005	100,000	15,582	9,000	6,582	93,418
13	2006					
14	2007					
15	2008					
16	2009					
17	2010					
18	2011					
19	2012					
20	2013					
21	2014					
22						
23	Totals					
24						
25						

	Option 1	2	3	4	5	6	7	8	9
Rate	9%	8%	10%	9%	8%	10%	9%	8%	10%
Years	10	10	10	7	7	7	13	13	13
Payment	15,582								
Total interest	55,820								

Spreadsheet Tips

1. Excel will calculate an installment loan payment. The interest rate (%), number of periods (nper), and amount borrowed or otherwise known as present value (PV) must be entered in the payment formula. The formula for the payment is =PMT(rate,nper,pv). The rate, number of periods, and amount borrowed (present value) may be entered as actual amounts or referenced to other cells. In the preceding spreadsheet, the payment formula can be either =PMT(9%,10,100000) or =PMT(B4,B5,B3). In our case, the latter is preferred so that variables can be altered in the spreadsheet without also having to rewrite the payment formula. Notice that the payment is a negative number.
2. Using positive numbers is preferred in the amortization schedule. The loan payment (cell B6) in the loan information section shows up as a negative number. Any reference to it in the amortization schedule should be preceded by a minus sign to convert it to a positive number. For example, the formula in cell C12 for the cash payment is =−B6.
3. Recall that to copy a fixed number, a $ sign must be positioned before the column letter and row number. The complete formula then for cell C12 is =−$B$6.

ATC 10–10 SPREADSHEET ANALYSIS *Mastering Excel (Appendix)*

Wise Company was started on January 1, 2004, when it issued 20-year, 10 percent, $200,000 face value bonds at a price of 90. Interest is payable annually at December 31 of each year. Wise immediately purchased land with the proceeds (cash received) from the bond issue. Wise leased the land for $27,000 cash per year. The lease revenue payments are due every December 31.

Required

Set up the following horizontal statements model on a blank spreadsheet. The CFS Activity column is for the classifications operating, financing, or investing.

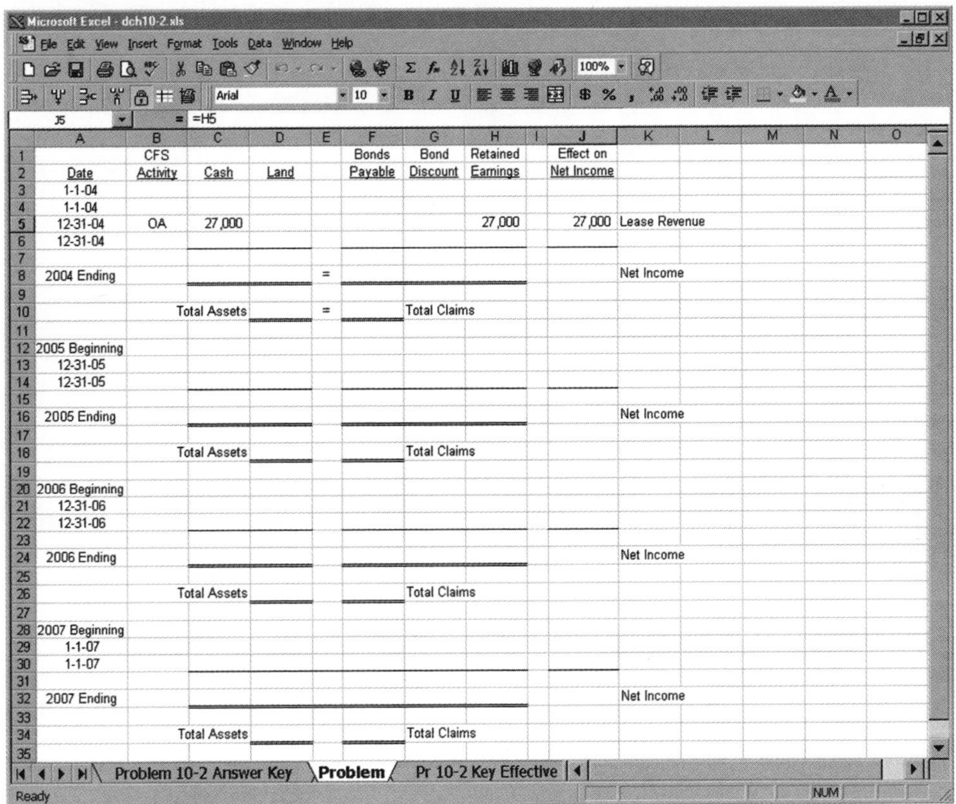

Microsoft Excel - dch10-2.xls

J5 = =H5

Date	CFS Activity	Cash	Land		Bonds Payable	Bond Discount	Retained Earnings	Effect on Net Income	
1-1-04									
1-1-04									
12-31-04	OA	27,000					27,000	27,000	Lease Revenue
12-31-04									
2004 Ending				=					Net Income
	Total Assets			=		Total Claims			
2005 Beginning									
12-31-05									
12-31-05									
2005 Ending									Net Income
	Total Assets					Total Claims			
2006 Beginning									
12-31-06									
12-31-06									
2006 Ending									Net Income
	Total Assets					Total Claims			
2007 Beginning									
1-1-07									
1-1-07									
2007 Ending									Net Income
	Total Assets					Total Claims			

Problem 10-2 Answer Key | Problem | Pr 10-2 Key Effective

a. Enter the effects of the 2004 transactions. Assume that both the interest and lease payments occurred on December 31. Notice that the entry for the lease has already been entered as an example. Calculate the ending balances.
b. Enter the effects of the 2005 transactions. Assume that both the interest and lease payments occurred on December 31. Calculate the ending balances.
c. Enter the effects of the 2006 transactions. Assume that both the interest and lease payments occurred on December 31. Calculate the ending balances.
d. On January 1, 2007, Wise Company sold the land for $190,000 cash. Immediately after the sale of the land, Wise repurchased its bond at a price of 93. Assume that no other accounting events occurred during 2007. Enter in the effects of the 2007 balances. Calculate the ending balances.

Chapter 11

Accounting for Equity Transactions

Learning Objectives

After completing this chapter, you should be able to:

1. Identify the different types of business organizations by analyzing financial statements.

2. Explain the characteristics of major types of shares issued by corporations.

3. Describe the accounting treatment for different types of shares issued by corporations.

4. Explain the effects of a declaration and payment of cash dividends on a company's financial statements.

5. Explain the effects of stock dividends and stock splits on a company's financial statements.

6. Explain how accounting information can be useful in making investment decisions.

the *curious* accountant

Imagine that a rich uncle wanted to reward you for outstanding performance in your first accounting course, so he gave you $15,000 to invest in the shares of one company. You narrowed your choice to two companies. After reviewing their recent annual reports, you developed the following information:

Mystery Company A: This company has been in existence for about four years and has never made a profit; in fact, it has net losses totalling more than $36 million. Each year of its existence, its net loss has been much larger than the loss of the year before. The shares are selling for about $100 per share, so you can buy 150 shares. A friend has told you it was a "sure winner," especially at its current price.

Mystery Company B: This company has been in existence more than 100 years and has made a profit most years. In the most recent three years, its operating income totalled over $22 *billion*, and it paid dividends of over $9 *billion*. This company's shares are trading for about $75 per share, so you can buy 200 shares of it. Your friend has said it is a company "your grandfather should own."

The descriptions apply to real-world companies, the names of which are revealed later. Based on the information provided, which company's shares would you buy? See page 463 for more information.

Appearance of Capital Structure in Financial Statements

LO1

Identify the different types of business organizations by analyzing financial statements.

So far, we have used generic terms to reflect capital structure in financial statements. The term *equity* has been used to describe the total ownership interest in the business. This interest has been divided into two categories: (1) *contributed capital*, which represents owner investments, and (2) *retained earnings*, which measures the capital generated through operating activities. Although these two elements are present in all forms of business organization, they are shown in significantly different formats, depending on the type of business for which a set of financial reports is being prepared.

Presentation of Equity in Proprietorships

On the balance sheets of proprietorships, common shares and retained earnings are combined in a single Capital account. To illustrate, assume that Worthington Sole Proprietorship was started on January 1, 2007, when it acquired a $5,000 capital contribution from its owner, Phil Worthington. During the first year of operation, the company generated $4,000 of cash revenues, incurred $2,500 of cash expenses, and distributed $1,000 cash to the owner. Exhibit 11–1 shows the December 31, 2007, financial statements for Worthington's company. Looking at the *capital statement* (sometimes called a *statement of owner's equity*), note that in accounting for proprietorships, distributions are called **withdrawals**. The other unique feature you should verify is the combination of the $5,000 capital acquisition and the retained earnings of $500 ($1,500 net income − $1,000 withdrawal) into a single equity account called *Capital*. More specifically, note the $5,500 ($5,000 + $500) balances in the capital account on both the statement of owner's equity and the balance sheet.

Presentation of Equity in Partnerships

The format for presenting partnership equity in financial statements is similar to that used for proprietorships. For example, the Capital account includes both acquired capital and retained earnings. The only significant difference is that a separate capital account is used to reflect the amount of ownership interest of each partner in the business.

To illustrate, assume that Sara Slater and Jill Johnson decided to form a partnership. The partnership acquired $2,000 of capital from Slater and $4,000 from Johnson. The partnership agreement called for an annual distribution equal to 10 percent of acquired capital. The remaining amount of earnings was retained in the business and added to each partner's capital account on an equal basis. The partnership was formed on January 1, 2007. During 2007, the company earned $5,000 of cash revenue and incurred $3,000 of cash expenses, resulting in net income of $2,000 ($5,000 − $3,000). In accordance with the partnership agreement, Slater received a $200 ($2,000 × 0.10) cash withdrawal, while Johnson's withdrawal was $400 ($4,000 × 0.10). The remaining $1,400 of income was retained in the business and divided equally, thereby resulting in a $700 addition to each partner's capital account.

Exhibit 11–1

WORTHINGTON SOLE PROPRIETORSHIP
Financial Statements
December 31, 2007

Income Statement		Statement of Owner's Equity		Balance Sheet	
Revenue	$4,000	Worthington, Capital, Jan. 1	$ 0	Assets	
Expenses	2,500	Plus: Investment by Owner	5,000	Cash	$5,500
Net Income	$1,500	Plus: Net Income	1,500	Owners's Equity	
		Less: Withdrawal by Owner	(1,000)	Worthington, Capital	$5,500
		Worthington, Capital, Dec. 31	5,500		

Exhibit 11–2

SLATER AND JOHNSON PARTNERSHIP
Financial Statements
December 31, 2007

Income Statement		Statement of Partners' Equity		Balance Sheet	
Revenue	$5,000	Beginning Capital Balance	$ 0	Assets	
Expenses	3,000	Plus: Investment by Partners	6,000	Cash	$7,400
Net Income	$2,000	Plus: Net Income	2,000	Partners' Equity	
		Less: Withdrawals by Partners	(600)	Slater, Capital	$2,700
		Ending Capital Balance	$ 7,400	Johnson, Capital	4,700
				Total Partners' Equity	$7,400

Exhibit 11–2 shows the financial statements for the Slater and Johnson partnership. Again, note that the word *withdrawal* is used to label the distributions made to the partners. Also note that the balance sheet contains a *separate capital account* for each partner. Each capital account includes the amount of the partner's invested capital plus her proportionate share of income less amounts withdrawn for personal use.

Presentation of Equity in Corporations

Capital structures of corporations are considerably more complicated than proprietorships and partnerships. The rest of this chapter is devoted to some of the more prevalent features of the corporate structure.

Weiss Company was started on January 1, 2004, when it acquired $50,000 cash from its owner. During 2004 the company earned $72,000 of net income. Explain how the equity section of Weiss's December 31, 2004, balance sheet would differ if the company were a proprietorship rather than a corporation.

Answer *Proprietorship* records combine capital acquisitions from the owner and earnings from operating the business in a single capital account. In contrast, *corporation* records separate capital acquisitions from the owners and earnings from operating the business. If Weiss were a proprietorship, the equity section of the year-end balance sheet would report a single capital component of $122,000. If Weiss were a corporation, the equity section would report two separate equity components, most likely common shares of $50,000 and retained earnings of $72,000.

Characteristics of Capital Shares

LO2 Explain the characteristics of major types of shares issued by corporations.

A number of terms are associated with shares. Some terms are used to identify different values that are commonly assigned to shares; other terms pertain to the number of shares that a corporation has the authority to issue versus the number that it has actually issued. There are also terms that describe different classes of shares. These terms are used to distinguish the rights and privileges assigned to the different owners of the same corporation (not all shareholders are treated the same way). Knowledge of the meanings of these terms is essential to an understanding of corporations' accounting practices.

Par Value

Historically, the **par value** of a share has represented the maximum liability of the investor. The par value is multiplied by the number of shares issued; the resulting figure represents the minimum amount of assets that should be maintained as protection for creditors. This figure is known as the amount of **legal capital**. *Legal capital* as defined by par value has come to have very little relevance to investors or creditors. As a result, many jurisdictions, including the province of Ontario and the federal government, allow the issuance of no-par shares.

Stated Value

No-par shares may have a stated value. Like par value, the **stated value** is an amount that is arbitrarily assigned by the board of directors. It also has little relevance to investors and creditors. For accounting purposes, par-value and stated-value shares are treated exactly the same. When a share has no par or stated value, there are slight differences in treatment. These differences will be made clear later, when the procedures required for recognizing par values in financial statements are covered.

Other Valuation Terminology

The price that must be paid to purchase a share is called the **market value**. There is no relationship between market value and par value. The sales price of a share may be more or less than the par value. Another term often associated with shares is *book value*. The **book value per share** is determined by dividing the total shareholders' equity (assets − liabilities) by the number of shares issued. The book value is different from the market value because equity is measured mainly in historical dollars rather than in current values.

Authorized, Issued, and Outstanding Shares

Several terms are used to distinguish the number of shares available for issue from those that have been issued to shareholders. **Authorized shares** refer to the number of shares the corporation is approved to issue. When blocks of shares are sold to the public, they become **issued shares**. Often, for reasons we discuss later, a corporation may buy back some of its own shares. These are known as **treasury shares**, and although they remain issued, they are no longer outstanding. Thus, **outstanding shares** are defined as shares owned by outside parties, or total issued shares minus treasury shares. For example, assume that a company that is authorized to issue 150 shares issues 100 shares and then buys 20 treasury shares. There are 150 shares authorized, 100 shares issued, and 80 shares outstanding.

Classes of Shares

The corporate charter defines the number of shares authorized, the par value if any, and the classes of shares that a corporation can issue. Although there are many variations in the types of shares that may be sold, most issues can be classified as either *common* or *preferred*. If only one class of shares is issued, they are known as **common shares**. Common shareholders generally possess several rights, including these five: (1) the right to buy and sell shares, (2) the right to share in the distribution of profits, (3) the right to share in the distribution of corporate assets in the case of liquidation, (4) the right to vote on significant matters that affect the corporate charter, and (5) the right to participate in the

answers to the *curious* accountant

Mystery Company A is Webmethods, Inc. (as of July 2001). Webmethods provides infrastructure software and services to companies engaged in business-to-business commerce. The company was incorporated in 1996. On February 11, 2000, its shares were sold to the public in an *initial public offering (IPO)* at $35. The first day its shares traded on NASDAQ, it opened at $195; during that day, it sold for as high as $215 per share. Obviously, the people trading Webmethods' shares were not paying much attention to accounting data. Instead, they were focusing on what the company might become, and many were simply speculating based on the hype the company's IPO had generated. The stock market does not always behave rationally. By the end of February 2000, Webmethods' share price had hit $336, but by July 2001, it was down to around $15.

Mystery Company B is Phillip Morris Companies, Inc. (as of July 2001). Of course, only the future will tell which company will be the better investment.

selection of directors. Common shareholders are considered the true owners of a corporation. On one hand, they bear the ultimate risk of losing their investment if the company is forced to liquidate; on the other hand, they are the main beneficiaries when a corporation prospers.

Preferred Shares

Holders of **preferred shares** receive some form of preferential treatment relative to common shareholders. To receive special privileges in some areas, preferred shareholders often give up rights in other areas. Usually, preferred shareholders have no right to vote at shareholders' meetings, and the size of the distributions they are entitled to receive is often limited. Some of the common preferences assigned to preferred shareholders are as follows:

1. *Preference as to assets*. Often there is a liquidation value associated with preferred shares. In case of bankruptcy, the amount of liquidation value must be paid to the preferred shareholders before distributions can be made to common shareholders. However, the preferred shareholder claims still fall behind those of the creditors.
2. *Preference as to dividends.* Distributions to shareholders are commonly called **dividends**. Preferred shareholders are often guaranteed the right to receive dividends before common shareholders. The amount of the preferred dividend is normally stated on the share certificate. It may be stated in an absolute dollar value per share (such as $5 per share) or as a percentage of the par value. Most preferred shares have **cumulative dividends**, meaning that if a corporation cannot pay the preferred dividend in any year, the dividend is not lost but begins to accumulate. Cumulative dividends that have not been paid are called **dividends in arrears**. Once the firm can pay dividends, the arrearages must be paid first. Noncumulative preferred shares are not seen often because much of the attraction of purchasing preferred shares is lost if past dividends do not accumulate.

To illustrate the effects of preferred dividends, consider this situation. Dillion Incorporated has the following shares outstanding:

Preferred shares, 4%, $10 par	10,000 shares
Common shares, $10 par	20,000 shares

Assume that the preferred share dividend has not been paid for two years. If Dillion distributes $22,000 to the two classes, how much will each receive? The answer will vary according to whether the preferred shares are cumulative or not.

Allocation of Distribution for Cumulative Preferred Shares

	To Preferred	To Common	Total
Dividends in arrears	$ 8,000	$ 0	
Current year's dividends	4,000	10,000	
Total distribution	$12,000	$10,000	$22,000

Allocation of Distribution for Noncumulative Preferred Shares

	To Preferred	To Common	Total
Dividends in arrears	$ 0	$ 0	
Current year's dividends	4,000	18,000	
Total distribution	$ 4,000	$18,000	$22,000

The yearly dividend for preferred shares is $4,000, calculated as 0.04 × $10 par × 10,000 shares. If the preferred shares are cumulative, the $8,000 in arrears must be paid first. The $4,000 for the current year's dividend is paid next. The remaining $10,000 goes to common shareholders. If the preferred shares are noncumulative, the $8,000 of dividends from past periods is ignored. This year's preferred dividend is paid first, with the remainder going to common.

Several of the other features that may be considered for preferences are the right to participate in distributions beyond those established as the amount of the preferred dividend, the right to convert preferred shares to common shares or bonds, and the potential for having the preferred shares called (repurchased) by the corporation. A detailed discussion of these topics is left to more advanced courses.

Check Yourself 11.2

On January 1, 2006, Janelle Company's shareholders' equity was as follows:

Preferred shares, $4, cumulative, 100,000 shares authorized, 2,000 shares issued	$200,000
Common shares, no par, 1,000,000 shares authorized, 300,000 shares issued	600,000
Total capital shares	$800,000

During the year, a $30,000 dividend was declared. The preferred dividends are two years in arrears. How much will each class of shares receive? How would your answer change if the preferred shares were noncumulative?

Answer The preferred dividend rate is $4 so the preferred shareholders should receive a dividend of $8,000 (2,000 shares × $4 per share) each year. Since the dividends are two years in arrears, the preferred shareholders will be owed $16,000 for past dividends and an additional $8,000 for the current year's dividend. Therefore, the preferred shareholders will receive a total dividend of $24,000. The common shareholders will receive the remaining balance of $6,000 ($30,000 − $24,000).

If the preferred shares were noncumulative, the preferred shareholders would only receive $8,000 for their current year entitlement. The remaining balance of $22,000 ($30,000 − $8,000) would be distributed to the common shareholders.

Accounting for Share Transactions on the Day of Issue

Shares Issued at Par Value

LO3 Describe the accounting treatment for different types of shares issued by corporations.

Methods of recording the initial issue of shares vary depending on whether the shares have a par value, a stated value, or no par value. When either a par or stated value exists, this amount is recorded in the share account. Any amount above the par or stated value is recorded in the **Contributed Capital in Excess account**. Therefore, the total amount invested by the owners is divided between two separate equity accounts. To illustrate, assume that Nelson Incorporated has been authorized to issue 250 common shares. During 2007, Nelson Incorporated issues 100 shares of $10 par common shares for $22 per share. The event increases assets and shareholders' equity by $2,200 ($22 × 100 shares). The increase in shareholders' equity is divided into two parts, with one part representing the $1,000 of par value (100 shares × $10 per share) and the remaining $1,200 ($2,200 − $1,000) pertaining to the additional amount that was contributed in excess of the par value. The income statement is not affected. The $2,200 cash inflow is shown in the financing activities section of the cash flow statement. The effects on the financial statements and the journal entry necessary to record the event are as follows:

Assets	=	Liab.	+	Equity			Rev.	−	Exp.	=	Net Inc.	Cash Flow Statement
Cash	=	Liab.	+	Com. Sh.	+	CC in Excess						
2,000	=	NA	+	1,000	+	1,200	NA	−	NA	=	NA	2,200 FA

Account Title	Debit	Credit
Cash	2,200	
Common Shares, $10 Par Value		1,000
Contributed Capital in Excess of Par Value—Common		1,200

The legal capital of the corporation is $1,000, which is the par value of the common shares. The number of shares issued can be easily determined by dividing the total amount in the common shares account by the par value ($1,000 ÷ $10 = 100 shares). Remember, however, that the full amount that has been paid for the shares includes both the amount recorded in the Common Shares account and the amount in the Contributed Capital in Excess of Par or Stated Value account.

Share Classification

Nelson Incorporated obtains authorization to issue 400 Class B, $20 par value common shares. The company issues 150 shares at $25 per share. The event acts to increase assets and shareholders' equity by $3,750 ($25 × 150 shares). The increase in shareholders' equity is divided into two parts, with one representing the $3,000 of par value (150 shares × $20 per shares) and the remaining $750 ($3,750 − $3,000) pertaining to the additional amount paid in excess of the par value. The income statement is not affected. The $3,750 cash inflow is shown in the financing activities section of the cash flow statement. The effects on the financial statements and the journal entry necessary to record the event are as follows:

Assets	=	Liab.	+	Equity			Rev.	−	Exp.	=	Net Inc.	Cash Flow Statement
Cash	=	Liab.	+	Com. Sh.	+	CC in Excess						
3,750	=	NA	+	3,000	+	750	NA	−	NA	=	NA	3,750 FA

Account Title	Debit	Credit
Cash	3,750	
Common Shares, Class B, $20 Par Value		3,000
Contributed Capital in Excess of Par Value—Common		750

As the preceding event suggests, companies can have many classes of common shares. The specific rights and privileges associated with each class are described in the individual share certificates.

Shares Issued at Stated Value

Assume that Nelson issues 100 preferred shares with a stated value of $10 per share. The preferred shares pay a 7 percent cumulative dividend. Assume here an issue price of $22 per share. The effect on the financial statements is identical to that described for the issue of the $10 par value common shares. The journal entry changes only to reflect the name of the different class.

Assets	=	Liab.	+	Equity			Rev.	−	Exp.	=	Net Inc.	Cash Flow Statement
Cash	=	Liab.	+	Pref. Sh.	+	CC in Excess						
2,200	=	NA	+	1,000	+	1,200	NA	−	NA	=	NA	2,200 FA

Account Title	Debit	Credit
Cash	2,200	
Preferred Shares, $10 Stated Value, 7% cumulative		1,000
Contributed Capital in Excess of Stated Value—Preferred		1,200

Shares Issued at No-Par Value

When no-par shares are issued (no par or stated value is provided), then the entire amount is added to the share capital account. Assume that Nelson Incorporated issues 100 no-par value common shares at $22 per share. As in the previous two examples, the event acts to increase assets and shareholders' equity by $2,200. The effects on the financial statements and the journal entry required to record the event are shown here:

Assets	=	Liab.	+	Equity			Rev.	−	Exp.	=	Net Inc.	Cash Flow Statement
Cash	=	Liab.	+	Com. Sh.	+	CC in Excess						
2,200	=	NA	+	2,200	+	NA	NA	−	NA	=	NA	2,200 FA

Account Title	Debit	Credit
Cash	2,200	
Common Shares, No Par		2,200

Financial Statement Presentation

Exhibit 11–3 shows the balance sheet of Nelson Incorporated right after the four issues of shares just described. The exhibit assumes that Nelson earned and retained $5,000 of cash income during 2007. Notice that the share accounts are presented first, followed by the contributed capital in excess accounts. Another popular format is to group accounts by the type of share classification, with the paid excess accounts shown along with their associated share accounts. A properly constructed shareholders' equity section includes complete descriptions of the share classifications, as shown in Exhibit 11–3. But, in practice, many companies simply combine the different classes into a single account and provide the detailed information in the notes to the financial statements. Do not be confused by the fact that reporting formats vary widely in practice.

Exhibit 11–3

NELSON INCORPORATED Balance Sheet January 1, 2007	
Assets	
Cash	$15,350
Shareholders' Equity	
Contributed Capital	
Share Capital	
Preferred Shares, $10 stated value, 7% cumulative, 300 shares authorized, 100 issued and outstanding	$ 1,000
Common Shares, $10 par value, 250 shares authorized, 100 shares issued and outstanding	1,000
Common Shares, Class B, $20 par value, 400 shares authorized, 150 issued and outstanding	3,000
Common Shares, No Par, 150 shares authorized, 100 issued and outstanding	2,200
Total Share Capital	$ 7,200
Additional Contributed Capital	
Contributed Capital in Excess of Stated Value—Preferred	1,200
Contributed Capital in Excess of Par—Common	1,200
Contributed Capital in Excess of Par—Class B Common	750
Total Contributed Capital	$10,350
Retained Earnings	5,000
Total Shareholders' Equity	$15,350

Cash Dividend

A corporation generates net income for the benefit of its owners. If the company retains the income, the price of the shares should increase to reflect the increase in the value of the firm. Alternatively, firms can distribute the income to their owners directly through the payment of cash dividends. Three important dates are associated with cash dividends: *declaration date, date of record*, and *payment date*. To illustrate the accounting treatment for a cash dividend, consider these circumstances. On November 1, 2007, Nelson Incorporated declares a cash dividend on the 100 shares of its $10 stated value preferred shares. The dividend will be paid to the shareholders of record as of December 15, 2007. The cash payment will be made on January 30, 2008.

Declaration Date

LO4 Explain the effects of a declaration and payment of cash dividends on a company's financial statements.

November 1, 2007, is the **declaration date**. On this day, the chairperson of the board of Nelson Incorporated issued a press release to notify shareholders and other interested parties that a 7 percent cash dividend will be paid on the company's preferred shares. Although corporations don't have to declare dividends, they are legally obligated to pay those dividends that have been declared. Therefore, a liability is recognized on the date of declaration. The increase in liabilities is offset by a decrease in Retained Earnings. The income statement and cash flow statement are not affected. The effect of the *declaration* of the $70 ($10 × 0.07 × 100 shares) dividend on the financial statements and the journal entry necessary to record it are as follows:

Assets	=	Liab.	+	Equity			Rev.	−	Exp.	=	Net Inc.	Cash Flow Statement
	=			Com. Sh.	+	Ret. Earn.						
NA	=	70	+	NA	+	(70)	NA	−	NA	=	NA	NA

Account Title	Debit	Credit
Retained Earnings	70	
Dividends Payable		70

Date of Record

The cash dividend will be paid to the investors who own the preferred shares, as of the **date of record**. Any share sold after the date of record but before the payment date is said to be traded **ex-dividend**, or sold without the benefit of the upcoming dividend. Since the date of record is merely a cutoff date, it does not affect the financial statements.

Payment Date

The corporation mails the dividend to the shareholders on the **payment date**. This event is treated the same as the payment of any other liability. The asset Cash and the liability Dividends Payable both decrease. The income statement is not affected. The cash outflow is shown in the financing activities section of the cash flow statement. The effect of the cash payment on the financial statements and the journal entry for recording it are as follows:

Assets	=	Liab.	+	Equity			Rev.	−	Exp.	=	Net Inc.	Cash Flow Statement
	=			Com. Sh.	+	Ret. Earn.						
(70)	=	(70)	+	NA	+	NA	NA	−	NA	=	NA	(70) FA

Account Title	Debit	Credit
Dividends Payable	70	
Cash		70

LO5 Explain the effects of stock dividends and stock splits on a company's financial statements.

Stock Dividend

Instead of distributing cash to shareholders, a company may choose to distribute shares. There are two main reasons that a firm might decide to distribute a **stock dividend**:

1. There may not be enough funds available for a cash dividend, but the company wants to reward its shareholders in some way.
2. The price of the shares in the market may be getting so high that potential investors are discouraged from purchasing it.

To illustrate, assume that Nelson Incorporated decides to issue a 10 percent stock dividend on the 150 shares of its class B common shares that carry a \$20 par value. Nelson will issue 15 new shares (150 shares × 0.10). Assume that the distribution is made at a time when the shares market value is \$30. In this case, the stock dividend will act to transfer \$450 (\$30 × [150 shares × 0.10]) from the Retained Earnings account to the contributed capital section of the balance sheet. This is an equity exchange transaction. The income statement and cash flow statement are not affected. The effect of the stock dividend on the financial statements and the journal entry for recording it are as follows:

Assets	=	Liab.	+	Equity					Rev.	−	Exp.	=	Net Inc.	Cash Flow Statement
	=			Com. Sh.	+	CC in Excess	+	Ret. Earn.						
NA	=	NA	+	300	+	150	+	(450)	NA	−	NA	=	NA	NA

Account Title	Debit	Credit
Retained Earnings	450	
Common Shares, Class B,\$20 Par Value		300
Contributed Capital in Excess of Par Value—Class B Common		150

The logic behind the accounting treatment for stock dividends may be clarified by observing the fact that the end result of issuing a stock dividend is the same as it would be if the company had issued the common shares for the market price and then used the funds to pay the cash dividends. This should be apparent from a review of the following journal entries. To make it easier to see, the offsetting entries to the Cash account are marked with strikethroughs to show that their elimination produces the same result as the issuance of a stock dividend.

Account Title	Debit	Credit
~~Cash~~	~~450~~	
Common Shares, Class B $20 Par Value		300
Contributed Capital in Excess of Par Value—Class B Common		150
Retained Earnings	450	
~~Cash~~		~~450~~

Notice that assets are not affected by the stock dividend. However, the number of shares increases. Since there is a larger number of shares representing the ownership interest in the same amount of assets, the market value per share of the company's shares normally declines when a stock dividend is distributed. This result makes the shares more affordable and so may increase the demand for the shares. For this reason, a company's shares may not decline in exact proportion to the number of new shares issued.

Stock Split

A more dynamic way of lowering the market price of a corporation's shares is through a **stock split**. A stock split removes the old shares from the books and replaces them with new shares. For example, if Nelson Incorporated declares a 2-for-1 stock split on the 165 shares (150 original issue plus 15 shares issued from the stock dividend) of the class B common shares, a notation is made in the accounting records that the old $20 par value shares were replaced with 330 shares of $10 par value shares. Investors who owned the 165 shares of old common would now own 330 shares of the new common. Since the 330 shares represent the same ownership interest as the 165 shares previously represented, the market value (price) per share should be one-half as much as it was before the split. However, as with a stock dividend, the lower price will probably create demand for the shares. Therefore, the drop in market price is likely to be less dramatic than the increase in the number of shares. In other words, doubling the number of shares will cause the price to fall to a point that is slightly more than one-half the value that existed before the split. If the shares were selling for $30 per share before the 2-for-1 split, they may sell for $15.50 after the split.

Financial Statement Presentation

Exhibit 11–4 contains the December 31, 2007, balance sheet for Nelson Incorporated. The balance sheet reflects the 11 equity transactions that Nelson completed during 2007. These events are summarized here for your convenience in analyzing the effect of each event on the balance sheet. (All transactions—except those affecting only equity accounts—are assumed to be cash transactions.)

1. Issued 100 shares of $10 par value common shares at a market price of $22 per share.
2. Issued 150 shares of class B $20 par value common shares at a market price of $25 per share.
3. Issued 100 $10 stated value preferred shares at a market price of $22 per share.
4. Issued 100 no-par common shares at a market price of $22 per share.
5. Earned and retained $5,000 cash from operations.
6. Declared and paid a $70 cash dividend on the preferred shares.

Exhibit 11–4

NELSON INCORPORATED Balance Sheet December 31, 2007	
Assets	
Cash	$ 15,280
Shareholders' Equity	
Contributed Capital	
Share Capital	
Preferred Shares, $10 Stated Value, 7% cumulative, 300 shares authorized, 100 issued and outstanding	$ 1,000
Common Shares, $10 Par Value, 250 shares authorized, 100 shares issued and outstanding	1,000
Common Shares, Class B, $20 Par Value, 400 shares authorized, 150 issued and outstanding	3,300
Common Shares, No Par, 150 shares authorized, 100 issued and outstanding	2,200
	$ 7,500
Additional Contributed Capital	
Contributed Capital in Excess of Stated Value—Preferred	1,200
Contributed Capital in Excess of Par—Common	1,200
Contributed Capital in Excess of Par—Class B Common	900
Total Share Capital	$10,800
Retained Earnings	4,480
Total Shareholders' Equity	$15,280

7. Issued a 10 percent stock dividend on the 150 outstanding class B common shares that carried a $20 par value (15 additional shares). At the time of issue, the market price was $30 per share. There is a total of 165 (150 + 15) shares outstanding after the stock dividend.
8. Issued a 2-for-1 stock split on the 165 class B common shares. After this transaction, there are 330 shares outstanding of the class B common shares with a $10 par value.

Assessment of Potential Investment Returns

LO6 Explain how accounting information can be useful in making investment decisions.

Why does an investor acquire the shares of a particular company? Of course, the ultimate objective of any investment is to make money. However, money can be made in a variety of ways. Shareholders benefit when the companies they own generate profits. The profits may be distributed directly to the owners in the form of dividends. Alternatively, the business may choose to retain its earnings, whereupon the value of the shareholder's investment (market price of the shares) should increase.

Receiving Dividends

Will a company pay dividends in the future? Accounting information can help answer this question. First, the financial statements show whether dividends were paid in the past. Usually, a history of dividend payment is an indicator of future dividend payments. Also, to pay future dividends, the company must have cash. Although there is always uncertainty about the future, financial statements, especially the cash flow statement, can help investors assess the probability of a company's future cash flows.

Note that very good reasons exist for a company not to pay dividends. A more thorough explanation of whether a company should pay dividends is a topic for finance courses, but do not assume that just because dividends were not paid, a company's shares are less desirable to investors. Businesses that are not paying dividends may be reinvesting the money in the company. If the company is earning a return on assets of 20 percent, it is wiser to reinvest available cash than to pay dividends to shareholders who would put the money in a bank account paying 6 percent interest.

Understanding the Price-Earnings Ratio

There is a ratio that can provide some insight into how analysts view the future prospects of a company relative to its current net income. This ratio is called the **price-earnings ratio** and is defined as

$$\frac{\text{Selling price of 1 share}}{\text{Earnings per share}^*}$$

This ratio, usually referred to as the **P/E ratio**, is one of only two ratios shown in stock price listings in newspapers such as *The Globe and Mail*. As a general rule, the higher the P/E ratio, the more optimistic investors are about a company's future. In other words, investors are willing to pay higher prices for the shares of companies if the investors believe that the company will perform well (earnings will grow rapidly) in the future. If a company currently has negative earnings per share, its P/E ratio is not computed.

The following information pertains to Jackson Incorporated:

As of December 31,	2003	2004
Market price per share	$72.28	$27.30
Earnings per share	2.78	1.82

Calculate the P/E ratios for 2003 and 2004. What do these ratios suggest about investor confidence in Jackson's future earning capacity?

Answer

The P/E ratio for 2003 is 26 times ($72.28 ÷ $2.78) and for 2004 is 15 times ($27.30 ÷ $1.82). The decrease in the P/E ratio suggests that investor confidence in Jackson's ability to generate earnings has declined.

Exercising Control

Investors may also make money by influencing or controlling the operations of a business. There are several ways that an investor can benefit by exercising some control over a company. As one example, consider a power company that uses coal to produce electricity. The power company may purchase some of the common shares of a mining company to help ensure the stable supply of the coal it needs to operate its electric business. What percentage of the mining company's shares does the power company need to acquire in order to exercise significant control over the mining company? The answer depends on how many people own shares in the mining company and how the number of shares is distributed among the shareholders.

The more people who own a company's shares, the more *widely held* the company is said to be. If ownership is concentrated in the hands of a few persons, the company is said to be *closely held*. Generally, the more widely held the shares of a company, the smaller the percentage that must be acquired to exercise significant control. Accounting information can help determine how many shares

* *Earnings per share* (EPS) can be computed under a variety of assumptions. Indeed, the reporting of earnings per share in financial statements is a complicated task requiring the application of many technical accounting rules. However, for the purposes of this text, earnings per share is shown in its simplest form, which is net income divided by the number of common shares outstanding.

are needed to exercise control. However, financial statements do not contain all of the information needed. For example, the financial statements disclose the total number of shares outstanding, but the statements normally contain very little information about the number of shareholders and even less information regarding the nature of the relationships between shareholders. Information regarding such relationships is critically important because related shareholders, whether bound by family or business interests, might exercise control by voting as a block.

---

a look back

If you wished to start a business, one of the first things you must do is to raise equity financing; you must have money to make money. Although you may wish to borrow money, lenders are unlikely to make loans to businesses without some degree of owner financing. Therefore, equity financing is critical to virtually all profit-oriented businesses. The purpose of this chapter has been to examine some of the issues related to accounting for equity transactions.

Ownership interest in corporations may be evidenced by a variety of financial instruments. A corporation can issue different classes of common shares and preferred shares. In general, *common shares* provide the widest range of privileges including the right to vote and participate in earnings. *Preferred shareholders* often give up the right to vote to receive other benefits such as the right to receive preference in the payment of dividends or the return of assets upon liquidation. Shares may be issued at *par value or stated value*, both of which are legal requirements that relate to the amount of capital that must be maintained in the corporation. Corporations may also issue *no-par shares* that avoid many of the legal requirements associated with par or stated value shares.

Companies may issue *stock splits* or *stock dividends*. The result of these transactions is to increase the number of shares representing the same ownership interest in the net assets of a company. The per share market value usually drops when a company engages in stock splits or dividends.

Beginning with Chapter 6, this course has been moving systematically down the balance sheet accounts. Along the way you have seen how each of these balance sheet accounts interacts with related accounts on the income statement. For example, when Chapter 8 examined the balance sheet effects of different methods of accounting for *inventory*, it also examined the related effects on *cost of goods sold*, which appears on the income statement. Equity is the last section on the balance sheet.

a look forward

Chapter 12 presents a more detailed explanation of the cash flow statement than has been presented in the past chapters. The format of the cash flow statement that has been used to this point has been somewhat informal, although its informational content is very valid. Chapter 12 not only presents additional details about the cash flow statement but also examines the statement in the formal format used by most real-world companies.

SELF-STUDY REVIEW PROBLEM

Edwards, Inc., experienced the following events:

1. Issued common shares for cash.
2. Declared a cash dividend.
3. Issued noncumulative preferred shares for cash.
4. Distributed a stock dividend.
5. Distributed a 2-for-1 stock split.
6. Issued cumulative preferred shares for cash.
7. Paid a cash dividend that had previously been declared.

Required

Show the effect of each event on the elements of the financial statements using a horizontal statements model like the one shown here. Use + for increase, − for decrease, and NA for not affected. In the Cash Flow Statement column, indicate whether the item is an operating activity (OA), investing activity (IA), or a financing activity (FA). The first transaction is entered as an example.

Event No.	Assets	=	Liab.	+	Equity	Rev.	−	Exp.	=	Net Inc.	Cash Flow Statement
1	+		NA		+	NA		NA		NA	+ FA

Solution to Self-Study Review Problem

Event No.	Assets	=	Liab.	+	Equity	Rev.	−	Exp.	=	Net Inc.	Cash Flow Statement
1	+		NA		+	NA		NA		NA	+ FA
2	NA		+		−	NA		NA		NA	NA
3	+		NA		+	NA		NA		NA	+ FA
4	NA		NA		− +	NA		NA		NA	NA
5	NA		NA		NA	NA		NA		NA	NA
6	+		NA		+	NA		NA		NA	+ FA
7	−		−		NA	NA		NA		NA	− FA

KEY TERMS

authorized shares *462*
book value per share *462*
common shares *462*
contributed capital in excess account *465*
cumulative dividends *463*
date of record *468*
declaration date *467*
dividends *463*
dividends in arrears *463*
ex-dividend *468*
issued shares *462*
legal capital *462*
market value *462*
outstanding shares *462*
par value *461*
payment date *468*
preferred shares *463*
price-earnings (P/E) ratio *471*
stated value *462*
stock dividend *468*
stock split *469*
treasury shares *462*
withdrawals *460*

QUESTIONS

1. What are the similarities and differences in the equity structure of a sole proprietorship, a partnership, and a corporation?
2. What is the meaning of each of the following terms with respect to the corporate form of organization?
   a. Legal capital
   b. Par value
   c. Stated value
   d. Market value
   e. Book value
   f. Authorized shares
   g. Issued shares
   h. Outstanding shares
   i. Treasury shares
   j. Common shares
   k. Preferred shares
   l. Dividends
3. What is the difference between cumulative preferred shares and noncumulative preferred shares?
4. What are no-par shares? How are they recorded in the accounting records?
5. Assume that Best Co. has issued and outstanding 1,000 shares of $100 par value, 10 percent, cumulative preferred shares. What is the dividend per share? If the preferred dividend is two years in arrears, what total amount of dividends must be paid before the common shareholders can receive any dividends?
6. If Best Co. issued 10,000 shares of $20 stated value common for $30 per share, what amount is credited to the Common Shares account? What amount of cash is received?
7. What is the difference between par value and stated value?
8. What is the importance of the declaration date, record date, and payment date in conjunction with corporate dividends?
9. What is the difference between a stock dividend and a stock split?
10. What are the primary reasons that a company would choose to distribute a stock dividend instead of a cash dividend?
11. What is the primary reason that a company would declare a stock split?
12. If Best Co. had 10,000 common shares outstanding and declared a 5-for-1 stock split, how many shares would then be outstanding after the split?
13. What is meant by *equity financing*?
14. What is meant by *debt financing*?
15. What are some reasons that a corporation might not pay dividends?
16. What does the price-earnings ratio generally indicate about a company?

EXERCISES

L.O. 1 EXERCISE 11–1 *Effect of Accounting Events on the Financial Statements of a Sole Proprietorship*

A sole proprietorship was started on January 1, 2005, when it received $50,000 cash from Ed Simms, the owner. During 2005, the company earned $25,000 in cash revenues and paid $14,500 in cash expenses. Simms withdrew $1,500 cash from the business during 2005.

Required
Prepare an income statement, statement of owners' equity, balance sheet, and cash flow statement for Simms Company's 2005 fiscal year.

L.O. 1 EXERCISE 11–2 *Effect of Accounting Events on the Financial Statements of a Partnership*

Bruce Bailey and Roy Clark started the BC partnership on January 1, 2004. The business acquired $40,000 cash from Bailey and $75,000 from Clark. During 2004, the partnership earned $75,000 in cash revenues and paid $36,000 for cash expenses. Bailey withdrew $1,000 cash from the business, and Clark withdrew $3,000 cash. The net income was allocated to the capital accounts of the two partners in proportion to the amounts of their original investments in the business.

Required
Prepare an income statement, statement of partners' equity, balance sheet, and cash flow statement for the BC partnership for the 2004 fiscal year.

L.O. 1 EXERCISE 11–3 *Effect of Accounting Events on the Financial Statements of a Corporation*

Hill Corporation was started with the issue of 2,000 shares for cash on January 1, 2005 at a market price of $22 per share. During 2005, the company earned $46,000 in cash revenues and paid $34,000 for cash expenses. Also a $2,500 cash dividend was paid to the shareholders.

Required
Prepare an income statement, statement of shareholders' equity, balance sheet, and cash flow statement for Hill Corporation's 2005 fiscal year.

L.O. 3 EXERCISE 11–4 *Effect of Issuing Common Shares on the Balance Sheet*

Newly formed Health-Max Corporation has 50,000 shares of $5 stated value common authorized. On March 1, 2006, Health-Max issued 8,000 shares for $15 per share. On May 2 the company issued an additional 15,000 shares for $22 per share. Health-Max was not affected by other events during 2006.

Required

a. Record the transactions in a horizontal statements model like the following one. In the Cash Flow Statement column, indicate whether the item is an operating activity (OA), investing activity (IA), or financing activity (FA). Use NA to indicate that an element was not affected by the event.

Assets	=	Equity			Rev. − Exp. = Net inc.	Cash Flow Statement
Cash	=	Com. Sh.	+	CC in Excess		

b. Determine the amount Health-Max would report for common shares on the December 31, 2006, balance sheet.
c. Determine the amount Health-Max would report for contributed capital in excess of stated value.
d. What is the total amount of capital contributed by the owners?
e. What amount of total assets would Health-Max report on the December 31, 2006, balance sheet?
f. Prepare journal entries to record the March 1 and May 2 transactions.

EXERCISE 11–5 *Recording and Reporting Common and Preferred Share Transactions* L.O. 3, 4

Meyer, Inc., was organized on June 5, 2007. It was authorized to issue 400,000 common shares and 50,000 shares of $2 cumulative class A preferred. The following share transactions pertain to Meyer, Inc., during 2007:

1. Issued 20,000 common shares for $9 per share.
2. Issued 5,000 class A preferred shares for $22 per share.
3. Declared a cash dividend of $15,000.

Required

a. Prepare general journal entries for these transactions.

b. Prepare the shareholders' equity section of the balance sheet immediately after these transactions. Assume retained earnings were $100,000 before these transactions.

EXERCISE 11–6 *Effect of Common and Preferred Shares on the Horizontal Statements Model* L.O. 3, 4

Irwin Corporation issued 2,000 common shares for $25 per share. Irwin also issued 1,000 shares of $5 preferred shares at $70 per share. A dividend of $14,000 was declared.

Required

a. Record these events in a horizontal statements model like the following one. In the Cash Flow Statement column, indicate whether the item is an operating activity (OA), investing activity (IA), or financing activity (FA). Use NA to indicate that an element was not affected by the event.

Assets	=	Equity					Rev. − Exp. = Net Inc.	Cash Flow Statement
Cash	=	Pref. Sh.	+	Com. Sh.	+	Ret. Earn.		

b. Prepare journal entries to record these transactions.

EXERCISE 11–7 *Issuing Shares for Assets Other than Cash* L.O. 3

Jana Corporation was formed when it issued common shares to two of its shareholders. Jana issued 3,000 common shares to Marco Byron in exchange for $36,000 cash (the issue price was $12 per share). Jana also issued 2,000 shares to Simon Jones in exchange for a one-year-old delivery van on the same day. Jones had originally paid $35,000 for the van.

Required

a. What was the market value of the delivery van on the date of the share issue?

b. Show the effect of the two share issues on Jana's books in a horizontal statements model like the following one. In the Cash Flow Statement column, indicate whether the item is an operating activity (OA), investing activity (IA), or financing activity (FA). Use NA to indicate that an element was not affected by the event.

Assets			=	Equity			Rev. − Exp. = Net Inc.	Cash Flow Statement
Cash	+	Van	=	Com. Sh.	+	Ret. Earn.		

EXERCISE 11–8 *Effect of Cash Dividends on Financial Statements* L.O. 4

On October 1, 2005, Med Corporation declared a $75,000 cash dividend to be paid on December 30 to shareholders of record on November 20.

Required

a. Record the events occurring on October 1, November 20, and December 30 in a horizontal statements model like the following one. In the Cash Flow Statement column, indicate whether the item is an operating activity (OA), investing activity (IA), or financing activity (FA).

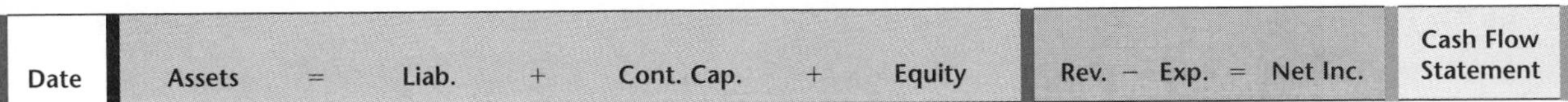

Date	Assets	=	Liab.	+	Cont. Cap.	+	Equity	Rev.	−	Exp.	=	Net Inc.	Cash Flow Statement

b. Prepare journal entries for all events associated with the dividend.

L.O. 4 EXERCISE 11–9 *Accounting for Cumulative Preferred Dividends*

When Earles Corporation was organized in January 2003, it immediately issued 1,000 shares of $50 stated value, 8 percent, cumulative preferred shares and 20,000 common shares. The corporation has never paid a dividend. The company's earnings history is as follows: 2003, net loss of $15,000; 2004, net income of $75,000.

Required

a. How much are the dividends in arrears as of January 1, 2004?
b. Assume that the board of directors declares a $20,000 cash dividend at the end of 2004 (remember that the 2003 and 2004 preferred dividends are due). How will the dividend be divided between the preferred and common shareholders?

L.O. 4 EXERCISE 11–10 *Cash Dividends for Preferred and Common Shareholders*

Ace Corporation had the following shares issued and outstanding at January 1, 2006:

1. 200,000 common shares.
2. 20,000 shares of $50 stated value, 8 percent, noncumulative preferred shares.

On May 10, Ace Corporation declared the annual cash dividend on its 20,000 preferred shares and a $1 per share dividend for the common shareholders. The dividends will be paid on June 15 to the shareholders of record on May 30.

Required

a. Determine the total amount of dividends to be paid to the preferred shareholders and common shareholders.
b. Prepare general journal entries to record the declaration and payment of the cash dividends (be sure to date your entries).

L.O. 4 EXERCISE 11–11 *Cash Dividends: Common and Preferred Shares*

Ming Corp., had the following shares issued and outstanding at January 1, 2006:

1. 100,000 shares of no-par common shares.
2. 20,000 shares of $3 cumulative preferred shares. (Dividends are in arrears for one year, 2005.)

On February 1, 2006, Ming declared a $120,000 cash dividend to be paid March 31 to shareholders of record on March 10.

Required

a. What amount of dividends will be paid to the preferred shareholders versus the common shareholders?
b. Prepare the journal entries required for these transactions. (Be sure to include the dates of the entries.)

L.O. 5 EXERCISE 11–12 *Accounting for Stock Dividends*

Nichols Corporation issued a 4 percent stock dividend on its 20,000 common shares. At the time of the dividend, the market value was $35 per share.

Required

a. Compute the amount of the stock dividend.
b. Show the effects of the stock dividend on the financial statements using a horizontal statements model like the following one.

Assets	=	Liab.	+	Com. Sh.	+	Ret. Earn.	Rev.	−	Exp.	=	Net Inc.	Cash Flow Statement

c. Prepare the journal entry to record the stock dividend.

EXERCISE 11–13 *Determining the Effects of Stock Splits on the Accounting Records* **L.O. 5**

The market value of Chan Corporation's common shares had become excessively high. The shares were currently selling for $160 per share. To reduce the market price of the common shares, Chan declared a 2-for-1 stock split for the 200,000 shares outstanding.

Required

a. How will Chan Corporation's books be affected by the stock split?
b. Determine the number of common shares outstanding and the par value after the split.
c. Explain how the market value of the stock will be affected by the stock split.

EXERCISE 11–14 *Using the P/E Ratio* **L.O. 6**

During 2007, Frontier Corporation and Upton Corporation reported net incomes of $60,000 and $112,000, respectively. Both companies had 15,000 common shares issued and outstanding. The market price per share for Frontier was $70 while Upton's sold for $90 per share.

Required

a. Determine the P/E ratio for each company.
b. Based on the P/E ratios computed in Requirement *a*, which company do investors believe has more potential for growth in income?

PROBLEMS—SERIES A

PROBLEM 11–1A *Effect of Business Structure on Financial Statements* **L.O. 1**

MMX Company was started on January 1, 2007, when the owners invested $300,000 cash in the business. During 2007, the company earned cash revenues of $80,000 and incurred cash expenses of $52,000. The company also distributed cash of $10,000.

Required

Prepare a 2007 income statement, statement of equity, balance sheet, and cash flow statement using each of the following assumptions. (Consider each assumption separately.)

a. MMX is a sole proprietorship owned by Martin Mayer.
b. MMX is a partnership with two partners, Martin Mayer and Kay Mitchell. Mayer invested $200,000 and Mitchell invested $100,000 of the $300,000 cash that was used to start the business. Mitchell was expected to assume the vast majority of the responsibility for operating the business. The partnership agreement called for Mitchell to receive 70 percent of the profits and Mayer the remaining 30 percent. With regard to the $10,000 distributions, Mitchell withdrew $4,000 from the business and Mayer withdrew $6,000.
c. MMX is a corporation. The owners were issued 12,000 common shares when they invested the $300,000 cash in the business.

PROBLEM 11–2A *Recording and Reporting Share Transactions and Cash Dividends across Two Accounting Cycles* **L.O. 3, 4**

Oak Corporation was authorized to issue 50,000 common shares and 10,000 shares of $8 cumulative preferred. Oak Corporation completed the following transactions during its first two years of operation:

2008

Jan.	2	Issued 20,000 common shares for $8 per share.
	15	Issued 4,000 preferred shares for $130 per share.
Feb.	14	Issued 10,000 common shares for $9 per share.
Dec.	31	During the year, earned $270,000 of cash revenues and paid $160,000 of cash expenses.
	31	Declared the cash dividend on outstanding shares of preferred shares for 2008. The dividend will be paid on January 31 to shareholders of record on January 15, 2009.
	31	Closed revenue and expense accounts to the retained earnings account.

2009

Jan. 31 Paid the cash dividend declared on December 31, 2008.
Mar. 1 Issued 2,000 preferred shares for $150 per share.
Dec. 31 During the year, earned $250,000 of cash revenues and paid $175,000 of cash expenses.
31 Declared the dividend on the preferred shares and a $0.20 per share dividend on the common shares.
31 Closed revenue and expense accounts.

Required

a. Prepare journal entries for these transactions for 2008 and 2009.
b. Prepare the shareholders' equity section of the balance sheet at December 31, 2008.
c. Prepare the balance sheet at December 31, 2009.

L.O. 3, 4, 5 PROBLEM 11–3A *Recording and Reporting Stock Dividends*

Granger Corp. completed the following transactions in 2004, the first year of operation:

1. Issued 15,000 common shares for $40 per share.
2. Issued 5,000 shares of $2 preferred at $50 per share.
3. Paid the annual cash dividend to preferred shareholders.
4. Issued a 5 percent stock dividend on the common shares. The market value at the dividend declaration date was $50 per share.
5. Later that year, issued a 2-for-1 split on the 15,750 outstanding common shares.
6. Earned $210,000 of cash revenues and paid $128,000 of cash expenses.

Required

a. Record each of these events in a horizontal statements model like the following one. In the Cash Flow Statement column, indicate whether the item is an operating activity (OA), investing activity (IA), or financing activity (FA). Use NA to indicate that an element is not affected by the event.

Assets	=	Liab.	+	Equity					Rev.	−	Exp.	=	Net Inc.	Cash Flow Statement
Cash	=	Div. Pay	+	Pr. Sh.	+	Com. Sh.	+	Ret. Earn.						

b. Record the 2004 transactions in general journal form.
c. Prepare the shareholders' equity section of the balance sheet at the end of 2004.

L.O. 3, 5 PROBLEM 11–4A *Analyzing the Shareholders' Equity Section of the Balance Sheet*

The shareholders' equity section of the balance sheet for Excite Company at December 31, 2007, is as follows:

Shareholders' Equity		
Contributed Capital		
Preferred Shares, $6 Par Value, $2 cumulative,		
250,000 shares authorized,		
30,000 shares issued and outstanding	$600,000	
Common Shares, $10 Stated Value,		
750,000 shares authorized,		
? shares issued and outstanding	500,000	
Contributed Capital in Excess of Stated Value—Common	200,000	
Total Contributed Capital		$1,300,000
Retained Earnings		250,000
Total Shareholders' Equity		$1,550,000

Note: The market value is $25 per common share, and $22 per preferred share.

Required

a. How many common shares are issued?
b. What was the average issue price (price for which the shares were issued) of the common shares?
c. Explain the difference between the issue price and the market price of the common shares.
d. If Excite declared a 2-for-1 stock split on the common shares, how many shares would be outstanding after the split? What amount would be transferred from the retained earnings account because of the stock split? Theoretically, what would be the market price of the common shares immediately after the stock split?

PROBLEM 11–5A *Effects of Equity Transactions on Financial Statements*

L.O. 3, 4, 5, 6

The following events were experienced by Abbot, Inc.:

1. Issued common shares for cash.
2. Issued noncumulative preferred shares.
3. Distributed a stock dividend.
4. Declared a cash dividend.
5. Paid the cash dividend declared in Event 4.
6. Issued cumulative preferred shares.
7. Distributed a 2-for-1 stock split on the common shares.

Required

Show the effect of each event on the elements of the financial statements using a horizontal statements model like the following one. Use + for increase, − for decrease, and NA for not affected. In the Cash Flow Statement column, indicate whether the item is an operating activity (OA), investing activity (IA), or financing activity (FA). The first transaction is entered as an example.

Event No.	Assets	=	Liab.	+	Equity	Rev.	−	Exp.	=	Net Inc.	Cash Flow Statement
1	+		NA		+	NA	−	NA	=	NA	+ FA

PROBLEMS—SERIES B

PROBLEM 11–1B *Effect of Business Structure on Financial Statements*

L.O. 1

Calloway Company was started on January 1, 2009, when it acquired $40,000 cash from the owners. During 2009, the company earned cash revenues of $18,000 and incurred cash expenses of $12,500. The company also paid cash distributions of $3,000.

Required

Prepare a 2009 income statement, statement of equity, balance sheet, and cash flow statement under each of the following assumptions. (Consider each assumption separately.)

a. Calloway is a sole proprietorship owned by Macy Calloway.
b. Calloway is a partnership with two partners, Macy Calloway and Artie Calloway. Macy Calloway invested $25,000 and Artie Calloway invested $15,000 of the $40,000 cash that was used to start the business. A. Calloway was expected to assume the vast majority of the responsibility for operating the business. The partnership agreement called for A. Calloway to receive 60 percent of the profits and M. Calloway to get the remaining 40 percent. With regard to the $3,000 distribution, A. Calloway withdrew $1,200 from the business and M. Calloway withdrew $1,800.
c. Calloway is a corporation. It issued 5,000 common shares for $40,000 cash to start the business.

PROBLEM 11–2B *Recording and Reporting Share Transactions and Cash Dividends across Two Accounting Cycles*

L.O. 3, 4

Hamby Corporation received a charter that authorized the issuance of 100,000 common shares and 50,000 shares of $5 cumulative preferred. Hamby Corporation completed the following transactions during its first two years of operation.

2008

Jan. 5 Sold 10,000 common shares for $28 per share.
12 Sold 1,000 preferred shares for $70 per share.
Apr. 5 Sold 40,000 common shares for $40 per share.
Dec. 31 During the year, earned $170,000 in cash revenue and paid $110,000 for cash expenses.
31 Declared the cash dividend on the outstanding shares of preferred shares for 2008. The dividend will be paid on February 15 to shareholders of record on January 10, 2009. Closed the revenue, expense, and dividend accounts to the retained earnings account.

2009

Feb. 15 Paid the cash dividend declared on December 31, 2008.
Mar. 3 Sold 10,000 preferred shares for $78 per share.
Dec. 31 During the year, earned $210,000 in cash revenues and paid $140,000 for cash expenses.
31 Declared the annual dividend on the preferred shares and a $0.60 per share dividend on the common shares. The dividends will be paid on February 15 to shareholders of record on January 10, 2010.
31 Closed revenue, expense, and dividend accounts to the retained earnings account.

Required

a. Prepare journal entries for these transactions for 2008 and 2009.
b. Prepare the balance sheets at December 31, 2008 and 2009.
c. How many common shares had been *issued* at the end of 2008? At the end of 2009?

L.O. 3, 4, 5 PROBLEM 11–3B *Recording and Reporting Stock Dividends*

Deaton Co. completed the following transactions in 2006, the first year of operation:

1. Issued 20,000 common shares for $10 per share.
2. Issued 5,000 $1 preferred shares for $20 per share (no shares were issued prior to this transaction).
3. Paid a cash dividend of $5,000 to preferred shareholders.
4. Issued a 10 percent stock dividend on the common shares. The market value at the dividend declaration date was $15 per share.
5. Later that year, issued a 2-for-1 split on the shares of outstanding common shares. The market price at that time was $35 per share.
6. Produced $145,000 of cash revenues and incurred $97,000 of cash expenses.

Required

a. Record each of the six events in a horizontal statements model like the following one. In the Cash Flow Statement column, indicate whether the item is an operating activity (OA), investing activity (IA), or financing activity (FA). Use NA to indicate that an element is not affected by the event.

Assets =	Liab. +		Equity		Rev. − Exp. = Net Inc.	Cash Flow Statement
Cash =	Div. Pay +	Pr. Sh. +	Com. Sh. +	Ret. Earn.		

b. Record the 2006 transactions in general journal form.
c. Prepare the shareholders' equity section of the balance sheet at the end of 2006. (Include all necessary information.)
d. Theoretically, what is the market value of the common shares after the stock split?

PROBLEM 11–4B *Analyzing the Shareholders' Equity Section of the Balance Sheet*

L.O. 3, 5

The shareholders' equity section of the balance sheet for Cross Electric Co. at December 31, 2005, is as follows:

Shareholders' Equity		
Contributed Capital		
Preferred Shares, ? Stated Value, 8% cumulative,		
100,000 shares authorized,		
5,000 shares issued and outstanding	$ 250,000	
Common Shares		
200,000 shares authorized,		
100,000 shares issued and outstanding	2,500,000	
Contributed Capital in Excess of Stated Value—Preferred	100,000	
Total Contributed Capital		$2,850,000
Retained Earnings		500,000
Total Shareholders' Equity		$3,350,000

Note: The market value per share of the common shares is $36, and the market value per share of the preferred shares is $75.

Required

a. What is the stated value of the preferred shares?
b. What is the dividend per share on the preferred shares?
c. What was the average issue price per share (price for which the shares were issued) of the common shares?
d. If Cross declares a 3-for-1 stock split on the common shares, how many shares will be outstanding after the split? What amount will be transferred from the retained earnings account because of the stock split? Theoretically, what will be the market price of the common shares immediately after the stock split?

PROBLEM 11–5B *Effects of Equity Transactions on Financial Statements*

L.O. 3, 4, 5

The following events were experienced by Baskin, Inc.

1. Issued common shares for cash.
2. Declared a cash dividend.
3. Issued cumulative preferred shares.
4. Issued noncumulative preferred shares.
5. Distributed a stock dividend.
6. Distributed a 2-for-1 stock split on the common shares.
7. Paid a cash dividend that was previously declared.

Required

Show the effect of each event on the elements of the financial statements using a horizontal statements model like the following one. Use + for increase, − for decrease, and NA for not affected. In the Cash Flow Statement column, indicate whether the item is an operating activity (OA), investing activity (IA), or financing activity (FA). The first transaction is entered as an example.

Event No.	Assets	=	Liab.	+	Equity	Rev.	−	Exp.	=	Net Inc.	Cash Flow Statement
1	+		NA		+	NA	−	NA	=	NA	+ FA

ANALYZE, THINK, COMMUNICATE

ATC 11–1 BUSINESS APPLICATIONS CASE *Bombardier's Annual Report*

Using the Bombardier financial statements in Appendix B, answer the following questions:

Required

a. What classes of shares are authorized by Bombardier?
b. How many common shares were outstanding as of January 31, 2001? January 31, 2002?
c. Did Bombardier pay any cash dividends in 2002? If so, how much?
d. Using the consolidated statement of shareholders' equity, determine why the number of common shares outstanding increased or decreased from 2001 to 2002.
e. What information, if any, was disclosed about stock splits, stock dividends, or treasury shares.

ATC 11–2 GROUP ASSIGNMENT *Missing Information*

Listed here are the shareholders' equity sections of three public companies for years ending 2000 and 1999:

	2000	1999
Wendy's (dollar amounts are presented in thousands)		
Shareholders' Equity		
Common shares, ?? Stated Value per share, authorized: 200,000,000; 136,188,000 in 2000 and 134,856,000 in 1999 shares issued, respectively	$ 12,074	$ 11,941
Capital in Excess of Stated Value	423,144	398,580
Retained Earnings	1,211,015	1,068,883
Accumulated Other Comprehensive Expense	(27,133)	(14,443)
Treasury Shares, at cost: 21,978,000 in 2000; 16,626,000 shares in 1999	(492,957)	(399,522)
Coca-Cola (dollar amounts are presented in millions)		
Shareholders' Equity		
Common Shares, ?? Par Value per share, authorized: 5,600,000,000; issued: 3,481,882,834 shares in 2000 and 3,466,371,904 shares in 1999	870	861
Capital Surplus	3,196	2,584
Retained Earnings	21,265	20,773
Accumulated Other Comprehensive Income	(2,722)	(1,551)
Treasury Shares, at cost: (997,121,427 shares in 2000; 994,796,786 shares in 1999)	(13,293)	(13,160)
Harley Davidson (dollar amounts are presented in thousands)		
Shareholders' Equity		
Common shares, ?? Par Value per share, authorized: 200,000,000, issued: 321,185,567 in 2000 and 318,586,144 shares in 1999	3,210	3,184
Additional Paid-in Capital	285,390	234,948
Retained Earnings	1,431,017	1,113,376
Accumulated Other Comprehensive Income	308	(2,067)
Treasury Shares, at cost: 19,114,822 for 2000 and 15,863,518 for 1999	(313,994)	(187,992)
Unearned Compensation	(276)	(369)

Required

a. Divide the class in three sections and divide each section into groups of three to five students. Assign each section one of the companies.

Group Tasks

Based on the company assigned to your group, answer the following questions.

b. What is the per share par or stated value of the common shares in 2000?
c. What was the average issue price of the common shares for each year?
d. How many shares are outstanding at the end of each year?
e. What is the average cost per share of the treasury shares?

f. Do the data suggest that your company was profitable in 2000?
g. Can you determine the amount of net income from the information given? What is missing?
h. What is the total shareholders' equity of your company for each year?

Class Discussion

i. Have each group select a representative to present the information about its company. Compare the share issue price and the par or stated value of the companies.
j. Compare the average issue price to the current market price for each of the companies. Speculate about what might cause the difference.

REAL-WORLD CASE *Computing P/E Ratios for Four Companies* ATC 11–3

Many companies grant certain members of management stock options that allow them to purchase designated amounts of shares for less than its market price. These arrangements are referred to as *share compensation plans* and are intended to help the company retain high-quality management and to encourage management to increase the market value of the company's shares.

Listed here are data from four different companies that grant stock options to members of their management. The data are based on information provided in the companies' annual reports.

Sears Canada	
Basic EPS as reported on the fiscal year 2000 income statement	$ 3.89
Basic EPS if share compensation is deducted	3.77
Selling price of the company's shares on Dec 7, 2001	45.00
Hudson's Bay Company	
Basic EPS as reported on the fiscal year 2001 income statement	$ 1.60
Basic EPS if share compensation is deducted	1.47
Selling price of the company's shares on Dec 7, 2001	13.60
Microsoft	
Basic EPS as reported on the fiscal year 2001 income statement	$ 1.38
Basic EPS if share compensation is deducted	1.32
Selling price of the company's shares on Dec 7, 2001	68.47
Oracle Corporation	
Basic EPS as reported on the fiscal year 2001 income statement	$ 0.44
Basic EPS if share compensation is deducted	0.46
Selling price of the company's shares on Dec 7, 2001	15.85

Required

a. Compute each company's P/E ratio on December 7, 2001, based on (1) EPS as reported and (2) EPS with share compensation deducted. You will have eight P/E ratios.
b. Assuming these companies are representative of their respective industries (department stores and software companies), what conclusions can you draw from the data provided and from your P/E computations? Write a brief report presenting your conclusions and the reasons for them.

BUSINESS APPLICATIONS CASE *Finding Stock Market Information* ATC 11–4

This problem requires stock price quotations for the Toronto Stock Exchange, the New York Stock Exchange, and NASDAQ. These are available in the business sections of many daily newspapers, including *The National Post* and *The Globe and Mail*. Stock prices are also available on electronic data services such as globeinvestor.com.

Required

For each company listed here, provide the requested information as of Thursday of last week. (*Hint:* Information about Thursday's stock market is in Friday's newspaper.)

Name of Company	Stock Exchange Where Listed	Closing Price	P/E Ratio
Indigo Books & Music Inc.			
Laidlaw Inc.			
Magna International Inc.			
Yahoo			
Xerox			

ATC 11–5 BUSINESS APPLICATIONS CASE *Using the P/E Ratio*

During 2007, Geolock Corporation and Minerals Corporation reported net incomes of $8,000 and $9,400, respectively. Each company had 2,000 common shares issued and outstanding. The market price per share of Geolock was $48; Minerals' shares sold for $94 per share.

Required

a. Determine the P/E ratio for each company.
b. Based on the P/E ratios computed in Requirement *a*, which company do investors believe has more potential for growth in income?

ATC 11–6 WRITING ASSIGNMENT *Comparison of Organizational Forms*

Jim Baku and Scott Hanson are thinking about opening a new restaurant. Baku has extensive marketing experience but does not know that much about food preparation. However, Hanson is an excellent chef. Both will work in the business, but Baku will provide most of the funds necessary to start the business. At this time, they cannot decide whether to operate the business as a partnership or a corporation.

Required

Prepare a written memo to Baku and Hanson describing the advantages and disadvantages of each organizational form. Also, from the limited information provided, recommend the organizational form you think they should use.

ATC 11–7 ETHICAL DILEMMA *Bad News versus Very Bad News*

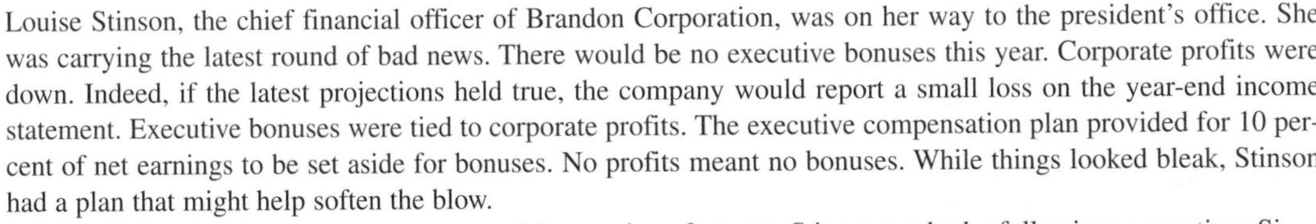

Louise Stinson, the chief financial officer of Brandon Corporation, was on her way to the president's office. She was carrying the latest round of bad news. There would be no executive bonuses this year. Corporate profits were down. Indeed, if the latest projections held true, the company would report a small loss on the year-end income statement. Executive bonuses were tied to corporate profits. The executive compensation plan provided for 10 percent of net earnings to be set aside for bonuses. No profits meant no bonuses. While things looked bleak, Stinson had a plan that might help soften the blow.

After informing the company president of the earnings forecast, Stinson made the following suggestion: Since the company was going to report a loss anyway, why not report a big loss? She reasoned that the directors and shareholders would not be much more angry if the company reported a large loss than if it reported a small one. There were several questionable assets that could be written down in the current year. This would increase the current year's loss but would reduce expenses in subsequent accounting periods. For example, the company was carrying damaged inventory that was estimated to have a value of $2,500,000. If this estimate were revised to $500,000, the company would have to recognize a $2,000,000 loss in the current year. However, next year when the goods were sold, the expense for cost of goods sold would be $2,000,000 less and profits would be higher by that amount. Although the directors would be angry this year, they would certainly be happy next year. The strategy would also have the benefit of adding $200,000 to next year's executive bonus pool ($2,000,000 × 0.10). As well, it could not hurt this year's bonus pool because there would be no pool this year since the company was going to report a loss.

Some of the other items that Stinson is considering include (1) converting from straight-line to accelerated amortization, (2) increasing the percentage of receivables estimated to be uncollectible in the current year and lowering the percentage in the following year, and (3) raising the percentage of estimated warranty claims in the current period and lowering it in the following period. Finally, Stinson notes that two of the company's department stores have been experiencing losses. The company could sell these stores this year and thereby improve earnings next year. Stinson admits that the sale would result in significant losses this year, but she smiles as she thinks of next year's bonus cheque.

Required

a. Explain how each of the three numbered strategies for increasing the amount of the current year's loss would affect the shareholders' equity section of the balance sheet in the current year. How would the other elements of the balance sheet be affected?
b. If Stinson's strategy were effectively implemented, how would it affect the shareholders' equity in subsequent accounting periods?
c. Comment on the ethical implications of running the company for the sake of management (maximization of bonuses) versus the maximization of return to shareholders.
d. Formulate a bonus plan that will motivate managers to maximize the value of the firm instead of motivating them to manipulate the reporting process.
e. How would Stinson's strategy of overstating the amount of the reported loss in the current year affect the company's current P/E ratio?

SEDAR DATABASE *Analyzing Maple Leaf's Equity Structure* ATC 11–8

Required

Using the most current annual report available on SEDAR, answer the following questions about Maple Leaf Foods for the most recent year reported. (Maple Leaf Foods is a leader in prepared meat products, flour-based products, and livestock and pet foods.) Instructions for using SEDAR are in Appendix A.

a. What is the *book value* of Maple Leaf's shareholders' equity that is shown on the company's balance sheet?
b. What was Maple Leaf's earnings per share?
c. Does Maple Leaf have any treasury shares? If so, how many treasury shares does the company hold?
d. Why do the shares of a company such as Maple Leaf have a market value that is higher than its book value?

SPREADSHEET ANALYSIS *Using Excel* ATC 11–9

Annette's Accessories had the following shares issued and outstanding at January 1, 2005.

150,000 Common Shares
10,000 Shares of $50 Stated Value, 8%, Cumulative Preferred Shares

On March 5, 2005, Annette's declared a $100,000 cash dividend to be paid March 31 to shareholders of record on March 21.

Required

Set up a spreadsheet to calculate the total amount of dividends to be paid to preferred and common shareholders under the following alternative situations:

a. No dividends are in arrears for preferred shareholders.
b. One year's worth of dividends is in arrears for preferred shareholders.
c. Two years' worth of dividends is in arrears for preferred shareholders.
d. Instead of a $100,000 dividend, Annette's paid a $70,000 dividend and one year of dividends was in arrears.

Spreadsheet Tips

The spreadsheet on page 486 provides one method of setting up formulas for all possible alternatives. The spreadsheet also reflects the results of Requirement *a*.

Notice the use of the IF function. The IF function looks like =F(condition, true, false). To use the IF function, first describe a certain condition to Excel. Next indicate the desired result if that condition is found to be true. Finally, indicate the desired result if that condition is found to be false. Notice in cell C4 of the spreadsheet (dividends in arrears distributed to preferred shareholders) that the condition provided is B4<B3, which is asking whether the dividends in arrears are less than the total dividend. If this condition is true, the formula indicates to display B4, which is the amount of the dividends in arrears. If the condition is false, the formula indicates that B3 should be displayed, which is the total amount of the dividend.

The IF function can also be used to determine the amount of the current dividend distributed to preferred shareholders, the amount available for common shareholders, and the dividends in arrears after the dividend.

Microsoft Excel - dch11-1.xls

File Edit View Insert Format Tools Data Window Help

C4 = =IF(B4<B3,B4,B3)

	A	B	C	D
1	**Alternative 1- Formulas**		Distribution to Shareholders	
2			Preferred	Common
3	Total dividend declared	100000		
4	Preferred Dividends in Arrears	0	=IF(B4<B3,B4,B3)	
5	Current Preferred Dividend	=500000*8%	=IF(B5<B3-C4,B5,B3-C4)	
6	Available & Distributed to Common	=IF(B3-C4-C5>0,B3-C4-C5,0)		=B6
7	Total	=B3-B4-B5-B6	=SUM(C4:C5)	=D6
8				
9	Dividends in Arrears	=IF(B7<0,B7,0)		
10				
11	**Alternative 1- Actual Numbers**		Distribution to Shareholders	
12			Preferred	Common
13	Total dividend declared	100000		
14	Preferred Dividends in Arrears	0	0	
15	Current Preferred Dividend	40000	40000	
16	Available & Distributed to Common	60000		60000
17	Total	0	40000	60000
18				
19	Dividends in Arrears	0		
20				
21				

ATC 11–10 SPREADSHEET ASSIGNMENT *Mastering Excel*

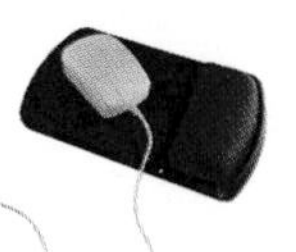

Required

Complete Requirement *a* of Problem 11–3B using an Excel spreadsheet.

Chapter 12

Cash Flow Statement

Learning Objectives

After completing this chapter, you should be able to:

1. Identify the types of business events that are reported in the three sections of the cash flow statement.

2. Convert an accrual account balance to its cash equivalent.

3. Prepare a cash flow statement using the T-account method.

4. Explain how cash flow from operating activities reported under the indirect method differs from that reported under the direct method.

5. Explain how the classifications used on the cash flow statement could provide misleading information to decision makers.

the *curious* accountant

Priceline.com began operations in April 1998 and first sold its shares to the public on March 30, 1999. By the end of 2000, the company had cumulative net losses of more than US$1.4 billion. Even though its sales grew from US$35 million in 1998 to more than US$1 billion in 2000, it did not make a profit in any of those years. How can a company lose so much money and still be able to pay its bills? See page 493 for the answer.

The cash flow statement explains how a company obtained and used cash during some period. The sources of cash are known as ***cash inflows****, and the uses are called* ***cash outflows****. The statement classifies cash receipts (inflows) and payments (outflows) into three categories: operating activities, investing activities, and financing activities. The following sections define these activities and outline the types of cash flows that are normally classified under each category.*

Cash Flow Statement

Operating Activities

LO1

Identify the types of business events that are reported in the three sections of the cash flow statement.

Operating activities include cash inflows and outflows generated by running (operating) the business. Some of the specific items that are shown under this section are as follows:

1. Cash receipts from sales, commissions, fees, and receipts from interest and dividends.
2. Cash payments for inventories, salaries, operating expenses, interest, and taxes.

Note that *gains* and *losses* are not included in this section. The total cash collected from the sale of assets is included in the investing activities section.

Investing Activities

Investing activities include cash flows generated through a company's purchase or sale of long-term operational assets, investments in other companies, and lending activities. Some items included in this section follow:

1. Cash receipts from the sale of property, plant, equipment or of short-term investments as well as the collection of loans.
2. Cash payments used to purchase property, plant, equipment or short-term investments as well as loans made to others.

Financing Activities

Financing activities include cash inflows and outflows associated with the company's own equity transactions or its borrowing activities. The following are some items appearing under the financing activities section:

1. Cash receipts from the issue of shares and borrowed funds.
2. Cash payments for the purchase of treasury shares, repayment of debt, and payment of dividends.

When you are trying to classify transactions into one of the three categories, it is helpful to note that the identification of the proper category depends on the company's perspective rather than on the type of account being considered. For example, a transaction involving common shares is considered an investing activity if the company is purchasing or selling its investment in another company's common shares. In contrast, common share transactions are classified as financing activities if the company is issuing its own shares or is buying back its own shares (treasury shares). Similarly, the receipt of dividends is classified as an operating activity, but the payment of dividends is classified as a financing activity. As well, lending cash is an investing activity, and borrowing cash is a financing activity. Therefore, proper classification centres on the behaviour of the company involved rather than on the type of instrument being used.

Noncash Investing and Financing Transactions

Companies sometimes engage in significant **noncash investing and financing transactions**. For example, a company may issue some of its common shares in exchange for the title to a plot of land. Similarly, a company could accept a mortgage obligation in exchange for the title of ownership to a building (a 100 percent owner-financed exchange). Since these types of transactions do not involve the exchange of cash, they cannot be included as cash receipts or payments on the cash flow statement. However, the Canadian Institute of Chartered Accountants (CICA) has concluded that full and fair reporting requires the disclosure of all material investing and financing activities regardless of whether they involve the exchange of cash. Therefore, the CICA requires that the cash flow statement include note disclosure of noncash investing and financing activities.

Exhibit 12–1

WESTERN COMPANY Cash Flow Statement For the Year Ended 2007		
Cash Flows from Operating Activities		
Plus: List of Individual Inflows	$XXX	
Less: List of Individual Outflows	(XXX)	
Net Increase (Decrease) from Operating Activities		$XXX
Cash Flows from Investing Activities		
Plus: List of Individual Inflows	XXX	
Less: List of Individual Outflows	(XXX)	
Net Increase (Decrease) from Investing Activities		XXX
Cash Flows from Financing Activities		
Plus: List of Individual Inflows	XXX	
Less: List of Individual Outflows	(XXX)	
Net Increase (Decrease) from Financing Activities		XXX
Net Increase (Decrease) in Cash		XXX
Plus: Beginning Cash Balance		XXX
Ending Cash Balance		$XXX

Reporting Format for Cash Flow Statement

The cash flow statement is arranged with operating activities shown first, investing activities second, and financing activities last. Under each category, individual cash inflows are shown first, with cash outflows being subtracted and the net difference being carried forward. Exhibit 12–1 demonstrates this format of statement presentation.

Converting from Accrual to Cash-Basis Accounting

The operating activities section of the cash flow statement is essentially a cash-basis income statement. Since accounting records are normally maintained on an accrual basis, data based on accruals and deferrals must be converted to cash equivalents to determine the amount of cash flow from operating activities. The following section discusses the conversion process.

LO2
Convert an accrual account balance to its cash equivalent.

Operating Activities

Converting Accruals to Cash

Accrual accounting is the process by which revenues and expenses are recognized before cash is exchanged. When accrual accounting is applied, revenue and expense items recognized in the current period may have cash consequences in a later period. As well, revenue and expense items recognized in a past period may result in cash receipts or payments that materialize in the current period. Therefore, the amount of cash receipts and payments realized during any particular accounting period may be larger or smaller than the amount of revenue and expense recognized during that period. The following section discusses the adjustments needed to convert accrual accounting to cash-basis accounting.

Revenue Transactions With regard to **revenue transactions**, the application of accrual accounting means that some revenue is likely to be reported on the income statement before the cash is received. The amount of revenue recognized is normally different from the amount of cash that the company realizes in any particular accounting period. Some customers purchase goods or services in the current accounting period but pay for them in a later period. Other customers may pay cash in the current period for goods or services purchased in a prior period. As a result, the cash received may be more or less than the amount of revenue recognized.

To convert revenue recognized to the corresponding amount of cash collected, one must analyze both the amount of revenue appearing on the income statement and the change in the balance of the accounts receivable account. For example, assume that a company reported $500 of revenue on its income statement. As well, assume that during the accounting period at hand, the beginning and ending balances in the company's Accounts Receivable account were $100 and $160, respectively. Therefore, the balance in the receivables account increased by $60 ($160 − $100). Taking this into consideration, we can conclude that $60 of the $500 in sales was not collected in cash. Therefore, the amount of cash collected must have been $440 ($500 − $60).

LO3 Prepare a cash flow statement using the T-account method.

The conclusion that $440 of cash was collected from the revenue transactions was derived through logic. This conclusion can be confirmed through a process commonly called the T-account method. The **T-account method** begins with the opening of the Accounts Receivable T-account with the appropriate beginning and ending balances displayed. Here, the beginning balance is $100, and the ending balance is $160. Next, a $500 debit is added to the account to record the recognition of the revenue. The resulting T-account is as follows:

	Accounts Receivable	
Beginning Balance	100	
Debit to Record Sales	500	?
Ending Balance	160	

Mathematically, adding $500 to a beginning balance of $100 does not result in an ending balance of $160. A $440 credit to the receivables account would be required to arrive at the $160 ending balance. Since cash collections result in credits to the Accounts Receivable account, it can be assumed that the Cash account was debited when the receivables account was credited. The analysis of the T-account also leads us to conclude that $440 of cash was collected as a result of activities associated with the generation of revenue.

Expense Transactions Accrual accounting results in the recognition of **expense transactions** before the payment of cash occurs. This means that a liability is normally recorded at the time the expense is recognized. The liability is later reduced as cash payments are made. This means the amount of accrued expense displayed on the income statement must be analyzed in conjunction with any change in the balance of the related liability account in determining the amount of cash outflow associated with the expense recognition. For example, assume that a company reports $200 of utilities expense on its income statement. As well, assume that the beginning and ending balances in the Utilities Payable account are $70 and $40, respectively. All this implies that the company not only made payments to cover the use of the utilities in the current period but also paid an additional $30 ($70 − $40) to reduce the obligations of prior periods. The amount of cash outflow associated with utility use is $230 ($200 + $30).

The T-account method can also be used to verify the $230 cash payment. A T-account for Utilities Payable is opened with beginning and ending balances placed in the account. Also, a credit amounting to $200 is made to the account to reflect the recognition of the current period's utility expense. The resultant T-account appears as follows:

Utilities Payable		
	70	Beginning Balance
?	200	Credit to Record Expense
	40	Ending Balance

First, it should be remembered that GAAP requires that earnings and losses be computed on an accrual basis. A company can have negative earnings and still have positive cash flows from operating activities. This was not the case at Priceline.com, however. From 1998 through 2000, the company's cash flows from operating activities totalled a negative US$122.9 million. Although this is much less than the US$1.4 billion cumulative losses the company incurred during the same period, it still does not pay the bills.

Priceline.com, like many new companies, was able to stay in business because of the cash it raised through financing activities. These cash flows were a positive US$325.9 million for 1998 through 2000. The company also had some significant noncash transactions. Exhibit 12–2 presents Priceline.com's cash flow statement from the first three years of its life.

Exhibit 12–2

PRICELINE.COM INCORPORATED
Cash Flow Statement
(in thousands of $US)

	Year Ended December 31		
	2000	**1999**	**1998**
Operating Activities			
Net loss	$(315,145)	$(1,055,090)	$(112,243)
Adjustments to reconcile net loss to net cash used in operating activities			
Depreciation and amortization	17,385	5,348	1,860
Provision for uncollectible accounts	7,354	3,127	581
Warrant costs	8,595	1,189,111	67,866
Webhouse warrant	189,000	(189,000)	—
Net loss on disposal of fixed assets	12,398	—	—
Net loss on sale of equity investments	2,558	—	—
Asset impairment	4,886	—	—
Compensation expense arising from deferred share awards	1,711	—	—
Changes in assets and liabilities			
Accounts receivable	7,401	(29,617)	(4,757)
Prepaid expenses and other current assets	1,194	(12,043)	(1,922)
Related party receivables	(3,484)	—	—
Accounts payable and accrued expenses	45,155	28,470	8,300
Other	1,276	(3,331)	112
Net cash used in operating activities	(19,716)	(63,025)	(40,203)
Investing Activities			
Additions to property and equipment	(37,320)	(27,416)	(6,607)
Purchase of convertible notes and warrants of licencees	(25,676)	(2,000)	
Proceeds from sales/maturities of investments	31,101	—	—
Funding of restricted cash and bank term deposits	(4,779)	(8,789)	(680)
Investment in marketable securities	(5,000)	(38,771)	
Net cash used in investing activities	(41,674)	(76,976)	(7,287)

Continued

Financing Activities			
Related party payable	—	—	(1,072)
Issuance of long-term debt	—	—	1,000
Payment of long-term debt	—	(1,000)	
Principal payments under capital lease obligations	—	(25)	(22)
Issuance of common shares and subscription units	14,031	211,816	26,495
Payment received on shareholder note	—	—	250
Issuance of Series A convertible preferred shares	—	—	20,000
Issuance of Series B convertible preferred shares	—	—	54,415
Net cash provided by financing activities	14,031	210,791	101,066
Net increase (decrease) in cash and cash equivalents	(47,359)	70,790	53,576
Cash and cash equivalents, beginning of period	124,383	53,593	17
Cash and cash equivalents, end of period	$ 77,024	$ 124,383	$ 53,593
Supplemental Cash Flow Information			
Cash paid during the period for interest	$ 4	$ 37	$ 61

Mathematical logic dictates that a $230 debit is required to arrive at the $40 ending balance ($70 + $200 − $230 = $40). Since debits to payable accounts are normally offset by credits to the Cash account, the T-account analysis indicates that cash outflows associated with utility expenses amounted to $230.

Hammer, Inc., had a beginning balance of $22,400 in its Accounts Receivable account. During the accounting period, Hammer earned $234,700 of revenue on account. The ending balance in the Accounts Receivable account was $18,200. Based on this information alone, determine the amount of cash received from revenue transactions. In what section of the cash flow statement would this cash flow appear?

Answer

Beginning accounts receivable balance	$ 22,400
Plus: Revenue earned on account during the period	234,700
Receivables available for collection	257,100
Less: Ending accounts receivable balance	(18,200)
Cash collected from receivables (revenue)	$238,900

Cash received from revenue transactions appears in the operating activities section of the cash flow statement.

Converting Deferrals to Cash

Deferral transactions are events in which cash receipts or payments occur before the associated revenue or expense is recognized. Since revenue and expense recognition occurs in one accounting period and the associated cash receipts and payments occur in a different accounting period, differences arise between income reported in the financial statements and the cash-basis income. The following section discusses the procedures for converting deferrals to their cash-basis equivalents.

Revenue Transactions When cash is collected before the earnings process is completed, a company incurs an obligation (liability) to provide goods or services at some future date. The revenue associated with the cash receipt is recognized in a later period when the work is accomplished. As a result, *the amount of revenue reported on the income statement and the amount of cash receipts normally differ*. The conversion of deferrals to cash requires an analysis of the amount of revenue reported and the change in the balance of the liability account, *Unearned Revenue*. For example, assume the amount of revenue recognized was $400 and that the Unearned Revenue account increased from a beginning balance of $80 to an ending balance of $110. The increase in the liability account implies that the company received cash in excess of the amount of the revenue recognized. Not only did the company earn the $400 of revenue reported on the income statement, but it also received $30 ($110 − $80), for which it became obligated to provide goods and services in a future period. Therefore, cash receipts associated with earnings activities amounted to $430 ($400 + $30).

An analysis of the T-account for unearned revenue confirms the receipt of $430 cash. The Unearned Revenue account is opened with the appropriate beginning and ending balances. A debit is made to the account to record the recognition of $400 of revenue. The resulting account looks like this:

	Unearned Revenue		
		80	Beginning Balance
Debit to Recognize Revenue	400	?	
		110	Ending Balance

Clearly, $430 must have been added to the beginning balance of $80 so that when the $400 debit entry was subtracted, the resulting ending balance was $110. Credit entries to the Unearned Revenue account are normally offset by corresponding debits to the Cash account; this suggests that $430 of cash receipts was associated with revenue activities.

Expense Transactions Very often, companies pay cash for goods or services that are not used right away. The cost of the goods or services is normally capitalized in an asset account at the time the cash payment is made. The assets are then expensed in later periods when the goods or services are used for earning revenue. Thus, some items paid for in prior periods are expensed in the current period, while other items that are paid for in the current period are not expensed until later periods. *Remember, the amount of cash outflows normally differs from the amount of expense recognized for any given accounting period.*

To convert recognized expenses to cash flows, we must analyze the amount of change in the balance of certain asset accounts as well as the amount of corresponding expense recognized on the income statement. For example, assume that the beginning and ending balances in the Prepaid Rent account are $60 and $80, respectively, and that the amount of reported rent expense is $800. This suggests that the company not only paid enough cash to cover the $800 of recognized expense but also paid an additional $20 ($80 − $60). Therefore, the cash outflow associated with the rent payments amounted to $820 ($800 + $20).

We can confirm the cash outflow of $820 for rent payments through T-account analysis. The beginning and ending balances are placed in a T-account for prepaid rent. We then credit the account to reflect the rent expense recognition of $800. The resulting T-account looks like this:

	Prepaid Rent		
Beginning Balance	60		
	?	800	Credit to Recognize Expense
Ending Balance	80		

To have an ending balance of $80, there must have been an $820 debit to the account ($60 + $820 − $800 = $80). Since a debit to the Prepaid Rent account is normally offset by a credit to Cash, the analysis confirms that the cash outflow associated with rent payments is $820.

Investing Activities

Determining cash flow from investing activities may also require us to analyze changes in the beginning and ending account balances along with certain income statement data. For example, assume that the

Land account had a beginning and ending balance of $900 and $300, respectively. As well, assume that the income statement contained the recognition of a $200 gain on the sale of land. The $600 ($900 − $300) decline in the book value of the land suggests that the land was sold. The gain from the income statement implies that the land was sold for $200 more than its book value. Thus, the analysis suggests that the land was sold for $800 ($600 + $200) cash. Note that the amount of cash flow is different from the amount of gain appearing on the income statement. Indeed, the full $800 cash inflow appears in the investing activities section of the cash flow statement. The operating activities section of the statement is not affected by the gain from the land sale.

We can verify the amount of cash inflow ($800) from investing activities through the T-account method. An analysis of the beginning and ending balances in the Land account suggests that land costing $600 ($900 beginning balance − $300 ending balance) was sold. This amount, coupled with the $200 gain shown in the Retained Earnings account, suggests that $800 cash was collected from the sale. The appropriate T-accounts look like this:

Cash		Land		Retained Earnings	
?		900	600		200
		300			

Possibly, the company could have received some resource other than cash when the land was sold. However, other alternative explanations would be discovered when the other balance sheet accounts were analyzed.

Financing Activities

Cash flow from financing activities can often be determined by simply analyzing the change in the balances of liability and shareholders' equity accounts. For example, an increase in bond liabilities from $500 to $800 implies that the company issued new bonds that resulted in the receipt of $300 cash. This conclusion can be supported by an analysis using the T-account method. A T-account is opened with the beginning and ending balances looking like this:

Bonds Payable		
	500	Beginning Balance
	?	
	800	Ending Balance

A $300 credit must be added to the $500 opening balance to arrive at the $800 ending balance. Since cash normally increases when bond liabilities increase, the analysis supports the conclusion that $300 of cash inflow was derived from the incurrence of debt.

Other explanations are also possible. Perhaps some of the company's shareholders decided to exchange their equity securities for debt securities. Or the company may have been willing to incur the obligation in exchange for some asset (property, plant, or equipment) other than cash.

Comprehensive Example Using the T-Account Approach

LO3

Prepare a cash flow statement using the T-account method.

The preceding discussion emphasized the need to analyze financial statements and supporting data when preparing a cash flow statement. The beginning and ending balances in the accounts being analyzed can be drawn from two successive balance sheets. The revenues, expenses, gains, and losses can be found on the income statement. Also, notes to the financial statements may contain information needed to

Exhibit 12–3

THE NEW SOUTH CORPORATION
Comparative Balance Sheets
December 31

	2004	2005
Current Assets		
Cash	$ 400	$ 900
Accounts Receivable	1,200	1,000
Interest Receivable	300	400
Inventory	8,200	8,900
Prepaid Insurance	1,400	1,100
Total Current Assets	11,500	12,300
Long-Term Assets		
Investments, Long-Term	3,500	5,100
Equipment	4,600	5,400
Less: Accumulated Amortization	(1,200)	(900)
Land	6,000	8,500
Total Long-Term Assets	12,900	18,100
Total Assets	$24,400	$30,400
Current Liabilities		
Accounts Payable—Inventory Purchases	$ 1,100	$ 800
Salaries Payable	900	1,000
Other Operating Expenses Payable	1,300	1,500
Interest Payable	500	300
Unearned Rent Revenue	1,600	600
Total Current Liabilities	5,400	4,200
Long-Term Liabilities		
Mortgage Payable	0	2,500
Bonds Payable	4,000	1,000
Total Long-Term Liabilities	4,000	3,500
Shareholders' Equity		
Common Shares	8,000	10,000
Retained Earnings	7,000	12,700
Total Shareholders' Equity	15,000	22,700
Total Liabilities and Shareholders' Equity	$24,400	$30,400

identify noncash transactions. Exhibits 12–3 and 12–4 are the balance sheets, income statement, and additional information needed to prepare a cash flow statement.

Preparation of the Cash Flow Statement

Begin the analysis of the financial statements by opening a T-account for each item on the balance sheet. Enter the beginning and ending balances for each item into the T-accounts. Use the 2004 balance sheet (see Exhibit 12–3) to determine the beginning balance of each account and the 2005 balance sheet to get the ending balance. The Cash account should be large enough to be divided into three components, representing cash flows from operating, investing, and financing activities. Exhibit 12–5 (page 499) contains a full set of T-accounts with all analytical transactions included. Each transaction is labelled with a lower-case letter. Since some analysis requires more than one entry, each letter is also followed by a number, which permits detailed labelling for each transaction. The following section explains each transaction in full detail.

Exhibit 12–4

THE NEW SOUTH CORPORATION
Income Statement
For the Period Ended December 31, 2005

Sales		$20,600
Cost of Goods Sold		(10,500)
Gross Profit		10,100
Operating Expenses		
Amortization Expense	$ 800	
Salaries Expense	2,700	
Insurance Expense	600	
Other Operating Expenses	1,400	
Total Operating Expenses		(5,500)
Operating Income		4,600
Other Operating Income—Rent Revenue		2,400
Total Operating Income		7,000
Nonoperating Revenue and Expenses		
Interest Revenue	700	
Interest Expense	(400)	
Loss on Sale of Equipment	(100)	
Total Nonoperating Items		200
Net Income		$ 7,200

Additional information:

1. The corporation sold equipment for $300 cash. This equipment had an original cost of $1,500 and accumulated amortization of $1,100 at the time of the sale.
2. The corporation issued a $2,500 mortgage note in exchange for land.
3. There was a $1,500 cash dividend paid during the accounting period.

Cash Flows from Operating Activities

Cash flow from operating activities is essentially a cash-basis income statement. Since accrual accounting is normally used in preparing formal financial statements, we have to convert the income statement data to cash equivalents. Thus, each item on the income statement should be analyzed separately to assess its effect on cash flow.

Cash Receipts from Sales

The first item on the income statement is $20,600 of sales revenue. Assuming that all sales transactions were on account, the entry to record sales would have required a debit to Accounts Receivable and a credit to Sales Revenue. Because the T-account analysis includes only balance sheet accounts and sales revenue acts to increase Retained Earnings, the entry to record sales in the T-accounts is shown as a debit to Accounts Receivable and a credit to Retained Earnings. This entry is labelled (a1) in Exhibit 12–5. After the sales revenue transaction is recorded, we can determine the cash inflow from sales by analyzing the Accounts Receivable T-account. Note that the beginning balance of $1,200 plus the debit to receivables of $20,600 resulting from sales transactions suggests that $21,800 of receivables was available for collection. Since the ending balance in the receivables account amounts to $1,000, there must have been $20,800 ($21,800 − $1,000) of receivables collected. This cash inflow is recognized with a debit to the Cash account under the operating activities section and a credit to the Accounts Receivable account. This entry is labelled (a2) in Exhibit 12–5.

Exhibit 12–5 *Balance Sheet T-Accounts*

Assets = Liabilities + Shareholders' Equity

Assets

Cash

Bal.	400		

Operating Activities

(a2)	20,800	11,500	(b3)
(g2)	1,400	2,600	(d2)
(h2)	600	300	(e2)
		1,200	(f2)
		600	(i2)

Investing Activities

(k1)	300	1,600	(j1)
		2,300	(l1)

Financing Activities

(o1)	2,000	3,000	(n1)
		1,500	(p1)
Bal.	900		

Accounts Receivable

Bal.	1,200	20,800	(a2)
(a1)	20,600		
Bal.	1,000		

Interest Receivable

Bal.	300	600	(h2)
(h1)	700		
Bal.	400		

Inventory

Bal.	8,200	10,500	(b1)
(b2)	11,200		
Bal.	8,900		

Prepaid Insurance

Bal.	1,400	600	(e1)
(e2)	300		
Bal.	1,100		

Investments

Bal.	3,500		
(j1)	1,600		
Bal.	5,100		

Equipment

Bal.	4,600	1,500	(k1)
(l1)	2,300		
Bal.	5,400		

Accumulated Amortization

(k1)	1,100	1,200	Bal.
		800	(c1)
		900	Bal.

Land

Bal.	6,000		
(m1)	2,500		
Bal.	8,500		

Liabilities

Accounts Payable—Inventory

(b3)	11,500	1,100	Bal.
		11,200	(b2)
		800	Bal.

Salaries Payable

(d2)	2,600	900	Bal.
		2,700	(d1)
		1,000	Bal.

Operating Exp. Payable

(f2)	1,200	1,300	Bal.
		1,400	(f1)
		1,500	Bal.

Interest Payable

(i1)	600	500	Bal.
		400	(i1)
		300	Bal.

Unearned Rent Revenue

(g1)	2,400	1,600	Bal.
		1,400	(g2)
		600	Bal.

Mortgage Payable

		0	Bal.
		2,500	(m1)
		2,500	Bal.

Bonds Payable

(n1)	3,000	4,000	Bal.
		1,000	Bal.

Shareholders' Equity

Common Shares

		8,000	Bal.
		2,000	(o1)
		10,000	Bal.

Retained Earnings

(b1)	10,500	7,000	Bal.
(c1)	800	20,600	(a1)
(d1)	2,700	2,400	(g1)
(e1)	600	700	(h1)
(f1)	1,400		
(i1)	400		
(k1)	100		
(p1)	1,500		
		12,700	Bal.

The preceding discussion introduces several practices that apply to the analysis of all cash flows from operating activities. First, note that all revenue, expense, gain, and loss transactions ultimately affect the Retained Earnings account. Therefore, to reconcile the beginning and ending balances in Retained Earnings, we post all income statement items directly to the Retained Earnings account. Second, the determination of when to stop the analysis depends on the reconciliation between the beginning and ending account balances. Here, the analysis of Accounts Receivable stopped with the $20,800 credit because the beginning balance plus the debit and minus the credit equalled the ending balance. The analysis of the account is completed because the beginning and ending balances have been reconciled (the change in the account has been fully explained). The analysis for the entire statement is completed when the beginning and ending balances in all the balance sheet accounts are reconciled. Since many of the balance sheet accounts remain to be reconciled, the cash flow analysis in this case will continue.

Cash Payments for Inventory Purchases

It is helpful to make two simplifying assumptions in analyzing cash payments for inventory purchases. First, assume that the company employs the perpetual inventory method; second, assume that all purchases are made on account. On the basis of these assumptions, the entry to record the cost of goods sold ($10,500, as shown on the income statement in Exhibit 12–4) would have required a credit to the Inventory account and a debit to Retained Earnings (cost of goods sold). This entry is labelled (b1) in the exhibit. This entry only partly explains the change in the beginning and ending balances of the Inventory account. A closer analysis of this account suggests that some inventory must have been purchased. Given that the beginning balance in the Inventory account was $8,200 and that $10,500 of inventory cost was transferred to cost of goods sold, it is logical to assume that $11,200 of inventory was purchased to arrive at the ending Inventory balance of $8,900. The entry to record the inventory purchase, labelled (b2), includes a debt to Inventory and a credit to Accounts Payable. This entry completes the explanation of the change in the beginning and ending balances but only partly explains the change in the beginning and ending balances in the Accounts Payable account. Given a beginning balance in Accounts Payable of $1,100 and additional purchases on account amounting to $11,200, there must have been $12,300 of accounts payable available for payment. Since the ending balance in the Accounts Payable account amounted to $800, there must have been cash payments of $11,500 ($12,300 − $800). The entry to record this cash outflow, labelled (b3), includes a credit to the operating activities section of the Cash account and a debit to the Accounts Payable account.

Noncash Effects of Amortization

The next item on the income statement is amortization expense. Amortization expense is a noncash charge against revenues. In other words, no cash changes hands at the time the amortization expense is recorded. Indeed, the entry to record amortization expense (c1) includes a debit to Retained Earnings (amortization expense) and a credit to Accumulated Amortization. This entry only partly explains the change in accumulated amortization, indicating that further analysis is required. However, cash flow consequences associated with long-term assets and their respective contra-accounts affect the investing activities section of the cash flow statement. Therefore, further analysis is delayed until investing activities are considered. At this stage, the analysis of cash flows from operating activities continues.

Cash Payments for Salaries

The entry to record $2,700 of salary expense includes a debit to Retained Earnings (salary expense) and a credit to Salaries Payable. This entry, labelled (d1), partly explains the change in beginning and ending balances in the Salaries Payable account. The beginning balance of $900 plus the $2,700 increase for the current period's expense suggests that there were $3,600 of salaries available for payment during the period. Since the ending balance amounted to $1,000, there must have been a cash payment for salaries amounting to $2,600 ($3,600 − $1,000). The entry to record the cash payment for salaries includes a debit to the Salaries Payable account and a credit to the operating activities section of the Cash account. This entry is labelled (d2) in the exhibit.

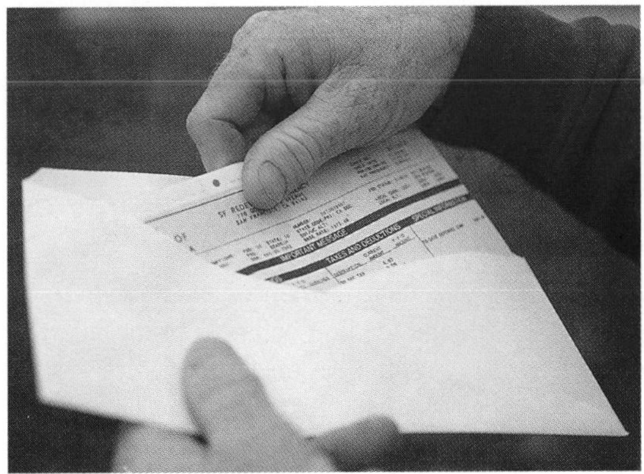

Cash Payments for Insurance

The entry to record $600 of insurance expense requires a debit to Retained Earnings (insurance expense) and a credit to Prepaid Insurance. This entry, labelled (e1), partly explains the change in the beginning and ending balances in the Prepaid Insurance account. The beginning balance of $1,400 less the reduction of $600 associated with the recognition of insurance expense suggests an ending balance of $800. However, the balance sheet shows an actual ending balance of $1,100. A purchase of $300 ($1,100 − $800) of prepaid insurance must have been made during the accounting period. The cash outflow for the purchase of insurance is labelled (e2) and includes a debit to the Prepaid Insurance account and a credit to the operating activities section of the cash flow statement.

Cash Payments for Other Operating Expenses

The $1,400 of other operating expenses appearing on the income statement is recorded in the T-accounts with a debit to Retained Earnings and a credit to the Operating Expenses Payable account. This entry, labelled (f1), partly explains the change in the beginning and ending balances in the Operating Expenses Payable account. Given a beginning balance of $1,300 and the $1,400 addition for current expenses, the total amount available for payment was $2,700 ($1,300 + $1,400). Since the ending balance amounted to $1,500, the cash payments must have amounted to $1,200 ($2,700 − $1,500). The entry to record the cash payment is labelled (f2) and includes a debit to the Operating Expenses Payable account and a credit to the operating activities section of the Cash account.

Cash Receipts for Rent

The entry to record $2,400 of rent revenue includes a debit to the Unearned Rent Revenue account and a credit to the Retained Earnings account. This entry, labelled (g1), partly explains the change in the beginning and ending balances in the Unearned Rent Revenue account. The beginning balance of $1,600 less the $2,400 reduction caused by the recognition of the rent revenue suggests that there must have been a credit (increase) in the account in order to arrive at an ending balance of $600. Since increases in the unearned account are offset by increases in cash, collections must have been equal to $1,400 ($1,600 + $1,400 − $2,400 = $600). The required entry for the cash receipt includes a credit to the Unearned Rent Revenue account and a debit to the operating activities section of the Cash account. This entry is labelled (g2) in Exhibit 12–5.

Cash Receipts from Interest

The entry to record $700 of interest revenue includes a debit to the Interest Receivable account and a credit to Retained Earnings (interest revenue). This entry, labelled (h1), partially explains the change in the beginning and ending balances in the Interest Receivable account. Given the beginning balance of $300 plus the $700 debit created through the recognition of interest revenue, the receivables account indicates that there was $1,000 ($300 + $700) of interest receivables available for collection. The ending balance of $400 implies that $600 ($1,000 − $400) of cash was collected. The entry to record this cash inflow is labelled (h2) and includes a credit to Interest Receivable and a debit to the operating activities section of the Cash account.

Cash Payments for Interest

The entry to record $400 of interest expense is labelled (i1) and includes a debit to Retained Earnings (interest expense) and a credit to Interest Payable. The entry partly explains the change in the beginning and ending balances in the Interest Payable account. The beginning balance of $500 plus the $400 that resulted from the recognition of interest expense suggests that there was $900 of interest obligations available for payment. The ending balance of $300 implies that $600 ($900 − $300) was paid in cash. The entry to recognize the cash outflow for this interest payment is labelled (i2) and includes a debit to the Interest Payable account and a credit to the operating activities section of the Cash account.

Noncash Effects of Loss

The loss on the sale of equipment does not affect cash flows from operating activities. The full proceeds from the sale constitute the amount of cash flow. The amount of any loss or gain is irrelevant. Indeed, the sale involves the disposal of an investment and so is shown under the investing activities section. Cash flow from operating activities is not affected by gains or losses on the disposal of long-term assets.

Completion of Analysis of Operating Activities

Since no other items appear on the income statement, the conversion process from accrual to cash is completed. The operating activities section of the Cash account contains all the cash receipts and payments necessary to determine the net cash flow from operations. This information is placed into the formal cash flow statement (presented later in the chapter). With the completion of the assessment of cash flow from operating activities, the analysis proceeds to the cash flow effects associated with investing activities.

Q Magazine, Inc., reported $234,800 of revenue for the month. At the beginning of the month, its Unearned Revenue account had a balance of $78,000. At the end of the month, the account had a balance of $67,000. Based on this information alone, determine the amount of cash received from revenue.

Answer

The Unearned Revenue account decreased by $11,000 ($78,000 − $67,000). This decrease in unearned revenue would have coincided with an increase in revenue that did not involve receiving cash. As a result, $11,000 of the revenue earned had no effect on cash flow during this month. To determine the cash received from revenue, subtract the noncash increase from reported revenue. Cash received from revenue is $223,800 ($234,800 − $11,000).

Cash Flows from Investing Activities

Investing activities generally involve the acquisition (purchase) or disposal (sale) of long-term assets. The analysis of cash flows from investing activities centres on changes from the beginning to the ending balances of long-term assets.

Cash Payments to Purchase Investments

The first long-term asset shown on the balance sheets is Investments. An analysis of this asset account indicates that the balance in the account increased from $3,500 at the beginning of the period to $5,100 at the end of the period. The most reasonable explanation for this increase is that the corporation purchased additional securities in the amount of $1,600 ($5,100 − $3,500). In the absence of information to the contrary, we assume that the purchase was made with cash. The entry to record the purchase includes a debit to the Investments account and a credit to the investing activities section of the Cash account. This entry is coded (j1) in Exhibit 12–5.

Cash Receipts from Sale of Equipment

The next asset on the balance sheets is Equipment. Our earlier review of the income statement disclosed a loss on the sale of equipment, which suggests that some equipment was sold during the period. This sale is expected to result in a cash inflow in the amount of the sales price. The additional information at the bottom of the income statement discloses that equipment costing $1,500 with accumulated amortization of $1,100 was sold for $300. The difference between the $400 ($1,500 − $1,100) net book value and the $300 sales price explains the $100 loss on the income statement. The cash receipt from the sale is $300. The original cost, accumulated amortization, and loss do not affect cash flow. The entry to recognize the cash receipt includes a debit to the investing section of the Cash account, a debit to Retained Earnings (loss), a debit to the Accumulated Amortization account, and a credit to the Equipment account. The entry is labelled (k1) in the exhibit.

Cash Payments to Purchase Equipment

The sale of equipment partly explains the change in the beginning and ending balances in the Equipment account. However, further analysis suggests that some equipment must have been purchased. A beginning balance of $4,600 less $1,500 for the equipment that was sold suggests that $2,300 of equipment must have been purchased in order to arrive at the ending balance of $5,400 ($4,600 − $1,500 + $2,300 = $5,400). The cash payment necessary to purchase the equipment is labelled (l1) and includes a debit to the Equipment account and a credit to the investing activities section of the Cash account.

Noncash Transaction for Land Acquisition

The Land account increased from a beginning balance of $6,000 to an ending balance of $8,500, thereby suggesting that $2,500 ($8,500 − $6,000) of land was acquired during the accounting period. The additional information at the bottom of the income statement discloses that the corporation acquired this land by issuing a mortgage. Therefore, no cash consequences are associated with the transaction. The transaction recording this event is labelled (m1) in Exhibit 12–5.

Since all long-term asset accounts have been reconciled, the analysis of cash flows from investing activities is completed. The process continues with an assessment of cash flows associated with financing activities.

Cash Flows from Financing Activities

The long-term liability and shareholders' equity sections of the balance sheets are analyzed to assess the cash flows from financing activities. Note that the first long-term liability account on the balance sheet is Mortgage Payable. The change in this account was explained in the analysis of the land acquisition, discussed earlier in this chapter. Therefore, the analysis of cash flows continues with the change in the Bond Liability account.

reality bytes

How was Air Canada able to increase its number of aircraft without spending any cash? The answer can be found in the company's cash flow statement. The investing section of this statement states, "Proceeds from sale and leaseback of assets." This item coupled with the notes to the financial statements indicates that 15 aircraft were acquired with capital lease obligations. In other words, Air Canada obtained these aircraft by agreeing to pay for them later.

Cash Payment for Bonds

The balance in the Bonds Payable account decreased from $4,000 to $1,000. In the absence of information to the contrary, it is logical to assume that $3,000 ($4,000 − $1,000) was paid to reduce bond liabilities. The entry to record the cash outflow includes a debit to the Bonds Payable account and a credit to the financing activities section of the Cash account. This entry is coded (n1) in the exhibit.

Cash Receipt from Share Issue

The balance in the Common Shares account increased from $8,000 to $10,000. In the absence of information to the contrary, it is logical to assume that $2,000 ($10,000 − $8,000) of cash was collected as proceeds from the issuance of common shares. The entry to record this cash inflow is labelled (o1) and includes a credit to Common Shares and a debit to the financing activities section of the Cash account.

Cash Payments for Dividends

Finally, additional information at the bottom of the income statement discloses a cash dividend of $1,500. The transaction to record this cash outflow includes a debit to the Retained Earnings account and a credit to the financing activities section of the Cash account. It is labelled (p1) in Exhibit 12–5.

Presenting Information in the Cash Flow Statement

Since all income statement items have been analyzed, changes in balance sheet accounts have been explained, and all additional information has been considered, the analytical process is completed. The data in the T-account for cash must now be organized in appropriate financial statement format. Recall that cash flow from operations is presented first, cash flow from investing activities second, and cash flow from financing activities third. Noncash investing and financing activities are shown in the notes to the financial statements. Exhibit 12–6 presents a cash flow statement.

Exhibit 12–6

THE NEW SOUTH CORPORATION Cash Flow Statement For the Year Ended December 31, 2005			
Cash Flows from Operating Activities			
Cash Receipts from			
Sales	$20,800		
Rent	1,400		
Interest	600		
Total Cash Inflows		$22,800	
Cash Payments for			
Inventory Purchases	11,500		
Salaries	2,600		
Insurance	300		
Other Operating Expenses	1,200		
Interest	600		
Total Cash Outflows		(16,200)	
Net Cash Flow from Operating Activities			$ 6,600
Cash Flows from Investing Activities			
Inflow from Sale of Equipment		300	
Outflow to Purchase Marketable Securities		(1,600)	
Outflow to Purchase Equipment		(2,300)	
Net Cash Flow from Investing Activities			(3,600)
Cash Flows from Financing Activities			
Inflow from Share Issue		2,000	
Outflow to Repay Debt		(3,000)	
Outflow for Dividends		(1,500)	
Net Cash Flow from Financing Activities			(2,500)
Net Increase in Cash			500
Plus: Beginning Cash Balance			400
Ending Cash Balance			$ 900

Cash Flow Statement Presented under the Indirect Method

LO4 Explain how cash flow from operating activities reported under the indirect method differs from that reported under the direct method.

Up to now, the cash flow statement has been presented in accordance with the **direct method**. The direct method is intuitively logical and is the method recommended by the CICA. Even so, most companies use an alternative known as the **indirect method**. The difference between the two methods is in the presentation of the operating activities section. The indirect method uses net income as reported on the income statement as the starting point. The method proceeds by showing the adjustments necessary to convert the accrual-based net income figure to a cash-basis equivalent. The conversion process can be accomplished by applying three basic rules, which are discussed next.

An increase in the balance of the Accounts Receivable account would suggest that not all sales were collected in cash. The amount of revenue shown on the income statement would overstate the amount of cash collections. Therefore, we must subtract the amount of the increase in the receivables account from the amount of net income to convert the income figure to a cash-equivalent basis. Similarly, a decrease in the receivables balance has to be added to the net income figure. Extending this logic to all current asset accounts results in the first general rule of the conversion process. **Rule 1: Increases in current assets are deducted from net income, and decreases in current assets are added to net income.**

The opposite logic applies to current liabilities. For example, an increase in accounts payable suggests that not all expenses were paid in cash. Therefore, it is necessary to add the increase in the payables account to the amount of net income to convert the income figure to a cash-equivalent basis. Conversely, decreases in payable accounts are deducted from net income. Extending the logic to all the current liability accounts produces the second general rule of the conversion process. **Rule 2: Increases in current liabilities are added to net income, and decreases in current liabilities are deducted from net income.**

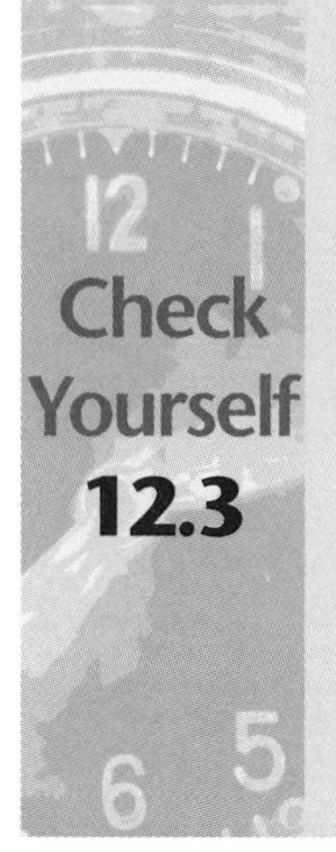

The following account balances were drawn from the accounting records of Loeb, Inc.

Account Title	Beginning Balance	Ending Balance
Prepaid Rent	$4,200	$3,000
Interest Payable	$2,900	$2,650

Loeb reported $7,400 of net income during the accounting period. Based on this information alone, determine the amount of cash flow from operating activities.

Answer Answer Based on Rule 1, the $1,200 decrease ($3,000 − $4,200) in Prepaid Rent (current asset) must be added to net income to determine the amount of cash flow from operating activities. Rule 2 requires that the $250 decrease ($2,650 − $2,900) in Interest Payable (current liability) must be deducted from net income. The cash flow from operating activities must be $8,350 ($7,400 + $1,200 − $250). Note that paying interest is defined as an operating activity and should not be confused with dividend payments, which are classified as financing activities.

Finally, note that some expense and revenue transactions do not have cash consequences. For example, although amortization is reported as an expense, it does not require the payment of cash. Similarly, losses and gains reported on the income statement do not have consequences that are reported in the operating activities section of the cash flow statement. **Rule 3: All noncash expenses and losses are added to net income, and all noncash revenue and gains are subtracted from net income.**

Arley Company's income statement reported net income (in millions) of $326 for the year. The income statement included amortization expense of $45 and a net loss on the sale of disposable assets of $22. Based on this information alone, determine the net cash flow from operating activities.

Answer Based on Rule 3, both the amortization expense and the loss would have to be added to net income to determine cash flow from operating activities. Net cash flow from operating activities would be $393 ($326 + $45 + $22).

These three general rules apply only to items affecting operating activities. For example, Rule 2 does not apply to an increase or decrease in the current liability account for dividends because dividend payments are considered to be financing activities rather than operating activities. Some degree of judgment must be exercised in applying the three general rules of conversion.

Exhibit 12–7 shows the presentation of a cash flow statement under the indirect method. The statement was constructed by applying the three general rules of conversion to the data for The New South Corporation shown in Exhibits 12–3 and 12–4. Notice that the only difference between the statement presented under the indirect method (Exhibit 12–7) and the statement shown under the direct method (Exhibit 12–6) is the cash flow from operating activities section. Cash flows from investing and financing activities and the schedule of noncash items are not affected by the alternative reporting format.

Exhibit 12–7

THE NEW SOUTH CORPORATION
Cash Flow Statement (Indirect Method)
For the Year Ended December 31, 2005

Cash Flows from Operating Activities		
Net Income	$7,200	
Plus: Decreases in Current Assets and Increases in Current Liabilities		
Decrease in Accounts Receivable	200	
Decrease in Prepaid Insurance	300	
Increase in Salaries Payable	100	
Increase in Other Operating Expenses Payable	200	
Less: Increases in Current Assets and Decreases in Current Liabilities		
Increase in Interest Receivable	(100)	
Increase in Inventory	(700)	
Decrease in Accounts Payable for Inventory Purchases	(300)	
Decrease in Interest Payable	(200)	
Decrease in Unearned Rent Revenue	(1,000)	
Plus: Noncash Charges		
Amortization Expense	800	
Loss on Sale of Equipment	100	
Net Cash Flow from Operating Activities		$6,600
Cash Flows from Investing Activities		
Inflow from Sale of Equipment	300	
Outflow to Purchase Investments	(1,600)	
Outflow to Purchase Equipment	(2,300)	
Net Cash Flow from Investing Activities		(3,600)
Cash Flows from Financing Activities		
Inflow from Share Issue	2,000	
Outflow to Repay Debt	(3,000)	
Outflow for Dividends	(1,500)	
Net Cash Flow from Financing Activities		(2,500)
Net Increase in Cash		500
Plus: Beginning Cash Balance		400
Ending Cash Balance		$ 900

Consequences of Growth on Cash Flow

LO5 Explain how the classifications used on the cash flow statement could provide misleading information to decision makers.

Why do decision makers in business need a cash flow statement? Why is the information provided on the income statement not sufficient? Although it is true that the income statement shows how well a business is doing on an accrual basis, it does not show what is happening with cash. Understanding the cash flows of a business is extremely important because cash is used to pay the bills. A company, especially one that is growing rapidly, can have substantial earnings but be short of cash because it must buy goods before they are sold, and it may not receive cash payment until months after revenue is recognized on an accrual basis. To illustrate, assume that you want to go into the business of selling computers. You borrow $2,000 and use the money to purchase two computers that cost $1,000 each. Assume as well that you sell one of the computers on account for $1,500. At this point, if you had a payment due on your loan, you would be unable to pay the amount due. Even though you had a net income of $500 (revenue of $1,500 − cost of goods sold of $1,000), you would have no cash until you collected the $1,500 cash due from the account receivable.

Real-World Data

The cash flow statement often provides a picture of business activity that would otherwise be lost in the complexities of accrual accounting. For example, consider the effects of restructuring charges on operating income versus cash flow experienced by IBM Corporation. For 1991, 1992, and 1993 combined, IBM reported operating *losses* (before taxes) of more than US$17.9 *billion*. During this same period, it reported "restructuring charges" of more than US$24 billion. Therefore, without the restructuring charges, IBM would have reported operating *profits* of about US$6 billion (before taxes). Are restructuring charges an indication of something bad or something good? Who knows? Different financial analysts have different opinions about this issue. There is something about IBM's performance during these years that can be more easily understood. The company produced over US$21 billion in positive cash flow from operating activities. It had no trouble paying its bills.

Exhibit 12–8 is a comparison of the income from operations and the cash flow from operating activities for four real-world companies from different industries for the 1998, 1999, and 2000 fiscal years.

Exhibit 12–8 *Net Income versus Cash Flow from Operations (Amounts in millions)*

	Company	2000	1999	1998
Deere & Co.	Net income	$ (64)	$ 486	$ 239
	Cash flow from operations	1,113	1,080	1,434
Boeing	Net income	2,128	2,309	1,120
	Cash flow from operations	5,942	6,224	2,415
Mattel	Net income	170	108	328
	Cash flow from operations	555	430	586
Call-Net Enterprises	Net income	(399)	(237)	16
	Cash flow from operations	(81)	(74)	139

Several things can be observed from Exhibit 12–8. First, notice that in each case cash flow from operating activities is higher than income from operations. This condition is true for many real-world companies because amortization, a noncash expense, is usually significant. The most dramatic example of this is for Deere in 2000. Even though Deere reported a *net loss* of $64 million, it generated *positive cash flow from operations* of more than $1 *billion*. This difference between cash flow from operations and income helps explain how some companies can have significant losses over a few years and continue to stay in business and pay their bills.

How can Call-Net Enterprises stay in business when the company has incurred both net losses and negative cash flow from operations for the past three years? The answer comes from looking at the remaining sections of the cash flow statement. Investing activities caused a small outflow of approximately $5 million. Financing activities in the prior year generated a total of $987 million with $985.8 million from the issuing of notes payable and $1.2 million generated from the issuance of common shares.

The conclusion one must reach about using the cash flow statement is the same as that for using the balance sheet or the income statement. Users cannot simply look at the numbers. They must analyze the numbers based on a knowledge of the particular business being examined.

Accounting alone cannot tell a businessperson how to make a decision. Making good business decisions requires an understanding of the business in question, the environmental and economic factors affecting the operation of that business, and the accounting concepts on which the financial statements of that business are based.

a look back

Throughout this course, you have been asked to consider many different accounting events that occur in the business world. In many cases, you were asked to consider the effects these events have on a company's balance sheet, income statement, and cash flow statement. By now, you should be aware that each of the financial statements shows a different, but equally important, view of the financial situation of the company in question.

This chapter provided a more detailed examination of only one financial statement, the cash flow statement. The chapter presented a more comprehensive review of how an accrual accounting system relates to a cash-based accounting system. It is important that you understand not only both systems but also how the two systems relate to each other. This is the reason that a formal cash flow statement begins with a reconciliation of net income, an accrual measurement, to net cash flow from operating activities, a cash measurement. Finally, this chapter explained how the idiosyncrasies of classifying cash events as operating, investing, or financing activities requires analysis and understanding of the financial information to reach correct conclusions.

a look forward

This chapter probably completes your first course in accounting. We sincerely hope that this text has provided you a meaningful learning experience that will serve you well as you progress through your academic training and your ultimate career. Good luck and best wishes!

SELF-STUDY REVIEW PROBLEM

The following financial statements pertain to Schlemmer Company.

BALANCE SHEETS December 31	2008	2009
Assests		
Cash	$ 2,800	$48,400
Accounts Receivable	1,200	2,200
Inventory	6,000	5,600
Equipment	22,000	18,000
Accumulated Amortization—Equip.	(17,400)	(13,650)
Land	10,400	17,200
Total Assets	$25,000	$77,750
Liabilities and Shareholders' Equity		
Accounts Payable	$ 4,200	$ 5,200
Long-Term Debt	6,400	5,600
Common Shares	10,000	19,400
Retained Earnings	4,400	47,550
Total Liabilities and Shareholders' Equity	$25,000	$77,750

INCOME STATEMENT For the Year Ended December 31, 2004	
Sales Revenue	$67,300
Cost of Goods Sold	(24,100)
Gross Profit	43,200
Amortization Expense	(1,250)
Operating Income	41,950
Gain on Sale of Equipment	2,900
Loss on Disposal of Land	(100)
Net Income	$44,750

Additional Data

1. During 2004 the company sold equipment for $8,900 that had originally cost $11,000. Accumulated amortization on this equipment was $5,000 at the time of sale. Also, the company purchased equipment for $7,000.
2. The company sold for $2,500 land that had cost $2,600, resulting in the recognition of a $100 loss. Also, common shares were issued in exchange for land valued at $9,400 at the time of the exchange.
3. The company declared and paid dividends of $1,600.

Required

a. Use T-accounts to analyze the preceding data.
b. Using the direct method, prepare in good form a cash flow statement for the year ended December 31, 2004.

Transactions Legend

a1. Revenue, $67,300.
a2. Collection of accounts receivable, $66,300 ($1,200 + $67,300 − $2,200).
b1. Cost of goods sold, $24,100.
b2. Inventory purchases, $23,700 ($5,600 + $24,100 − $6,000).
b3. Payments for inventory purchases, $22,700 ($4,200 + $23,700 − $5,200).
c1. Amortization expense, $1,250 (noncash).
d1. Sale of equipment, $8,900; cost of equipment sold, $11,000; accumulated amortization on equipment sold, $5,000.
d2. Purchase of equipment, $7,000.
e1. Sale of land, $2,500; cost of land sold, $2,600.
f1. Issue of shares in exchange for land, $9,400.
g1. Paid dividends, $1,600.
h1. Paid off portion of long-term debt, $800.

Solution to Requirement a

SCHLEMMER COMPANY
T-Accounts

Assets = Liabilities + Equity

Cash

Bal.	2,800	b3	22,700
a2	66,300	d2	7,000
d1	8,900	g1	1,600
e1	2,500	h1	800
Bal.	48,400		

Accounts Receivable

Bal.	1,200		
a1	67,300	a2	66,300
Bal.	2,200		

Inventory

Bal.	6,000	b1	24,100
b2	23,700		
Bal.	5,600		

Land

Bal.	10,400	e1	2,600
f1	9,400		
Bal.	17,200		

Accounts Payable

b3	22,700	Bal.	4,200
		b2	23,700
		Bal.	5,200

Long-Term Debt

h1	800	Bal.	6,400
		Bal.	5,600

Common Shares

		Bal.	10,000
		f1	9,400
		Bal.	19,400

Retained Earnings

b1	24,100	Bal.	4,400
c1	1,250	a1	67,300
e1	100	d1	2,900
g1	1,600		
		Bal.	47,550

Equipment

	Debit		Credit
Bal.	22,000	d1	11,000
d2	7,000		
Bal.	18,000		

Accumulated Amortization

	Debit		Credit
d1	5,000	Bal.	17,400
		c1	1,250
		Bal.	13,650

Solution to Requirement a

SCHLEMMER COMPANY Cash Flow Statement For the Year Ended December 31, 2004		
Cash Flows from Operating Activities		
Cash Receipts from Customers	$66,300	
Cash Payments for Inventory Purchases	(22,700)	
Net Cash Flow Provided by Operating Activities		$43,600
Cash Flows from Investing Activities		
Inflow from Sale of Equipment	8,900	
Inflow from Sale of Land	2,500	
Outflow to Purchase Equipment	(7,000)	
Net Cash Flow Provided by Investing Activities		4,400
Cash Flows from Financing Activities		
Outflow for Dividends	(1,600)	
Outflow for Repayment of Debt	(800)	
Net Cash Flow Used by Financing Activities		(2,400)
Net Increase in Cash		45,600
Plus: Beginning Cash Balance		2,800
Ending Cash Balance		$48,400

KEY TERMS

accrual accounting *491*
cash inflows *489*
cash outflows *489*
deferral transactions *494*
direct method *505*
expense transactions *492*
financing activities *490*
indirect method *505*
investing activities *490*
noncash investing and financing transactions *490*
operating activities *490*
revenue transactions *492*
T-account method *492*

QUESTIONS

1. What is the purpose of the cash flow statement?
2. What are the three categories of cash flows reported on the cash flow statement? Discuss each and give an example of an inflow and an outflow for each category.
3. What are noncash investing and financing activities? Provide an example. How are such transactions shown on the cash flow statement?
4. Best Company had beginning accounts receivable of $12,000 and ending accounts receivable of $14,000. If total sales were $110,000, what amount of cash was collected?
5. Best Company's Utilities Payable account had a beginning balance of $3,300 and an ending balance of $5,200. Utilities expense reported on the income statement was $87,000. What was the amount of cash paid for utilities for the period?
6. Best Company had a balance in the Unearned Revenue account of $4,300 at the beginning of the period and an ending balance of $5,700. If the portion of unearned revenue Best recognized as earned during the period was $15,600, what amount of cash did Best collect?

7. Which of the following activities are financing activities?
   a. Payment of accounts payable.
   b. Payment of interest on bonds payable.
   c. Sale of common shares.
   d. Sale of preferred shares at a premium.
   e. Payment of a cash dividend.
8. Does amortization expense affect net cash flow? Explain.
9. If Best Company sold land that cost $4,200 at a $500 gain, how much cash did it collect from the sale of land?
10. If Best Company sold office equipment that originally cost $7,500 and had $7,200 of accumulated amortization at a $100 loss, what was the selling price for the office equipment?
11. In which section of the cash flow statement would the following transactions be reported?
    a. Cash receipt of interest income.
    b. Cash purchase of investments.
    c. Cash purchase of equipment.
    d. Cash sale of merchandise.
    e. Cash sale of common shares.
    f. Payment of interest expense.
    g. Cash proceeds from loan.
    h. Cash payment on bonds payable.
    i. Cash receipt from sale of old equipment.
    j. Cash payment for operating expenses.
12. What is the difference between preparing the cash flow statement using the direct approach and using the indirect approach?
13. Which method (direct or indirect) of presenting the cash flow statement is more intuitively logical? Why?
14. What is the major advantage of using the indirect method to present the cash flow statement?
15. What is the advantage of using the direct method to present the cash flow statement?
16. How would Best Company report the following transactions on the cash flow statement?
    a. Purchased new equipment for $46,000 cash.
    b. Sold old equipment for $8,700 cash. The equipment had a net book value of $4,900.
17. Can a company report negative net cash flows from operating activities for the year on the cash flow statement but still have positive net income on the income statement? Explain.

EXERCISES

L.O. 1 EXERCISE 12–1 *Classifying Cash Flows into Categories—Direct Method*

Required

Identify whether the cash flows in the following list should be classified as operating activities, investing activities, or financing activities on the cash flow statement (assume the use of the direct method).

a. Acquired cash from issue of common shares.
b. Provided services for cash.
c. Acquired cash by issuing a note payable.
d. Paid cash for interest.
e. Paid cash dividends.
f. Paid cash to settle note payable.
g. Sold land for cash.
h. Paid cash to purchase a computer.
i. Paid cash for employee compensation.
j. Received cash interest from a bond investment.
k. Recognized amortization expense.

L.O. 1 EXERCISE 12–2 *Cash Outflows from Operating Activities—Direct Method*

Required

Which of the following transactions produce cash outflows from operating activities (assume the use of the direct method)?

a. Cash payment to purchase inventory.
b. Cash payment for equipment.
c. Cash receipt from collecting accounts receivable.
d. Cash receipt from sale of land.
e. Cash payment for dividends.
f. Cash payment to settle an account payable.

EXERCISE 12–3 *Using Account Balances to Determine Cash Flows from Operating Activities—Direct Method* **L.O. 2**

The following account balances are available for Pae Company for 2004.

Account Title	Beginning of Year	End of Year
Accounts Receivable	$23,000	$21,000
Interest Receivable	5,000	7,000
Accounts Payable	28,000	25,000
Salaries Payable	10,000	11,000

Other Information for 2004

Sales on Account	$646,000
Interest Income	24,000
Operating Expenses	270,000
Salaries Expense for the Year	172,000

Required

(*Hint*: It may be helpful to assume that all revenues and expenses are on account.)

a. Compute the amount of cash *inflow* from operating activities.

b. Compute the amount of cash *outflow* from operating activities.

EXERCISE 12–4 *Using Account Balances to Determine Cash Flow from Operating Activities—Direct Method* **L.O. 2**

The following account balances were available for Jefferson Enterprises for 2006.

Account Title	Beginning of Year	End of Year
Unearned Revenue	$4,000	$6,000
Prepaid Rent	2,200	2,500

During the year, $65,000 of unearned revenue was recognized as having been earned. Rent expense for the period was $12,000. Jefferson Enterprises maintains its books on the accrual basis.

Required

Using T-accounts and the preceding information, determine the amount of cash inflow from revenue and cash outflow for rent.

EXERCISE 12–5 *Using Account Balances to Determine Cash Flow from Investing Activities* **L.O. 2**

The following account information pertains to Kallapur Company for 2005.

Land			Short-Term Investments		
Bal.	38,000	24,000	Bal.	78,000	49,000
	127,000			139,000	
Bal.	141,000		Bal.	168,000	

The income statement reported a $3,000 loss on the sale of land and a $2,500 gain on the sale of short-term investments.

Required

Prepare the investing activities section of the 2005 cash flow statement.

L.O. 2, 3 EXERCISE 12–6 *Using Account Balances to Determine Cash Flow from Financing Activities*

The following account balances pertain to Kilgore, Inc., for 2006.

Bonds Payable	
	Bal. 245,000
150,000	
	Bal. 95,000

Common Shares	
	Bal. 368,000
	200,000
	Bal. 568,000

Preferred Shares	
	Bal. 90,000
	60,000
	Bal. 150,000

Required
Prepare the financing activities section of the 2006 cash flow statement.

L.O. 2, 3 EXERCISE 12–7 *Using Account Balances to Determine Cash Outflow for Inventory Purchases*

The following account information pertains to Gupta Company, which uses the perpetual inventory method and purchases all inventory on account.

Inventory	
Bal. 67,000	
?	376,000
Bal. 72,000	

Accounts Payable	
	Bal. 49,000
?	?
	Bal. 47,000

Required
Compute the amount of cash paid for the purchase of inventory.

L.O. 2, 4 EXERCISE 12–8 *Using Account Balances to Determine Cash Flow from Operating Activities—Indirect Method*

Altec Company presents its cash flow statement using the indirect method. The following accounts and corresponding balances were drawn from Altec's accounting records for the period.

Account Title	Beginning Balances	Ending Balances
Accounts Receivable	$24,000	$22,600
Prepaid Rent	1,650	1,950
Interest Receivable	900	700
Accounts Payable	10,200	8,850
Salaries Payable	2,700	2,950
Unearned Revenue	2,000	2,450

Net income for the period was $43,000.

Required
Using the preceding information, compute the net cash flow from operating activities using the indirect method.

L.O. 2, 3, 4 EXERCISE 12–9 *Using Account Balances to Determine Cash Flow from Operating Activities—Direct and Indirect Methods*

The following account balances are from Hutton Company's accounting records. Assume Hutton had no investing or financing transactions during 2008.

December 31	2007	2008
Cash	$65,000	$114,200
Accounts Receivable	75,000	77,000
Prepaid Rent	1,200	800
Accounts Payable	33,000	37,000
Utilities Payable	15,600	18,800
Sales Revenue		$272,000
Operating Expenses		(168,000)
Utilities Expense		(36,400)
Rent Expense		(24,000)
Net Income		$ 43,600

Required

a. Prepare the operating activities section of the 2008 cash flow statement using the direct method.
b. Prepare the operating activities section of the 2008 cash flow statement using the indirect method.

EXERCISE 12–10 *Interpreting Cash Flow Statement Information*

L.O. 3, 5

The following selected transactions pertain to Armstrong Corporation for 2004:

1. Paid $23,400 cash to purchase delivery equipment.
2. Sold delivery equipment for $2,900. The equipment had originally cost $15,000 and had accumulated amortization of $13,000.
3. Borrowed $40,000 cash by issuing bonds at face value.
4. Purchased a building that cost $180,000. Paid $50,000 cash and issued a mortgage for the remaining $130,000.
5. Exchanged common shares for machinery valued at $64,900.

Required

a. Prepare the appropriate sections of the 2004 cash flow statement.
b. Explain how a company could spend more cash on investing activities than it collected from financing activities during the same accounting period.

PROBLEMS—SERIES A

PROBLEM 12–1A *Classifying Cash Flows*

L.O. 1

Required

Classify each of the following transactions as an operating activity (OA), an investing activity (IA), a financing activity (FA), or a noncash transaction (NT).

a. Bought land with cash.
b. Collected cash from accounts receivable.
c. Issued common shares for cash.
d. Repaid principal and interest on a note payable.
e. Declared a stock split.
f. Purchased inventory with cash.
g. Recorded amortization of goodwill.
h. Paid insurance with cash.
i. Issued a note payable in exchange for equipment.
j. Recorded amortization expense.
k. Provided services for cash.
l. Purchased investments with cash.
m. Paid cash for rent.
n. Received interest on note receivable.
o. Paid cash for salaries.
p. Received advance payment for services.

q. Paid a cash dividend.
r. Provided services on account.
s. Purchased office supplies on account.

L.O. 2, 3 PROBLEM 12–2A *Using Transaction Data to Prepare a Cash Flow Statement*

Store Company engaged in the following transactions during the 2006 accounting period. The beginning cash balance was $32,300.

1. Credit sales were $250,000. The beginning receivables balance was $95,000 and the ending balance was $103,000.
2. Salaries expense for the period was $56,000. The beginning salaries payable balance was $3,500 and the ending balance was $2,000.
3. Other operating expenses for the period were $125,000. The beginning operating expense payable balance was $4,500 and the ending balance was $9,600.
4. Recorded $19,500 of amortization expense. The beginning and ending balances in the Accumulated Amortization account were $14,000 and $33,500, respectively.
5. The Equipment account had beginning and ending balances of $210,000 and $240,000, respectively. The increase was caused by the cash purchase of equipment.
6. The beginning and ending balances in the Notes Payable account were $50,000 and $150,000, respectively. The increase was caused by additional cash borrowing.
7. There was $6,000 of interest expense reported on the income statement. The beginning and ending balances in the Interest Payable account were $1,200 and $1,000, respectively.
8. The beginning and ending Merchandise Inventory account balances were $90,000 and $108,000, respectively. The company sold merchandise with a cost of $156,000 (cost of goods sold for the period was $156,000). The beginning and ending balances of Accounts Payable were $9,500 and $11,500, respectively.
9. The beginning and ending balances of Notes Receivable were $2,500 and $10,000, respectively. The increase resulted from a cash loan to one of the company's employees.
10. The beginning and ending balances of the Common Shares account were $100,000 and $125,000, respectively. The increase was caused by the issue of common shares for cash.
11. Land had beginning and ending balances of $50,000 and $41,000, respectively. Land that cost $9,000 was sold for $14,700, resulting in a gain of $5,700.
12. The tax expense for the period was $7,700. The Tax Payable account had a $950 beginning balance and an $875 ending balance.
13. The Investments account had beginning and ending balances of $25,000 and $29,000, respectively. The company purchased investments for $18,000 cash during the period, and investments that cost $14,000 were sold for $9,000, resulting in a $5,000 loss.

Required

Convert the preceding information to cash-equivalent data and prepare a cash flow statement.

L.O. 2, 3 PROBLEM 12–3A *Using Financial Statement Data to Determine Cash Flow from Operating Activities*

The following account information is available for Big Sky Company for 2004:

Account Title	Beginning of Year	End of Year
Accounts Receivable	$20,000	$24,000
Merchandise Inventory	58,000	56,000
Prepaid Insurance	24,000	2,000
Accounts Payable (Inventory)	20,000	21,000
Salaries Payable	4,200	2,800

Other Information

1. Sales for the period were $175,000.
2. Purchases of merchandise for the period were $85,000.
3. Insurance expense for the period was $42,000.
4. Other operating expenses (all cash) were $26,000.
5. Salary expense was $35,000.

Required

a. Compute the net cash flow from operating activities.
b. Prepare the cash flow from the operating activities section of the cash flow statement.

PROBLEM 12–4A *Using Financial Statement Data to Determine Cash Flow from Investing Activities* **L.O. 2, 3**

The following information pertaining to investing activities is available for Chico Company for 2005:

Account Title	Beginning of Year	End of Year
Land	$ 90,000	$110,000
Machinery and Equipment	425,000	510,000
Investments	112,000	75,000

Other Information for 2005

1. Investments were sold at book value. No gain or loss was recognized.
2. Machinery was purchased for $110,000. Old machinery with a net book value of $5,000 (cost of $25,000, accumulated amortization of $20,000) was sold for $8,000.

Required

a. Compute the net cash flow from investing activities.
b. Prepare the cash flow from investing activities section of the cash flow statement.

PROBLEM 12–5A *Using Financial Statement Data to Determine Cash Flow from Financing Activities* **L.O. 2, 3**

The following information pertaining to financing activities is available for Tiger Company for 2004:

Account Title	Beginning of Year	End of Year
Bonds Payable	$300,000	$190,000
Common Shares	200,000	250,000
Preferred Shares	75,000	125,000

Other Information

1. Dividends paid during the period amounted to $45,000.
2. No new funds were borrowed during the period.

Required

a. Compute the net cash flow from financing activities for 2004.
b. Prepare the cash flow from the financing activities section of the cash flow statement.

PROBLEM 12–6A *Using Financial Statements to Prepare a Cash Flow Statement—Direct Method* **L.O. 2, 3**

The following financial statements were drawn from the records of Pacific Company.

Balance Sheet as of December 31	2005	2006
Assets		
Cash	$ 2,800	$24,200
Accounts Receivable	1,200	2,000
Inventory	6,000	6,400
Equipment	42,000	19,000
Accumulated Amortization—Equipment	(17,400)	(9,000)
Land	10,400	18,400
Total Assets	$45,000	$61,000
Liabilities and Shareholders' Equity		
Accounts Payable	$ 4,200	$ 2,600
Long-Term Debt	6,400	2,800
Common Shares	10,000	22,000
Retained Earnings	24,000	33,600
Total Liabilities and Shareholders' Equity	$45,000	$61,000

Income Statement for the Year Ended December 31, 2006	
Sales Revenue	$35,700
Cost of Goods Sold	(14,150)
Gross Profit	21,550
Amortization Expense	(3,600)
Operating Income	17,950
Gain on Sale of Equipment	500
Loss on Disposal of Land	(50)
Net Income	$18,400

Additional Data

1. During 2006, the company sold equipment for $18,500; it had originally cost $30,000. Accumulated amortization on this equipment was $12,000 at the time of the sale. Also, the company purchased equipment for $7,000 cash.
2. The company sold land that had cost $4,000. This land was sold for $3,950, resulting in the recognition of a $50 loss. Also, common shares were issued in exchange for title to land that was valued at $12,000 at the time of exchange.
3. Paid dividends of $9,200.

Required

Use the T-account method to analyze the data and prepare a cash flow statement.

L.O. 2, 3 **PROBLEM 12–7A** ***Using Financial Statements to Prepare a Cash Flow Statement—Direct Method***

The following financial statements were drawn from the records of Raceway Sports:

Balance Sheet as of December 31	2005	2006
Assets		
Cash	$ 28,200	$123,600
Accounts Receivable	66,000	57,000
Inventory	114,000	126,000
Notes Receivable	30,000	0
Equipment	255,000	147,000
Accumulated Amortization—Equipment	(141,000)	(74,740)
Land	52,500	82,500
Total Assets	$404,700	$461,360
Liabilities and Shareholders' Equity		
Accounts Payable	$ 48,600	42,000
Salaries Payable	24,000	30,000
Utilities Payable	1,200	600
Interest Payable	1,800	0
Note Payable	60,000	0
Common Shares	240,000	300,000
Retained Earnings	29,100	88,760
Total Liabilities and Shareholders' Equity	$404,700	$461,360

Income Statement for the Year Ended December 31, 2006	
Sales Revenue	$ 580,000
Cost of Goods Sold	(288,000)
Gross Profit	292,000
Operating Expenses	
Salary Expense	(184,000)
Amortization Expense	(17,740)
Utilities Expense	(12,200)
Operating Income	78,060
Nonoperating Items	
Interest Expense	(3,000)
Gain or (Loss)	(1,800)
Net Income	$ 73,260

Additional Information

1. Sold equipment costing $108,000 with accumulated amortization of $84,000 for $22,200 cash.
2. Paid a $13,600 cash dividend to owners.

Required

Use the T-account method to analyze the data and prepare a cash flow statement.

PROBLEM 12–8A *Using Financial Statements to Prepare a Cash Flow Statement—Indirect Method* **L.O. 2, 4**

The comparative balance sheets for Redwood Corporation for 2003 and 2004 follow:

Balance Sheet as of December 31	2003	2004
Assets		
Cash	$ 40,600	$ 68,800
Accounts Receivable	22,000	30,000
Merchandise Inventory	176,000	160,000
Prepaid Rent	4,800	2,400
Equipment	288,000	256,000
Accumulated Amortization	(236,000)	(146,800)
Land	80,000	192,000
Total Assets	$375,400	$562,400
Liabilities		
Accounts Payable (Inventory)	$ 76,000	$ 67,000
Salaries Payable	24,000	28,000
Shareholders' Equity		
Common Shares	200,000	250,000
Retained Earnings	75,400	217,400
Total Liabilities and Shareholders' Equity	$375,400	$562,400

Income Statement for the Year Ended December 31, 2004	
Sales	$1,500,000
Cost of Goods Sold	(797,200)
Gross Profit	702,800
Operating Expenses	
Amortization Expense	(22,800)
Rent Expense	(24,000)
Salaries Expense	(256,000)
Other Operating Expenses	(258,000)
Net Income	$ 142,000

Other Information

1. Purchased land for $112,000.
2. Purchased new equipment for $100,000.
3. Sold old equipment that cost $132,000 with accumulated amortization of $112,000 for $20,000 cash.
4. Issued common shares for $50,000.

Required

Prepare the cash flow statement for 2004, using the indirect method.

PROBLEMS—SERIES B

L.O. 1 PROBLEM 12–1B *Classifying Cash Flows*

Required

Classify each of the following as an operating activity (OA), an investing activity (IA), or a financing activity (FA) cash flow, or a noncash transaction (NT).

a. Paid cash for operating expenses.
b. Wrote off an uncollectible account receivable using the allowance method.
c. Wrote off an uncollectible account receivable using the direct write-off method.

d. Issued common shares for cash.
e. Declared a stock split.
f. Issued a mortgage to purchase a building
g. Purchased equipment with cash.
h. Repaid the principal balance on a note payable.
i. Made a cash payment for the balance due in the Dividends Payable account.
j. Received a cash dividend from investments.
k. Purchased supplies on account.
l. Collected cash from accounts receivable.
m. Accrued warranty expense.
n. Borrowed cash by issuing a bond.
o. Loaned cash to a business associate.
p. Paid cash for interest expense.
q. Incurred a loss on the sale of equipment.
r. Wrote down inventory because the year-end physical count was less than the balance in the Inventory account.
s. Paid cash to purchase inventory.

PROBLEM 12–2B *Using Transaction Data to Prepare a Cash Flow Statement* **L.O. 2, 3**

Greenstein Company engaged in the following transactions during 2008. The beginning cash balance was $86,000.

1. Credit sales were $548,000. The beginning receivables balance was $128,000 and the ending balance was $90,000.
2. Salaries expense for 2003 was $232,000. The beginning salaries payable balance was $16,000 and the ending balance was $8,000.
3. Other operating expenses for 2003 were $236,000. The beginning operating Expense Payable balance was $16,000 and the ending balance was $10,000.
4. Recorded $30,000 of amortization expense. The beginning and ending balances in the Accumulated Amortization account were $12,000 and $42,000, respectively.
5. The Equipment account had beginning and ending balances of $44,000 and $56,000, respectively. The increase was caused by the cash purchase of equipment.
6. The beginning and ending balances in the Notes Payable account were $44,000 and $36,000, respectively. The decrease was caused by the cash repayment of debt.
7. There was $4,600 of interest expense reported on the income statement. The beginning and ending balances in the Interest Payable account were $8,400 and $7,500, respectively.
8. The beginning and ending Merchandise Inventory account balances were $22,000 and $29,400, respectively. The company sold merchandise with a cost of $83,600. The beginning and ending balances of Accounts Payable were $8,000 and $6,400, respectively.
9. The beginning and ending balances of Notes Receivable were $100,000 and $60,000, respectively. The decline resulted from the cash collection of a portion of the receivable.
10. The beginning and ending balances of the Common Shares account were $120,000 and $160,000, respectively. The increase was caused by the issue of common shares for cash.
11. Land had beginning and ending balances of $24,000 and $14,000, respectively. Land that cost $10,000 was sold for $6,000, resulting in a loss of $4,000.
12. The tax expense for 2003 was $6,600. The Tax Payable account had a $2,400 beginning balance and a $2,200 ending balance.
13. The Investments account had beginning and ending balances of $20,000 and $60,000, respectively. The company purchased investments for $50,000 cash during 2008, and investments that cost $10,000 were sold for $22,000, resulting in a $12,000 gain.

Required

Convert the preceding information to cash-equivalent data and prepare a cash flow statement.

PROBLEM 12–3B *Using Financial Statement Data to Determine Cash Flow from Operating Activities* **L.O. 2, 3**

The following account information is available for Gables Auto Supplies for 2008:

Account Title	Beginning of Year	End of Year
Accounts Receivable	$ 17,800	$ 21,000
Merchandise Inventory	136,000	142,000
Prepaid Insurance	1,600	1,200
Accounts Payable (Inventory)	18,800	19,600
Salaries Payable	6,400	5,800

Other Information

1. Sales for the period were $248,000.
2. Purchases of merchandise for the period were $186,000.
3. Insurance expense for the period was $8,000.
4. Other operating expenses (all cash) were $27,400.
5. Salary expense was $42,600.

Required

a. Compute the net cash flow from operating activities.
b. Prepare the cash flow from the operating activities section of the cash flow statement.

L.O. 2, 3 PROBLEM 12–4B *Using Financial Statement Data to Determine Cash Flow from Investing Activities*

The following information pertaining to investing activities is available for Tony's Flea Markets, Inc., for 2007.

Account Title	Beginning of Year	End of Year
Land	$ 42,000	$ 34,000
Trucks and Equipment	162,000	170,000
Investments	66,000	51,200

Other Information for 2007

1. Tony's sold investments at book value. No gain or loss was recognized.
2. Trucks were purchased for $40,000. Old trucks with a cost of $32,000 and accumulated amortization of $24,000 were sold for $11,000.
3. Land that cost $8,000 was sold for $10,000.

Required

a. Compute the net cash flow from investing activities.
b. Prepare the cash flow from the investing activities section of the cash flow statement.

L.O. 2, 3 PROBLEM 12–5B *Using Financial Statement Data to Determine Cash Flow from Financing Activities*

The following information pertaining to financing activities is available for Engineered Components Company for 2008.

Account Title	Beginning of Year	End of Year
Bonds Payable	$170,000	$180,000
Common Shares	210,000	280,000
Preferred Shares	84,000	116,000

Other Information

1. Dividends paid during the period amounted to $28,000.
2. Additional funds of $40,000 were borrowed during the period by issuing bonds.

Required

a. Compute the net cash flow from financing activities for 2008.
b. Prepare the cash flow from the financing activities section of the cash flow statement.

PROBLEM 12–6B *Using Financial Statements to Prepare a Cash Flow Statement—Direct Method* **L.O. 2, 3**

The following financial statements were drawn from the records of Healthy Products Co.

Balance Sheet as of December 31	2005	2006
Assets		
Cash	$ 1,900	$16,120
Accounts Receivable	2,000	2,400
Inventory	2,600	2,000
Equipment	17,100	13,700
Accumulated Amortization—Equipment	(12,950)	(11,300)
Land	8,000	13,000
Total Assets	$18,690	$35,920
Liabilities and Shareholders' Equity		
Accounts Payable	$ 2,400	$ 3,600
Long-Term Debt	4,000	3,200
Common Shares	10,000	17,000
Retained Earnings	2,290	12,120
Total Liabilities and Shareholders'Equity	$18,690	$35,920

Income Statement for the Year Ended December 31, 2006	
Sales Revenue	$17,480
Cost of Goods Sold	(6,200)
Gross Profit	11,280
Amortization Expense	(1,750)
Operating Income	9,530
Gain on Sale of Equipment	1,800
Loss on Disposal of Land	(600)
Net Income	$10,730

Additional Data

1. During 2006, the company sold equipment for $6,800; it had originally cost $8,400. Accumulated amortization on this equipment was $3,400 at the time of the sale. Also, the company purchased equipment for $5,000 cash.
2. The company sold land that had cost $2,000. This land was sold for $1,400, resulting in the recognition of a $600 loss. Also, common shares were issued in exchange for title to land that was valued at $7,000 at the time of exchange.
3. Paid dividends of $900.

Required

Use the T-account method to analyze the data and prepare a cash flow statement.

PROBLEM 12–7B *Using Financial Statements to Prepare a Cash Flow Statement—Direct Method* **L.O. 2, 3**

The following financial statements were drawn from the records of Norton Materials, Inc.

Balance Sheet as of December 31	2005	2006
Assets		
Cash	$ 14,100	$ 94,300
Accounts Receivable	40,000	36,000
Inventory	64,000	72,000
Notes Receivable	16,000	0
Equipment	170,000	98,000
Accumulated Amortization—Equipment	(94,000)	(47,800)
Land	30,000	46,000
Total Assets	$240,100	$298,500
Liabilities and Shareholders' Equity		
Accounts Payable	$ 26,400	24,000
Salaries Payable	10,000	15,000
Utilities Payable	1,400	800
Interest Payable	1,000	0
Note Payable	24,000	0
Common Shares	110,000	150,000
Retained Earnings	67,300	108,700
Total Liabilities and Shareholders' Equity	$240,100	$298,500

Income Statement for the Year Ended December 31, 2006	
Sales Revenue	$ 300,000
Cost of Goods Sold	(144,000)
Gross Profit	156,000
Operating Expenses	
Salary Expense	(88,000)
Amortization Expense	(9,800)
Utilities Expense	(6,400)
Operating Income	51,800
Nonoperating Items	
Interest Expense	(2,400)
Loss on Disposal	(800)
Net Income	$ 48,600

Additional Information

1. Sold equipment costing $72,000 with accumulated amortization of $56,000 for $15,200 cash.
2. Paid a $7,200 cash dividend to owners.

Required

Use the T-account method to analyze the data and prepare a cash flow statement.

L.O. 2, 4 PROBLEM 12–8B ***Using Financial Statements to Prepare a Cash Flow Statement—Indirect Method***

The comparative balance sheets for Lind Beauty Products, Inc., for 2007 and 2008 follow:

Balance Sheet as of December 31	2007	2008
Assets		
Cash	$ 48,400	$ 6,300
Accounts Receivable	7,260	10,200
Merchandise Inventory	56,000	45,200
Prepaid Rent	2,140	700
Equipment	144,000	140,000
Accumulated Amortization	(118,000)	(73,400)
Land	50,000	116,000
Total Assets	$189,800	$245,000
Liabilities and Shareholders' Equity		
Accounts Payable (Inventory)	$ 40,000	$ 37,200
Salaries Payable	10,600	12,200
Shareholders' Equity		
Common Shares	120,000	150,000
Retained Earnings	19,200	45,600
Total Liabilities and Shareholders' Equity	$189,800	$245,000

Income Statement for the Year Ended December 31, 2008	
Sales	$480,000
Cost of Goods Sold	(264,000)
Gross Profit	216,000
Operating Expenses	
Amortization Expense	(11,400)
Rent Expense	(7,000)
Salaries Expense	(95,200)
Other Operating Expenses	(76,000)
Net Income	$ 26,400

Other Information

1. Purchased land for $66,000.
2. Purchased new equipment for $62,000.
3. Sold old equipment that cost $66,000 with accumulated amortization of $56,000 for $10,000 cash.
4. Issued common shares for $30,000.

Required

Prepare the cash flow statement for 2008 using the indirect method.

ANALYZE, THINK, COMMUNICATE

BUSINESS APPLICATION CASE *Bombardier's Annual Report* **ATC 12–1**

Required

Using Bombardier's annual report in Appendix B, answer the following questions:

a. Does Bombardier use the direct or indirect method for preparing the cash flow statement? How did you know this?
b. What were the main sources of cash from operating activities? From investing activities? From financing activities?
c. What were the main uses of cash from operating activities? From investing activities? From financing activities?
d. What was the amount of dividends paid for 2002? For 2001? On which two statements did this information appear?

ATC 12–2 GROUP ASSIGNMENT *Preparing a Cash Flow Statement*

The following financial statements and information are available for Blythe Industries, Inc.

Balance Sheet as of December 31	2006	2007
Assets		
Cash	$120,600	$ 160,200
Accounts Receivable	85,000	103,200
Inventory	171,800	186,400
Investments	220,000	284,000
Equipment	490,000	650,000
Accumulated Amortization	(240,000)	(310,000)
Land	120,000	80,000
Total Assets	$967,400	$1,153,800
Liabilities and Shareholders' Equity		
Liabilities		
Accounts Payable (Inventory)	$ 66,200	$ 36,400
Notes Payable—Long-Term	250,000	230,000
Bonds Payable	100,000	200,000
Total Liabilities	416,200	466,400
Shareholders' Equity		
Common Shares	200,000	240,000
Preferred Shares	100,000	110,000
Total Share Capital	300,000	350,000
Retained Earnings	251,200	337,400
Total Shareholders' Equity	$551,200	$ 687,400
Total Liabilities and Shareholders' Equity	$967,400	$1,153,800

Income Statement for 2007		
Sales Revenue		$1,050,000
Cost of Goods Sold		(766,500)
Gross Profit		283,500
Operating Expenses		
Supplies Expense	$20,400	
Salaries Expense	92,000	
Amortization Expense	90,000	
Total Operating Expenses		202,400
Operating Income		81,100
Nonoperating Items		
Interest Expense		(16,000)
Gain from the Sale of Investments		30,000
Gain from the Sale of Land and Equipment		12,000
Net Income		$ 107,100

Additional Information

1. Sold land that cost $40,000 for $44,000.
2. Sold equipment that cost $30,000 and had accumulated amortization of $20,000 for $18,000.
3. Purchased new equipment for $190,000.
4. Sold investments that cost $40,000 for $70,000.
5. Purchased new investments for $104,000.
6. Paid $20,000 on the principal of the long-term note.
7. Paid off a $100,000 bond issue and issued new bonds for $200,000.
8. Issued some new common shares.
9. Issued some new preferred shares.
10. Paid dividends. (*Note:* The only transactions to affect retained earnings were net income and dividends.)

Required

a. Organize the class into three sections, and divide each section into groups of three to five students. Assign each section of groups an activity section of the cash flow statement (operating activities, investing activities, or financing activities).

Group Task

Prepare your assigned portion of the cash flow statement. Have a representative of your section put your activity section of the cash flow statement on the board. As each adds its information on the board, the full cash flow statement will be presented.

Class Discussion

Have the class finish the cash flow statement by computing the net change in cash. Also have the class answer the following questions:

b. How many preferred shares were issued if the issue price was $50 per share?
c. How many common shares were issued if the shares have a stated value of $4?
d. What was the net book value of the equipment sold?

WRITING ASSIGNMENT *Explaining Discrepancies between Cash Flow and Operating Income* ATC 12–3

The following selected information was drawn from the records of Fleming Company:

Assets	2002	2003
Accounts Receivable	$ 400,000	$ 840,200
Merchandise Inventory	720,000	1,480,000
Equipment	1,484,000	1,861,200
Accumulated Amortization	(312,000)	(402,400)

Fleming is experiencing cash flow problems. Even though it reported significant increases in operating income, operating activities produced a net cash outflow. Recent financial forecasts predict that Fleming will have insufficient cash to pay its current liabilities within three months.

Required

Write a response explaining Fleming's cash shortage. Include a recommendation to remedy the problem.

ETHICAL DILEMMA *Would I Lie to You?* ATC 12–4

Andy and Jean Crocket are involved in divorce proceedings. When discussing a property settlement, Andy told Jean that he should take over their investment in an apartment complex because she would be unable to absorb the loss that the apartments are generating. Jean was somewhat distrustful and asked Andy to support his contention. He produced the following income statement:

CROCKET APARTMENTS Income Statements For the Year Ended December 31, 2008		
Rent Revenue		$580,000
Less: Expenses		
Amortization Expense	$280,000	
Interest Expense	184,000	
Operating Expense	88,000	
Management Fees	56,000	
Total Expenses		(608,000)
Net Loss		$ (28,000)

All revenue is earned on account. Interest and operating expenses are incurred on account. Management fees are paid in cash. The following accounts and balances were drawn from the 2007 and 2008 year-end balance sheets.

Account Title	2007	2008
Rent Receivable	$40,000	$44,000
Interest Payable	12,000	18,000
Accounts Payable (Oper. Exp.)	6,000	4,000

Jean is reluctant to give up the apartments but feels that she must because her present salary is only $40,000 per year. She says that if she takes the apartments, the $28,000 loss would absorb a significant portion of her salary, leaving her only $12,000 with which to support herself. She tells you that while the figures seem to support her husband's arguments, she believes that she is failing to see something. She knows that she and her husband collected a $20,000 distribution from the business on December 1, 2008. Also, $150,000 cash was paid in 2008 to reduce the principal balance on a mortgage that was taken out to finance the purchase of the apartments two years ago. Finally, $24,000 cash was paid during 2008 to purchase a computer system used in the business. She wonders, "If the apartments are losing money, where is my husband getting all the cash to make these payments?"

Required

a. Prepare a cash flow statement for the 2008 accounting period.
b. Compare the cash flow statement prepared in Requirement *a* with the income statement, and provide Jean Crocket with recommendations.

ATC 12–5 SPREADSHEET ANALYSIS *Preparing a Cash Flow Statement Using the Direct Method*

Refer to the information in Problem 12–8A. Solve for the cash flow statement using the direct method. Instead of using the T-account method, set up the following spreadsheet to work through the analysis. The Debit/Credit entries are very similar to the T-account method except that they are entered onto a spreadsheet. Two distinct differences are as follows:

1. Instead of making entries on row 2 for Cash, cash entries are made beginning on row 24 under the heading Cash Transactions.
2. Entries for Retained Earnings are made on rows 15 through 20 since there are numerous revenue and expense entries to that account.

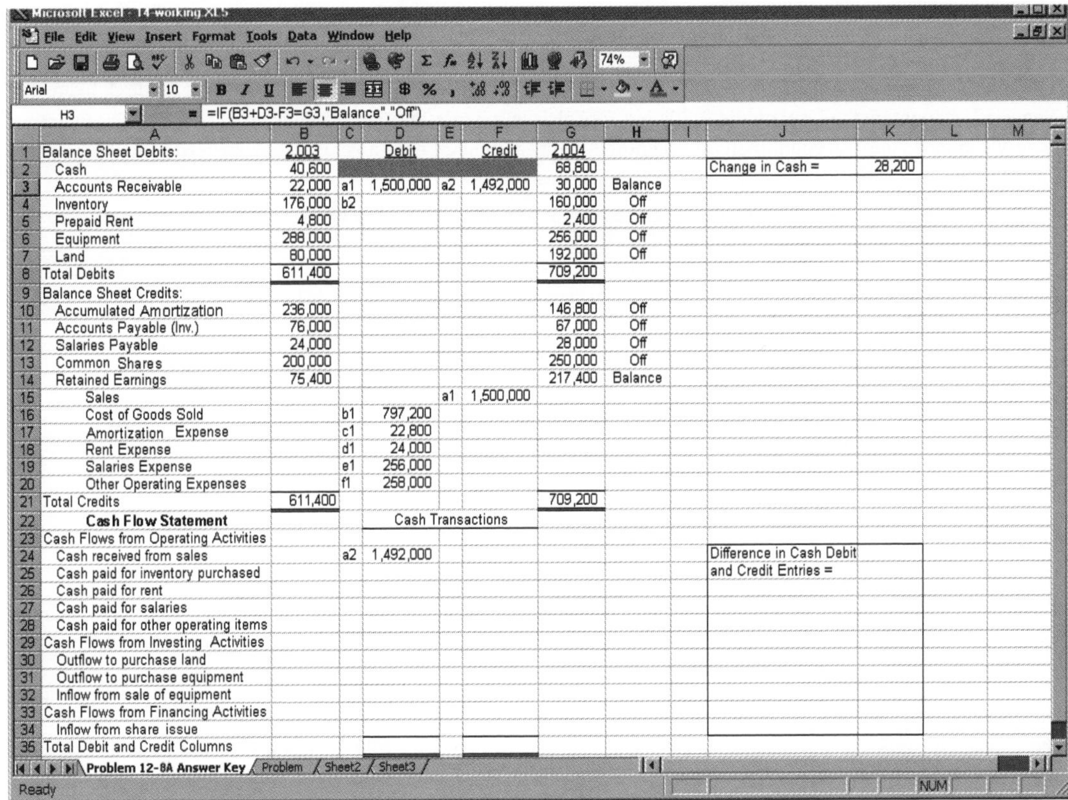

Microsoft Excel - 14-working.XLS

H3 = =IF(B3+D3-F3=G3,"Balance","Off")

	A	B	C	D	E	F	G	H	I	J	K
1	Balance Sheet Debits:	2,003		Debit		Credit	2,004				
2	Cash	40,600					68,800			Change in Cash =	28,200
3	Accounts Receivable	22,000	a1	1,500,000	a2	1,492,000	30,000	Balance			
4	Inventory	176,000	b2				160,000	Off			
5	Prepaid Rent	4,800					2,400	Off			
6	Equipment	288,000					256,000	Off			
7	Land	80,000					192,000	Off			
8	Total Debits	611,400					709,200				
9	Balance Sheet Credits:										
10	Accumulated Amortization	236,000					146,800	Off			
11	Accounts Payable (Inv.)	76,000					67,000	Off			
12	Salaries Payable	24,000					28,000	Off			
13	Common Shares	200,000					250,000	Off			
14	Retained Earnings	75,400					217,400	Balance			
15	Sales				a1	1,500,000					
16	Cost of Goods Sold		b1	797,200							
17	Amortization Expense		c1	22,800							
18	Rent Expense		d1	24,000							
19	Salaries Expense		e1	256,000							
20	Other Operating Expenses		f1	258,000							
21	Total Credits	611,400					709,200				
22	**Cash Flow Statement**			Cash Transactions							
23	Cash Flows from Operating Activities										
24	Cash received from sales		a2	1,492,000						Difference in Cash Debit and Credit Entries =	
25	Cash paid for inventory purchased										
26	Cash paid for rent										
27	Cash paid for salaries										
28	Cash paid for other operating items										
29	Cash Flows from Investing Activities										
30	Outflow to purchase land										
31	Outflow to purchase equipment										
32	Inflow from sale of equipment										
33	Cash Flows from Financing Activities										
34	Inflow from share issue										
35	Total Debit and Credit Columns										

Problem 12-8A Answer Key / Problem / Sheet2 / Sheet3

Required

a. Enter information in Column A.

b. Enter the beginning balance sheet amounts in Column B and ending balances in Column G. Total the debits and credits for each column.

c. To prevent erroneous entries to Cash in row 2, darken the area in Columns C through F.

d. In Columns C through F, record entries for the revenue and expenses and then the related conversions to cash flow. The first entry (a1) and (a2) converting Sales to Cash Received from Sales has been provided for you. So has the labelling for the expense entries (b1 through f1).

e. Record the four entries from the Other Information provided in Problem 12–8A. These are investing and financing activities.

f. In Column H, set up the IF function to determine whether the balance sheet accounts are in balance or not ("off"). Cell H3 for Accounts Receivable is provided for you. Cell H3 can be copied to all the balance sheet debit accounts. The balance sheet credit account formulas will differ given the different debit/credit rules for those accounts. The formula for Retained Earnings will need to include rows 14 through 20. *When the word "Balance" is reflected in every balance sheet cell in column H, the spreadsheet analysis is complete.* For more information on the IF function, refer to Spreadsheet Tips in ATC 11–9 in Chapter 11.

g. Total the Debit and Credit columns to ensure that the two columns are equal.

h. As a final check, beginning in cell J2, compute the change in the Cash account by subtracting the beginning balance from the ending balance. The difference will equal $28,200. Also beginning in cell J24, compute the difference in the debit and credit cash entries in rows 24 through 34. The difference should also equal $28,200.

Spreadsheet Tip

Darken cells by highlighting the cells to be darkened. Select Format and then Cells. Click on the tab titled Patterns and choose a colour.

ATC 12–6 SPREADSHEET ANALYSIS *Preparing a Cash Flow Statement Using the Indirect Method*

(*Note:* If you completed ATC 12–5, that spreadsheet can be modified to complete this problem.)

Refer to the information in Problem 12–8A. Solve for the cash flow statement using the indirect method. Instead of using the T-account method, set up the following spreadsheet to work through the analysis. The Debit/Credit entries are very similar to the T-account method except that they are entered onto a spreadsheet. Instead of making entries on row 2 for Cash, Cash Flow entries are made beginning on row 18.

Microsoft Excel - 14-mastering.XLS

H3 = =IF(B3+D3-F3=G3,"Balance","Off")

	A	B	C	D	E	F	G	H	I	J	K
1	Balance Sheet Debits:	2,003		Debit		Credit	2,004				
2	Cash	40,600					68,800			Change in Cash =	28,200
3	Accounts Receivable	22,000	(c)	8,000			30,000	Balance			
4	Inventory	176,000					160,000	Off			
5	Prepaid Rent	4,800					2,400	Off			
6	Equipment	288,000					256,000	Off			
7	Land	80,000					192,000	Off			
8	Total Debits	611,400					709,200				
9	Balance Sheet Credits:										
10	Accumulated Amortization	236,000			(b)	22,800	146,800	Off			
11	Accounts Payable (Inv.)	76,000					67,000	Off			
12	Salaries Payable	24,000					28,000	Off			
13	Common Shares	200,000					250,000	Off			
14	Retained Earnings	75,400			(a)	142,000	217,400	Balance			
15	Total Credits	611,400					709,200				
16	**Cash Flow Statement**										
17	Cash Flows from Operating Activities										
18	Net Income		(a)	142,000						Difference in Cash Debit	
19	Plus Noncash Charges									and Credit Entries =	
20	Amortization Expense		(b)	22,800							
21	Changes in Current Assets & Liab.										
22	Increase in Accounts Receivable				(c)	8,000					
23	Decrease in Inventory										
24	Decrease in Prepaid Rent										
25	Decrease in Accounts Payable										
26	Increase in Salaries Payable										
27	Cash Flows from Investing Activities										
28	Outflow to purchase land										
29	Outflow to purchase equipment										
30	Inflow from sale of equipment										
31	Cash Flows from Financing Activities										
32	Inflow from share issue										
33	Total Debit and Credit Columns			172,800		172,800					
34											
35											

Problem 12-8A Answer Key / Problem / Sheet2 / Sheet3

Required

a. Enter information in Column A.

b. Enter the beginning balance sheet amounts in Column B and ending balances in Column G. Total the debits and credits for each column.

c. To prevent erroneous entries to Cash in row 2, darken the area in Columns C through F.

d. Record the entry for Net Income. This is entry (a) provided.

e. Record the entry for Amortization expense. This is entry (b) provided.

f. Record the entries for the changes in current assets and liabilities. The entry for the change in Accounts Receivable has been provided and is referenced as entry (c).

g. Record the four entries from the Other Information provided in Problem 12–8A. These are the investing and financing activities.

h. In Column H set up the IF function to determine whether the balance sheet accounts are in balance or not ("off"). Cell H3 for Accounts Receivable is provided for you. Cell H3 can be copied to all the balance sheet debit accounts. The balance sheet credit account formulas will differ given the different debit/credit rules for those accounts. *When the word "Balance" is reflected in every balance sheet cell in column H, the spreadsheet analysis is complete.* For more information on the IF function, refer to Spreadsheet Tips in ATC 11–9 in Chapter 11.

i. Total the Debit and Credit columns to ensure that the two columns are equal.

j. As a final check, beginning in cell J2, compute the change in the Cash account by subtracting the beginning balance from the ending balance. The difference will equal $28,200. Also beginning in cell J18, compute the difference in the debit and credit cash entries in rows 18 through 32. The difference should also equal $28,200.

Accessing the SEDAR Database through the Internet

Successful business managers need many different skills, including communication, interpersonal, computer, and analytical skills. Most business students become very aware of the data analysis skills used in accounting, but they may not be as aware of the importance of "data finding" skills. There are many sources of accounting and financial data. The more sources you are able to use, the better.

One very important source of accounting information is the SEDAR database. Others are probably available at your school through the library or business school network. Your accounting instructor will be able to identify these for you and make suggestions regarding their use. By making the effort to learn to use electronic databases, you will enhance your abilities as a future manager and your marketability as a business graduate.

SEDAR, which stands for the System for Electronic Document Analysis and Retrieval, has been used since January 1, 1997, to electronically file securities-related information with the Canadian Securities Administrators. The Canadian Depository for Securities has developed this innovative Web site to make public securities filings easily accessible to all. Use it to find and retrieve SEDAR public securities filings and company/mutual fund profiles, as well as read the latest news about SEDAR. You will find that the SEDAR site is very user friendly.

These instructions assume that you know how to access and use an Internet navigator, such as Netscape. After you activate the navigator program on your computer, follow the instructions to retrieve data from SEDAR as outlined below. Be aware that Web sites on the Internet are updated and changed regularly. Accordingly, be prepared for differences between the following instructions and what appears on your computer screen. Any major changes in accessing SEDAR will be posted on the Online Learning Centre that accompanies this text (at www.mcgrawhill.ca/college/edmonds). Take comfort in the fact that changes are normally designed to simplify user access. If you encounter a conflict between the following instructions and the instructions provided in the SEDAR interface, remember that SEDAR is more current and should take precedence over the following instructions:

1. To connect to SEDAR, type in the following address: http://www.sedar.com.
2. After the SEDAR home page screen appears, click on About SEDAR. This section provides relevant information concerning the System for Electronic Document Analysis and Retrieval (SEDAR). A list appearing on the left side of the screen allows you to choose a variety of links, including the background of SEDAR and frequently asked questions.
3. You can access all publicly traded companies by clicking on the link Company Profiles. The public companies are listed in alphabetical order, so if you know the first letter of the name of the company and click on it, all public companies starting with that letter will appear. This information is also available for mutual fund groups as well.
4. Another way of accessing company information is by using the Search Database link. Again you can search for either public companies or mutual fund groups. This search function allows you to find specific documents by company name, industry grouping, or date. Documents include annual reports, financial statements, management discussion and analysis, press releases, and a variety of other documents.

5. Access the documents of your choice by clicking on the link. If you wish to save any of the documents, you can do so by using the File Save As command.

6. Good Luck! If you have never used the Internet before, you will find that it contains an incredible amount of stuff. Some of this stuff, such as the SEDAR database, actually contains useful information. However, you will also find that the Internet is often very slow and frustrating, especially during the middle of business days. Using SEDAR during off-hours is more enjoyable and efficient.

Let's use the SEDAR system to find the latest information for Bombardier Inc.:

1. Access SEDAR and click on Company Profiles. Click on the letter B in the Public Companies box.

2. Scroll down the list of companies until you find Bombardier Inc. Click on the link. You are now on the Bombardier profile screen. Here you can obtain general information about the company such as its location, size, year-end date, exchanges the shares are traded on, who the independent auditors are, and so on.

3. At the bottom of the screen, you can find a View button. Click on this button to view the company's documents. A list of all public documents filed with SEDAR appears in chronological order. To access any of the documents, just click on the link.

4. The audited financial statements usually get posted at the beginning of April. Click on the most current data available and review the financial statements.

Bombardier Annual Report

ANNUAL REPORT YEAR ENDED JANUARY 31, 2002

DEFINING OUR FUTURE

BOMBARDIER

BOMBARDIER

MANAGEMENT'S RESPONSIBILITY FOR FINANCIAL REPORTING

The accompanying financial statements of **Bombardier Inc.** and all the information in this Annual Report are the responsibility of Management and have been approved by the Board of Directors.

The financial statements have been prepared by Management in accordance with Canadian generally accepted accounting principles. The financial statements include some amounts that are based on estimates and judgments. Management has determined such amounts on a reasonable basis in order to ensure that the financial statements are presented fairly, in all material respects. Financial information used elsewhere in the Annual Report is consistent with that in the financial statements.

Bombardier Inc.'s policy is to maintain systems of internal accounting and administrative controls of high quality, consistent with reasonable cost. Such systems are designed to provide reasonable assurance that the financial information is relevant, accurate and reliable and that the Corporation's assets are appropriately accounted for and adequately safeguarded.

The Board of Directors is responsible for ensuring that Management fulfils its responsibilities for financial reporting and is ultimately responsible for reviewing and approving the financial statements. The Board carries out this responsibility principally through its Audit Committee.

The Audit Committee is appointed by the Board and is comprised of a majority of outside Directors. The committee meets periodically with Management, as well as the internal auditors and the external auditors, to discuss internal controls over the financial reporting process, auditing matters and financial reporting issues, to satisfy itself that each party is properly discharging its responsibilities and to review the financial statements and the external auditors' report. The committee reports its findings to the Board for consideration by the Board when it approves the financial statements for issuance to the shareholders.

The financial statements have been audited by Ernst & Young LLP, the external auditors, in accordance with Canadian generally accepted auditing standards on behalf of the shareholders. The external auditors have full and free access to the Audit Committee.

(signed)

Louis Morin, CA
Senior Vice President and Chief Financial Officer
March 19, 2002

AUDITORS' REPORT

TO THE SHAREHOLDERS OF BOMBARDIER INC.

We have audited the consolidated balance sheets of **Bombardier Inc.** as at January 31, 2002 and 2001 and the consolidated statements of income, shareholders' equity and cash flows for the years then ended. These financial statements are the responsibility of the Corporation's Management. Our responsibility is to express an opinion on these financial statements based on our audits.

We conducted our audits in accordance with Canadian generally accepted auditing standards. Those standards require that we plan and perform an audit to obtain reasonable assurance whether the financial statements are free of material misstatement. An audit includes examining, on a test basis, evidence supporting the amounts and disclosures in the financial statements. An audit also includes assessing the accounting principles used and significant estimates made by Management, as well as evaluating the overall financial statement presentation.

In our opinion, these consolidated financial statements present fairly, in all material respects, the financial position of the Corporation as at January 31, 2002 and 2001 and the results of its operations and its cash flows for the years then ended in accordance withCanadian generally accepted accounting principles.

(signed)

Ernest & Young LLP
Chartered Accountants
Montréal, Canada
February 26, 2002
(except for note 28, which is as at March 8, 2002)

CONSOLIDATED BALANCE SHEETS

As at January 31, 2002 and 2001 (millions of Canadian dollars)		Bombardier Inc. consolidated		Bombardier		BC	
	Notes	2002	2001	2002	2001	2002	2001
Assets							
Cash and cash equivalents		**$ 462.8**	$ 1,373.9	**$ 462.8**	$ 1,358.8	**$ –**	$ 15.1
Receivables	3	**1,902.1**	851.2	**1,590.7**	626.5	**311.4**	224.7
Finance receivables	4	**6,461.7**	7,202.7	**63.4**	62.0	**6,398.3**	7,140.7
Assets under operating leases	5	**1,831.2**	1,768.1	**–**	–	**1,831.2**	1,768.1
Inventories	6	**8,956.5**	6,413.7	**8,956.5**	6,413.7	**–**	–
Property, plant and equipment	7	**3,408.4**	2,090.9	**3,245.3**	1,958.1	**163.1**	132.8
Goodwill	8	**2,712.9**	–	**2,712.9**	–	**–**	–
Investment in and advances to BC		**–**	–	**1,363.0**	1,581.5	**–**	–
Other assets	9	**2,017.0**	703.8	**1,456.4**	421.6	**560.6**	282.2
		$27,752.6	$20,404.3	**$19,851.0**	$12,422.2	**$9,264.6**	$9,563.6
Liabilities							
Short-term borrowings	10	**$ 3,037.0**	$ 2,531.2	**$ 1,341.7**	$ –	**$1,695.3**	$2,531.2
Advances from Bombardier		**–**	–	**–**	–	**20.0**	205.5
Accounts payable and accrued liabilities	11	**7,779.4**	4,036.6	**7,360.9**	3,840.0	**418.5**	196.6
Advances and progress billings in excess of related costs	6	**3,019.0**	2,362.8	**3,019.0**	2,362.8	**–**	–
Long-term debt	12	**7,857.7**	6,131.2	**2,080.7**	879.4	**5,777.0**	5,251.8
Other liabilities	13	**1,969.5**	1,530.1	**1,958.7**	1,527.6	**10.8**	2.5
		23,662.6	16,591.9	**15,761.0**	8,609.8	**7,921.6**	8,187.6
Shareholders' equity (Investment in BC)		**4,090.0**	3,812.4	**4,090.0**	3,812.4	**1,343.0**	1,376.0
		$27,752.6	$20,404.3	**$19,851.0**	$12,422.2	**$9,264.6**	$9,563.6

The accompanying summary of significant accounting policies and notes are an integral part of these Consolidated Financial Statements and provide information on the financial statement presentation.

On behalf of the Board of Directors,

(signed)

Robert E. Brown
Director

(signed)

Donald C. Lowe
Director

CONSOLIDATED STATEMENTS OF SHAREHOLDERS' EQUITY

For the years ended January 31, 2002 and 2001 (millions of Canadian dollars)	Notes	2002 Number (in thousands)	2002 Amount	2001 Number (in thousands)	2001 Amount
SHARE CAPITAL	14				
Preferred shares – Series 2		12,000	$ 300.0	12,000	$ 300.0
Common shares					
Class A (Multiple Voting) Shares					
Balance at beginning of year		347,426	48.1	351,594	48.6
Redemption of shares		–	–	(4,015)	(0.5)
Converted to Class B		(5,059)	(0.7)	(153)	–
Balance at end of year		342,367	47.4	347,426	48.1
Class B (Subordinate Voting) Shares					
Balance at beginning of year		1,018,625	821.9	1,026,024	813.7
Issued under the share option plans	15	4,720	26.2	4,299	17.6
Redemption of shares		–	–	(11,851)	(9.4)
Converted from Class A		5,059	0.7	153	–
Balance at end of year		1,028,404	848.8	1,018,625	821.9
Balance at end of year – common shares		1,370,771	896.2	1,366,051	870.0
Total – share capital			1,196.2		1,170.0
RETAINED EARNINGS					
Balance at beginning of year			2,660.0		2,392.5
Effect of change of accounting policy for employee future benefits			–		(210.6)
Balance at beginning of year – adjusted			2,660.0		2,181.9
Net income			390.9		975.4
Dividends:					
Preferred shares			(16.5)		(16.5)
Common shares			(248.0)		(186.3)
Excess of redemption price of common shares over stated value			–		(293.9)
Other			(1.1)		(0.6)
Balance at end of year			2,785.3		2,660.0
Deferred translation adjustment			108.5		(17.6)
Total – shareholders' equity			$4,090.0		$3,812.4

The accompanying summary of significant accounting policies and notes are an integral part of these Consolidated Financial Statements and provide information on the financial statement presentation.

CONSOLIDATED STATEMENTS OF INCOME

For the years ended January 31, 2002 and 2001
(millions of Canadian dollars, except per share amounts)

		Bombardier Inc. consolidated		Bombardier		BC	
	Notes	2002	2001	2002	2001	2002	2001
Revenues	26	**$21,633.8**	$15,943.7	**$21,056.4**	$15,274.2	**$ 966.8**	$935.9
Cost of sales and operating expenses	17, 18	**19,480.6**	14,323.9	**18,954.1**	13,594.7	**915.9**	995.6
Depreciation and amortization	26	**467.1**	302.3	**322.1**	210.0	**145.0**	92.3
Interest expense	18	**182.0**	108.2	**182.0**	69.8	**–**	38.4
Other income	19, 26	**(170.6)**	(218.6)	**(35.1)**	(43.6)	**(135.5)**	(175.0)
Net loss (income) from BC before BC's special items		**–**	–	**(24.6)**	9.1	**–**	–
		19,959.1	14,515.8	**19,398.5**	13,840.0	**925.4**	951.3
Income (loss) before special items, income taxes and goodwill amortization		**1,674.7**	1,427.9	**1,657.9**	1,434.2	**41.4**	(15.4)
Special items	20	**1,070.2**	29.7	**812.8**	(2.1)	**662.5**	79.5
Income (loss) before income taxes and goodwill amortization		**604.5**	1,398.2	**845.1**	1,436.3	**(621.1)**	(94.9)
Income taxes	21	**167.0**	422.8	**407.6**	460.9	**(240.6)**	(38.1)
Income (loss) before goodwill amortization		**437.5**	975.4	**437.5**	975.4	**(380.5)**	(56.8)
Goodwill amortization		**46.6**	–	**46.6**	–	**–**	–
Net income (loss)		**$ 390.9**	$ 975.4	**$ 390.9**	$ 975.4	**$(380.5)**	$ (56.8)
Earnings per share:	16						
Basic		**$ 0.27**	$ 0.70				
Diluted		**$ 0.27**	$ 0.69				
Earnings per share, before goodwill amortization:	16						
Basic		**$ 0.31**	$ 0.70				
Diluted		**$ 0.30**	$ 0.69				

The accompanying summary of significant accounting policies and notes are an integral part of these Consolidated Financial Statements and provide information on the financial statement presentation.

CONSOLIDATED STATEMENTS OF CASH FLOWS

For the years ended January 31, 2002 and 2001
(millions of Canadian dollars)

	Notes	Bombardier Inc. consolidated 2002	Bombardier Inc. consolidated 2001	Bombardier 2002	Bombardier 2001	BC 2002	BC 2001
Operating activities							
Net income (loss)		**$ 390.9**	$ 975.4	**$ 390.9**	$ 975.4	**$ (380.5)**	$ (56.8)
Non-cash items:							
Depreciation and amortization		**513.7**	302.3	**368.7**	210.0	**145.0**	92.3
Net loss from BC		**–**	–	**380.5**	56.8	**–**	–
Provision for credit losses	4	**117.5**	150.8	**–**	–	**117.5**	150.8
Deferred income taxes	21	**34.1**	271.8	**273.5**	350.0	**(239.4)**	(78.2)
Special items	20	**1,070.2**	29.7	**407.7**	(49.8)	**662.5**	79.5
Net changes in non-cash balances related to operations	22	**(2,815.0)**	(830.1)	**(2,703.7)**	(629.4)	**(111.3)**	(200.7)
Cash flows from operating activities		**(688.6)**	899.9	**(882.4)**	913.0	**193.8**	(13.1)
Investing activities							
Additions to property, plant and equipment		**(838.8)**	(415.1)	**(789.8)**	(395.4)	**(49.0)**	(19.7)
Net investment in finance receivables		**(869.7)**	(1,061.7)	**(1.5)**	(4.8)	**(868.2)**	(1,056.9)
Additions to assets under operating leases		**(1,021.1)**	(2,201.0)	**–**	–	**(1,021.1)**	(2,201.0)
Disposal of assets under operating leases		**924.2**	1,427.5	**–**	–	**924.2**	1,427.5
Business acquisitions, net of cash acquired	2	**(979.8)**	–	**(979.8)**	–	**–**	–
Disposal of businesses	20	**–**	66.1	**–**	66.1	**–**	–
Investment in and advances to BC		**–**	–	**(90.4)**	(77.5)	**90.4**	77.5
Other		**(122.5)**	(60.9)	**(80.6)**	(14.0)	**(41.9)**	(46.9)
Cash flows from investing activities		**(2,907.7)**	(2,245.1)	**(1,942.1)**	(425.6)	**(965.6)**	(1,819.5)
Financing activities							
Net variation in short-term borrowings		**26.0**	458.1	**986.5**	–	**(960.5)**	458.1
Proceeds from issuance of long-term debt		**3,881.9**	1,425.3	**1,210.4**	38.4	**2,671.5**	1,386.9
Repayment of long-term debt		**(1,009.7)**	(220.2)	**(48.4)**	(139.0)	**(961.3)**	(81.2)
Issuance of shares, net of related costs		**26.2**	17.6	**26.2**	17.6	**–**	–
Redemption of shares	14	**–**	(303.8)	**–**	(303.8)	**–**	–
Dividends paid		**(264.5)**	(202.8)	**(264.5)**	(202.8)	**–**	–
Cash flows from financing activities		**2,659.9**	1,174.2	**1,910.2**	(589.6)	**749.7**	1,763.8
Effect of exchange rate changes on cash and cash equivalents		**25.3**	(119.1)	**18.3**	(87.7)	**7.0**	(31.4)
Net decrease in cash and cash equivalents		**(911.1)**	(290.1)	**(896.0)**	(189.9)	**(15.1)**	(100.2)
Cash and cash equivalents at beginning of year		**1,373.9**	1,664.0	**1,358.8**	1,548.7	**15.1**	115.3
Cash and cash equivalents at end of year		**$ 462.8**	$ 1,373.9	**$ 462.8**	$ 1,358.8	**$ –**	$ 15.1
Supplemental information							
Cash paid for – interest		**$ 477.3**	$ 582.2				
– income taxes		**$ 79.8**	$ 76.0				

The accompanying summary of significant accounting policies and notes are an integral part of these Consolidated Financial Statements and provide information on the financial statement presentation.

SUMMARY OF SIGNIFICANT ACCOUNTING POLICIES

For the years ended January 31, 2002 and 2001

CONSOLIDATED FINANCIAL STATEMENT PRESENTATION

Bombardier Inc. is incorporated under the laws of Canada. The consolidated balance sheets are unclassified because Bombardier Inc. and its subsidiaries (the "Corporation") carry out their operations in four distinct segments, each one characterized by a specific operating cycle. Financial services and real estate activities, being distinct from Bombardier's other activities, are shown in a separate column (BC) in the Consolidated Financial Statements.

The following describes the columns shown in these financial statements:

BOMBARDIER INC. CONSOLIDATED

This column represents all of the activities of the Corporation on a consolidated basis, after elimination of balances and transactions between Bombardier and BC.

BOMBARDIER

This column represents the activities of the Corporation's three manufacturing segments (aerospace, transportation and recreational products). These segments are grouped and referred to as "Bombardier" and intercompany transactions and balances within this column have been eliminated. Bombardier's investment in BC is accounted for, in this column, under the equity method and comprises BC's equity and subordinated debt of Bombardier in BC.

BC

Bombardier Capital (BC) represents the financial services and real estate activities of the Corporation. Intercompany transactions and balances within BC have been eliminated.

BOMBARDIER INC. CONSOLIDATED SIGNIFICANT ACCOUNTING POLICIES

BASIS OF CONSOLIDATION

The consolidated financial statements include the accounts of Bombardier Inc. and its subsidiaries, substantially all of which are wholly-owned. They also include the Corporation's proportionate share of its joint ventures. Most legal entities of the transportation segment use a December 31 fiscal year-end. As a result, the Corporation consolidates these operations with a one month lag with the remainder of its operations.

USE OF ESTIMATES

The preparation of financial statements in conformity with Canadian generally accepted accounting principles requires Management to make estimates and assumptions that affect the reported amounts of assets and liabilities, disclosure of contingent assets and liabilities and the reported amounts of revenues and expenses. Actual results could differ from these estimates.

TRANSLATION OF FOREIGN CURRENCIES

Foreign operations are classified as integrated or self-sustaining. All significant foreign investees are classified as self-sustaining entities.

BOMBARDIER INC. CONSOLIDATED
SIGNIFICANT ACCOUNTING POLICIES (cont'd)

[A] SELF-SUSTAINING FOREIGN OPERATIONS

All assets and liabilities are translated at exchange rates in effect at year-end. Revenues and expenses are translated at the average rates of exchange for the period. The resulting net gains or losses are shown under "Deferred translation adjustment" in shareholders' equity.

[B] ACCOUNTS IN FOREIGN CURRENCIES

Accounts in foreign currencies, including integrated foreign investees, are translated using the temporal method. Under this method, monetary balance sheet items are translated at the rates of exchange in effect at year-end and non-monetary items are translated at historical exchange rates. Revenues and expenses (other than depreciation and amortization, which are translated at the same rates as the related assets) are translated at the rates in effect on the transaction dates or at the average rates of exchange for the period. Translation gains or losses are included in the statement of income, except those related to the translation of long-term debt, which are deferred and amortized to income over the remaining life of the related debt on a straight-line basis, and those related to debt designated as an effective hedge of the Corporation's net investment in self-sustaining foreign operations, which are shown under "Deferred translation adjustment" in shareholders' equity.

CASH AND CASH EQUIVALENTS

Cash and cash equivalents consist of cash and highly liquid investments which have maturities of less than three months at the date of acquisition. These securities are only with investment grade financial institutions.

PROPERTY, PLANT AND EQUIPMENT

Property, plant and equipment are recorded at cost. Depreciation is computed under the straight-line method over the following estimated useful lives:

Buildings	10 to 40 years
Equipment	2 to 15 years
Other	3 to 20 years

Depreciation of assets under construction and development commences when they are ready for their intended use.

INCOME TAXES

Income taxes are provided for using the liability method. Under this method, deferred income tax assets and liabilities are determined based on all significant differences between the carrying amounts and tax bases of assets and liabilities using substantively enacted tax rates and laws expected to be in effect when the differences reverse.

EARNINGS PER SHARE

Basic earnings per share and basic earnings per share before goodwill amortization are computed based on net income less dividends on preferred shares and net income before goodwill amortization less dividends on preferred shares, respectively, divided by the weighted average number of Class A (Multiple Voting) Shares and Class B (Subordinate Voting) Shares outstanding during the year. Diluted earnings per share are computed using the treasury stock method, giving effect to the exercise of all dilutive elements.

BOMBARDIER INC. CONSOLIDATED
SIGNIFICANT ACCOUNTING POLICIES (cont'd)

EMPLOYEE FUTURE BENEFITS

The cost of pension and other post-retirement benefits earned by employees is actuarially determined using the projected benefit method prorated on service and Management's best estimate of expected plan investment performance, salary escalation, retirement ages of employees and health care costs. Plan obligations are discounted using current market interest rates and plan assets are presented at fair value. The excess of net actuarial gains and losses over 10% of the greater of the benefit obligation and the fair value of plan assets is amortized to income over the estimated average remaining service life of participants.

ALLOWANCE FOR CREDIT LOSSES

Finance receivables and trade receivables are classified as impaired when, in the opinion of Management, there is reasonable doubt as to the ultimate collectibility of a portion of principal and interest. Accrual of interest income is suspended when the account becomes 90 days delinquent or may be suspended earlier if collection of an account becomes doubtful.

The Corporation maintains an allowance for credit losses in an amount sufficient to provide adequate protection against losses. The level of allowance is based on Management's assessment of the risks associated with each of the Corporation's portfolios, including loss and recovery experience, industry performance and the impact of current and projected economic conditions.

DERIVATIVE FINANCIAL INSTRUMENTS

The Corporation is party to a number of derivative financial instruments, mainly foreign exchange contracts, interest-rate swap agreements and cross-currency interest rate swap agreements used to manage currency and interest rate risks. Gains and losses on foreign exchange contracts entered into to hedge future transactions are deferred and included in the measurement of the related foreign currency transactions. Payments and receipts under interest-rate and cross-currency interest rate swap agreements are recognized as adjustments to interest expense.

ENVIRONMENTAL OBLIGATIONS

Liabilities are recorded when environmental claims or remedial efforts are probable, and the costs can be reasonably estimated. Environmental expenditures that relate to current operations are expensed or capitalized as appropriate. Expenditures that relate to an existing condition caused by past operations, and which do not contribute to future revenue generation, are expensed.

SHARE-BASED PLANS

The issuance of options under the Corporation's share option plans is treated as a capital transaction for accounting purposes. Accordingly, the issuance of options does not give rise to compensation expense in the Consolidated Financial Statements of the Corporation.

The Corporation's contributions to the employee share purchase plan are accounted for in the same manner as the related employee payroll costs.

BOMBARDIER
SIGNIFICANT ACCOUNTING POLICIES

REVENUE RECOGNITION

Revenues from long-term contracts are recognized using the percentage-of-completion method of accounting in accordance with Statement of Position 81-1 "Accounting for Performance of Construction-Type and Certain Production-Type Contracts", published by the American Institute of Certified Public Accountants (AICPA). For the transportation segment, the degree of completion is mostly determined by comparing the costs incurred to the total costs anticipated for the entire contract, excluding costs that are not representative of the measure of performance, or based on the units of delivery method when more appropriate.

Estimated revenues from long-term contracts include future revenues from claims when it is probable that such claims, resulting from work performed for customers in addition to the work contemplated in the original contracts, will result in additional revenues in an amount that can be reliably estimated.

New business aircraft contracts are segmented between green aircraft (i.e. before interiors and optional avionics are installed) and completion of interiors. Revenues are recognized based on green aircraft deliveries and upon final acceptance of interiors by the customers.

Revenues from the sale of commercial aircraft, fractional interests in business aircraft and other products and services are recognized upon delivery of products or when the services are rendered.

COST OF SALES

▪ AEROSPACE PROGRAMS

Cost of sales for commercial and business aircraft is determined under the program accounting method at the estimated average unit cost computed as a percentage of the sale price of the aircraft. The estimated average unit cost under program accounting is calculated by applying to the sale price of each aircraft the ratio of total estimated production costs for the entire program over the estimated sale price of all aircraft in the program. Non-recurring costs are amortized over a predetermined number of aircraft. In the early stages of a program, a constant gross margin before amortization of non-recurring costs is achieved by deferring a portion of the actual costs incurred for each unit delivered. This excess over average production costs is recovered from sales of aircraft anticipated to be produced later at lower-than-average costs, as a result of the learning curve concept which anticipates a predictable decrease in unit costs as tasks and production techniques become more efficient through repetition and Management action.

Commercial and business aircraft programs are based on long-term delivery forecasts, normally for quantities in excess of contractually firm orders. For new programs, the program quantity is initially based on an established number of units representing what Management believes is a conservative estimate of the number of units to be sold.

Estimates of revenues, unit production costs and delivery periods associated with forecasted orders are an integral component of program accounting, and Management's ability to reasonably estimate these amounts is a requirement for the use of program accounting. Management periodically reviews its assumptions as to the size of the various programs, the estimated period over which the units will be delivered, the estimated future costs and revenues associated with the programs. Adjustments of estimates are accounted for prospectively with the exception of anticipated losses on specific programs which are recognized immediately in the period when losses are anticipated.

▪ LONG-TERM CONTRACTS

Cost of sales for long-term contracts is established based on the estimated total contract costs, including material, direct labour and manufacturing overhead costs in relation to the percentage of completion. The effect of changes to total estimated profit for each contract is recognized in the period in which the determination is made and losses, if any, are fully recognized when anticipated.

BOMBARDIER
SIGNIFICANT ACCOUNTING POLICIES (cont'd)

INVENTORY VALUATION

▪ LONG-TERM CONTRACTS

Long-term contract inventory is mostly computed under the percentage-of-completion method of accounting or under the units of delivery method when more appropriate. It includes material, direct labour, related manufacturing overhead costs and, in the case of contracts accounted for using the percentage-of-completion method, estimated margins.

▪ AEROSPACE PROGRAMS

Inventory costs determined under the program accounting method include raw materials, direct labour and related manufacturing overhead as well as non-recurring costs (development, pre-production and tooling costs), and excess over average production costs.

Non-recurring costs related to the early stages of the design of a modified or new aircraft are expensed until the results from the technical feasibility study and the market analysis of the program justify the deferral of these costs. Subsequent non-recurring costs are capitalized to the related program to the extent that their recovery can be regarded as reasonably assured.

▪ OTHER INVENTORIES

Raw materials, work in process and finished products, other than those included in long-term contracts and aerospace programs, are valued at the lower of cost (specific cost, average cost or first-in, first-out depending on the segment) and replacement cost (raw materials) or net realizable value. The cost of work in process and finished products includes the cost of raw materials, direct labour and related manufacturing overhead.

▪ ADVANCES AND PROGRESS BILLINGS

Advances received and progress billings on long-term contracts and aerospace programs are deducted from related costs in inventories. Advances and progress billings in excess of related contract costs are shown as liabilities.

GOODWILL

Goodwill represents the difference between the purchase price, including acquisition costs, of businesses acquired and the fair value of the identifiable net assets acquired. Goodwill is amortized on a straight-line basis over its useful life over 40 years. The carrying value of goodwill is reviewed periodically for impairment based on an estimate of the undiscounted cash flows of the related acquired businesses over the remaining period of amortization. Effective February 1, 2002, the Corporation prospectively adopted the new recommendations of the Canadian Institute of Chartered Accountants (CICA) relating to goodwill and other intangible assets and therefore ceased amortizing goodwill as of that date and adopted the goodwill impairment model introduced by the new accounting rules.

INTANGIBLE ASSETS

Intangible assets represent the cost of acquired licences, patents and trademarks and are amortized over their estimated useful lives, not exceeding 20 years. The carrying value of intangible assets is reviewed periodically for impairment based on an estimate of the undiscounted cash flows over the remaining period of amortization.

BC

SIGNIFICANT ACCOUNTING POLICIES

INTEREST INCOME

Interest income related to finance receivables is recognized on an accrual basis computed on the average daily finance receivables balance outstanding and is recorded in revenues.

SALES OF FINANCE RECEIVABLES

Since April 1, 2001, transfers of finance receivables in securitization transactions are recognized as sales when BC is deemed to have surrendered control over these assets and consideration other than beneficial interests in the transferred assets was received by BC. Assets retained may include interest-only strips, subordinated tranches of securities, servicing rights, overcollateralization amounts and cash reserve accounts, all of which are included in retained interests in the securitized receivables. When the transfer is considered a sale, BC derecognizes all assets sold, recognizes at fair value the assets received and the liabilities incurred and records the gain or loss on the sale in other income. Such gain or loss depends in part on the previous carrying amount of the financial assets involved in the transfer, allocated between the assets sold and the retained interests based on their relative fair values at the date of transfer. Fair values are obtained from quoted market prices, when available. However, quotes are generally not available for retained interests and BC generally estimates fair values based on the present value of future expected cash flows using Management's best estimates for credit losses, rate of prepayment, forward yield curves, and discount rates commensurate with the risks involved.

Prior to April 1, 2001, finance receivables transferred were recognized as sales when the significant risks and rewards of ownership were transferred to the purchaser. Transactions entered into prior to April 1, 2001 or completed subsequently pursuant to a commitment made prior to April 1, 2001, were accounted for under the former accounting standard.

DEFERRED ORIGINATION COSTS

BC defers the direct origination costs of finance receivables. These costs are amortized on a yield basis over the expected term of the finance receivables.

LEASE RECEIVABLES

Assets leased under terms which transfer substantially all of the benefits and risks of ownership to customers are accounted for as direct financing leases. Income is recognized over the terms of the applicable leases in a manner that produces a const ant rate of return on the lease investment and is recorded in revenues.

ASSETS UNDER OPERATING LEASES

Assets under operating leases are recorded at the lower of cost and net recoverable value. Depreciation is computed under the straight-line method over periods representing their estimated useful lives. BC's rental income from assets under operating leases is recognized over the life of the lease on a straight-line basis.

NOTES TO CONSOLIDATED FINANCIAL STATEMENTS

For the years ended January 31, 2002 and 2001
(tabular figures in millions of Canadian dollars,
except share capital and share option plans)

1. CHANGES IN ACCOUNTING POLICIES

EARNINGS PER SHARE

Effective February 1, 2001, the Corporation retroactively adopted the new recommendations published by the CICA relating to the method of calculation and the presentation and disclosure requirements for earnings per share. The new recommendations, which are essentially aligned with the requirements of the U.S. Financial Accounting Standards Board Statement No. 128 on this subject, require the use of the treasury stock method instead of the imputed earnings method for calculating diluted earnings per share. The impact of the adoption of the new recommendations on the computation of basic and diluted earnings per share is not material for the current and prior years.

TRANSFER OF RECEIVABLES

Effective April 1, 2001, the Corporation prospectively adopted the new CICA recommendations applicable to the transfer of receivables. The new recommendations are essentially consistent with the requirements of the U.S. Financial Accounting Standards Board Statement No. 140. The effect of adopting the new recommendations on the Corporation's consolidated income, financial position and cash flows is not material for the current year.

2. BUSINESS ACQUISITIONS

ADTRANZ

Effective May 1, 2001, the Corporation acquired from DaimlerChrysler AG (DaimlerChrysler) of Stuttgart, Germany, all of the common shares of its subsidiary DaimlerChrysler Rail Systems GmbH (Adtranz) based in Berlin, an integrated manufacturer of transportation equipment, for a cash consideration of $725.0 million US ($1.1 billion). The terms of the sale and purchase agreement (SPA) provide for a purchase price based on the carrying value of the adjusted net assets acquired as at April 30, 2001 (Net Asset Amount) as determined under U.S. generally accepted accounting principles (U.S. GAAP). The SPA also contemplates a maximum purchase price adjustment of €150.0 million, provided that the minimum Net Asset Amount was delivered at closing of the transaction. Under the SPA, on April 30, 2001, DaimlerChrysler made contractual representations and guarantees to the Corporation, including a written confirmation that the minimum level of Net Asset Amount was met.

Starting in May 2001, Adtranz, under the ownership of the Corporation, prepared its April 30, 2001 closing balance sheet under U.S. GAAP in accordance with the provisions of the SPA for the purpose of establishing the Net Asset Amount. The resulting Net Asset Amount did not meet the minimum value contemplated in the SPA due to significant adjustments pertaining to the application of U.S. GAAP and unrecorded costs required to complete contracts with third parties. The SPA provides for a negotiation procedure, and, if warranted, for an arbitration process.

Discussions with DaimlerChrysler have failed to result in an agreement on the value of the Net Asset Amount at closing and, accordingly, the Corporation has notified DaimlerChrysler that it will file a claim against it for damages under the arbitration process governed by the rules of arbitration of the International Chamber of Commerce, as set forth in the SPA. The Corporation's claim will be in the order of €1.0 billion ($1.4 billion). The claim for damages is largely based on material breaches of contractual representations and guarantees, including a significant deficiency in the Net Asset Amount. The ultimate outcome of the above-mentioned disagreement cannot be determined at this time. Bombardier has recorded an initial adjustment of $205.6 million (€150.0 million) as a reduction of goodwill in connection with the purchase price adjustment clause of the SPA. Resolution of the claim in excess of €150.0 million will be accounted for as an additional reduction of goodwill.

2. BUSINESS ACQUISITIONS (cont'd)

This acquisition has been recorded under the purchase method of accounting. The financial results of operations of Adtranz have been consolidated with those of the Corporation as of May 1, 2001. The allocation of the preliminary purchase price, including estimated acquisition costs of $40.0 million, to the net assets acquired at fair value is as follows:

Cash and cash equivalents	**$ 279.5**
Receivables	**1,195.3**
Inventories (net of advances of $1,145.2)	**618.0**
Property, plant and equipment	**729.1**
Deferred income taxes	**823.5**
Other assets	**396.2**
	4,041.6
Intercompany balance with DaimlerChrysler	**(374.3)**
Accounts payable and accrued liabilities	**(3,231.0)**
Advances and progress billings in excess of related costs	**(1,571.0)**
Long-term debt	**(29.1)**
Other liabilities	**(428.2)**
	(5,633.6)
Identifiable net assets at fair value	**(1,592.0)**
Goodwill	**2,764.2**
Purchase consideration	**$ 1,172.2**

Management has established the preliminary purchase price allocation taking into account all relevant information at the time of preparing these Consolidated Financial Statements. However, the preliminary purchase price allocation is subject to further refinements. A provision for restructuring costs amounting to $189.2 million, of which $78.1 million relates to the write-down of acquired property, plant and equipment, has been recorded in the purchase equation. The remaining amount of the provision relates to anticipated employee severance and other involuntary termination costs as well as other exit costs.

The Corporation has not recognized, in its preliminary purchase price allocation, future income tax benefits amounting to approximately $645.0 million, relating to acquired losses for tax purposes and other deductible temporary differences. Any subsequent recognition of these unrecorded future income tax benefits will be recorded as a reduction of goodwill related to this acquisition.

2. BUSINESS ACQUISITIONS (cont'd)

OMC

On March 9, 2001, the Corporation acquired for a cash consideration of $53.8 million US ($83.3 million), before acquisition costs of $3.8 million, most of the net assets of the engine manufacturing operations of Outboard Marine Corporation (OMC). This acquisition occured following OMC's and certain of its subsidiaries' filing, on December 22, 2000, of a voluntary petition for relief under Chapter 11 of the U.S. Bankruptcy Code. OMC was a leading manufacturer of engines built to service the boat industry and the acquired assets include the Evinrude and Johnson outboard marine engine brands and Ficht fuel-injection technology.

Net assets acquired at fair value	
Receivables	$ 8.3
Inventories	76.3
Property, plant and equipment	73.8
	158.4
Accounts payable and accrued liabilities	(71.3)
Purchase consideration	$ 87.1

3. RECEIVABLES

Bombardier's receivables essentially comprise trade accounts receivable. These receivables were concentrated in the transportation and aerospace segments (86% and 9%, respectively, as at January 31, 2002; 73% and 22%, respectively, as at January 31, 2001) and were mainly located in Europe and in North America (72% and 19%, respectively, as at January 31, 2002; 54% and 39%, respectively, as at January 31, 2001).

4. FINANCE RECEIVABLES

	2002			2001		
	Total	Weighted average maturity (months)	Weighted average rate (%)	Total	Weighted average maturity (months)	Weighted average rate (%)
BC						
Commercial						
– Loans	$1,164.4	58	6.9	$1,166.7	61	9.2
– Receivables	2,481.7	12	4.6	1,670.5	12	8.6
– Lease receivables	504.6	35	5.9	342.0	36	8.9
	4,150.7	28	5.4	3,179.2	32	8.9
Floor plan						
– Receivables	973.7	6	9.6	972.1	6	11.4
	5,124.4			4,151.3		
Allowance for credit losses	(32.3)			(22.2)		
Total – continued portfolios	5,092.1			4,129.1		
Discontinued portfolios [(1)]						
Manufactured housing loans	630.7	267	11.7	2,067.6	315	10.7
Consumer loans	443.9	98	11.5	274.9	91	13.5
Other [(2)]						
– Loans	131.5			169.0		
– Lease receivables	341.1			610.9		
	472.6	28	8.6	779.9	36	8.9
	1,547.2			3,122.4		
Allowance for credit losses	(241.0)			(110.8)		
Total - discontinued portfolios	1,306.2			3,011.6		
	6,398.3			7,140.7		
Bombardier						
Finance receivables	63.4			62.0		
Total	$6,461.7			$ 7,202.7		

(1) During the year ended January 31, 2002, Management decided to exit the manufactured housing and consumer finance activities. As a result, these portfolios have been reclassified as discontinued portfolios.

(2) Include the technology management and finance, mid-market equipment commercial finance and small ticket finance portfolios.

4. FINANCE RECEIVABLES (cont'd)

PRODUCT DESCRIPTION – BC

[i] Commercial loans and receivables

Commercial loans and receivables include aircraft, transportation and industrial equipment loans and receivables mostly related to third-party financing of business aircraft and related products, railcar financing and interim financing of commercial aircraft. Receivables mostly arise from the factoring of the Bombardier manufacturing segments' receivables from third parties. They are generally collateralized by the related assets.

[ii] Floor plan receivables

Floor plan receivables arise mainly from the financing of products owned by retailers and are collateralized by the related inventory as well as generally secured by repurchase agreements with distributors or manufacturers. In case of default, BC may repossess the products from a retailer within a time period specified in the agreement and may require the distributors or manufacturers to repurchase them for a cash consideration equal to the outstanding balance.

During the year ended January 31, 2001, BC purchased two portfolios of floor plan receivables for a cash consideration of $107.4 million.

[iii] Manufactured housing loans

Manufactured housing loans consist of contractual promises by the buyers of manufactured housing units in the United States to pay amounts owed under retail installment sales contracts. BC obtains a security interest in the housing units purchased.

In connection with BC's decision to exit completely from the manufactured housing finance activity as described in note 20, modifications were made to certain securitization transactions for manufactured housing portfolios. As a result, these portfolios, previously securitized and accounted for as financing transactions, and their corresponding asset-backed bonds recorded as long-term debt, are no longer presented on the Corporation's balance sheet.

[iv] Consumer loans

Consumer loans relate primarily to the financing of third-party recreational products in the form of revolving credit and installment loans secured by the related recreational products to consumers in the United States. This portfolio was discontinued during the year ended January 31, 2002.

[v] Lease receivables

Lease receivables consist of the following:

	2002	2001
Total minimum lease payments	**$ 955.2**	$1,072.2
Unearned income	**(144.3)**	(176.8)
Unguaranteed residual value	**34.8**	57.5
	$ 845.7	$ 952.9

The minimum lease payments for the next five years are as follows: 2003 – $473.3 million; 2004 – $160.6 million; 2005 – $98.5 million; 2006 – $58.1 million and 2007 – $52.4 million.

[vi] Credit facilities

BC has provided certain of its third-party customers with lines of credit totalling $703.0 million and $2,582.0 million US as at January 31, 2002 ($796.0 million and $2,589.5 million US as at January 31, 2001). The unused portion of these facilities amounted to $268.9 million and $1,055.7 million US as at January 31, 2002 ($414.2 million and $1,042.0 million US as at January 31, 2001).

4. FINANCE RECEIVABLES (cont'd)

ALLOWANCE FOR CREDIT LOSSES

Changes in the allowance for credit losses were as follows:

	2002	2001
Balance at beginning of year	**$ 133.0**	$ 56.5
Provision for credit losses	**657.9**	230.3
Amounts charged off – net of recoveries	**(517.6)**	(153.8)
Balance at end of year	**$ 273.3**	$ 133.0

The provision for credit losses included a special charge of $540.4 million for the year ended January 31, 2002 and $79.5 million for the year ended January 31, 2001 as described in note 20.

Impaired finance receivables amounted to $106.1 million and $187.5 million as at January 31, 2002 for continued and discontinued portfolios respectively ($25.8 million and $356.4 million as at January 31, 2001). Repossessed assets amounted to $41.3 million and $84.1 million as at January 31, 2002 and 2001 respectively. The allowance for credit losses has been established after taking into consideration expected recoveries from impaired finance receivable collections of principal and interest and from collateral realizations.

GEOGRAPHIC DISTRIBUTION – BC

The geographic distribution of BC's finance receivables, before allowance for credit losses, was as follows:

2002	Canada	United States	Western Europe	Other	Total
Loans	**$ 149.6**	**$ 1,792.5**	**$ 288.3**	**$ 140.1**	**$ 2,370.5**
Receivables	**1,145.0**	**2,090.6**	**219.8**	**–**	**3,455.4**
Lease receivables	**105.8**	**470.1**	**145.7**	**124.1**	**845.7**
	$1,400.4	**$4,353.2**	**$ 653.8**	**$ 264.2**	**$ 6,671.6**

2001	Canada	United States	Western Europe	Other	Total
Loans	$ 515.5	$2,821.8	$ 90.9	$250.0	$3,678.2
Receivables	1,001.5	1,500.9	140.2	–	2,642.6
Lease receivables	163.1	672.4	23.5	93.9	952.9
	$1,680.1	$4,995.1	$254.6	$343.9	$ 7,273.7

No single customer represented more than 10% of BC's finance receivables as at January 31, 2002 and 2001.

SECURITIZATIONS AND OTHER TRANSFERS OF RECEIVABLES

BC periodically sells finance receivables to third-party special purpose entities (SPEs). The SPEs issue various asset-backed securities representing interests in the assets transferred. During the years ended January 31, 2002 and 2001, BC sold $3,860.0 million and $4,106.7 million of floor plan finance receivables to revolving securitization SPEs. In addition to the finance receivables presented on its balance sheet, BC was servicing $1,890.7 million as at January 31, 2002 ($1,969.4 million as at January 31, 2001) of securitized floor plan finance receivables. It also continues to service $313.8 million as at January 31, 2002 ($1,335.1 million as at January 31, 2001) of finance receivables related to securitized discontinued portfolios. In addition, an amount of $2,635.3 million as at January 31, 2002 of manufactured housing loans in public securitization vehicles are serviced by BC but are not considered assets under management, following Management's September 26, 2001 decision to exit this business.

4. FINANCE RECEIVABLES (cont'd)

BC retains interests in the finance receivables sold to SPEs, including interest-only strips (representing the present value of the SPEs' expected future excess cash flows), subordinated tranches of securities, servicing rights, overcollateralization amounts, cash reserve accounts and transferor interests. BC retained interests amounting to $827.5 million as at January 31, 2002 ($674.0 million as at January 31, 2001) in the finance receivables sold to SPEs. BC records fee income in connection with the retained servicing rights. BC's retained interests are presented with the related finance receivable portfolios.

BC provides credit enhancements in order to achieve certain credit ratings for the asset-backed securities issued by the SPEs by way of subordination of a portion of its retained interests. Credit enhancements amounted to $621.9 million as at January 31, 2002. The holders of asset-backed securities and the securitization SPEs have no recourse to BC's other assets.

In addition, BC services a portfolio of lease receivables sold to third parties related to its discontinued technology management and finance portfolio, amounting to $89.9 million as at January 31, 2002 ($194.2 million as at January 31, 2001).

5. ASSETS UNDER OPERATING LEASES

BC's assets under operating leases were as follows:

	2002	2001
Aircraft		
– Business	**$1,133.0**	$1,032.2
– Commercial	**645.2**	521.8
Freight cars – Assets held for resale	**81.0**	184.0
Industrial equipment	**61.7**	25.2
Discontinued portfolios (note 4)	**88.7**	94.4
	2,009.6	1,857.6
Accumulated depreciation	**(178.4)**	(89.5)
	$1,831.2	$1,768.1

Freight cars held temporarily, pending their financing through sale and leaseback transactions, are presented as assets held for resale. For the purpose of establishing the assets under management, the portfolio of off-balance sheet freight cars amounted to $1,067.9 million as at January 31, 2002 ($917.8 million as at January 31, 2001) which represents the net present value of the minimum lease payments of $1,974.4 million as at January 31, 2002 ($1,737.7 million as at January 31, 2001), pursuant to sale and leaseback transactions disclosed in note 25 [B].

The weighted average maturity of the operating leases was 52 months as at January 31, 2002 (53 months as at January 31, 2001).

Depreciation of assets under operating leases was $132.4 million for the year ended January 31, 2002 ($81.8 million for the year ended January 31, 2001) and is included in depreciation and amortization.

6. INVENTORIES

	2002	2001
Raw materials and work in process	**$ 545.4**	$ 395.0
Long-term contracts and aerospace programs	**7,087.8**	5,436.9
Finished products	**1,323.3**	581.8
	$8,956.5	$6,413.7

6. INVENTORIES (cont'd)

AEROSPACE PROGRAMS

Inventory costs include non-recurring and excess over average production costs for which recovery depends on future firm customer orders. As at January 31, 2002, costs to be recovered from future firm customer orders amounted to $2,498.4 million ($2,137.0 million as at January 31, 2001) for programs under commercial production. For programs not yet under commercial production, namely the Bombardier Continental, the Bombardier Global 5000 and the Bombardier CRJ900, non-recurring costs amounted to $433.5 million as at January 31, 2002 ($233.6 million as at January 31, 2001 for the Bombardier Continental and the Bombardier CRJ900).

Anticipated proceeds from future sales of aircraft for each program exceeded the related costs in inventory as at January 31, 2002 and 2001, plus the estimated additional non-recurring and production costs still to be incurred for each program. However, substantial amounts of unrecoverable costs may eventually be charged to expense in a given year if fewer than the aircraft program quantity are sold, the proceeds from future sales of aircraft are lower than those currently estimated, or the costs to be incurred to complete the programs exceed current estimates. During the year ended January 31, 2002, an amount of $264.0 million of non-recurring costs for the Bombardier Q400 aircraft was written off (see note 20).

ADVANCES AND PROGRESS BILLINGS

Under certain contracts, title to inventories is vested in the customer as the work is performed in accordance with contractual arrangements and industry practice. In addition, in the normal conduct of its operations, the Corporation provides performance bonds, bank guarantees and other forms of guarantees to customers, mainly in the transportation segment, as security for advances received from customers pending performance under certain contracts. In accordance with industry practice, the Corporation remains liable to the purchasers for the usual contractor's obligations relating to contract completion in accordance with predetermined specifications, timely delivery and product performance.

Costs incurred and accrued margins related to long-term contracts and costs incurred related to ongoing aerospace programs amounted to $11,693.2 million as at January 31, 2002 ($9,485.3 million as at January 31, 2001). Advances received and progress billings on long-term contracts and ongoing aerospace programs amounted to $7,624.4 million as at January 31, 2002 ($6,411.2 million as at January 31, 2001) of which $3,019.0 million represents a liability disclosed as advances and progress billings in excess of related costs as at January 31, 2002 ($2,362.8 million as at January 31, 2001).

7. PROPERTY, PLANT AND EQUIPMENT

	2002		2001	
	Cost	**Accumulated depreciation**	Cost	Accumulated depreciation
Bombardier				
Land	**$ 213.8**	**$ –**	$ 109.9	$ –
Buildings	**2,062.2**	**417.1**	1,251.7	347.3
Equipment	**2,295.3**	**1,162.7**	1,867.2	1,071.3
Other	**367.5**	**113.7**	205.5	57.6
	4,938.8	**1,693.5**	3,434.3	1,476.2
BC	**213.7**	**50.6**	172.5	39.7
	5,152.5	**$1,744.1**	3,606.8	$1,515.9
Accumulated depreciation	**(1,744.1)**		(1,515.9)	
	$3,408.4		$ 2,090.9	

Included in the above are assets under construction and development amounting to $357.2 million as at January 31, 2002 ($360.2 million as at January 31, 2001).

8. GOODWILL

Goodwill amounted to $2,712.9 million, net of accumulated amortization of $45.7 million, as at January 31, 2002 (nil as at January 31, 2001). Goodwill is related to the Adtranz acquisition as described in note 2.

9. OTHER ASSETS

	2002		2001	
	Bombardier	**BC**	Bombardier	BC
Licences, patents and trademarks (net of accumulated amortization of $12.3 million)	**$ 257.2**	**$ –**	$ –	$ –
Deferred income taxes	**583.2**	**325.5**	109.5	72.3
Prepaid expenses	**159.9**	**86.7**	96.4	75.9
Accrued benefit asset	**246.4**	**–**	146.6	–
Other	**209.7**	**148.4**	69.1	134.0
	$1,456.4	**$560.6**	$421.6	$282.2

10. SHORT-TERM BORROWINGS

	2002	2001
Bombardier	**$1,341.7**	$ –
BC	**1,695.3**	2,531.2
	$ 3,037.0	$2,531.2

Under banking syndicate agreements, Bombardier Inc. and some of its subsidiaries must maintain certain financial ratios, a condition which had been met as at January 31, 2002 and 2001.

10. SHORT-TERM BORROWINGS (cont'd)

BOMBARDIER

Bombardier's credit facilities and borrowings as well as their rates and maturities were as follows:

							2002
	Available			Drawn		Rate	Maturity
		Cash	Currency component	Letters of credit	Year-end	Average for the year	
Credit facilities:							
European	$2,325.9	$ 414.9	€300.0	$ 985.7	3.6%	4.2%	2006
North American	1,750.0	165.4		145.5	2.2%	3.7%	2003-2006
	$4,075.9	580.3		$ 1,131.2			
Borrowings:							
Notes		761.4	€200.0 ¥20,000.0		2.4%	2.7%	2003
		$1,341.7					

						2001
	Available		Drawn		Rate	Maturity
		Cash	Letters of credit	Year-end	Average for the year	
Credit facilities:						
European	$2,373.7	$ –	$1,190.1	–	6.3%	2006
North American	1,750.0	–	346.6	–	6.0%	2002-2006
	$4,123.7	$ –	$1,536.7			

The European facility can be used to issue bank guarantees and letters of credit or to draw advances in various freely convertible currencies up to a maximum amount of €1.7 billion or its equivalent in other currencies. Advances drawn under the facility bear interest at variable rates based on Euribor or LIBOR.

During the year ended January 31, 2002, the Corporation renewed the committed 364-day, $750.0 million portion of its syndicated North American bank credit facility until September 2002. Amounts may be drawn under the North American facility in Canadian or U.S. dollars or in euros at variable rates based on the Canadian prime rate, U.S. base rate, LIBOR, or banker's acceptance discount rate or the facility may be used for the issuance of letters of credit. The facility may also be used as a liquidity back-up for the Corporation's $1.0 billion Commercial Paper program.

In August 2001, Bombardier Inc. issued $250.0 million of 13-month floating-rate notes in the Canadian market and Bombardier Corporation, a wholly-owned subsidiary of the Corporation, issued $518.3 million (€200.0 million and ¥20.0 billion) of 13-month floating-rate notes in the Euromarket.

In addition, standby letters of credit were assumed as a result of the Adtranz acquisition described in note 2, amounting to $2,449.4 million as at January 31, 2002 and Bombardier had $1,213.9 million of outstanding letters of credit as at January 31, 2002 ($703.1 million as at January 31, 2001) in addition to the outstanding letters of credit shown in the table above.

10. SHORT-TERM BORROWINGS (cont'd)

BC

BC's credit facilities and their rates and maturities were as follows:

						2002
	Available	Drawn		Rate		Maturity
		Cash	US $ component	Year-end	Average for the year	
Credit facilities:						
Revolving lines	**$2,610.8**	**$ 1,277.3**	**$749.5**	**2.1%**	**4.3%**	**2003-2006**
Bank loans	**286.6**	**215.3**	**95.0**	**2.9%**	**4.6%**	**2003**
Other	**796.3**	**202.7**	**124.4**	**2.0%**	**2.6%**	**2003**
	$3,693.7	**$1,695.3**				

						2001
	Available	Drawn		Rate		Maturity
		Cash	US $ component	Year-end	Average for the year	
Credit facilities:						
Revolving lines	$2,500.0	$2,221.5	$1,431.7	7.0%	6.7%	2002-2006
Bank loans	142.5	142.5	95.0	6.2%	7.2%	2002
Other	240.0	167.2	23.6	6.4%	6.5%	2002
	$2,882.5	$2,531.2				

REVOLVING LINES

Bombardier Capital Inc. has a $1.9 billion ($1.2 billion US) committed, unsecured, revolving credit facility with a syndicate of banks (the "U.S. Facility"). This facility is composed of two equal tranches: a 364-day tranche maturing September 2002 and a 5-year tranche maturing July 10, 2005. Bombardier Capital Ltd. has a $700.0 million committed, unsecured, revolving, 364-day credit facility with a syndicate of banks (the "Canadian Facility") maturing in September 2002. They also serve as liquidity back-up for the borrowers' respective commercial paper programs for a maximum amount of $1.9 billion ($1.2 billion US) for Bombardier Capital Inc. and $700.0 million for Bombardier Capital Ltd.

Under the U.S. Facility, amounts may be drawn at variable rates based on the U.S. base rate or LIBOR, while, under the Canadian Facility amounts may be drawn in Canadian dollars or U.S. dollars at variable rates based on the Canadian prime rate, U.S. base rate, LI BOR or banker's acceptance discount rate. The outstanding amounts under these facilities included $1,277.3 million as at January 31, 2002 ($2,221.5 million as at January 31, 2001) of commercial paper borrowings, with maturities of up to six months.

11. ACCOUNTS PAYABLE AND ACCRUED LIABILITIES

		2002		2001
	Bombardier	BC	Bombardier	BC
Accounts payable	**$2,990.2**	**$ 94.7**	$1,868.8	$ 62.6
Payroll related liabilities	**447.7**	**0.3**	358.8	0.6
Accrued liabilities	**3,923.0**	**323.5**	1,612.4	133.4
	$ 7,360.9	**$418.5**	$3,840.0	$196.6

12. LONG-TERM DEBT

The Corporation's long-term debts and their average rates and maturities were as follows:

				2002
	$	Currency component	Average rate	Maturity
Bombardier				
Debentures	1,527.6	€500.0 £175.0	6.4 %	2004-2027
Notes	315.4	$ 167.3 US	6.6 %	2004-2012
Other loans	237.7	$ 64.9 US €32.6	4.0 %	2003-2029
	2,080.7			
BC				
Notes	5,047.0	$2,730.0 US	3.0 %	2003-2008
Capital Trust Securities	310.5	$ 195.0 US	2.4 %	2033
Debentures	250.0	–	2.9 %	2004
Other loans	169.5	$ 70.0 US	6.6 %	2003-2017
	5,777.0			
	7,857.7			

				2001
	$	Currency component	Average rate	Maturity
Bombardier				
Debentures	450.0	–	7.4 %	2004-2027
Notes	312.9	$ 175.9 US	6.6 %	2004-2012
Other loans	116.5	$ 10.8 US	4.5 %	2002-2029
	879.4			
BC				
Notes	3,025.0	$1,750.0 US	7.0 %	2002-2006
Asset-backed bonds	1,490.1	$ 993.4 US	7.8 %	2002-2030
Capital Trust Securities	300.0	$ 200.0 US	7.1 %	2033
Debentures	250.0	–	7.2 %	2004
Other loans	186.7	$ 84.1 US	8.3 %	2002-2017
	5,251.8			
	6,131.2			

12. LONG-TERM DEBT (cont'd)

BC's Capital Trust Securities bear interest at variable rates based on LIBOR unless remarketed as a junior fixed rate Subordinated Security. As at January 31, 2002, the remainder of the Corporation's long-term debt bears interest at fixed rates except for $172.1 million of Bombardier's other loans, $1,360.1 million of BC's notes and $26.0 million of other loans ($52.7 million of Bombardier's other loans, $525.0 million of BC's notes and $142.5 million of asset-backed bonds as at January 31, 2001).

Average rates are based on year-end balances and interest rates, after giving effect to the $5,683.9 million of interest-rate and cross-currency interest rate swap agreements ($2,941.3 million as at January 31, 2001) described in note 23.

As of January 31, 2002, BC no longer presents the asset-backed bonds related to the discontinued manufactured housing portfolios previously securitized to third parties on its balance sheet (see note 4).

The repayment requirements on the long-term debt during the next five years are as follows:

	Bombardier Inc. consolidated	Bombardier	BC
2003	$2,234.4	$ 50.3	$2,184.1
2004	1,394.1	184.3	1,209.8
2005	757.6	24.5	733.1
2006	585.4	257.2	328.2
2007	1,479.4	559.2	920.2

As at January 31, 2002 and 2001, the Corporation had complied with the restrictive covenants contained in its various financing agreements.

13. OTHER LIABILITIES

	2002		2001	
	Bombardier	BC	Bombardier	BC
Income taxes payable	$ 29.1	$ 2.6	$ 91.1	$0.2
Accrued benefit liability	1,036.2	3.3	492.1	2.3
Deferred income taxes	868.0	4.9	944.4	–
Other	25.4	–	–	–
	$1,958.7	$10.8	$1,527.6	$2.5

14. SHARE CAPITAL

PREFERRED SHARES

An unlimited number of preferred shares, without nominal or par value, issuable in series, of which the following series have been authorized:

12,000,000 Series 2 Cumulative Redeemable Preferred Shares, non-voting, redeemable at the Corporation's option at $25.00 per share on August 1, 2002 or at $25.50 per share thereafter, convertible on a one-for-one basis on August 1, 2002 and on August 1 of every fifth year thereafter into Series 3 Cumulative Redeemable Preferred Shares. On a conversion date, if the Corporation determines after having taken into account all shares tendered for conversion by holders that there would be less than 1,000,000 outstanding Series 2 Preferred Shares, such remaining number shall automatically be converted into an equal number of Series 3 Preferred Shares. Additionally, if the Corporation determines that on any conversion date, there would be less than 1,000,000 outstanding Series 3 Preferred Shares, then no Series 2 Preferred Shares may be converted. Until July 31, 2002, the quarterly dividend rate is equal to $0.34375 per share. Thereafter, floating adjustable cumulative preferential cash dividends will be payable monthly, if declared, commencing on August 1, 2002, with the annual floating dividend rate equal to 80% of the Canadian prime rate. The dividend rate will float in relation to changes in the prime rate and will be adjusted upwards or downwards on a monthly basis to a monthly maximum of 4% if the trading price of the Series 2 Preferred Shares is less than $24.90 per share or more than $25.10 per share; and

12,000,000 Series 3 Cumulative Redeemable Preferred Shares, non-voting, redeemable at the Corporation's option at $25.00 per share on August 1, 2007 and on August 1 of every fifth year thereafter, convertible on a one-for-one basis at the option of the holder on August 1, 2007 and on August 1 of every fifth year thereafter into Series 2 Cumulative Redeemable Preferred Shares. On a conversion date, if the Corporation determines after having taken into account all shares tendered for conversion by holders that there would be less than 1,000,000 outstanding Series 3 Preferred Shares, such remaining number shall automatically be converted into an equal number of Series 2 Preferred Shares. Additionally, if the Corporation determines that on any conversion date there would be less than 1,000,000 outstanding Series 2 Preferred Shares, then no Series 3 Preferred Shares may be converted. The initial dividend, if declared, will be payable on October 31, 2002 and the quarterly dividend rate will be fixed by the Corporation at least 45 days before the initial dividend, for the first five-year period. Each five-year fixed dividend rate selected by the Corporation shall not be less than 80% of the Government of Canada bond yield as defined in the Articles of Amendment creating the Series 3 Preferred Shares.

COMMON SHARES

1,792,000,000 Class A (Multiple Voting) Shares, without nominal or par value, 10 votes each, convertible at the option of the holder into one Class B (Subordinate Voting) Share; and

1,792,000,000 Class B (Subordinate Voting) Shares, without nominal or par value, one vote each, with an annual non-cumulative preferential dividend of $0.001563 per share, and convertible, at the option of the holder, into one Class A (Multiple Voting) Share, after the occurrence of one of the following events: (i) an offer made to Class A (Multiple Voting) shareholders is accepted by the present controlling shareholder (the Bombardier family); (ii) such controlling shareholder ceases to hold more than 50% of all outstanding Class A (Multiple Voting) Shares of the Corporation.

SHARE REPURCHASE

During the year ended January 31, 2001, the Corporation repurchased 15,866,300 shares of its common shares for an aggregate purchase price of $303.8 million.

15. SHARE-BASED PLANS

SHARE OPTION PLANS

Under share option plans, options are granted to key employees and directors to purchase Class B (Subordinate Voting) Shares. Of the 135,782,688 Class B (Subordinate Voting) Shares initially reserved for issuance, 71,013,694 were available for issuance under these share option plans as at January 31, 2002. The exercise price is equal to the average of the closing prices on the stock exchange during the five trading days preceding the date on which the option was granted. These options vest at 25% per year during a period commencing two years following the grant date, except for 348,000 outstanding options granted to directors which vest at 20% per year commencing on the grant date. The options terminate no later than 10 years after the grant date.

The summarized information on options issued and outstanding as at January 31, 2002 is as follows:

	Issued and outstanding			Exercisable	
Exercise price range	**Number of options**	**Average remaining life (years)**	**Average exercise price**	**Number of options**	**Average exercise price**
$0 to $5	16,630,466	2.79	$ 3.57	16,630,466	$ 3.57
$6 to $10	13,507,768	6.46	9.10	4,324,915	8.14
$11 to $15	3,072,750	7.52	11.27	1,148,750	11.26
$16 to $20	4,285,000	8.21	18.62	–	–
$21 to $25	6,346,000	9.23	21.99	–	–
	43,841,984			22,104,131	

The number of options has varied as follows:

	2002		2001	
	Number of options	**Average exercise price**	Number of options	Average exercise price
Balance at beginning of year	44,227,634	$ 8.14	44,727,660	$ 6.36
Granted	5,827,000	21.68	5,747,500	19.72
Exercised	(4,720,150)	5.55	(4,299,020)	4.11
Cancelled	(1,492,500)	16.15	(1,948,506)	10.31
Balance at end of year	43,841,984	$ 9.95	44,227,634	$ 8.14
Options exercisable at end of year	22,104,131	$ 4.86	19,048,837	$ 3.84

EMPLOYEE SHARE PURCHASE PLAN

Under the Employee Share Purchase Plan, employees of the Corporation may set aside funds through payroll deductions for an amount up to a maximum of 20% of their base salary subject to a yearly maximum of $30,000 per employee. The Corporation contributes to the plan an amount equal to 20% of the employees' contributions. The contributions are used to purchase Class B (Subordinate Voting) Shares of the Corporation in the open market. The Corporation's contribution to the plan for the year ended January 31, 2002 amounted to $14.1 million ($11.5 million for the year ended January 31, 2001).

16. EARNINGS PER SHARE

The number of shares and options are expressed in thousands.

	2002	2001
Basic and diluted earnings per share		
Net income	$ 390.9	$ 975.4
Preferred share dividends after tax	17.6	17.1
Net income available to common shareholders	$ 373.3	$ 958.3
Weighted average number of common shares outstanding	1,368,516	1,369,021
Stock options	21,683	27,378
Weighted average diluted number of common shares outstanding	1,390,199	1,396,399
Basic	$ 0.27	$ 0.70
Diluted	$ 0.27	$ 0.69
Basic and diluted earnings per share, before goodwill amortization		
Income before goodwill amortization	$ 437.5	$ 975.4
Preferred share dividends after tax	17.6	17.1
Income before goodwill amortization available to common shareholders	$ 419.9	$ 958.3
Basic	$ 0.31	$ 0.70
Diluted	$ 0.30	$ 0.69

For the year ended January 31, 2002, a total of 9,119 stock options were excluded from the calculation of diluted earnings per share since the exercise price of these options exceeded the average market value of the Corporation's common shares for the year.

17. RESEARCH AND DEVELOPMENT EXPENSES

Bombardier's cost of sales and operating expenses include research and development expenses amounting to $233.5 million for the year ended January 31, 2002 ($123.4 million for the year ended January 31, 2001) excluding those incurred under contracts and programs.

18. INTEREST EXPENSE

	2002		2001	
	Bombardier	BC	Bombardier	BC
Long-term debt	$123.4	$320.0	$ 72.2	$321.8
Short-term borrowings	58.6	101.2	36.0	177.2
	182.0	421.2	108.2	499.0
Allocated to BC	–	–	(38.4)	38.4
	$182.0	$421.2	$ 69.8	$ 537.4

BC's interest expense of $421.2 million for the year ended January 31, 2002 ($499.0 million for the year ended January 31, 2001) is classified as cost of sales and operating expenses.

19. OTHER INCOME

Other income includes the following:

	2002	2001
BC		
Gain on sale of finance receivables	$ 51.7	$ 82.9
Servicing and other fees	66.5	52.3
Other	17.3	39.8
	135.5	175.0
Bombardier		
Interests	35.1	43.6
	$170.6	$218.6

20. SPECIAL ITEMS

The Corporation recorded the following special items:

	2002	2001
Aerospace	$ 333.5	$(49.8)
Transportation	74.2	–
BC	662.5	79.5
Special items, pre-tax	1,070.2	29.7
Income taxes on BC special items	(257.4)	(31.8)
Special items of Bombardier[(1)]	812.8	(2.1)
Income taxes on Bombardier's special items	(121.2)	5.8
Special items, after tax	$ 691.6	$ 3.7

(1) After equity pick-up of BC's net income

FOR THE YEAR ENDED JANUARY 31, 2002

On September 26, 2001, the Corporation recorded a special charge of $264.0 million related to the write-off of the carrying value of the non-recurring costs of the Bombardier Q400 program in the aerospace segment. This charge is due to the overall outlook of the turboprop aircraft market. In addition, the Corporation reduced employment levels, production rates and deliveries in this segment to adjust to current market conditions. As a result, a $69.5 million special charge for severance and other involuntary termination benefits was recorded during the year ended January 31, 2002.

The Corporation also recorded a special charge of $74.2 million during the fourth quarter in the transportation segment for restructuring costs related to severance and other involuntary termination costs and to the write-down in the value of certain manufacturing assets in Europe and North America. These charges result from the integration of the transportation manufacturing operations with those of Adtranz. In addition to these restructuring costs, restructuring costs amounting to $189.2 million have been provided for in the Adtranz preliminary purchase price allocation (see note 2).

20. SPECIAL ITEMS (cont'd)

In addition, the Corporation discontinued loan origination activities for the manufactured housing and the consumer products finance businesses for the BC segment. As a result of this decision and the slowdown of the U.S. economy which negatively affected the credit quality of the portfolios related to these businesses, BC recorded a special charge of $540.4 million related to the impairment of the value of these on- and off-balance sheet portfolios. BC also incurred charges of $122.1 million for the write-down of the value of other assets related to the discontinued portfolios and for other related restructuring charges.

FOR THE YEAR ENDED JANUARY 31, 2001

During the quarter ended July 31, 2000, the Corporation sold Bombardier Services (UK) Limited's defense service business, including its wholly-owned subsidiary Airwork Ltd., an operation located in the United Kingdom. The net sale proceeds of $66.1 million resulted in a net gain of $49.8 million.

A special charge of $79.5 million has been provided for during the quarter ended April 30, 2000, related to additional provision for credit losses for BC's small ticket finance portfolio.

21. INCOME TAXES

The reconciliation of income taxes computed at the Canadian statutory rates to income tax expense was as follows:

	2002		2001	
	$	%	$	%
Income taxes calculated at statutory rates	**214.0**	**38.4**	553.2	39.6
Increase (decrease) resulting from:				
Manufacturing and processing credit	**(53.1)**	**(9.5)**	(69.4)	(5.0)
Income tax rates differential of foreign investees	**(51.9)**	**(9.3)**	(45.7)	(3.3)
Non-recognition of tax benefits related to foreign investees' losses and temporary differences	**75.2**	**13.5**	20.4	1.5
Recognition of previously unrecorded tax benefits	**(2.7)**	**(0.5)**	(16.4)	(1.2)
Tax-exempt items	**11.2**	**2.0**	(26.5)	(1.9)
Effect of income tax rate changes	**(40.8)**	**(7.3)**	–	–
Other	**15.1**	**2.6**	7.2	0.5
	167.0	**29.9**	422.8	30.2
Current income taxes	**132.9**		151.0	
Deferred income taxes				
– Temporary differences	**77.6**		288.2	
– Effect of income tax rate changes	**(40.8)**		–	
– Recognition of previously unrecorded tax benefits	**(2.7)**		(16.4)	
	167.0		422.8	

21. INCOME TAXES (cont'd)

Deferred income taxes reflect the net tax effects of temporary differences between the carrying amounts of assets and liabilities for financial reporting purposes and the amounts used for income tax purposes. Significant components of the Corporation's deferred income tax asset (liability) as at January 31 were as follows:

	2002	2001
Inventories	**$ (1,156.6)**	$ (1,175.0)
Loss carryforwards	**2,011.7**	702.7
Warranty and other provisions	**469.0**	179.3
Finance receivables	**169.2**	77.4
Assets under operating leases	**(281.9)**	(203.2)
Accrued benefit liability	**262.1**	114.0
Property, plant and equipment	**47.5**	(1.0)
Intangible assets	**(91.3)**	–
Other	**(164.1)**	(110.9)
	1,265.6	(416.7)
Valuation allowance	**(1,229.8)**	(345.9)
Net amount	**$ 35.8**	$ (762.6)

The net amount of deferred income tax is presented on the Corporation's balance sheet as follows:

	2002	2001
Deferred income tax liability	**$ (872.9)**	$ (944.4)
Deferred income tax asset	**908.7**	181.8
Net amount	**$ 35.8**	$ (762.6)

Losses carried forward and other deductions which are available to reduce future taxable income of certain European subsidiaries for which no related income tax benefits have been recognized amounted to $3,373.0 million as at January 31, 2002 ($849.5 million as at January 31, 2001), mostly with no specified expiry dates, of which $1,880.0 million are related to the Adtranz acquisition and $400.0 million has resulted from the favourable outcome of a tax audit.

Undistributed earnings of the Corporation's foreign subsidiaries are considered to be indefinitely reinvested and, accordingly, no provision for income taxes has been provided thereon. Upon distribution of those earnings in the form of dividends or otherwise, the Corporation may be subject to withholding taxes.

22. NET CHANGES IN NON-CASH BALANCES RELATED TO OPERATIONS

The net changes in non-cash balances related to operations were as follows:

	2002	2001
Bombardier		
Receivables	**$ 239.4**	$ (76.5)
Inventories	**(2,112.5)**	(1,057.2)
Accounts payable and accrued liabilities	**105.9**	745.0
Income taxes payable	**(78.9)**	21.8
Advances and progress billings in excess of related costs	**(914.8)**	(273.9)
Other	**57.2**	11.4
	(2,703.7)	(629.4)
BC		
Receivables	**(119.3)**	(154.0)
Accounts payable and accrued liabilities	**23.8**	(13.4)
Other	**(15.8)**	(33.3)
	(111.3)	(200.7)
	$(2,815.0)	$ (830.1)

23. FINANCIAL INSTRUMENTS

[A] DERIVATIVE FINANCIAL INSTRUMENTS

The Corporation uses derivative financial instruments to manage foreign exchange risk and interest rate fluctuations. The Corporation does not trade in derivatives for speculative purposes.

Foreign exchange contracts

The Corporation enters into foreign exchange contracts to hedge future cash flows in various currencies whereby it sells or buys specific amounts of currencies at predetermined dates and exchange rates. These contracts are matched with anticipated operational cash flows in various currencies, the amount of which are estimated based on existing orders from customers, current conditions in the Corporation's markets and past experience.

The following table sets out the notional amounts outstanding under foreign exchange contracts, the average contractual exchange rates and the settlement periods of these contracts. The amounts represent U.S. dollars to be paid (to be received) against other currencies as at January 31:

		2002			2001	
Maturity	**Cdn $**	**£**	**€**	Cdn $	£	€
Less than 1 year	**2,798.3**	**995.5**	**162.1**	3,118.8	810.0	190.2
	(184.3)	**–**	**(100.7)**	(813.4)	–	(57.6)
Weighted average rate	**1.50**	**0.68**	**1.06**	1.47	0.65	0.96
	(1.52)	**–**	**(1.14)**	(1.49)	–	(0.89)
One to three years	**1,316.5**	**402.0**	**28.7**	2,547.9	994.7	–
	(25.4)	**–**	**(55.5)**	(328.9)	–	–
Weighted average rate	**1.55**	**0.67**	**1.13**	1.49	0.66	–
	(1.45)	**–**	**(1.09)**	(1.48)	–	–

23. FINANCIAL INSTRUMENTS (cont'd)

In addition, the Corporation is party to foreign exchange contracts for the sale of sterling pounds against the euro amounting to £372.9 million at an average rate of 1.62 as at January 31, 2002 (£11.1 million at an average rate of 1.56 as at January 31, 2001) and to various other contracts mostly involving exchanges of Western European currencies having an equivalent total nominal value of $2,138.1 million as at January 31, 2002 ($327.5 million as at January 31, 2001).

The Corporation also entered into a forward exchange contract to hedge the reimbursement of the principal amount of a floating-rate note denominated in yen which was issued in August 2001. As at January 31, 2002, the notional amount of the contract was of ¥20.0 billion at a rate of 0.0121.

Interest-rate swap agreements – BC

BC enters into interest-rate swap agreements to convert from fixed to variable interest rates certain long-term debts and certain finance receivables. As at January 31, 2002 and 2001, the interest-rate swap agreements were as follows:

2002

Purpose	Notional amount	(US $ component)	Range of fixed rates	Variable rates	Maturity
Asset hedge	$1,308.3	($ 702.6)	5.1% - 8.7%	LIBOR or Banker's Acceptance	2003-2016
Debt hedge	$5,057.5	($ 2,925.0)	4.9% - 6.8%	LIBOR or Banker's Acceptance	2003-2008

2001

Purpose	Notional amount	(US $ component)	Range of fixed rates	Variable rates	Maturity
Asset hedge	$1,700.7	($ 964.6)	5.0% - 8.7%	LIBOR or Banker's Acceptance	2002-2018
Debt hedge	$2,691.3	($ 1,527.5)	5.1% - 7.0%	LIBOR or Banker's Acceptance	2002-2006

Cross-currency interest rate swap agreements – BC

BC enters into cross-currency interest rate swap agreements that modify the characteristics of certain long-term debts from the Canadian dollar to the U.S. dollar and, for the year ended January 31, 2002, from the yen to the U.S. dollar. These contracts also change the interest rate from fixed to variable to match the variable interest of its finance receivables. The notional amount of the cross-currency interest rate swap agreements outstanding as at January 31, 2002 was an equivalent of $626.4 million ($250.0 million as at January 31, 2001). These contracts mature in 2003 to 2007.

[B] FAIR VALUE OF FINANCIAL INSTRUMENTS

The following methods and assumptions were used in estimating the fair value of financial instruments:

Cash and cash equivalents, receivables, short-term borrowings and accounts payable and accrued liabilities: The carrying amounts reported in the balance sheet approximate the fair values of these items due to their short-term nature.

Finance receivables: The fair values of variable-rate finance receivables that reprice frequently and have no significant change in credit risk approximate the carrying values. The fair values of fixed-rate finance receivables are estimated using discounted cash flow analyses, using interest rates offered for finance receivables with similar terms to borrowers of similar credit quality. The fair value of finance receivables as at January 31, 2002 was $6,499.2 million compared to a carrying amount of $6,461.7 million ($7,123.0 million compared to $7,202.7 million as at January 31, 2001).

23. FINANCIAL INSTRUMENTS (cont'd)

Long-term debt: The fair values of long-term debt are estimated using public quotations or discounted cash flow analyses, based on current corresponding borrowing rates for similar types of borrowing arrangements. The fair value of long-term debt as at January 31, 2002 was $7,980.6 million compared to a carrying amount of $7,857.7 million ($6,248.2 million compared to $6,131.2 million as at January 31, 2001).

Foreign exchange contracts and interest-rate and cross-currency interest rate swap agreements: The fair values generally reflect the estimated amounts that the Corporation would receive on settlement of favourable contracts or be required to pay to terminate unfavourable contracts at the reporting dates. Investment dealers' quotes or quotes from the Corporation's bankers are available for substantially all of the Corporation's foreign exchange contracts and interest-rate and cross-currency interest rate swap agreements.

	2002	2001
Fair values of foreign exchange contracts		
Favourable	**$ 34.7**	$ 59.8
Unfavourable	**$574.5**	$275.0
Fair values of interest-rate and cross-currency interest rate swap agreements		
Favourable	**$153.6**	$ 60.1
Unfavourable	**$ 83.8**	$ 28.2

Credit support and guarantees: The determination of the fair values of bank guarantees and other forms of guarantees related to long-term contracts is not practicable within the constraints of timeliness and cost but such guarantees usually decrease in value in relation to the percentage of completion of the related contracts and usually expire without being exercised. The fair values of credit support and guarantees provided to purchasers of manufactured products are not readily determinable.

[C] CREDIT RISK

In addition to the credit risk described elsewhere in these Consolidated Financial Statements, the Corporation is subject to risk related to the off-balance sheet nature of derivative financial instruments, whereby counterparty failure would result in economic losses on favourable contracts. However, the counterparties to these derivative financial instruments are major financial institutions which the Corporation anticipates will satisfy their obligations under the contracts.

24. EMPLOYEE FUTURE BENEFITS

The Corporation sponsors several defined benefit registered and non-registered pension plans and other post-retirement benefit plans for its employees.

The significant actuarial assumptions adopted to determine the Corporation's accrued benefit obligations are as follows (weighted-average assumptions as at the December 31 measurement date preceding the fiscal year-end):

	2002		2001	
	Pension Benefits	**Other Benefits**	Pension Benefits	Other Benefits
Discount rate	**6.10%**	**6.63%**	6.70%	7.09%
Expected long-term rate of return on plan assets	**8.00%**	**–**	8.00%	–
Rate of compensation increase	**3.78%**	**4.08%**	4.25%	4.60%
Health care cost trend	**–**	**5.11%**	–	5.39%

24. EMPLOYEE FUTURE BENEFITS (cont'd)

In Canada, a 8.5% annual rate of increase in the per capita cost of covered health care benefits was assumed for the year ending January 31, 2003. This rate is assumed to decrease gradually to 5.50% for fiscal 2006 and to remain at that level thereafter. In other countries, the health care cost trend remains constant.

The following tables give effect to the acquisition of Adtranz described in note 2 and provide a reconciliation of the changes in the plans' accrued benefit obligations and fair value of assets and a statement of the funded status as at December 31 measurement date preceding the fiscal year-end:

	2002		2001	
	Pension Benefits	Other Benefits	Pension Benefits	Other Benefits
Accrued benefit obligations				
Obligation at beginning of year	$ 2,886.8	$ 242.5	$ 2,600.8	$ 214.0
Current service cost	158.3	14.7	108.8	12.3
Employee contributions	50.4	–	35.6	–
Interest cost	264.6	18.0	177.6	16.1
Plan amendments	21.6	–	63.6	–
Actuarial loss (gain)	172.1	(0.7)	59.7	9.2
Benefits paid	(182.7)	(12.2)	(106.4)	(9.8)
Business acquisition	1,559.8	14.8	–	–
Curtailment	(15.9)	(8.1)	–	–
Effect of foreign currency exchange rate changes	72.6	3.4	(52.9)	0.7
Obligation at end of year	$ 4,987.6	$ 272.4	$ 2,886.8	$ 242.5

	2002		2001	
	Pension Benefits	Other Benefits	Pension Benefits	Other Benefits
Plan assets				
Fair value at beginning of year	$ 2,488.7	$ –	$ 2,531.9	$ –
Actual return on plan assets	(335.9)	–	12.2	–
Employer contributions	88.5	–	63.8	–
Employee contributions	50.4	–	35.6	–
Benefits paid	(182.7)	–	(106.4)	–
Business acquisition	1,206.7	–	–	–
Effect of foreign currency exchange rate changes	62.7	–	(48.4)	–
Fair value at end of year	$ 3,378.4	$ –	$ 2,488.7	$ –
Funded status				
Plan deficit	$(1,609.2)	$ (272.4)	$ (398.1)	$(242.5)
Unrecognized amounts	1,081.8 [1]	6.7	282.8	10.0
Net recognized amount	$ (527.4)	$ (265.7)	$ (115.3)	$(232.5)

[1] Includes an amount of $999.0 million for actuarial loss and $76.7 million for prior service costs.

24. EMPLOYEE FUTURE BENEFITS (cont'd)

The following table provides the amounts recognized in the balance sheet as at January 31:

	2002		2001	
	Pension Benefits	Other Benefits	Pension Benefits	Other Benefits
Accrued benefit asset	$ 246.4	$ –	$ 146.6	$ –
Accrued benefit liability	(773.8)	(265.7)	(261.9)	(232.5)
Net amount recognized	$ (527.4)	$ (265.7)	$ (115.3)	$ (232.5)

The accrued benefit obligations and fair value of plan assets, for pension plans with accrued benefit obligations in excess of plan assets, were $4,777.3 million and $3,140.4 million respectively, as at January 31, 2002 ($2,247.4 million and $1,807.3 million as at January 31, 2001 respectively). The Corporation's plans for post-retirement benefits other than pensions are all unfunded.

Plan assets include $16.7 million of common shares of the Corporation.

The following table provides components of the net benefit plan cost for the year ended January 31:

	2002		2001	
	Pension Benefits	Other Benefits	Pension Benefits	Other Benefits
Current service cost	$ 158.3	$ 14.7	$ 108.8	$ 12.3
Interest cost	264.6	18.0	177.6	16.1
Expected return on plan assets	(281.8)	–	(198.8)	–
Amortization of prior service costs	7.0	–	–	–
Amortization of net actuarial loss	0.1	0.3	–	–
Curtailment gain	(1.3)	(5.2)	–	–
Special termination benefits	3.6	–	–	–
Other	1.4	–	1.9	–
Net benefit plan cost	$ 151.9	$ 27.8	$ 89.5	$ 28.4

25. COMMITMENTS AND CONTINGENCIES

In addition to the commitments and contingencies described elsewhere in these Consolidated Financial Statements, the Corporation is subject to the following:

[A] GUARANTEES

In connection with the sale of aircraft, Bombardier provides financial support in the form of guarantees of third-party financing, lease payments, advances as well as services related to the remarketing of aircraft. The off-balance sheet credit risk from these guarantees, maturing in different periods up to 2019, were as follows as at January 31:

	2002	2001
Maximum credit risk	$ 917.4	$ 722.3
Less: provisions	405.8	283.5
Off-balance sheet risk	511.6	438.8
Less: net benefit of the estimated resale value	422.3	350.2
Net credit risk	$ 89.3	$ 88.6

25. COMMITMENTS AND CONTINGENCIES (cont'd)

The net credit risk represents the unrecorded portion of Bombardier's estimated exposure to losses from potential defaults from third-party purchasers under legally binding agreements, after giving effect to the net benefit of the estimated resale value.

As at January 31, 2002, Bombardier was also committed in relation to guarantees on future sales of aircraft for an amount of $215.0 million after deducting the net benefit of the estimated resale value amounting to $521.0 million ($260.8 million after deducting the net benefit of the estimated resale value amounting to $332.7 million as at January 31, 2001). The provision in relation with these guarantees, if any, will be recorded at the time of the corresponding sale of aircraft.

Substantially all financial support involving potential credit risk is with commercial airline customers. Maximum credit risk relating to two commercial airline customers accounted for 15% each of the total maximum credit risk as at January 31, 2002. This concentration resulted from consolidation in the U.S. commercial airline industry.

At the expiry date of certain financing and lease agreements, Bombardier has provided guarantees of the residual value of aircraft and transportation equipment. Certain of these guarantees can only be called upon if the above credit risk guarantees have not been called upon. The Corporation estimates its exposure under the residual value guarantees based on independent third-party appraisals of the future value of the related equipment at the time the guarantees are callable. The Corporation's expected losses under these guarantees are not significant as at January 31, 2002.

[B] SALE AND LEASEBACK

BC and Bombardier concluded third-party sale and leaseback transactions regarding freight cars and aircraft respectively which in most instances were simultaneously leased to operators. Details of minimum lease payments as at January 31, 2002 were as follows:

2003	**$ 309.1**
2004	**109.4**
2005	**101.0**
2006	**101.2**
2007	**101.0**
Thereafter	**1,469.7**
	$2,191.4

Minimum lease payments include $1,974.3 million for freight cars and $217.1 million for aircraft.

Minimum sub-lease rentals from operators and the net benefit of the estimated resale value of the equipment approximate the amount of minimum lease payments. Expected minimum sub-lease rentals from operators include the amounts from contracted and anticipated sub-leases. The amount for anticipated sub-leases of $1,584.1 million has been calculated taking into account current and expected future market conditions for each type of equipment. The total amount of the net benefit of the estimated resale value of the equipment included in the expected receipts was $193.0 million.

The net benefit of the estimated resale value, used in the calculation of the net credit risk related to the guarantees provided on sales of aircraft and in the expected receipts in relation to sale and leaseback transactions of equipment, represents the anticipated fair value based upon analyses conducted by third parties.

[C] OPERATING LEASES

The Corporation leases buildings and equipment and assumes operating lease obligations on trade-in aircraft for which the total minimum lease payments amount to $1,591.7 million. The annual minimum lease payments for the next five years are as follows: 2003 – $252.8 million; 2004 – $215.7 million; 2005 – $180.2 million; 2006 – $149.7 million and 2007 – $122.4 million.

25. COMMITMENTS AND CONTINGENCIES (cont'd)

[D] CLAIMS

The Corporation has notified DaimlerChrysler that it will file a claim in the order of €1.0 billion ($1.4 billion) in connection with the acquisition of Adtranz as described in note 2.

On November 8, 2001, the Corporation filed a claim against Amtrak in the United States District Court for the District of Columbia. The claim seeks damages in excess of $200.0 million US ($317.5 million) as compensation for additional costs incurred during execution of the Acela high-speed trainsets and locomotives contracts, including costs incurred as a result of Amtrak's failure to upgrade its infrastructure to accommodate the new equipment. On December 3, 2001, Amtrak filed a Motion to Dismiss alleging that the Corporation had failed to follow contractual dispute resolution procedures. The Corporation has vigorously contested the Motion to Dismiss, which is currently pending before the Court.

[E] LITIGATIONS

The Corporation is defendant in certain legal cases currently pending before various courts in relation to product liability and contract disputes with customers and other third parties.

The Corporation intends to vigorously defend its position in these matters. Management believes the Corporation has set up adequate provisions to cover potential losses and amounts not recoverable under insurance coverage, if any, in relation to these legal actions.

26. RECLASSIFICATION

Certain of the 2001 figures have been reclassified to conform to the presentation adopted in 2002. The most significant changes consist in the presentation of interest income of Bombardier as other income and the reclassification of gain on sale of finance receivables, servicing and other fees and other income of BC from revenues to other income. In addition, BC's depreciation expense related to assets under operating leases previously presented against revenues is now included in depreciation and amortization.

27. SEGMENT DISCLOSURE

The Corporation operates in the four reportable segments described below. Each reportable segment offers different products and services, requires different technology and marketing strategies and is headed by a president and chief operating officer.

The aerospace segment is engaged in the design, manufacture and sale of business and regional aircraft for individuals, corporations as well as commercial airline customers. It is also engaged in the manufacture of major airframe components for aircraft designed and built by other American and European aircraft manufacturers. In addition, it provides commercial and military aviation services, including technical services and pilot training.

The transportation segment is the global leader in the rail equipment manufacturing and servicing industry. Its wide range of products includes passenger railcars and complete rail transportation systems. It also manufactures locomotives, freight cars, propulsion and train control systems and provides signalling equipment and systems.

The recreational products segment is responsible for developing, manufacturing and marketing snowmobiles, watercraft, boats, all-terrain vehicles, utility vehicles and engines.

27. SEGMENT DISCLOSURE (cont'd)

The capital segment (BC) includes financial services and real estate activities. The financial services offer secured financing and leasing solutions to manufacturers, retailers and other commercial businesses, primarily in North American markets. BC is also offering full-service maintenance and/or management services to owners and users of freight cars in North American markets. BC also services the discontinued portfolios described in note 4. The real estate activities of this segment consist in selling land to real estate developers and renting office buildings to Bombardier.

The accounting policies of the segments are the same as those described in the Summary of Significant Accounting Policies. Management evaluates performance based on income or loss before special items, income taxes and goodwill amortization. Intersegment services are accounted for at current market prices as if the services were provided to third parties.

Corporate interest costs are allocated to the manufacturing segments based on each segment's net assets and most corporate office charges are allocated based on each segment's revenues. Net assets exclude cash and cash equivalents, investment in and advances to BC and deferred income taxes and are net of accounts payable and accrued liabilities, advances and progress billings in excess of related costs and accrued benefit liability and other.

Effective February 1, 2001, the Corporation ceased allocation of corporate interest charges to the BC segment. The new allocation basis is now used by Management in evaluating performance and making operating decisions for each segment. The effect of this modification was a decrease of interest expense allocated to the BC segment of $36.2 million for the year. The corresponding increase in the allocation of interest expense has been mostly borne by the aerospace segment.

The table containing the detailed segmented data is shown on the following page.

28. SUBSEQUENT EVENT

On March 8, 2002, the Corporation issued 9,400,000 Series 4 Cumulative Redeemable Preferred Shares carrying a fixed cumulative preferential cash dividend of 6.25% per annum, payable quarterly. The net proceeds of the issuance, amounting to approximately $227.6 million, have been used to repay short-term borrowings.

Photo Credits

Chapter 1

p. 3 PhotoDisc; **p. 7** Bob Daemmrich; **p. 25** Joseph Nettis/Stock Boston; **p. 25** PhotoDisc; **p. 25** PhotoDisc; **p. 25** Courtesy of Bombardier.

Chapter 2

p. 54 CP (Kevin Frayer); **p. 61** AP Photo/Stuart Ramson; **p. 62** Robert Rathe/Stock Boston.

Chapter 3

p. 91 Summer Productions; **p. 92** Michael Newman/PhotoEdit.

Chapter 4

p. 131 Messer Schmidt/eStock Photography/Picture Quest; **p. 153** AP Photo/Chad Rachman.

Chapter 5

p. 189 Stock/CP Archives; **p. 212** Ovak Arslanian.

Chapter 6

p. 235 CP (Marcos Townsend); **p. 272** Superstock.

Chapter 7

p. 277 Richard L. Miller/Stock Boston; **p. 290** Spencer Grant/PhotoEdit; **p. 300** PhotoDisc.

Chapter 8

p. 329 Stock/CP Archives; **p. 338** Dick Durrance II/Woodfin Camp & Associates; **p. 340** Richard Pasley/Stock Boston; **p. 342** Roger Rossmeyer/CORBIS.

Chapter 9

p. 365 PhotoDisc; **p. 387** AP Photo/Tsugufumi Matsumoto.

Chapter 10

p. 411 EyeWire Collection; **p. 419** Associated Press AP; **p. 425** AP Photo/*Battle Creek Enquirer*, Scott Erskine.

Chapter 11

p. 459 Najlah Feanny/Stock Boston; **p. 462** BD Lamphere/Stock Boston.

Chapter 12

p. 489 Najlah Feanny/Stock Boston; **p. 501** Bonnie Kamin/PhotoEdit.

accelerated amortization methods Amortization methods that recognize amortization expense more rapidly in the early stages of an asset's life than in the later stages of its life. p. 369

account Record used for the classification and summary of transaction data. p. 9

account balance Difference between total debits and total credits in an account. p. 132

accounting Service-based profession that provides reliable and relevant financial information useful in making decisions. p. 3

accounting controls Procedures designed to safeguard assets and to ensure accuracy and reliability of the accounting records and reports. p. 235

accounting cycle A cycle consisting of these stages: recording accounting data, adjusting the accounts, preparing the financial statements, and closing the nominal accounts; when one accounting cycle ends, a new one begins. p. 65

accounting equation Expression of the relationship between the assets and the claims on those assets. p. 10

accounting event Economic occurrence that causes changes in an enterprise's assets, liabilities, and/or equity. p. 13

accounting period Span of time covered by the financial statements, normally one year, but may be semiannually, quarterly, and monthly. p. 17

accounts receivable Expected future cash receipts arising from permitting customers to buy now and pay later; usually are small with a short term to maturity. pp. 54, 277

accounts receivable turnover ratio Financial ratio that measures how fast accounts receivable are turned into cash; computed by dividing sales by accounts receivable. p. 302

accrual Recognition of events before exchanging cash. p. 54

accrual accounting Method of accounting that records the effects of accounting events in the period in which such events occur regardless of when cash is exchanged. pp. 53, 491

accumulated amortization Contra asset account that indicates the sum of all amortization expense recognized for an asset since the date of acquisition. pp. 94, 371

adjusted cash balance Actual balance of cash owned by a company at the close of business on the date of the bank statement. p. 244

adjusting entry Entry that updates account balances prior to preparing financial statements. p. 62

administrative controls Procedures designed to evaluate performance and the degree of compliance with a firm's policies and public laws. p. 235

adverse opinion Audit opinion for a set of financial statements issued by a professional accountant that means that part of or all of the financial statements are not in compliance with GAAP and the auditors believe this non-compliance would be material to the average prudent investor. p. 69

allocation Recognition of expense by systematic assignment of the cost of an asset to periods of use. p. 91

allowance Reduction in the selling price of goods extended to the buyer because the goods are defective or of lower quality than the buyer ordered and to encourage a buyer to keep merchandise that would otherwise be returned. p. 197

allowance for doubtful accounts Contra asset account that contains an amount equal to the accounts receivable that are expected to be uncollectible. p. 279

allowance method of accounting for bad debts Method of accounting for bad debts in which bad debts are estimated and expensed in the same period in which the corresponding sales are recognized. The receivables are reported in the financial statements at net realizable value (the amount expected to be collected in cash). p. 278

amortization Method of systematically allocating the costs of tangible and intangible assets to expense over their useful lives; also term for converting the discount on a note to interest expense over a designated period. pp. 293, 433

amortization of loan Systematic repayment of principal and interest over the life of a loan. p. 413

amortization expense Portion of the original cost of a long-term tangible asset allocated to an expense account in a given period. p. 94

annual report Document in which an organization provides information to shareholders, usually on an annual basis. p. 25

annuity Series of equal payments made over a specified number of periods. p. 431

articles of incorporation Items on an application filed for the formation of a corporation; contains such information as the corporation's name, its purpose, its location, its expected life, provisions for its share capital, and a list of the members of its board of directors. p. 5

asset Economic resource used by a business for the production of revenue. p. 9

asset exchange transaction A transaction that decreases one asset while increasing another asset so that total assets do not change; for example, the purchase of land with cash. p. 55

asset/expense adjustment Adjusting entry that decreases assets and increases expenses. p. 143

asset source transaction Transaction that increases an asset and a claim on assets; three types of asset source transactions are acquired from owners (equity), borrowed from creditors (liabilities), or earned through operations (revenues). pp. 13, 54

asset/revenue adjustment Adjusting entry that increases assets and revenues. p. 141

asset use transaction Transaction that decreases an asset and a claim on assets; the three types are distributions (transferred to owners), liabilities (used to pay creditors), or expenses (used to operate the business). p. 55

audit Detailed examination of a company's financial statements and the documents that support the information presented in these statements. p. 68

audit around the computer Procedure in which auditors provide input that is expected to result in a designated output and then tests the system by comparing the actual output with the expected output. p. 239

authorized shares Number of shares that the corporation is approved to issue. p. 462

average days in inventory ratio (sometimes called average number of days to sell inventory ratio) Financial ratio that measures the average number of days that inventory stays in stock before being sold. p. 340

average number of days to collect accounts receivable Length of the average collection period for accounts receivable; computed by dividing 365 (or 366) by the accounts receivable turnover ratio. p. 302

bad debts expense Expense associated with uncollectible accounts receivable; amount recognized may be estimated using the allowance method, or actual losses may be recorded using the direct write-off method. p. 279

balance sheet Statement that lists the assets of a business and the corresponding claims (liabilities and equity) on those assets. p. 18

bank reconciliation Schedule that identifies and notes differences between the cash balance reported by the bank and the cash balance in the firm's accounting records. p. 244

bank statement Statement issued by a bank (usually monthly) that denotes all activity in the bank account for that period. p. 243

bank statement credit memo Memo that describes an increase in the account balance. p. 243

bank statement debit memo Memo that describes a decrease in the account balance. p. 243

basket purchase Acquisition of several assets in a single transaction with no specific cost attributed to each asset. p. 368

bearer or coupon bonds Also called unregistered bonds; bonds for which interest and principal payments are made to anyone who holds and redeems the interest coupon. p. 420

board of directors Group of individuals elected by the shareholders of a corporation to oversee its operations. p. 6

bond Debt security used to obtain long-term financing in which a company borrows funds from a number of lenders, called bondholders; usually issued in denominations of $1,000. p. 419

bond discount Difference between the selling price and the face amount of a bond sold for less than the face amount. p. 425

bond indenture Bond contract that specifies the stated rate of interest and the face value of the bond as well as other contractual provisions. p. 419

bond premium Difference between the selling price and the face amount of the bond that is sold for more than the face amount. p. 436

book value per share Determined by dividing the total shareholders' equity by the number of shares issued. p. 462

books of original entry Journals in which a transaction is first recorded. p. 148

call premium Difference between the call price (the price that must be paid for a called bond) and the face amount of the bond. p. 420

call price Specified price that must be paid for bonds that are called; usually higher than the face amount of the bonds. p. 437

callable bonds Bonds that include a feature allowing the issuer to pay them off prior to maturity. p. 420

Canada pension plan (CPP) A pension plan established by the federal government to which most employees contribute during their working years. p. 298

capital cost allowance A declining balance of amortization required by the Canadian Income Tax Act for tax reporting purposes. p. 278

capital expenditures (on an existing asset) Substantial amounts of funds spent to improve an asset's quality or to extend its life. p. 379

capitalized Recorded cost in an asset account until the item is used to produce revenue. p. 109

carrying value Face amount of a bond liability less any unamortized bond discount or plus any unamortized bond premium. p. 432

cash Coins, currency, cheques, balances in chequing and certain savings accounts, money orders, bank drafts, term deposit, and other items that are payable on demand. p. 240

cash discount Discount offered on merchandise sold to encourage prompt payment; offered by sellers of merchandise and represent sales discounts to the seller when they are used and purchase discounts to the purchaser of the merchandise. p. 197

cash flow statement Statement that explains how a business obtained and used cash during an accounting period. p. 11

cash inflows Sources of cash. p. 489

cash outflows Uses of cash. p. 489

cash short and over Account used to record the amount of cash shortages or overages; shortages are considered expenses and overages are considered revenues. p. 248

certified cheque Cheque guaranteed by a bank to be drawn on an account having funds sufficient to pay the cheque. p. 245

chart of accounts List of all ledger accounts and their corresponding account numbers. p. 146

cheques Prenumbered forms, sometimes multicopy, with the name of the business issuing them preprinted on the face, indicating to whom they are paid, the amount of the payment, and the transaction date. p. 242

claims Owners' and creditors' interests in a business's assets. p. 9

claims exchange transaction Transaction that decreases one claim and increases another so that total claims do not change. For example, the accrual of interest expense is a claims exchange transaction; liabilities increase, and the recognition of the expense causes retained earnings (equity) to decrease. p. 55

classified balance sheet Balance sheet that distinguishes between current and noncurrent items. p. 252

closing entries Entries used to transfer the balances in the revenue, expense, and dividends accounts to the Retained Earnings account at the end of the accounting period. pp. 59, 149

closing the accounts or closing Process of transferring balances from nominal accounts (Revenue, Expense, and Dividends) to the permanent account (Retained Earnings). p. 18

code of professional conduct A set of guidelines established by professional accountants to promote high ethical conduct among their membership. p. 70

collateral for loans Assets pledged as security for a loan. p. 416

common size financial statements Financial statements in which amounts are converted to percentages to allow a better comparison of period-to-period and company-to-company financial data since all information is placed on a common basis. p. 206

common shares Basic class of share capital that carries no preferences as to claims on assets or dividends, certificates that evidence ownership in a company. pp. 10, 462

compound interest Practice of reinvesting interest so that interest is earned on interest as well as on the initial principal. p. 427

compounding Earning interest on interest. p. 429

concept of materiality Concept that recognizes practical limits in financial reporting by allowing flexible handling of matters not considered material; information considered material if the decisions of a reasonable person would be influenced by its omission or misstatement. p. 97

continuity Concept that describes the fact that a corporation's life may extend well beyond the time at which any particular shareholder decides to retire or to sell his or her shares. p. 6

contra account Account that normally has a balance opposite to that of the other accounts in a particular category (Accumulated Amortization is classified as an asset, but it normally has a credit balance). p. 143

contra asset account Account subtracted from another account with which it is associated; has the effect of reducing the asset account with which it is associated. pp. 94, 371

contra liability account Account reported in the liability section of the balance sheet that has a debit balance; reduces total liabilities. A discount on a Note Payable is an example of a contra liability account. p. 292

contributed capital in excess account Any amount above the par or stated value is recorded in this account when the shares are issued. p. 465

convertible bonds Bonds that can be converted (exchanged) to an ownership interest (shares) in the corporation. p. 420

copyright Legal protection of writings, musical compositions, and other intellectual property for the exclusive use of the creator or persons assigned the right by the creator. p. 483

corporation Legal entity separate from its owners; formed when a group of individuals with a common purpose join together in an organization according to provincial or federal laws. p. 4

cost of goods available for sale Total costs paid to obtain goods and to make them ready for sale, including the cost of beginning inventory plus purchases and transportation-in costs, less purchase returns and allowances and purchase discounts. p. 190

cost of goods sold Total cost incurred for the goods sold during a specific accounting period. p. 190

credit Entry that increases liability and equity accounts or decreases asset accounts. p. 132

cumulative dividends Preferred dividends that accumulate from year to year until paid. p. 463

current (short-term) asset Asset that will be converted to cash or consumed within one year or an operating cycle, whichever is longer. p. 251

current (short-term) liability Obligation due within one year or an operating cycle, whichever is longer. p. 252

current ratio Financial ratio that measures the relationship between current assets and current liabilities; determined by dividing current assets by current liabilities, with the result expressed in decimal format. p. 253

date of record Date that establishes who will receive the dividend payment: Shareholders who actually own the shares on the record date will be paid the dividend even if the shares are sold before the dividend is paid. p. 468

debenture Unsecured bond issued based on the general credit of the organization. p. 419

debit Entry that increases asset accounts or decreases liability and equity accounts. p. 132

debt to assets ratio Financial ratio that measures a company's level of risk. p. 107

declaration date Date on which the board of directors actually declares a dividend. p. 467

deferral Recognition of revenue or expense in a period after the cash is exchanged. p. 91

deferral transactions Accounting transactions in which cash payments or receipts occur before the associated expense or revenue is recognized. p. 494

delivery expense See transportation-out. p. 198

deposit ticket Bank form that accompanies cheques and cash deposited into a bank account; normally specifies the account number, name of the account, and a record of the cheques and cash being deposited. p. 242

deposits in transit Deposits recorded in a depositor's books but not received and recorded by the bank. p. 244

direct method Method of preparing the statement of cash flows that reports the total cash receipts and cash payments from each of the major categories of activities (collections from customers, payment to suppliers). p. 505

direct write-off method Method of recognizing bad debts expense only when accounts are determined to be uncollectible. p. 287

disclaimer of audit opinion Position that an auditor can take with respect to financial statements when there is not enough information to confirm compliance or noncompliance with GAAP; is neither positive nor negative. p. 70

dividend Transfer of wealth from a business to its owners. pp. 11, 463

dividends in arrears Cumulative dividends on preferred shares that have not been paid; must be paid prior to paying dividends to common shareholders. p. 463

double taxation Policy to tax corporate profits distributed to owners twice, once when the income is reported on the corporation's income tax return and again when the dividends are reported on the individual's return. p. 5

double-declining balance amortization Amortization method that recognizes larger amounts of amortization in the early stages of an asset's life and progressively smaller amounts as the asset ages. p. 373

double-entry accounting (bookkeeping) Method of keeping records that provides a system of checks and balances by recording transactions in a dual format. pp. 14, 132

effective interest rate Yield rate of bonds, which is usually equal to the market rate of interest on the day the bonds are sold. p. 424

effective interest rate method Method of amortizing bond discounts and premiums that computes interest based on the carrying value of liability. As the liability increases or decreases, the amount of interest expense also increases or decreases. p. 438

elements Primary components of financial statements including assets, liabilities, equity, revenue, expenses, gains, and losses. p. 9

employment insurance (EI) A fund created to help employees through difficult times when they become unemployed. p. 298

entity Specific unit (individual, business, or institution) for which the accountant records and reports economic information; has boundaries that are distinct and separate from those of the owners, creditors, managers, and employees. p. 24

equity Portion of assets remaining after the creditors' claims have been satisfied (Assets = Liabilities + Equity); also called residual interest or net assets. p. 9

estimated useful life An estimate of the length of time an asset will be in service. p. 369

ex-dividend Shares traded after the date of record but before the payment date; does not receive the benefit of the upcoming dividend. p. 468

expense(s) Assets used in the process of generating revenues. (expanded definition) Decrease in assets or increase in liabilities that occurs in the process of generating revenue. pp. 11, 67

expense transactions Transactions completed in the process of operating a business that decrease assets or increase liabilities. p. 492

extraordinary items Items of income and expense that are unusual and rarely occur and that are set apart from operating income on the income statement. p. 437

face value Amount of the bond to be paid back (to the bondholders) at maturity. p. 419

fidelity bond Insurance policy that a company buys to insure itself against loss due to employee dishonesty. p. 236

financial accounting Accounting information designed to satisfy the needs of an organization's external users, including business owners, creditors, and government agencies. p. 7

financial audit Detailed examination of a company's financial statements and the documents that support the information presented in those statements; includes a verification process that tests the reliability of the underlying accounting system used to produce the financial reports. p. 69

financial leverage Concept of increasing earnings through debt financing; investment of money at a higher rate than that paid to borrow the money. pp. 108, 419

financial resources Money or credit arrangements supplied to a business by investors (owners) and creditors. p. 5

financial statements Primary means of communicating the financial information of an organization to the external users. The four general-purpose financial statements are the income statement, statement of equity, balance sheet, and cash flow statement. p. 8

financing activities Cash transactions associated with owners and creditors; also one of the three categories of cash inflows and outflows shown on the cash flow statement. This category of cash activities shows the amount of cash provided by these resource providers and the amount of cash that is returned to them. pp. 11, 490

first-in, first-out (FIFO) cost flow method Inventory cost flow method that treats the first items purchased as first items sold for the purpose of computing cost of goods sold. p. 330

fiscal year Year for which a company's accounting records are kept. p. 131

fixed interest rate Interest rate (charge for the use of money) that does not change over the life of the loan. p. 413

FOB (free on board) destination point Term that designates the seller as the responsible party for freight costs (transportation-in costs). p. 196

FOB (free on board) shipping point Term that designates the buyer as the responsible party for freight costs (transportation-in costs). p. 196

franchise Exclusive right to sell products or perform services in certain geographic areas. p. 383

future value Amount an investment will be worth at some point in the future, assuming a specified interest rate and the reinvestment of interest each period that it is earned. p. 430

gains Increases in assets or decreases in liabilities that result from peripheral or incidental transactions. p. 103

general authority Policies and procedures that apply across different levels of a company's management, such as everyone flies coach class. p. 237

general journal Journal in which all types of accounting transactions can be entered but is commonly used to record adjusting and closing entries and unusual types of transactions. p. 148

general ledger Complete set of accounts used in accounting systems. p. 16

generally accepted accounting principles (GAAP) Rules and regulations that accountants agree to follow when preparing financial reports for public distribution. p. 8

going concern assumption Assumption that a company will continue to operate indefinitely, will pay its obligations and should therefore report those obligations at their full face value in the financial statements. p. 278

goodwill Added value of a successful business that is attributable to factors—reputation, location, and superior products—that enable the business to earn above-average profits; stated differently, the excess paid for an existing business over the appraised value of the net assets. p. 367

gross profit Difference between sales revenue and cost of goods sold; the amount a company makes from selling goods before subtracting operating expenses. p. 190

gross profit method Method of estimating ending inventory that assumes that the percentage of gross profit to sales remains relatively stable from one accounting period to the next. p. 345

gross profit percentage Expression of gross profit as a percentage of sales computed by dividing gross profit by net sales; the amount of each dollar of sales that is profit before deducting any operating expenses. p. 206

half-year rule A tax rule that allows only one-half of the first years' amortization to be claimed, regardless of when the asset was purchased. This rule is applied when using the capital cost allowance method for amortization. p. 378

historical cost Actual price paid for an asset when it was purchased. p. 94

historical cost concept Requires assets to be recorded at the amount paid for them. p. 367

horizontal statements model Arrangement of a set of financial statements horizontally across a sheet of paper. p. 13

imprest basis Description of the periodic replenishment of a fund to maintain it at its specified original amount. p. 249

income from operations Income determined by subtracting operating expenses from operating revenues. Gains and losses and other peripheral activities are added to or subtracted from income from operations to determine net income or loss. p. 103

income Added value created in transforming resources into more desirable states. p. 4

income statement Statement that measures the difference between the asset increases and the asset decreases associated with running a business. This definition is expanded in subsequent chapters as additional relationships among the elements of the financial statements are introduced. p. 11

independent auditor Professional accountant licensed to perform audits who is independent of the company being audited. p. 69

indirect method Method of preparing the cash flow statement that uses the net income from the income statement as a starting point for the reporting of cash flow from operating activities. The adjustments necessary to convert accrual-based net income to a cash-equivalent basis are shown in the operating activities section of the cash flow statement. p. 505

intangible assets Assets that may be represented by pieces of paper or contracts that appear tangible; however, the true value of an intangible asset lies in the rights and privileges extended to its owners. p. 366

interest-bearing notes Notes that require the payment of the face value plus accrued interest at maturity. p. 292

internal controls A company's policies and procedures designed to reduce the opportunity for fraud and to provide reasonable assurance that its objectives will be accomplished. pp. 71, 235

inventory Supply of goods that is in the process of being made or is finished and ready for sale; also describes stockpiles of goods used in the business (office supplies, cleaning supplies). p. 189

inventory cost flow methods Methods used to allocate the cost of goods available for sale between cost of goods sold and inventory. p. 329

inventory turnover Ratio of cost of goods sold to inventory that indicates how many times a year the average inventory is sold (turned over). p. 340

investing activities One of the three categories of cash inflows and outflows shown on the cash flow statement; include cash received and spent by the business on productive assets and investments in the debt and equity of other companies. pp. 11, 490

investment Commitment of assets (usually cash) by a business to acquire other assets that will be used to produce revenue. p. 61

issued shares Shares sold to the public. p. 462

issuer of a bond Party that issues the bond (the borrower). p. 418

issuer of a note Individual or business borrowing funds (the party receiving the cash when a note is issued). pp. 66, 292

journal Book of original entry in which accounting data are entered chronologically before posting to the ledger accounts. p. 148

last-in, first-out (LIFO) cost flow method Inventory cost flow method that treats the last items purchased as the first items sold for the purpose of computing cost of goods sold. p. 330

ledger Collection of all accounts used by a business; primary information source for the financial statements. p. 146

legal capital Amount of assets that should be maintained as protection for creditors; the number of shares multiplied by the par value. p. 462

liabilities Obligations of a business to relinquish assets, provide services, or accept other obligations. p. 9

liability/expense adjustment Adjusting entry that increases liabilities and expenses. p. 142

liability/revenue adjustment Adjusting entry that decreases liabilities and increases revenue. p. 145

limited liability Concept that investors in a corporation may not be held personally liable for the actions of the corporation (the creditors cannot lay claim to the owners' personal assets as payment for the corporation's debts). p. 6

line of credit Preapproved credit arrangement with a lending institution in which a business can borrow money by simply writing a cheque up to the approved limit. p. 416

liquidity Ability to convert assets to cash quickly and meet short-term obligations. pp. 18, 252

long-term notes payable A form of debt financing, issued by banks or other financial institutions, that have maturities of two or more years, requiring periodic payments of principal and interest. p. 414

long-term operational assets Assets used by a business to generate revenue; condition of being used distinguishes them from assets that are sold (inventory) and assets that are held (investments). p. 365

losses Decreases in assets or increases in liabilities that result from peripheral or incidental transactions. p. 103

lower-of-cost-or-market rule Accounting principle of reporting inventories at market value if their value declined below their cost, regardless of the cause. p. 338

management's discussion and analysis (MD&A) Section of the annual report that management uses to explain many different aspects of the company's past performance and future plans. p. 154

managerial accounting Branch of accounting that provides information useful to internal decision makers and managers in operating an organization. p. 7

manufacturing companies Makers of goods sold to customers. p. 24

market Gathering of people or organizations for the purpose of buying and selling resources. p. 4

market interest rate Current interest rate available on a wide range of alternative investments. p. 425

market value The price that must be paid to purchase a share; also called fair value. p. 462

matching principle Process of matching expenses with the revenues they produce; three ways to match expenses with revenues include: matching expenses directly to revenues; matching expenses to the period in which they are incurred; and matching expenses systematically with revenues. pp. 62, 97

materiality A concept permitting companies to ignore insignificant items if their impact on the financial statements is immaterial. p. 287

material error Error or other reporting problem that, if known, would have influenced the decision of an average, prudent investor. p. 69

merchandise inventory Supply of finished goods held for resale to customers. p. 189

merchandising businesses Companies that buy and sell merchandise inventory. pp. 24, 189

mortgage bond Type of secured bond that conditionally transfers title of a designated piece of property to the bondholder until the bond is paid. p. 419

multistep income statement Income statement format that matches particular revenue items with related expense items and distinguishes between recurring operating activities and nonoperating items such as gains and losses. p. 202

natural resources Mineral deposits, oil and gas reserves, and reserves of timber, mines, and quarries are examples; sometimes called wasting assets because their value wastes away as the resources are removed. p. 366

net assets Portion of the assets remaining after the creditors' claims have been satisfied (Assets = Liabilities + Net assets); also called equity or residual interest. p. 9

net book value Historical (original) cost of an asset minus the accumulated amortization; alternatively, the unamortized amount to date. pp. 94, 379

net income Increase in net assets resulting from operating activities. p. 11

net income percentage Another term for return on sales. Refer to return on sales for the definition. p. 207

net loss Decrease in net assets resulting from operating activities. p. 11

net pay An employee's gross pay less statutory deductions and less voluntary deductions. p.298

net realizable value Face amount of receivables less an allowance for accounts whose collection is doubtful (amount actually expected to be collected). p. 278

nominal accounts Accounts that contain information applicable to a single accounting period; sometimes called temporary accounts. p. 18

non-cash investing and financing transactions Business transactions that do not directly affect cash, such as exchanging shares for land or purchasing property by using a mortgage and that are reported as both an inflow and outflow in a note referenced to the cash flow statement. p. 490

non-sufficient-funds (NSF) cheque Customer's cheque deposited but returned by the bank on which it was drawn because the customer did not have enough funds in its account to pay the cheque. p. 244

note payable Liability that results from the execution of a legal document called a note that describes technical terms, including interest charges, maturity date, collateral, and so on. p. 66

notes receivable Notes that evidence rights to receive cash in the future; usually specify the maturity date, rate of interest, and other credit terms. p. 277

notes to the financial statements Explanations of the information in the financial statements such as estimates used and options allowable under GAAP that have been chosen. p. 153

operating activities One of the three categories of cash inflows and outflows shown on the cash flow statement; show the amount of cash generated by revenue and the amount of cash spent for expenses. pp. 12, 490

operating cycle Time required to turn cash into inventory, inventory into receivables, and receivables back to cash. p. 251

opportunity cost Income given up by choosing one alternative over another; for example, the wage a working student forgoes to attend class. p. 208

outstanding cheques Cheques deducted from the depositor's cash account balance but not yet presented to the bank for payment. p. 245

outstanding shares Shares owned by outside parties; normally the amount of shares issued less the amount of treasury shares. p. 462

par value Arbitrary value assigned to a share by the board of directors. p. 461

partnership Business entity owned by at least two people who share talents, capital, and the risks of the business. p. 4

partnership agreement Legal document that defines the responsibilities of each partner and describes the division of income and losses. p. 4

patent Legal right granted by the Canadian Intellectual Property office ensuring a company or an individual the exclusive right to a product or process. p. 382

payment date Date on which a dividend is actually paid. p. 468

period costs Expenses matched to the period in which they are incurred regardless of when cash payments for them are made; costs that cannot be directly traced to products but are usually recognized as expenses in the period in which they are incurred. pp. 60, 190

periodic inventory system Method of accounting for changes in the Inventory account only at the end of the accounting period. p. 191

peripheral (incidental) transactions Transactions that do not arise from ordinary business operations. p. 103

permanent accounts Accounts that contain information transferred from one accounting period to the next. p. 18

perpetual inventory system Method of accounting for inventories that increases the Inventory account each time merchandise is purchased and decreases it each time merchandise is sold. p. 191

petty cash fund Small amount of cash set aside in a fund to pay for small outflows for which writing cheques is not practical. p. 249

physical flow of goods Physical movement of goods through the business; normally a FIFO flow so that the first goods purchased are the first goods delivered to customers, thereby reducing the likelihood of obsolete inventory. p. 330

post-closing trial balance A trial balance prepared after adjusting entries are recorded and posted to ensure the accuracy of the posting process. p. 152

posting Process of transferring information from journals to ledgers. p. 148

preferred shares Shares that receive some form of preferential treatment (usually as to dividends) over common shares; normally have no voting rights. p. 463

present value Current value of some investment amount that is expected to be received at some specified future time. p. 428

price-earnings (P/E) ratio Ratio of the selling price per share to the earnings per share; generally, a higher P/E ratio indicates that investors are optimistic about a company's future. pp. 21, 471

principal Amount of cash actually borrowed. p. 292

privately held corporation A corporation held by a few individuals. p. 5

procedures manual Manual that sets forth the accounting procedures to be followed. p. 237

product cost Inventory costs directly traceable to the product including the cost to acquire goods or make them ready for sale. p. 190

productive assets Assets used to operate the business; frequently called capital assets. p. 11

property, plant, and equipment Category of assets, sometimes called plant assets, used to produce products or to carry on the administrative and selling functions of a business; includes machinery and equipment, buildings, and land. p. 366

purchase discount Reduction in the gross price of merchandise extended under the condition that the purchaser pay cash for the merchandise within a stated time (usually within 10 days of the date of the sale). p. 197

qualified opinion Opinion issued by a professional accountant that falls between an unqualified opinion (see later definition) and an adverse opinion; means that for the most part, the company's financial statements are in compliance with GAAP, but the auditors have reservations about something in the statements or have other reasons not to give a fully unqualified opinion; reasons that a qualified opinion is being issued are explained in the auditor's report. p. 70

realization A term that usually refers to transactions that involve the collection or payment of cash. p. 53

recognition Recording an accounting event in the financial statements. p. 53

registered bonds Bonds for which the issuing company keeps a record of the names and addresses of the bondholders and pays interest and principal payments directly to the registered owners. p. 420

relative fair market value method Method of assigning value to individual assets acquired in a basket purchase in which each asset is assigned a percentage of the total price paid for all assets. The percentage assigned equals the market value of a particular asset divided by the total of the market values of all assets acquired in the basket purchase. p. 368

reporting entities The particular business or other organization for which financial statements are prepared. p. 8

residual interest Portion of the assets remaining after the creditors' claims have been satisfied (Assets = Liabilities + Residual Interest); also called *equity* or *net assets*. p. 9

residual (salvage) value The estimate of the value of an asset at the end of its useful life; the expected selling price of the asset at that time. p. 369

restrictive covenants Special provisions specified in the bond contract that are designed to prohibit management from taking certain actions that place bondholders at risk. p. 416

retail companies Companies that sell goods to consumers. p. 189

retained earnings Increase in equity that results from the retention of assets obtained through the operation of the business. p. 10

return on sales Percent of net income generated by each $1 of sales; computed by dividing net income by net sales. p. 207

return on assets ratio Ratio that measures the relationship between the level of net income and the size of the investment in assets. p. 106

return on equity ratio Ratio that measures the relationship between the amount of net income and the shareholders' equity of a company. p. 108

revenue Increase in assets or a decrease in liabilities that results from the operating activities of the business. pp. 11, 67

revenue transactions Transactions completed in the process of operating a business that increase assets or decrease liabilities. p. 492

salaries payable Amounts of future cash payments owed to employees for services that have already been performed. p. 55

salary An employee's annualized lump-sum amount when he/she is hired. p. 297

schedule of cost of goods sold Schedule that reflects the computation of the amount of the cost of goods sold under the periodic inventory system; an internal report not shown in the formal financial statements. p. 210

secured bonds Bonds secured by specific identifiable assets. p. 419

selling and administrative costs Costs that cannot be directly traced to products that are recognized as expenses in the period in which they are incurred. Examples include advertising expense and rent expense. p. 190

separation of duties Internal control feature of, whenever possible, assigning the functions of authorization, recording, and custody to different individuals. p. 236

serial bonds Bonds that mature at specified intervals throughout the life of the total issue. p. 420

service charges Fees charged by bank for services performed or a penalty for the depositor's failing to maintain a specified minimum cash balance throughout the period. p. 244

service organizations Organizations—accountants, lawyers, and dry cleaners—that provide services to consumers. p. 24

share certificate Evidence of ownership interest issued when an investor contributes assets to a corporation; describes the rights and privileges that accompany ownership. p. 5

shareholders Owners of a corporation. p. 5

shareholders' equity Represents the portion of the assets that is owned by the shareholders. p. 10

signature card Bank form that records the bank account number and the signatures of the people authorized to write cheques on an account. p. 242

simple interest Interest computed by multiplying the principal by the interest rate by the number of periods. Interest earned in a period is not added to the principal, so that no interest is earned on the interest of previous periods. p. 429

single-step income statement Single comparison between total revenues and total expenses. p. 202

sinking fund Fund to which the issuer annually contributes to ensure the availability of cash for the payment of the face amount on maturity date. p. 420

sole proprietorship Business (usually small) owned by one person. p. 4

solvency Ability of a business to pay liabilities in the long run. p. 252

source document Document such as a cash register tape, invoice, time card, or cheque stub that provides accounting information to be recorded in the accounting journals and ledgers. p. 148

special journals Journals designed to improve the efficiency of recording specific types of repetitive transactions. p. 148

specific authorizations Policies and procedures that apply to designated levels of management, such as the policy that the right to approve overtime pay may apply only to the plant manager. p. 237

specific identification Inventory method that allocates costs between cost of goods sold and ending inventory using the cost of the specific goods sold or retained in the business. p. 330

spread Difference between the rate a bank pays to obtain money (interest paid on savings accounts) and the rate that the bank earns on money it lends to borrowers. p. 418

stakeholders Parties interested in the operations of a business, including owners, lenders, employees, suppliers, customers, and government agencies. p. 4

stated interest rate Rate of interest specified in the bond contract that will be paid at specified intervals over the life of the bond. p. 419

stated value Arbitrary value assigned to a share by the board of directors. p. 462

statement of shareholders' equity Statement that summarizes the transactions occurring during the accounting period that affected the owners' equity p. 17

stock dividend Proportionate distribution of additional shares by the declaring corporation. p. 468

stock split Proportionate increase in the number of outstanding shares; designed to reduce the market value of the stock and its par value. p. 469

straight-line amortization Method of amortization that allocates bond discount or premium in equal amounts to each period over the life of the bond. p. 433

straight-line amortization Method of computing amortization that allocates the cost of an asset to expense in equal amounts over its life. p. 369

straight-line method Allocation method computed by subtracting the residual value from the cost and then dividing by the number of years of useful life. p. 94

subordinated debentures Unsecured bonds that have a lower priority than general creditors, that are paid off after the general creditors are paid in the case of liquidation. p. 369

systematic allocation Process of spreading the cost of an asset over several accounting periods in an orderly manner. p. 97

T-account Simplified account form, named for its shape, with the account title placed at the top of a horizontal bar, debit entries listed on the left side of the vertical bar, and credit entries shown on the right side. p. 131

T-account method Method of determining net cash flows by analyzing beginning and ending balances on the balance sheet and inferring the period's transactions from the income statement. p. 492

tangible assets Assets that can be touched such as equipment, machinery, natural resources, and land. p. 366

temporary accounts Accounts used to collect information for a single accounting period (usually revenue, expense, and distribution accounts). p. 18

term bonds Bonds in an issue that mature on a specified date in the future. p. 420

times interest earned ratio Ratio that computes how many times a company would be able to pay its interest by using the amount of earnings available to make interest payments; amount of earnings is net income before interest and income taxes. p. 427

trademark Name or symbol that identifies a company or an individual product. p. 382

transaction Particular event that involves the transfer of something of value between two entities. p. 13

transferability Concept referring to the practice of dividing the ownership of corporations into small units that are represented by shares, which permit the easy exchange of ownership interests. p. 6

transportation-in (freight-in) Cost of freight on goods purchased under terms FOB shipping point that is usually added to the cost of inventory and is a product cost. p. 196

transportation-out (freight-out) Freight cost for goods delivered to customers under terms FOB destination; a period cost expensed when it is incurred. p. 198

treasury shares Shares first issued to the public and then bought back by the corporation. p. 462

trial balance List of ledger accounts and their balances that provides a check on the mathematical accuracy of the recording process. p. 152

2/10, n/30 Term indicating that the seller will give the purchaser a 2-percent discount on the gross invoice price if the purchaser pays cash for the merchandise within 10 days from the date of purchase. p. 197

unadjusted bank balance Ending cash balance reported by the bank as of the date of the bank statement. p. 244

unadjusted book balance Balance of the Cash account as of the date of the reconciliation before making any adjustments. p. 244

undepreciated capital cost (UCC) The balance remaining to be amortized when the capital cost allowance method of amortization is used for tax purposes. It represents the net book value for tax purposes. p. 378

unearned revenue Revenue for which cash has been collected but the service has not yet been performed. p. 92

units-of-activity amortization Amortization method based on a measure of activity rather than a measure of time, for example, an automobile may be amortized based on the expected kilometres to be driven rather than on a specific number of years. p. 376

unqualified opinion Opinion on financial statements audited by a professional accountant that means the auditor believes the financial statements are in compliance with GAAP. p. 69

unregistered bonds Also called coupon or bearer bonds; bonds for which no record of the holder of the bond is kept. p. 420

unsecured bonds Also known as debentures, bonds issued on the general credit of the organization. p. 419

unsubordinated debentures Unsecured bonds that have equal claims with the general creditors. p. 419

users Individuals or organizations that use financial information for decision making. p. 4

value-added tax The additional value attached to goods sold or services provided to customers. p. 305

variable interest rate Interest rate that fluctuates (may change) from period to period over the life of the loan. p. 413

vertical statements model Arrangement of a full set of financial statements on a single page with account titles arranged from the top to the bottom of the page. p. 20

voluntarily disclosing Professional responsibility to clients that forbids professional accountants from voluntarily disclosing information obtained as a result of their client–accountant relationships. p. 70

voucher Internally generated document that includes spaces for recording transaction data and designated authorizations. p. 249

wage A per diem basis using hours worked or units produced as the factor to calculate the employee's pay for the time period. p. 297

warranty Promise to correct a deficiency or dissatisfaction in quality, quantity, or performance of a product or service sold. p. 289

weighted-average cost flow method Inventory cost flow method in which the cost allocated between inventory and cost of goods sold is based on the average cost per unit, which is determined by dividing total costs of goods available for sale during the accounting period by total units available for sale during the period. If the average is recomputed each time a purchase is made, the result is called a moving average. p. 330

wholesale companies Companies that sell goods to other businesses. p. 189

withdrawals Distributions to the owners of proprietorships and partnerships. p. 460

Index

E

F

G

H

I